THE PRISONER SOCIETY

CLARENDON STUDIES IN CRIMINOLOGY

Published under the auspices of the Institute of Criminology,
University of Cambridge; the Mannheim Centre, London School of
Economics; and the Centre for Criminological Research,
University of Oxford.

GENERAL EDITOR: IAN LOADER
(*University of Oxford*)

EDITORS: MANUEL EISNER ALISON LIEBLING, AND
PER-OLOF WIKSTRÖM
(*University of Cambridge*)

JILL PEAY AND TIM NEWBURN
(*London School of Economics*)

LUCIA ZEDNER AND JULIAN ROBERTS
(*University of Oxford*)

Recent titles in this series:

**Black Police Associations: An Analysis of Race and
Ethnicity within Constabularies**
Holdaway

Making Sense of Penal Change
Daems

**Punishing Persistent Offenders: Exploring
Community and Offender Perspections**
Roberts

**When Children Kill Children:
Penal Populism and Political Culture**
Green

Criminal Lives: Family Life, Employment, and Offending
Godfrey, Cox, and Farrall

The Prisoner Society

Power, Adaptation, and Social Life
in an English Prison

BEN CREWE
Institute of Criminology,
University of Cambridge

OXFORD
UNIVERSITY PRESS

OXFORD
UNIVERSITY PRESS

Great Clarendon Street, Oxford OX2 6DP

Oxford University Press is a department of the University of Oxford.
It furthers the University's objective of excellence in research, scholarship,
and education by publishing worldwide in

Oxford New York

Auckland Cape Town Dar es Salaam Hong Kong Karachi
Kuala Lumpur Madrid Melbourne Mexico City Nairobi
New Delhi Shanghai Taipei Toronto

With offices in

Argentina Austria Brazil Chile Czech Republic France Greece
Guatemala Hungary Italy Japan Poland Portugal Singapore
South Korea Switzerland Thailand Turkey Ukraine Vietnam

Oxford is a registered trade mark of Oxford University Press
in the UK and in certain other countries

Published in the United States
by Oxford University Press Inc., New York

British Library Cataloguing in Publication Data

Data available

Library of Congress Cataloging in Publication Data

Crewe, Ben.
  The prisoner society : power, adaptation, and social life in an English prison/Ben Crewe.
     p. cm.
  Includes bibliographical references and index.
  ISBN 978-0-19-957796-5 (hardback : alk. paper)
1. Prisons—Great Britain. 2. Prisoners—Great Britain. 3. Prison psychology—Great
Britain. I. Title.
  HV9647.C67 2009
  365'.942—dc22

                                                              2009027942

Typeset by Macmillan Publishing Soultions
Printed in Great Britain
on acid-free paper by
CPI Antony Rowe, Chippenham, Wiltshire

ISBN 978-0-19-957796-5

1 3 5 7 9 10 8 6 4 2

General Editor's Introduction

Clarendon Studies in Criminology aims to provide a forum for outstanding empirical and theoretical work in all aspects of criminology and criminal justice broadly understood. The editors welcome excellent PhD work, as well as submissions from established scholars. The Series was inaugurated in 1994, with Roger Hood at its first General Editor, following discussions between Oxford University Press and three Criminology Centres. It is edited under the auspices of these three Criminological Centres: the Cambridge Institute of Criminology, the Mannheim Centre for Criminology at the London School of Economics, and the Oxford Centre for Criminology. Each supplies members of the Editorial Board.

Ben Crewe's carefully crafted book, *The Prisoner Society: Power, Adaptation, and Social Life in an English Prison,* contributes significantly to a longstanding but neglected tradition of key sociological studies of the prison. As Loïc Wacquant argued, 'the ethnography of the prison...went into eclipse at the very moment when it was most urgently needed'. Ben Crewe revisits and renews this tradition, describing the prison's culture and social organization, and prisoners' adaptations to it, richly and with dexterity. He shows how the prison sentence is 'reconstituted' by prisoners, as they struggle with, against, and adapt to, the institution's logic, aims, and techniques. They do this creatively and in distinctive ways. Unusually, Crewe takes full account of prisoners' pre-prison biographies and identities, as well as of the managerial context in which the prison exists, in his classification of prisoners' adaptive styles. They become 'players', 'pragmatists', 'enthusiasts', 'stoics', or 'retreatists', and the deprivations of imprisonment take on particular meanings as a result. The author illustrates how penal power operates closely, in both more subtle and more overt ways, when compared to a formerly more authoritarian era. He describes its current shape as 'neo-paternalistic'. Drawing on extensive ethnographic fieldwork, Crewe describes the new pains, frustrations, and deprivations of imprisonment, the new techniques of psychological survival, and the new social world of the modern prison.

This clearly written and thoroughly researched book examines several new dimensions of prison life in an engaging and scholarly way. The editors welcome this important addition to the Series.

Alison Liebling
University of Cambridge,
February 2009

Acknowledgements

This book began as a three-year New Career Development Fellowship in the Social Sciences, awarded by the Nuffield Foundation (award NCF/00076/G). I thank them sincerely for being a generous and obliging funder. I am also grateful to the Prison Service of England and Wales, for providing indirect financial support in subsequent years, and for taking a continued interest in the study without insisting on any kind of control over the direction or dissemination of the research findings.

Peter Bennett first consented to the research taking place in HMP Wellingborough and has remained a champion of the work during the process of research and writing. His faith in the intellectual value of the project has helped to sustain my own. Jim Lewis was extremely kind in agreeing to continue hosting the research, at a time when it must have been tempting to decline politely. Paul Cawkwell, likewise, has been accommodating and encouraging throughout. Thanks are also due to Louise Taylor, who allowed me to do my pilot study at HMP Stafford, and a number of other practitioners, whose interest and access over the years have made the empirical work possible, and have sharpened my thinking considerably.

A large number of academics have offered insight, encouragement, and intellectual sustenance along the way. Some will not realize they have done so, but by providing positive (and sometimes critical) feedback about the nature and content of the study, they have all contributed to its development. These include Keith Bottomley, Eamonn Carrabine, Tomer Einat, Loraine Gelsthorpe, Dave Green, Mark Halsey, Richard Harding, John Irwin, Yvonne Jewkes, Lila Kazemian, Anna King, Roy King, Candace Kruttschnitt, Fergus McNeill, Sean Nixon, Ian O'Donnell, Coretta Phillips, Gwen Robinson, Richard Sparks, Alisa Stevens, Thomas Ugelvik and Richard Young, and a number of colleagues at the Institute of Criminology and beyond. Apologies to anyone I have omitted, and to all those who have had to endure discussions of what the book's title should be. Shadd Maruna deserves a special mention for providing ongoing support and for demonstrating

viii   Acknowledgements

what an academic can be. Most of all, I am deeply grateful to
Alison Liebling, who took something of a risk in agreeing to be
the senior partner in my postdoctoral research proposal. Since we
first met in summer 2000, she has been an exemplary mentor, and
a model of academic integrity. Our discussions over many years
about prisons, academic life, and the world beyond have been
hugely formative, and the study has benefited enormously from
her input.

Alison has also built up a Prisons Research Centre in whose
rigorous, humanistic culture I have always felt at home. Its
members have provided stimulation and friendship in one form
or another since I arrived at the Institute in 2001. These include
Helen Arnold, Leonidas Cheliotis, Leon Digard, Deborah Drake,
Linda Durie, Vicky Gadd, Joel Harvey, Ann Phillips, and Sarah
Tait. Clare McLean and Susie Hulley have both been excellent
company and first-rate colleagues during the many weeks we have
spent together doing fieldwork on a more recent project. They
have made the difficult work and dodgy hotels a lot more enjoyable. Sara Snell and Jennifer Cartwright have also been a pleasure
to work with.

Draft versions of the book were read by a number of people, and
I am grateful to them for their patience and generally positive comments. Sarah Tait and Geraldine Tait deserve particular credit for
their extremely detailed and beautifully acerbic copy-editing. Guy
Shefer raised a number of valuable questions about the tone and
tenor of some passages. Abigail Wild and Ruth Armstrong also
provided important feedback on some sections. Jamie Bennett,
Peter Bennett, and Peter Wright also found time to cast their eyes
over late drafts of the final manuscript, and all offered generous,
constructive commentary. The three assessors to whom Oxford
University Press sent the completed manuscript were not only very
kind in their reviews, but positive enough to assist me in defending the book's length. The detail is important, and I hope that it
does not detract from the analysis.

A great debt of thanks is owed to the staff and prisoners who
were living and working in HMP Wellingborough during my
fieldwork period. Almost all of them were friendly and helpful,
despite the strains of the environment. Particular mention should
be made of Jason Warr, whom I have now interviewed, taught,
and supervised since we first met, in very different contexts. He
has been generous throughout—negotiating some difficult and

sometimes surreal situations with considerable tact—and has always given honest, incisive feedback.

The book draws on arguments and insights first developed in a number of existing publications, including articles in *Punishment and Society*, *The British Journal of Criminology*, and *The Howard Journal of Criminal Justice*. I am grateful to their publishers for granting permission to reuse some passages and quotations.

Finally, I would like to thank my family for their love and support, and Nicole Martin for everything she has brought to my life in the last few years. The book is dedicated to Ruby, Esther, and Hannah, who at the moment think that prison is 'for people who are bad', but I hope, in time, will see that the truth is more complex.

Table of Contents

1

Introduction

Just when the experience of imprisonment is becoming a normal pathway for significant portions of the population, the pathways of knowledge that made the experience of incarceration visible are closing.... The whole question of the prison social order appears distant from the concerns of both social science and prison management.... Inmate society, represented centrally in the discourses of both prison sociology and prison literature, seems to be disappearing from public view. (Simon 2000: 285–302)

Observational studies depicting the everyday world of inmates all but vanished just as the United States was settling into mass incarceration and other advanced countries were gingerly clearing their own road towards the penal state. *The ethnography of the prison thus went into eclipse at the very moment when it was most urgently needed* on both scientific and political grounds. (Wacquant 2002: 385)

Imprisonment is the ultimate sanction of the state in nearly all Western nations, and its use in the developed world has risen considerably in recent years (Walmsley 2005). The prison occupies a central place in the politics of crime control and has become a normal social destination for growing numbers of citizens. At the same time, it has retreated from public view and academic scrutiny (Bosworth and Sparks 2000; Simon 2000; Wacquant 2002; Liebling 2004). Prisons are no longer built in city centres, as looming warnings of the consequences of crime, but on secluded sites, removed from the conurbations that feed them (Pratt 2002). Meanwhile, their innards have become increasingly obscured. While the aims and techniques of imprisonment have changed significantly, their social outcomes and effects are little known. At a moment when it seems essential to understand what imprisonment is and what it does, research into the prison's interior life has become somewhat scarce. In the terms of one prominent scholar, prison ethnography—in the United States (US) at least—is 'not merely an endangered species but a virtually extinct one' (Wacquant 2002: 385).

Observers of the penological scene in the US have identified a number of reasons for the decline in academic interest: low levels of government research funding; the practical demands of intensive fieldwork; the unappealing nature of the research site; the stringency of ethical approval committees within universities; and the comparative ease and kudos of conducting research on related issues, such as sentencing patterns and prison population trends (Simon 2000; Wacquant 2002). Prisons have become less enthusiastic research partners, in some countries at least. In the early years of prison sociology, knowledge of the prison's internal social dynamics was considered vital for the development of a rational and effective penal system. Many prison scholars worked within or alongside the system, sometimes as psychologists, counsellors, or classification sociologists within the establishments they wrote about (Pollock 1997; Wacquant 2002). Donald Clemmer, for example, conducted his fieldwork for *The Prison Community* (1940) while employed at Menard prison, and went on to be the director of the District of Columbia's prison system and the head of the American Correctional Association (Simon 2000). Gresham Sykes gained access to Trenton prison, the subject of *The Society of Captives* (1958), by developing a close relationship with its warden, whom he had asked to contribute to his criminology course at Princeton (Sykes 1995). The classic studies that resulted—focusing on issues such as inmate roles, norms, and leadership—were highly influential in informing attempts by prison officials to design rehabilitative interventions and maintain order.

In many jurisdictions, particularly the US, there is now less interest in governing prisons through these social and interpersonal mechanisms. In some states, and in many prisons, reformist ambitions are negligible.[1] Relationships between staff and prisoners are minimal. Officers serve mainly as enforcers of compliance or as faceless instruments in sterile regimes that deliver services with little interaction or humanity. In such post-social prisons (DiIulio 1987), there is little to gain and much more to lose in granting access to researchers. Where prisoners are merely contained or

---

[1] It is important to note that prison philosophies and conditions are extremely varied within the US. Much of the writing about American prisons has been based on the particularities of the Californian prison system, which is notoriously squalid, overcrowded, and violent.

controlled, their values and relationships are of little concern to prison officials. In the UK—and elsewhere in Europe—interest in the prison's social world has not been abandoned. Officers are encouraged to build relationships with prisoners, in the interests of decency, safety, and security. Attempts are made to regulate prison cultures and regimes so as to diminish some of the burdens of incarceration and reduce conflict between prisoners. The huge 'warehouse' prisons described by Irwin (2005) and Wacquant (2002), in which prisoners are primarily seen as toxic units to be stored and managed at minimum cost, are not (yet) a reality. Nonetheless, while managerial data about the 'performance' of prisons are plentiful, there is much less sociological knowledge about their ordinary social characteristics: their arrangements of power, their social structures, the intricacies of their cultures, their mundane pains, and the behaviours and adaptations that they generate.

Based on a case study of an English prison, HMP Wellingborough, this book provides an account of these rather neglected dimensions of modern imprisonment. It seeks to expose and dissect the prison's social anatomy, to illuminate the experiences that occur within it, and to relate these both to prisoners' prior lives and to the aims, means, and conditions of the institution—in this case, a medium-security or Category-C men's training prison, known colloquially as a 'Cat-C'. In its focus and method, the book aims to revisit and help renew the tradition of prison ethnography (see *inter alia*, Clemmer 1940/1958; Sykes 1958; Morris and Morris 1963; Mathieson 1965; Jacobs 1977; Carroll 1974; King and Elliott 1977; Genders and Player 1995; Owen 1998). Patched together, the studies within this tradition constitute a bright but ragged backdrop of knowledge: rich, colourful and highly elaborate in places, yet patchy, uneven and with some conspicuous holes. Most have focused on a single establishment, with depth of analysis and richness of detail taking precedence over breadth. Generalizability has been willingly sacrificed for an approach that can pierce the skin of the institution, penetrate official descriptions, and show the interconnections between apparently discrete elements of the prison's social structure. These studies have mapped the penal terrain selectively and sporadically, making meaningful comparisons between them problematic. Given that they span different eras and contexts, the variations in their findings are unsurprising. Yet there are also consistencies in their findings—recurring social patterns and tendencies. There is no such thing as '*The* Prison' (Sparks *et al.* 1996) but, as early theorists argued, imprisonment entails some more-or-less 'intrinsic' pains, deprivations and conditions, and these factors influence the prison's culture and social organization.

The degree to which these in-built properties of imprisonment mould the prison experience is one of the key debates of the discipline, and remains an empirical question. Many early studies, exemplified by Sykes's (1958) *The Society of Captives* (but also McCorkle and Korn 1954; Garabedian 1963), presupposed the primacy of the institution in structuring the world within it. By the 1950s, the prevailing assumption of the discipline was that phenomena such as the prisoner hierarchy and interpersonal loyalty were outcomes of the inherent qualities of confinement and 'products of official and unofficial administrative policies' (Cressey 1958: viii). Sykes argued that the 'inmate code' arose as a collective response to the deprivations of imprisonment, which it alleviated through the promotion of mutual aid, loyalty, and collective self-esteem. Other scholars demonstrated that the nature of this code depended on the particular goals of the institution (Grusky 1959; Berk 1966; Street *et al.* 1966). Where prisons were treatment-oriented rather than custody-oriented, the values and behaviour of prisoners were less 'oppositional'. In such perspectives—labelled 'deprivation' or 'indigenous' theories—the prison was seen as a virtually self-contained system whose social properties required little reference to the external community.

Later studies did not dispute that the prisoner society was a 'response to problems of imprisonment', but questioned 'the emphasis given to the notion that solutions to these problems are found within the prison' (Irwin and Cressey 1962: 145). Prisoner culture was instead seen as a version of criminal cultures and subcultural norms 'imported' from the outside community. In *Stateville*, Jacobs (1977) showed how Chicago gangs had transplanted patterns of leadership, loyalty, and conflict virtually wholesale into the prison environment. The prison's social structures *reproduced* those of the urban ghetto, its code reflected the values of the street, and its frustrations were mitigated by the psychological, social, and material support provided by the gangs rather than a collective code of behaviour. Management ideologies and prisoner expectations were likewise shaped by broad social currents, shifts in political culture, and legal interventions into the prison.

The prison walls were porous and permeable, and institutions could not insulate themselves from these external forces.[2]

The importation–deprivation framework can be related to *individual adaptations* to imprisonment as well as the prison's *culture and social structure* (and the two are of course connected). Conceptions of the prison as an organization cut-off from the outside world assumed a particular model of prisoner socialization. Individuals entered an institution of domination, whose official aims involved refashioning their identities and whose informal social mechanisms remoulded them almost irresistibly into new and unfamiliar roles and relationships. Individuals did not capitulate entirely to these processes (Goffman 1961). But it was taken for granted that, in their adjustments to imprisonment, prisoners were subordinate to the social and institutional forces to which they were subjected. To adjust and survive meant acting in new ways, indeed, being a different kind of person. The social roles available to prisoners were defined by the needs of the environment: the need to cope with sexual and material deprivation, to recapture social status, to claw back some autonomy and to ensure one's personal safety. These roles were conveyed by labels that were allocated to prisoners by their peers, and which structured their subsequent behaviour (Garabedian 1963). As Sykes (1995: 78) explained, his experience in the army had shaped a belief that: 'for better or worse, people often became whatever they were assigned, regardless of personal proclivities or skills'.[3]

---

[2] Nor can we consider the world *outside* the prison to be isolated from the cultural and 'collateral effects' of incarceration. Some scholars have recently noted that the era of mass incarceration in the US turns the prison into a 'shaping institution for whole sectors of the population' (Garland 2001: 2). Attention should be focused not only on how external forces *flow in*, nor how the prison impacts upon the individuals within it, but how its effects *flow out*: the social consequences that result when some populations and communities are so ravaged by the 'war on crime' and its penal consequences. Others have argued that divisions between the prison and the ghetto have been virtually obliterated (Wacquant 2000; 2001). The prison and its culture are neither appendages to nor reflections of a separate world outside. Rather, they form part of a 'carceral continuum' (Wacquant 2001) that regulates a social underclass that is superfluous to the neo-liberal economy. In such readings, as the cultures of the prison and the street mesh and merge, questions about their relative impact on each other become almost obsolete.

[3] Influential studies in social psychology, in particular Milgram's (1963) research on obedience to authority and the Stanford Prison Experiment (see Haney *et al.* 1973), added weight to the notion that individuals easily submitted to institutional roles and authority.

Variations in the degree to which prisoners took up the values of their new world could be explained by factors such as the amount of time they were exposed to them and the relative hardship of the environment (Wheeler 1961; and see Akers *et al.* 1977; Thomas 1977). Why prisoners with similar carceral histories occupied different roles—that is, why certain prisoners adopted some roles rather than others—was harder to explain.

Importation theories could account far more adequately for the distinctions between prisoners' adaptations, by pointing to the role of personal histories, prior orientations, and future expectations in shaping prison conduct. Pre-prison identities were not dispossessed completely by the institution, or entirely surrendered. They were drawn upon to navigate its demands. The work of Irwin and Cressey (1962) and Jacobs (1974; 1977) also gave some sense of how imprisonment was subjectively experienced: how social positions and cultural assumptions informed different perceptions of the prison environment e.g. the status of officers, the value of institutional rewards, and so on. Yet the degree to which prisoners acted knowingly, strategically, and self-consciously in adopting their roles was not always apparent in such work. Although early importation studies disputed the implication that prisoners were blank slates upon which institutional roles could be inscribed, at times they too presented prisoners rather facelessly, as carriers of external roles and cultures that seemed just to *flow through* them into the prison.[4] The place of *agency*—the capacity of individuals actively to shape their environment—in the adaptive process remained elusive. Likewise, the lived realities of imprisonment were not often illuminated.

The subjective experience of imprisonment is now better documented, in prisoner autobiographies (e.g. Boyle 1977, 1984; Shannon and Morgan 1996; Smith 2004; James 2003; Warr 2008) and in academic studies (e.g. Cohen and Taylor 1972; Toch 1992; Medlicott 2001; Jewkes 2005a, 2005b; Harvey 2007). Such accounts have provided considerable insight into how incarceration feels and how prisoners interpret and negotiate its terms and obligations. They have shown how acts that are apparently trivial can represent assertions of selfhood (Bosworth 1999; McEvoy 2001), and how seemingly irrational practices have meaning to the

---

[4] It is instructive in this respect that these were labelled theories of 'cultural drift' (see Jacobs 1974).

people who engage in them (Carrabine 2004). However, few studies have provided a joined-up analysis of the connections between individual acts and experiences and the institutional contexts where they occur (although see Jewkes 2002 and Kruttschnitt and Gartner 2005). Put more simply, there is little systematic knowledge of how prisoners actively live out their sentences within the constraints of the environment.

This book seeks to address the issues outlined above. First, it is a book about *power*: how it is deployed by the institution, and with what ambitions and techniques; and how it is experienced and reconstituted by prisoners in their everyday practices. It asks what attitudes, behaviours, and relationships the prison both promotes and inhibits, what it rewards and punishes, with what logic, and through which means. It provides an empirical analysis of what Liebling (2004: 484) has called 'the largely undocumented penal project of the last decade or so: to eliminate residual resistance and secure a new mode of compliance'. But it does not assume that this mission has been successful or that prisoners are rendered docile by the strategies of the institution, potent though they are. In this respect, it explores the 'dialectic of control' (Giddens 1984: 16; and see Sparks *et al.* 1996) between the institution and its inhabitants: the perpetual struggle that is the prison's essential dynamic. It is the struggle by one side for order and compliance and by the other for autonomy, influence, and self-assertion.

Second, the book is a study of *adaptation*. It explores how the behaviour of individual prisoners is shaped both by institutional imperatives and by the values and orientations that they carry into the sentence. It shows how, within the terms delimited by the institution, prisoners reflect on their circumstances, evaluate their options, and make decisions about how to 'do time' in ways that relate to their pre-prison characteristics.[5] Here, the book seeks to

---

[5] It is important to emphasize that agency is not the same as autonomy or free will. As conceived in recent social theory (for example, Giddens 1984; Bourdieu 1972), agency is structurally constituted, such that it tends to reproduce existing structures, particularly in its pre-conscious forms (what Giddens labels 'practical consciousness' and Bourdieu calls the 'habitus') but always holds the possibility of transforming them or finding 'creative' ways of existing within them. There is little work on imprisonment that shows how, in their purposeful actions and particular dispositions, prisoners both reproduce and transform the social structures of the prison *and* the outside community.

move beyond the stale impasse of the importation–deprivation debate to provide a more nuanced description than those that can be offered in quantitative studies of prison culture and conduct. It illustrates in some detail *how* these processes work: how structural, institutional, and external determinants interrelate in practice, and do so differently for different individuals, creating a variety of adaptive outcomes. It is because prisoners confront the penal regime with such a range of backgrounds, expectations and sentence conditions that they experience and adjust to different pains and deprivations, contest different aspects of the regime, discard and maintain their identities to different extents, and develop different kinds of social relationships.

The *social world* that comprises these adaptations is the book's third main focus. Here, the framework of the study is most apparent. In analysing the prison's hierarchy, social relationships, and everyday culture, it takes into account three main influences: first, the prison's structural imperatives i.e. its more or less inherent conditions and the social requirements these produce; second, its institutional culture, function, and policies, e.g. its role as a Cat-C prison, its ethos, practices, and techniques, and the frustrations and pressures that these generate; and, third, the ideologies and inclinations that are imported into the environment by prisoners. These include views on masculinity and status, sentiments of shame and defiance, and histories of addiction and power that are themselves structured by biographical, social and criminal experiences. The ambition is to provide a comprehensive sociological analysis of the prison. Like the studies from which it has drawn most inspiration, the analysis also illustrates the links between the prison's social components. These include its mundane system of norms, its patterns of leadership, loyalty, and affiliation, its tendencies towards order and disorder, and its institutional characteristics. The prison is not a self-contained social domain in the manner that some of its early students suggested, but it remains fruitful to think of it, to some degree, as an 'organic inter-related whole' (Clemmer 1958: 322). Without seeing its elements in reference to each other, the day-to-day exploits of the landings become free-floating acts disembedded from their wider context and determinants.

A further aim of the book is to capture a particular moment in penal history, to provide a sociological snapshot of the prison in what could be considered the 'managerial' or 'late-modern' era (but does not necessarily require such epochal labels). Institutional politics, culture, and power relations are worthy of analysis in themselves. Prisons are complex, conflicted organizations, whose dynamics are rarely exposed, even though they reveal important dimensions of state practice and authority. Their specific organizational qualities also mould the world of prisoners, and have created some distinctive new pains and frustrations. The book explicitly relates prison social life to the terms of contemporary imprisonment. In effect, it asks how shifts in the penal and political climate have been translated into a particular arrangement of policies and practices, and explores how these arrangements serve to condition the new society of captives. As Carrabine (2000; 2004) and Sparks *et al.* (1996) have noted, few studies have successfully traced this relationship between the prison's political logic—what it is *for*—and its internal dynamics—what it is *like* (although see Jacobs 1977; Kruttschnitt and Gartner 2005). In doing so, this book provides a ground-level analysis that should complement recent accounts of modern penality (Garland and Young 1983; Garland 2001a; Pratt 2002; Wacquant 2000; 2001a, 2001b) and more specific descriptions of the history and moral performance of Her Majesty's Prison Service (Liebling 2004).[6]

It is here that the book commences, in Chapter 2, where the scene is set for the empirical analysis that follows. The chapter outlines the broad trends that have shaped modern imprisonment in recent decades, developments in the Prison Service since the early 1990s, and the history and functions of HMP Wellingborough, an establishment that can be seen as a typical prison of its kind. Through these descriptions, the chapter discusses shifts in the aims, means and strategies of imprisonment, and the manner in which these shifts framed the priorities and concerns of the prison under study.

Chapter 3 documents in more detail the culture and ethos of HMP Wellingborough, exploring how the ideologies and techniques of modern imprisonment were translated in practice. The chapter focuses in particular on staff attitudes and practices, and the prison's overall value culture: its moral and emotional climate. It describes the orientation of staff towards prisoners as a form of benign indifference, and discusses the somewhat fractious

---

[6] The term Prison Service is used hereafter to denote the Prison Service of England and Wales.

relationships between uniformed staff and governors. The aim is to indicate the balance and location of power within the establishment and to depict the experiences and outcomes of power for staff.

The concern of Chapter 4 is to provide a detailed description of the form and flow of power, as it was applied to Wellingborough's prisoners. The chapter begins by outlining the modes of power that can be used to achieve order and compliance, and outlines how these have featured in sociological studies of imprisonment. Prisoner testimonies are then used to convey the nature and location of power in HMP Wellingborough: its scope, targets, qualities and objectives. The chapter shows how a range of policies and mechanisms—including staff-prisoner relationships, early release and earned privilege schemes, mandatory drug testing, and psychological expertise—constituted a particular form of power, which can be characterized as a form of 'neo-paternalism'. It argues that this form was both 'soft' and 'hard', both muted and oppressive, both remote and highly gripping. It combined a welfarist concern with rehabilitation and decency, a neo-liberal emphasis on responsibility and self-regulation, and an authoritarian impulse of control and compliance. Its aim was not so much to make prisoners meekly passive or merely obedient but to inculcate in them a kind of enthusiastic engagement with the terms of the regime. In this respect, while being less authoritarian and less destructive than its previous guises, it was demanding, invasive and unforgiving: 'tight', as well as 'deep' (Downes 1988) and 'heavy' (King and McDermott 1995). The accompanying burdens of this power formation—some of the new pains of imprisonment—are discussed further in the book's conclusion.

The issue of how prisoners engaged with this form of power is taken up in Chapter 5. As David Garland has noted (1996; 1997) to describe power's intentions without observing its effects is to paint only half a picture. The chapter elaborates in some depth a range of adaptive outcomes. These were not types of prisoner *per se*, but particular kinds of responses or strategies that were linked both to prisoners' particular backgrounds and to the adaptive positions that the institution promoted. This typology reveals significant differences between prisoners in relation to a range of attitudes and behaviours: the main deprivations that they experienced and thus sought to alleviate; the reasons for their compliance; the sources of their resentment; the outlets they used to express frustration and hostility; their views of staff and of the prison as a criminal justice organization; their engagement with officers and the wider system of power; their future plans and preferences for 'doing time'. The chapter concludes by discussing how the prison's power formation contributed to a particular model of social order and dissent: a relatively atomized community, where open defiance was rare and resistance largely took forms that were individualized and surreptitious. It also discusses the fluidity of prison behaviour, illustrating how institutional practices and changing self-conceptions could contribute to significant shifts in adaptive styles.

The second half of the book—Chapters 6 to 8—explores the shape and complexity of prisoner culture and social life, and tries to convey its daily texture, structure and experience. It shows how Wellingborough's everyday social world was shaped by the interplay of structural, institutional, cultural, and biographical factors. Exploring in turn the prisoner hierarchy, social relationships between prisoners, and the everyday culture of the prisoner community, it shows how the prison incited as well as constrained particular patterns of social organization through its intrinsic conditions, its institutional character, and its policies and practices. These factors set the parameters within which imported characteristics took their various forms. Chapter 6 documents power relations between prisoners, unpicking the determinants and consequences of status and stigma. Chapter 7 describes the structure of social relationships within the prison, the inducements and impediments to friendship formation, the bases and nature of interpersonal loyalties and affiliations, and the relationships within and between primary and secondary groups. Chapter 8 examines other aspects of everyday social life and culture, focusing in particular on the informal economy and drug culture, issues of interpersonal politics and conflict, the prisoner value system and emotional rules, and the public and private sentiments of the prisoner society. Throughout, these chapters illustrate how the prison's inherent and institutional conditions created competing pressures—broadly, to 'individualize' and to 'socialize', to restrict and to develop allegiances, relationships and interactions. These pressures (and the frustrations they represented) weighed upon and were weighed up by different prisoners in different ways, according to their values, needs, expectations and particular penal predicaments. Thus, through the use of the typology, each chapter highlights the considerable diversity within the prisoner world in terms of attitudes towards and commitments to friendship, trade, and the prisoner value system.

The book is a study of a single Cat-C prison at a particular point in time. It makes no claims to widespread generalizability as such. The hope is that, by exposing the prison's social components and examining its constituent parts, it may provide a framework for analysis that can be employed in other circumstances and can shed light both on the similarities between prison social systems and the reasons why they differ. First and foremost, it is an attempt to open up the prison to sociological analysis and help drag its inner life out of the 'dark zone of knowledge and power' (Simon 2000: 285).

2

The Penal Context and History

'Don't believe anyone who says that the contribution of Cat-C prisons is in any way easier or less important than that of other types of establishment', declared Phil Wheatley, Director General of the Prison Service, at the annual conference of Cat-C governors, in March 2003. Category-C prisons, he stated were, '[the] workhorses of the service'. Closing the meeting, Wheatley summarized the condition of the estate and the challenges of the coming year. Foremost among them was overcrowding, a problem with multiple implications. With the system at full capacity, many prisoners would have to be located far from their homes. It would be harder than normal to transfer 'difficult prisoners' to other establishments. The need to free up places at the more secure end of the system would also mean that Cat-C prisons would be handling some men only recently held in high-security establishments, where staffing was much higher and regimes considerably more restricted. To keep the system functioning, governors would need to move prisoners to open conditions 'pretty damn quick' and ignore the temptation to hang onto their most compliant prisoners. According to one area manager, under such pressures, Cat-C prisons were becoming increasingly like 'transit camps'.

The main risk of overcrowding was instability, and Wheatley emphasized the blend of measures that managers would need to take to reinforce compliance and secure control: the leverage provided by the incentives and earned privileges (IEP) scheme should be used to maximum effect; regimes should be predictable; prisoners should feel that they were benefiting from the treatment and training opportunities available in this branch of the estate; and, to avoid triggering discontent, fairness and positive relationships between staff and prisoners should be at the heart of daily treatment.

Meanwhile, Cat-C prisons would need to avoid being distracted from their other objectives. Resettlement work—the focus of the previous year's conference—and 'decency'—one of the watchwords of the Prison Service since the late 1990s—were vital not only in the service of internal order, but as ends in themselves. Wheatley declared his vision for a 'professional service', treating prisoners humanely, making 'evidence-based interventions', and ensuring that staff felt rewarded and recognized. 'Performance management'—the theme of the 2003 conference—remained the core mechanism of ensuring that prisons met these responsibilities. In a context of strained resources and private sector competition, it would be a 'very interesting year'.

Wheatley had stopped at HMP Wellingborough en route to the conference, and drew upon the visit to illustrate his speech. Wellingborough, he commented, was managing a number of fairly recent Category-A prisoners. It was feeling the strain of acute overcrowding in the Midlands, taking disgruntled prisoners from beyond its normal ambit. It was suffering from staffing problems, in part because new recruits were being diverted to new prison accommodation, constructed to ease the overcrowding crisis. Wheatley noted that prisoners in Wellingborough were not only aware of this problem, they were 'talking like the POA [Prison Officers Association]: "we're short-staffed. What are you gonna do about it?"'. At the same time, he stated, the prison had 'worthwhile staff, doing a wide range of work and working with prisoners better than ever before'.

In Wellingborough's morning meeting two days later, the senior management team was briefed on the Director General's visit and the conference. Jim Lewis, the prison's governing governor,[1] reiterated the key messages of Wheatley's speech. Deputy Governor Paul Cawkwell reported that he had described Wellingborough as a 'very good prison that could be an excellent prison' and had recognized its urgent need for more staff. Wellingborough's concerns were partly defined by local issues, but these were framed by the context and issues that Wheatley's speech had captured.

The Penal Landscape

By the start of the decade, chronic overcrowding had become the defining problem of the prison system, and the first issue on the everyday agenda of its senior managers. At over 73,000 in 2003,

---

[1] 'Governing governor' or 'number one governor': the governor in overall charge of a prison.

the average prison population was the highest then on record, around 28,000 more than a decade earlier, when numbers had begun to climb following a period of relative stability. Population pressures generated daily logistical crises in terms of cell provision and systemic efficiency. In addition, by stretching resources and moving prisoners to wherever space was available, overcrowding exacerbated the most damaging aspects of imprisonment, aggravated its normal frustrations, and hampered attempts to be humane and productive.

This rise in the prison population related more to an increase in punishment than an increase in crime, with longer sentences being applied for serious offences, and a greater use of custodial punishment for relatively minor convictions. Such trends were emblematic of the re-emergence of the prison in Western nations as a 'seemingly indispensable pillar of contemporary social order' (Garland 2001b: 14), reflecting a long-term transition from a culture of penal-welfarism to one of control, retribution, and penal populism.[2] The resurgence of the prison, and the form of its return, had not been expected. In the 1970s, penal-welfarism was the ideological spine of criminal justice, within a political discourse of social inclusion and citizenship (ibid.). Since the prison appeared costly, ineffective, and highly repressive as a mechanism of behavioural change and reintegration (Martinson 1974; Lipton et al. 1975; Bottoms 1995), if anything, the expectation was that its use would recede and its conditions would liberalize (Garland 2001a). But what began as a progressive critique of the failings of incarceration and the overuse of state coercion was quickly recast in a more retributive mould. Increasing public wealth, widening inequalities and declining social solidarities resulted in rising crime rates and a more punitive attitude towards those people who threatened the security and affluence of the prosperous. The professional middle classes, traditionally the natural allies of welfarism, felt besieged on the one side by crime and on the other by a tax system which seemed incapable of either aiding or regulating the unruly urban underclass (ibid.; Feeley and Simon 1992; Wacquant 2000, 2001a). Instead of becoming critiques of

---

[2] Needless to say, although some general patterns are discernible, penal trends are not globally uniform. There are substantial differences not only between the penal cultures and sensibilities of Europe and the US, but also within these continents (see e.g. Pratt 2002; Jones and Newburn 2006).

the prison's institutional existence, the failings of the prison led to a scaling down of its social ambitions and a shift in its means and conditions (Garland 1996).

The consequences of these shifting sensibilities have been complex. Garland (2001) suggests that while confidence in the prison's rehabilitative capacity has diminished, it satisfies more voluble demands that it incapacitates cheaply and effectively, and fulfils an expressive role as the symbol of collective reprisal (see also Pratt 2002; Feeley and Simon 1992). In part, it is argued, this reflects a change in the notion of the 'the criminal'. Offenders are less often perceived as victims of social deprivation who merit civic support and welfare interventions. Instead, they are more likely to be seen as dangerous individuals responsible for their own criminality and culpable for the suffering of others. With the interests of prisoners relegated below those of public security, treatment programmes and rehabilitative interventions are targeted less at the needs of the offending individual and his or her social conditions, but at safeguarding the public body (Garland 2001a; Robinson 2008). Strands of welfarism remain (Zedner 2002), indeed, they take on revised forms in practices such as restorative justice, 'resettlement' policies, 'offender management' and targeted interventions (Hutchinson 2006; Robinson 2008). But the organizing logic of the system has been reconstituted: from rehabilitation as a right of the offender, with the aim of social inclusion, to risk-management and social control in the service of the 'law-abiding majority'.

According to many accounts, then, imprisonment thus becomes a means of social exclusion rather than integration. Both physically and symbolically, the prison screens the lawful from the dangerous. Its increasing fortification helps to make sure that its occupants are expunged from the consciousness of the public. Ensuring that prisoners remain quarantined becomes more important than rendering them educated and employable (Feeley and Simon 1992). For Wacquant (2000, 2001a, 2001b), writing primarily about the US, this serves the interests of an economy in which the urban poor have become superfluous. That the American 'warehouse prison' does little beyond containment and control is indicative of its role as the primary means of managing and neutralizing an apparently irredeemable underclass (Simon 1993). Money is drained from welfare intervention to penal provision (Beckett and Western 2001). Accordingly, as the shield of the welfare state retracts, the penal canopy is stretched over the domains and disorders that are no longer sheltered or treated by what Wacquant (2001b) calls the 'left-hand' of the state. The prison comes to function as a carceral depot for the mentally ill, the drug- and alcoholic-addicted, and for the ghetto inhabitants whose life chances have been devastated by the spirals of incarceration that have emaciated their communities (Garland 2001b; Wacquant 2001a).

The prison has also been subjected to a number of reforms focused around effectiveness and efficiency. These reforms are aimed not at the elimination of crime but at making it manageable through 'systemic coordination' (Feeley and Simon 1992: 455) and 'technocratic intervention' (Cheliotis 2006: 315). They stem from a view that penal-welfarism was an expensive failure based on misplaced ideological commitment to a *social* mode of governance (Garland 2001a; O'Malley 1999). This entailed a belief that crime had social roots and social solutions, and that prisons themselves were best governed by understanding the social energies of the inmate society—its relationships, forces and interests (Simon 2000). The replacement for this is a mode of governance whose core logic is *economic*. One part of this framework is a more forceful insistence on the financial accountability and frugality of government institutions. Imprisonment should be cheap, cost-effective and able to justify itself to a parsimonious public—hence the appeal of incapacitation over rehabilitation (O'Malley 1999). According to this logic, it should also learn from commercial practices or have its functions contracted out to the private sector if viable and economical.

Another part of this new logic employs the language and techniques of economic production to prison administration. Described as 'managerialism' (e.g. McLaughlin and Muncie 2000) or 'new penology' (Feeley and Simon 1992)—the differences need not be explored here—this is a 'pragmatic, future-oriented, technologically supported approach to the management of organisations' (Liebling 2004: 377), in which the primary organizational focus is shifted from ends and outcomes to processes, systems, and outputs. For prisons, this means new and intensified forms of self-scrutiny and measurement, most notably in the shape of performance targets and internal audits that check compliance with organizational standards. Aided by information technology, these targets are set according to national frameworks and are appraised from the organizational nerve centre.

Many commentators have argued that this performance culture limits the prison's moral ambitions, decoupling the institution from social ends and implications (Feeley and Simon 1992; Nellis 2001), or mollifying calls for alternatives to prison by making imprisonment seem like a painless, neutral, or moral practice (Cheliotis 2008). These critics claim that managerialism encourages an obsession with smooth efficiency and internal, measurable processes, evaluating what the organization '*does*, rather than what, if anything, it *achieves*' (Garland 1996: 458, italics in original). Resettlement aims, for example, may be judged in terms of the provision of offending behaviour courses and work placements regardless of their quality or their impact on recidivism. Establishments become judged against their own standards, but the question of how these standards relate to moral questions and social goals may become obscured. However, performance management also carries a number of moral advantages. As Cheliotis (2006: 329) acknowledges, systemic efficiency may lead to the 'effective delivery of individuals' entitlements' and the minimization of discrimination in institutional decision-making. It places brakes on rogue management and can empower attempts to challenge traditional cultures. The defence of managerialism therefore argues that, if measures are set correctly and if a naïve fixation on targets can be avoided, it can be used as a means to humanitarian ends.

However it is regarded, the implications of managerialism for criminal justice personnel are the same. The centralization of decision-making, strict organizational oversight, and the tightening and formalization of guidelines means that both managers and their staff have less discretion to make localized decisions, to act against the grain, and to challenge or ignore the directives that come from above.[3] The era of maverick governors and individual fiefdoms has passed (Bryans 2007; Liebling 2004).

This mode of governance also has consequences for prisoners. Feeley and Simon (1992) argue that, rather than being dealt with as individual cases and diagnosed according to clinical need, prisoners are managed and assessed as 'units' using actuarial, predictive techniques. These calculate risk and dangerousness at the level of aggregate groups, within which prisoners are located on

---

[3] Although strictly speaking a singular noun, the term 'staff' is used as a plural form in this book.

the basis of personal variables. It is the management of the system, and the containment of risky sub-populations within it, that is prioritized. The neo-liberal logic that underwrites managerialism (and forms of 'governmental power' emerging throughout the field of crime control) is also applied to the discipline and reform of individual prisoners (Garland 1997; and see Foucault 1977, 1982, 1991). As fits the shift from welfarism to an ideology of individual responsibility and self-management, the prisoner is addressed as 'an entrepreneur of his own personal development, rather than an objectivized or infantilized client upon whom therapeutic solutions are imposed' (Garland 1997: 191). Responsibility for the causes and solutions of offending moves from the state towards the individual (Hannah-Moffat 2005).

Within these trends are a number of contradictions: between the demand for public protection at any cost and the insistence on frugality (Garland 2001a); between discourses of authoritarianism and ideologies that stress the need for prisoners to 'self-manage'; and between systems that are explicitly punitive, those that are merely incapacitating, and those that continue to pursue rehabilitative goals. O'Malley (1999) argues that these inconsistencies are indicative of two discernible currents within modern penality. One is neo-liberal and stresses individual responsibility, enterprise, accountability, and efficiency. The other is neo-conservative, emphasizing discipline, punishment, and state authority. It is the friction between them that helps account for the volatile and unpredictable nature of penal policy development. This also leaves room for alternative forms of penal practice, such as those committed to rehabilitation (O'Malley 1999), and for ideological constellations that combine old currents in novel forms. Along similar lines, Hutchinson (2006) criticizes accounts of penal change that imply some kind of decisive break between two discrete eras of rehabilitation and punishment. Such accounts—he argues—underplay the elements and undercurrents of retribution/coercion that existed in the period of welfarism, and overstate the demise and disappearance of reformist ambitions in recent years. Certainly, whatever lip service was paid to rehabilitative ideals in the British post-war period, the reality of prison life was often brutal, austere, and deeply punitive.

That rehabilitative ambitions have persisted in UK penality is also a reminder that general trends in penal politics cannot account for the specific character of national jurisdictions (Garland 2001a;

Jones and Newburn 2006). The kind of broad description provided above is inevitably partial and schematic. In the UK, for example, incarceration rates have not risen on the same meteoric trajectory as in the US, nor has the penal net been cast so disproportionately over minority ethnic populations. Likewise, although the prisons of England and Wales serve as storage zones for a number of social problems that are inadequately addressed in the community—in particular, mental illness and drug addiction—domestic welfare structures have been stripped away to a much lesser degree than in the US. Furthermore, as Liebling states, 'the reinvention of the prison has an internal as well as an external dynamic' (Liebling 2004: 40). Imprisonment's local terrain is shaped but not fully determined by the forces of macro-social change. It is also influenced by organizational politics, professional values, personal priorities, and historical contingencies.

The Local Terrain: The Prison System of England and Wales

The Strangeways Riot and the associated disturbances of 1990 provided the most significant point of departure for the formation of penal values and policy in the decade that followed. The period before the riots had seen the beginnings of institutional reform and increasing rumination on the aims and means of imprisonment (Bottoms 1990; Liebling 2004). Ironically, in Strangeways, the rise in prisoner expectations that regime improvements had brought about, and the placement of a reformist governor into a prison with a deeply intransigent culture, may have contributed to the disorder that followed (Carrabine 2004). But the extent of reform had been modest, and its value base unclear. Lord Woolf's (2001) Report on the disturbances affirmed that prisoner grievances across the system were forged by chronic overcrowding, unsanitary conditions, and indecent treatment by staff. Woolf's recommendations ranged from specific measures such as revised grievance procedures, improved sanitation, more constructive regimes, and better contact with families to an ambitious reform agenda, which would see a more integrated criminal justice system (CJS) and accredited standards throughout the Prison Service (Liebling 2004; Scott 2007).

Woolf also highlighted the need for clarity of purpose. Given that the aims of imprisonment—punishment, deterrence, incapacitation, and rehabilitation—appear contradictory, and its operational goals—security, order, decency etc—also seem conflictual, it is unsurprising that definitional clarity is difficult to achieve, let alone to translate into practice. Woolf's formula was 'security, control and justice', the latter term referring to humanity, fairness, and due process. In a context of liberal penal thinking, it was around this term that political discourse and institutional practice crystallized. Woolf's recommendations were broadly welcomed by penologists and commentators, and were accepted by the government (Liebling 2004). Arguably, they were broadly in line with internal Prison Service thinking, as represented by Ian Dunbar's influential book *A Sense of Direction* (1985). Galvanized into a process of relegitimation, the Prison Service placed renewed emphasis on the need for positive regimes, humane conditions, and good staff-prisoner relations. Prisons were fitted with telephones; provisions and conditions for visits were extended and improved; home leave opportunities were expanded. Officers were given a clear message that prisoners should be treated with respect and civility, and that this was the means by which order should be achieved.

As Liebling (2004) shows, it was in this equation of order and justice that the seeds of the punitive backlash were sown. The notion of a more respectful and humane prison became conflated with lax indulgence. In some establishments, officers avoided conflict and stopped asserting their authority; the supervision of prisoners was minimal. Levels of drug use, assaults, and escapes escalated. When a number of escapes occurred from high-security establishments, it became apparent that they had been made possible by the chronic under-enforcement of rules, based on the fear of disorder and the desire to ensure 'good' relationships. Despite Woolf's insistence on the importance of security, the misapplication of his message meant that, in practice, containment was eclipsed by other concerns.

By the mid-1990s, the Conservative Home Secretary, Michael Howard, needed little persuasion that the system's value-base should be overhauled. His instincts were highly anti-liberal, and they now converged with the evident disarray of the Prison Service and with a political moment when public sentiments were ripe for punitive exploitation. A new phase in penal policy and ideology was established. There was to be less reticence about using the prison as a means of incapacitation, even if this led to a significant rise in the population. In the service of deterrence, prisons were to be 'decent but austere', the latter word overriding the former. The balance of power was to be swung back to staff, without apology.

Liebling (2004) defines the ensuing period, from 1995–1999, as a time of recovery and safety, but one during which the politicized agenda of security of control continued to predominate (see Carlen 1998). It was in this context—on the basis of a remoulded penal sensibility—that a range of new policies was implemented. Woolf had proposed a number of situational measures, including smaller and more manageable wings, whose implementation was designed to prevent the outbreak and spread of unrest. These were now augmented with increased perimeter security, enhanced internal surveillance (e.g. CCTV), and further limits on prisoner movements around establishments. The prison 'tightened up' in other ways: prisoners were allowed fewer personal goods, visitors could no longer hand in property, and temporary release provisions became more restricted. Meanwhile, Woolf's vision of a system of high basic standards and rights, with extra incentives on top, was reshaped into a 'more punitive and restrictive' system of 'sticks and carrots' (Liebling 2004: 30). Entitlements were redefined as privileges. This policy—a form of governmental power which will be analysed in Chapter 4—was typified by the IEP scheme, launched in 1995, which gave prisoners the opportunity to earn benefits (such as in-cell television, more visits, and greater private spending) on the basis of good behaviour. In a similar vein, the introduction of mandatory drug testing had a somewhat authoritarian bent, designed not to aid prisoner detoxification, nor merely to regulate prisoner behaviour, but also to discipline those whose conduct fell outside acceptable boundaries.

Informed by the messages emanating from the political centre, these years also saw a shift in the moral culture of imprisonment. Among prisoners, perceptions of fairness and justice fell (Liebling 2004). In some establishments, staff violence returned. In contrast to the preceding period, the signal events of the time—most infamously, a female prisoner giving birth while shackled to a prison officer—shocked the public not because they indicated penal laxity, but rather harshness and inhumanity. When Martin Narey took over as Director General of the Prison Service in 1999, under a Labour government, he sought to re-insert a moral vocabulary to the prison domain. Centred on the notion of 'decency', this meant challenging staff racism and brutality, enhancing race relations among staff and prisoners, emphasizing the need for humane treatment, improving healthcare provision and standards of hygiene and treating prisoner suicides as a measure of the system's failure or success.

It also meant defining the prison as a place of reformation. Under Narey's stewardship, rehabilitation and 'resettlement' returned to the forefront of penal vernacular. Narey was a committed proponent of education and offending behaviour courses, and, on the basis of some initially encouraging research findings (Friendship *et al.* 2002), he expanded the number of cognitive behavioural programmes (e.g. the reasoning and rehabilitation (R&R) course). Within mainstream prison education, Narey promoted key skills and literacy. In the area of drugs, increased emphasis was placed upon detoxification and treatment. In 1999, a service known as counselling, advice, referral, assessment, and throughcare (CARAT) was placed in every prison in England and Wales. But this was not woolly liberalism, nor was it a return to the post-Woolf blueprint. 'Failing prisons' and their governors were managed robustly. Despite the increasing involvement in prisons of external agencies (in particular charities working on housing and employment issues), regimes did not 'open up' or liberalize. A preoccupation with issues of 'risk' meant that trust and innovation rarely trumped risk-aversion. From around 2002, resettlement began to take a backseat as public protection took the wheel of penal policy. Security remained a dominant concern—although senior practitioners argued that improvements in control and security enabled prisons to focus on decent treatment and reducing reoffending. As coming chapters will detail, there was no retraction of policies that sought to discipline prisoner behaviour, fragment collective interests, limit movements and possessions, and place upon prisoners much of the responsibility for their progression and conditions. Power remained firmly in the hands of the prison, with the principal goals being compliance, containment, and order.

The context of these developments is worth further elaboration. There was no shift in the *means* of prison administration. Bureaucratic managerialism had been the primary mode of operation since the late 1980s, and the main engine of organizational transformation. Performance targets had been established in 1992, to assist long-term planning, provide clarity for practitioners and offer a standardized measure of institutional outcomes; biennial process audits were introduced in 1995 (Liebling 2004). By the end of the decade, there was no change in these methods or in the intended dynamic of perpetual improvement. If anything, under Narey, the pace and scale of reform accelerated. Private sector competition became all the more entrenched as a means of forcing union modernization and promoting innovation and efficiency throughout the service. From 2001, all prisons were gauged according to a 'weighted scorecard', based on performance data, costs and progress, and designed to generate internal competition. Underperforming prisons were threatened with market testing (bidding to maintain their own contracts against private sector companies), or performance improvement plans.

Attempts were made during this period to tailor targets to a more liberal-humanitarian agenda. From 1998, the basis of targets shifted somewhat from 'inputs' to 'outcomes'; and in 2003, targets were introduced in relation to healthcare and suicide reduction (Liebling 2004). Meanwhile, the Prison Service's Standards Audit Unit augmented its practices with a 'quality of life survey' that had been developed to evaluate the dimensions of prison life that existing measures failed to address—'softer' outcomes such as respect, humanity, fairness, and personal development (ibid.). At the same time, rehabilitative ambitions were circumscribed by the managerial framework and subsumed to other interests (Scott 2007). In education, the focus on key skills and certificated qualifications—rather than arts, citizenship and more complex forms of self-improvement—partly reflected this preoccupation with what could be demonstrated and evaluated. Similarly, the standardization and accreditation of offending behaviour groupwork was consistent with a managerial culture of promoting interventions that were quantifiable and measurably effective. Most courses had a cognitive basis and were designed to modify modes of thinking and behaviour (Wilkinson 2005; Tong and Farrington 2006). Understanding the individual and dealing with underlying psycho-social issues was not the prime concern; one-to-one counselling was rare. The growth in the scope and power of psychological expertise in prisons was not in the service of prisoners and their personal problems, but primarily in the interests of public protection (see Chapter 4). Reducing reoffending and keeping the public safe required that rehabilitation occurred within 'an appropriate punitive envelope' (Halliday

2001: ii). Increasingly, prisoners became sites of potential risk rather than justice (Feeley and Simon 1992). The language of individual rights was eclipsed by a language of administration.

In the sphere of criminal justice, there had been little change in the political climate. Both main political parties continued to scrabble for the macho penal high-ground, creating a bi-partisan rhetorical chorus of 'tough' sentencing. The public was invoked simplistically as punitive and vengeful.[4] The progressive strands of New Labour policy on crime and justice were stated quietly, with qualifications, or were given little public airing. In relation to prisons, the need to 'reassure the public' and avoid negative publicity were the paramount concerns. In the government's public pronouncements, 'prisoner rights' were subordinated to those of 'victims', 'the public' and 'the law-abiding majority', as if these were simple distinctions. There was no return to the language of 'austerity' or to the 'prison works' mantra of the mid 1990s; and the government recognized the need for the system to have some legitimacy in the eyes of prisoners. But nor was there any hint of decarceration—the reduction of prison numbers. Narey saw overcrowding and under-resourcing as obstacles to the system achieving its ends, but he accepted a need to be accountable to 'public opinion' and the constraints set by pocket-book voting. In his public declarations, he expressed considerable optimism about what the prison could achieve, both for the prisoner and for society at large in terms of reducing reoffending.

This phase of penal politics—the time during which the Wellingborough study took place (2002–03)—can be characterized in various ways. For its proponents, including many new-breed practitioners, it represented a moral version of managerialism. It satisfied external demands to contain prisoners securely and cost-effectively, while fulfilling internal ambitions by delivering entitlements and decency. It set clear standards and provided mechanisms of accountability that were vital in an environment that could so easily 'go wrong'. 'Show me a prison achieving all its key performance indicators [KPIs][5] and I will show you a prison

---

[4] Research suggests that members of the public are not as punitive as newspapers and politicians tend to suggest, particularly when they are informed about the realities of criminal justice policy and are encouraged to reflect on matters of crime and punishment (see Hough and Roberts 1998).

[5] KPIs: key performance indicators; KPTs: key performance targets.

which is also treating prisoners with dignity', Narey declared (2001: 5), embodying this position. For some critics—including many old-style liberal governors—the external demands on the prison and its humanitarian proclamations were contradictory. The Service might be committed to human rights, improving race relations, and reducing distress, but such ends were unachievable with a rising population, limited resources, and the ascendance of security, compliance and control as the supreme requirements of the system. Managerialism fulfilled these latter demands more effectively than it guaranteed fairness and decency. For other critics, there was an inherent contradiction between managerial means and humanitarian ends, with the former always smothering the latter and lapsing into faceless, instrumental bureaucracy. From this perspective, Narey's equation was back-to-front: the focus should be creating decent prisons, and these prisons would meet well-toned measures. To chase targets on the assumption that this would deliver decency was a doomed exercise in bureaucratic myopia. How prisoners themselves experienced the managerial prison—or, to be precise, a particular prison of the era—is one of the main subjects of this book.

Summarizing the period, Liebling (2004) has used the terms 'effectiveness-plus' and 'neo-rehabilitation'. The first conveys the insistence on making the sentence 'effective' and the system efficient while relegitimating the prison through moral principles and practices. The second suggests that new versions of rehabilitation reflect the neo-liberal ideologies that have come to prominence throughout criminal justice and the wider political domain. Here, rehabilitation is conceived not as the responsibility of the state alone, or as something to be either imposed or merely offered, but something that the offender should take up willingly (Garland 1997; Hannah-Moffat 2001). But this definition of commitment betrays the complexity of this mode of rehabilitation, and exposes the coercive and instrumental means by which it is realized. As coming chapters illustrate, this is rehabilitation with edge.

In due course, the book will return to this form of governmental power, and to a more detailed analysis of how penal power has been reconfigured in practice by the developments outlined above. The purpose thus far has been to illustrate the context in which HMP Wellingborough operated: the values that framed its aims and the techniques used to achieve them. As Liebling notes (2004: 456), these have been combined in complex, conflicting and shifting ways: 'the tensions and oscillations between bureaucratic-managerial, punitive, and humanitarian values throughout this period have been striking'. The contradictions between goals of custody, retribution, and rehabilitation are a perennial concern throughout the prison estate. But they are perhaps most apparent within the Cat-C system, where prisoners are geared up for release under conditions where trust and autonomy remain limited, and where the outside world feels increasingly tangible, but the walls and fences still loom large.

The Category-C estate

In 2003, with around 18,000 places in thirty-three establishments, the Cat-C estate managed the bulk of convicted adult males and almost a quarter of the prison population in England and Wales. The system of categorization was based on the likelihood and consequences of escape, with prisoners placed into four categories from A to D. Category-C prisoners were 'those who cannot be trusted in open conditions, but who do not have the ability or resources to make a determined escape attempt' (Mountbatten 1966). Prisons were allowed to hold prisoners of lower categories than their institutional designation, which meant that Cat-D prisoners could be held in Cat-C establishments if population pressures and logistical considerations required it.

Category-C prisons varied considerably in terms of age, size, design, accommodation type, and level of physical security. Some establishments were acknowledged to be more secure and restricted than others, and more capable of handling potentially disruptive prisoners.[6] Relative to higher-security prisons, Cat-Cs had lower staffing ratios, lower costs (£20,060 per prisoner per year in 2002–2003, compared to £24,385 in category B prisons), and—despite

[6] Research into a 1994 riot at HMP Wymott suggested that certain prisoners were more likely than others to commit disciplinary offences, and that disturbances were more likely in establishments where such prisoners formed a high proportion of the population. These prisoners, known as 'Score 3s' were men aged under 25 at the time of conviction, serving sentences for burglary or robbery, and sentenced to less than four years. The Prison Service assessed how capable each establishment was of holding Score 3 prisoners, based on accommodation type (cells, dormitories), ease of supervision (relating to design and sight-lines), internal security (i.e. gates and zonal fencing), site size and dispersal, and special programmes (Marshall 1997). A prison's rating determined the proportion of Score 3s it was allowed to hold as a percentage of its certified normal accommodation.

a fortification programme since 2000—less imposing perimeter security (Dymond-White 2003).[7]

With the organization of the prison system based on security considerations and their attendant costs (as opposed to reintegration needs, for example), the existence of regimes that allowed greater autonomy was a by-product of other logics. Although, by definition, the security level of Category-C prisons differed from Cat-Bs, their official *remit* did not. The greater freedoms and opportunities found in these establishments derived from the aim to hold prisoners in facilities that were the least secure (and therefore least costly) as was possible given the need to prevent escapes. As Phil Wheatley, Director General of the Prison Service, explained:

It is about security basically, not about care and treatment.... It's not anything other than a cheaper way of delivering security.... It's very wasteful and very wrong to hold prisoners in higher security conditions than they need. [But] the judgment is about how we prevent people from escaping, that's what it really is about (Wheatley 2003).

It was consistent with this logic that the Category-C estate had only nominal 'functional management' (i.e. separate and dedicated management structure and oversight).[8] According to Wheatley, such an approach would risk Cat-Cs becoming 'sealed off' from surrounding prisons. This would undermine attempts to manage smoothly the sentence progression of prisoners within their local areas, and would make it more difficult for area managers to deal with issues of security, control and population pressure within their jurisdictions. With Cat-Cs thus integrated into the rest of the prison system, senior managers believed that the expertise required to run them was no different from what was demanded elsewhere in the estate (Wheatley 2003). This belief was also indicative of the increasing standardization of prison governance in recent years.

For prisoners, the Cat-C prison represented a transitional point of the sentence. Compared to the Cat-B 'Locals' from which

[7] Escapes from Cat-Cs were uncommon, with only two recorded across the estate in 2002–2003.

[8] At the time of study, one area manager held the title of 'Category-C policy lead'. His responsibilities included monitoring performance and the impact of policies across the Category-C estate. However, the realities of overseeing a large area office meant that it was difficult to fulfil this role (Dymond-White 2003).

many prisoners were allocated, there were more opportunities for education, training, and personal development.[9] Compared to the more secure Cat-B training prisons from which other prisoners had progressed, these opportunities were not necessarily better quality, but they did feel more relevant. Cat-C was the stage when prisoners could meaningfully contemplate re-entering the community or moving on to open establishments (Cat-Ds) where regimes offered much greater autonomy. Emphasis was placed on helping prisoners to find work and housing on release, and ensuring that family relationships could be maintained and developed. Prisoners were expected to demonstrate the personal responsibility and trustworthiness that less stringent security measures and lighter supervision required—for example, by developing life skills, addressing offending behaviour, and managing everyday conduct (e.g. getting to work on time, keeping cells clean) without the more oppressive oversight that characterized more secure conditions. In the Category-C estate in particular, the years before 2003 had seen a forceful assertion of the 'resettlement agenda' and a greater expectation that prisoners participated actively in their personal development and life management.

However, in terms of the freedoms that they allowed, and the amount of contact with the outside world that they permitted, Cat-C prisons were far closer to the Cat-Bs that supplied them than to the Cat-Ds they fed. External security was conspicuous, and had been enhanced in recent years not only to prevent escapes, but to stop drugs being thrown into establishments over perimeter fences. Concerns about drugs had also led to a greater use of CCTV, the introduction of a pin-phone system allowing greater scrutiny of calls, and improved intelligence links with local police forces. Internal security measures had also been strengthened to counter the threat of disturbances, particularly following a number of concerted incidents in the Cat-C estate in the 1990s. Compared to Cat-Bs, control was meant to be rooted less in the physical environment and direct supervision than in good relationships, active regimes, and 'dynamic security'— 'security resulting from well developed staff-inmate relationships

---

[9] Local prisons hold prisoners who are remanded in custody prior to or during trial, convicted prisoners with short sentences, and prisoners awaiting allocation to training establishments.

and an active regime' (Marshall 1997: 4).[10] However, with so many measures to restrict prisoners' movements, monitor their behaviour, and reinforce to them their captive status, prisoners regularly complained that Cat-C conditions did not indicate trust (Dymond-White 2003), and that their distinction from Cat-Bs was negligible.

Cat-C staff across the estate complained about inadequate resourcing, population pressures which hindered programme delivery and destabilized the population, and performance pressures which encouraged income generation and a maximization of employment figures rather than constructive work and meaningful training (Dymond-White 2003). Managers identified a number of reasons why Cat-C prisons failed to meet their ideals: physical plants and facilities were often poor; training opportunities could not always be tailored to the needs of the local economy or the expectations of prisoners; the allocation of prisoners could not always ensure that they were located close to the communities into which they would be released (a problem exacerbated by overcrowding); and staff retention and recruitment was difficult, with high-quality middle managers in particularly short supply, such that ideas and inspiration tended to be concentrated at senior levels. Good principal officers and senior officers were often given too much work, or were promoted too rapidly (interview, area manager).[11] Many of these problems were salient in Wellingborough, although the form they took was shaped by the prison's history, and the particularities of its culture, character, and preoccupations.

HMP Wellingborough

At the time of study, Wellingborough was a medium-sized prison, with certified normal accommodation for 516 prisoners, a limit it met throughout the fieldwork period. There were seven residential wings. E-wing had been constructed in the early 1970s, and served as an induction wing. F and G-wings had been built in

---

[10] Official documents also emphasized the role of 'meaningful incentives', such as improved accommodation, specialist programmes, work opportunities, and good facilities in securing consent.

[11] Principal officers are the highest-ranking uniformed staff, and are classified, along with senior officers, as 'middle managers'.

1999 and were used as the prison's voluntary testing unit (VTU). This VTU formed a separate block from the prison's main residential buildings, and had its own exercise yard. Wings A–E were housed in the prison's main building, linked by a corridor around which the education department was based. Most prisoners accessed the prison gym, workshops, kitchen, and visits room via this throughfare.

F and G were modern, quick-build versions of the classic Victorian prison design, with the landings and walkways visible from the centre. Although there were small areas at the end of each floor where phones were located and prisoners could sit around small tables, the main social areas were the ground floors, where there were pool tables, table tennis tables, and dart boards. Both F and G had three landings, and could hold ninety prisoners each in single cells. Wings A–D were designed in the shape of an H-block, with E-wing running separately below the bottom of the 'H'. Each had two residential landings, which could not be observed from other floors, split into three spurs. On these wings, the ground floor had no residential function other than one shared cell, but contained a food servery and small dining area, showers, staff offices, and recreational rooms for prisoners containing pool and table tennis tables. E-wing had two long landings, cut off from the ground floor where there were similar recreational facilities, a food servery, staff offices, and two rooms for induction training. The cells on A–E wings were smaller, darker and less well-ventilated than those on the VTU. All had internal sanitation (in-cell sinks and toilets). On E-wing, where most cells were shared by two prisoners, the toilet was in a small room separated from the main cell. On other wings, the toilet was located within the main cell-space. E-wing's capacity was around 100 prisoners. Wings A and B held up to fifty-eight prisoners each, and C and D up to sixty-six each, almost all in single cells. D-wing was for life-sentence and long-term prisoners deemed suitable for medium-security conditions.

In a 1997 Home Office research paper, Wellingborough was used as an example of establishments at the mid-point of the Cat-C security range: with 'moderate/good structural integrity, semi-secure or secure accommodation, and moderately dispersed layouts' (Marshall, 1997: 4). The prison's perimeter security was a metal fence (rather than a wall), topped with barbed wire and cameras. Prisoners were allowed to move unescorted from their wings to work and education, although officers and operational support grades (OSGs) were positioned along the main route to supervise mass movement, and this route did not touch the prison's external boundaries. At other times, prisoners could move around the prison unsupervised, but only with approval from staff, and via locked gates that only staff could open. Exercise in the prison's two yards was overseen by stationary officers. During association periods, prisoners were obliged to stay on their wings unless going to the gym, chapel, or evening education classes.[12]

Wellingborough offered vocational training and qualifications of various forms, including construction, welding, motorcycle care, horticulture, and kitchen work. There were also workshops where prisoners repaired supermarket trolleys, recycled the prison's waste, and placed small toys into plastic eggs for vending machines. The prison also had an IT workshop and working kitchens. Education was provided full-time, part-time, and in evening classes, covering a wide subject curriculum including philosophy, yoga, and foreign languages. Physical education was provided as a full-time course and as a recreational activity. Wages varied from £5 to £16 per week, with the most being offered for kitchen jobs, followed by trolley repair. Prisoners were able to spend private cash of between £5 and £15 per week, depending on their privilege level.

All prisoners in Wellingborough were sentenced. The majority (61 per cent) were serving sentences of between two and six years. Ten per cent were on life sentences or sentences of over ten years, and 12 per cent were sentenced to less than two years. The most common offences were burglary (23 per cent), drugs offences (20 per cent), robbery (14 per cent), violence against the person

[12] The standard prison day was as follows: all prisoners were unlocked at around 8am. At 8.30am, those involved in work, education, or courses left their wings, or began their work as wing cleaners or painters. Unemployed prisoners were at this point locked back in their cells. This period finished at 11.30am, at which point prisoners returned to their wings, or were unlocked from cells, allowing them to socialize on the wing or spend half an hour on morning exercise. Lunch was served on the wings at around 12.00pm. At 12.30pm, prisoners were locked up for an hour, while staff took their lunch hour. Between 1.30pm and 4.30pm, prisoners returned to their main activity, before being locked up again for an hour. The evening meal was served at 5.30pm—at this point, 'breakfast packs' were also handed out—from which time prisoners were free to associate on the wings (or participate in off-wing activities) until shortly after 8.00pm, when they were locked up until the following day.

(11 per cent), murder, driving offences, and theft and handling. Almost 60 per cent of prisoners were aged between twenty-one and twenty-nine; over 30 per cent were between thirty and thirty-nine. Most prisoners were from East Anglia and the Midlands. Fifty were foreign nationals (less than 10 per cent). Of all prisoners, 48 per cent were Church of England or Catholic. Seventy-three per cent declared themselves 'White British'; 19 per cent were Black African, Black Caribbean or Black Other, and around 5 per cent were Asian Indian, Asian Pakistani, or Asian Other;[13] 10 per cent were Muslim, 2.5 per cent Buddhist, and 1 per cent Sikh.

Institutional History and Development

HMP Wellingborough opened in 1963, on a 56-acre site on the outskirts of the small East Midlands town (pop. circa 50,000) from which it took its name. It was architecturally unobtrusive— visible from the dual carriageway that brought cars past the town, but otherwise an out-of-sight appendage to its suburbs. For twenty years, it operated as a borstal and then, in different guises, as a Young Offenders Institution until 1990, when it briefly held prisoners decanted from HMP Grendon, which was undergoing refurbishment. Thereafter, Wellingborough operated as a Cat-C training prison for adult, sentenced males.

These transitions set the terms for many of the problems of the following decade. As a borstal, Wellingborough had been 'extraordinarily traditional: reasonably humane, but [with] a very firm framework, with staff very much in control' (senior officer). Young offenders had been more boisterous than adult males, but also more deferential to authority and more respectful of the strict rules and boundaries with which the youth system operated. The therapeutic ethos of Grendon was highly alien to this, and the adult population that the prison held from this time was more recalcitrant in the face of staff authority.[14] Staff were left 'in bewilderment' (former governor), uncertain about their role and nervous about how to deploy their power.

---

[13] The term 'Asian' is used within this book to refer to prisoners whose ethnic origins were in the Indian sub-continent.

[14] HMP Grendon is unique within the England and Wales prison system in being the only establishment that functions as a democratic therapeutic community across all wings.

Their eventual reaction was to dig in, 'begin to develop an identity' (ibid.) and resist management attempts to transform Wellingborough into a kind of vocational college within a custodial setting. When a new management team took over the prison around 1993, it gave staff little confidence or security. The team was led by an experienced and well-liked governor, who, in his opening address to staff, said that he had reached the peak of his ambition and planned to remain at the prison until his retirement. Officers resented governors who they perceived as careerists, using the prison as a springboard for personal gain (a tendency they associated with new-style managers). But they were also critical of managers who appeared to lack the ambition that careerism engendered. Some staff interpreted the new governor's speech as a declaration that he was simply looking to 'kill time' (senior officer), and his management team failed to enthuse the workforce or impose its will on the prison.

As a consequence, power reportedly amassed in several areas: first, to a stratum of principal officers who exploited the lack of management oversight of staff detailing, and who were, by all accounts, 'running the jail' during this period.[15] As one governor recalled:

You had people making decisions here that made the hair stand up on the back of my neck: a principal officer was signing a licence to put a prisoner out on licence.... It should be the governing governor or the deputy governor or a governor of equal grade..., but that kind of decision was made as a matter of course, and the principal officer would make the decision knowing that they had no intention of passing it up the chain: '[Their view was:] this is my jail and you're not messing with my jail'. And a governor would walk into an area and they could openly challenge: 'what are you doing here, what do you want?' (Governor)

Second, power was apparently yielded to the prison's POA committee, which became increasingly intransigent about reforming work practices and developing the prison regime. Third, it accrued to prisoners, who had been granted relatively free movement, but with little structure or oversight. One officer recalled that: 'it got

[15] 'The Detail' or 'detail office' was where staff rotas and leave were organized ('detailing'). In the past, this had been done through a system of informal reciprocity: officers were given leave and time off on the condition that they were prepared to do late or weekend shifts. This informality—which reflected the 'homely' culture of the prison—contributed to accusations of 'rampant cronyism' and 'corruption' made by several officers when describing the mid to late 1990s. One member of senior staff claimed that it was 'just accepted that people would basically pre-book sickness—[i.e.] "its your turn to have a day off today"'.

to be a dangerous place for inmates and staff. There were gangs of people roaming the corridors. Awful…awful it were. It surprised me that no one actually got killed.' Staff felt they had neither control nor support, and began to take unilateral decisions to lock off wings (and prevent free movement) to regain some sense of power.

The period also saw a number of escapes from the prison. According to one member of staff, escapes had occurred in the past due to attempts to 'push out' the regime, for example, by allowing prisoners to use the sports fields. This, he argued, constituted a 'balanced risk' between liberty and security (of the kind that was acceptable during the period, although unimaginable by the time of the study). The more recent escapes, it was claimed, occurred due to basic security lapses: 'There'd be mesh sheets that would be three metres [high], that you could put against the fence and climb up; there'd be just a dozen sheets of that lying in the yard, not tethered to anything.' In 1998, Wellingborough was declared a prison in need of 'special managerial attention', with the emphasis on its management. An Inspectorate report in March corroborated concerns about the prison's quality and performance. Shortly after, Edd Willetts took over as governing governor at Wellingborough.

The style of the outgoing governor had been 'soft and amiable'. Willetts, who had worked at Wellingborough as an Assistant Governor and as the Deputy Governor, was known as a 'fixer' and a firm leader. Brought in to turn the prison around, Willetts was given the authority to overhaul the prison's management team. 'We found a place that was completely and utterly out of control.… Out of control in managerial terms', Willetts recalled. Systems and structures were not in place, the regime for prisoners was poor, and personal officer work was not being conducted. Willetts prided himself on his leadership skills, motivational ability, and a robust management style. He did not present himself as 'a systems man', but considered himself capable of creating a culture in which systems would be established and maintained by others. Within a short period of time, he challenged lax and improper practices, increased positive activity for prisoners, and negotiated a new staff profile (precipitating a showdown with the prison's POA leader, who was subsequently removed from office by union members).

The staff who remained in Wellingborough during Willetts' tenure remembered him as authoritarian but effective: 'Not everybody agreed with him, and maybe people hated him [but] he sorted this place out, gave it direction, and [brought it] screaming and kicking into the real world of what a prison should be' (senior officer). Officers saw his methods as tough, but most acknowledged that they were necessary and that the staff most hurt by them deserved their treatment. The majority felt that the prison had been transformed, that power had been restored to staff, and that practices and processes had been tightened up. A standards and security audit in June 2000 noted the significant effort that had gone into raising the prison's performance, while an unannounced inspection the following month commended the prison's governing team and staff on the improvements they had achieved. In the preface to this report, Chief Inspector Sir David Ramsbotham described Wellingborough as 'an example of all that is best about the Prison Service—dedicated staff doing their best for and on behalf of the public, based on assessments of what is likely to contribute most to a prisoner not re-offending on return to the community' (HMCIP 2000: 4).

Willetts left Wellingborough in May 2000. His successor was Peter Bennett, previously the Governor of HMP Nottingham and a Prison Service Assistant Governor since the mid-1980s. Bennett represented a generation of liberal-humanitarian governors who were primarily interested in the welfare of individual prisoners, and who used explicitly moral language to describe their work. A self-confessed 'woolly liberal', he had joined the Prison Service in 1983 with idealistic aspirations about what the job could achieve, but with deep ambivalence about entering what he saw at the time as a regressive organization: 'there were lots of associations with the Prison Service being racist, and being hard and cruel and everything else, [and initially] all of those stereotypes seemed to be totally and utterly confirmed'. Before entering the Service, he had completed a PhD in social anthropology, and he retained an air of benign academic eccentricity. His manner was thoughtful but confident, a style which some saw as friendly and 'fluffy' and others as reserved and inscrutable.

Bennett described his philosophy of staff management as follows:

I like to govern by means of a kind of invisible contract that you will do this for the prison and for me, and I'll make sure that you're a happy person and you'll be comfortable and that you're safe. I don't like the idea of people coming to work being scared or frightened or worried about what's going happen in the day.

It was this approach to leadership—one that emphasized support and personal relationships—that Bennett was asked to deploy at Wellingborough. The prison's turnaround under Willetts had required firm management, but there were concerns that the governing team had been too bullish and autocratic, keeping too much power to itself, and leaving uniformed staff feeling bruised and untrusted. Bennett's aim was to 'consolidate and de-alienate': to soothe the feelings of the workforce, without allowing sloppiness or the over-assertion of staff authority. Officers on long-term sick were coaxed back into work, the system of staff reports was improved, and efforts were made to make uniformed staff feel more appreciated. Attempts were also made to formalize and make more transparent the workings of the detail office, which had become the most confrontational site in the prison—one of the places where the power struggle between managers and staff was most apparent.

Bennett was also briefed to strengthen the cultural components of the regime. With the prison back under management control and the POA 'stunned into quiet efficiency' (former governor), attention could be given to areas such as race relations, the drug and anti-bullying strategies, and the IEP scheme.[16] This suited Bennett's inclination to be more 'culture-oriented' than 'systems-oriented'. He recognized the importance of performance management, and liked to 'latch on to that quite a lot to get things done'. At the same time, he was dubious about statistical measurement, believing that it could stifle creativity, and preferred to raise performance by changing a prison's overall ethos.[17]

A key part of Bennett's method was to 'use the drugs strategy to run the prison'. Despite his misgivings about target culture, he recognized the advantage of having a clear measure of progress around which all staff could energize, particularly at a time when rates of drug-taking were high. As well as providing

[16] A Standards and Security Audit in Spring 2002 highlighted strengths and improvements in the prison's race relations policies, drugs strategy, sentence management and planning, and security procedures (HMP SAU 2002).

[17] 'I've got to be measured to an extent, but in reality I want to rebel against it sometimes, and say, "well look, I can achieve that outcome, I can be successful, even though that doesn't measure very well and because I don't want to concentrate on how much bloody mail we respond to in seven days or whatever, and that's a lower priority for me".... Overall, I've delivered pretty well on the KPTs and so on, but sometimes I do put another priority in, instead of that.' (Peter Bennett)

a sense of purpose, the policy was aimed at making the prison safer and more ordered. Reduced levels of bullying and assault would be of mutual benefit to staff and prisoners. Meanwhile, with help from outside agencies, prisoners would be more capable of tackling the drug habits that lay behind many of their problems. Complementing this approach, which Bennett believed 'covered the whole of the Prison Service mission statement', he sought to build on the prison's strengths in the area of security (including very good relations with the local police). This would reduce the flow of drugs into the prison and would be popular with uniformed staff. Bennett reasoned that, once staff and prisoners felt secure, the developments he desired most would be easier to implement and would compensate for a more secure regime:

Prisoners often say to me 'this is a Cat-B prison', in terms of security. What I would say is that by having a prison that is controlled, you can make it a much fairer prison, and you can introduce lovely things for prisoners where they gain self-esteem et cetera, et cetera. You can have good offending behaviour programmes, you can get your writer-in-residence, and you can have a Youth and Community project,[18] you can introduce all these projects and allow all these initiatives to develop, and prisoners can do that simply because you feel fairly secure and safe and because staff feel better about it and are prepared then to develop the prisoner programmes more.

Bennett had been left with an able and confident management team, but its disintegration was the main difficulty of his tenure. While he was on holiday and without forewarning, two governors including his deputy left Wellingborough to join Willetts at HMP Holloway; two more were promoted to other establishments. The management team that remained—at one point, only four governors—was depleted and divided. Bennett brought in Paul Cawkwell as his deputy, a governor who he believed would complement his own strengths and weaknesses. In particular, Cawkwell was more performance-oriented than Bennett, and Bennett hoped that by placing him in charge of target delivery and financial planning, he would free himself to push his strategic vision for the establishment (in particular, the drugs strategy,

---

[18] The Youth and Community Project used prisoners (and some ex-offenders) to give presentations to school pupils and college students warning them of the dangers of drugs and crime.

the HOPE project and the Youth and Community project).[19] He also hoped that Cawkwell would manage some of the growing divisions within the senior management team. However, before Cawkwell started work at the prison, Bennett announced his own departure. The circumstances were unfortunate. Having pledged, in a full staff meeting, that he intended to remain at Wellingborough for at least two years, the following week he was offered the governor's post at HMP Grendon—the only job he would have taken at the time, and one for which his philosophy was well suited.

After a period during which Cawkwell took charge of the prison and pushed through a new staff profile, a new governor was put in place in October 2002 (when the fieldwork began). Jim Lewis came from Glen Parva Young Offenders Institution, where he had been the Deputy Governor and, for a period, the Acting Governor. Lewis had joined the Prison Service in 1986, initially as a basic grade officer, but with the intention of rising through the ranks to a management position. His father had been a prison officer, and, during the recession of the mid-1980s, Lewis had been attracted by the job security and conditions that he knew the Service could offer: 'There was nothing much [at the time] about a crusade, about prisoners or making things better; it was just going into a world that I knew something about, in very uncertain times.'

Despite the pragmatism of his initial motives, Lewis had soon become committed to the moral dimensions of his job: 'making sure that people have their rights, that people are treated properly, whoever they are, and [that] you do things for the right reasons and the right way'. His first post, at HMP Grendon, had convinced him of the value of respect and fairness in staff-prisoner relations. He also stressed the structural dimensions of decency: 'having enough sets of underpants, having enough time out of cell, not [sending] you up and down the country with no notice—very difficult things in the current situation [of overcrowding]'.

---

[19] The High Offender Partnership Enterprise (HOPE) project was a multi-agency initiative involving the prison, and local police, probation and drug and alcohol services. It was directed at persistent offenders whose crimes related to drug abuse, and its aim was to help reintegrate these men through intensive treatment within the prison's VTU and then on release. In prison, participants underwent frequent drug tests and drug counselling, and were given advice on housing, employment and family support. Counselling, treatment and testing continued in the community on release, and were closely monitored by local police.

Members of his senior management team consistently remarked on his integrity and his commitment to the Prison Service's moral agenda.

Such values were reflected in Lewis's personal style. He was open, thoughtful and consultative, and his manner was low-key, but he was 'single-minded' in the pursuit of his goals and used target culture to pursue them: '[my style] does have underneath it a bedrock of performance—we still have to achieve what we are here to achieve'. Relative to Bennett, he was more performance-oriented and more convinced that targets could provide direction and help achieve moral ends: 'there is no doubt in my mind that, since performance management, we have become better at doing what we should be doing. In all the prisons I have worked in, the performance is better than it was previously because of this.' Likewise, Lewis was more systems-oriented than his predecessor—less focused on liberal projects and individual care than on the systematic delivery of a humane regime. Nonetheless, he was lucid about the limitations of measurement and the dangers of excessive managerialism, and was sceptical that moral treatment was achievable through targets alone. Although very comfortable with the aims and philosophy of the Prison Service, Lewis was also uneasy about the disparity between these ideals and what was achievable in practice given overcrowding and tight resourcing.

In his interview for the post, Lewis spoke to the national issues of the period, emphasizing the need to prioritize prisoner resettlement while maintaining a safe and predictable regime. Preparing prisoners more effectively for release meant addressing their needs and establishing greater links with outside agencies (police, probation, drug agencies, resettlement organizations), but the prison's custodial imperatives remained paramount. On local issues, Lewis had been briefed that the prison's performance had tailed off slightly, but that it was a relatively efficient and happy establishment. Once in post, he discovered a prison that was ostensibly friendly, with little overt conflict, but which harboured a range of problems and resentments that had sedimented over previous years.[20]

---

[20] An independent consultant, brought in to gauge staff concerns, reported with surprise that the prison appeared a relaxed institution, but that the complaints he heard from staff were the same as those he heard when at large Local prisons with much more difficult populations, more complex tasks, and more dilapidated facilities.

The first of these was the state of the senior management team, which had little stability or confidence, and little corporate memory on which to draw. Most governors were new to their roles, and all were over-burdened with work due to the unfilled posts around them. In addition to the other recent changes in management, Bennett's departure had left officers feeling insecure and in need of direction. The incumbent governors were perceived by uniformed staff as 'nice people' with decent values and good intentions, but not the strong, purposeful leaders that they wanted.

Lewis had also inherited a serious staffing shortage. In March 2002, an external resources review had demanded almost £300,000 of efficiency savings. Most of this took the form of staff cuts. Governors acknowledged that, on paper, the prison could be run with fewer staff. However, with many officers already on long-term sick, the prison's active workforce was smaller than official figures suggested. The staffing predicament was exacerbated by a number of factors. First, recruitment was difficult. The area was economically vibrant, with low unemployment and high living costs, but no outer-London pay weighting. Second, the Prison Service had recently changed its recruitment procedures, allocating staff centrally instead of allowing establishments to shape their own staffing. Wellingborough had no new accommodation on which to base its appeal for a more generous staff allocation. Meanwhile, through the imposition of an unpopular work profile (in October 2002) and Cawkwell's strong management of industrial relations, Wellingborough was doing better than most prisons in keeping wings open, maintaining its regime, delivering against targets, and minimizing the hours of overtime it owed to staff. As one governor noted—and as I discuss in more depth below—the prison 'was a victim of its own success'. The impression it gave to its area manager was that it was coping with its staffing level. In truth, it was struggling, with staff feeling increasingly alienated.

A further set of difficulties was caused by the prison's recent management culture. Bennett had increased the amount of authority at lower levels of the organization, and had made staff feel more valued by senior managers. However, with governors reluctant to hand back control to uniformed staff, the devolution of power had been partial and cautious. Principal officers appreciated a more supportive culture, but remained frustrated at being excluded from senior decisions. Many officers felt bullied and beleaguered. Under Cawkwell—whose style was polite but uncompromising—some claimed that the prison had reverted back to management by autocracy. This feeling was intensified by the firm style of the centralized detail office, whose power increased at a time of staff shortages, when shift and leave decisions were all the more significant for staff.

This situation had a number of effects. Officers and line managers felt over-managed, distrusted, and uncertain. They felt 'browbeaten' by managers, yet they had little stability at senior levels from which to take guidance. The result was nervousness about making decisions and using initiative, and a vacuum of power among the prison's middle-management strata. Incoming governors were stunned by the kinds of judgments that senior officers consulted them on and the actions for which they asked permission: updating the rota for the Listeners scheme, for example, and deciding whether to admit visitors who had forgotten to bring identification.[21] The absence of confident authority on the residential units was compounded by the nature of staff shortages. Middle management had been hit particularly hard by resource cuts. Senior officers now covered two wings rather than one when on duty, leaving many officers feeling adrift. With so many going sick, senior officers were frequently forced to 'act down' to cover basic grade responsibilities. In turn, POs and governors were assuming duties normally carried out by less senior staff. The residential governor, for example, was maintaining anti-bullying and suicide prevention strategies in order to prevent them from stagnating. With normal working structures in this way subsiding, and managers disillusioned, meetings went unarranged and systems of staff management and training faltered.

A second outcome was a decline in the morale of uniformed staff during the period of research, and an increase in their resentment about treatment and conditions (in particular, the difficulty of obtaining ad hoc leave). Much of this was directed at the detail manager and the deputy governor, who faced daily, overt antipathy. Discontent also took shape in an increasingly antagonistic POA committee, whose resurgence

---

[21] The Listeners Scheme trains prisoners to offer confidential support to their peers, with backing and guidance from The Samaritans.

represented a return of suppressed sentiments. Bennett had left 'without having healed all the bruises' of the previous era, and his departure had left the skeletal management team vulnerable to resistance. Lewis had mistaken the POA's initial lack of resistance for assent: 'when in fact what I should perhaps have presumed was a build up of resentment and bitterness'. His style of caution and collaboration were at odds with the more direct methods of his deputy. The POA committee was left feeling distrustful and impatient, and was increasingly aware that divisions within the governing team could be exploited. When it began to vent its frustrations—many of which Lewis acknowledged as legitimate—it did so with considerable animosity, resulting in a number of fairly acrimonious battles about policies such as the staffing of evening exercise.

Low morale was expressed through staff practices and attitudes. On the wings, many staff retreated to the offices, and carried out their duties with little enthusiasm or attention to detail. Roll checks often had to be redone, disrupting the prison's routine. Security procedures were carried out casually. During the early phases of the study, the prison was dirty and littered. Practices on the wings were sloppy. Many staff felt that managers had little interest in their concerns or in the pressures and realities of their working lives. Bennett's priorities had lain beyond the residential areas of the prison, for example, in recreational education and the Youth and Community project. As he acknowledged, he had not been a particularly visible governor, and had spent less time on the wings than in some other areas of the prison. While the education staff had adored him, the uniformed staff were more ambivalent. Officers were impatient for clear, visible management, but also for nurture and appreciation.[22] With Lewis taking time to find his feet and recruit more staff, officers continued to

---

[22] One governor observed that uniformed staff seemed to carry a cultural memory of the time when the prison served as a total institution for officers, who lived in prison houses maintained by prison works staff, had their lawns cut by prison gardeners, and socialized in the prison mess. The prison was a place of nurture as well as work. Another commented that staff wanted 'to be pampered' and expected governing governors to be 'father figures'. It is interesting in this regard that maternal and paternal language is often used within prisons. Carrabine (2004), for example, mentions that HMP Strangeways was nicknamed 'The Lady' by its uniformed staff, and that governors often describe officers and prisoners as behaving like sibling rivals.

feel alienated and undervalued, and took little pride in their core responsibilities.[23]

Once in post, Lewis therefore found himself fighting a number of unexpected fires and handling a far greater workload than he had envisaged. He was making decisions which 'should have been a matter of policy. At one point I just felt that everything was landing on my desk for the whole jail.' Although he knew that his role was to provide the prison's strategic direction rather than handle low-level logistical problems, he was keen to 'find out what was going on. [And] I didn't seem to have anybody else who was doing it.' On top of his initial aspirations for the prison, he had to recruit more officers, prevent existing staff from leaving, improve communication, bolster his governing team, rebuild basic structures and clarify lines of responsibility. Operationally, his main priority was to keep the regime going without locking down wings. However, staffing problems meant that 'it was very hard just to cover the basic work'. Doing so, and maintaining a predictable regime, meant taking officers from areas such as drug work, induction training, resettlement and sentence planning to work on the wings: 'everything is done at the cost of something else' (Lewis).

An Inspectorate report published in October 2003 summarized the state of the prison thus. Wellingborough was a safe and respectful establishment, with good reception and induction procedures, a strong education department, good security procedures, a relatively low rate of drug use (a positive rate of 5.4 per cent), some innovative programmes (such as HOPE and

---

[23] A staff quality of prison life survey was conducted by the author and colleagues in August 2002. Wellingborough's scores were contrasted with those of Highpoint South, a prison considered similar to Wellingborough. Wellingborough scored less well on all dimensions apart from 'safety and security', and 'sympathy for vulnerable prisoners'. Scores were notably poor on 'opportunities to use initiative', 'level of responsibility and authority', 'involvement in decision-making', and 'loyalty to the prison, governors and the Prison Service'. Perhaps most strikingly, officers reported higher levels of trust in prisoners than in governors, and said they felt more respected by prisoners than by line managers and governors. In their responses to open-ended questions, the most frequently-made comments related to poor communication, lack of respect from management, and lack of management continuity. In carrying out the survey, it was notable that officers were paranoid about issues of confidentiality, claiming that 'governors would do anything they can to trace it back to individuals'.

the Youth and Community Project), and a growing emphasis on resettlement work.[24]

However, Wellingborough was not meeting its role as a training prison. Work spaces existed for 68 per cent of prisoners, but only half were in work or education at any one time. The rest were locked in their cells for long periods. Wages for education and courses were considerably lower than for menial workshop labour, discouraging prisoners from taking up more productive activity. The report acknowledged that the 'training' role was undermined by the rate of prisoner turnover: 43 per cent of prisoners were in the establishment for less than one month, and only 15 per cent for more than a year, making resettlement work difficult. But several areas of weakness directly reflected the prison's staffing problems. Race relations policy and procedures had been neglected, resettlement work had languished, and anti-bullying work was not being done effectively. Some officers had not been allocated time for personal officer work since November 2002, and almost 40 per cent of prisoners said they had never met their personal officer. The system for dealing with the needs of lifers had faltered, and town visits were no longer occurring. The CARAT team was understaffed. There were long delays in the handing out of property. Release on temporary licence was being underused (with only nine between January and June 2003), although Home Detention Curfew (HDC, or 'tagging') was being used more effectively.

The report also commented on staff-prisoner relations, which were described as 'relaxed and friendly'. Of prisoners, 70 per cent, had said there was a member of staff to whom they could turn for help and 65 per cent that staff treated them 'well' or 'very well'. At the same time, the report noted that 'there were few signs of staff initiating contact or challenging prisoners' behaviour in any

[24] 79 per cent of prisoners had never felt unsafe while at Wellingborough, a figure well above the average for training prisons (67 per cent). One in five prisoners had been victimized by another prisoner, primarily in the form of remarks, rather than physical abuse (which made up only a quarter of cases). 17 per cent reported having been victimized by staff, mainly through insults about where they were from or their race/ethnicity. No prisoners reported physical abuse from officers. Force was used relatively little, only fourteen times since January 2003, with control and restraint techniques employed on seven of those occasions.

positive way'.[25] Officers had told the inspection team that they felt themselves becoming merely 'turnkeys' (HMCIP 2003: 14). Reporting the Inspection team's initial feedback to a full staff meeting, Lewis stressed that there were many pockets of good practice but that the prison was not meeting its potential. Staff-prisoner relations remained fairly positive, he said, yet staff seemed unaware that the quality of these relationships constituted work of which they should be proud.

Conclusion

Students of the prison have consistently argued that its goals are mutually incompatible, and that the pursuit of any one aim is likely to compromise others. In the US, it is argued, as the prison has been re-invented as the essential institution not just of criminal justice but political governance in general (Wacquant 2001b; Simon 2007), rehabilitation has been discarded in the interest of cut-price containment and public retribution. Some of the more 'catastrophic' (Hutchinson 2006) announcements of the death of welfarism and the emergence of the 'warehouse' prison apply in some parts of the US and Europe more than others.

The UK terrain has been shaped in some distinctive ways. By the early years of the 2000s, a penal pendulum that had swung a number of times in the previous decade had slowed. It rested in a position that combined elements of neo-liberalism, authoritarianism, and welfarism. Prisons should be safe and constructive, and treatment should be fair, respectful, and legal. The institution should encourage prisoners to take responsibility for their offending behaviour, to tackle their addictions, and to prepare themselves for release. Yet the interests of the public pre-dominated. The need for the prison to justify itself to external stakeholders took precedence over its need to legitimize itself to its inhabitants.

[25] A quality of prison life survey, carried out with prisoners by the author and colleagues at the start of the fieldwork period in August 2002 suggested similar strengths and weaknesses. Wellingborough scored well on 'respect', 'safety', 'dignity', 'entry into custody', 'development (family)', 'drugs strategy', and 'care for the vulnerable', but poorly on 'trust' and 'development (programmes)'. Relative to three other Cat-C training prisons, including one high-performing establishment, one prison considered to be performing poorly, and one seen as relatively similar to Wellingborough, the prison was the second-best rated establishment.

The rights of prisoners were weighed up against increasingly stringent notions of public protection. Riots and escapes were publicly intolerable, holding the system hostage to political embarrassment, even when measures of security and compliance appeared increasingly restrictive and illiberal. Safety-first was the dominant principle of the estate. Interventions served the interests of 'reducing re-offending' as much as they targeted individual needs and wellbeing. Ambitions to reform and contain were to be met while budgets were increasingly scrutinized for potential savings, and without upsetting public demands that imprisonment should not be 'easy'.

In theory then, decency and legitimacy should rise *at the same time* as prisons should become more secure, more controlled, and more confident that those they released would not threaten public property and safety. And these aims should be met as the system moved steadily and predictably towards full capacity, and as heavier sentencing reduced the possibilities of efficiency savings (Brownlee 1998). In short, prisons had the task of achieving more, with greater numbers of people and tighter resources. Questions about the feasibility of these aims, their potential inconsistencies, and the appropriate trade-offs between them seemed to slide out of political debate and policy discourse. (Once concerns about security have ratcheted up relevant measures, it appears more difficult to ratchet them down.) There was little sense that the prison was practically and symbolically overloaded, and little public outcry from practitioners about the demands of their brief. As the chapter that follows suggests, governors felt unable to speak out against or challenge the increasing burdens of their post.

Wellingborough's priorities reflected shifts in national policies and priorities. Security procedures tightened, power was returned to staff, systems were stabilized, and matters of interpersonal and material decency returned to the agenda. These priorities were clearly prescribed and tightly managed from the organizational centre. The prison's problems likewise echoed those found across the prison estate: over-crowding, under-resourcing, conflict between uniformed staff and governors, changes in management personnel, an unstable prisoner population often located far from home, and the difficulties of fulfilling the functions of a 'training prison' within the constraints of policy and budget. Governors operated within fairly narrow parameters. In Wellingborough, the styles and characteristics of individual governors—to caricature somewhat, the gentleman governor, the fixer-leader, the liberal-humanitarian, and the modern manager—were subordinate to national decrees and priorities in shaping the prison's strategic objectives. At the same time, the prison's everyday culture, ethos, and power dynamics were not reducible to national patterns. These features require further elaboration.

3

Institutional Culture and Power in HMP Wellingborough

Sparks *et al.* (1996: 306) argue that most overviews of penal problems lack 'any developed awareness of the ways in which the broad outlines of policy and the local construction of social relations in prison interact'. The aim of the previous chapter was to draw the general contours of recent penality and provide some detail about the history, function, and priorities of HMP Wellingborough. The aim of this chapter is to take a step from the general to the specific—to move from policy abstractions, official declarations and matters of context to more concrete issues of how power and culture took shape in the prison.

The chapter begins by characterizing Wellingborough's general ethos, and moves on to outline the views and practices that were characteristic of its uniformed workforce. It describes how organizational aims (such as decency, control, and rehabilitation) and techniques (in particular, targets) were perceived by uniformed staff and managers, how both groups experienced their authority, and how relationships with prisoners were structured by these factors. The chapter explains some of the pressures and constraints on the prison's workforce, describes the relationships between staff strata, and presents an initial analysis of the nature and location of institutional power. These features of the prison are then linked to specific institutional factors and more general characteristics of the managerial era.

Wellingborough's Culture, Values, and Practices

HMP Wellingborough did not have a strong identity within the Prison Service. It was not known to be either consistently high-achieving or under-performing; it had experienced no major incidents, and, unlike some Cat-Cs, it did not carry a reputation as a 'dumping ground' or 'punishment prison'. Staff often commented that the prison was seen as something of a 'sleepy hollow', serving an area with few large cities and sited on an anonymous edge of a small town. The prison was often said to have a 'family feel'. An uncommonly high number of staff were related to or in relationships with each other, and many had only worked at Wellingborough during their prison careers. The prison also had a relatively high proportion of female officers (almost 30 per cent) and operational support grades (OSGs), giving it a less macho feel than many other establishments.

Wellingborough's uniformed workforce was well balanced in terms of age, with some notable differences between the orientations of staff of different experience. Many older officers were nostalgic for an earlier era of imprisonment and for the clear lines of authority of the past. These officers often held prisoners in low esteem, emphasizing their greed and moral turpitude and supporting the maintenance of a clear status distinction between prisoners and staff. Many felt that the regime was too 'soft', and that prisoners were being 'spoon-fed'. Despite these views, they were not the brusque, indifferent 'dinosaurs' dominant in many establishments, nor the 'hardline' staff who imposed rules to the letter (see McLean and Liebling 2008). Some were exceptional at dealing with prisoners, handling volatile situations and ensuring the calm maintenance of the daily routine. Many attributed this 'jailcraft' to the prison's borstal days and to years of 'life experience', often accumulated through time in the armed forces. They bemoaned the inexperience of younger officers, who they saw as socially naïve, careless in their use of authority, and incapable of using discretion appropriately. As one old-timer lamented:

They seem more concerned with getting the computer right, rather than talking to inmates. If it says so, they do it. If it doesn't, [they'll] nick them. Never mind about talking to them to find out what's wrong. There are some that wouldn't give [prisoners] the time of day.

These older officers frequently complained that 'paperwork and computer work' had become more important than 'getting on that landing, and going and talking to them'. In this respect, they felt out of touch with developments in custodial work. Some were recognized by their colleagues as having excellent interpersonal skills that compensated somewhat for their other deficiencies. Others were regarded as lazy and half-hearted (Crawley 2004a), doing little more than drinking tea and tiding things over until shifts were completed.

These 'avoiders' (Liebling and Price 2001) and officers with punitive personal views separated private feelings from professional behaviour by invoking ideas of public duty and loyalty to the Service.[1] Such officers saw their work in vocational terms, as a 'job for life'—an attitude that could engender loyalty but could also signify a somewhat static notion of what the job should entail. Terms of this kind were used far less often by younger and more recent recruits. These officers were more likely to have entered the Prison Service from light industry and service sectors than from the military (see Crawley 2004a). The majority described their initial motivations for entering prison work in instrumental terms, as a way of 'paying the mortgage' and securing a good pension. Many saw the Prison Service as one among a number of career providers that might offer job satisfaction and personal development, but would be discarded if it failed to do so (see Sennett 1998; Bauman 2000). Such officers rarely expressed pride in the uniform or a strong sense of corporate loyalty:

I've never even thought about being proud of it. I just come in, do my work, do whatever I can for other people and go home.

Some officers talk about having a kind of loyalty to the service and a pride in the ....

I've got no loyalty...it's all about my own self. [I like to do] a good day's work, but I don't even think about doing a service to the Queen, to the country, anything like that, it's all about me, how it makes me feel, you know.

For these younger staff, decency was grounded as much in a personal sense of what constituted moral behaviour as in a professional notion of service. Some were the most committed and professional staff in the establishment. Few reported having joined in order to 'make a difference', but a number operated with drive and humanity, which they attributed to private values about what effort and treatment was 'right'. Other young officers—both

---

[1] It was these officers who most often bemoaned the invisibility of their labour, and the lack of public recognition that they were in effect an 'emergency service' (see Crawley and Crawley 2008). They were also most sensitive to issues of symbolic recognition, for example, the fact that, at the time of study, the Golden Jubilee Medal could be awarded to members of the Armed Forces, and the three main emergency services, but not to Prison Service staff.

male and female—were highly rule-governed, operating without punitive 'edge' but with little empathy or diplomacy.

The tone of Wellingborough's staff-prisoner relations was set by the benign cohort of its experienced workforce, and was maintained through mundane conversation and censure. Derision was expressed for officers who shirked responsibilities, who cherished their power unduly, and who ignored or alienated prisoners. Excessive machismo was also ridiculed. Officers on one wing mocked the posturings of those officers 'who swagger around as if they've got a pole stuck up their arse'.[2] A new recruit was reprimanded for starting a shift by announcing that it was 'time to let the animals out of their cages'. As colleagues discussed after the event, language of that kind was not part of Wellingborough's ethos.

It was in such ways that a basic degree of interpersonal respect was embedded throughout Wellingborough's culture (see HMCIP 2000; 2003). In its reception unit, the area of the prison where culture is first set, the tone was polite and informal. Prisoners were not coldly 'processed', nor was their status and powerlessness deliberately reinforced.[3] 'You *know* you're in prison when you're being called by your second name', one prisoner commented. Many prisoners remarked that the procedure was less dehumanizing than in most establishments, and commented that this typified initial encounters with officers. 'This is the only prison I've ever been in where they treat you with respect before you treat them', one prisoner observed. On the induction wing, officers took pride in 'giving a chance' to prisoners with records for non-compliance, and celebrated their ability to 'break the cycle' of mutual mistrust. It was rare to hear officers using abusive language towards

---

[2] This is not to say the officer culture was not, in all manner of ways, fairly macho. Many officers took pride in activities such as burping and yelling as loudly as possible to gain prisoners' attention. At lunchtime, while education staff tended to use the prison's gym to play badminton or short-tennis, officers were more likely to push weights. Several were training for 'hard-man' and triathlon events. Conversations revolved around sport, DIY, sexual innuendo, and domestic issues such as personal finances, television, the news, holidays, and the politics of the prison. Female as well as male officers participated in these conversations and practices.

[3] This was in contrast to reception procedures I had observed several months earlier in another Cat-C training prison, where prisoners were left in little doubt that officers were in charge and underwent a much more deliberate process of status degradation.

prisoners, provocation was very uncommon, and wings never felt acutely tense. Prisoners frequently contrasted the friendliness of Wellingborough officers with the culture of more traditional Cat-Cs, where 'screws go round speaking to you with attitude, and calling you wanker and dickhead, and names like that' (Leon).[4]

Wellingborough was consistently described as a 'laid-back' and 'easy-going' establishment:

This is one of the best jails I've ever been in. The first impression, and the attitude of staff, you're on first name terms with most of the staff and they're quite relaxed. (Alfie)

It's laid back. It's like a different world compared to other jails. When I first come here I couldn't believe how the officers were, I couldn't believe how they spoke to you—they spoke to you like normal people; if you wanted help on something they'd go and find out for you. (Dom)

The officers here are very easy-going. Whereas [prison X] is a screws' nick: they'll just bust in anybody's cell on the slightest whim. And they'll be carried off and you'll never see them again. Here they're a bit more laid back and a lot more easygoing. (Noah)

Relative to other prisons, Wellingborough was not an authoritarian establishment. Officers sought to persuade rather than threaten prisoners into everyday compliance, and took satisfaction from the informal relationships that they cultivated. 'Direct orders' were uncommon, reversion to force (through official techniques of 'control and restraint') was rare, and staff did not 'get on your back'.[5] For many prisoners, it was 'a soft jail, but in a good way' (prisoner, fieldwork notes)—a place where one would not be provoked into conflict.

Prisoners attributed Wellingborough's relaxed atmosphere to a number of factors beside staff attitudes. Excluding a phase at the start of the fieldwork, the prison was not awash with drugs, making it considerably less edgy than many establishments ('street jails'). Second, it was a prison where all men except those on the 'basic' privilege level were allowed to wear their own clothes.[6]

---

[4] 'Screws': a derogatory term for officers.

[5] In HMP Stafford, adjudications often related to the use of staff authority, with prisoners frequently charged for disobeying lawful orders e.g. to go to work. Such charges were very rare at HMP Wellingborough, illustrating this difference in the use of power.

[6] In most prisons, the IEP scheme operates with three levels: basic, standard, and enhanced.

This policy had a significant impact on prisoners' self-perceptions and their view of their environment: 'it just makes you feel yourself; you feel more at home in your own clothes' (Leon). The use of such vocabulary also related to more formal features of the regime. Evening exercise was rarely cancelled, and—unlike some other Cat-Cs—there were not strict rules about where prisoners could stand or how they should address staff.[7]

However, prisoners consistently complained that Wellingborough's regime was restricted and that they had expected 'a bit more freedom' (Connor). Exercise areas were small, there were few opportunities to get fresh air, and prisoners could not mingle on other wings during evening exercise. As in many other Cat-Cs, in the shadow of barbed-wire fences, the prison had large grounds, but these were off-limits to prisoners except in special circumstances.[8] Many commented that, in terms of perimeter security and freedom of movement, the differences between Wellingborough and most Cat-Bs were negligible: 'the only difference is you can walk to work by yourself. You can walk along the corridor. But you're not getting any more trust really' (Ross).[9] Prisoners arriving from Cat-B training prisons felt that life in Cat-Cs was pettier and more repressive, and that Cat-B staff had given them more 'slack': '[they] don't get on your back [in Cat-B], because they don't want riots, they don't want trouble' (Nathan).

Prisoners arriving from Cat-B training prisons were also bemused to find that they were not allowed to use tools or make items that had not been barred in higher-security prisons. Den complained that he was not allowed to have a pottery mask, 'in case I try to escape!' 'Security' was considered the meta-excuse of the institution. Staff were certainly preoccupied with security issues. Any decrease in the number of Security Information Reports

---

[7] In some other Cat-Cs, prisoners were given evening association only on alternate days; and in one Cat-C at which many prisoners had spent time, prisoners were disciplined if they stepped over lines painted onto the floor without permission.

[8] On one occasion, prisoners had the frustration of being locked up to allow staff to play an inter-prison football match on a pitch that was visible to them from their cells, but to which their access was highly restricted.

[9] Matt joked about the number of fences that surrounded the wings: 'it's like the Grand National or something. You'd fucking bleed to death before you got out over there!'

was interpreted as a failure of staff to be sufficiently alert. Many officers assumed that all prisoners were 'up to no good': 'Ninety-five per cent have security reports written on them, and the rest we just haven't caught yet!', a security officer commented.

Terms such as 'relaxed' and 'laid back' were also used by officers, intimating both the positive and negative aspects of Wellingborough's culture. First, this vocabulary signalled a reluctance to question established ways of operating and a comfort in the prison's traditions. One senior officer outlined this tendency as follows:

You can have [bedding] posted in, but you can't have it handed in on a visit. Why? Nobody can answer that question. 'Ooh, well we don't do it like that.' They're very backward looking. They will say 'oh, we used to do it this way and it worked.' You can tell [most] staff have never worked anywhere other than Wellingborough. They're very...dogmatic, very set in their ways.

Second, it reflected a slightly lethargic culture, in which officers were slow to take initiative and resolve problems. [10] Staff at all levels of the prison identified this ethos—'a mañana type attitude—things don't always get done as quickly as they might' (senior officer)—as part of the 'Wellingborough way'. The following example was given by a senior officer:

We've got eight [new prisoners] coming in. So I rang the VTU, and they went 'oh, we haven't got any TVs. If they want to come down they're going to have to know they haven't got any TVs'. 'Well why haven't you got any TVs?' 'Well, they broke them'. 'Well why haven't you fixed them then?' 'Well we've been told we've got to wait until April'. 'How long have you known that you haven't got any TV's?' 'Oh, a week' 'So why didn't you try to get them repaired?' 'Well it's not our job.' In this prison, staff do not use their own initiative. Basic stuff doesn't get done.

Although Wellingborough's officer culture was largely benign, this took a passive rather than active form. Bennett had noted that staff harboured fewer negative attitudes than in most prisons, and expressed less kneejerk resistance to change. Lewis observed a similar desire among officers to 'do a good job, by and large', and a genuine interest in prisoner welfare. Wellingborough certainly did

---

[10] One prisoner claimed that, when he and his fellow wing workers had pointed out that there were no clean pillowcases for the weekly kit change, officers had walked away, stating that 'all we're here to do is bang everyone up'.

not have a traditional culture of obstruction to reform, antipathy to prisoners, and engrained suspicion of governors. But nor was it a dynamic or purposeful prison, where officers were proactive in assisting prisoners—particularly once staff morale began to wane. On the one hand then, officers did not stonewall prisoner complaints, and were normally helpful in response to questions and requests. As Jordan noted: 'If you ask for something to be checked up, it usually gets done. Sometimes it gets done months later, but it usually gets done in the end. Whereas in every other prison I've been in it doesn't get done at all'. On the other hand, this was a reactive—at its worst, a rather inert—form of assistance: 'If you don't put yourself out there and tell them what you want, you don't get it. They'll just leave you', said Connor; 'We have to fucking scream to get the[ir] attention', Zack declared.

Many officers did little to make themselves available to prisoners. On evening association, staff were rarely seen on the landings and mingled very little with prisoners in recreational areas. Dynamic officers stood out against the prevailing culture of the wings. As one highly motivated officer commented:[11]

Certain officers are quite content to lean against the radiator all day or sit on a chair [with] a cup of tea. [My view is] If you hear the cell bell going off here, don't just turn it off and then come back in. If you're going to turn it off you've got to answer it. I do fall out with officers quite a lot over their lack of enthusiasm.

Despite the high rate of prisoner inactivity, officers appeared unconcerned about finding ways to get prisoners out of their cells. This inertia was particularly striking on E-wing, where 'pods' in which activity could have been organized sat empty, and prisoners often waited several weeks before being allocated to work or education.[12] Such failures were partly systemic. As the newly

[11] In a quality of prison life survey conducted by the Prison Service Standards Audit Unit in May 2004—some months after the fieldwork period had ended— prisoners remained unhappy about the inaccessibility and lack of help from staff, long waiting lists for work, the amount of time spent in cells, and the prison's security level. As was consistent with previous reports, prisoners were positive about the levels of property and possessions that the prison allowed, in-cell TV, the prison's gym, education facilities and courses, the induction programme, and relationships with staff.

[12] Shortly after the fieldwork period ended, some of the prison's more menial work was moved from a workshop onto the induction wing in order to provide at least some activity for incoming prisoners.

appointed Head of Learning and Skills noted, the prison did little to tap into its own potential: 'we have workshops where we train people in carpentry and painting and decorating, but we always call in outside contractors to do the work'.

Third, uniformed staff at Wellingborough lacked a vision of 'performance' and 'service-delivery'. Officers understood the need for targets, audits, and public sector efficiency.[13] But the majority were either unaware of the targets by which the prison was evaluated, or saw little relationship between these targets and their everyday practices. As a senior officer observed:

On ground level I'd say we don't take a lot of notice of KPIs or KPTs at all. We do what we need to do on a daily basis to get through. Some of the targets, they are made to do things right, you know, a lot of stuff used to be [too lax]. [But] I wouldn't think prisoners are beneficiaries of it. I mean you speak to staff about KPIs and KPTs and they just glaze over. It means nothing to them. I suppose it is good to see how you perform against other Cat-Cs, but it doesn't affect us on a day to day basis, it doesn't affect how we do our job, the only thing it makes a difference to is the governors—whether they get a big budget or not.

In part, the cynicism expressed here reflected an awareness of the creative means with which some targets were achieved. Prisoners were sent to one workshop regardless of whether there was work to be done, allowing them to be marked down as 'in work' even if they were playing cards for most of the day. Senior managers were also sceptical of certain aspects of target culture. One governor outlined the flaws in resettlement targets, noting that there was no means of validating prisoners' claims about their employment status on release. Another explained that 'certain targets are being reached but at the expense of others. We do get a bit bogged down sometimes making sure that there's an audit trail'.

Whatever their reservations, governors were the institutional enforcers of target culture. In the eyes of uniformed staff, they were inextricably associated with performance management. This contributed significantly to widespread mistrust about their motives and expertise. A typical belief—here expressed somewhat extremely—was that governors were 'people with no idea of what it is like on the ground floor, who make arbitrary decisions on things they don't understand on information they're

---

[13] Many were proud citizens but reluctant taxpayers.

given by people who have never been in prison' (senior officer). This cynicism was exacerbated by the feeling that targets were being pursued at the expense of staff welfare, and that they were unachievable given the meagre resources being allocated in their pursuit.[14] Many officers believed that governors were preoccupied with targets because of links to earnings: 'it affects their money and their bonus'. Most saw management as highly self-interested: '[They're] on the side of furthering their career. I don't think they're out to improve prisoners' lives; they never stay at one prison for more than two or three years' (officer interviews).

Officers recognized that governors operated under stringent financial constraints and that the prison's staffing situation could not be resolved instantaneously. Nonetheless, they felt aggrieved at bearing the burdens of management decisions, and complained that governors were failing to protect them from the pressures of the institutional world above them. As one officer protested: 'it's all right them saying, "we know you're one [officer] short today, but can you open up and run the wing", because it reflects on their performance. But they're not the ones actually on the landings, [facing] any repercussions.' In such situations, officers exaggerated the risks that lean staffing entailed. Wellingborough was very safe, relative to other prisons, with no history of unrest and a low rate of staff assaults. Such protests signalled an emotional climate of under-appreciation, insecurity, neediness, and neurosis more than they reflected actual risks of physical assault.[15]

Officers were also sceptical about the official language of decency and rehabilitation. This was not because they were opposed to rehabilitative practices or the fundamentals of decent treatment. On the contrary, most officers supported the provision of better training and education facilities, particularly in the interests

---

[14] 'We've got to have targets. We have to have goals and aims, without them we've got nothing. But the goals and aims should be targets for us to achieve if we had the facilities, it shouldn't be targets to be achieved at the cost of the sanity of a member of staff, which is what we're getting. Has anybody wondered why you've got thirteen, fourteen staff on long-term sick? It's not a coincidence, it coincides with the fact that we never lock a wing up, staff are all owed hours, they're asked to come in and work, they're bullied, cajoled, threatened in some cases. The numbers don't add up. You know, and somebody's authorizing this' (senior officer).

[15] Evidence from recent research (Liebling et al. 2005) has shown that staff perceptions of safety are related less to assault levels than issues such as trust in senior management and confidence in one's occupational role.

of public protection. In particular, the idea of 'preventing the next victim' held considerable appeal to uniformed staff. Most also recognized that prisoners deserved dignified and respectful treatment. What they resented was the disparity between rhetoric and reality: a language of rehabilitation when they saw prisoners working in inadequate and outdated workshops, and a discourse of decency at a time of funding cuts and overcrowding. The deficiencies of Wellingborough's provision were also apparent to most prisoners: 'if it was about rehabilitation you wouldn't have fucking stupid jobs like [trolley fixing] where they pay a lot of money for doing fuck all, and then education paying you half of that' (Callum).

Staff of all grades complained that senior prison service personnel expected decency to be delivered without providing the resources to enable it. 'I am only allowed to deliver the basics because that's all I can get resourced for', noted one principal officer. One governor provided a more expansive description:

The problem we've got as a service is obviously the population pressures, which really has a massive impact on what we can deliver. [...] Over the last four or five years we've been making cutbacks and economies, and yet the population has still increased. I think we're getting to a stage where we're struggling to make any more economies, [especially] if we're [talking about] actually doing something purposeful with prisoners. Because you can play numbers around till you're blue in the face, and you can hit targets, but if they're meaningless targets, and they're just number crunching, then it's a really pointless exercise, and we can only do so much quality work with the [number of] people that we've got.

For uniformed staff, the same perceptions were exacerbated by a perception that managers were so focused on performance targets that they were blind to the moral realities of the landings. A senior officer highlighted this disjuncture as follows:

When I can't give a new inmate a pillowcase because we haven't got any because we haven't got any money left in the budget, that's disgraceful. It's not decency is it? You know, we can't even provide these people with pillowcases and proper clean bedding every week, but we're supposed to be a model of public sector reform. In theory we do provide a clean pillowcase every week, clean towels. In practice we tend not to, but they'll tell you we do. If you went up and saw a manager and said 'do they get clean pillowcases?' he'd say 'yeah, every week'. I told [a governor] at the weekend that we hadn't had clean pillowcases for five weeks. 'Yes you have'; 'No we haven't'. 'The laundry said you have'. 'Well I'm telling you we haven't'. They listen to what they want to hear.

Wing officers explained the daily struggles of delivering decency: of guaranteeing that non-smokers were not sharing cells with smokers when there was no spare cell capacity, to give a minor example. Decent treatment was easier in theory than practice, officers argued: 'Nobody gets in [Martin Narey's] space and calls him a tosser and abuses him. If they did he might understand what it feels like' (senior officer).

Such a statement was telling in indicating the limitations of decency within the prison. Although decent treatment was a taken-for-granted part of Wellingborough's ethos, the definition of decency was not explicit, nor was it articulated in moral terms. Little thought was given to *why* good relations mattered, or how they could be assured in situations when it might be easier to abandon them i.e. when prisoners were abusive or highly demanding. The version of decency that uniformed staff articulated was primarily *instrumental*: 'if we're talking nicely to each other it's really hard for one of them to break my jaw' (senior officer); 'it's a lot easier to speak to people than fight with people' (officer). This is not to suggest that officers were indifferent to the moral dimensions of imprisonment. Officers recognized the legitimacy of prisoners' basic expectations to be able to maintain contact with their families, to live in decent and safe conditions, and to be treated with civility. Most rehearsed the dictum that incarceration served '*as* not *for* punishment'. Acts of concern and compassion were common. Yet concern and compassion were not entrenched parts of officer culture, and although officers generally treated prisoners with respect, they were not particularly sympathetic to prisoners' frustrations. This represented a somewhat foreshortened sense of decency.

Courteous interactions also concealed more punitive, censorious sentiments. Most officers viewed crime as an individual choice. Punishment was seen as just desserts for immoral or impulsive conduct. As one officer explained:

[Prisoners whinge that] 'the food's crap, I can't get in touch with my girl-friend'. My stock answer is 'well, you knew that when you committed your crime'. Prison can't be that harsh and that bad if they can go out and re-offend and come back. I'm of the opinion [that] we all have the choice.

Prisoners' complaints and excuses were frequently dismissed through the adage that 'we all have problems in life'. Such direct comparisons of predicament reflected a perception among officers that governors were more concerned about prisoner welfare than staff issues. Managerial decisions were seen as zero-sum equations, whereby anything that benefited one party worked to the detriment of the other. One senior officer decried a situation where officers could not always get leave to attend family funerals, 'cos prisoners have to come out to play table tennis. If that would have been an inmate, they'd have gone—and none of us have got sentences. They forget that!' When feeling collectively undervalued, officers thus compared their plight to that of prisoners. One complained that the staff showers had been faulty for several weeks, whereas 'if it'd been this lot, it would've been sorted straightaway'. Another declared himself irritated that he was 'being asked to do things for people who are morally inferior' (fieldwork notes). 'Human rights' were generally seen as a liberal indulgence. Such sentiments—although not universal—were indicative of a common belief that prisoners were less eligible for decent treatment than people who upheld the law.[16] They also illustrated the failure of Wellingborough's management team to convince officers that improvements in the quality of life for prisoners were likely to improve the working lives of staff.

There were other indications of a more disrespectful streak within officer culture. In backstage areas, officers often used highly derogatory language about prisoners, describing them as 'shitbags' or 'arses', and joking about the concerns of vulnerable individuals. Such terms were rarely used in public exchanges with prisoners, and care for the vulnerable was good, illustrating the complex relationship between front and backstage behaviour.[17] But the careless use of language betrayed a widespread perception that prisoners were lesser social objects. Explaining the prison's rules to a group of new arrivals, one officer turned to me and stated, at audible volume, that 'to you and me this might be simple, but to this lot it isn't'. A group of incoming prisoners was described as 'rejects from the Lincoln riot' while they stood by. Officers often discussed the 'mentality' of 'inmates' in highly generic terms, oblivious that they were objectifying the prisoners working silently around them.

[16] It is interesting to note that prisoners and staff shared a belief that the other party were 'volunteers' within the institution, and therefore had no cause to complain about their conditions.

[17] Officers performed to each other as well as to prisoners, and it was not clear which performances reflected their real views. Furthermore, as Crawley (2004) argues, the dark humour of the prison can arguably be seen as a coping mechanism in the same way that it is in other forms of frontline work, such as nursing.

In front of the servery workers, two officers claimed that their habit of making jokes as each prisoner collected his food made them: 'all feel a bit special. Most of them don't understand it, but they like it!'[18] Many prisoners became inured to these mundane incivilities—signs of their denuded social status.

Incivilities were supplemented by a tendency for officers to misconceive 'banter' as a form of egalitarian exchange. One explained that he liked to joke with prisoners that: 'all inmates are shitbags but some are better than others. [I] call them bastards, nonces and everything else.[19] It might sound a bit harsh, [but] it's in fun, and they swear at me. It's part of my banter!' Some prisoners did enjoy such exchanges, but many resented being allocated generic nicknames ('Jock' for a Scot, 'Scouser' for anyone from Liverpool, etc) and being addressed in ways that presumed their desire to engage in pseudo-friendly dialogue.[20] Many officers failed to recognize that banter was often predicated on power differentials, and that such conditions could make it condescending and insulting—an aspect of domination. Here, the use of power was careless.

Elsewhere, it was telling that officers were resistant to practices that would symbolically reduce the status differential between themselves and prisoners. There was considerable opposition to addressing prisoners by their preferred names.[21] Most officers were happy to use first names or nicknames once familiarity had been established, but they tended to do so on their own terms and in ways that were not reciprocal. Most felt that prisoners should not call them by their names until that right was 'earned'.

---

[18] On one occasion, when trying to rearrange a prisoner interview by phoning from one wing to another, I asked to speak to the prisoner in question, rather than communicate with him via the officer who had answered the phone, next to whom he was standing. Although the officer was happy to hand the phone to the prisoner, an E-wing officer who overheard my request was dumbfounded: speaking to a prisoner in this way was 'just not done'. The incident exposed some of the contradictions between the prison's claims to encourage responsibility and autonomy and some of its routine practices.

[19] 'Nonce' is a derogatory term for a sex-offender.

[20] 'Certain screws, they're cracking a joke with you, you know, "watch yourself, Scouser's about, put your hands on your wallets". I mean, it does play on my mind, that, a bit. They just start stereotyping me. It shouldn't be done, whether it's a joke or not. I don't turn round and say "watch yourself, there's a screw about". It's not right. He's here to do his job not to pass judgement on me'. (Ross)

[21] Even at senior levels and in management meetings, prisoners were often referred to by surnames alone.

Some officers also reinforced moral distance by pointing out that they had come from similar backgrounds as prisoners but had resisted criminal temptations and chosen lawful pathways in life.

Further, although officers were committed to judging prisoners on the basis of present rather than past behaviour, the corollary of this ethos was that respect was to some degree withheld from prisoners who were difficult or abusive:

Respect is earned, respect is never given freely, yeah? I can treat with humanity, dignity and respect somebody who isn't standing in my face and calling me a useless wanker. [But] You can't respect somebody who does nothing but abuse you because you do what you're supposed to do. Respect is earned (senior officer).

Some of them don't deserve [sympathy], because they're total arses towards you, you know, you try and help them and they just sort of blank you. And then about a week later they might come to you and I'll say 'look, you didn't want to know last week ...' (wing officer).

Both prisoners and officers saw respect as the outcome of reciprocal behaviour. However each believed that the onus was on the other to set the terms of interpersonal engagement. For prisoners, this related to the power imbalances of the prison—the sense that it was officers who had more scope to create either good or bad relationships, and that staff should appreciate their frustrations (Liebling 2001). In contrast, officers saw the issue in terms of status, role, and morality (and saw symbols of these things, such as their uniform, as the keystones of respect, whereas prisoners emphasized interpersonal qualities, such as decency and humanity): as the possessors of legitimate and moral authority, respect was rightfully theirs. It was for prisoners to prove their own moral worth.

Officer culture and power

Wellingborough officers were not generally militant and did not share with their union leaders nostalgia for the era of austerity and staff power.[22] Indeed, the POA was seen by many of its own

[22] It was interesting to note that the POA's leading members gravitated towards working in the segregation unit. In part, this was due to a macho attraction to working in the prison's 'difficult' areas. It also reflected the appeal of having limited prisoner contact, and working in a zone where power differentials between staff and prisoners were especially clear-cut. Relationships and treatment in the segregation unit were good, but were predicated on prisoners accepting their subordinate status.

members as out-of-touch and self-interested. As was the case across the service (Bennett and Wahidin 2008), most officers joined the union for benefits relating to insurance, legal representation and financial services advice rather than for political purposes. Many felt more loyal to their wing colleagues than to the uniformed force as a whole. Older officers begrudged this absence of team spirit and camaraderie. Some attributed this to government legislation that had made industrial action illegal, and to the fragmentation of staff interests (ibid.). In particular, they resented the growing number of 'nine-to-fivers' whose interests differed from those of shift-working wing officers. Others blamed younger officers who they saw as more individualistic than veteran staff and more compliant in the face of management power.

The lack of solidarity was reflected in the willingness of officers to extend their working hours in order to stem staff shortages, and in the frequency with which some uniformed staff 'went sick' to shirk work or obtain time off. Both were individualistic responses which undermined the potential for collective resistance and only exacerbated the staffing crisis for colleagues. As staff bitterness increased, the POA had become an influential mouthpiece, but it had insufficient influence to persuade officers to sacrifice personal for collective goals. Most officers had little faith that the union could take on the muscle of senior managers. Nationally, the mood was similar, as the threat of privatization pushed the POA and the Prison Service management board into a state of 'uneasy partnership' (Bennett and Wahidin 2008).

Officers were aware that it was their lack of united resistance, and their individual decisions to patch up a leaking system, that sustained their frustrations. Many were conflicted by this knowledge and by the tensions between personal and professional loyalties:

Take contracted hours: there are some that say we shouldn't be doing them because it's making the prison worse.[23] If you're coming in doing extra hours, you're actually helping the prison to continue to run even though we're short of staff. There are others that believe, 'well, this extra money is actually helping my life become better; it's helping my day to day life become easier, and therefore, if it's there legitimately, there's no reason

[23] 'Contracted hours': a scheme by which staff could agree to work beyond their normal hours for extra pay.

why I shouldn't be doing it'. I'm in agreement that if there are people that are helping the system run by doing contracted hours, [managers] might never feel that they should put the officers in place to do the job. But I also agree that as the head of a household it's up to me to earn what I can, to provide for my family, so if I've got the time and ability to do extra hours and earn extra money, I think that nobody should be standing in my way for me to do it.

Significantly, most decisions to extend contracted hours resulted from commitments to personal earnings rather than loyalty to the establishment or the Prison Service.

The POA also had little influence on many everyday decisions. As Chapter 4 explains in more detail, individual wing staff had considerable discretion and responsibility, but relatively little collective influence to set policy, determine the regime or make operational decisions. Power lay elsewhere: with the security department, which dominated decision-making on work allocations, cell searches and transfers from the prison ('they're the ones with the knowledge, they're getting all the sexy information all the time'); with the detail office ('cos they're holding what people need'); and with the governors and 'money-men' who, in the eyes of the uniformed workforce, held sway over landing life while being sheltered from its realities:

Half-way through the month we've got no toilet rolls. Why? Because some civvy has made a decision [that] it would cut costs. We've got to provide them with bedding, clothing and all the other things that they need, to be told we haven't got any. Why not? Because the head finance man said we can't keep them on the shelf. So what am I supposed to give him? Is the head finance man going to come down and tell these guys they can't have them? Well, no he isn't, [he's] in his office. It's okay sitting up there and saying we've got to save £1,000 this month, we'll save it by not having any towels, except that the knock-on of that is me and my staff have to fight the inmate who we can't give any towels to, because he rightly thinks he's entitled to them. (senior officer)

Wing staff believed that decisions about resources were foisted upon them without consultation or consideration. On most operational issues, they were powerless to act without consulting their superiors. To place a violent or vulnerable prisoner in the segregation unit required permission from a principal officer, for example. Such measures were interpreted as signs of management mistrust and indifference.

Only the most senior uniformed rank had sufficient authority to make decisions that had collective consequences for prisoners, as one principal officer identified:

The prisoners know the rank system—I'm the one that's got the power to make their life a misery and make their life not a misery. [I can] close the association room, whereas the officers have not got the authority to do that, because the first thing the governor will say is 'who told you to do that?'

Thus, power was formally located at the higher end of the organization. Yet principal officers described an absence of power and leadership: 'no-one's running the place. There's no real power anywhere. There's little bit of power pockets all over the place, but no-one is taking the bull by the horns and saying "right, let's drive this way".'

Power, authority, and staff-prisoner relationships

The main problems that officers reported related not to prisoners, but to senior managers, the Prison Service and the political context. Even without the acute staff shortages that affected Wellingborough during the time of study, officers would have been more concerned with national issues (such as pay and status) than the demands of managing prisoners. Indeed, in the eyes of all staff, the great majority of prisoners were highly submissive. 'I've never met a more compliant bunch of prisoners than we've got here', one governor declared. Another described prisoners as 'very, very compliant'. Staff who had worked in other establishments commented that officers who complained about working life at Wellingborough had no idea what work in other prisons could be like, in terms of heavy workloads, management 'bullying', and difficulties with prisoners.[24] Nonetheless, there was no doubt that officers in Wellingborough felt powerless and demoralized: 'at breaking point:...overworked and underpaid and overstretched' (senior officer).[25]

---

[24] As one officer said: 'it does make me cringe sometimes when I see the lads in reception here and the workload that they [complain about]: "oh, we're snowed under with this".'

[25] The same senior officer reported that members of his team were crying in the wing office at least twice a week. There were reports of tearful breakdowns among at least three middle managers during my period of fieldwork.

The consequences were manifold. Their weak collective power meant that officers did not feel over-confident, and were not offhand or dismissive with prisoners. 'They manage [them] rather than barking orders at them', observed one principal officer. In this respect, staff powerlessness contributed to the informal nature of staff-prisoner relations. However, as staff became disillusioned they turned increasingly to formal means of using authority. Prisoners were steered into using written applications ('apps') for complaints that could have been dealt with in person. Meanwhile, officers side-stepped their formal duties, passing responsibilities up the institutional hierarchy, as Jim Lewis explained:

Something might come straight up to me as an application for a prisoner to go on release for something. It's my decision [ultimately] whether he goes or not, but the prisoner should have made an application for that, [which] should have generated an application form for that releasing licence. [That] should have been written up by his personal officer, there should have been a security report on it, [and] some indication of what the need was for the leave period, and then that should have been considered by a board and the board should have made the recommendation, and *then* I would have considered the outcome. Instead I was getting it first hand and having to send back for all of those things.

Officers also became increasingly reactive, reporting prisoner activity rather than supervising it. One governor was dumb-founded to receive a security report from an officer noting his suspicions about the presence of 'hooch' [illicitly-brewed alcohol] in a cell—something that could have been handled directly through a cell-search. When officers did come across disciplinary infractions, they used formal authority with inappropriate zeal, giving prisoners 'strikes' instead of using discretion.[26] Such mech-anisms maximized punitive 'effectiveness' with minimal effort and bureaucracy, as one officer explained:

If I'd nicked him on adjudication, he'd get a caution, which is done and finished with, or he'll get a stoppage of half a canteen for one week and it's finished. If this guy's going to be an arsehole over a period of time, as opposed to getting seven or eight nickings where nothing's happening to him or he's losing half his canteen, you give him three strikes and he'll be put on basic for twenty-eight days, which means he's locked up more obviously [and he] loses his telly. It's a bigger punishment, it hurts them

[26] A 'strike': an official behaviour warning. In Wellingborough, a prisoner who received three strikes moved down one privilege level on the IEP scheme.

more. Rightly or wrongly we have to use whatever we can to try and get at them. So yeah, the staff here won't nick inmates for what they used to nick them for six months ago, but they'll strike them instead. It's not worth the paperwork.

In part, this kind of officer behaviour related to the removal from governors of the power to add extra days to prisoners' sentences. This authority had been passed to independent external adjudicators, in whose judgment (i.e. severity) officers had little faith. It also indicated the petty, sometimes vindictive use of authority, particularly on the VTU, where prisoners received strikes for very minor infringements such as putting up makeshift curtains or picking food from meal trays before returning to their cells.[27] Each of these examples indicated an absence of strong line management and a deficit in healthy authority on the prison's landings.

In summary, while officers maintained relatively relaxed relations with prisoners, feelings of resignation led them to disengage from interpersonal work and resort to formal power to manage the wings. Retreat was a way of resisting managerial authority and offsetting feelings of powerlessness. In effect, officers embraced the role of the faceless turnkey that they felt the job had become, and did so in ways that undermined institutional aims. Elsewhere, resistance was more active. In some instances, it involved the illegitimate use of formal rules and procedures. One senior officer advised a prisoner who was demanding to see a governor (in order to sort out his gym sessions) that the only way this was possible was if he was sent to the prison's segregation unit, which would require him to refuse to 'bang up'.[28] Another form of resistance was to pursue institutional goals via illegitimate means, as illustrated in the following example:

The governor rings me up and says: 'I need some paperwork done' [for prisoners]. But I'm not able to give the officer time to do that. Personal officer time is not profiled for in this prison. But we still are expected to

---

[27] The rule that prisoners could not eat on the landings had been made on health and safety grounds to stop prisoners from eating their entire meals in communal areas. Its aim was not to ban *any* kind of eating in these areas.

[28] This was advice which intensely irritated his colleagues in the segregation unit, who had to do the paperwork for a prisoner who did not need to be there. It also made life more difficult for colleagues on his wing, who were faced with many more prisoners threatening to refuse to enter their cells in order to get an audience with the governor.

do all these forms [otherwise] you start getting upset prisoners who're putting request and complaints in, and eventually it'll probably come back to me. [So] basically we cook the books, I've closed X-Wing and Y-Wing down in [recent months] to get urgent paperwork done. The governor doesn't know...

So once you've let everyone off to work and education...

... Yeah, the rest just stay locked up. In the evening we have activity patrols, so we'll cancel one of the activity patrols—you've got some urgent paperwork to get done, stay on the wing and get it done and we'll cover a different way. Basically we're cutting corners all the time, we're making a bad system work.

Both examples were acts where uniformed staff circumvented approved procedures to meet ends that they felt were otherwise unachievable. Both also exploited—and illuminated—the distance between management goals and those of its frontline representatives. The examples were interesting for other reasons: the first because it represented a form of collusion between uniformed staff and prisoners; the second because, in 'making a bad system work', it perpetuated the very system to which staff were opposed.

Collusion, Accommodation, and the Ironies of Power

Overcrowding and staff discontent placed considerable strain on Wellingborough's functions and relationships.[29] Prisoners felt neglected, and were deeply frustrated at the lack of personal officer time. Despite Lewis's commitment to curtailing the regime as little as possible, wings could not always be staffed for evening exercise or association. The need to have officers in core positions also meant that important but expendable activities such as group-based drug work, induction talks, and resettlement interviews were often cancelled. Despite such issues—and despite what officers suspected was the premature categorization of Cat-B prisoners as Cat-Cs to make room further up the system—Wellingborough

---

[29] By the time of the study, the prison was receiving around twenty prisoners per week—a higher turnover than Cat-Cs were designed to manage. In the past, prisoners had only been eligible to come to Wellingborough if they had more than nine months of their sentence left to run. By 2003, population pressures were such that this rule was no longer applicable.

experienced no serious or concerted control problems. Rates of staff-prisoner assaults remained very low. Minor problems had occurred when overcrowding drafts had compelled the prison to accept a large number of prisoners from the West Midlands, who were angered to be so far from home; and petitions about food quality had occasionally threatened to ignite into larger issues. In general though, most policies went publicly unchallenged. In spite of their discontent, prisoners remained—or at least appeared—highly compliant.

Officers were proud of their ability to defuse prisoner frustrations and manage under difficult circumstances. Yet, in talking up the imminence of prisoner revolt while also quelling it, they highlighted a paradox. Dissent and disturbances were highly undesirable for officers, for anger would be directed against them or they would be its frontline victims. Yet in the absence of visible resistance—if the prison remained ostensibly calm, despite lower staffing—staff complaints were less likely to be taken seriously.

Without effective outlets, officer discontent was expressed in collusive forms. When wing staff had to tell prisoners that evening association was cancelled, they made a point of disclaiming responsibility for the decision. Explanations on wing notice boards brusquely cited staff shortages, pointing an accusatory finger at management. When prisoners expressed annoyance, officers openly endorsed their feelings and vented their own frustrations. These actions testified to the shared interests of those who worked the landings and those who lived on them. They also illustrated a sentiment shared by staff and prisoners that the world beyond the wings was indifferent to their concerns and stacked against their interests. Like prisoners, many officers described themselves as treated like 'numbers' rather than individuals, and saw the prison as a place that rewarded you only 'if your face fits'.[30]

As Phil Wheatley had noted in his speech to the Cat-C conference, some prisoners spoke out on behalf of the plight of officers. They did so not only for reasons of self-interest (i.e. because they suffered when officers were stretched), but because they identified

---

[30] Sharing a physical and cultural location, officers also appropriated strands of prisoner language to depict their working conditions. Thus, they emphasized the need to 'front' in order to stop others from 'taking liberties', and described colleagues who left work through stress as 'fraggled out' (see Chapter 6).

with the stresses that officers conveyed. 'In some instances', summarized one governor, 'it's them against us—prisoners *and* staff'.

As another governor acknowledged, such alliances were inadvertently promoted by target culture:

The wings are perhaps the most easily ignored area, because we don't get problems from them, because the prisoners are compliant, and because the auditor says we've got the right posters in the right places and the right ticks in the right boxes. So actually it's all too easy to forget the wings, to forget the staff on them, to forget their lot.

There were other examples of this mutual sympathy and interest. When food was substandard, or when handed-in items were slow to be passed on to prisoners, officers encouraged prisoners to lodge official grievances. These were failures of service-delivery, which prisoners felt were not the responsibility of officers.[31] Prisoners and wing staff recognized that, in many respects, neither had the capacity to solve the problems that most exercised the other.

Governors and power

In the eyes of wing staff, Wellingborough was 'a governors' jail— the POA have got nothing here' (senior officer). Yet, just as officers argued that power resided in the upper branches of the institution, governors reported that their main problems and frustrations derived from the organizational world above them. In part, these were financial constraints over which governors had little control. One explained his feeling that budget cuts were increasingly undermining the aims of senior management and changing the nature of the job, turning it into an exercise in creative butchery:

We've gone through the meat, we've gone through the fat, we've gone through the bone, we're now into the bone marrow, but [The Centre is] still expecting us to make year on year savings. Whatever saving we make something's got to go. You can only do a set amount of work with a certain amount of resources.

Lewis highlighted similar pressures. He had 'a great deal of discretion in running the establishment', but felt that this was diminishing. A growing part of the prison's budget was hypothecated for

---

[31] It should be said, however, that these problems were more often the fault of officers than prisoners realized. Some officers claimed helplessness because it was easier to do so than to resolve problems.

specific services, such as offending behaviour programmes, education, and drug treatment. At the same time, managerial expectations meant that, while his financial and operational discretion contracted, the pressure on him to deliver was heightened. The Prison Service was also 'increasingly demanding of *particular ways* of doing things', requiring that offending behaviour programmes were homogenous and accredited, and imposing orders and instructions from above on all manner of policies and practices. The ease with which performance data could be accessed held governors to account for their failures while limiting their room for manoeuvre (Carlen 2005). Financial limits, then, were coupled with restrictions on the nature and scope of management. Accountability and responsibility were high, but autonomy was limited.

For governors, the experience of power was highly ambivalent, as one member of the senior management team indicated:

> On a day-to-day basis, I have enormous power. I'm the arbiter on whether or not a member of staff gets an order to extend [their shift], or whether ninety prisoners are locked up involuntarily. [But] I don't know strategically if I have that much power at all. My job is in making sure that the Governor's strategy is being relayed and being delivered. I know the route we're taking. [But] I don't feel that I've got any power at all to influence that. We're not in a position to say 'pull back'.

Several points merit expansion. There was an important distinction between the everyday power wielded by governors and their capacity to define the shape, direction, and uses of this power. Governors (and principal officers) had *operational* responsibility for decisions of great significance for those below them, and the prison's hierarchical structure meant that they often felt extremely commanding. Yet they did not hold enough political or *allocative* power (Murdock 1982) to alter the general terms by which the institution functioned. One governor believed that he could 'at a stroke, cure most of the ills of this prison, if I was given my target staffing figure'. Without such power, and operating under such constraints, the governing role was one of technical management as much as professional expertise. The job description was 'almost robotic: [it] says to manage this area of the prison to the best of my capability' (governor). As is suggestive of Foucault (1977), power operated *through* personnel at all levels. For both governors and officers, as much as power was exercised, it often felt 'elsewhere' and was never truly in their possession.

With so much power being channelled through them, governors felt in highly invidious positions. One described himself as being 'under siege, from all quarters', with officers and senior managers asserting conflicting demands and both groups looking to him to resolve them. Lewis conveyed deep frustration about being held to account for issues over which he had little control:

I do think that it's unfair that people blame me for us not having enough staff because I've been recruiting as fast as I possibly can do. But people feel frustrated and they have to vent their frustration somewhere, and where do you vent it? It's not the senior officer's fault and it's not the principal officer's fault and it's not the visits' [staff] fault, it must be the governor's fault, you know. It's certainly the governor's responsibility [even] if it's not the governor's fault. I have railed against some of those things as well, and have railed against the fact that I've not got a settled team here.

But you're not cross with anyone in particular?

No. There is nobody for you to be cross with.

Lewis's declaration of powerlessness resonated in striking ways with prisoners' complaints about the elusiveness and anonymity of penal power, as coming chapters will show. It illustrated the way that, as for officers, managerialism could feel harsh and oppressive to those who were its institutional representatives. More importantly, for current purposes, it captured the constrained agency of the governor's role. Like officers, governors felt that they bore a disproportionate level of responsibility relative to their autonomy. They too sometimes appealed to prisoners to understand their predicament, as one governor explained in relation to evening exercise:

We knew that we would never be able to sustain it, we tried to build on the good relationships between staff and prisoners here and say 'look, you know we're short staffed, you know that we find it difficult to do things, but we're going to make this effort and we can't do it all the time, but we will do it whenever we can'. And most people seem to have taken to that, and we've had to cancel on a number of occasions and there's not been a great backlash against it, because I think [there's] an acceptance that that's the way of the world and we're doing what we can.

Such pleas for empathy indicated the possibility of understanding between prisoners and their custodians. But the supplication of governors to prisoners was born of weakness, not the search for normative consensus as such. At the same time, it pointed to an alliance of interests within the institution: not divisions between different strata in the prison, but a line of division between the institution and the world above it.

Even the governor most committed to the performance agenda described his need to function in bad faith: 'I'm paid to get on with this and even the bits that I don't like, the Brussels sprouts on the plate, I've got to eat. There's lots of Brussels sprout eating that we have to do.' Governors felt bound by corporate responsibility to implement the orders of their seniors regardless of personal reservations and frustrations about resourcing. Not least, they recognized that their seniors were as constrained as they were in setting the agenda for their actions. Moreover, governors were no less pragmatic about their professional actions than officers, and knew that defiance was not indulged:

If I was to say, 'no, this is stupid and we're not doing it', then they would simply move me out and put someone else in.

I think you have to be in line with the performance culture because it's the only game in town. If you were in a governing position and you didn't play their game, you wouldn't remain in the governing position for very long.

Despite their frustrations and reservations, then, governors were highly compliant in the face of managerial power.

This acquiescence had some ironic qualities. Wellingborough's governors had been so successful in managing the POA into submission that they had diminished the capacity to achieve their own ends. Like officers, without organized pressure from below, managers could not illustrate to their seniors that their claims to need more staff were valid:

I have at numerous times over the year had to prop up the POA and say 'challenge me over this will you, and I'll give ground'. The POA could and should be doing [things] that would influence a Governor and force their hand and still allow a Governor to keep corporate responsibility. It [should] be very difficult to champion an argument that says Wellingborough [should] be sending someone to Ashwell prison this week to help sustain the regime there, when we're twelve officers short *here*. Yet the POA aren't challenging us over it. The Area Manager will see that the POA aren't challenging it, therefore it's obviously not perceived as a problem here. They should have 'failed to agree' over it and said, 'you're not doing it and we want a consultation process', but they didn't.

As suggested here, by running the prison 'effectively' (i.e. keeping within the budget, meeting targets, maintaining the regime), and fulfilling a particular vision of institutional success, governors could perpetuate problems that edged beneath the managerialist radar, and could foment frustrations that would return to haunt them.[32] They were also placed in positions where they were disliked by staff for imposing agendas whose flaws they were well aware of.

The distribution of power in Wellingborough made it possible for governors to suppress staff discontent, or push it into forms (such as staff sickness) that remained 'managerial' rather than systemic problems. It was difficult to envisage resourcing issues being challenged or negotiated without a corporate, consensual, or collusive approach to industrial relations. These issues could not be resolved within the institution itself—indeed, many could not easily be resolved by the Prison Service at all—and required power to be exerted outside the establishment. But the divergence of interests between governors and uniformed staff made such strategies difficult. For governors, meeting targets within budget was the *sine qua non* of their employment, and this generally meant minimizing staff costs. For officers, targets were false idols. To them, 'failing prisons' seemed to benefit more than establishments that successfully struggled to meet official expectations or effectively performed high-performance. As one senior officer complained:

If we lock down a wing because of staff shortages, the area manager has to be notified. We don't do that. So they think everything's wonderful. Littlehey loses one member of staff and closes down a wing. We lose five and somehow manage by swapping shifts and coming in. Littlehey will be given extra funding for more staff, Littlehey will be given probably overtime. We don't get any of this because somehow we cope, and the fact that we cope is a great credit to us. We manage to keep the lid on it, [but] because we keep the lid on it we're going to be punished.

For those officers who saw targets being met while the prison's spirit and procedures crumbled, failure appeared a more desirable option.

---

[32] As with uniformed staff, the human costs of this situation were apparent. Asked to recall his last good day at work during the previous few weeks, one governor replied that he would struggle to identify 'a good moment'.

Conclusion

The first aim of this chapter has been to provide a description of Wellingborough's institutional culture and staff attitudes, and to explore how power was distributed between and experienced by governors and uniformed staff. It has suggested that, despite their enormous capacity to determine the quality of prison life for prisoners, uniformed staff did not perceive themselves to be powerful figures in institutional life. As a group, they were demoralized and fragmented. Managerial reforms had winched power to higher levels of the organization, eroding their collective influence. Many officers felt un-trusted, out of touch with institutional aims, and alienated from organizational decision-making. Cynicism about management motives and methods was widespread. Resentment was partly based on a feeling that managers cared more about prisoner wellbeing than staff concerns, and were fixated on (what were considered) abstract and meaningless 'targets' while indifferent to the nature of the 'real work' that took place on the landings. Many frontline staff were also bitter about discrepancies between the rhetoric and realities of penal ambitions. Overcrowding and taut resourcing exacerbated a perception that expectations were unachievable. Despite the considerable discretion that they were able to wield, most uniformed staff felt increasingly rule-bound, constrained by rigid lines of accountability, formalized procedures, 'human rights' and grievance procedures. In the absence of effective collective means of channelling their views and frustrations, these staff expressed their discontent by disengaging from interpersonal work or going sick—forms of resistance that disadvantaged their own co-workers, as well as prisoners and senior managers.

In spite of their authority and influence, governors felt little more autonomous and barely more in control of the institutional agenda. Most highlighted an important distinction between the high levels of responsibility and accountability they carried and the shrinking autonomy of their role in a context where control, oversight, and audit were increasingly centralized (see Bryans 2007). They were managed lightly, but their agency was highly constrained by the knowledge that they could act only within certain parameters. For senior managers as well as staff, it felt as though power resided above them, and seemed that they had to shoulder organizational problems and emotional expectations whose solutions were beyond their control. Governors also shared with the uniformed workforce the sense that it was increasingly difficult to meet management demands without compromising some aspects of quality. Like them, they often claimed to be managed with little organizational sympathy, and felt that their options to challenge their seniors and assert their views were highly circumscribed. In the belief that resisting the management agenda was futile unless they could wield the discontent of another party—ideally, one whose concerns would enter the field of vision of senior Prison Service managers—they were highly compliant in following organizational goals.

Ultimately, and ironically, therefore, governors and officers felt equally disempowered by the absence of visible discontent among *prisoners*. These pervasive feelings of powerlessness were intensified by the knowledge that, by coping in difficult circumstances, one's problems were more likely to be perpetuated than resolved. All parties felt complicit in their own disgruntlement. As the chapters that follow will show, there were striking parallels between these feelings of resigned self-management among staff and those expressed by prisoners. In terms of sympathies, allegiance and conflict, the prison was jointed and dislocated in unexpected ways, with deceptive fissures and connections.

Uniformed staff expressed as much hostility and cynicism about governors as they did about prisoners (see Liebling 2004), with whom they shared space and developed tacit alliances through a shared perception of managerial neglect. Likewise, governors spent more time managing staff than prisoners. It was extremely difficult to maintain a positive relationship with uniformed staff while promoting a vision for the establishment that was implicitly critical of their position. The culture among officers was a hindrance to governors' moral ambitions, but alienating uniformed staff risked making things worse.

Although they were conditioned by the prison's specific institutional history, these patterns and problems also reflected more generic characteristics of the times. Across the system, schisms between governors and uniformed staff were the norm rather than the exception.[33] As in most prisons in the early years of the decade, Wellingborough's management turnover was rapid and its priorities changed frequently. In some prisons, POA

---

[33] In some prisons, governors report that some officers blank them or audibly call them 'wankers' when they walk around the wings.

committees retained the collective power that had elsewhere been siphoned to higher echelons of the organization, but the collective disunity of Wellingborough's uniformed staff mirrored general, national tendencies (Bennett and Wahidin 2008). It also reflected long-term shifts in the nature of prison management (Liebling 2004; Carlen 2005). Centralized control had been tightened in part because of the moral deficiencies and abuses that a less firmly managed system had allowed in previous decades. Senior managers justified increased scrutiny and accountability by arguing that imprisonment, more than other domains, necessitated rather autocratic management, not so much of prisoners but staff. Inevitably though, the layers of audit that this view produces can imply a lack of faith in the expertise of professionals, who often felt restricted, controlled, and disempowered even while they recognized the benefits of oversight. As Foucault (1977) argued, the supervisors as well as the supervised are under surveillance, disciplined and enmeshed by the system of power.

This chapter's second aim has been to show how institutional culture and dynamics gave shape to staff-prisoner relations and determined how power was exercised on prisoners. Wellingborough's culture was largely benign, and staff sought to use relationships rather than more coercive strategies in the service of order. Officers were not provocative or intrusive in their use of power. In this respect, it was a relatively easy prison in which to 'do time'. However, it was a less good place in which to get things done. Wellingborough was not a dynamic prison, in which staff took initiative or had a wider vision of service-delivery. Prisoners received little help as well as little hassle. Nor was it an establishment in which authority was always used with confidence. Practices were rather casual, and relaxed relationships concealed an underbelly of disdain, indifference, and moral superciliousness. As staff morale dropped, these sentiments surfaced. Decent relationships had lacked a solid normative basis, and their foundations were shallow. Officers retreated to their offices and resorted increasingly to the use of formal power rather than interpersonal discretion. As the next chapter explains, compliance was not achieved through either technique alone, but through a range of power strategies that combined in practice to form a distinctive arrangement of power.

4

Power

The prison has long been considered an exemplary site for the study of power, order, and resistance (*inter alia* Sykes 1958; Sparks *et al.* 1996; Carrabine 2004). In some work, it has been considered emblematic of forms of power in society at large (Foucault 1977). Elsewhere, it has been examined as a case study of total power. Sykes (1958) bracketed the penitentiary with the concentration camp and the labour colony, noting that each was 'a social system in which an attempt is made to create and maintain total or almost total social control' (Sykes 1958: xiv). Certainly, the prison is an arena where differentials in power—the capacity to achieve intended outcomes—are more glaringly evident than in most social domains. Indeed, imprisonment is often implied in illustrations of extremes in social powerlessness: 'only a person who is kept totally confined and controlled does not participate in the dialectic of control' (Giddens 1982: 39).

Yet in probing the social realities of this 'new leviathan', Sykes highlighted an essential discrepancy between the unparalleled level of power apparently at the disposal of the institution and the defects in its dominative grip:

Far from being omnipotent rulers who have crushed all signs of rebellion against the regime, the custodians are engaged in a continuous struggle to maintain order—and it is a struggle in which the custodians frequently fail. (Sykes 1958: 42)

Sparks *et al.* (1996: 2) concur that the 'maintenance of order is a *perennial problem*' in prisons. Obstacles to the accomplishment of order appear inherent to institutions that confine people against their will in circumstances they are highly unlikely to enjoy (Sykes 1958), and demand of them behaviour patterns they would not naturally embrace. In such conditions, even if its terms cannot easily be altered, penal power is unlikely to go uncontested. In prison, order, control, and influence are thus matters of considerable energy and constant struggle.

Lorna Rhodes (2001: 66) has argued that 'a large and growing body of work alludes to, but does not explore, the prison as a central site for the exercise of disciplinary power'. This book explores the two domains of power that affect prisoners. The first is represented by the institution and its officials; the second by the prisoner community. Previous chapters have given some sense of the general aims, means, and functions of modern imprisonment. The following two chapters seek to describe the specific processes by which power was exercised by the institution and experienced, negotiated, and resisted in practice by prisoners. Specifically, this chapter describes the nature and intentions of power in HMP Wellingborough as comprised by a number of policies and practices. Chapter 6 explores the effects of these forms of power, exploring how different prisoners complied with, adapted to, and transformed their techniques and ambitions.

The chapter begins by outlining the elementary forms of power in prison—the four principal means by which order and other effects can be achieved. Order is not the sole aim of penal power, but it is the *sine qua non* of the system: the basis on which other aims, such as rehabilitation or repentance, are predicated. The chapter goes on to discuss how, in the pursuit of order and compliance, these forms of power can be employed and combined in a number of ways. These combinations have consequences for prison social life and individual adaptations that cannot simply be read off from formal intentions, but are clearly related to the terms and techniques of power. It is these terms and techniques that the chapter then elaborates, providing a detailed account of how they were manifested in HMP Wellingborough and how they formed a specific regime of everyday power—a form of 'neo-paternalism' that combined elements of neo-liberalism, authoritarianism, and welfarism.

The Elementary Forms of Social Power

Social and penal theorists have highlighted four main mechanisms of power, order, and compliance (e.g. Scott 2001; Bottoms 2002; Carrabine 2005). The first of these is *coercion*, which includes physical constraint, force, threat, and deprivation. All prisons are, in the last instance, coercive institutions, even if naked power is not immediately visible in their everyday operation. As Cover (1986: 1607) notes succinctly, 'most prisoners walk into prison because they know they will be dragged or beaten into prison if they do not walk'. Equally, were the walls to be demolished, the gates to be unlocked, and the state to shrug its shoulders, there are few prisoners who would remain in their cells voluntarily—although I will suggest that there may be a few. In such respects, coercion is the bulwark of the penal institution, both in literal and figurative terms. The distinction between the threat of force and its actual application is important here, for it is through the former—as a 'final persuader'—that coercion functions most effectively (Wrong 2002: 26). The knowledge that, if need be, tanks could surround the prison or one could be placed in segregation or transferred to another establishment is normally sufficient for such measures not to be required. Likewise, casual threats (e.g. about the consequences of disobedience) and tacit warnings (that evening exercise will be cancelled unless troublemakers are identified) often precede or preclude the resort to formal coercive measures.

While the resort to violence or physical constraint implies a failure of 'softer' forms of power, it also reinforces the credibility of threat and may thereby diminish the future need for such 'hard' deployments of power.[1] It is rare though, in any context, for power-holders to rest solely on hard versions (although see Scraton *et al.* 1991), for, in its rawest form, coercion is a provocative, inefficient, and illegitimate means of enforcing order. As Sykes (1958) noted, violence can easily spiral out of control and the constant application of force is highly disruptive to a complex institution. Nonetheless, 'lighter' forms of coercion can be built into the prison's everyday routines and structures, in the form of situational control measures that restrict free movement and constrain social opportunities. In 'super-max' prisons, for example, the almost total isolation of prisoners and the routine use of handcuffs, leg irons, and other direct forms of restraint represent an almost total reliance on coercive forms of power without the use of actual violence (King 2005). In general though, hard power is converted into softer means and it is through these means that routine compliance is achieved.

---

[1] It is partly because of this paradox that riots may take such unpredictable turns. The use of force reinforces to prisoners the power at the disposal of the state, while at the same time it confirms to prisoners that the other tools of the prison authorities have failed and that the normal order of things has been profoundly disrupted.

One of these means, and the second form of social power, is *manipulation* or *inducement*: the appeal to self-interest, or the orchestration of needs and desires. The depriving nature of imprisonment means that this mechanism operates in complex ways. If conditions are such that the prisoner's circumstances can barely be worsened and little can be offered to improve them, the rewards and punishments offered by the prison may have little persuasive influence (Sykes 1958). Indeed, incentives and disincentives may be subverted by their official status and the alternative meanings assigned to them within prisoner subculture. If being punished achieves a perverse kind of kudos among prisoners, it may become desirable, while rewards may draw stigma. Rational choice models of prisoner behaviour may be flawed for other reasons. Prisoners may not understand incentive schemes, may struggle to conform to their terms, may be indifferent to what they offer, and may perceive them to be implemented unfairly and unpredictably (see Liebling *et al.* 1999; Bottoms 2003).

At the same time, in the spartan context of the prison, the significance of apparently trivial rewards can be amplified (Mathieson 1965). As Goffman (1961) noted, when personal possessions, identity, and autonomy are restricted, items that seem minor or are taken for granted in the outside world—a jar of coffee, the right to smoke, the opportunity to watch television, small amounts of extra spending money—can become levers through which behaviour can be adjusted. These minor perks can be tendered illicitly as well as through official policies. That is, staff may distribute minor privileges to prisoners in order to procure their compliance or may underenforce sanctions in order to keep the peace (Sykes 1958). Everyday relations between staff and prisoners are often characterized more by these kinds of negotiations than by the stringent application of formal rules. The routine use of discretion in the interpretation of regulations and in the distribution of privileges represents a bureaucratic grey area, one which can be dangerously extra-legal (Scott 2006) or a necessary and often benign compromise that enhances the prison's 'legitimacy' (see below) (Liebling and Price 2001). There is considerable scope for the semi-formal allocation of rewards and punishments. When formal incentives hold out the prospect of freedom, for example, through early release schemes and home leaves, their appeal is likely to be all the more potent.

The third form of power or source of compliance is *habit, ritual* or *fatalistic resignation*. Compliance and other effects can be born out of the sense that there are no alternatives and that one's subordination is inevitable and unalterable. Within society at large, this may derive from an inability to imagine alternative social possibilities ('this is the way the world works; how else could things be?') or to conceive of strategies of transformation ('what can I do to change things?'). Often, it is an outcome of the mundane necessities of survival that monopolize the energies of most people at the expense of radical action (Abercrombie *et al.* 1990). Compliance is a product of what Marx called the 'dull compulsion' of economic relations—the need to work, eat, and get on with the banal imperative of daily subsistence. It is a mode of power whose essential form is the 'taken-for-granted'—the dimensions of everyday life that are undertaken without conscious reflection. Rituals and routines are crucial here, for they reinforce fatalism at the same time as they manifest it. Mundane repetition socializes habits, while symbolic representations signify to subordinates the naturalness of their predicament. Through timetabling, regimentation, and spatial organization, constraint is instilled in both the body and the psyche (Foucault 1977). Compliance becomes almost automatic.

In prison, the sense that one is powerless to alter one's *general* situation—that of being incarcerated—is almost always completely realistic (Carrabine 2005). In terms of more mundane matters, such as the everyday observance of rules, resigned and habitual forms of compliance are less assured, for the possibilities for minor dissent are considerable. Nonetheless, the prison is replete with symbolic reminders of institutional dominance and the futility of resistance. Reception to prison is a case point of ritual degradation whereby the loss of status and autonomy that imprisonment entails is made clear through a range of procedures, from body searches and showering to the surrendering of personal possessions, and the assignment of numbers and uniform (Garfinkel 1956; Goffman 1961).[2] Throughout the sentence, directives on speech and behaviour, the regulation of normal tasks such as washing and spending money, the withholding of information, the visibility of security cameras and fences, the sheer presence of

---

[2] Even when these processes are not intentionally degrading, they still have the effect of communicating to prisoners that they are submitting their normal status as free citizens.

uniformed custodians, and the stultifying routine all contribute to a generalized sense of powerlessness and the inevitable, unchangeable nature of captivity.

The distinction between power that is taken-for-granted and power that is accepted as just or legitimate is crucial here (Sparks *et al.* 1996; Carrabine 2005), for it marks the difference between ritual or habit and *normative justification* or *commitment*—the fourth mechanism of compliance. Normative compliance is based upon shared values, rather than rituals or rewards, and takes three forms. The first is personal morality: the belief that a form of behaviour is morally right *per se* or that an injunction is consistent with personal ethics. The second form is what Bottoms (2002) calls 'attachment leading to compliance'. Here, compliance is not the outcome of personal belief as such, but derives from the values of someone else to whom one has some loyalty or commitment. Thus, one might pledge to give up taking drugs because a partner considers it morally wrong.

The third means by which norms play a role in achieving outcomes is through 'legitimacy': the assent of the governed to the right of those in power to ordain their behaviour. As defined here, legitimacy represents normative acceptance rather than normative consensus. Personal beliefs may be at odds with a particular rule or command, but if an order comes from an authority that is deemed legitimate, it will be followed out of a commitment to its source rather than its content (Wrong 2002: 49). The relationship between legitimacy and personal morality is complex, and there are situations in which each may trump the other. Conscientious objectors place their own morality above the orders of the state, while most drivers who stick to the speed limit do so not because they think the limit is appropriate, but because they accept that personal behaviour should conform to the decrees of a legitimate legal authority. The suggestion of obligation is clear here, but should not be mistaken for coercion, for it is out of a normative rather than enforced commitment to authority that compliance is secured.

In relation to the prison, it is easy to assume that normative commitment plays little role in the accomplishment of order and other ends. Sykes, for example, argued that prisoners lacked any 'inner moral compulsion to obey' (1958: 48), and critics of the prison have emphasized the structural features of imprisonment, such as its profoundly undemocratic character, which make legitimacy almost impossible to achieve (Scraton *et al.* 1990; Sim

1994b). More recently though, while theorists of penal order have continued to argue that *absolute consensualism* is very hard to achieve in prison (where the wishes of prisoners are the same as those of prison officials and prisoners will want to do what is expected of them independently of reward, force, or habit), a number have highlighted the means by which authority in prison can be experienced as more or less legitimate (Sparks *et al.* 1996; Liebling 2004). This relates partly to whether an institution is considered justifiable within society i.e. whether it holds power legitimately. It also depends on *the way* that power is exercised: the degree to which it is exercised in accordance with formal rules and conforms to broad principles of justice—principles that are shared by the governors and the governed. It is in this respect, in terms of the manner of one's treatment, that some consensus can be found, for there is a moral palette on which staff and prisoners can agree. Where prisoners feel that power is being exercised fairly and their treatment is respectful, they are more likely to grant it legitimacy and therefore accept its demands even when these run counter to personal wishes (Sparks *et al.* 1996; and see Tyler 1990). In this formulation, legitimacy is conditional. It must be reconstituted perpetually through the moral dimensions of routine interactions and procedures (Sparks *et al.* 1996; Liebling 2004).

Although these forms of social power have been presented as discrete entities, the divisions between them are fuzzy. Once socialized into certain views, people may act upon them habitually. In such cases, their normative content is only 'latent' (Bottoms 2002). When someone desists from an activity for the sake of someone they care about, if the fear of losing that person plays some role in the decision, normative, and self-interested motives become blurred (ibid.). In prisons, situational control measures like CCTV and secure corridors are ostensibly coercive, but as prisoners become habituated to their presence, their primary effect is to signify institutional dominance and the impossibility of escape. The vast majority of prisoners do not routinely check that the locks, bolts, and bars of their cells are solid. Rather, they simply become resigned to the unbreachable nature of the carceral environment. Meanwhile, instrumental forms of power can transmute into coercive ones. The threat of withdrawing privileges is experienced as a punishment once one's baseline of expectations changes (Wrong 2002). Thus, inducement bleeds into coercion. Elsewhere, threats and veiled suggestions constitute forms of 'psychic violence' (ibid. 28) that are continuous with both coercion and fatalistic resignation.

Certain forms of power are associated with certain penal ambitions. Thus, coercion and routine are linked with authoritarianism and incapacitation; legitimacy with welfarism and rehabilitation; and economic inducement with neo-liberalism. However, these are not necessary alignments. The 'separate and silent' model, instituted in the nineteenth century in the UK at HMP Pentonville and in the US in Philadelphia, sought to promote spiritual reflection and reform through coercive restrictions in movement. There are also more and less authoritarian ways to encourage 'responsibility', as this chapter will show.

Power and Order

Sykes (1958) argued that the forms of power that could accomplish order in most environments were deficient within the special domain of the prison. Prisoners had no 'internal sense of duty'—that is, no normative motivation—to comply; the prison's rewards were meagre, and its punishments were either counter-productive or could do little to worsen the prisoner's predicament; the use of coercion was perilous and unwieldy. The power of officers was also compromised. Staff were outnumbered by prisoners and keen to maintain positive relationships with them, particularly given the potential for riots, when prisoners might look to settle scores. They were dependent on those they guarded to carry out the prison's daily tasks and make them appear competent. To write up all rule infractions was time-consuming, risked generating resentment, and gave an unwanted appearance of having a disordered wing.

Sykes considered these defects in the prison's supremacy to be virtually intrinsic and to belie the prison's apparently limitless formal power. Order was not achieved through the official mechanisms of coercion and reward that one might expect to predominate in such totalitarian institutions. Instead, he argued, it was accomplished through an in-built tendency for accommodation or compromise between the governors and the governed. In return for general obedience, officers turned a blind eye to minor rule infractions. Meanwhile, they induced compliance by passing goods and information to inmate leaders, who in turn dispensed these privileges within the inmate population. This arrangement helped the maintenance of order in three linked ways: by relieving the everyday tensions of prison life; by sweetening into compliance prisoners who were potentially unruly; and by reinforcing the status of inmate leaders while giving them a stake in maintaining institutional stability by smoothing and discouraging unrest. Institutional stability was an outcome of an informal, collective, pragmatic negotiation; power functioned *through* the norms and hierarchy of the prisoner community.

Sykes's study should be placed in context, for the means of accomplishing order are historically contingent. Informal accommodation and collective self-regulation among prisoners were outcomes of the specific terms of the post-war American prison, where prisoners mixed relatively freely and were integrated into the daily maintenance of the establishment, while guards did little more than patrol the prison's perimeter to prevent escapes (Irwin 2005). But, despite Sykes's claims, this model of order was not inevitable. Mathieson's (1965) study of Norwegian imprisonment provided empirical confirmation that incentives could be highly potent, particularly where prisoners were too disorganized to assert power collectively and force compromise on the part of the custodians. Jacobs' (1977) account of Stateville corroborated two key points. The first is that the prison is embedded in wider society, and this shapes the means by which it exerts power. More specifically, the transition of the American prison from an authoritarian autocracy to a more bureaucratic organization reflected shifts in wider sensibilities: demands for greater external legitimacy, for institutional accountability, and for some recognition of prisoners' rights.

Prisoners are part of this wider society, and as their expectations shift, the terms by which power is exerted are unlikely to remain static. As Sparks *et al.* (1996) note, power virtually always seeks legitimation, and this 'depends upon some degree of consonance with externally prevailing sensibilities' (Sparks *et al.* 1996: 310). Power therefore requires *some* negotiation with those who are subjected to it, whether this is with their values (e.g. what they are prepared to put up with) or the social power that they can generate within the prison.[3] As Jacobs (1977) outlined, the capacity of prison gangs to alleviate many of the pains of imprisonment meant that the Sykesian model of informal accommodation was no longer viable. Certainly, mechanisms of power and order are shaped by

---

[3] Whether this can be said of the most extreme penal regimes is a different matter, although even in super-max establishments, prisoners have at least some legally enshrined rights.

a dialectic between the intentions of those who deploy them and the responses of those on whom they are imposed. Indeed, forms of power are 'devised, elaborated, and justified' with resistance in mind (Scott 1990: 111). Prison officials speculate constantly on how prisoners will respond to decisions. In summary, as the context of imprisonment changes, and as prison populations vary, so too do the means of organizing and exercising power.

There is great variation in the means by which order can be successfully realized, even with similar populations. Prisons with democratic-therapeutic communities, such as Barlinnie and Grendon, have attained high levels of legitimacy despite dealing with prisoners considered highly recalcitrant (see Boyle 1984; Cooke 1989; Genders and Player 1995; and Sparks *et al.* 1996), while super-max prisons come close to embodying a complete control-coercion model of order in dealing with 'the worst of the worst' (King 1991, 1999; Rhodes 2004). However, even in these extreme cases, where it is especially apparent that one source of order is dominant, establishments do not rely on a single mechanism alone (Carrabine 2005). Coercive environments can, in theory, be more economical with other forces. In practice, though, they are unlikely to generate smooth compliance unless supported by other means. Even in the super-max prison, coercive measures are supplemented by routines (albeit ones that are exceptionally oppressive). In the consistency of their service delivery, their programmes and the relative safety they provide for prisoners, they may also generate a minimal level of legitimacy (King 1991).

Conversely, in prison therapeutic communities—often considered the most legitimate regimes in the system—prisoners comply in part because they know that they could easily be sent back to less liberal establishments. The threat of being 'shipped out' thus looms over what appears to be a relatively uncoercive regime. That compliance within medium-security American prisons is now achieved in part through the fear of transfer to super-max conditions indicates the need to evaluate modes of order *across* prison estates as well as within single establishments.[4] More

---

[4] In the UK, certain establishments, such as Dartmoor and Wandsworth have traditionally been seen as 'punishment nicks', where prisoners are sent to be 'taught a lesson'. As such, they have formed part of the control mechanism in less punitive prisons, where staff may explicitly remind prisoners that their continuing residence relies on their obedience.

significantly, for current purposes, the point is to emphasize that the vast majority of prisons cannot be characterized through simple notions of coercion or consent (Carrabine 2004, 2005), and that almost all prisons blend the forms of power outlined above. In any one establishment, power is exercised and order is achieved through multiple means.

This complicates questions about the *outcomes* of power. Outcomes are to some degree predictable at the poles of the system. Although coercion and consent are both capable of generating ordered environments, they arouse very different levels of *frustration* (see Wrong 2002: 47–52). Prisoner autobiographies—generally written by men at the penal 'deep-end'—provide ample testimony that violent regimes tend to provoke seething resentment at best and violent counter-conduct at worst. They also illustrate that, when placed in more legitimate environments, prisoners previously considered uncontrollable and irrational behave very differently (Boyle 1984; and see Cooke 1989; Sim 1994a; Sparks 2002). McEvoy's (2001) study of paramilitary imprisonment in Northern Ireland supports the notion that the strategies of the institution set the parameters of resistance, generating greater confrontation the more 'hardline' their form. The nature of institutional power clearly conditions forms of adaptation, compliance, resistance, and resentment, and does so especially sharply in extreme circumstances.

Yet these responses are rarely straightforward. Penal history is replete with examples of liberal intentions failing to produce happy compliance. The lifting of *Stateville's* authoritarian lid increased rather than diminished antipathy and violence, emboldening a prisoner community that was increasingly antagonistic towards the prison authorities (Jacobs 1977). Carrabine (2004) describes a similar process in the build-up to the Strangeways disturbance in 1990. Regime improvements failed to address fundamental grievances in full, while creating new frustrations and providing greater opportunities for them to be ventilated. In both cases, management attempts at liberalization were implemented reluctantly, partially, and unevenly by uniformed staff. The messy confluence of bureaucratic management, militaristic authoritarianism, and reformist ambition opened spaces for reactions that were plainly not envisaged.

The first contention here is that prisons are extremely complicated organizations, where management goals are mediated by staff and prisoners in ways that often have unforeseen effects. The second is that, where several forms of power are combined and conjoined, their consequences are hard to predict. This is not to say that these consequences are arbitrary, merely that they cannot be assumed from the formal properties of power alone. *Prisons and the Problem of Order* (Sparks *et al.* 1996) illustrates this lucidly, demonstrating how important differences between two English maximum-security prisons, including the number and form of violent incidents, the size of the informal economy, and the basis of legitimacy, related in complex ways to their different models of accomplishing order. Long Lartin was ostensibly the more 'liberal' prison, with more relaxed relationships between prisoners and staff, and a less tightly controlled regime. However, compared to Albany, its delivery of services was less consistent, and there were fewer restraints on the activities of more boisterous and predatory prisoners. Among prisoners, backstage violence, and victimization were common, often linked to the prison's more extensive system of illicit trade. Albany was a more authoritarian and oppressive establishment, and was in some respects less legitimate than Long Lartin. Tensions between prisoners and staff were higher than in Long Lartin, and there were more minor disciplinary infractions and assaults on staff. However, older prisoners who sought a quiet and predictable existence 'welcomed its restraining effect on the noisiness and bumptiousness of the younger majority' (1996: 317). Meanwhile, Albany prisoners 'drew a rather sharp distinction between the regime as such and the staff who administered it, whom they considered in the main to be reasonable [and] fair,' (Sparks *et al.* 1996: 317). Through the particularities of their cultures and practices, and the different levers they used to promote order, each prison produced different kinds of disorder, resentment, and social adaptation. The point is that these outcomes could be traced to their different arrangements of power, but, at the same time, the relationship between intentions and outcomes was far from straightforward.

Two further issues are crucial to the analysis that follows. The first is that legitimacy has a number of different facets. Sparks *et al.* (1996) list these as fair procedures, consistent outcomes, the behaviour of prison officials, and basic regime conditions. It is quite possible for institutions to be legitimate in some ways but not others. A prison may be procedurally fair but impersonal, or consistent but materially depriving. The second argument is that different prisoners will morally evaluate the prison, and grant it normative assent, in different ways. What feels unfair, impersonal, or indecent to one prisoner can feel fair and humane to another. As Sparks *et al.* (1996) suggest (without much further discussion), the same prison may be experienced by one prisoner as restrictive and by another as consistent, or by one prisoner as relaxed and another as unsafe. Such sentiments will also operate in relation to different levels of the institution. A prisoner might think that officers are administering a system fairly, but that the system is morally bankrupt; another may feel that individual officers are disrespectful, but that officers in general are the moral guardians of society and are generally worthy of respect. This does not preclude the moral evaluation of prisons in terms of how fair or humane they are in general (see Liebling 2004). It means that there is always variation within the prisoner community in terms of how these matters are perceived—how legitimacy is *individually* granted.

This is not just a matter of directly experienced institutional treatment, but also personal norms and values: one's views about the functions of imprisonment and the moral status of authority figures, for example. Political prisoners are more likely than other prisoners to align themselves normatively against state institutions and representatives, but they may well recognize the decency of individual officers.[5] To employ an example used by Sparks *et al.*, although most prisoners would not dispute the right of staff to patrol exercise yards, others might well do. When one considers the legitimacy of an institution, it is not enough to focus only on what the institution contributes i.e. how power is arranged and employed. There is also a need to explore the attitudes and expectations that are imported into the institution. These may reflect media representations, the reported experiences of significant others, or broader anti-authority sentiments (see Smith 2007). To summarize, there is always a subjective element to the granting of legitimacy, and this means that it will be conferred or withheld in various different ways.

Forms of power based on inducement, routine, and coercion will likewise have differential 'bite' or impact.[6] The pull of incentives

[5] A clear example here is Nelson Mandela, who formed a friendship with at least one of his guards while imprisoned on Robben Island (Mandela 1994).

[6] Thanks are due here to Richard Jones of Edinburgh University for this succinct phrase.

will depend on a prisoner's material needs and expectations—how much money s/he receives from outside the prison and how much s/he requires to 'make do'. Perceptions of agency and powerlessness will relate to psychological resources such as feelings of self-efficacy and inventiveness. Prisoners have different preferences: for structure, safety, flexibility, autonomy, and so on (Toch 1992). Some become hardened to violence and isolation in ways that others do not, such that fears of coercion and segregation will also vary. The key point here is that these basic forms of power are experienced in different ways, and whether individual prisoners are enticed, coerced, habituated, or persuaded into compliance will vary according to a range of factors that they *import* into the environment. To summarize further, in any one prison, order is not achieved homogenously. Power is deployed in multiple ways (Carrabine 2004) and different prisoners are addressed, engaged, and provoked by different components and combinations of power. 'Some may obey rules from fear, while others might support them out of habit or loyalty. They may even be obedient because they believe in the legitimacy of regulations in their own right' (Bosworth and Carrabine 2005: 506).

Very little work has explored these issues systematically. Sparks *et al.* (1996) note that differences in compliance relate to prior socialization, but in their work, as in most studies of power and order, the main unit of analysis is the wing or institution. Little is said to explain individual variance in compliance or resistance—the focus is *social* order in general rather than *individual* conformity (see also Carrabine 2004). It is clear from other work that, within any one institution, concerns and frustrations are differentiated according to ethnicity (Johnson 1976; Toch 1992; Cheliotis and Liebling 2006), age (Crawley 2005) and other variables; and that there are multiple experiences of prison life, which reflect identities, behaviours and characteristics carried from the external community. Many typologies of adaptation have emphasized the role of these imported variables in determining different ways of doing time, attitudes to the prison authorities, and orientations to other prisoners (Irwin and Cressey 1962; Irwin 1970, 1985; Cohen and Taylor 1972; Jacobs 1977). However, in these kinds of studies, compliance with institutional ends has rarely been the focus. Virtually no research has sought to relate the specific form of institutional power to different kinds of adaptation and resistance, or has untangled the different interactions of indigenous, institutional and imported factors in these processes.

In recent years, the best study of this kind has been conducted by Kruttschnitt and Gartner (2005), whose research compares adaptive styles and social life in two contemporary Californian women's prisons, and in the same prison at different points in time. Kruttschnitt and Gartner show how, since the 1960s, female prisoners have become more self-reliant, more distrustful of staff and other prisoners, and more socially isolated, with fewer friendships and less peer solidarity. These shifts reflect the 'refigurement' of women's imprisonment in the mould of the 'new penology': the movement to a more austere system, focused more on personal responsibility than rehabilitation, with fewer concessions to gender difference, less attention to the individual, and an emphasis on compliance rather than personal transformation. In accordance with these shifts, the nature of dissent has altered (although the continuing existence of homosexual activity represents an enduring mode of resistance). There are fewer means of challenging the system as an individual, but legal action has become more common. Meanwhile, the prison's concern with conformity rather than normalization means that obedience has become simpler and there are fewer points of provocation.

Second, Kruttschnitt and Gartner show that, even when controlling for background and sentence attributes, the nature of the institution has 'a significant and sizeable impact' (2005: 140) on how women 'do time'. In the prison that was more representative of the new penology, trust was lower and social life more restricted. Most women lived in fairly alienated states, as they tried to cope with a harsh regime. In this context, certain adaptations were more likely—those of the 'convict' and the 'isolate'. Both adaptations involved troubled relationships with staff and social withdrawal, reflecting the difficulties of negotiating the prison's regime. In the more traditional and less punitive establishment, adaptations were more diverse. The environment was less destructive of imported attributes, and there were more 'adapted' prisoners who had positive relationships with staff and other prisoners, and felt some sense of control in their everyday lives. The general point should be clear: the study of prison social life and adaptation requires an analysis of institutional conditions, for these conditions shape—without fully determining—patterns of prison adjustment, and the degree to which imported variables can be expressed.

Resistance

Perhaps one reason why studies of compliance and resistance have been uncommon is that the level of consent and legitimacy that an establishment produces is not easy to decipher. In the first place, the value of subjective accounts of subordination can be questioned. Even in the most unjust circumstances, some subordinates express negligible resentment and will grant legitimacy to their oppressors (the phenomenon of the 'the contented slave'). Consent can be manufactured (Gramsci 1971), and it may be psychologically preferable to embrace one's powerlessness than to torment oneself with the daily recognition of one's subjection. The logic of such perspectives is that a situation of apparent consensus could represent total ideological domination as much as normative harmony. However, such concerns may be overstated. Evidence suggests that such pure forms of 'false consciousness' are almost never achieved. At most, subordinates are likely to hold a 'dual consciousness' (Abercrombie *et al.* 1980; Scott 1990), where even if they grant lip service in public to the notion that their predicament is deserved, in private and in their 'common-sense' discourse they recognize its unfairness. In prison, where the terms of inequality are so stark and where the depredations are so direct, it seems particularly unlikely that subordinates might misrecognize illegitimate practices as legitimate ones. Prisoners are highly sensitive to poor treatment, unfairness, and minor acts of illegitimacy.

The difficulty, therefore, is not that sentiments of resistance might not exist, but that they can be hard to excavate. As Scott (1990: 199) asserts throughout *Domination and the Arts of Resistance*, there is an 'immense political terrain [between] quiescence and revolt' and to seek out only public defiance and open rebellion as indications of frustration is to reduce resistance to its most extreme and ostentatious manifestations. Where power differentials are acute and the punishments for dissent are severe, subordinates are unlikely to flaunt their opposition or pursue their grievances blatantly. Unless they are confident of overturning their domination, it is more prudent for them when in public either to rehearse hegemonic discourse or to negotiate using its terms. In such situations, one finds a 'public transcript' that is relatively smooth and apparently consensual, yet it is almost impossible to gauge what this represents. It could mean ideological concord (in which dominant norms are held sincerely, or have been internalized), or rather fear, fatalism, or the performance of consent. Certainly, the use by the powerless of the terms of the dominant should not be taken as a straightforward indication of defeat or submission. The use of prevailing discourse to haggle with the system may be highly effective, as well as prudential. It is far easier for power-holders to deflect attacks that use oppositional terms than to dismiss those that deploy their own standards and values, for to do the latter would risk exposing their own ideological bankruptcy.

Here then, subordinates make pragmatic use of the contestable space that always exists where terms must be interpreted, rules implemented, and discretion exercised. Yet however polite their opposition and however much they concede to the discourse of the power-holders, these public contestations are still relatively brazen displays of disagreement. Under conditions of domination, it would be naïve not to look beyond public discourse for signs of dissent. At their most concealed, these may be limited to the 'hidden transcript', expressed in the relative safety of private spaces, 'outside the intimidating gaze of power' (Scott 1990: 18). In these offstage spaces one finds expressions of irreverence and self-assertion, fantasies of revenge, outbursts of rage, and imagined inversions of normal power relations. A further realm exists between this completely secluded domain—in which resentment can be freely expressed—and the public zones where prisoners are censorious but conciliatory. Here, there exists a 'politics of disguise and anonymity that takes place in public view but is designed to have a double meaning or to shield the identity of the actors' (ibid. 19). This is a sphere where contempt is concealed and expressed simultaneously, through the skilled performance of humility and the secretion of coded insults into the public transcript.

This continuum of political discourse, which ranges from bold, open defiance at one end to private frustration at the other, provides a useful framework through which resistance in prison can be classified. The most explicit forms of prison dissent are riots and protests. At their most extreme, these are organized attempts to overturn the function and logic of the system (Useem and Kimball 1989; Scraton *et al.* 1991; Colvin 1992; Carrabine 2004). As well as through these attempts at rupture, institutional power can be resisted in perpetual forms, through ongoing and overt expressions of hostility, and the constant threat of collective rebellion.

The basis for such efforts may be a shared set of oppositional values generated by common predicament (Sykes 1958)—what might be referred to as structural solidarity. Collective power can also stem from values imported from networks and organizations located outside the prison (Jacobs 1977). Most notably, prisoners can be galvanized into purposeful action by political convictions, particularly when these are reinforced and supported by a wider ideological community. In Northern Ireland, for example, paramilitary prisoners gained incremental control over the prison's public spaces in part by making threats to staff safety through the use of external contacts (McEvoy 2001). Shared political commitments also provided the will and solidarity to sustain long-term hunger strikes and dirty protests. Such strategies, along with escape attempts and certain forms of legal action, represent conscious challenges to state power (see also Buntman 2003).

Mathiesen's (1965) study supports Scott's assertion that, to be effective, power does not need to be either collective or oppositional. Lacking a cohesive value system, and dependent upon staff for a range of highly desired privileges, the prisoner community that Mathieson described was 'atomized' and highly divided. Prisoners had little choice but to accept ostensibly the terms of their captors, and to make personal representations from within prevailing ideology. But by chastizing officials for not conforming to their own stated norms—for imposing rules too literally and being insufficiently flexible, *or* for veering from the rulebook and being inconsistent and unfair—prisoners could exert considerable influence over their custodians and take advantage of the inherent weaknesses of bureaucratic domination.

Other forms of resistance in prison take the more privatized and ambiguous forms that Scott highlights: seething anger, expressed only among trusted associates; collective dreams of retribution, cloaked insults, and so on. As studies of women's imprisonment in particular have demonstrated, acts and gestures that are apparently trivial—backstage jokes, the use of in-group language, choices of dress—often represent assertions of agency and identity, personal forms of subversion, and contestations of the meanings and definitions imposed by the institution (Bosworth 1999; Bosworth and Carrabine 2001). Resistance is not limited to its more explosive and organized manifestations, for its minor and mundane expressions are the skirmishes that help maintain personal integrity and draw the boundaries of institutional power.

Nonetheless, questions should be asked about what counts as resistance as opposed to survival, coping or the maintenance of mental and physical integrity (see Cohen and Taylor 1972; Buntman 2003). Resistance and coping exist on the same spectrum of activities, but should not be confused (McEvoy 2001). If resistance is defined as *any* expression of agency or identity, the danger is that all acts are flattened out into the same thing, whatever their aims, scope, and consequences, and regardless of their context. The pursuit of education is a completely different thing depending on whether it fulfils or subverts institutional aims. Similarly, where the stated aim of the prison system is to maintain rather than obliterate individuality and personal integrity, expressions of agency cannot necessarily be seen as assertions 'against' the system. Buntman's (2003: 237) characterization of resistance as 'actions and practices designed to dilute, circumvent, or eliminate the imposition of unwelcome power' is thus a useful baseline definition, allowing at least some consideration of intentions, outcomes, and the dialectic of power between dominant and subordinate parties. Scott (1990: 92) offers a more nuanced way to evaluate the intensity of resistant practices. The least radical step is to criticize some of the dominant class for violating their own principles; then to aim accusations at the entire stratum of rulers; the most extreme position 'repudiates the principles by which the dominant stratum justifies its dominance' (ibid.). Whether in public or offstage, almost all forms of critique can be assessed through this schema.

The analysis of resistance is also enhanced when acts can be placed within the context of the prison's social world. As I discuss below, forms of individual resistance require social support or toleration, and whether they aggregate depends on social factors such as the extent to which subordinates are mutually dependent and socially cohesive, share a common experience of domination, and can change their status by other means (Scott 1990). Some studies of resistance emphasize subjective meaning but give little sense of these social factors or of the forms of power that help shape resistant practices. The objects of analysis are thus left disembedded and decontextualized. Questions of why power is resisted in particular ways, at particular times, and by particular people cannot easily be answered. A more comprehensive account of the differential forms of resistance and compliance requires an analysis of the nature of power, the social context, and the experiences and expectations of individual prisoners.

The Nature of Modern Penal Power

You don't exist right up against the authoritarian wall, you exist some-where away from it, and there is a buffer zone in-between. If you start pushing for things, all of a sudden you hit up against that. You couldn't live with that shield or wall or whatever on you all the time because it would breed a greater resentment than there already is.... There are cer-tain things that you're never gonna get, there are other things where you can undermine or erode that authoritarian block. But [mainly] you live in a buffer zone between it, so you might not [hit it]. Then all of a sudden, *bang*, you will hit up against the wall.... Back in the day the system was pure authority, there was no give in it. [You] were banging up against it, so you did get things like riots, you did get things that was problems, you did get the very us/them division, which has been eroded over the years to a certain degree. That shield has been removed slightly from your everyday contact with the prison, which makes it easier to cope with. It also makes it less likely to kick off, because there are other ways round it: you have other recourses, other ways of retreating from hostilities. (Nathan)

Previous chapters have sketched broad changes in the aims and functions of Western imprisonment, and have outlined the shift-ing priorities of the Prison Service since the 1990s. Put briefly, following a period of liberalization and relegitimation in the years following the Woolf report, events in the mid-90s propelled a focus on security and control throughout the rest of the decade. A punitive swing in the political climate also drove a tightening-up of regimes and an emphasis on individual responsibility. Policies such as the Incentives and Earned Privileges Scheme and Mandatory Drug Testing embodied these shifts, linking rewards, punishments, and sentence progression to compliant behaviour. By the end of the decade, a moral lexicon of decency and respect had been appended to these concerns, and there was a resumed emphasis on rehabilitation. Indeed, in the period immediately prior to the study, 'resettlement' had become the watchword of the Service. But the refocusing of priorities towards risk reduction and public protection was ever more conspicuous, channelling rehabilitative impulses into particular forms. Discourses of wel-farism and decency, authority and control, and personal responsi-bility and accountability thus co-existed not just within the same system, but, as this chapter will elaborate, within specific pol-icies, creating a particular formation of power on the prison land-ings. These policies and sensibilities took form in particular ways within HMP Wellingborough. The prison's culture was benign and—compared to many other Cat-C prisons—it was persuasive rather than coercive in its methods of control. At the same time, it was a prison that rather lacked vision and dynamism. At times, (and particularly as the research went on) prisoner treatment was indifferent and unengaged. It was in this context that policies were implemented and power was refined.

The diminishment of pure authority

The description of a past culture of 'pure authority'—as described in the quotation above—referenced a considerable shift in the tone of the landings and the manner by which uniformed staff exercised their power. There was no recourse to the deliberate intimidation and sheer thuggery that was a common feature of regimes in the past (King and McDermott 1990; Smith 2004; Sim 2008).[7] In earlier times, such threats were central to the mainten-ance of order. As George noted, a prison's segregation unit was 'a fearsome place—you did not wanna go down the block cos you knew you'd be curled up in the corner nursing bruises within the hour, and that's how they enforced control'. Gerry concurred that, years earlier, breaking rules meant 'a good likelihood you were going to get battered'. He also highlighted the manner in which officers had inflamed frustrations through their indiffer-ence to prisoner concerns:

There was no such thing as telephones, and the staff had to ring up [for you]. You couldn't go to a member of staff, because he'd say 'ah, do one' [i.e. go away]. Your wife's in hospital, or your child's in hospital, and he'd say 'yeah, I'll do it later', when it was important for them to do it now. It was confrontational. There was one situation where a con came to an officer, in front of quite a number of cons, and he's crying, and he says 'boss, [I don't know if you know, but] my mum's died and nobody's told me'. The officer says 'I don't know that one. You sing it, and I'll hum it'. That was confrontational.

Wellingborough's culture was not characterized by exchanges of this kind. Treatment was sometimes poor and indifferent, but officers did not operate with the unaccountable callousness of the past—willfully abusing their power, mishandling prisoners'

---

[7] None of this is to suggest that these things do not still occur in some prisons (as HMCIP reports and investigations into prisons such as Wandsworth, Wormwood Scrubs, and Portland have shown in recent years).

property, 'not answering bells, holding back letters, delaying an escort to a visit' (King and McDermott 1990: 457; and see McDermott and King 1988; Scraton *et al.* 1991). As the previous chapter explained, officers were not necessarily proactive in their pursuit of prisoner welfare, but neither did they seek to antagonize or humiliate prisoners or completely ignore their concerns.

The humanization of staff culture relates in part to cultural factors and practices of staff recruitment. Officers now go through formalized vetting procedures, including competence-based assessments and job simulation exercises, and their training places emphasis on issues such as interpersonal skills, respect for others, communication and care, as well as traditional aspects of the officer role such as maintaining safety and security (McHugh *et al.* 2008). Filtering out those applicants unwilling or incapable of interacting or empathizing with prisoners has been a significant aim of such policies (although one that is not always fulfilled, and may be undermined by the realities of officer training (Crawley 2004a; Arnold 2005; 2008)). The introduction of female staff has diluted some of the more abrasive aspects of 'canteen culture' (Fielding 1994). Messages from the organizational centre have encouraged governors to deal robustly with staff brutality. In theory, the formalization of control and restraint procedures means that force is used more carefully and there is less recourse to intimidation. A more challenging approach towards recalcitrant POA committees, alongside the threat of privatization, has eroded some of the traditional sources of indifference and disengagement among uniformed staff. Meanwhile, efforts have been made to mirror more adequately the ethnic make-up of prisoners in the staffing of prisons, with efforts made to recruit more minority ethnic staff (McHugh *et al.* 2008). In Wellingborough, few uniformed personnel were ex-armed forces (see Liebling and Price 2001; Crawley 2004a), and those who were did not cling to a militaristic model of discipline and order. The vast majority of officers were approachable and reasonable—as Harvey summarized, 'if you talk to an officer in the right way, you get things done'.

The relative absence of caustic resentment or 'toxic hostility' (Sim 2008) on Wellingborough's landings also reflects a range of long-term improvements in material decency across the prison system. Experienced prisoners contrasted an era of austerity and unsanitary conditions, when 'nobody had radios [and] it was piss buckets, with three of you to a cell' to one of 'stereos, flasks for water, where [you] can have trainers and clothes sent in' (Noah). Standards of food, hygiene, and comfort, although still wretched in some establishments, have undoubtedly got better;[8] and life on the wings has been normalized considerably through the introduction of telephones, in-cell television, and the possibility of wearing one's own clothing. As Jim Lewis noted—and as Chapter 2 sketched out broadly—the last twenty years has also seen great strides in terms of 'positive interventions': 'When I first joined the Prison Service, we were not doing anything to address offending behaviour in any systematic way. Things like family ties, visits, resettlement, offending behaviour programme, drug treatment are all much, much better.' To this could be added improvements in first night care, gym facilities, and educational provision.

In terms of basic conditions and opportunities, then, the baseline of legitimacy has been raised significantly, as George summarized:

Physically, a lot of the frustrations have gone. There was an old saying, I don't hear it anymore, I used to hear it a lot: 'there's three things you don't mess with, and that's food, visits and mail'. Those were the three things that prisoners were concerned about. But now we've got so much more: physically, there's no problem. It's a lot more civilised, a lot better.

Changes in living standards and officer culture have been achieved through structural as well as cultural means. As previous chapters have outlined, managerialist reforms have relocated power to higher levels of the prison (see also Bryans 2007). Strategies of audit and centralized command have enhanced control over the lower levels of the organization (Liebling 2004; Carlen 2005; Cheliotis 2006). To a much greater degree, prisons are 'run to policy'. Decision-making practices have been homogenized, procedures and entitlements have been published openly (in forms that are theoretically accessible to prisoners), and managers are held responsible for institutional conformity to standards. There are also clear grievance procedures for prisoners.

---

[8] 'The food, generally, is a lot better. When I was in Liverpool prison for six months I went hungry. I did actually really go hungry, cos the food was [that] bad' (George)

One consequence is that the authority of officers is structured and made accountable in ways that make deviations from policy and blatant misuses of power more difficult.[9] In the past, these aberrations and abuses had been common, as George recalled: 'prison clothes used to be used as a weapon by staff. If they didn't like you, you'd find you'd been given a shirt with no buttons on, or a pair of trousers that came down to here.' Other prisoners reported being refused showers, denied exercise, and having food spat upon (see also Scraton *et al.* 1991). In Wellingborough, such visible digressions were now less conceivable, in part because its staff culture mitigated against them, but also because officer power was so closely contained through formal scrutiny, over-sight, and an ever-tighter management grip on staff behaviour.

The relocation and dispersal of power

A second, linked outcome has been that, in terms of *organizational* decision-making, the power of uniformed staff has to some degree been eroded and supplanted. Until the 1990s, it was normal for new receptions to prison to be forcefully reminded that officers' authority was absolute and that uniformed staff 'ran the prison'. As one principal officer recalled, 'somebody would say: "while you're in prison, there is only one rule, and that's *do as you are told by prison officers*"' (see also King and McDermott 1988). Pete recounted that officers had 'been gods: they had the power of life or death'. Gerry concurred that 'they had control of the whole prison. They did whatever they wanted, and the governor backed them.' Governors themselves told stories of their relative powerlessness in times gone by, for example, being intimidated by uniformed staff not to enter certain areas of the prison, such as segregation units.

In Wellingborough, as in all but the most traditional establish-ments, such descriptions no longer applied. Decisions about the prison's regime, timetable and operations—for example, whether to cancel evening association or how to organize visits—were based on centralized targets and taken at management level. Officers were consulted on these strategic decisions, but they no longer represented the power base of the organization. Collectively,

---

[9] As King and McDermott (1989) demonstrated, in the 1980s, Prison Service senior managers had little grip on many vital aspects of the system.

their weight was diminished.[10] As in all prisons, judgments about recategorization and release were based partly on feedback from wing staff. Ultimately too though, these decisions were made at higher levels and were influenced most by input from specialist staff such as psychologists and probation officers.

The bureaucratization of officer authority, its relative softening, and the dispossession of power from the prison landings (the removal of the 'authoritarian wall' from everyday contact, to refer back to an earlier quotation) have significantly reconfigured the nature and experience of power for prisoners. The basic relationship with uniformed staff and the perception of their role have been altered significantly. From the viewpoint of Wellingborough's wings, organizational power did not reside with basic grade officers. These staff made the prison run, but they did not run the prison. They *implemented* the system of power, and they remained its frontline representatives, but they did not *embody* it. Power flowed through officers, and the way in which they used it was a principal determinant of the prison's legitimacy and survivability (see Liebling 2004; Sparks *et al.* 1996), but they were not its ultimate possessors.

Notably then, officers were often excluded from descriptions of 'The System' and were often seen as peripheral figures in its organization. Nathan commented that officers seemed to 'feel marginalized, adrift from the system; they're no longer an amalgamated part of it'. Although attitudes to officers varied—as Chapter 6 explains in more detail—criticism rarely targeted their collective use of power or tarnished them in blanket terms. Rather, it reflected individual behaviour, their role in systemic failings and their status as representatives of authority. In this respect, officers were conduits rather than controllers of organizational power: 'just doing a job' or 'paying their mortgage', rather than 'the enemy' or 'callous zoo keepers' (McDermott and King, 1988: 361; and see below). Put more pejoratively, they were 'like robots— they're programmed to give certain answers' (Matt). Inevitably, frustrations were often vented at officers, but few prisoners held

---

[10] One incident in the prison, when the perimeter fence security system failed, illustrated the hierarchy of decision-making among staff. Wing officers were given only basic information about the situation, and were not consulted on how to deal with it. Decisions were made by a team consisting of the prison's governors and three principal officers.

them responsible for the injustices and inefficiencies of a system determined well above their heads.

Discretion, relationships, and incentives: 'soft power'

This should not be taken to suggest that officers were powerless or that they were merely vessels of institutional power. At the same time as their collective influence within penal organizations has diminished, as the 'street-level bureaucrats' of the system (Lipsky 1983), officers still wielded considerable *discretionary* authority.[11] To a large degree, this discretion was accidental, an inevitable result of the need for frontline personnel to translate policy into practice, and—within certain boundaries—to interpret and implement a multitude of organizational rules and procedures (see Liebling and Price 2001). As Cheliotis (2008: 254) summarizes, 'what escapes the supervisory gaze of the "system", no matter how Orwellian that may be, is the panoply of personal values and idiosyncratic meanings that individual decision-makers bring to their decisions'. Elsewhere, policies such as the IEP scheme were designed to hand discretionary power to landing staff, giving them considerable influence to determine the everyday lifestyles of individual prisoners (Bottoms 2003).[12] In these respects, the 'buffer zone' was a domain of personal discretion and localized autonomy.

In Wellingborough, as in other areas of criminal justice work (Lynch 1998; Lucken 1998; Robinson 2002), this discretion was put to a number of uses. Discretion can function for or against legitimacy (Liebling 2000). At times, it was employed to bypass inefficiencies, enable prisoners to back down from confrontation without losing face, reduce needless tensions, and to make exceptions for prisoners who were vulnerable.[13] In such ways, officers

---

[11] The differences in prisoner life quality at establishments with the same functions and populations show how significant this discretion can be (Liebling 2004).

[12] Decisions to place or keep prisoners on the basic privilege level could not be taken by officers alone, and had to be endorsed by Principal Officers or more senior managers, except in exceptional circumstances agreed by the Area Manager.

[13] Examples included a prisoner who had exhausted his phone credits being allowed to use the staff office to contact an ill relative; and another, who was always in debt, being permitted to use extra private cash to purchase tobacco, to prevent him sliding into further arrears.

both under- and over-used the legal power at their disposal in ways that were consistent with notions of natural justice. Elsewhere, they used discretion in the service of institutional calm, recognizing the value of tolerating minor infringements in exchange for general goodwill (Sykes 1958). Prior to starting cell searches, for example, it was common for officers to give prisoners time to dispose of illicit goods or borrowed items. Some such compromises were accepted by management as part of what one governor called an 'unwritten code' that tacitly accepted that 'it's okay to brew hooch, but it's not okay to assault staff'.

However, the discretionary element of staff power was 'a mixed bonus' (Den), with a number of consequences. At one extreme, officers could remove or deny privileges, withhold entitlements, and enforce rules unfairly and inconsistently. In this regard, policies such as IEP have facilitated new forms of punishment. Abuses take place less often through behaviour which steps *outside* the rules of the system—for example, through physical brutality or deliberate psychological persecution (MacDonald and Sim 1978; Scraton *et al.* 1991). Instead, they occur within its bureaucratic folds, through distortions of policy and procedure: exaggerated suspicions, misuse of the IEP system, and other such acts, whose iniquities cannot be easily discerned, let alone proved.

Even when staff sought to use discretionary power responsibly, the role of personal judgment meant that relationships were inherently precarious. For officers, the exercise of bureaucratic authority was fraught with difficulties, always open to challenge (Mathieson 1965). Indeed, uncertainty and ambiguity were intrinsic features of the 'sticky' relationships between prisoners and staff that modern policies encouraged. Since officers differed in their use of authority, with some more inclined than others to grant small favours, chase up requests, and help with job placements, positive relationships with staff could be highly beneficial to a prisoner's living standards. And since prisoners also relied on staff for privilege decisions and wing reports, the dynamic between staff and prisoners was far from one of pure voluntarism. Social distance was reduced by necessity. Among prisoners, cordial relations with officers therefore incurred little stigma or suspicion. There were limits to what could be legitimately discussed with uniformed staff. Nonetheless, it was normal for prisoners to chat with officers on the landings or joke with them while waiting to move off the wings. This represented a significant change from an era where there were few practical or social reasons to mix with wing staff, as Alexis described:

Years ago, if you was seen hanging around the office, you was a grass, you was no good.[14] [Now] the staff that we've got, they are friendly and open, so if you're seen talking to them it's not misconstrued. People do their own thing. (Alexis)

Meanwhile, policies of 'dynamic security' encouraged officers to interact with prisoners in order both to identify their concerns, and detect and inhibit the roots of discontent. 'Decency' was fused with control, producing a form of power that was supple and discreet.

Inevitably, these relationships were complex and compromised, for while they melded humanity and authority, the latter tended to triumph if the two came into tension. In certain respects, for prisoners, the incitement to interact with staff functioned coercively. If one wanted to progress, getting on with staff was less a matter of choice than compulsion. The relationships this invited could thus be instrumental, disingenuous, and highly unstable. Charlie's comparison with the past emphasized a customary frustration of the modern era: 'they were stricter then, but it were easier as well, because you knew where you stood. Now you have a joke and a laugh with a screw, and he'll nick you the next fucking minute.' Connor agreed that: 'they'll be nice to you one minute, then they'll just turn and basically want to nick you'. These were common statements, which underlined the fragility of relationships that combined intimacy and power. For some prisoners, there was more psychological comfort in 'knowing your enemy' than in a form of shallow rapport whose latent functions were exposed when officers imposed their authority. Relations with female staff were all the more volatile. Many prisoners struggled to maintain appropriate psychological boundaries with female officers, and the intensity of their attachments led to extreme emotional reactions when discipline supplanted friendliness (Crewe 2006a; Tait 2008).

Just as relationships with staff were imbued with power, so too were policies of material improvement. These improvements—and the general raising of material standards—should not be underestimated in terms of the difference they have made to normalizing the prison environment. Yet, as some prisoners recognized,

---

[14] A 'grass': a prisoner who informs on his or her peers. In the US, a 'snitch'.

despite their ostensible benevolence, they also served as core components of penal control (see also Jewkes 2002).

A lot of the things the prisons implement over the years, yes, it might be rehabilitative but it's also controlling. The courses they implement, the fact that they give you TVs, they really are control mechanisms, and people buy into that. (Nathan)

People are scared. They're all chasing things now. And like I said, they don't want to upset the apple cart. They don't want to have the TV taken off them. [The prison's] saying to you, 'we'll give you that but you've got to do this for us'.... They give you so much now, but they only give you things which they can take back off you.... All this 'enhanced', 'standard', 'basic', it's a good thing in the long run because prison did need this change, where they gave you a bit more. But the prison system will only give you stuff which they can take away from you. (Darren)

Such comments recognized a tension between the enhancement of legitimacy achieved by penal reforms and the coercive dimensions of incentive schemes that granted benefits in ways that were conditional and differentiated.[15] The formal aims of the IEP scheme were to reward individual compliance, to encourage hard work and responsible behaviour, and to create a more orderly, disciplined environment (Liebling *et al.* 1999; Bottoms 2003). In sociological terms, the policy aspired to reduce the feelings of material deprivation that could inflame unrest, while making compliance more effective than collective action in enhancing living standards. Ideally then, prisoners were incorporated into the prison's opportunity structures, and seduced away from illicit sources of goods and services. Power would be transferred from the prisoner community to the prison machinery. Moreover, while all prisoners would be given an interest in compliance, the scheme would splinter collective interests. Both the motivations and the potential for peer solidarity would be reduced (see Chapter 5).

Shifts in the political climate during the 1990s had altered the tenor of the IEP scheme in significant ways. Initially, it had been envisaged partly as a way of supporting 'the development of constructive and positive regime provision' (Bottoms 1993: 112). By the time of implementation, its emphasis was more coercive. Rights had been reconceived as privileges, the notion

---

[15] It is interesting to note that Liebling *et al.* (1997) found that prisoners felt that the IEP scheme was fair in principle but not in implementation, and that it was unsuccessful in its aim of improving prisoner behaviour.

of 'minimum standards' was no longer a key priority, and the policy's punitive role had been clearly foregrounded. Matt's complaints conveyed this more coercive spirit: 'it's alright havin carrots, but there's no point having carrots if somebody's behind it with a big stick'. Comforts could also serve as a substitute for reasonable treatment and explanation: 'if you wanna complain about something, you can't. They don't wanna know, they say "look at everything we've gave ya".... They expect me to be grateful cos they gave me something' (Matt).

Meanwhile, the linking of opportunities with compliance extended the *amount* and *intensity* of power available to the prison authorities. 'They can hit you with a stick a lot fuckin harder', said Matt, 'they've got more stick to wield'. Prison officers in particular were empowered by their role in the IEP process. For prisoners, the more significant factor was the smooth efficiency of this power: the way it worked upon their material desires. Prisoners repeatedly testified to the coercive effects that material inducements produced, once expectations adjusted to new privileges. The fear of 'losing things' loomed large in testimonies of compliance:

TV matters now. When I was first on this wing, we never had TVs, so I used to read more then and sleep more. TV weren't really an issue. You missed it but you never had one. Now you've got one, when they take it away, that's a head fuck. (Kai)

Before, nothing could be taken off ya. You didn't have nothing, so they couldn't do nothing, but now if you spend time in the block, you lose your TV—and, as I say, once you've had that, you get used to it. (Alexis)

Most officers acknowledged the coercive potential of incentives, in the sense that they knew they were effective levers for ensuring prisoner compliance. Yet they also considered the IEP scheme to be excessively generous. Indeed, their complaints about what prisoners were allowed revealed the prevalence of attitudes of 'less eligibility'.[16] Staff less often recognized that the prison's beneficence and its power to punish were inextricable. Inducements ranged from material goods to sentence progression, forming an extensive web of enticement. Moreover, being an 'enhanced' prisoner was not only an incentive in itself—a source of current provision (in-cell

---

[16] Less eligibility in this context refers to the belief that conditions in prison should not be better than those in the outside world.

television, extra visits, association time, etc). It was also desirable because it represented an official status label that helped accelerate the journey towards freedom: 'It looks better on my record later on' (Stephen). Since these inducements could be withheld or withdrawn, and progress towards release could thus be slowed, the might of the stick and the appeal of the carrot could not easily be separated. The potency of the prison's enticements was what made them so sharply double-edged, and so encompassing. The situation was 'more diplomatic; [but] they always balance it in their favour.... The system has the monopoly. They own all the cards' (Darren). This was government by self-interest, relationships, and discretion: 'soft power'.

The texture of bureaucratic power

The complexity of staff-prisoner relations was emblematic of a more general ambiguity that was built into the form of bureaucratic power. In the same way that prisoners highlighted the difficulties of knowing the precise limits of acceptable conduct with staff, their testimonies repeatedly contrasted a regime of clarity, when there were 'lines you did not cross' and 'rules written in stone' (Pete) (and see Carrabine 2004), with contemporary circumstances where boundaries were blurred and expectations unclear. Darren provided a particularly insightful analogy to convey how the parameters of action had been reconfigured:

[In the past] the rules was tight but at the same time it was relaxed because you knew exactly how far you could go. It's like getting a piece of elastic band, pulling it, and you know if you pull it a bit further it's going to snap. [Now] you have the same elastic band and pull it and pull it and pull it and not know when it's going to snap.

As portrayed here, the authoritarian prison of the past was oppressive but predictable. In comparison, modern imprisonment was less restrictive but more difficult to navigate. Tommy argued in similar terms that while in the past the penalties for disobedience had been brutal, it had at least been apparent what disobedience entailed: 'The violence in the prisons—you had to cross that line. [It] was only there if you went out and looked for it.' Staff corroborated these reminiscences of a bygone culture that was harsher but less ambiguous. In the words of one governor: 'the line was well drawn, and if the prisoner overstepped the line, he would suffer the consequences. There was very little consideration, it never wavered. But it also meant there were less areas of conflict.'

The point here is not to evaluate claims about which era was preferable (especially since there were elements of machismo in the idealization of starker forms of power), but to bring into relief how power on the landings has been reshaped. The idea of bureaucratic rule is that power is applied more fairly and that 'penal decisions [are] more easily subjected to the various demands for accountability' (Aas 2004: 384). In Wellingborough, however, its application was typical of frontline bureaucracies, with rules employed and procedures explained in ways that were often erratic and inconsistent. Knowing what to conform to was not straightforward (Kruttschnitt and Gartner 2005):

> We're supposed to go to chapel every evening. We don't go, and some of the officers know we don't go. They've seen us in the library, and they let it go a couple of times. [Then] one time they come in pissed off and say 'you're nicked'. Years ago you'd have been nicked anyway, straightaway, no question asked and down the block. (Darren)

> You knew where you stood [even though] it was a harder time than it is now. Today's prison, one day, you go and ask for something and you'll be given a reasonable answer. The next day, you'll go and ask and be told a pack of lies to confuse you. They let one man do one thing, but the next man they say 'no'. (Tommy)

> A-shift can allow you to do this and do that. B-shift will go, 'oh, we're having none of that'. So you don't know where the fuck you are. (Pete)

Such quotations highlighted the ontological insecurities that discretion could engender, and which rendered the external environment unreliable and unpredictable (see also Sparks *et al.* 1996: Chapter 5). Comments that the prison experience depended on whether 'your face fits'—a motto of the modern prison—highlighted a significant downside of bureaucratic discretion (see Toch 1992). In the eyes of prisoners, the logic of decision-making was often opaque, and seemed to depend on personal relationships with staff. For a minority of prisoners who had experienced the certainties and hostilities of the past, the lack of clear authority in the contemporary prison was perceived as a psychological threat— 'head games' (Alexis).[17] For the majority, as Darren suggested, its character was confusing and capricious—'softer but shitter'

---

[17] Sparks (2002: 561) describes prisoners in Barlinnie reflecting on the 'elemental', almost serene, simplicity of the deep-end of the penal system, where lines of solidarity and enmity were unambiguous.

(Kieran), or, in Pete's terms, 'easier but hard. It's a piece of piss, but it's not *hard*, it's intolerable. You just cannot get anything done.'

Likewise, prisoners frequently contrasted a past era of few rights and expectations with one where comforts and opportunities were available, but never guaranteed:

In the past, you could ask for something, and you knew the answer. The answer was always 'no', so you didn't expect nothing. There was no delusions, no dangling carrots in front of my face saying 'if you do this, you will be rewarded at the end of it'—but every time you get closer, they move the goalposts. (Tommy)

Many prisoners spoke a similar language of 'hoops', 'hurdles', and 'obstacles'—a sense that the prison was deliberately making it difficult for them to advance. Not all shared such negative perceptions of the prison's opportunity structures. But Tommy's quotation pointed to the comfort that could be taken from the certainty of low expectations. Discretion required faith in others; pure authority made no promise that hope was worthwhile.

Meanwhile, for most prisoners, the form and location of power were highly obscure. The prison was 'run by staff', yet since organizational power no longer resided with its frontline representatives, it was difficult to identify where the base was located or how to affect it. 'Nobody runs it, I suppose', shrugged Gerry, 'I haven't the foggiest idea'. Pete expressed similar uncertainty:

The staff were gods in them [old] days. You could say 'I want such and such' and he [had] the power to give it you. He didn't have to go anywhere. He didn't have to fill an app in. The power doesn't lie with the screw no more. The screw can't make a decision no more. A screw has to go to his line manager. [Now] There is no such thing as a god to go to. It's within the guidelines. [But] Those guidelines are manoeuvrable.

Pete pointed to the difficulties of getting things done when certain kinds of authority had been dispersed from the landings. As the following chapter elucidates in more detail, this dispersal of power and its diffusion within the establishment was not experienced homogenously. Indeed, many prisoners did not notice the means by which power operated upon them at all, despite knowing that their behaviour was restricted and that they had little scope to negotiate the terms that governed them. For other prisoners, power was not imperceptible but intangible. It operated from locations that made it almost impossible to affect. The system functioned anonymously, unreachably, and inflexibly (Foucault 1977), like 'a spider's web without the spider' (Said 1983: 221):[18]

You get to a certain level within a prison that you never meet, the people that actually run the prison. That's the wall, the shield. If I'm dealing with an officer I'm dealing with another person, I can talk to them, I can manipulate them, or I can negotiate with them. Once you get beyond that, it's a faceless contact, you can't actually get to em: security, the administration, even the governors. You can't actually get anything but superficial contact. (Nathan)

There's definitely a brick wall there, and you hit the brick wall then that's it, no further. The system, or the people who administer the system, will never ever change anything for an individual prisoner's benefit. If the system says 'no' then it is 'no', no matter what it is. (George)

It was in this respect, as a bureaucratic machine, that authority was encountered as an immoveable 'wall'. The system appeared faceless, and its decisions (e.g. about home leave or a prisoner's right to personal property) felt almost impossible to challenge through interpersonal negotiation or direct appeals to humanity. For prisoners, then, the humanization of staff culture was offset by what was widely perceived as a hardening of the world beyond the wings.

Dealings with this systemic machinery were fraught with difficulty. The advantages of bureaucratic procedures should not be overlooked, in terms of the relative transparency and consistency that they can achieve, and the formal opportunities they provide for prisoners to pursue grievances. In practice, however, 'paperwork' was the institutional black hole into which problems could be cast without further explanation. Decisions about job allocations and early release were often simply attributed to 'security', with little further explanation but with significant and enduring consequences. Prisoners were left with little certainty of what such terms meant and what could be done to address them. Processes were complicated and long-winded. Requests, complaints, and applications passed through a number of institutional hands before resolution, but prisoners were often left with little sense of their progress:

They pass it along to the governors, and the governors seem to take their time about what they've got to do, or they've got loads of work to do. It's just a general run-around with everyone. Everyone's got so much

---

[18] With apologies for taking this term somewhat out of context.

to do. And the thing is, they blame each other for it. So then you start wondering who you're going to be angry with. The only people you can directly be angry with is the officers on the wing. And sometimes you don't know whether to believe them or not. They can stand there and say 'Yeah, I've done your paperwork. Your paperwork's gone'. And you've got to believe them. You don't get a slip off the governor saying 'I've got your review paperwork here and I'm reviewing it and I'll let you know in due course, seven days', you don't hear anything like that. (Den)

Observations of this kind were common. 'Sometimes paperwork can be a help, or sometimes it can be a hindrance, because it's going from one person to another, then back to admin and into the other necessary places it needs to go. Paperwork can get lost' (Dave). When paperwork went missing or moved slowly, prisoners were left unsure of what was happening, who was to blame and what could be done about it. 'I've waited and waited, put in a request and complaint, and you don't even get an answer from that. Where has [it] gone? How do you know it's even gone to anybody?' (Harvey).

For officers, this was exploitable territory. Once Wellingborough's wing staff had retreated from informal contact with prisoners, and increasingly dealt with prisoner concerns through formal channels, they could absolve themselves of responsibility for inactivity by hiding in the shadows of the bureaucratic process. By encouraging prisoners to use applications, shovelling work to higher levels, or falsely claiming to have passed work to appropriate personnel in order to buy themselves time, they overstated their powerlessness in ways that prisoners could do little to challenge. Those mechanisms designed to enhance legitimacy served instead to create feelings of frustration and fatalism. They created rather than resolved problems; they exacerbated prisoners' feelings of powerlessness; and they contributed to the facelessness of the system. As Ashley summarized: 'Nowadays everything's done with forms. There's more paperwork and less prison officer contact'.

Such complaints signalled other dimensions of everyday power. When officers had held the capacity to make the decisions about which prisoners cared most, the experience of power was direct and 'honest', even when confrontational. With officers often serving as the messengers of decisions made off the wings, or contributing to reports and assessments that were conveyed on paper, contemporary power had a less reliable quality:

Now, it's more a manipulative form of confrontation. Before, he'd tell you in front of your face. [Now] he'll write it in a report. He won't talk to you. He'll give you the report, and when you've got the report, he's not in the prison, he's on holiday for a week. (Gerry)

First then, power was *indirect*, operating 'behind your back' rather than through face-to-face contact. For many prisoners, as with discretionary inconsistency, this was experienced as a form of dishonesty and 'disrespect'—a sly and unmanly form of power. Several experienced prisoners expressed nostalgia for an era of 'straightforward' verbal confrontation, where 'knowing where you stood' meant unstifled communication. As the following quotations suggest, frank exchanges and 'letting off steam' (Cohen and Taylor 1972: 84) were now considered hazardous:

You have to be so careful of the words you say. Because otherwise it could get called up on one of your interviews—your 'areas of concern'. [Back then] you could tell a screw to fuck off and he'd tell you to fuck off. You knew where you stood. (Pete)

If you say to a screw, 'fuck off, you're a dickhead', you might think that was just said in the heat of the moment, that it's forgotten the next day. [But] That officer's got your file out and he's wrote, 'confrontation with Smith, he didn't like what I was telling him, told me to fuck off and called me a dickhead'. If you come up for a decent job in the prison, they'll pull your file, 'Oh, we ain't giving him that job. He's disrespectful to staff'. Everything you do, and everything you say is put down on paper, in your file. (Danny)

Second, power was *deferred*, with delayed repercussions that could not be anticipated. Conflicts could end, yet their effects (in terms of privilege level or sentence progression) could persist: 'if you cause an argument', said Asif, 'you're not going to get what you want later out of the sentence'. In claiming, however hyperbolically, that staff violence was preferable to being 'killed off on file', prisoners emphasized the difference between punishments that were immediate, predictable and short-lived in their consequences, and those whose outcomes were long-lasting or took effect at an unpredictable point in the future. As Darren summarized: 'a kicking was over in fifteen minutes. Your pain's over five minutes after it's happened. [Now] you haven't got your telly for a month. They're prolonging it.'

Such comments underlined the shifts in power that have characterized imprisonment in the last two decades of the twentieth century. To a large degree, bureaucratic management and psychological power have replaced coercive authoritarianism. They also hinted at the distinctive grip and potency that these new forms of power entailed. As Stephen noted, 'in the old days, they could fuck you up with their fists. Now they can fuck you up with their pen. The power of the pen is really mighty in prison nowadays.' In the words of another prisoner, 'they can ruin your life with a stroke of a pen'. Despite its civilizing appearance, then, shifts in the form of power were not experienced as a simple diminution of authority, but a different form of discipline and control—one with complex psychological dimensions (see Foucault 1977).

'Psychological Power'

The role of psychological expertise

Two related trends, outlined in earlier chapters, have led to the growing prominence within prisons of psychological staff and expertise. The first is the shift to a less forgiving attitude towards offenders, and the growing emphasis throughout criminal justice on public protection. The second is the re-emergence of belief in rehabilitation, albeit in a limited guise, following a period of widespread pessimism about the possibilities of offender treatment (see Martinson 1974). Under this new orthodoxy, frequently referred to as 'what works?' or 'evidence-based practice', resources are focused on specific kinds of interventions, largely highly structured cognitive-behavioural programmes designed to enhance interpersonal skills and address cognitive deficits (McGuire 1995). As is consistent with the punitive turn, this renaissance in rehabilitative provision is oriented to public security, with prisoners' psychological 'needs' narrowly defined according to what is deemed desirable for the public rather than what prisoners might require to enhance their psychological wellbeing or address their social needs (Thomas-Peter 2006; Hannah-Moffat 2001, 2005).[19] Reflecting this focus, the overwhelming majority of psychological staff in

---

[19] Senior Prison Service psychology staff recognize that terms such as 'criminogenic need' are problematic not only because they are jargonistic and are often misunderstood and misused, but also because they only target personal and emotional factors and can do little to address the social problems that also drive offending (see Towl 2003, 2006).

the correctional services of England and Wales are forensic rather than clinical in training (Home Office 2003).

The result of these developments is that, in prisons and probation, the field of forensic psychology is 'booming' (Towl 2003: 1); it has 'never... been more influential' (Thomas-Peter 2006: 24). The increasing emphasis on assessing and reducing 'risk' has raised the need for psychological work both to deal with prisoners with indeterminate sentences, and to organize and oversee the widespread provision of structured intervention programmes (Towl 2003, 2007). These programmes have expanded significantly since their introduction in prisons in 1996. The chief responsibilities of prison psychologists are to conduct risk assessments, recommend and manage appropriate interventions, and provide psychological reports for the Parole Board and other judicial bodies. Psychology staff may be involved in a number of other areas, including the planning and evaluation of resettlement work, organizational change and health-related interventions. They also have considerable responsibility for the development and delivery of suicide awareness and suicide prevention strategies, and the assessment and management of suicidal and self-harming behaviour. However, the role of psychologists in the alleviation of psychological distress and the promotion of individual wellbeing is limited. Psychiatric and counselling services are available to prisoners with severe mental health problems, but these services are highly limited (in Wellingborough, a consultant psychiatrist attended the prison one day per week).

When prisoners in Wellingborough referred to 'psychologists' and psychological power, they denoted a range of experiences and interventions. Life-sentence prisoners had a range of dealings with psychology staff throughout their sentences. Early in the sentence of a lifer, a psychologist conducted an analysis of the prisoner's index offence and offending behaviour to form a summary of 'risk factors' and 'needs'. These assessments helped to establish a sentence plan specifying the targets and interventions required for movement towards release. These might include stipulations to gain education and employment skills, deal with drug and alcohol problems, and address cognitive and emotional 'deficits'—in relation to interpersonal skills, anger management, anxiety and depression, etc—through individual and group-work, carried out or overseen by psychology staff. This initial assessment formed the basis for subsequent reviews, which monitored progress on risk factors based upon attitudes towards one's offence, insight into offence-related problems, and in-prison behaviour (Willmot 1999; Crighton and Bailey 2006). Recategorization, and therefore movement to lower-security conditions, was dependent on these reviews, to which psychologists contributed reports that carried considerable weight. Each lifer then had a Parole Board review three years prior to tariff expiry to consider transfer to open conditions, with subsequent reviews every two years to monitor progress until the point of release. At this stage, the main considerations were risk of absconding and risk of harm to self or others.

Parole Board reviews also determined whether early release would be granted to prisoners with fixed sentences of over four years. However, prisoners with such terms were unlikely to have the kinds of individual assessments with psychologists that lifers underwent. For these prisoners, as for lifers and prisoners on shorter-sentences, psychological judgments were expressed primarily through reports submitted by treatment managers—often but not always psychologists—after the completion of offending behaviour courses. Likewise, prisoners on non-parole sentences were unlikely to have contact with psychology staff outside the context of such programmes (for example, the 'Reasoning and Rehabilitation' course). For such prisoners, references to 'psychology' were shorthand for the reports presented by uniformed staff, workshop instructors, probation officers, and other staff at institutional hearings to determine IEP, recategorization, home leave, or HDC decisions.[20] Psychological power, then, entailed the set of written submissions that, for all prisoners, structured the path towards freedom.

Experienced prisoners frequently commented on the ascendance of psychological expertise in prison and the shift in its focus:

When I first came away, the psychologist was there if you'd got problems, to talk to. She wasn't there to write reports, she wasn't there to judge you, she wasn't there to write reports and manipulate you, she was there to help

[20] In some establishments, a psychologist sat on the HDC committee, but there was considerable variation in committee composition between establishments. Psychologists might also attend committees if there were particular issues or prisoners about which or whom their comments had relevance. HDC boards included probation and psychology staff, a wing or senior officer, and a governor grade who made the final recommendation.

you if you needed help. Now that attitude's not there. They are there to write reports on you, they are there to judge you, they are there to fucking try and manipulate you. Your interests, your needs are pretty much last on the list. That's the perception of it. This is why a lot of psychologists are held in nothing other than suspicion. Probation the same: you went from probation officers being someone who would help you get this and that, to someone who was involved in keeping you in prison, making assessments on your suitability and your character. (Nathan)

Psychologists have taken over prisons in the last ten years. In the eighties, you never saw a psychologist. [Now] If a psychologist says you've addressed your offending behaviour, and you genuinely appear to be making progress with life and going straight, then that gets you out. If a psychologist says the opposite of that, that keeps you in. (Stephen)

Remarks of this kind pointed to a number of features of psychological and professional power as experienced by a large proportion of Wellingborough's prisoners.[21] The shift in concern from prisoner welfare to public protection positioned almost all specialist staff as agents of an extensive and repressive network of disciplinary power.[22] Both probation and psychology staff wielded forms of authority that branded them, in the eyes of many prisoners, as instruments of state punishment and obstacles to progress. Although some prisoners singled-out probation officers—normally, those working outside the prison—as sources of genuine support, distinctions were often not made between these professional groupings. Here then, the dispersal of power away from the wings did not represent its repeal or dissipation so much as its *diffusion* and *expansion*.

In terms of specialist expertise and assistance, prisoners had very few allies or outlets. Few members of staff were exempted from suspicion and mistrust. Significantly, although those who were excluded—education staff, CARAT workers, and members

---

[21] It is possible that one reason why life sentence prisoners emphasized an apparent shift in the emphasis of psychological intervention is that the tone of the interventions they faced altered over the course of their sentence. Early on, reports tended to emphasize personal problems and used less secure conditions as a target towards which the prisoner should work. As the prisoner approached release, risk to the public moved more closely into focus, and reports focused more on factors liable to *prevent* release.

[22] It is interesting to note the ordering of the following statement: 'There are a range of stakeholders who may be deemed the recipients (directly or indirectly) of psychological services; the public, victims of crime, prison and probation staff and offenders—each may be viewed as stakeholders' (Towl 2003: 6).

of the chaplaincy—could contribute to reports used in parole decisions and were able to place prisoners on disciplinary charges, their roles within the prison were explicitly welfare-oriented and they spoke a distinctive language of care, concern, and individual wellbeing. Prisoners saw education staff in particular as genuinely committed to their personal development and sympathetic to their concerns. These staff also did not carry the cultural cynicism or evaluative functions that tainted prisoners' interactions with other specialists. Nathan compared the resulting relationships as follows:

With officers, it's a professional relationship. With prison psychology, there's always boundaries. With education staff, there is still boundaries but in a different way. Because it's in a sort of non-judgmental way, which makes it a closer, more personal relationship. I know full well that at some time that psychologist is gonna be writing reports. With teachers that's not there.

Within the education department, many prisoners found sanctuary from the stresses of life on the wings and from the normal terms on which staff-prisoner relations were founded. Prisoners often commented that the education block was one of the few zones within the institution that didn't 'feel like prison'. Certainly the tone within the classrooms had a feel closer to a further education college than a custodial establishment. To a large degree, the more trustful and intimate relations that could be found here were fostered by an explicit belief among education staff in the sanctity of student-teacher relations, regardless of the context. They were also encouraged by a range of messages that teachers conveyed, both consciously and unconsciously, about their attitude towards uniformed staff and the institution. Some teachers handed round biscuits during breaks in classes or paid for art resources from their own incomes; others shared a certain amount of personal information and showed sustained interest in the personal lives of their students; many expressed despair at the rigidity with which some officers enforced the rules and the formality with which they treated prisoners. In return, prisoners were protective of education staff in ways that applied to few other prison personnel: 'They don't deserve to get shit from inmates', Zack asserted. 'That's another rule [among prisoners]: don't abuse the education staff.'

Psychologists were not accorded the same value. Most prisoners had little objection to psychological insight *per se*. A large proportion expressed concerns about mental health issues and longed for help to deal with deep-rooted personal problems such as bereavements and childhood abuse, and with the psychological roots of their offending behaviour. Indeed, many prisoners embraced a terminology of 'criminogenic need' that indicated their absorption of institutional discourse. These prisoners located their problems in personal cognition, and yearned for a kind of correctional injection that would cure their 'defects'. Other prisoners were less subsumed by official discourse, but questioned their psychological health or moral core—'...what kind of person I am'. These men sought diagnoses that could provide insight into their personalities and patterns of crime.[23] Yet, as George explained, the opportunities to explore and address these issues outside the boundaries of institutional power were limited:

> They may *isolate* difficulties that you're having, but they don't *help* you with them. They will observe how you handle those difficulties, how you come to terms with them. You are given the opportunity to speak to a counsellor or somebody if you feel you're having problems, but it will all end up in a report. (George)

Prisoners were crying out for neutral forms of intervention and explanation. Yet the system left little room for unpartisan judgment. Personal problems—alcoholism, schizophrenia, anxiety, obsessive-compulsive disorder, unspecified anger—were quickly subsumed into institutional discourse, and transformed from needs to risks in the interests of public protection (see Hannah-Moffat 2005). This focus left gaping holes in therapeutic provision, and provided a stark symbolic message to prisoners about their debased social status.

---

[23] 'Sometimes I have trouble understanding myself. Because in prison, you have to adapt to the way things go on in prison. And because you adapt, I think you lose part of yourself. I've done so many things in my life—I've gone into the Army, I've travelled a bit, I've tried a few jobs, and I've been in prison—I don't really see what kind of person I am. Am I a good person? Am I a bad person? So it would be nice for somebody to say to me really, you know, everything you've been through, you're still a good person. You might have done some bad things but you are a good person. Or have somebody say to me, 'you're a bastard basically, you're just a sociopath'. I haven't sort of found myself and it would be nice to try and find that out before I leave.' (Den)

The nature of psychological power

Although parole and recategorization decisions were based on reports made by a range of prison personnel, psychologists were held most responsible for determining their outcomes and therefore bore the brunt of prisoners' resentments.[24] In part, this reflected the relative weight that the Parole Board attached to psychological assessments, as evidenced in the feedback that prisoners received when given a 'knockback'. But the strength and direction of feeling about psychological power—which was highly intense and almost universally negative—was related to its *form* and *reach*. As Nathan observed, in these respects, it differed significantly from the terms of mundane authority:

[In terms of] The day-to-day concerns, most prisoners know what to expect, they know the rules that they're living within, so they accept that. They accept the day-to-day authority that they're under. When it comes to probation and psychology, because it's not to do with the day-to-day things, it's to do with the effects on your *life*, the effects of you getting out, it's a deeper type of power [from] the every day situation: I think it's felt more profoundly.

As this quotation clearly indicates, the force of psychological power lay in its capacity to determine future plans and possibilities. Rather than appropriating the past, like the traditional sentence, it predicted and prevented possible futures. In this respect, it was a form of 'pre-punishment' (Zedner 2007), which functioned like a supplementary sentence rather than part of the initial punishment, decreeing a further bloc of liberty of which the prisoner could be deprived. Since most prisoners found everyday conditions more or less acceptable, this more fundamental deprivation of freedom carried all the more significance. More than any other staff within the prison, it was psychologists who held the key to captivity or release. As lifers and prisoners with parole sentences repeatedly observed, 'To get out, my paperwork's got to be right.' Much of the criticism aimed at officers also related to their use of

---

[24] Progress reports for lifers were made by people including the lifer manager, wing manager and the prisoner's personal officer, his probation officer, psychologist and psychiatrist (where relevant), his education officer or activity supervisor, and, if appropriate, the chaplain and medical staff. Although, in principle, psychologists had no more sway than other staff in determining the outcome of these reports, it was generally recognized that, in practice, their representations carried more weight than anyone else's (senior Prison Service psychologist, pers. comm.).

paperwork: negative and petty comments, or incomplete files that delayed proceedings.

Nathan's observation also signalled the difference between a form of authority that was at least broadly knowable and predictable, and (as with bureaucratic power) a mode of power that was much harder to decipher. Although prisoners understood the general factors that fed into parole decisions and risk assessments—most importantly, whether progress had been made in addressing risk factors and the causes of offending behaviour—the formulae by which such decisions were made were so imprecise as to render the process highly obscure. Cases were considered on individual merit, and assessments of personality, risk, and future behaviour were based on interpretations and projections that were inevitably subjective. This is despite recent attempts by the Prison Service to curb the amount of discretion that psychologists can employ. In the past, risk assessments were based almost entirely on professional judgment and discretion, using free-ranging clinical interviews and case file reviews (Clark 1999). However, since evidence suggested that this method was unreliable in predicting future offending—with some practitioners' predictions being 'consistently in the wrong direction' (Crighton 2005: 55)—the Prison Service has drawn increasingly on more reliable, structured and empirical risk-assessment tools to forecast behaviour such as violence and to diagnose disorders such as psychopathy. As Aas (2004) has argued, unstructured professional knowledge has come to be seen as a source of unpredictability and disorder.

Subjectivity remains an issue, however. First, psychologists make choices about which assessment tools to employ; second, inputting data into structured models still requires a degree of 'translation' and often relies on personal judgments (for example, whether a prisoner is 'promiscuous' or has had 'many' short-term sexual relationships) (Crighton 2005); third, with tools such as the revised psychopathy checklist (PCL-R), there is no consensus on what score marks the boundary between normal and classifiable behaviour; fourth, diagnostic conclusions still need to be related to a prisoner's risk of reoffending rather than seen in isolation; finally, because even the most reliable tools produce a large number of false positives and false negatives—prisoners caught in the diagnostic net who are not real risks, and those who get through the diagnostic filter but do reoffend.

Here, a significant problem is that actuarial tools are predictive of groups rather than individuals. Based on a prisoner's record, a psychologist can be confident that there is, say, an 80 per cent likelihood that s/he will reoffend, but cannot tell whether s/he is one of the individuals who falls into the 80 per cent who will or the 20 per cent who will not. Despite the use of a combination of clinical and actuarial tools, a supervision system aimed at regulating discretion, and inter-rater reliability tests designed to ensure consistency in the use of structured tools, psychologists recognize that there is 'always going to be a degree of subjectivity' in their evaluations. As one senior practitioner has summarized, 'psychologists sometimes find themselves coming to very different conclusions from their colleagues about the risk presented by individual offenders' (Wilmott 2003: 111).

That psychological power had such influence but also such subjective dimensions made its authority all the harder for many prisoners to accept. As they saw it, discrepancies between assessments made at different establishments were clear evidence of scientific fallibility:

A lot of [my reports/assessments] have been very contradictory: what was a problem in one prison isn't a problem in another prison. I'm not very communicative with staff here, really, but much the same as in prison X. But whereas down there it was seen as a major problem [and an] anti-authoritarian attitude, here it's seen very positively: I don't make unreasonable demands on the time of staff; 'very polite, gets on with his work, presents no control problems'. It's the same situation, just totally different interpretations. (George)

Many trainee psychologists and psychological assistants were 'young white women predominately from higher socio-economic groups' (Home Office 2003: 4). This was a further source of aggravation for some prisoners, who felt resentful that their lives were being determined by people to whom, outside prison, they would not allow themselves to be subordinated. More often, prisoners were simply sceptical of the diagnostic expertise of junior psychology staff, and struggled to take direction from course tutors who they felt had little life experience: 'they know nothing about drugs, or the reasons for taking drugs. They're trying to teach you something that you know back to front and they know nothing about' (Callum). When programmes relied on course manuals, prisoners perceived their rigidity as a sign that course content was inflexible, that the expertise of tutors was superficial, and that tutors were what Thomas-Peter (2006: 32) has called '"programme drones", little more than replaceable cogs in the programme machine'.[25] When young psychologists used structured risk-assessment tools, the effects were similar. Rigid procedures implied that psychological expertise was shallow and personality could be distilled into a checklist of features. In such a system, many prisoners felt like mere objects to be fed into the institutional machinery.

For the majority of prisoners, the bases on which decisions were made were unclear, inconsistent, or unreasonable. Some challenged the validity of using in-prison behaviour as a proxy measure of future risk (see Hannah-Moffat 2005).

> I should be judged 'am I a threat to society?' I'm only a threat to the prison system. I realise that I've done wrong and should be in prison. If I spend the rest of my life in prison because of the murder I've committed, then that's fair enough by me. But I shouldn't be kept in because somebody doesn't like my attitude.... What I am inside and outside are two different people. How I conduct myself in here, I have to conduct myself like this to survive. (Pete)

Pete drew attention to the difference between conforming to the rules of an institution and adhering to the laws of society. Prisoners who queried orders, questioned staff authority, or did not assent meekly to the terms of the system (often having been taught assertiveness skills in prison courses) and then found themselves described in wing reports as aggressive or refractory saw no necessary relationship between such behaviours and the notions of 'risk to life and limb' around which assessments were meant to be based. Like Pete, they emphasized the prison's responsibility for inciting their assertions, for provoking their frustrations, and for socializing them into hardened and forceful identities over the course of long sentences. For these prisoners, the distorted environment of the prison bore little relation to the world outside and was an inadequate laboratory in which to gauge their behaviour. When challenges to power were logical, valid and non-violent—as they very often were—it seemed questionable that they were not

---

[25] Courses such as R&R and enhanced thinking skills (ETS) had to be run according to strict guidelines, as laid out in manuals based on the original, Canadian version of the course, and were video-recorded to ensure compliance and consistency with this model.

seen as illustrations of the kinds of healthy, critical faculties that might serve prisoners well outside prison. For long-term prisoners especially, to adapt 'successfully' to imprisonment was psychologically maladaptive and was a poor grounding for the realities of the free community (see Jamieson and Grounds 2005).

Psychologists recognized that the relevance of in-prison behaviour was limited and case-specific (see Clark *et al.* 1993).[26] Officers were well placed to comment on offence-paralleling behaviour, but they were not always well informed about what kind of behaviour was relevant to such judgments. Whether a 'neat and tidy cell'—the kind of thing that an officer might include in a report—was an indication of healthy self-respect or excessive self-control was a complex matter. The degree to which such matters were relevant to 'risk' depended on the particular prisoner and his offending history. Likewise, psychologists would primarily be interested in whether a prisoner was involved in drug culture if drugs were related to his offending behaviour, or if he were insisting that he no longer had anything to do with drugs. Officers often hypothesized about the parallels between institutional behaviour and potential offending, frequently including details on wing reports that prisoners felt were immaterial (and which governors on HDC boards often, but not always, chose to ignore). Martin challenged the relevance of submissions on his wing report that he was 'high up in my own peer group, [and] I don't get on with certain inmates'. Pete likewise complained that 'you're judged by the company you keep. If you're having it with somebody that's taking drugs, you're done by association.'[27]

Prisoners thus resented both the logic of assessment—'if I'm carrying on that bad, why aren't I getting no strikes, why aren't I on basic?' (Martin)—and the breadth of behaviours that were policed—'they want to pick and choose your friends for you' (Martin). Whether or not officers' speculations were discounted, and regardless of the sophistication with which psychologists sifted information about in-prison behaviour, the impact of psychological power was the same: most prisoners felt that all areas of their life—the people with whom they walked on the exercise

[26] Decisions about release on temporary licence (ROTL) had to be considered independently of IEP level, because they were about need for and purpose of leave, and therefore risk rather than institutional behaviour.

[27] 'Having it': mixing with.

yard, how they socialized with other prisoners and staff, the posters they had on their walls, their reading material, whether they received visits, who they wrote to, their interests and aspirations—were baselessly under scrutiny, and regulated themselves accordingly. The risks of not doing so were too great to ignore. In such respects, psychological power was *all-encompassing*, working like a panoptical gaze, with effects beyond its direct point of focus (Foucault 1977).

The legitimacy of psychological expertise was also undermined by apparent inconsistencies in judgments about recategorization, HDC and parole. Aaron's complaint was typical: 'Jones got his tagging with twenty-seven nickings. I didn't have one for sixteen months, and they can't even explain to me why [I didn't get my tag]. All I want to know is why other people have got it.' Again, the point here is not to judge the integrity of these decisions—although there was little doubt that governors exercised discretion in ways that made decisions inconsistent and potentially extra-legal (see Scott 2006)[28] —but to draw attention to how their terms were perceived on the wings. In this respect, psychological power lacked the very transparency and accountability that bureaucratic government is supposed to advance. Decisions seemed arbitrary, particularly to those prisoners who did not grasp the distinction between in-prison behaviour and the risk of future offending, and who therefore assumed that if they stayed out of trouble, decisions would go their way. As I discuss shortly, such passive compliance had little bearing on risk reduction and did not match the institutional template of ideal behaviour.

In a similar vein, the institutional preoccupation with channelling risk reduction through offending behaviour courses meant that there was considerable uncertainty among prisoners about how risk could be addressed outside the framework of structured programmes. Prisoners deemed ineligible for courses expressed confusion when they discovered that this did not mean that they had satisfied demands to reduce their risk factors, as Darren's experience illustrated:

I went for the R and R course and they asked me all these questions and they said, 'well, you haven't got enough defects to do the course, we don't

---

[28] One governor (not employed at Wellingborough) disclosed concerns that many of his peers had little grasp of the details of Prison Service orders/instructions, and habitually acted in ways that contravened legal principles.

feel that you'll benefit from it'. They said to me, 'that's as good as a pass'. [But] my parole papers come back and it says 'you haven't done enough courses'.

The likelihood here was that the Parole Board had not insisted that further courses needed to be sat, but that, to diminish risk suffi- ciently, Darren needed to engage in work that went *beyond* what cognitive programmes could provide (for example, one-to-one interventions or drug-counselling). That Darren had conflated these recommendations was precisely the point: the institu- tional fixation on structured group-work meant that, to prison- ers, 'courses' were the keystone of release. At times, the enforced demand to get onto courses had an almost hysterical feel.

Prisoners who had good records while inside and had completed all their recommended courses but were still considered high-risk shone light on the system's conservatism. They also came to doubt the prison's faith in its proclaimed ideology of rehabilitation:

I've [only] had three nickings in four years, and the Home Office has decided I'm still at risk. Well what do they know about me to decide whether I'm a risk or not? Cos they're looking on past performances, and I'm not here for my past performances, I'm here for what I done for *this* [sentence]. This is a system where you're told that you can rehabilitate— I'm changing, but then they turn round and say because of things I done ten years ago, I'm not gonna get something now. I'm like: 'Hold on a minute, what you're really saying is your system don't work'. And if it don't work, what's the point in me trying? (Alexis)

For these men, the prison claimed to believe in change, but was fixated on the actions of the past. As Attrill and Liell (2007) also report, many prisoners felt trapped by events that they considered outdated. Tommy's history provided an extreme example. Many years earlier, a recommendation for release had been overruled, and he had been obliged instead to take a number of offending behaviour courses. Having done so, and finally gained Cat-D status, he had been returned to more secure conditions because of a mistake which he considered unrepresentative of his general behaviour:[29]

I've spent twenty years in the system and everyone has said 'he has good relationship skills, and doesn't need this course'. And then, because of

---

[29] Tommy may still be in prison, and, to protect his identity, it would be wrong to provide further details of this incident.

one incident, I have to spend years doing courses in that area. Yes, it was a mistake. But that is not who I am.... All my reports say I've done every offending behaviour course, I'm a nice person, I'm polite, I don't present a risk. Yet the parole board picked up on two incidents and used that as an excuse to keep me in prison. (Tommy)

As a result of this incident, Tommy had been given a label—of not being sufficiently open or honest—that continued to hold back his release, and which, from his perspective, bore no relation to proper considerations of risk:

Everything should centre on whether you're a risk to the public. If you're not, they've no grounds to keep you in. With me, they're saying that the likelihood of me committing any offence is very low. I'm not a risk. Yet the answer they give me this time is that I've got to go back to Cat-D conditions because [of what happened] six years ago. And I can't accept that answer.... I'm being judged on moral and social issues, rather than risk. The minute that they look at how long over tariff I am, they assume I must have done something major wrong. They can't find it in any of my records. But they're reluctant to sign their name to that release. (Tommy)

Through such descriptions, prisoners highlighted the difficulties of proving change and shedding psychological labels in a politicized context of caution. In philosophical terms, preventive forms of punishment can only be justified based on certainty that a future event will occur, for otherwise they close the windows of opportunity for individuals to change (Zedner 2007). In a context preoccupied with public protection over individual rights, the failure of actuarial assessment to provide this certainty was not the priority. Its logic was preventive, calculating into the future rather than on the basis of past behaviour. In this respect, psychological power was highly unforgiving.

This quality was reinforced by its means of record. Once committed to file, negative assessments and comments could not be erased, and tainted judgments of future acts while overshadowing routine positive behaviour. As one psychologist noted, anything on record had to be addressed, regardless of whether it would show up in a present assessment: 'once you refer someone onto a programme, that's on their record, and if they don't do it the reference is still there: "why didn't you do that in 1993 when it was offered to you?"'. Diagnostic records, as well as 'security files', were highly adhesive and therefore highly enduring. Given the environment, it was far easier for prisoners to make mistakes that confirmed institutional labels than to dispel them (see also Attrill and Liell 2007).

> They might, in a year, say 'his attitude's changed'. But they'll still have the bad comments. [And] what real good can you do in here? You turn up to work on time, you're polite, tidy, your cell's clean. Little things like that aren't on your file. But 'he spoke to me out of hand at the servery', they'll pick up on that. Then when you go for a home leave, or D-cat, or even a good job, they'll pull this magic file out with all the bad comments in it. (Tyler)

> You have one minor incident and they'll go write it in the file. That's gonna catch up with you in two or three years time: a silly little incident, every few months, a minor indiscretion.... You're in prison! You've just got the hump, or you've slept badly. But you add em all together and they show a pattern of something that's not really there. (Alexis)

Prisoners who were prepared to make concerted and visible efforts to show expiation or reform could appear transformed. As Tyler suggested though, those unwilling to make such exertions had few means of illustrating change through their routine conduct. Small acts of anger caused damage that sustained patience could not necessarily repair.

In these respects, psychological power was also highly *absolutist*. It offered little clemency for human errors which—as in Tommy's case—were hard to equate with criminal risk, and it left little room for ambivalence or ambiguity. Files did not always place acts in the context of prison life—with all its stresses and temptations—or personal narratives, with their developmental complexities (Aas 2004). Admissions of internal conflicts or tensions risked being pathologized and deemed problematic. To express legitimate and realistic concerns about being dragged back into reoffending or about forming relationships on release was to place one's freedom in jeopardy. This was particularly the case if 'protective strategies' were unavailable to manage the basis of a prisoner's anxieties i.e. if there were no courses available to address his particular issues. Thus, regardless of a prisoner's own efforts, limits to institutional resources and psychological knowledge could inhibit his chances of release. The consequences of rehabilitative deficiencies fell onto prisoners, who were held responsible for their 'risk factors' whether or not means were available to address them (Thomas-Peter 2006). In practice, unsure about what fears they could safely divulge, and concerned that they could snag themselves in their own net of risk factors, many prisoners withheld their worries. The identities that they presented to psychologists were more confident and secure than their inner realities.

Psychological reports also felt highly *partial*. Prisoners complained that wing files presented 'one-sided' and questionable accounts of incidents, without allowing the opportunity for rectification. It was certainly common in conversation for officers to make lay diagnoses about prisoners ('he's got a personality disorder') or provide specious interpretations of their behaviours. More significantly, many prisoners (primarily those on longer sentences) were ascribed paper identities and 'criminogenic factors' that they considered highly spurious. Darren laughed at being told that his 'pattern of crime' had not changed despite a sixteen-year gap between his current and previous convictions. Other prisoners emphasized the discrepancies between the patterns observed on paper and the complexities of lived experience. When prisoners like Tommy complained that judgments did not capture who they 'really were', they implicitly identified the limits of actuarial prediction and the lack of interest in individuality that psychological tools exhibited.

Although psychological judgments functioned primarily to define prisoners' futures, they also had significant and insidious effects on their current lives. In being subjected to psychological discourse, long-term prisoners were forced to accept (or, at least, accept the consequences of) meanings and categories that were at odds with self-perceptions. As Gerry's frustrations conveyed, self-definitions and subjective experiences were often bulldozed by psychological discourse, forcing prisoners to adopt a bi-focal view of themselves:

My life doesn't go parallel with theirs. The system has forced me to draw to their level, how *they* see things and deal with things, rather than helping me deal with things in my own way, in my own personality, in my own mistakes, weaknesses, difficulties. They've taken me off that road, and forced their opinion, their understanding onto me.... They're only interested in their own decision-making. You go through [your] sentence, and everybody's telling you to be open and honest, and when you do, they don't believe you. *Their* truth they can handle. Not the prisoner's truth.

Gerry's description was unusually emotive. Nonetheless, it captured the uncompromising nature of psychological assessment and its objectifying qualities. Some prisoners complained that reports were written about them by people they had never met. Labels of misogyny or psychopathy could not help but annihilate the complexities of personality, carving identity into psychologically manageable, disaggregated units (see Thomas-Peter 2006). These judgments were based not on who prisoners were but what they had done.[30] In terms of achieving release, these were the master-categories by which prisoners were addressed and their identities 'fixed' (Aas 2004). A prisoner could be a talented painter or a good father, but relative to psychological tags, such attributes were made to feel irrelevant. Risk-assessment tools were insensitive to narrative progression, social context, and holistic understandings of identity. Instead, life histories were required to fit into parameters provided by the database and the abstract vocabulary that standardization necessitated (Aas 2004). For long-term prisoners, for whom maintaining some control over personal integrity and identity was a paramount concern (Cohen and Taylor 1972; and see Chapter 7), to have one's experience and identity 'formalized and institutionalized' (George) in these ways was a pain of major significance. For long-term prisoners, psychological processes such as these were among the mortifications and abasements of the modern prison (cf. Goffman 1961).

There was little room to negotiate such terms or present alternative interpretations of past actions. Prisoners had various means of challenging psychological assessments: by correcting factual inaccuracies, by making their own representations to the Parole Board, by obtaining assessments from external (non-Prison Service) psychologists, and by disputing directly the conclusions of psychology staff. However, such strategies were limited in effect and potentially hazardous. Parole Boards gave little credibility to prisoners' representations and were often sceptical of the true independence of external psychologists. Similarly, while they noted prisoners' views, Prison Service psychologists were highly unlikely to change their minds based on their defences. Indeed, it was more likely that prisoners' arguments would confirm existing diagnoses: 'to be honest, they might be getting themselves deeper into trouble, because their evidence may be so wrong or add weight to what I was [already] talking about' (senior psychologist). Here, the imbalance in power between prisoners and psychology staff

---

[30] Ronan, a prisoner aware of his acute schizophrenia, expressed his view of psychological expertise succinctly: 'psychiatrists are more mad than me—they're off their fucking heads'.

was brought into sharp relief. Prisoners' subjective experiences were invariably discounted, while professional expertise was accorded respect. For prisoners, this logic was profoundly objectifying (see Attrill and Liell 2007).

For the prison, these imbalances could be counter-productive in their consequences. Specialist staff demanded accounts of honesty and sincerity, but the power that they wielded made such accounts highly risky and hindered truthful disclosure. Prisoners who publicly maintained alternative 'truths' about their characters or their 'criminogenic factors' risked appearing non-compliant or unable to come to terms with their offending behaviour. Given the prevailing institutional language, alternative representations were in effect unintelligible. As Foucault argues (1977), resistance becomes seen as 'unrecognizable', irrational behaviour, part of the justification for further treatment. For prisoners who privately rejected institutional labels, the prison thus suppressed truth and invited deception. Darren—who was refused parole soon afterwards—provided a good example of how truth had become a dangerous language:

When I got interviewed for the drug courses, they said to me 'we don't want you to come on these courses just so we can cross the t's and dot the i's. We want you to benefit'. I just—maybe it was the wrong thing—but I told the truth: I wouldn't have benefited. They could speak to me for twenty-four hours a day, seven days a week, but as soon as I walk out of them gates, this is forgotten about. It doesn't matter how many courses I've done, it's forgotten about.

Other prisoners complained along similar lines. If they were honest about not regretting their crimes, they were less likely to obtain parole; but if they second-guessed institutional discourse they could be caught out by their lies: 'I said "I was put under pressure by other people to do the violence", and they said "so what makes us think that when you're on home leave, you're not going to be influenced again"' (Pierce). Few truths were acceptable to the system, leaving many prisoners in performative limbo.

Offending behaviour programmes

Offending behaviour programmes shared almost all of the wider characteristics of psychological power and promoted similar consequences. To qualify for accreditation, courses needed to be standardized, open to empirical measurement, clearly effective, and efficiently deliverable to a maximum number of offenders.[31] Interventions were thus limited by a logic that was managerial and pragmatic (Thomas-Peter 2006). Long-term, humanistic, psychological therapies were unsuitable for this framework (Crighton 2006), and many prisoners fell outside the borders of provision. In relation to the R&R course, this group included offenders with severe learning difficulties or severe psychological disorders (Thomas and Jackson 2003), as well as those with few discernible cognitive problems.

To prisoners, such limitations could feel senseless and discriminatory. Bradley recounted being 'told that I was *too* violent to go on a violence prevention course—how the fuck does that work?' Many prisoners genuinely sought self-discovery, and were disappointed to be told they had 'not got enough deficits [or] enough issues to deal with' for the courses on offer (Ross). The degree to which many prisoners submitted to a discourse that saw criminality as an outcome of defects in individual cognition was striking. Other prisoners had little normative interest to sit courses, but, in their mania to fulfil sentence plan requirements, tried to squeeze their characters into institutional categories or conform to official labels. Such prisoners despaired when told they were ineligible for course attendance. These men felt that they were effectively being penalized for *not* having obvious defects, or for having problems that the institution deemed too costly or difficult to treat. When courses had long waiting lists, or there were none relevant to one's index offence (e.g. arson), prisoners were again disadvantaged by factors beyond their control.

Prisoners were also acutely aware of the power of programme reports. After one R&R session, several men crowded around the programme facilitator, asking what she had been 'looking for' in the day's questions. 'Just give us a clue! Don't leave the session like that', asked one prisoner, in plaintive terms. Each scrambled to look at the comments that had been written under their

---

[31] Questions remain about the impact of offending-behaviour programmes. Much of the evidence for their effectiveness has come from evaluations of programmes outside prison, and much of the research on prison-based programmes has suggested that effects are small (Wilkinson 2005; although see Tong and Farrington 2006 for a more positive appraisal). Offenders may be a particularly difficult group to treat, and the prison environment is not conducive to treatment interventions (Losel 1995). It certainly seems likely that courses will be more effective in prisons with positive cultures than in establishments that do not display the traits and behaviours that they are attempting to teach.

name. One prisoner, awaiting a parole interview the following week, complained that 'all they've written is I'm "quiet"' (field-work notes). His concerns captured the feeling that the difference between freedom and captivity could rest on such terms.

Within the institution, official discourse showed little aware-ness of either the fallibility or impact of psychological discourse (see Fox 1999). In contrast, senior Prison Service psychologists were aware of the problems of uncritically celebrating the disci-pline's ascendance within late-modern corrections—the dangers of a narrow approach to rehabilitation, of relatively unfettered power, of dividing offenders' problems 'into those we have an in-tention to change and those we do not' (Thomas-Peter 2006: 34). Likewise, they recognized the risks of treating prisoners as objects rather than subjects, and bearing a veil of noble intervention that masked a culture in which the real needs of offenders were often buried beneath calls for public protection at all costs. One psych-ologist summarized such fears thus:

I think that when we were a small number of staff and didn't do pro-grammes left, right and centre, as a professional group we had a much better grasp of the professional requirement for us to manage that power imbalance—the things you can do to try to make it better, even though it's always going be there. I think now that we put prisoners through pro-grammes, we *do to* prisoners a lot more, we don't *do with* prisoners. And I think that's one of the dangers to me with programmes. We put people through this [group-work] process, and you don't always think about who does fall off the edge.... People are going to fall down the side of that for all sorts of reasons.... We're doing these things to people, and that's not the world I was brought up in. We used to work *with* people.

Programme content was demanding and ideologically rigid, as some facilitators acknowledged. Role-plays assumed a rational-choice agent, unconstrained by, or resistant to, the kinds of pressures that dominated the cultures and communities to which prisoners would return—pressures to maintain 'face' and 'reputation', not to back down in the face of provocation, and never to appear passive (see Fox 1999). In the course classrooms then, many prisoners functioned with a kind of dual consciousness. They often recognized that the behaviours advanced by the course had merit in principle, yet saw them as bearing little relevance to their lives. In Den's terms:

They're trying to get you to act in a way that you would never act, that no human being would ever do. If you're put in a confrontational situ-ation you ain't going to ask a man to stop because you don't want to fight him—he is trying to hit you. If you're backed in a corner you're going to have to fight your way out. They're trying to say 'no, you don't do things like that, you have to talk to this person'. And they can't get into their heads that you *can't do it*. It's not real. And they'll sit and argue with you. And they've got to be right, you can't be seen as being given your own view, you have to [take] *their* view. And I can't comply like that. There's too many ifs, whats, and buts to everything. There's too many questions for me to sit back and just accept that one person's opinion. If we lived like that, we'd be machines.

Den's complaints highlighted the perception that psychological discourse was highly partial and its truths unyielding. Disputing programme assumptions was almost impossible—a further sign of one's 'thinking errors' or 'cognitive distortions' (Fox 1999; Maruna and Mann 2006). There was no room within programme discourse for prisoners to expound accepted sociological explanations for their offending trajectories. There were few options to understand oneself and one's options on alternative grounds— those which took into account the culture of the inner city, accepted that some problems were psychiatric or socio-economic, or simply allowed more dialogic debate about appropriate courses of action.[32] In its efforts to subjectify prisoners into risk-free identities, psychological power was thus experienced by some men as deeply oppressive. Some felt that that they were expected to become almost inhuman—robotic prototypes of responsible citizenship. Living up to these expectations felt almost impossible: in the terms of some prisoners, like being 'set up to fail'. At the same time, as the following chapter describes in more detail, it is important to note that many prisoners were far more positive about courses and what they gained from attending them.

With its formidable force, psychological power also risked confirming its own assumptions, and promoting lies instead of truths. Thus, Martin argued that, because he was seen on record as 'some violent beast', to be perceived as 'honest' he was forced within classes to give answers that confirmed that identity. Working through a particular role-play, which asked prisoners how they would react if they bumped into an ex-girlfriend with

---

[32] One ageing lifer claimed that he had been told by a probation officer that his plan for release—'to get a bus pass'—was not sufficiently positive. 'As a double murderer, I might struggle to get work', he said dryly. Some psychologists and course facilitators were more aware than others of some of the flaws in their professional discourse.

a new boyfriend, his suggestions that he would simply 'say hello' were disbelieved: 'so I just said "alright then, I'd buy him a drink and I'd glass him", and [the tutor said] "that's what I thought you'd do"'. Several prisoners reported being advised by officers to 'start off by acting like a prick' (fieldwork notes) and then show improvement, following the institutional narrative of engagement and reform. Further, the institutional emphasis on meeting performance targets for course graduates fuelled a perception that courses served to promote superficial presentations of self. As Pete complained, 'the system wants to see you on paper, whether you've taken a blind bit of notice... or gone through the motions. It's quite easy to sit there and tell them what they want to hear.' To meet bureaucratic imperatives, compliance needed to be visibly demonstrated and formally recorded, almost regardless of its underlying sincerity.

The model performance over the course of a programme was one of personal progress and transformation (see Fox 1999). The ideal subject was the prisoner capable of being emancipated from his unthinking, irrational, wayward self into the rational self-governing agent that lay within. In essence then, cognitive group-work addressed the offender by appealing to an essential 'good side' that its selection policy ensured was amenable. Those whose rationality was already considered deficient or who were irredeemably 'misguided' were excluded from participation. This logic, whereby prisoners were liberated from their own irrational interests for the sake of a wider majority, represented a form of authoritarian paternalism. Course attendance typified a doctrine in which prisoners were nominally free to choose their actions, but suffered if their decisions were not aligned with institutional objectives (Fox 1999; Carlen 2005). As Den described:

Jail doesn't say you *have* to do these courses. But if you do, you've got a better chance of getting your parole.... If you don't do them, they hold that over you.... I wouldn't do R and R, [and they said] that I wasn't complying with the rules of the system. But it's not in the rules to do R and R. As soon as you go there, they tell you it's voluntary.

There were understandable reasons for not wanting to attend programmes. Many prisoners saw them as simplistic and irrelevant or had taken the same courses years earlier or on previous sentences. However they were expressed, these objections made little difference to institutional conclusions: non-attendance was a sign of non-compliance. Such judgments vividly exposed the hard edges of voluntarism and rehabilitation.

Neo-Paternalism

The softening of everyday authority and the dispersal of power to specialist and bureaucratic staff did not represent a simple evacuation of power from the prison landings. Rather, it entailed a transformation in the means by which power was imposed. In the past, it was enforced more directly, through staff presence and interventions. In relation to institutional order and discipline, officers were strict in their pursuit of obedience and submission. Beyond this, where activities were deemed unthreatening to staff control, prisoners were granted considerable autonomy. In some prisons during the 1980s and early 1990s, residential zones were 'no go areas' for staff, with prisoners draping blankets over the ends of landings to symbolize their dominion and conceal their activities of drug-taking, drinking, and 'exploitation...and strong-arming of various kinds' (McDermott and King 1988: 364).

In such a context, despite the need for prisoners to conform to petty regulations and to endure poor conditions, the social world of prisoners was a zone of relative autonomy from the reaches of power. Likewise, little was expected of prisoners in terms of engagement with the system or personal transformation. As Matt explained:

You used to be just left to your own devices. It was less comfortable but you had more freedom. You didn't have all these fucking Reasoning and Rehabilitation and all these drug courses and all that. As long as you didn't give them no bother, they didn't care. They'd just move you through the system, for an easy life.

This was a penal doctrine that, while authoritarian and exacting in policing disobedience, made little attempt to penetrate the mind or target the psyche. The lines of acceptable conduct were clearly marked and monitored by direct surveillance. In Wellingborough, by contrast, the regulation of behaviour did not rely on external supervision—indeed, during association periods, staff visibility on the landings was minimal and periodic. But the grasp of power was not restricted by the limitations of interpersonal surveillance. Here, the 'buffer zone' between the prisoner and the bare face of staff control was the sphere where the captive was expected to self-govern without direct intervention: to be, in Foucault's (1977: 203) terms, 'the principle of his own subjection'.

The key techniques of this modality of power were mandatory drug testing, the IEP scheme, cell searches, and the forms of psychological power described above. Operating at distance, these tools meant that personal oversight was not required for prisoners to be gripped tightly by mechanisms of control. Power of this kind had no embodiment, no sovereign face, and little discernible 'weight' as such. Drugs could be taken privately but discovered through testing some days later. And with surveillance for reports an ongoing matter, based on conduct and 'attitude' rather than mere compliance, prisoners were required to self-monitor not only during direct exchanges with officers, but perpetually and with little certainty of outcomes. Prisoners often commented that staff were not 'in your face' or 'on your back' (Olly), but this lack of intervention was not an absence of power. As Isaac noted, 'you hardly ever see them, but they're running the show. When push comes to shove, they're the ones that do your reports.'

The transfer of responsibility from the institution to the individual is highly significant, and represents a shift in the rationality of crime control (Hannah-Moffat 2001; 2005; Kruttschnitt and Gartner 2005; Garland 1997). Prisoners have always 'self-governed' to some degree, to disguise illicit activity or reduce the points of friction with the institution. But this imperative has intensified, giving the achievement of order an apparently automatic quality. Whereas McDermott and King (1988: 362) described the need for officers to 'order 100 men to stop watching television or to leave the football field and return to their cells', in Wellingborough, prisoners required little chivvying or cajoling to conform to the regime. As Darren highlighted, prisoners were not subjected to orders so much as the agents of their own incarceration:

The screws [used to] let you know: 'you step over that line, and I'll have you'. These days, they'll let you step over the line. They'll give you enough rope to hang yourself. You can just tie yourself up and then kill yourself with it. [You] think 'well, fuck me, [I've done this] loads of times, why haven't you nicked me before?'

Darren's quotation indicated the insecurities that went with 'responsibilization'. When behaviour was patrolled by staff, the enemy was clear and the main onus on the prisoner was to stay out of trouble. With prisoners held responsible under the IEP scheme for a wide range of conduct, the burdens imposed on the individual and the sites of responsibility were multiplied: 'like walking on eggshells', prisoners often commented. There was more to manage and monitor, and more to get wrong. Being a prisoner was a more complex task:

Before you just did your time and you got out. There was nothing required of you, except to go to work. Whereas now it's down to the slightest little thing, it's all tied in. Like there's a notice out there, 'don't fill a bucket from the hot water tap or you get a strike' You get three strikes, you're knocked down a level, you might lose your TV, [or] a couple of visits. Right down to the slightest little thing, it's all tied in to your behaviour. So right down to the sort of tiniest sort of forms of behaviour, it's all monitored; it's all tied in to your future. (George)

Even at the level of their social actions and identities, prisoners felt pressure to self-regulate. Kieran described the narrow parameters of acceptable conduct as a kind of social tightrope:

If you're keeping your head down, for instance, and you don't really mix with people, they'll say 'he's got a bit of an attitude problem'. If you're the opposite, and you hang around with people, you've 'got your fingers in all pies', you're up to no good.

Prisoners were held responsible for behaviours that were indicators of risk, rather than rule infractions as such, and were rewarded or punished for the minutiae of their everyday conduct. In these respects, by linking rewards to the details of daily behaviour, prison life was experienced not only as 'deep' (Downes 1988) or 'heavy' (King and McDermott 1995), but as 'tight': 'like a straitjacket' (Ross). As Elliott put it, the 'boundary of the bubble'—staff oversight and situational control—was less imposing and intimidating in a Cat-C than in high-security prisons, but 'to keep the bubble from bursting, it seems to be tighter. [They've got] control over you not with the bars [but] by saying: "look, you can get these things as long as you comply"'.

Since aspirations and desires were the basis of control, any inability to conform to the prison's expectations could be experienced as a form of self-denial—a failing in individual self-control as much as in institutional effectiveness. Meanwhile, the provision of cognitive behavioural courses designed to 'teach' responsibility reassigned liability for misbehaviour from the prison to the prisoner. 'They can say "well, he's had the opportunity, if he hasn't learned, it ain't our fault"' (Matt). Prisoners who had taken R&R courses were thus held doubly responsible for infractions—guilty of breaking the rules and of 'knowing better', despite having had little meaningful choice about signing up to the contracts that they were deemed to have breached (Jameson and Allison 1995; Crawford 2009).

George's quotation (above) indicated a related and significant shift in the expectations of the system. It was not enough to advance through the system invisibly, as a passive object. Avoiding trouble and 'toeing the line' was a necessary condition of progression. But a 'docile body' (Foucault 1977) or a 'blank mask' of compliance (Scott 1990) was insufficient to assure the swiftest journey to freedom. Rather, prisoners were required to demonstrate an active commitment to change and to engage with the system as enthusiastic partners in its project. Gaining enhanced status normally required prisoners to do 'something extra' for the prison that indicated such orientations i.e. join the Youth and Community project, work with handicapped children in the gym, or show special effort in some other area of activity.

For some prisoners, this demand for engagement was an advanced form of oppression. It represented the extension of control from the body to the mind and 'soul'. The logic of being punished for doing something *wrong* was easier to accept than the requirement to cultivate a certain kind of committed persona:

I haven't got the right attitude to get enhanced. I won't cause problems, but I won't jump to attention. To get enhanced, you've got to do a lot of arse-kissing. It's just not who I am. The way I look at it, I've been sent to prison, that's my punishment. We shouldn't be further punished unless we break rules. My privileges have been taken away from me already. As long as I keep to normal standards and don't cause problems, then I can't see where I'm going wrong. I'm just not prepared to do that little bit extra. (Jordan)

In noting the prison's ultimate desire for *commitment* as well as *compliance*, Jordan identified a fundamental shift in the kind of liberty that the prison provided. Prisons of the 1970s and '80s were generally highly authoritarian, and, despite an official discourse of 'training', welfare and rehabilitation, most offered little constructive activity and few meaningful opportunities for self-development. 'Positive liberty' (Berlin 1969), opportunities for self-realization and empowerment, was pitifully low. At the same time, *within* the prisoner world, 'negative liberty' (ibid.), the freedom from interference, was relatively high.

In current times, the situation is almost the opposite: improvements in terms of comforts, provisions, safety, and opportunities have supplanted the freedom to be left alone. Prisoners have more 'rights' and options, but less autonomy. Within the prisoner world, there is less negative liberty, both in physical and psychological terms. Officers themselves largely leave prisoners alone—particularly in Wellingborough, once morale had sagged—but there is little free movement within the prison (e.g. between wings) and there are an increasing number of psychological obstacles that prisoners must negotiate to attain their freedom with maximum speed. Positive liberty is undoubtedly higher, however. The prison has more purpose and provides prisoners with more opportunities. Room exists for the exercise of localized autonomy in terms of how the sentence is conducted. There are also significant strands of welfarism, for example, in the official commitment to 'decency', in the 'safer custody' agenda, and in the improved resources for prisoners with severe learning difficulties, drug problems, and mental health issues.[33]

But this is a narrowly defined version of opportunity and rehabilitation. It is filtered through the imperatives for efficiency and public protection, and its parameters are limited, with sharp edges that quickly become apparent if opportunities are not taken up or if behaviour does not suit institutional objectives. In such respects, depictions of the 'governmental power' that has been identified as a key mechanism of social and political rule in society at large appear highly relevant to the prison. Governmental power can be contrasted against both a welfarist conception of the individual as a passive recipient, and a disciplinary conception of power which exerts authority deductively—directly punishing subjects for breaching rules and boundaries. Rather, its preference is for an inductive version of power, which does not constrain, command or suppress the object, so much as incite, cultivate, and stimulate the subject. Through moral education and reward, governmental power seeks to foster individuals to become particular kinds of *agents* who self-govern actively and autonomously (Garland 1997; O'Malley 1997), without the need for external interventions or reminders of appropriate conduct.

---

[33] Most of these prisoners should not be in the CJS at all, but, tragically, they may find their needs better supported when under the wings of the penal state than in the community.

When successful, governmental power does not appear coercive. Individuals are not forced into choosing particular options, but steered into seeing personal goals and institutional objectives as analogous. They are trained and persuaded that, given the possibilities on offer, the best way to fulfil their personal ambitions, advance their interests and sate their desires is to take certain routes—routes that are consistent with the goals of the governing authorities. In its ideal form, decisions and identities that are made to 'make most sense' in terms of self-interest come to be experienced as normatively superior—the right way to be, as well as the most prudential. The individual is both addressed and cultivated as a 'rational agent', capable of weighing up available options and alternatives, but therefore held responsible for the consequences that emerge, even when these consequences are structured and determined by others (Garland 1997; Hannah-Moffat 2001).

The fact that options and consequences are structured from the start, and that the agent is urged and incited to 'exercise her freedom in a very specific fashion' (Dean 2006: 15), points to the tendentious nature of the autonomy that is really on offer (Crawford 2009). Autonomy and self-determination are *presupposed*, in that the individual 'must be free in order to exercise their authority' (Dean 2006: 165; Garland 1997), and there is a range of options for action. Yet the need to coach individuals to use their freedom responsibly—in the case of the prison, to take responsibility for the causes and solutions of their offending behaviour and 'risk'—is indicative of a highly structured form of freedom, a kind of *containment of the will*. As Rose notes, this involves a 'twin process of autonomisation plus responsibilisation—opening free space for the choices of individual actors while enwrapping these autonomised actors within new forms of control' (1999: xxiii).

Governmental power is associated with neo-liberalism, both inside and beyond the prison (Rose 1999; Dean 2006; Crawford 2009). In recent years, for example, users of the welfare state have been encouraged to see themselves as responsible, empowered agents able to raise themselves to less dependent social territory, rather than passive recipients destined to social submission. Contracts are entered into with the state, which promises services and benefits in return for subjects exercising their freedoms in particular ways (Rose 1999: 160). Subjects are deemed capable of knowing their preferences and sticking to their pledges of future conduct (Crawford 2009). But liberalism has always struggled with those citizens deemed incapable of 'responsible and prudential autonomy' (Dean 2006: 209), and even in its advanced forms, its coercive and paternalistic tendencies are made visible when agents do not align their choices with institutional goals or when self-monitoring fails (Hannah-Moffat 2001). In the free community, it is only at the margins that choices of conduct are bounded by the law and coercive interventions are considered acceptable (Rose 1999). In the prison, the discourse of public protection makes it easier not only to judge certain individuals as irrational, irresponsible or lacking in good judgment, but to justify violations of liberty and intrusions into private life that would be considered illegitimate elsewhere. Neo-liberalism and authoritarianism converge, with individuals exhorted to practice their freedom in ways that are defined by the dominant party, but then coercively policed to make sure that they decide to do so. The illusion of pure choice is more obvious.

In Wellingborough—as the chapter that follows shows more clearly—imprisonment was not experienced as a coercive imposition by those prisoners whose subjectivities were successfully engaged, harnessed, or transformed by institutional mechanisms. Its qualities were soft and unobtrusive. But noncompliance soon led to punitive sanctions (e.g. the denial of open visits, additions to the sentence, transfers to higher-security establishments). Resistant individuals were held responsible for behaviours that were indicative of poor self-governance and for breaking 'compacts' with the institution that they were given no option but to sign. Thus, the availability of drugs was such that the policy of drug testing appeared to test prisoners' capacity to *manage* their intake—allowing them to use drugs but holding them responsible for doing so. Prisoners who wanted to retain their enhanced status were required to submit to 'voluntary' drug tests, blurring the boundary between choice and necessity. With many jobs dependent on passing drug tests, the consequences of failing them reverberated widely, exposing the policy's disciplinary functions.

Course attendance was also voluntary, but prisoners who appeared uncommitted or insincere were sanctioned. Nonattendance had more severe consequences. As Derek summarized, 'you've got a choice, but if you don't go on them, you don't get out'. Opting out was not banned, but its costs made it highly imprudent. Those prisoners who did not volunteer for regular drug testing were, likewise, bound to create suspicion. Meanwhile, genuine effort was put into rehabilitative provision and prisoners were given options to engage in various ways with institutional opportunities, but these options were differentially rewarded, and those prisoners who rejected them entirely faced punitive consequences. Getting on with psychologists was, for many prisoners, a necessity: 'otherwise it can hold you back for x amount of years' (prisoner, fieldwork notes). By linking rewards and progression to behaviour, the IEP scheme, psychological reports, and mandatory drug testing incentivized prisoners to invest in institutionally desirable behaviour, and made them accountable for the terms of their confinement.

In this regard, the prison operated a form of what could be called 'authoritarian governmentality' (Dean 1999) or—perhaps more neatly—*neo-paternalism*. Its core was neo-liberal: a sphere of soft power and self-regulation. It offered paternalistic, almost protective support, stopping the prisoner from succumbing to inertia and preventing him from making hasty or uninformed decisions, while steering and inducing him towards 'sensible options' (as defined by the authorities), providing opportunities, and appealing to his 'better self'. In many respects, it offered decency, care, and assistance. But its perimeter was firmer and more coercive. If the prisoner did not want to be rehabilitated, if he chose not to conform to institutional demands, or if he could not recognize his 'best interests', then punishment and constraint—the 'authoritarian wall'—were not far away. The line between a guiding hand and a stiff, constraining grip was a fine one. There was little room for trust, for prisoners meaningfully to contest how their best interests were defined or to challenge the relative weight given to public interests over personal rights. The prison assumed not just the right but the responsibility to act upon the prisoner beyond the official terms of the sentence— the deprivation of liberty. In return, the prisoner was expected to participate enthusiastically in his own carceral management. In effect, he was encouraged—and, if necessary, nudged—along a thin precipice, with falls on each side. From the prisoner's vantage point, autonomy was offered with a smile, but backed by threat.

Conclusion

This chapter has described in some detail the nature and location of power in a modern prison. In explaining how it has been refigured in recent years, it has made a number of comparisons with the form of power in previous eras—here labelled 'authoritarian power' and defined loosely as the two decades preceding 1990. The table below provides a rudimentary conceptual overview of these differences. It is intended as a tool for comparative thinking rather than a definitive description.

Few prisons are likely to embody neo-paternalism. Some traditional Local prisons in the UK retain many of the characteristics of the more authoritarian era, as do many international prison systems. However, the globalization of penal practices, and techniques, such as incentive schemes, cognitive behavioural programmes, and dynamic security, means that the features of neo-paternalism should be recognizable well beyond the fences of HMP Wellingborough.

Table 4.1

Characteristics of power	Authoritarian power, circa 1970–1990	Neo-paternalism
Location	Close, immediate	Ubiquitous, yet distant, elusive, intangible
Character	Embodied, obtrusive	Faceless, invasive
Distribution	Concentrated (on landings)	Dispersed and diffuse
Implementation	Direct	Indirect
Effects	Immediate	Delayed
Form and feel	Heavy/hard	Soft, but tight, with hard edges
Reach	Limited	Pervasive
Expectations placed on the prisoner	Limited but strict	High but sometimes unclear
Institutional offerings	Few rights, informal rewards	Formalized incentives, differential privileges
Accountability	Minimal	Formal, bureaucratic
Balance of liberties	More freedoms ('negative liberty')	More rights and opportunities ('positive liberty')
Everyday consequences	Authoritarian clarity, austere certainty	Bureaucratic ambiguity, uncertainty

Table 4.1 *Continued*

Characteristics of power	Authoritarian power, circa 1970–1990	Neo-paternalism
Mode and means of staff authority	Rules, boundaries	Discretion, negotiation
Impact on prisoner community	Relative autonomy	No zones of autonomy, individualization
Site of transformation	Body, behaviour	Cognition, identity, 'soul'
Mode of discipline	Physical	Psychological
Logic of discipline	Deductive, corrective	Deductive, corrective, preventive
Primary form of power	Situational-coercive	Instrumental, neo-liberal
Institutional function	Containment	Neo-rehabilitation
Everyday aim	Obedience, compliance, submission	Active engagement, responsibility
Compliance via:	Institutional control	Individual self-government

In terms of its political character, contemporary penal power has neo-liberal, rehabilitative and authoritarian dimensions (see O'Malley 1999; Hannah-Moffat 2001).[34] It has not discarded its welfarist ambitions, and it is important not to downplay the degree to which decency has been embedded and legitimacy raised. Yet rehabilitation has a revised form that emphasizes personal rather than institutional responsibility for the regulation of the self (and see Robinson 2008). Situational control measures have been heightened, techniques of instrumental control have been strategically enhanced, and staff power has been reasserted through a disciplinary web that is robust, extensive and all-embracing (Liebling 2004; Simon 2000). Prisoners who step outside the bounds of acceptable conduct are sanctioned not through physical coercion but through techniques that bind their desires to institutional ambitions. The depth (Downes 1988), weight (King and McDermott 1995), and legitimacy of

[34] The balance of these dimensions—and the 'softness', 'hardness' and 'tightness' of a prison—will vary between establishments, according to function, staff culture, history, and other such factors.

imprisonment have each increased in some ways and decreased in others. The psychological burdens have shifted and, in some ways, intensified. Meanwhile, penal power now has another quality—'tightness'. This refers to much of what this chapter has described: the exacting demands of self-regulation, the experience of being judged and held responsible for all aspects of behaviour, and their consequences, and the feeling that power is ubiquitous and inescapable, yet hard to predict or decipher. It denotes the grip exercised by soft power, in particular the appeal to self-interest that induces prisoners to manage their own compliance. As the concluding chapter will discuss further, the distinctive new pains represented by 'tightness' are the outcome of the strategies of imprisonment rather than its intrinsic terms, and they have some significant consequences.

This is not, therefore, a simple diminishment of power, but its transformation and displacement from one form to another (Foucault 1977). Power of one kind has been removed from the wings—it would be insufficient now to assert that 'life in prison is essentially on the landings' (McDermott and King 1988: 359). In its systemic form, it is increasingly intangible. At the same time, it exercises a grip that is tighter, more potent and more invasive. Its terms are highly demanding. As Foucault anticipated, it is not concentrated in a particular location, but dispersed through specialist knowledge and expert authorities, operating in a manner that is 'light' (ibid.: 202) and 'non-corporal' (ibid.: 203), like an automatic, and anonymous piece of machinery. Its shift from direct to indirect techniques means that it requires a far greater degree of self-government while rendering the individual more responsible for its consequences, even when these are structured and determined by others. Power operates both at-a-distance and through the self. As a result, there is little autonomous space beyond the reach of power. At best, prisoners said, you could 'ride' the system, but it could not be ignored.

The need to 'engage with the system' meant that prisoners were in effect obliged to have an individual relationship with the system of power. These 'vertical' relationships with the institution had significant consequences for the 'horizontal' relationships that prisoners formed with each other. The prisoner social world, as described in Chapters 6 to 8, cannot be understood, therefore, without an account of individual styles of adaptation. These adaptations were structured by the form of penal power described in this chapter, but they cannot be assessed from an analysis of power alone. As Garland acknowledges, governmental projects are never fully realized in practice: 'the question of how prisoners *engage* with these practices, and the ways in which these practices do or do not actually shape prisoners' subjectivity and behaviour is a separate issue of great importance' (1997: 207).

5

Adaptation, Compliance, and Resistance

The wealth of typologies in prison sociology provides plentiful evidence that there is no single pattern by which individuals adjust to prison life. The basis of classification varies greatly between studies. So too do explanations for differences in experience and behaviour, and conceptions of the relative influence of the institution, the individual and the external environment in determining adaptive patterns. Many early studies of prison life highlighted the significance of 'indigenous' or institutional factors—such as the prison's organizational goals, the severity of its deprivations, and the way it administered power and privileges—in shaping the social roles available to prisoners (Grusky 1959, Berk 1966, Street *et al.* 1966).[1] Differences between prisoners were related (not always exclusively) to intrinsic characteristics of imprisonment, such as length of time exposed to the prisoner subculture (Clemmer 1940) or stage of sentence (Wheeler 1961). Prisoners were labelled according to prison-specific factors such as deviation from the 'inmate code' (Sykes 1958).[2] Roles were seen primarily as different ways of handling the pressures of imprisonment or managing the tension between the worlds of the institution and the free community (Goffman 1961).

The terminology of 'roles' reflected the belief that prisons generated certain social positions virtually regardless of the traits

[1] Reference in this book to 'adaptation' is not intended to suggest 'prisonisation' (Clemmer 1940), or a merely passive, accepting or 'tension-reducing' (Cohen and Taylor 1972: 132) response to imprisonment. Rather, it refers to the process of *adjusting* to the prison environment: the set of behaviours that a prisoner chooses or adopts within this domain.

[2] The word 'inmate' is employed when discussing the American prison literature, particularly the early prison ethnographies, because this was the term used in such studies. Elsewhere in this book, 'prisoner' is preferred because it is a more neutral, objective term. Although some Wellingborough prisoners referred to themselves as 'inmates', others felt that this connoted mental illness.

of those who entered them (Sykes 1995). According to these perspectives, the prison walls marked a decisive break with the outside community and surrounded an alien world with distinctive social positions, into which prisoners were 'socialized' or 'assimilated'. Imprisonment stripped prisoners of their identities, limiting their contact with external influences, restricting their physical and psychological autonomy, and providing a new set of rules, relationships, meanings, and rewards around which identity and behaviour were reconstituted. Although Sykes acknowledged that the differential adoption of roles was likely to be influenced by personality structures, his comments on this were rather cursory (Sykes and Messinger 1960). No attempt was made to elucidate how individual traits or cultural dispositions might influence prison conduct or might shape how particular positions within the inmate community could be consciously adopted.

Other theorists have emphasized the significance of 'imported' factors, such as criminal orientation and outlook (Irwin and Cressey 1962; Irwin 1970), attitude towards authority (Cohen and Taylor 1972), and race or ethnicity (Carroll 1974; Jacobs 1977) in determining differential responses towards incarceration: differences in relationships with staff, attitudes to drugs, violent misconduct and so on. Such studies do not deny that incarceration presents prisoners with specific kinds of social and psychological problems. However, they argue that the incoming prisoner is not wholly overwhelmed or over-written by the new world he or she enters. Rather, the problems of imprisonment are addressed and resolved through attitudes, cultures, networks and ideologies formed outside the institution, prior to imprisonment. These 'latent' orientations are not imported into the prison without amendment. Nonetheless, they provide the crucial ideological bridge between internal and external behaviour, and supply the social connections that enable involvement with particular social groups within the prison. Adaptations are thus seen as being in some way *consistent* with identities and values that pre-exist the prison experience. To some degree, the significance of these external factors in shaping adaptations is an outcome of prisons having become more porous and less repressive institutions.[3] As

---

[3] Although Clemmer's (1940) study of the prisoner community placed emphasis on external dispositions many years before the reforms that opened up prisons to outside forces.

they have become less depriving and have allowed prisoners more opportunities for outside contact, the generic identity of 'the convict' has diminished in importance and been superseded by a multitude of identities that had previously been suppressed (see Carroll 1974).

Importation exponents have tended to place more emphasis on the capacity of individuals to reflect upon the prison experience and choose, rather than merely accept, their place in the inmate world (see in particular Cohen and Taylor 1972). Even when they have not, their focus on 'types of person' rather than 'social roles' implies an interest in personality as well as institution. It is accepted now that the relationship between the two is complex or 'transactional' (Toch 1992; Toch and Adams 1989), that reactions to imprisonment are to some degree idiosyncratic (Bukstel and Kilmann 1980), and that the relationship between pre-prison factors and in-prison behaviour is variable, combining imported and indigenous components (Akers *et al.* 1974; Zamble and Porporino 1988). As Toch (1992: 2) notes: 'A given physical or social milieu is a different psychological environment for everyone who operates in it.'

Clearly, though—as Kruttschnitt and Gartner (2005) demonstrate—the institutional environment makes some adaptations more likely or 'available' than others. The history of the Scottish Special Units and the successes of prison therapeutic units and faith communities illustrate that, in particular penal contexts, individuals are given opportunities to escape their institutional histories: to be a different kind of prisoner. In other words, context matters, and any typology that presents prisoners in static terms fails to account for the fluidities in behaviour that can occur according to the institutional context (and the personal life-stage), albeit within the constraints of biography and personal resources.[4] Individuals are never *always* a particular kind of prisoner; nor are prisoner types universal. Indeed, any attempt to generalize about adaptations will struggle to cover the variety of penal settings where they occur and will fail to account for the range of imported factors through which adaptive possibilities are given form, shape, and substance.

Despite this, the prison literature suggests that a number of basic adaptive styles can be identified (the implication being

---

[4] With thanks to Richard Sparks for pushing me to clarify these issues.

that the conditions of imprisonment do make certain positions more likely). By combining the frameworks presented by Merton (1938) and Goffman (1961) (and see Schrag 1944), these can be bracketed as follows. First, some prisoners 'withdraw', 'retreat' or 'regress', focusing on immediate events and issues of 'self', and often isolating themselves from their peers. This includes obvious 'maladaptations', such as repeated self-mutilation or psychosis, but can also incorporate obsessive body-building and the deep absorption into art, education, or mere 'reverie' that can allow mental escape from institutional life (Clemmer 1940; Cohen and Taylor 1972; Boyle 1984).

Second, some prisoners actively rebel, engaging in organized and conscious resistance (Boyle 1977; McEvoy 2001), escape attempts (McVicar 1974), or concerted campaigns against prison conditions and practices (Cohen and Taylor 1972). In the UK, such activities tend to be concentrated within higher-security establishments, where the pains of imprisonment are more profound and prisoners are more likely to be desperately frustrated, personally resourceful and ideologically opposed to authority.

A third kind of adaptation is 'conformity' (Merton 1938) 'colonisation' or 'conversion' (Goffman 1961). Prisoners of this kind appear relatively content and comply with the demands of the system with apparent sincerity and enthusiasm. This category includes the 'centre-men', 'straights' and 'square johns' described in the early prison ethnographies, men who identified with conventional values prior to imprisonment. It also includes the category of 'gleaners' who Irwin (1970) identified as men seeking change and self-improvement through official programmes and structures. Several commentators argue that extreme forms of conversion—where prisoners internalize official definitions of their status and selfhood—are uncommon or merely superficial because they require that prisoners discard their values, abandon their claims to autonomous selfhood, and accept ideas of their inferior moral worth (Morris and Morris 1963; Carrabine 2005).

A fourth set of prisoners represents the 'innovators' that Merton described as men who accepted official objectives but rejected the institutional means of their attainment. To use Mathiesen's (1965) vocabulary, these are prisoners whose general stance is one of 'censoriousness' rather than normative opposition (c.f. Sykes 1958). 'Censoriousness' entails the criticism of those in power for not conforming to official standards or wider moral norms, or for pursuing institutional goals through the wrong means. These prisoners may include 'barrack room lawyers', or 'straight' prisoners who align themselves with pro-social values but see the prison as a deficient institution for the achievement of its stated aims.[5]

The majority of prisoners want to 'do their time and get out' (Carrabine 2004), and find ways of coping with imprisonment that involve neither extreme resistance nor complete acquiescence. Whether described as 'playing it cool' (Goffman 1961), 'doing time', or a particular form of 'ritualism' (Merton 1938; Morris and Morris 1963), this adaptation entails nominal but unenthusiastic conformity, aimed at making the prison experience as comfortable and conflict-free as possible. Prisoners in a sixth category are more active in seeking to manipulate the system (Morris and Morris 1963; King and Elliott 1977). They use their prison experience to exploit rules, work 'angles' and perform desired behaviour to prison officials while flouting it elsewhere. These prisoners do not necessarily cause 'trouble', and often use legitimate as well as illicit means to achieve their ends, but they do so outside the spirit of the system.

Typologies tend to underplay the degree to which adaptive positions can be strategic or provisional rather than fixed. Prisoners of all kinds may employ censoriousness at particular moments,[6] or may 'rebel', 'withdraw', or fully 'conform' at certain times in the sentence for tactical gain, because of changing life circumstances or when certain thresholds have been passed. The dilemma, therefore, is whether to characterize adaptive styles in the form of nouns or verbs: 'rebels' or 'rebellion', 'innovators' or 'innovation', and so on. The typology of adaptation provided in this chapter does the former. Not all prisoners fitted neatly or consistently into a single adaptive category, and the aim is not to suggest that styles of adaptation were static over the course of a sentence, let alone a carceral career. However, the great majority had a stable and classifiable orientation to the sentence at the time of the study and in the particular context of HMP Wellingborough. The focus of

---

[5] Bowker (1978) argues that 'merchants', 'politicians', and 'right guys' can be seen as innovators, because they pursue conventional goals of wealth, status, and power through illicit means. However, this seems to conflate *social* goals and more specific *institutional* goals.

[6] Regardless of the sincerity with which it is used, censoriousness is a highly effective means of contesting the terms of one's incarceration and blurring the moral divide between the prisoner and the state representative (Mathieson 1965).

the typology that follows is the interplay between the terms and imperatives of this institutional setting, and the values and dispositions that prisoners brought into this environment. The idea is not to presume the primacy of either biography or social structure, but to show their interaction. Likewise, the aim is to show the dynamics of agency and constraint—the manner in which prisoners chose to take up, reject, or refigure the opportunities, incentives and social positions that the prison made available.

The typology carries the normal drawbacks of typological analysis, but there are significant advantages in this descriptive style.[7] Although the social world cannot be carved up as cleanly as is always implied in typological work, an effective typology can draw attention to its contours and can provide a conceptual pathway through its terrain. Clear analysis requires some degree of simplification. Without some reduction into classes, the danger is that a complex social setting is presented as an undifferentiated mass of individual accounts with some hazy, central tendencies. One of the clear findings of this study is that there is no such thing as the typical prisoner or a single 'prison culture'. The typology seeks to provide a parsimonious description of variance within the prisoner world. It also allows comparisons to be made with other studies, whether of similar prisons, prisons in other jurisdictions, or other kinds of penal establishment.

One hazard of typological work is 'reification': the construction of abstract types with no empirical basis. Weberian (1949) 'ideal types' are often criticized on these grounds. As Bailey (1994: 19) argues though, this may be a misrepresentation of Weber's position, and ideal types can be seen as the 'clearest and purest example of the type, with no dull or damaged features'. Empirical cases are always likely to fall short of these clean specimens. In comparison, 'constructed types' (Becker 1940; McKinney 1954) place less emphasis on *accentuating* characteristics of the type and more on producing empirical 'approximations' from which real cases might deviate by being both more or less 'extreme'. The ideal type sits at the end of a continuum of values whereas the constructed type sits closer to the middle. In this chapter, the use

---

[7] Strictly speaking, a form of classification that begins empirically is known as a 'taxonomy' while one with a conceptual basis is a 'typology'. This study combines both, but the latter term is preferred because of its historical currency within prison sociology.

of case studies to illustrate each type demonstrates their empirical grounding and their lived authenticity. Nonetheless, these examples were chosen because they most closely captured the conceptually salient characteristics of each 'cell' of the typology. They were the exemplars relative to which most other prisoners within each category were less clearly illuminated.

As is common in ethnographic work, the construction of the typology was guided by conceptual priorities, but followed an inductive logic. As an adapted form of grounded theory (Glaser and Strauss 1967; Layder 1998), empirical clusters were identified prior to the development of conceptual labels,[8] but the identification of these groupings relied on direction from the literature described above. John Irwin's focus on criminal orientation and Cohen and Taylor's emphasis on attitudes towards authority merit acknowledgement here. Merton's typology of individual adaptations, as outlined in his (1938) article 'Social Structure and Anomie', was also influential in providing the initial conceptual framework through which the stock of disorganized data was strained.

The basic elements of Merton's framework are 'institutional norms' and 'culture goals' (1938: 673), or the appropriate *means* and the desired *ends* of a social environment. As such, it can be applied to almost any context. Merton provides a grid of adaptive possibilities (including conformity and deviance in terms of both means and ends) that can indicate how individuals act in any environment or institution. In suggesting a limited range of positions that individuals might take up, the framework has a clear structuralist bent. But Merton himself noted that adaptive styles related to cultural backgrounds and personalities (1938: 678). How structural positions take shape in practice clearly relates to imported factors—here, the late-modern context in which prisoners were socialized and the life experiences that shaped the transactions between individual and environment.

Merton's framework is apposite for the prison precisely because its core focus is individual compliance with institutional techniques and the achievement of institutional goals.[9] In the

---

[8] For clarity, I should state that the labels did not derive directly from the terminology used by prisoners themselves, nor from the language of staff.

[9] Cloward and Ohlin's (1960) *Delinquency and Opportunity* drew significantly on Merton's work, which Cloward had first employed in his doctoral analysis of adaptive styles in an army prison (see Bowker 1978).

managerial prison, increasing emphasis has been placed upon *institutional* conformity with particular methods of government and *individual* compliance with a specific set of institutional demands. The means of imprisonment are ever more regulated, and are tied to relevant ends for prisoners. In an earlier era, more concerned with containment than self-government, the relationship between everyday adaptations and institutional objectives was much looser and more tenuous. In the period when Sykes and Irwin were first writing, for example, as long as prisoners were not seeking to escape or causing disruption, there were few demands on them to adapt *in particular ways*.[10] Now that government—the direction of human conduct (Foucault 1982)—is a principal concern of the system, now that prisoners are addressed far more directly by techniques of institutional power, and now that their commitment to institutional objectives is more closely scrutinized, adaptive styles are intertwined with the mechanisms of institutional control. A 'relationship' of some kind with the institution is obligatory.

The typology that follows has five main parts. Prisoners are labelled[11] (1) *enthusiasts* (2) *pragmatists* (3) *stoics* (4) *retreatists* and (5) *players*. A further sub-category, the *disengaged*, is also discussed in this chapter, as is the small number of prisoners who appeared to be 'in transition' from one adaptive style to another.[12] The primary basis of classification is compliance with institutional means and goals. Each category of adaptation represents a different form of engagement with the system's demands for self-government and active engagement. Commitments to institutional imperatives ranged significantly, from normative enthusiasm to resigned pragmatism to hollow performance enacted as a form of resistance. The typology is ordered from most to least conformist, although the adaptive styles at its extremes are more easily positioned on this spectrum than those in its mid-section.

---

[10] The same is true in the modern 'warehouse prison', where prisoners are merely stored and emitted.

[11] I am aware of, and somewhat uncomfortable about, the regrettable irony that these categories impose another set of labels on a set of people already burdened by institutional definitions.

[12] Some indication is given of the approximate proportion of prisoners who occupied each adaptive category, but specific numbers are not included because the typology was constructed on the basis not only of formal interviews, but also very many informal discussions with prisoners, which were less easy to count.

Orientations were related to biographical experiences and future expectations, and took expression in a range of behaviours including attitudes to and relationships with staff, involvement in prison activities, and modes of resistance. Coming chapters will show how they also shaped and were manifested in aspects of the prisoner social world such as patterns of friendship and loyalty, commitments to prisoner values and involvement in the informal economy.

'Enthusiasts'

Carrabine (2005: 904–5) has commented that 'few prisoners embrace an ideology [...] that maintains that they are inferior and deserve their fate' (and see Morris and Morris 1963). It was certainly true that Wellingborough prisoners very rarely condemned themselves in terms that were absolute. However, a significant number (around one in five) denounced their past identities as morally shameful, provided testimonies that were suffused with guilt and self-reproach, and presented their current status as morally lowly captives as entirely warranted. Almost always, these were former drug addicts or alcoholics who attributed their crimes to selves that they had now shed, and who saw incarceration as an opportunity for self-improvement and moral reparation.

Luke and Ian were typical of this prisoner type. Luke—a roguish looking, thick-set, talkative prisoner—described his childhood as 'quite settled' until he was a teenager, when his parents separated and he moved with his mother and siblings to a rough area of a new town. His father was a strict disciplinarian, who would beat him with a whip until his legs bled. He left school aged 15, and received his first custodial sentence a year later, when he was sent to a 'brutal' detention centre. Now in his late thirties, he had been 'in and out of prison for fifteen years', mainly for relatively minor offences such as fraud, deception, and burglary.

During his previous sentence, as his relationship with the mother of his son faltered, Luke had attempted suicide: 'when I look back now, I can't believe I done it. But I was clinically depressed. And I found prison a very, very, lonely, horrible place.' Shortly after release, the relationship had ended, and although his ex-girlfriend had written to him at the start of his current term, he had told her to 'get on with her life; she's in the prime of her life. It would be wrong for me to try and hold her back, and quite naïve. You can't sustain a relationship in prison.' Luke did not want his son to visit him in prison—believing it was 'not right' to bring a child into the penal environment—and had not seen him for two years.

In the years before his current sentence, he had become a user of class A drugs, and had entered prison 'a nine-stone wreck, absolutely no good to society; [...] a crack and heroin addict. I was an habitual thief, living a terrible way of life.' Given a sentence of almost six years for a serious but non-violent offence, his primary aim during his sentence was to wean himself off drugs and re-establish his family ties:

When I was bad on drugs I don't suppose I was very nice as a person and it did affect my relationship with my family. And that is very important to me. My mum is getting on a bit now, I didn't want to let my mum see me like that. So when I got this prison sentence, I made a decision to keep away from drugs and pull myself back together.

Ian had grown up in a 'working class home', owned by his parents, both of whom were employed. His father was a violent alcoholic who used to beat him and his mother. When Ian was 14, his parents split up temporarily, and he moved in with his grandparents until he left school, at which point he worked as a salesman. At 14, he had begun to use cannabis—'it makes you sort of forget things that have happened'—and by 16 was addicted to amphetamines. He had first been imprisoned when aged 19, but his prison career accelerated when he started using crack and heroin three years later after separating from his girlfriend who had been unfaithful to him during a previous sentence. Now 29, Ian had been imprisoned on a number of occasions for domestic and commercial burglaries, carried out to feed his addiction. A mild and relatively introverted prisoner, he was currently serving a three and a half year sentence. As a consequence of his ex-girlfriend's drug addiction, their daughter now lived with his sister, a development that had 'turned my head around, made me realize I've got to look after her'.

Prisoners like Ian and Luke regarded imprisonment as a righteous intervention, not just a predictable outcome of offending. As well as accepting the legitimacy of their incarceration—as most prisoners ultimately do (Sparks *et al.* 1996)—they placed themselves on the same moral plane as that of the institution, whose motives they considered virtuous. This required a particular vision of self-identity: the 'good person' who had made 'bad decisions' or whose past acts did not represent 'the real me', or the 'lost soul' in search of spiritual redemption (see Maruna 2001). Through strenuous castigations of past acts and extensive deliberations on matters of conscience, they sought to distance themselves from the flawed, fallen selves of their past and prove their ethical substance. Zack, a former crack user and another typical enthusiast, rebuked himself for having been a 'ruthless, vicious, manipulative, obnoxious little bastard' at the height of his addiction, stealing from his family rather than looking after them following the death of his father. In berating himself for having taken 'the easy way out', it was significant that his language denoted a parallel identity and indicated his capacity for an alternative course of action. Describing the crime for which he had been sentenced, he underlined his feelings of guilt and the entrenched morality that represented his 'true self':

I really did feel shit for doing it. Because I knew there was an old lady who owned the house. And I thought 'no man, all the codes that you've always lived by, you just broke'. I really did genuinely, genuinely, genuinely feel shit about it.

Zack attributed his transformation to the recognition that 'everything in my life was not real. It was all false.' The way he was in prison—by his account, a compliant prisoner who protected the vulnerable, and was deeply committed to the Youth and Community Project—was his authentic persona: 'the real me. I've longed to be like this, for years.' Ian and Luke had similar self-narratives. Ian emphasized an upbringing that had taught him manners and morality, but had been corrupted by drug use. His original identity, he said, provided the compass by which he oriented his current existence in prison. Imprisonment was therefore welcomed for having restored his essential self:

When I was on the street and when I was on the heroin, I knew then that I was ready, I wanted to go to prison. I know it sounds mad but for me prison is the only place that you can get off the drugs. I'd just had enough. I didn't want to live the way I was living because *it wasn't me*. So when I got locked up it was sort of a godsend. [Emphasis added]

Luke explained:

[I] knew what I was doing was wrong. I knew right from wrong. Because I came from a good home. [...] I knew I was living a wrong, bad existence. And I felt I could do better than that, that I had better qualities in me than that which had been suppressed by the life I was leading. And I thought I should sort myself out and let my better qualities shine through. Because I'm a better person than that.

One reason, therefore, why the prison was considered a somewhat benign institution by these prisoners was that it helped them to rescue themselves from their 'bad' identities, and provided an opportunity for them to restore, cultivate, and exhibit what they considered their genuine selves. Within the prison, they fixated on projects that would demonstrate to their loved ones, to themselves, and to the law-abiding world with which they sought to identify that they were fundamentally 'good people' with prosocial aspirations. Typically, they aimed both to better themselves (through education, by learning skills, and by going on drug/ alcohol awareness or anger management courses) and to contribute to a wider notion of social good (for example, through the Youth and Community Project, or by getting involved in restorative justice or charity work). Most sought out victim awareness courses that would enable public apology and absolution, and work that would demonstrate trust and dedication.

Future plans involved making further amends, and promoting the wellbeing of the next generation—what Maruna (2001) refers to as 'generativity'. Ian wanted to work alongside the police in schools, warning children about the perils of drugs and crime: 'doing something good for the community and people outside, you know'. Zack wanted to mentor young offenders. Other *enthusiasts* hoped for jobs as drug counsellors and community workers, at the very least in 'honest business' (Luke). Most talked of moving away from hometowns and making a 'fresh start' somewhere they could get away from 'bad memories' (Kyle) and 'people who will get me into trouble' (Ian).[13] Zack's decision to commit to settle down with his girlfriend and his efforts to rebuild himself physically had clear symbolic functions in displaying his intention to rebrand himself.

Aspirations were expressed passionately and with absolute certainty. *Enthusiasts* had little doubt that they would succeed in going straight. Indeed, most exhibited an almost grandiose confidence

---

[13] Other prisoners' life stories indicated the ironic dangers of this stance, for, by refusing to stay in hostels occupied by drug users and petty offenders, they had found themselves homeless or in breach of licence conditions, and thus on the path back towards prison.

about their ability to forge their destinies—the kinds of narratives of unfettered agency that Maruna (2001) found were significant in aiding desistance. This discourse of self-efficacy and personal responsibility was recurrent among these prisoners. Some spoke almost evangelically about the need for prisoners to take control of their lives, exhorting their peers to desist from drug use and criminal activity and to reassess their personal values. Being clean and staying straight were committed to almost as new addictions. *Enthusiasts* often accosted prison visitors and non-custodial staff to inform them of the latest developments in their plans. Through these public pep talks, they reinforced their identities: like Foucauldian subjects, by telling their stories, they worked upon and reinscribed their selves. Much of their language echoed the terminology of offending behaviour courses and other cognitive programmes: setting 'goals' and 'objectives', 'being able to identify the problem', taking 'the right path' (see Fox 1999). 'It's up to you where you go again. Whether you go for a good life or a bad life', Zack argued. Furthermore, the descriptive labels of the prison's psychological discourse were often appropriated without cynicism. *Enthusiasts* frequently described themselves as 'high-risk' or 'prolific offenders', discussed their 'criminogenic needs', and complained that there were not enough available courses to match their enthusiasm.

Such language indicated the normative alignment between the aims and values of *enthusiasts* and those of the prison system. They supported the differentiation of prisoners according to privilege level or voluntary submission to drug testing, because it helped them to get away, spatially and symbolically, from what Luke called the 'idiots' and 'arseholes'. They had no complaints about mandatory drug testing (MDT), because they were keen to demonstrate their abstinence, or about the IEP scheme, which affirmed their efforts. Often, they complained that the prison's rules and IEP policies should be more stringent, to help demarcate the distinction between themselves and other prisoners. And they appreciated the prison's rehabilitative efforts, arguing that opportunities existed for anyone who wanted to change. 'The system does work if you let it', Zack argued. Luke compared his previous prison experiences to the current era, arguing that all his past sentences had been 'worthless':

All they've done is tried to punish me by locking me in a shit cell under shit conditions. [Now] I'm doing something worthwhile. For the first time in my life I'm *learning* something in prison that might benefit me in the outside world. [...] It was all one kind of life before. You was all in one big cauldron. Now there's a division where *if* you do toe the line, if you're the sort of prisoner who respects himself, who wants to get up and do something for themselves, you can. [...] There is a better kind of life in prison. [...] If you choose to take a good path in prison, doors will open for you.

The prison's increased legitimacy was signalled clearly here. Yet, as the language of choice suggested, it was important to these prisoners to be able to claim responsibility for their moral regeneration and self-development. 'It doesn't matter how many people sit round and say "oh, you should do this, you should do that"', argued Luke. 'It's up to me. You can't *make* someone want to change. You've got to want to change yourself. And that change has come from within me.' Zack likewise claimed that 'no-one's helped me change. I've had to recognize it all myself.' In this respect, they saw themselves as agents rather than subjects of power. Although the outcomes of their agency were consistent with institutional objectives, their compliance was presented as a means of personal reconstruction or making amends, rather than acquiescence to systemic demands. The prison was not considered a source or agent of compulsion, but a catalyst of change and a midwife of personal rebirth.

Enthusiasts resented any suggestion that their commitment was feigned, or that they would want to behave as anything other than decent, law-abiding people. Their ambivalence about imprisonment was apparent here, as they declared their determination not to submit to institutional culture: 'I refuse to act like an animal', declared Brian: 'I was raised to have manners, to have respect for people'. Ian expressed similar sentiments: 'Just because I'm in prison it doesn't mean to say that I've got to be an arsehole; it's not in my nature.' In the same manner, they insisted that they were not consciously regulating their natural behaviour in order to obtain early release and that their compliance did not require external regulation. Luke's comments typified this attitude of moral voluntarism: 'even if they opened the front gate now and said "go down the road, get a loaf of bread and come back" I would do it—I would go down the road, get a loaf of bread and come back'.

The degree to which *enthusiasts* normatively assented to the terms of the institution was confirmed by a number of statements of this kind. In many ways, they were the ideal, self-governing captives. 'I'm doing this for me, not for them' was a typical refrain. Arguably, this distinction between personal desire and institutional obligation was more symbolic than substantive. Nonetheless, there is a difference between normative commitment founded on personal morality ('ethics') and normative commitment based on the recognition of an authority's right to dictate behaviour (i.e. its legitimacy) (see Tyler 1990). Both were significant in ensuring the compliance of *enthusiasts*, who believed that they deserved to be in prison, embraced the prison's corrective ideology, accepted its moral rectitude, and generally saw the system as materially decent and fair. At times though, they prioritized personal integrity above absolute compliance with institutional authority, as Luke's testimony illustrated:

I won't go on a course unless I think it's going to benefit me.... I would like to show that I have looked at that area within myself, without being told to do it.... I can't not be me. When I go for my parole, I'm going to tell them straight. And if they don't give me it they don't give me it. It isn't going to make the slightest difference to me, because the development I've made personally within myself is so great, from what I came into prison to what I am now.... My idea [for parole] was not to do all their courses, but the ones that I felt was beneficial to me. Not what they told me to do, because of their statistics. When I tried to do ETS [Enhanced Thinking Skills], [my dissatisfaction] was a lot to do with the other people on the course. They were there for the sake of doing the course, not because they wanted to gain anything from it. They were just making up the numbers.

Enthusiasts were so determined to change, to do so autonomously (through 'free will' rather than compulsion), and to honour their 'real selves', that they could find themselves at odds with systemic prescriptions. Acts carried out as obligations could not illustrate their authentic commitment to change. Likewise, things that they perceived as insincere—the prison's statistical targets, and the motives of many of their peers—were stains on their own sincerity. 'Playing the game' was not an option if it meant being someone you were not. Such sentiments also illustrated the almost obsessive fixation with self-identity and self-exploration that is common among the 'born-again'.

Despite such moments of disillusion, *enthusiasts* rarely resisted institutional demands. They were generally driven by powerful loyalties to their families, partners or children outside, with whom they wanted to be reunited as soon as possible. Meanwhile, the enthusiasm they invested in their sentences was reinforced by the prison's reward structure. Normative motives to comply were thus bolstered through inducements and rewards (as Luke's comments that 'doors will open for you' suggested). Zack noted that 'there's two ways of doing prison sentences: an easy way and a hard way', and described his changed engagement with the system as follows:

There was an officer—I used to scratch his back, he used to scratch my back. And I used to get what I wanted. I used to get free range of the landing, and all that. But that was me, Mr Naïve. Now I'm not scratching their back at all. *I'm scratching my own back....* I've never been more compliant in all my life. And I'm getting more than I ever got out of the system [when I was] being manipulative, obnoxious, and kicking off. I'm getting what I want. I'm getting educational needs. I'm benefiting now, from everything that I'm doing. [Emphasis added]

Zack partly highlighted the shift in the primary means of accomplishing penal order from informal reciprocity (Sykes 1958) to the addressing of individual desire. By being rewarded for being a 'good prisoner', the identity and benefits of being a 'good person' were both reinforced. As also illustrated, 'responsibilised autonomy' (Garland 1997: 180) was effective in channelling behaviour in ways that were freely chosen and highly directed at the same time. In this respect, *enthusiasts* appeared both agents and subjects of power.

Throwing themselves into their pursuits, *enthusiasts* spent little time on their wings and had negligible involvement in the prison's informal economy.[14] They socialized in limited circles (see Chapter 7), fashioning lives that allowed them to 'let time go by', 'rebuild my life' and 'hide away from the realities of the worst side of prison life' (Luke). Indeed, they were often highly judgmental about other prisoners, deploying the normative language that infused their testimonies to censure their peers. 'I don't really look up to someone who's a murderer or an armed robber and think he's a tough guy', Ian explained: 'I think he's a big idiot. I won't do crimes like that.' Luke was equally at pains to differentiate his crime morally from more serious offences: 'I'm not saying that I'm an angel. I've [done a] terrible thing.

[14] Zack compared his everyday choices to those he would have made in the past: 'I'd go down the gym a lot, build myself up, get my fitness level peaking again, and know that once I get released, [the police] would have their hands full. [And] If I was doing drugs now, I'd be working in the workshops earning thirty quid a week to pay for my smack.'

But [some] people, they know what they're doing, they know it's wrong. My offence, I didn't mean to hurt anybody.' He also complained repeatedly about the values of those prisoners who did not share his commitment to change: 'people who just want to sit around taking drugs and have got no will, or just blatantly don't want to adhere to any kind of ruling, or buck the system, who just want to sit around and have a laugh with their mates, drink coffee, take drugs, and do as little as possible in prison and not try to improve themselves personally'. *Enthusiasts* thus presented themselves as both a 'better quality of prisoner' and a better kind of person, above the ignorance and immaturity of their peers.

The values implicit in this judgment corresponded with those of the institution. Burdened by guilt, much of the resentment that *enthusiasts* felt about their predicament was self-directed, rather than aimed at the prison authorities. Ian explained that he was 'here because of my own fault, nobody else's fault, they're just doing their job'. He was angry: 'at myself, for not being there for my family and messing up my life for the past ten years', and declared his loyalties not to other prisoners, but to his daughter and mother: 'so that's why I don't get in trouble'. Zack's priorities were: 'my family. My wife. And respecting the staff, and them respecting me.' *Enthusiasts* often expressed annoyance that other prisoners claimed that staff were lazy or malevolent. They identified as closely with staff as with other prisoners, and were more trustful of, and candid with, officers than they were with the majority of their peers: 'I'll stand here and talk to the officers rather than talk to some of the inmates', Ian noted. Kyle stated similar attitudes:

These lot look at them as their worst enemy. The way I see it, they're doing their job. I've got a lot of time and respect for officers and police officers, believe it or not. You always get the odd dickhead officer, but I've got a lot of respect for them. I could not do their job, not a fucking prayer. I could not come to work, put up with the shit that the inmates give the officers in here.

Relationships with male officers were often sincere and relaxed, based around shared interests and genuine 'connection'. Female officers provided opportunities to display charm and gain reassurance of masculine appeal. Zack sought to 'make sure that bit of charm's still there'; Ian's aim was to 'see if you can make them smile and stuff'. Other *enthusiasts* showed vulnerability and weakness with female officers that they hid from males. Female officers also served as surrogate versions of female family members, and were granted affection and 'protection' accordingly. Such orientations were forms of identity work, either validating 'normal' masculine status or providing symbolic reparation for past behaviour. Through these interactions with female staff, then, *enthusiasts* sought to reconstruct and maintain their self-images as good fathers, sons and husbands (Crewe 2006a).

As Kyle's quotation (above) showed, *enthusiasts* were not uniformly positive about uniformed staff. Although they accepted that their incarceration was legitimate, and that they should ungrudgingly endure its basic deprivations, they did not see why their treatment should be needlessly disrespectful. They were highly critical of officers who were rude, lazy, or careless with their power. Indeed, because they considered themselves moral arbiters and sponsors of the prison's moral agenda, they were all the more censorious of officers who failed to live up to high ethnical standards. Nonetheless, such officers were seen as 'bad apples' rather than emblems of a broader legitimacy deficit. As a stratum, officers were seen as fulfilling a vital function in difficult conditions, and as standing on the right side of the moral Rubicon. Committed to a discourse of 'mutual respect', in general, *enthusiasts* complied with reasonable expectations and made few attempts to deceive or manipulate staff.

It was in relation to systemic inefficiency that *enthusiasts* were most vocally critical. This included issues such as the late arrival of post, shortfalls in material provisions, slow responses to requests and applications, substandard work and education facilities, and the prison's failure to make available the rehabilitative programmes and resources (especially victim awareness courses) that *enthusiasts* demanded for their ventures in self-renewal. These were censorious forms of criticism (Mathiesen 1965), framed not through oppositional values, but in terms that were consistent with the means and ends of the institution. And although these grievances could be considerable, in general, they were repressed or were pursued in ways that sought to illustrate patience, self-control and respect for the prison establishment: cautiously and courteously, via sympathetic staff or through official channels. Bitter complaints and explosions into anger were uncommon. When they did occur, they were quickly followed by apologetic explanations and visible contrition.

'Pragmatists'

Around half of Wellingborough's prisoners complied for reasons that were mainly instrumental and fatalistic rather than normative. Although a rather disparate group, with a less consistent narrative than that of *enthusiasts*, prisoners of this kind shared a perception that the prison held a virtual monopoly on power and that to resist it was either impossible or imprudent. They could be divided into two relatively distinct groupings, within which there was further variation. The first group, *pragmatists*, tended to be young, low-level recidivists, serving short to medium-length sentences for violence and drug-related crimes such as burglary and robbery. The second group, *stoics*, were prisoners on much longer sentences, with rather different interests and identities, to which the chapter will return below.

Cameron was typical of a certain kind of *pragmatist*: the young 'tearaway' whose confidence hid a more complex interior life. An ebullient, white man, Cameron described being raised in a poor family in a large Northern town. He was abused by a family friend for several years from the age of 8, something for which he 'always blamed himself'. His father, a strict and abusive disciplinarian, left the family home when Cameron was 9, after which his mother began gambling heavily and went 'off the rails'. In school, Cameron bullied other children, and was expelled for beating up a teacher: 'he made me look a complete fool and he started being cheeky, so I punched him. Everyone was laughing in the class because he sent me out. I just felt like a prick and I didn't like it.' By fourteen, he had stopped attending school altogether, spending his time shoplifting, smoking cannabis, and joyriding. He soon began to commit violent robberies and received his first custodial sentence at the age of seventeen. In Young Offenders Institutions, he obtained respect through vicious bullying, about which he felt little compunction: 'That's life if you want to survive. That's the way things are. I didn't give a fuck, to be honest with you. I didn't really care.'

On release, his intentions were good, and he got himself a house and a job: 'I used to always have money, always have nice clothes.' Soon though, after a brief period on heroin and crack,

he began drinking, and started to commit acts of random violence, 'for no reason,...to have fun'. Although, when sober, he
felt bad about such acts, he repressed these feelings: 'because if
I start feeling worse and thinking about the bad things I'll get
depressed and end up flipping'. In prison, he struggled to control
his temper, venting his frustrations through use of the gym. He
maintained contact with his father, sister and young girlfriend,
describing visits as 'the only thing that keeps me going'. However,
such contact also exacerbated his stress. His emotional dependence made him feel 'like a cunt'. 'Now I'm the vulnerable one', he
acknowledged, having lost control of his emotions during a phone
call. His paranoia about his girlfriend's fidelity was such that he
banned her from going out more than once a week and constantly
questioned her movements. Meanwhile, he felt responsible for his
father's emotional instability:

Me coming to jail put a lot of stress on him, and my brother is a smackhead.[15] Every father's dream is, you know, they want their kids to make
it and that, but me and my brother, we don't seem to be doing anything
about it. We just commit crime and shit like that. I'd love to make him
proud.

Burdened by such anxieties, Cameron told his father nothing of
his frustrations in prison. Privately, he agonized about his volatility and his general mental state: 'I'm not normal, I don't think.
I've asked them if I can see psychiatrists or counsellors. Just to see
what's going on upstairs.' Despite these psychological problems,
Cameron gave a public impression of coping well with imprisonment, and was seen as 'one of the lads'.

Other *pragmatists* were low-status prisoners whose vulnerabilities were far more apparent, and who coped poorly both inside
prison and in the community.[16] One such prisoner was Colin, a
large, Afro-Caribbean man in his late thirties, serving a relatively
short sentence. Colin described his family background as 'typical
for a lot of people'. He had grown up in a small town near to
London, and had gone into care when his parents separated. After

[15] 'smackhead': heroin addict; 'smack': heroin; alternatively 'powder', 'brown'
or 'gear'.

[16] A number of prisoners within this category had been recalled to prison having
been out on licence, and struggled to understand why they had been re-incarcerated
for what felt like mistakes rather than offences: missing probation appointments
or stepping outside the terms of their licences.

a spell in an approved school,[17] he took up a number of manual jobs but 'felt closed in, y'know', and 'got into crime', mainly commercial burglaries, car thefts, and credit card fraud. Crime was 'a way of surviving.... I'm a hand to mouth man, spur of the moment thing'. Colin saw himself as 'no different from a tramp or a vagrant basically, I'm on the edge. And when I go out there I'm gonna do crime again.'

Colin had no family, explaining that he could 'not afford to'. He expressed fears that his social instability would have a 'knock-on effect' on any child. He was also psychologically vulnerable, stopping the interview at one point because of paranoia, and describing himself as having 'internal problems, so much that it is hard for me to explain it. I have a lot more stress than is necessary to cope with.' Within Wellingborough, on his tenth custodial sentence, he struggled to survive on his means. Without any private income from friends or family, he had to borrow money to fund his tobacco consumption and pleaded with other prisoners for cigarette papers. In the past, he had sold his food to raise money for such purposes. In Wellingborough, he earned very small amounts by 'mediating' between borrowers and lenders—in effect, finding out who needed 'items' and who had them to lend.[18]

Whether tearaways or poor copers, the compliance of *pragmatists* was founded on a blend of routine, resignation, and a pragmatic acceptance that self-government formed part of a reciprocal contract with the institution. First then, a number of testimonies signalled the role of sheer habit and conditioning in determining behaviour. Asked what motivated him to do what the prison wanted, Gavin replied that:

It's not about motivating. You've just got to do what you're told, don't you? It's like being at home again, it's like being with your parents. You do what they say. Bang up eight o'clock, bang up five o'clock, bang up flipping twelve o'clock. You become so used to it, you do the same thing day in, day out.

Gavin's parental metaphor was significant in illustrating how *pragmatists* took for granted the supremacy of staff. He also highlighted the manner whereby the symbolization of authority—here,

---

[17] An 'approved school': a residential institution for young offenders; in the US, a 'reform school'.

[18] 'items': goods used for trade, for example tobacco, phonecards, toiletries.

its reification through daily timetables and procedures—contributed to a sense of fatalism among *pragmatists* about their relative powerlessness. Connor conveyed a similar sense of helpless resignation in the face of the routine exhibition of institutional domination:

I just get on with it. That's all you can do.... They're always going to win.... [Officers] think they're higher than you, which I suppose they are. They're the bosses, we're the inmates. But they show that in silly little ways. Basically saying 'look, we can do this to you, you can't beat us. If we tell you to do something, you'll do it'.

And is that true? If they say something goes, does it go?

I'd say so, yeah.

As Cameron also summarized: 'The screws have got the power. The screws have got the keys and we're behind the doors at night; what they say goes.' Many *pragmatists* over-estimated the scope of officer domination, assuming that their surveillance techniques were more omniscient and sophisticated than they actually were. *Pragmatists* were also deeply aware of the measures that restricted their movements and the threat of being transferred to other establishments, where they might be further from home and would have to build from scratch the social and economic networks that aided their subsistence. 'Once you've finished kicking-off, you're going two hundred miles away to a different prison', said one prisoner. Coercive situational control measures thus encouraged these prisoners to stifle their frustrations.

This fatalistic orientation to doing time represented a practical rather than normative acceptance of subordination. Unlike *enthusiasts*, *pragmatists* did not dwell on their moral status or the legitimacy of their predicament. Nor did they pursue projects of personal transformation. They submitted with little thought to their situation and settled into passive routines, as their mundane descriptions of doing time illustrated: 'I don't make no fuss or nothing', declared Ellis, 'I've just plodded along with the sentence'; 'I just travel from day to day', said Harvey; 'you just settle down and get used to prison. I've done it for sixteen years', said Derek. In an environment where power was stacked so unevenly, where there were so many incentives to behave, and where resistance (as they perceived it) could only be counter-productive, such strategies appeared to represent the only sensible option:

If you fight against it, you don't get nothing. You lose no matter what. The only way you'll beat it is if you just go with the flow. You've just got to keep your head down basically. Just do your time and just get out, and don't let it get you down.... The best thing you can do is just do what they say. And no matter how much they annoy you, just grit your teeth and move on.... No matter what you do, you're still going to lose aren't you. You can't beat the system. The only time you beat it is when you get out. And you just play by their book. (Chris)

I think the best way is to just abide by their rules. I think that's the only way you're going to get anything off them, whether you're frustrated or want to kick off, sometimes it is best to just not show it and just try and abide by their rules and do things through the right channels. (Harvey)

This fatalism extended to *pragmatists*' perceptions of the prison's mechanisms of compliance. *Pragmatists* did not question drug testing; they took for granted that reports were being written about their behaviour; and they attended offending behaviour courses with little cynicism—for self-improvement and personal insight as much as obligation and sentence progression. Thus, Joey sat his course because 'it would help me to understand and it would help me try to go for parole', while Gavin sat his to help get parole and because: 'If I can learn to think before I actually say things [and] do things, then I think I'll be a much better person. I'll be able to get on a lot better and achieve a lot more in jail.' They spoke positively about programmes and courses, reporting that they had given them 'better insight, regarding the victims' (Ellis), improved their family relationships, and helped them understand their own thinking and behaviour. They sought out work that would teach them new skills, or would boost their earnings. To some degree, then, *pragmatists* were habituated into engagement. They did not embrace the prison's aspirations so much as allow its demands to flow through them and carry them on its tide.

Likewise, many *pragmatists* invested uncritically in the IEP scheme, seeking to enhance their living standards and make their sentences as comfortable or survivable as possible. Televisions and PlayStations served as vital 'bird-killers'.[19] Colin described television as making a 'phenomenal difference.... It eases the time, it

[19] 'Bird' was a common term for 'sentence' or 'prison-time' as well as woman or girlfriend.

brings you nearer the community, it eases the tension out of the brain'. Gym sessions helped in releasing frustrations as well as building physique; visits were vital sources of contact with girl-friends and young children; private cash allowed the purchase of supplementary foodstuffs and items such as grooming products and CD players which, in the eyes of many younger prisoners, denoted social status. For *pragmatists*, these were significant incentives to comply. Indeed, their importance was such that, although the potential for material dispossession was experienced as a significant threat, the prison's consumerist contract was perceived as legitimate: privileges were a fair deal for good behaviour. Those *pragmatists* who did resent the IEP system relied on it, and thus complied with it nonetheless.

In part, this unquestioning acceptance of the prison's compliance regime related to youth. Most *pragmatists* had considerable experience of custody, but none that included the era prior to IEP. The majority could not envision a system without conditional and differentiated living standards. Thus, while Cameron considered himself 'staunch', he could not think far beyond his material standards when pondering collective action:

You think: if we stick together, [they're] gonna take my enhanced off me and I'm going to lose my job. Is it worth the fucking risk for a fucking hot meal? I don't think so. I'll do me cold fucking meal. I'd rather keep my enhanced and make life a little bit easier.

Although this rationale was common among other prisoners, *pragmatists* were unusually motivated by considerations of their everyday conditions. Some recognized that the benefits of enhanced status went beyond official privileges. As Gavin noted: 'you get more favours and whatnot when it comes down to jobs. And when you go for your parole, home leave, D-Cat, transfer. It helps you, yes, of course.' Most were not especially strategic in the ways they sought out IEP status, so much as driven by need to maximize what they could obtain. Those, like Colin, who had experienced imprisonment in an era when much less was on offer recalled these conditions with dread. For these men, imprisonment was difficult enough whatever the circumstances:

Do you feel that you have control over your life in here?

No. I don't have no control over my life in here. My life is controlled very much by the system. Everything is controlled for me: the time I get in my cell, the time I wake up, dinner, time for shower, changing kit, everything is in control.... I haven't got dignity or power. I haven't got any power over anyone, apart from being the person I am.

Lacking economic and psychological resources ('inadequate', in the terms of many officers), these more vulnerable pragmatists relied on the prison's provisions to lessen the pains of imprisonment. 'I'm not content, I'm never gonna be content', Colin clarified, 'but the last thing I wanna do is to make any trouble for myself. Cos that means getting canteen wiped off, which then would make it harder on me, and then I start doing silly things.[20] So basically, yeah, I'm quite compliant.'

As also suggested here, for many *pragmatists*, compliance was not a simple matter of choice or effort. For those with mental health problems, the regime was difficult to follow. Many struggled to cope with regime inconsistencies. Colin explained that he was 'one of those persons who's always late'. He was often the last prisoner to get to his cell at the end of association periods—scurrying around trying to obtain tobacco or cigarette papers—or to come out of the shower or collect his dinner. He explained as follows:

It's not that I'm *bad*. I'm a bit, like, slow, to conform. When [I] come down for dinner, there's a big queue, and you have to wait five or ten minutes, and I think 'I can't be bothered doing this', so I think 'might as well wait ten minutes up here'. By the time I come down, my calculation is wrong.

Such behaviour was easily labelled as non-compliance. *Pragmatists* of this kind often gained strikes for infractions that resulted from their poor coping skills and vulnerabilities rather than any conscious attempt to be difficult. Some reacted in volatile ways to discretionary inconsistencies, perceiving them as deliberate slights: 'it's council estate mentality, you see everything as a threat' (prisoner, fieldwork notes). Others were penalized for the outcomes of their boisterousness and immaturity. Meanwhile, they were easily lured or manipulated into illicit activity, either through fear, naïvety or—more often—economic need. Colin was very aware that if he were placed on basic he would be 'escalating down a road where you're gonna feel bad and do [more] bad things'. Yet he was also required to get involved in petty illicit activity in order to make his prison experience more manageable.

[20] Here, Colin meant stealing from cells out of desperation.

Despite their general compliance, younger, more intelligent *pragmatists* were also active in the informal economy. 'Keeping your head down is actually a lot harder than it sounds', said Callum, 'everybody wants their little luxuries'. These men did not seek status or power through their dealings, which involved low-level trade in tobacco and drugs, and opportunistic thefts from the institution. Nor did they assign anti-institutional meaning to their trade activities. Instead, as was consistent with their general orientation, their actions were risks aimed at enhancing personal life quality. As Callum explained, contrasting *sub rosa* activity with explicit dissent, 'you weigh up the pros and cons. You'll get away with it more times than you'll get caught. [Whereas] if I'm protesting against something, that is going to cause a lot of trouble.'

In the same manner, *pragmatists* limited their involvement in the prisoner social world and curbed inclinations to express their frustrations. In relation to the former, to avoid being dragged into 'trouble', they restricted their social affiliations and put limits on the terms of their loyalty (see Chapter 7). In relation to the latter, although they were often discontent, they saw little point in challenging the system. 'Making a fuss gets you a nicking and then gets you nowhere', Declan commented. Other prisoners described their reasoning as follows:

I go home in three weeks. There is no way on earth you're going to get me in a protest about anything. If a screw turns around and tells me to do 600 press-ups in the bogs otherwise he's nicking me I'm off to do 600 press-ups. I'll hate him for making me do it, but I'll do it. (Callum)

All I want to do is go home on my [release] day.... I've done the fighting, I've done the answering back and that ain't got me anything apart from doing longer than what I should have to. This time I thought: 'just do it, if they ask you to do something just do it'. What have I got to lose? At least I know [that] when my date's up for release I'm going on that date. [If I comply] they can't stop me going home on my date. (Aaron)

The desire to be released on the due date was not an unusual aspiration. But this was a particularly significant motivation among *pragmatists*, either because they experienced imprisonment in such painful ways or because their longing to be reunited with family trumped the status issues that could motivate self-assertion and dissent among some other prisoners. Lifestyle circumstances and future expectations varied a great deal among *pragmatists*, but for those with young families, emotional attachments were highly significant in dampening inclinations to challenge the system and intensifying an attitude of submissive acceptance.

Aaron's view was also typical of *pragmatists* in its binary vision of compliance and resistance: 'kicking off' *or* 'keeping quiet'. Whereas some prisoners recognized alternative means of achieving their ends, *pragmatists* could conceive of few options beyond the most visible, explicit, and strategically naïve forms of resistance: 'smashing up' or barricading their cells, making threats of violence, 'giving attitude' or 'losing it' with members of staff. Most *pragmatists* struggled to see the precise ways that power operated on them and thus how resistance might take more sophisticated forms.[21] Significantly then, modes of dissent were shaped by the same sense of powerlessness that generally ensured compliance; they were the corollary of feelings that one had no other options. Largely, they were unplanned outbursts—about the late arrival of post, for example ('it's a *fucking* liberty!')—or were desperate attempts to obtain entitlements after legitimate channels failed to deliver. One prisoner, exasperated after accumulated visits with his wife had been delayed several times due to staff shortages, 'kicked off' in the hope of resolving his frustration by gaining access to a governor. The incident was striking for the consensus it achieved about the legitimacy of its aims despite the illegitimacy of its means. Staff acknowledged the prisoner's assertion that the prison had 'a duty to maintain prisoners' relationships' that it was not fulfilling. Meanwhile, the prisoner accepted that his violent outburst could not go unpunished: 'you know it's the wrong thing to do. [But] you go through all the right channels and still don't get what you need. [...] Sometimes it's the only way to make your point.'

The compliance of *pragmatists* was characterized primarily by economic pragmatism and fatalism. First then, to the extent that dissatisfaction was expressed at all, it was primarily about issues—such as getting trainers sent in and obtaining HDC—that confirmed the degree to which *pragmatists* accepted, and were actively assimilated into, the policies of self-interest designed to placate them. Power operated through the banal imperatives of daily subsistence, the desire to enhance living standards, and the

---

[21] Asked whether he ever played 'mind games' with people, Olly replied: 'I'm not really too smart, so I'm not really good at that psychology shit'.

longing to be reunited with partners and children as quickly as possible. Second, for *pragmatists*, the everyday terms of imprisonment were regarded as unalterable—or simply 'how it is'—more than they were accepted as legitimate (Carrabine 2004). But this is not to suggest an absence of legitimacy. *Pragmatists* were not committed enthusiasts of the regime, nor were they normatively aligned with the terms of the system, but they recognized the procedural, interpersonal, and material decency that it normally achieved.

This was evidenced in a number of ways, not least the relatively smooth nature of everyday interactions between *pragmatists* and staff. In arguing that 'the only way to manipulate [is to] show courtesy, show kindness, show reform' (Colin), *pragmatists* showed their faith in a discourse of mutual respect. 'Your power to them is politeness', said Chris: 'when we're being polite to them, they'll go out of their way to help us'. Some *pragmatists*, like Colin, found officers 'no bother whatsoever... quite relaxed', and assumed a stance of passive acceptance. Others were more demanding, but in terms that were measured and civil, and were active in developing instrumental relationships with uniformed staff. As Cameron explained: 'There's some, obviously, that I won't like. But I'll try and get on with every officer. Mainly to make my life easier so he don't get on my back.' These self-interested motives were not necessarily concealed: 'I'll give the landing a sweep. Or if they need something from a different wing, I'll say "I'll get that for you. Just remember it when the [parole] papers come in"' (Cameron).

This cultivation of good relationships with staff was partly an outcome of the discretionary power that allowed officers to allocate small privileges and make the IEP decisions on which *pragmatists* depended. It also showed the preference among *pragmatists* for using interpersonal rather than bureaucratic channels to pursue their ends. Some were too apathetic to use applications and request and complaint procedures. Others lacked confidence in their ability to use the system effectively. Many had little faith in its efficacy.

In front of other prisoners, younger *pragmatists* often expressed hostility towards officers. However, this was done principally out of bravado, and comments were quickly retracted when challenged. Very few held uniformly hostile attitudes towards officers or judged them through collective terms or definitions.

Rather, they tended to see officers as 'normal people' who were simply 'doing a job' without representing a wider ideological system. This also meant that, unlike *enthusiasts*, they did not automatically respect the symbolic authority of the officer position. Officers were guaranteed neither deference nor disdain. Many *pragmatists* expected respect to be offered before they would return it. Even when good relationships were formed, their maintenance required effort. Officers were judged as individuals, based on their interpersonal interactions. *Pragmatists* therefore expressed particularly sour views about officers whom they disliked, while also developing some relationships that were genuinely close and respectful. For vulnerable *pragmatists*, the warmth and support of officers was an essential element of psychological survival.

The disengaged

Disengaged prisoners—a sub-type—were *pragmatists* gone awry. They were men for whom, *in principle*, self-interest was the primary source of compliance, but for whom, *in practice*, and through various circumstances, incentives and disincentives had become insufficient or irrelevant. For some *disengaged* prisoners, this was because of external factors: not being able to give the prison a permanent address at which they could reside during their home detention curfew, or needing more time to sort out accommodation or patch up relationships. Others, such as Tyler, had been refused the rewards that would have provided motivation:

I've been turned down for parole, Ben, I feel that my chances for home leave are very limited, and to [get a] move to a different prison is going to be a struggle because of my previous record. What do you think you can really offer me in HMP Wellingborough? What goals have I got? What am I really supposed to do? I feel I'm locked in a very negative society.

Some prisoners anticipated such rebuffs and disengaged accordingly. Explaining why he refused to take courses, despite the impact of refusing, Billy said: 'you can do all your courses, behave yourself, talk to the screws all nice and pally, and you might get your parole, but you still might not'. As suggested here, to opt out in this manner was to release oneself from the burdens of impression-management. Confident that he would be refused a 'tagging', due to a prior absconcion and a poor disciplinary record, Marcus outlined the psychological compensation of disengagement:

I just don't like depending on them. I don't have to worry about keeping in his good books so he can give me a better life or he doesn't pad spin me.[22] I don't have to depend on fucking upsetting some member of staff.

Other *disengaged* prisoners considered the advantages of being 'enhanced' to be negligible relative to the effort required to obtain and maintain it. They were therefore happy to forego its benefits for the sake of their dignity.

For Darren, a Northern prisoner in a Midlands prison, punishments rather than incentives no longer had force:

I said to them, 'well, you can't send me no further from home, so you might as well take me today if you want. I'm not fucking bothered. Take me straight to Camp Hill' [on the Isle of Wight]. Because the damage has been done for me. They don't give me parole. They've told me basically I'm not getting home leave. They can't hurt me any more than what they've already done.

Some prisoners had lost faith in the prison's ability to deliver its pledges. Jordan described how he 'gave up trying to get stuff done a long time ago', after applications for Cat-D were repeatedly lost or unanswered:

You put in an app and it doesn't go anywhere for weeks on end. You've just got to go on repeating yourself and by the time you've got anywhere it's probably been about three or four months, because the apps take so long going through. You're waiting for an answer for so long, you're going to be out before you get an answer

Prisoners who saw how long it took, and how difficult it was, to be recategorized to open prisons likewise reconciled themselves to half-hearted compliance. Those who felt untrusted or ignored were also liable to give up their efforts: 'If I think people are suspicious, I think "fuck off" and then I don't make the effort. I wait for them, and they don't come....If I don't start to get help, I'm just gonna play the system.'

These positions were forms of fatalism born of submission to the prison's punitive potential (as with *stoics*) or to its rituals, routines, or rewards (as with *pragmatists*). Instead, they

[22] A 'pad spin': a cell search.

represented failures of the prison's incentive and opportunity structure to function effectively or correspond with some prisoners' interests and predicaments. The outcome though was a form of dormant or passive dissent, one that could easily slide into more active resistance, as later sections will discuss.

'Stoics'

Pragmatists perceived the terms of imprisonment as immutable but rarely described them as coercive. They had little awareness of how power operated upon them, and were relatively uncritical of the prison's incentive structure providing that it functioned fairly and effectively. *Stoics* were no less concerned about 'getting to the gate' and were equally resigned to the prison's domination. However, they were acutely aware of the strategies by which their compliance was accomplished, and were far more cynical about the mechanisms of power in which they were enmeshed. Despite this critical awareness, having spent years reaching medium-security conditions, *stoics* suppressed their frustrations and considered it sensible to comply or limit their complaints in order to hasten their sentence progression.[23]

Typically, stoics were life-sentence prisoners nearing release. George had been in prison for over twenty years for a crime he committed in his early twenties. He was raised in 'a very dysfunctional family', with a violent, alcoholic father, who committed suicide when George was young, and a 'highly volatile' mother, who had serious mental health issues and provided no emotional warmth. As a teenager, George became increasingly bitter and manipulative, and was expelled from school and taken into care. From the ages of 16 to 18, his lifestyle was relatively stable, and he held down a job in a factory, but he soon 'discovered booze', which both alleviated and aggravated his problems: 'all the crap from my childhood was still simmering away. I found myself very angry, very easily, and it was only the booze keeping the anger down.' He lost his job and home because of his heavy drinking, and began committing petty crime while living on the streets or in hostels. Given his first prison sentence

---

[23] Length of sentence is normally considered a 'deprivation' variable, yet for some prisoners, the time spent in prison was such that the experience of incarceration was built into personal identity.

at the age of 20, on release he resumed his cycle of drinking, living rough and offending. Within months he had committed a murder which showed 'how warped and amoral and unfeeling a person I'd become'.

Once convicted, he felt 'a great sense of peace and freedom; I'd got no responsibilities, all the anger was gone'. Initially, he refused to recognize the moral implications of his crime. Because of this stance, he was labelled a psychopath and sociopath by prison psychologists. Angry that he was being categorized in this manner without receiving help to deal with his issues, he had a nervous breakdown, and spent some time in a hospital cell: 'from their point of view, I was just an unstable and dangerous person who needed to be controlled. From my point of view, I was a very scared and immature individual, who didn't really understand what was happening to him.' Inspired by a sympathetic, non-judgmental member of staff, he began to recognize that 'the dysfunctional aspects of my upbringing were reasons why I turned out like I did, [but] they weren't justifications. [And] I was responsible for trying to sort out the person that they'd made me.' He started to look into his crime, and began to change from someone 'so emotionally stunted that I couldn't relate to other people, I wasn't even able to relate to myself as a human being', to someone capable of remorse, objectivity, and emotional connection, however limited. After some time, he was returned to a normal prison location, where he was a low-status prisoner, tolerated by his peers 'because I showed respect and didn't cause any problems to anybody'.

George's temper threshold was very low, and he would regularly smash up his cell when frustrated. To calm himself, and to deal with the stress of 'heavy-duty' prison, he would take valium, which he afforded by trading small amounts of cannabis. Otherwise, he tried to stay out of the prisoner world and keep his head down, although this was interpreted by staff as 'insubordination' and reported in files as an attitude of anti-authoritarianism. He was transferred to a prison-based therapeutic community, a positive experience which improved his social confidence: 'I came out of myself, basically; it was an environment that encouraged that, y'know, and I began to find my voice.' Expelled because staff believed he was subverting the therapeutic ethos, he returned to the Cat-B estate, where he struggled to obtain Cat-C status, due, at first, to his own volatility, and then, in his view, by systemic inefficiency and the outdated judgments of psychology staff:

[Since] 1995, I've just been standing still really. It's all been sort of on-going reviews, reports and knock-backs. I finally got Cat-C [and] was moved here four years ago. I've been here four years just marking time. In four years I've done three days' worth of courses, that's all I've been required to do. It's psychologists, basically. The old story: having to con-vince them that I'm not the person that I was, [and] get over all these labels that they put on me twenty years ago, y'know.... It's always been on the basis of a psychologist's report that the parole board have had to knock me back.

Tommy was also a lifer, and had been in prison since he was a teenager. He grew up in the North-West, where he was raised in children's homes from the age of 5, for reasons that had never been explained to him. The homes were a 'horrible experience', and Tommy struggled to settle at school, soon not bothering to turn up and living like a 'delinquent'. On entering prison after committing a murder, he was 'a young lad looking for something to prove' and hoped to use prison as an opportunity to develop a criminal career. He picked up a number of minor disciplinary charges for disobeying orders and using abusive language, and used drugs in prison, but, out of principle, never sold them. After a few years, he calmed down considerably, taking up education and changing his self-perception: 'I'm not a criminal. I'm not into crime. I've missed out so much on life that I want to go home and I want to enjoy it.' For many years, he had tried to spend his time in prison actively gaining positions of trust and trying to improve himself and develop as an adult: 'I do feel guilt, I do feel shame. It's something you never forget. But I've spent the last twenty years since trying to make my life better, trying to get away from that fact.'

Whereas *pragmatists* were primarily motivated by what they could *gain* from the system, and had a somewhat consumerist approach to the sentence, *stoics* were more concerned with what they might *lose* and with long-term goals rather than immediate conditions. Having spent years inside, they had been forced to make the prison into a home—a place of refuge and comfort. But the prison's material incentives were not their prime motives for compliance. Most *stoics* claimed to have coped well with more austere conditions, and did not fear an ascetic existence. Some claimed to be 'immune' from the prison's punitive potential. 'I don't take things for granted', Tommy asserted. 'These tellies, these associations, the bit of canteen they do give you: experience has taught me not to let them use it as a tool to influence me.... They could put me in the block for six months, a year, it wouldn't affect me one bit.' Others simply did not benefit from the majority of the privileges on offer, as George explained:

It doesn't really work for me. As a lifer who's done twenty years, who doesn't get visits, who doesn't receive private cash, there is no incentive within the structure of the incentive scheme for me to behave, really. My incentive is from within myself, y'know, I want to get out, as soon as possible, and that motivation doesn't come from what's going on around me. When they brought in voluntary [drug] tests to maintain your enhanced status, I had a chat with the PO who runs it. I said, 'there's no incentive for me to submit to the humiliation of a strip-search and a piss-test every month to maintain my enhanced status, cos I don't get anything out of it. I don't get visits, I don't get private cash, I don't benefit from the high level of private cash you can use, it's not worth it'. And he said, 'I can understand where you're coming from, but why not just do it anyway, [otherwise] it might look bad on your record'.

As suggested here, many of the benefits that the prison could offer were immaterial to *stoics* because of the time they had spent behind bars. In their experience, the IEP scheme was more coercive than seductive, a cause of considerable resentment. These prisoners worked towards enhanced status not because of the everyday rewards that accrued from it, but because they believed that 'being enhanced' was an institutional synonym for general behaviour that was fed into decisions about release and would 'look good later on'. This long-term target of freedom was considerably more important than short-term lifestyle goals; and it was the threat of being held back that was the primary inducement to conform. For *stoics*, then, the operation of power was primarily perceived in negative, coercive terms: there was little to gain from compliance, but much to lose from defiance or dissent—not just added days or loss of privileges, but sometimes years of supplementary captivity.

A second reason why *stoics* resented such coercive mechanisms of compliance was that they considered them unnecessary. 'It's not what they expect of me, it's what I expect of myself', said Tommy. Motivated by personal morality as well as the prospect of freedom, the majority of *stoics* had little desire to buck the system or cause trouble. Instead, they sought a quiet existence, looking to 'keep their heads down' in pursuits that were personally productive, such as education, art, and computer skills. At the same time, although they satisfied the prison's expectations of compliant behaviour, *stoics* did not strive to go beyond reasonable measures for the sake of appearances—to merely perform the prison's desired behaviour. For many such prisoners, it was difficult to sustain these performances or see prison as a matter of strategy. 'It's not a game', Tommy emphasized: 'This is my home. And that's where it differs. [To some prisoners] it's just a short stay, it is a game. But with me it's been my life, so I see it differently.' To perform or play games was to 'become part of the system'. Such views also reflected the considerable importance to most long-term prisoners of maintaining integrity, dignity, and control—of not being worn down by the system, and maintaining an authentic sense of self (Cohen and Taylor 1972). As Nathan argued, such aspirations had to be weighed up against the pragmatic imperative to submit: 'I wanna get out, but at the same time I'm not gonna compromise my integrity *to* get out. So it has been a careful balancing act between the two things.'

This balance was most evident in the detached but courteous relationships that *stoics* developed with uniformed staff. Some retained a categorical cynicism about officers, which they had absorbed while in higher-security prisons and in a more antagonistic era of staff-prisoner relationships. Generally, however, *stoics* appreciated the relative decency that Wellingborough officers showed in their daily interactions. 'I can honestly say that on my wing there's not one officer that I could have a bad word for', Tommy noted. They often expressed sympathy for officers, and were the prisoners most likely to condemn unjustified hostility towards uniformed and civilian staff. Nonetheless, they were wary of becoming too close to officers and did not seek to ingratiate themselves or cultivate friendly relationships. Rather, they preferred to maintain a form of polite, professional distance with both male and female officers, proffering respect with the expectation that it would be reciprocated. It was this distance, with its almost formalized civility, that enabled *stoics* to maintain their personal and public integrity without jeopardizing their progression towards release. They could not be accused by staff of disobedience or disrespect, nor by other prisoners of undue deference or over-enthusiasm.

Relations with officers also illustrated the form of legitimacy that underpinned *stoics*' compliance. Most Wellingborough officers—particularly those on the long-termers' wing—were perceived to 'listen to reason' (George), to handle their power with sensitivity, and to treat prisoners with respect. These traits were contrasted with the indifference and antagonism of the past. 'Generally speaking', George observed, 'they're much more approachable, much more willing to do their job [...] and you can talk about it if you've got any problems or difficulties'. Like *pragmatists*, *stoics* placed some trust in a shared language of decency and in official mechanisms of complaint, as Nathan indicated:

To be honest with you, I've found that if you come with a polite request, even if the officers can't help you, they tell you how to navigate the system. And when you make a formal request, as long as you're polite, [or it's] well written, you may not always get the answer you want but you won't get the 'oh you're a troublemaker'.

That many issues could be peacefully negotiated on the landings also pointed to the presence of certain forms of legitimacy in the daily relations of power. Regular D-wing officers appreciated the special difficulties of long-term imprisonment and were careful to explain and justify their decisions. In return, *stoics*' complaints about the regime (e.g. decisions to cancel evening exercise or raise canteen prices) and conditions (draughty cells, property entitlements) were normally expressed and resolved openly and politely. Physical and material conditions were perceived as reasonably decent: certainly an improvement on the past, when *stoics* recalled inedible food, bare and dirty cells, little access to telephones and showers, and arbitrary cancellations of visits, association, and exercise.[24]

For *stoics*, then, the prison met basic standards in terms of its regime and the conduct of its officials. But as Sparks *et al.* (1996) emphasize, institutions may fulfil some criteria of legitimacy while failing others. In this respect, deficits in some elements of legitimacy, and the role of fatalism in the daily dynamics of power, should not be understated. Since inducements had little hold on

[24] However, most *stoics* expressed disappointment that the amount of physical freedom they had was not much greater than in a Cat-B prison, and that higher up the system they had faced less interference from officers, been subject to fewer 'petty rules' in relation to clothing and conduct, and had been able to exercise more autonomy, for example, in cooking their own food.

stoics, the main sources of (and targets for) their frustrations were not located on the prison landings or in the form of prison officers. *Stoics* recognized that the power to make the decisions that affected them most profoundly—those relating to the promise of release—lay beyond the staff with whom they had regular contact. Instead, most grievances and frustrations stemmed from 'the system': its bureaucratic machinations, its reliance on psychological discourse, and the impersonal qualities that it exhibited. And whereas everyday treatment and conditions could, to some degree, be worked upon, the system of power was much harder to affect. Although *stoics* articulated a bitter transcript of frustration, they did so in backstage areas and pursued their grievances with extreme caution. In public, they were resigned to biting their tongues, swallowing some pride, and living with their own aggravation. Faced with circumstances that appeared unalterable or too hazardous to challenge, most were resigned to their own acquiescence. Everyday conditions were easy to tolerate, but the everyday frustrations that related to release and other systemic issues were resentfully endured.

These frustrations varied considerably. Most involved processes and outcomes relating to sentence planning, recategorization, town visits, preparing for release and other aspects of 'paperwork'. Den complained that he had been waiting for two years to receive a decision about going to a category D prison—'nobody's telling me anything'—and at having to push to have his file updated: 'it took me five or six sit-downs with my personal officer, and only because I collared him and said "you've got to listen to this"'. George had been waiting for over five months to obtain approval for a town visit, his first in three years, and was waiting for an answer from the parole board to which he had been legally entitled some weeks earlier. All his frustrations were centred on the speed of his progression: 'the waiting, the bureaucracy of it. The system grinds on in its own merry way, and nothing you can do can change it. Just waiting all the time. The wheels grind so slowly.' As noted earlier, like many lifers, his progress had been slowed by a series of psychological reports with which he took issue for being based on superficial contact, for contradicting each other, and for providing descriptions that felt partial and objectifying. Other *stoics* complained bitterly or despondently that judgments by psychologists and parole boards were based on institutional compliance and that this bore little relation to behaviour outside the prison; that psychological language assaulted their integrity; and that risk assessments were deeply conservative, expecting forms of behaviour that were very hard to achieve.

Tommy was several years beyond his tariff because of psychological assessments, and was in a state of deep despair about his predicament:

All that I need is an aim and a goal. If I've got an aim and a goal, then I can function. I can get on with things. When they take that away from me, then I just lose all hope. [...] I'm focused on the world out there. But it's getting over these hurdles in-between, to get out there, that I'm struggling with. [...] It's like I'm banging my head against a wall all the time. I get nowhere. [...] And to keep me in prison to do what? All my reports say I've done every offending behaviour course, I'm a nice person, I'm polite, I don't present a risk. When I got my parole board, I asked them 'if you send me back to Cat-D, what am I going to do there?' There's no courses I can do, basically, I'm just lost in the system again until my next parole.

The frustrations described here were two-fold. One was the sheer difficulty of navigating systemic requirements. In a system whose onus was active engagement, those prisoners who were not sure how to proceed were rather disadvantaged, as Tommy emphasized:

[When] you were [just] thrown behind the door, you knew that's where you were and that's where you stayed. And you could get on with it. [...] But now I go through the motions of doing everything right, for years without incident. I'll have one little incident and I'm back to square one. I'd rather just be behind my door. That was just being behind the door, and that way I'm not doing anything wrong.

The second frustration was the repeated raising of expectations. For *stoics* in particular, when targets were moved or long-term goals frustrated, it was easy to lose faith in the system and existential trust. When the system had been simpler and less exacting, there was at least some confidence in its predictable drudgery.

Criticisms of the system were pervasive. *Stoics* were the prisoners who were most cynical about the role of the IEP system, regarding it as a tool of control and a means of transforming rights into removable privileges: 'There's no carrots', said Nathan, 'it's all stick'. Courses were likewise viewed with considerable cynicism: exercises designed to give an outside appearance of rehabilitative effort, or 'for statistics' rather than to help prisoners or protect the public. Moreover, most *stoics* had been taking courses for years and felt little further enthusiasm to 'sort themselves out'.

Personal change was not attributed to the institution, at least not in a positive sense. As George noted, it occurred '*despite*' the pressures of the system, or, at best, through the 'room' provided by sustained incapacitation.

Relative to other prisoners, *stoics* were also particularly attuned to the tendencies of target culture to distort its own aims—for example, by sending prisoners to workshops whether there was work to do or not. Some prisoners were adamant that, in order to keep positive drug test figures low, the prison deliberately tested men who were known as non-users. *Stoics* rarely held conspiratorial views of the penal system—notions that it wanted them to fail, or that it was merely a self-serving system for the provision of criminal justice employment—but they despaired of its practical and ideological failings: its indifference, inefficiencies and the inconsistencies between its claims and realities.

As experienced prisoners, *stoics* were also acutely sensitive to the absurdities of bureaucracy. Den complained that he had been disciplined for possessing a forbidden article (a paintbrush), but that this had then been returned to him: 'What was the logic in doing that? If another officer comes off another wing, and it's my turn to have a search, they're doing me for the same thing. "Can I have my days back please?" "No, because you had a forbidden article". "Yeah, but you've given it back to me…".' Nathan protested that he was being moved in handcuffs to an open prison—which would have no fence and would allow him regular town visits. Asked if he could dispute the decision, he explained that: 'you can, but you don't get anywhere. It's like the authoritarian brick wall. I mean, *this is how it is*.'

Responses of this kind illustrated the fatalism that *stoics* expressed about the possibilities of exerting pressure on the system. Others used similar terms. 'You just see it as part of your position in this place', George explained. 'There's nothing you can do about it and to resist it will just cause you problems.' Tommy considered himself to be in a state of deep-freeze containment: 'It's not about punishment. I'm just existing. I switch off, and take one day at a time.' First, then, challenging decisions or making complaints was considered futile:

It doesn't matter how often you go down that office and ask what's happening. Nothing will be hurried up: it will go at the pace that it's supposed to go at. It doesn't matter how frustrated you get, there is no point in complaining, it will happen when it will happen. It's just the way the system is.... I don't ask for anything from the system. I never put applications in, I never ask to see the Board of Visitors, I never complain about anything. Because it's too much of a bloody hassle to be honest. It's form-filling, and explaining, and at the end you're probably gonna get a 'no' anyway. (George)

Second, as experienced prisoners had observed, overt dissent was dangerous and counter-productive:

I've seen people get up on roof tops, I've seen people kick off. At the end of the day it gets em fucking nowhere. It gets em [in] dispersal, it gets em in [Special Secure Units], it doesn't do em no favours. I've seen that, so the way that I've conducted myself in prison is different. I'll do it legally. At the end of the day, my fucking whole ambition is to get out. It's not to spend the rest of my fucking life stuck in one of these fucking shit holes. (Nathan)

So how do you make your voices heard about issues?

I don't. I just accept them. I don't let them walk over me, but I never let the little things bother me. Time and experience have taught me that if I complain about it, I'm labelled as a kick-off merchant or a ringleader or an inciter.... I just accept it. I don't like it, but I just accept it for what it is. (Tommy)

As Nathan suggested, *stoics* were extremely cautious in pursuing their grievances and objectives, doing so only through means that were officially recognized, and with care. George argued that the best way was 'to get staff onside, not to alienate them; it's to use the system as it's presented to you, even though it's a big paper chase. If you demand things, you won't get anything, obstacles will be put in your way.' Other *stoics* made sure only to ask for things to which they were entitled, and to do so infrequently, 'so that when I do ask it tends to be something that most people can see is fairly important' (Nathan). Those who used complaint procedures and legal channels (e.g. solicitors, the Prisons Ombudsman) to claim rights or accelerate processes did so after exhausting other options, and in ways that were not confrontational:

If I do ask for something I don't go in the office demanding this, that and the other. I make a polite request. If I don't get anywhere with the polite request I make a formal request. If I don't get anything with a formal request I'll make a formal request but this time maybe with a legal threat in it. If I don't get anywhere then, then I'll go outside the prison: solicitor, MP, whatever, just to exert pressure. (Nathan)

Stoics accepted that there were limits to what could be achieved through such methods, but feared being labelled 'trouble-makers'. They made courteous queries and sometimes assertive complaints about visits arrangements or property rules, but acquiesced completely when told that procedures were not subject to change. When polite petitions about food quality were ineffective, they took no further action. Third though, for some *stoics*, it was unclear how grievances could be pursued. As the previous chapter described, power was not invisible, but 'the system' was unreachable and inflexible to individual needs. 'Years ago I could fight it, I could challenge it', said Tommy, about parole decisions he could not understand. '[Now] I get sympathetic ears off the governors or the officers, but there's no legal process I can take to fight it.' When power operates at a distance, there are 'no buildings where the control desk of the system are lodged and which could be stormed and captured' (Bauman 2000: 5). Power is everywhere, yet there is no central power to resist. For *stoics*, this experience was especially familiar. Responsibility always lay 'somewhere else'. Since feelings of dissent had no clear target, and venting them publicly risked being 'killed off on file', they were suppressed or privatized—kept among trusted associates or expelled only behind cell doors.

For most *stoics*, this need to contain one's feelings and submit to the carceral machine was a frustration in itself, one that supplemented the daily humiliations of powerlessness. Whereas *pragmatists* were oblivious to the terms of their submission, and were not capable of imagining alternative arrangements, *stoics* were all too aware of how penal power operated and of how they capitulated to it. Often having been more defiant in the past, they could see how resistance could take shape. But with so much to lose from fighting the system, the temptation to resist itself had to be resisted. As Nathan explained, there was something 'deeply oppressive' in this conscious acquiescence and in participating in one's own carceral management:

There's always a sense that you *could* rebel, but you're responsible for staying there. For that to be made very overt—not being ordered to do stuff, but ordering yourself—is a burden. The burden of doing the sentence is not on the court or the prison, but on you. It's hard to bear, because it's hard to rebel or rail against. It means that your enemy becomes yourself, because there is no obvious enemy against whom you can protest.

Stoics therefore expressed resentment not only against the institution, but also against their own passivity and their incorporation into the apparatus of compliance.

Keeping out of trouble had implications for social life (as coming chapters show). *Stoics* had no desire to become embroiled in wing politics, trade, or social obligations. On the wings, they were loners, or picked their friends carefully. 'A lot of my friends are long-termers', Tommy explained. 'We just want to keep our heads down and get on with it.'

In accordance with their in-prison adaptations, *stoics* did not hold the same grandiose plans as their *enthusiast* peers. They were desperate for release, and confident that they would never reoffend, but after years of imprisonment their aims for the future were modest. 'I don't want anything big and massive', Tommy explained. 'I just want a job, a home. And that's all I've ever wanted.' George's expectations were equally unassuming. He recognized that he would be on the 'bottom rung of the ladder' in terms of employment prospects, and saw making friends only as a possibility. Other *stoics* had more optimism about their futures, but remained realistic about the chances of obtaining employment and re-integrating fully into society.

Such apprehensions were unsurprising. For prisoners like Tommy, who had experienced almost no adult life outside carceral institutions, 'real life' only began on release, yet it was impossible to envisage what such a life would entail. Indeed, long-term prisoners were so accustomed to the performances and repressions required in prison, and had aged so much within this distorted social environment, that they were often unsure who they would be once released. Nathan explained that the distance between his social mask and his true persona was no longer clear, and that he had no real connection to his pre-prison self:

I've done my maturing in prison so therefore the only person that exists out there is the immature kid that I was [all those] years ago. That person no longer exists, he is a dim and distant memory, and now all that exists is the person that I am now. I know that there is still a façade that I portray. Everyone does in prison. Now whether that means there is a sense of self behind the way that I portray myself, I don't know. This is something I can only explore once I'm out.

A second reason why *stoics* sought a quiet life was that they were anxious about their abilities to cope in the outside world. George described his town visits as having made him feel 'very dislocated;

more of an observer than a participant. I didn't feel connected with it in any way.' He also expressed concern about his capacity for interpersonal attachment:

Definitely over the years, I've become emotionally stunted.

'Stunted' as in you don't have emotions anymore?

Erm, well I do, but it's a very narrow range. I dunno… if perseverance is an emotion, if determination and frustration, hope, if that's an emotion. But other things, I don't know. It's difficult.… This has been my life for so long; it's very hard for me to feel any different.

Despite the kinds of profound consequences of long-term imprisonment evidenced here, *stoics* were neither the most damaged members of the prisoner community nor the most deeply resigned.

'Retreatists'

For another set of prisoners, resignation related even less to what the prison could offer, and much more to a fatalistic attitude to the self and the future. This small but distinctive set of prisoners (around one in fifteen) was highly compliant without either being actively seduced or directly subdued by the prison's mechanisms of power. These prisoners were former drug addicts who were not fatalistically resigned to the prison's dominance as such, but to life more generally.[25] They rejected, or sidestepped, both the means and ends of the institution (c.f. Merton 1938), engaging in minimal and selective ways with its incentive structure and declining its assumption that early release was the lodestar of the sentence.

Drugs and drug dependency were the recurrent themes of these prisoners' life narratives, and defined their adaptations to incarceration, as the testimonies of Alfie and Noah exemplified. Alfie grew up in a large family in a disadvantaged part of a Northern city. He described himself as a quiet, withdrawn child, who was abused at the age of 6 and lost his father two years later:

I don't even remember [the abuse], really. I know it happened but I sort of blanked it out, it's in the recesses of my mind.… I don't use it as a tool and say 'I was abused as a kid and that's why I'm so angry at society'. I'm more angry my father was taken away.

[25] Giddens (1991: 112) distinguishes between fatalism and stoicism as follows: 'stoicism [is] an attitude of strength in the face of life's trials and tribulations. A fatalistic outlook is one of resigned acceptance that events should be allowed to take their course'.

After his father's death, his mother turned to drink, as did some of his siblings—'drink is a big part of my family background'—while he had 'some sort of breakdown', for which he was prescribed valium. Hard to control, at fourteen he was sent to an approved school, followed by periods in a detention centre and a Young Offenders Institution. After a failed marriage in his early twenties, which ended when he received another sentence, he spent a happy period working for one of his brothers, but began to drink heavily and 'just became violent. I was fighting every second day'. Since this time, he estimated that he had spent no more than eleven consecutive months outside prison, mainly because of his addiction to heroin, which he had first used in prison to counteract boredom and anxiety:

I remember just sliding down the wall thinking 'oh my God'. It was just a euphoric feeling, nothing mattered. I was worried about [my] relationship with my first wife, a lot of stuff was going through my head, I was very pent up, and all my troubles just seemed to go away. I realised that heroin can take away all your problems in the short term; they're still there but you don't think about them as much. So that's the reason I've continued taking it, because my life has hurt me that much.

Opiate-dependent on release, he had begun living 'a desperate existence, living from hand to mouth' in order to try to provide for a previous partner to whom he had returned and their two children. Committing robberies and shoplifting, he was soon reconvicted, and 'came out to nothing. Two of my kids were in care, my life just fell apart.' Heroin, and the attempt to maintain his relationship, dominated his life from this point onwards, and the two were intertwined. His partner was also a heroin addict and a victim of child abuse—'that's why I can relate so much'—and their emotional and narcotic co-dependence dragged them repeatedly into spirals of addiction and offending. Together for sixteen years, Alfie said they had spent no more than five months together without the interruption of one of them going to prison. Now in his late thirties, he was serving a four-year sentence for robbery.

Noah was raised on a housing estate in a large city in the Midlands, in what he called a normal, loving, hardworking, but fairly poor family. Sport-mad as a child, he dreamed of becoming a footballer, but, from the age of fifteen, became distracted by girls and music. He left school, drifting happily in and out of work, and smoking and selling small quantities of cannabis. At seventeen, after getting involved with 'a group of lads', he served a short custodial sentence in a detention centre, which 'spun my world around': 'I come out of there hating people, a bit angry towards things.' After losing his flat and possessions while jailed, he moved back to his parents' house, working sporadically and dealing speed (amphetamines) and cannabis to fund his social life. At twenty, he met a woman with whom he moved to a flat and had a daughter.

After another short sentence for a crime in which he had little involvement, he repaired his relationship, moved to another city, and, for a while, held down a steady job. But once he became addicted to cocaine, he quickly lost his job, leading to arguments with his girlfriend and their eventual break-up. He returned to his home-city and began re-using speed: 'but on a different level', injecting it rather than taking it in the form of pills. Noah described his first amphetamine injection and its impact on his life as follows:

And then the rush came on. And I'm standing there thinking 'fucking what a rush.' Well that day was the biggest.... I've had some turns in my life, but from then on my life has proper been destroyed in drugs. And I mean proper. I have seen and done things since then which I would never dream I would see or do. From that first day my life just turned around. *Proper* turned around. When people [talk about] 'the dark side', I believe from that day on I did go into a dark side of drugs which I never thought existed.

To feed his habit, and despite another prison sentence, Noah began stealing from student accommodation. He was soon tempted into using crack cocaine, which accelerated and intensified his decline: 'what it took whizz and draw five or six years to do,[26] it took not even half a year for that crack to just bring me totally to my knees'. Descending into desperate addiction, he sold all his possessions, lost a significant amount of weight, developed massive paranoia, and exploited all his close friends and family:

All I could see was a tunnel and at the end of it was that [crack]-pipe. I didn't want to rip them off but I'd become so selfish, and mean, mean, mean. That was the sickest part of my life on drugs. I remember sitting down on main roads in town, and just thinking: 'I hope the police come and take me away.' And when the police finally caught me, I didn't run away, I fell into their arms, Ben. I was thinking 'please, lock me away. Just lock me away from this fucking stuff. Because I can't stop taking it'. For the first time I was in jail, I remember thinking: 'Thank God'.

[26] 'Whizz' and 'draw': amphetamines and cannabis.

Although he stayed off drugs while on that sentence, he returned to crack and crime immediately on release, and was soon arrested. On this occasion, he was bailed to a drug rehabilitation hostel, where he was 'transformed'. He remained drug-free for eight months, was given insight into his drug use, and regained his self-respect. Expecting to be given a non-custodial sentence, instead, he was sent to prison for almost two years: 'everything were back to front all of a sudden. I've done everything they said, and I'm in this fucking cell.' Returning to the rehab centre when freed, he was expelled after an argument with a woman with whom he had got involved—'when I seen her out in that bikini...it's a bit like the drugs, I'm just a sucker for it'. Although he once more took up crack and heroin, he did so much less fiercely than previously, until another relationship ended, and his return to heavy usage resulted in a further sentence. After staying clean throughout another term in prison, a probation mix-up led to him only being offered space in a night shelter, where he knew that drugs would be plentiful. Turning this down, he was left homeless, and very quickly returned to drug use and burglaries. Within six months, and now in his forties, he was arrested again, and given a six-year sentence.

Such life-stories resembled those of *enthusiasts* in a number of ways. Like them, *retreatists* were afflicted by guilt for their actions while on drugs, and—despite myriad social and personal misfortunes—did not seek to blame others for their predicaments. 'I've met people who have met with genuine accidents and end up here', Noah noted. 'But I've purposely gone out of my way to take drugs and burgle. I know what I did was wrong, and I did it. Nobody forced me to.' Alfie was equally lacking in self-pity: 'I class myself as a sensible person. I've no excuse whatsoever for why I haven't made more of my life.' Although he resented the 'untold effect' that prison had had on his life, and admitted that he suppressed underlying despair, his concerns were mainly for the hurt he had caused to his offence victims, and, in particular, his children:[27]

[They] know me by name only. They remember a thin, gaunt looking junkie getting dragged out of the house by coppers and that's the last recollection they've got of me.... I've neglected them for so long, I've never been there for them, I hardly know them, but I've still got the cheek to call

---

[27] 'In the last ten years, I've been hurting somebody every day, [physically] and financially. Sometimes in my pad at night, chilled out, I start thinking about the heartache I caused in my life.' (Alfie)

myself their father.... We were more concerned with making money to buy more heroin than going to see the kids. It's not something I'm proud of.

However, a significant difference between *enthusiasts* and *retreatists* was the support they received from people in the community. Whereas *enthusiasts* were determined to prove themselves to partners and family members who awaited their release, *retreatists* had negligible contact with the outside world, and thus no external audience to whom change could be demonstrated. Neither Alfie nor Noah received visits. Both were located some distance from their hometowns, and both had alienated almost everyone they cared about. Alfie's family had effectively 'disowned' him: 'they're under the impression I'm quite happy where I am, which might be true'. He interpreted his partner's failure to contact him following her own release from prison as an indication that their relationship was terminated. His sole communication beyond the prison was with another prisoner, with whom he exchanged letters when both were inside. This level of isolation was unusual, but illustrated the minimal social ties and support that all *retreatists* recounted. In terms of family and partners, there was little for them to return to.

As well as lacking an external focus for their future hopes, *retreatists* had little inner confidence that they could change their patterns of conduct. Whereas *enthusiasts* distanced themselves from their deeds by bifurcating their identities into 'bad' and 'good', or 'false' and 'authentic', *retreatists* were much less confident of these distinctions and were less sure that they would choose the 'right path' in the future. 'The day will come when I will be back out there again'. Noah mused. 'Then that's up to me, isn't it? It's that crossroads again. Which way am I going to go?' Alfie described himself as a self-destructive extremist, and could not imagine beating his demons outside prison: 'If I could stop taking drugs, stop drinking, I'd be fine, but I can't honestly sit here and say to you I think I could. I don't think I could stop taking drugs and drinking.' Noah said he had 'learned not to kid myself. I could stay clean every day in here, but it does me diddly-squat [i.e. nothing] out there unless I walk the walk.' In contrast to *enthusiasts*, who harnessed their temperaments in their projects of self-transformation, *retreatists* resigned themselves to being puppets of their addictive personalities. They were fearful of the future, tentative in their plans, and had little trust in themselves to control their impulses. Their designs were not grand visions of success and redemption, but rudimentary forms of contentment:

It doesn't matter what I do. Even if it's sweeping up somewhere, I'm not bothered. I can just get myself some furniture and just start to build my life up.... I can buy a little radio, I can buy a little telly.... And get meself just a normal bird, and just chill out for a bit. And I'd be happy with that—just a little place, you know what I mean? As long as the stuff in there's mine and I can open my door and can walk down the road with a bit of pride.... Just a normal bloke going to work and coming back. (Noah)

Alfie's image of his future, although perhaps realistic, presented a depressing account of his aspirations: 'I'll probably move into a bedsit, I'll have a couple of posters on the wall, my bed made, my telly in the corner. I'll probably make my bedsit into a cell because I'm quite happy with that.'

Alfie's quotation was also suggestive of his low expectations of the present. The degradations of life on the streets on drugs were such that *retreatists* had meagre demands within prison. Although they did not enjoy imprisonment, they appreciated the regularity of their sleeping patterns, meals, bowel movements, clean clothes and bedding, and the comforting simplicity of regimentation. While they recognized that such admissions were deeply depressing, in prison they felt more healthy and hygienic, more in touch with the world, more mentally stable, and more capable of normal relationships and conversation than they did as addicts outside.

Many of the conventional pains and deprivations of imprisonment were felt more keenly outside the institution than within it, as the following excerpts indicate:

You just become a slave. That's what druggies are. Just slaves to a drug. [I've] had nights where I daren't go out of my flat because I thought I was being followed. Or you're smoking [crack] with a son whose [mother has] just hustled the money [as a prostitute]. I suppose in a way I'm lucky. I know people who've died. So in a way, prison has saved me. It sounds crazy, but my quality of life at the moment is better. I'm eating. I'm sleeping in a clean bed. I'm getting clean clothes every day. And I've got some kind of order in my life. It sounds *mental*, don't it, to say that? But the life before I come in was just waking up, going out, burglaring people's houses, going round [other] people's houses letting them talk to me like shit because they knew I wanted money for crack. (Noah)

I don't have control over my life, heroin has control over my life. I hand the reins to heroin. It's in prison I'm able to control my life more, and I'm happier. I'm sensible enough to realise that the only thing I've treasured when I'm on the out is smack and in here I'm quite glad to see the back of it, glad to be deprived of that. (Alfie)

As suggested here, for such hardcore users, drug addiction meant social disrespect, moral squalor, physical degradation, material dispossession, lack of control and autonomy, psychological anxiety and ontological chaos. Prison was a respite from such mortifications (see Chapter 8), and from the temptations of the outside community. It was inside prison that these men felt safer, and more in control of their lives, however modestly. As Noah reported:

I still feel in control of myself and my emotions. We are powerless, but I still feel like I've got a bit of discipline in myself and in my life. And I earn money. I'm in control if I get myself up and keep myself tidy. Control if I keep my pad properly. Control [in] who I mix with.

This reversal of normal social yardsticks, alongside trepidation about the future, framed *retreatists'* everyday decisions and expectations. Like their hopes for the future, their current ambitions were simple: self-renewal rather than radical change, and inner peace rather than external validation. Noah liked to 'keep it simple, one day at a time. I don't even work for one day at a time. I work for meals. From dinner to tea. From tea till bedtime.' Alfie talked of his 'personal sentence plan. I just get my head down. I try and cause as little upset and unhappiness to people. I go with the flow.' They chose jobs that offered absorbing work or a pleasant working environment, or work that helped them make ends meet and afford the small luxuries that they could not supplement through private cash: 'mayonnaise in [my] cupboard, fresh milk every week, and noodles whenever I want' (Alfie). To boost their incomes further, they dabbled lightly in the informal economy, trading tobacco or brewing hooch in small quantities. When available, they smoked cannabis, but did not seek out heroin, well aware that they could not afford the amounts required to feed their prodigious narcotic appetites: 'I'd need about twenty of them, I would. And my mind's not that daft to realize that I couldn't keep it up. I haven't got that sort of money coming in.' In their minor illicit activities, they were neither cowed by the threat of being caught nor motivated by the notion of beating the system.

Nor too were they concerned about accumulating profit or status. Receiving no money from outside parties, their financial resources were insufficient for them to incur respect through their clothing or possessions. In any case, they had little interest in the judgments of their peers. As Noah implied, this reflected the modest goals they set for themselves, and the internal standards by which these goals were measured.

My happiness now, I feel, is in my soul. I know what I've done, and I know what I can do to put myself right. [What other people think] doesn't bother me. I'm not a person who thinks 'I haven't got this and that', because I have had it. I've [also] been homeless, so people's standards don't really mean a lot to me.

As fitted such ideals, they attached importance to 'conduct': being respectful and respectable in their everyday behaviour. They were surprised by the lack of dignity with which some prisoners conducted themselves, and the lack of attention some paid to making themselves and their cells presentable: 'They're forgetting they're living here', Alfie exclaimed tellingly. However, unlike *enthusiasts*—with their fervent sense of moral righteousness—*retreatists* were reluctant to pass judgment on other people. In relation both to their peers and the prison itself, they did little to assert themselves, keeping out of trouble and mixing in limited social circles.

Retreatists were liked by staff. They were obedient and courteous to male officers, and charming and chivalrous with female staff, whose honour they often defended against the approaches and accusations of other prisoners (see Crewe 2006a). They made few demands on staff time. 'I don't ask staff for anything much. I talk to staff, but I don't really chase them', said Alfie. 'They just let you get on with your thing', said Rhys. 'I'll say hello to them and I'll be polite. But I don't really talk to them that much.' *Retreatists* accepted the legitimacy of their punishment and the legitimate authority of the prison's representatives—'they're just doing their job' was the typical refrain—and they found their treatment and conditions relatively decent. Asked about hidden resistance, Alfie declared: 'I don't think anybody has got just cause for that. Honestly, in my experience with jails, this is one of the best jails I've ever been to.' In these respects then, the conformity of *retreatists* was partly an outcome of the prison's material and interpersonal legitimacy, and partly a reflection of their modest expectations.

In other respects, *retreatists* sidestepped the prison's mechanisms of power and disregarded its ends. With their muted daily ambitions and pessimistic projections of the future, they exhibited a form of personal fatalism that, although highly compliant, did not fulfil systemic expectations of active engagement. Prioritizing inner demons over external concerns, in effect, they sought personal reconstruction autonomously of the system. Although they were happy to take offending behaviour courses, they did so not to prove themselves to the prison authorities, but out of curiosity. They took drug tests without either enthusiasm or resentment. Everyday incentives had little potency and were dispassionately discounted. As Rhys explained: 'I don't want strikes, obviously, but it's not something I really think about'.

Retreatists had no desire for extra visits they would not receive nor for extra spending allowances for money they did not have. They did not want the disappointments and disruptions that occurred when hopes were pinned on things they might not get, which might be removed from them, or which they could not trust themselves to manage:

I'm not very bothered about Cat-D and all that business. I'd be tempted not to stay. So I'd be back to square one, I'd be on the run. I couldn't trust myself. I'll just keep myself in here for the time being.... I'll stay here till next March, and I'll take stock [then]. At the moment I'm on course: I've got my little bit of burn, I've got my little job, and I've got my little room.... I'm not going to bang my head on the wall for stuff that I'm not interested in, and don't want anyway. The way I look at it is, if I don't want a load there ain't a load to be took away from me. I'm not going to get upset because I'm not expecting anything. If I'm not expecting anything then my happiness is in myself and what I've built round [me]. (Noah)

People start talking about tagging, parole, home leaves in front of me, I either retract myself from the conversation or I'm not interested at all.... I'm content in my own existence. (Alfie)

Even the prison's most powerful incentives were effectively impotent. Alfie turned down his chance to apply for parole, explaining that he was: 'in no hurry to get out. It's fast and dangerous out there. I just want a bit more time. I don't want to get out there and go back to the life I had' (see Halsey 2006). Rhys expressed a similar position:

I'm not really going for Cat-D. I'm not really trying to reduce my sentence in any way. I've got seven police days which I could have put in for. But I don't really want them.... I could have got a tag, but I had no address, so I turned it down.... I'm not trying to—in a way—get out of jail. I just want to do my full sentence, and hopefully come out a better person.... Sort my head out. Get myself back to how I used to be before I got really badly into the drugs.

In such respects, *retreatists* were compliant *beyond* the system. They were aligned with the official discourses of the institution, but at the same time unengaged by them. In a system with a consumerist logic, not wanting anything was a source of threat. Passivity could represent a form of dissent as well as a form of compliance. As Alfie asked rhetorically, 'how can a prison have power over you when you're in no rush to get beyond the gate?'

'Players'

'Rituals of subordination...may be deployed both for purposes of manipulation and concealment', James Scott notes (1990: 35). A significant proportion of prisoners (around one in four) revealed that their public performances were precisely as Scott suggests: displays of compliance that were within the terms of institutional discourse but mocked the aims of the institution and masked backstage forms of resistance. These *players* were by no means content, nor did they see the establishment's material offerings as fair trade for compliance. Their normative commitment to the prison's aims was negligible. Indeed, they were normatively *opposed* to its practices and principles, and hostile to its staff. However, judging that the system could be neither ignored nor surmounted, they acted out the institutional script of active obedience in ways that were designed to subvert its aims and that disguised and promoted oppositional values and objectives. Behind such presentations were various forms of backstage resistance, including unstated contempt, fantasies of revenge, *sub rosa* activity invested with anti-institutional meaning (e.g. drug dealing; stealing from kitchens, workshops and classrooms) and active subversion (e.g. setting off fire alarms and buzzers). These adaptations were consistent with life narratives in which themes of power, agency, and masculine status predominated.

Ashley, an Afro-Caribbean prisoner in his late thirties, came from a large city in the Midlands, where he had been raised by a single mother alongside several siblings. He described his local neighbourhood as a multiracial 'ghetto', where criminal activity flourished: 'as soon as I stepped out of my front door, the first person I'd see is a prostitute and a pimp or a drug dealer'. He remembered having an anti-authority attitude from a young

age, never liking being told what to do and being expelled from
numerous schools for assaulting teachers. He also learned the instrumental value of fear—'a very strong weapon'—threatening
other children not to tell their parents about his disruptive activities at school in case they told his mother.

The relationship between violence and masculine power was
a recurring theme in Ashley's life narrative. Through fights between schools, he met other boys whose leadership qualities and
tastes for aggressive delinquency he identified with: 'if you've got
a lad who's leading fifty school-kids on a pitched battle, he's got
to have something about him, hasn't he?' On his estate, he mixed
with older men, admiring the local criminals—'men's men'—who
had 'respect for money' and whose violent lifestyles gave them
social and sexual kudos: 'I used to watch people tiptoe around
[them], and regardless of what anybody says, that's power.' For
Ashley, money was the elixir of status and a means of establishing
independence from his mother—a commanding figure to whom
he stated his adoration and pledged to support. At the age of 16,
alongside street robberies and football hooliganism, he began
working as a pimp, using fear to control his prostitutes and feeling little sympathy for their plight:

Being a pimp, you don't feel sorry for a bitch. She could be fucking dead
in some alleyway for all I cared.... As bad as it sounds—to be a pimp,
that's one of the coldest professions. That came naturally. I'd already got
my cold streak.

Ashley divided women into two categories: those within his family,
for whom he expressed undying love and loyalty, and those who
were 'just meat'—to be used for sex or money. In a similar manner, he would not commit to any of the mothers of his children,
but claimed deep commitment to the children themselves:

If they need anything, just ask and it's there. I don't want my kids to be
in the position I was in. I always want them to be aware that they can get
anything from dad.... I think I've spoiled them because a lot of the time I'm
not there. I'm always in prison. So I shower them with money and gifts.

The complex connections that Ashley made between love and
money were particularly apparent here. He described himself as
'a family man, at heart', and insisted that his reputation ensured
that his family had no troubles in terms of money or security.
Beyond these loyalties, his motto was highly individualistic: 'it's
every man for himself. If you've got something and I want it, I'm

taking it.' Ashley recognized the extreme nature of these categorizations and positions: 'I'm either black or white, there's no grey.
I might be exceptionally loving or extremely horrible.' Describing
the number of his friends who had died young, through various
forms of urban violence, he veered between sentimentality and
cool bravado: 'that's the life you live, isn't it? You live by the
sword and you may perish by it.'

Ashley's choice of crimes also signalled the value he attached to
certain forms of masculine status and agency.

> I haven't got the nerve to be a shoplifter.... Shoplifting, you're not in con-
> trol.... But I've got the nerve to come and rob the place blatantly. Stick
> a balaclava on and kick the fucking door off. I've only ever shoplifted
> one thing in my whole life, and I got caught. I never felt so shamed and
> embarrassed in my life.... The whole place stops. And they all look at you.
> I couldn't handle that. Whereas if I run into that same store, I'm in con-
> trol: 'Get on the fucking floor and do as you're told'. I like to be in control
> of what I do. Everybody wants to be in control. If you don't want to be
> in control, then you're submissive. And I find submissive people are very
> weak. And I'm not a submissive person.

Ashley received his first custodial sentence as an 18-year-old, an
experience that he recalled as a 'buzz', an initiation into criminal life, and a confirmation that 'violence could get you what
you wanted'. On release, he came out 'meaner' and started selling
drugs. He also began to carry a gun for the first time: 'it's amaz-
ing, the power of a gun. It gives you total power.' Having bullied
weaker prisoners as a Young Offender, he now took pleasure in
'seeing a bigger man cringe'. After another sentence, during which
he found out the value of drugs within prison, he developed a crack
habit, which led to further convictions for armed robberies.

Returning to drug dealing after a long term inside, the sentence
he was now serving stemmed from an attack on a rival drug supplier. Facing a life sentence if convicted of another violent offence,
although he was half-heartedly considering getting a normal job,
he envisaged returning to the drugs trade on release—'my method
is airtight. I don't think they could catch me.'[28] Although he
claimed to respect 'working people', he mocked the monotony of

---

[28] Ashley expressed his sense of invincibility when I presented him with my
consent form before the start of the interview. As I explained the terms of confidentiality (and although he did sign the form) he declared: 'I'm not really bothered.
No-one can't do me over so I ain't really bothered.'

working life and contrasted it with the autonomy and spontaneity of his lifestyle. In other respects, he sought to diminish the distinctions between his values and those of the apparently lawful, while defining himself as a 'survivor' rather than a criminal: 'There's a bit of criminal in everyone, isn't there? And aren't they just surviving? When Tony Blair goes home, Cherie's still fucking talking about getting the rent paid, you know what I'm saying?.'

Wilson was a twenty-five year-old prisoner, serving a five-year sentence for possession of drugs with intent to supply. His childhood had been unsettled, as he moved between his mother's council house in one city to his father's decrepit home in another. He recalled having to take responsibility for his own welfare and for his sister from the age of around ten—'I had a lot of responsibility, so to me I was a man from then. I don't feel I had a proper childhood.' His father was strict and sadistically violent, beating him for the slightest reasons and punishing him by dousing him with water and then locking him out of the house without any shoes—'I still carry that anger about', Wilson recognized.[29] When Wilson was thirteen, his father had demanded that he pay rent for food and lodgings (despite giving him the smallest bedroom in the house when a larger one was available—as Wilson remembered with bemusement and bitterness), which led to him shoplifting and loaning out his dinner money for interest. He enforced his debts through violence, and fought whenever he felt personally slighted—either disbelieved or disrespected. The roots of his hypersensitivity were clear:

I like to be heard, for someone to say, 'I believe you' for once, because my dad would never believe me.... I used to fight over the smallest little thing. If a man didn't pay me I'd beat him up. I knocked out a friend—for a joke he said something about my mum so I knocked him out. I beat up a kid, we were arguing over a pen or pencil. I just used to fight over silly things.

Leaving school without qualifications, Wilson continued to steal cars and shoplift, activities that provided income, social and

---

[29] Wilson recalled a number of acts of cruelty: 'The one that sticks out the most was when he got a Christmas hamper and he wasn't back yet, so I opened a can of chicken, heated it up in the microwave. When he came in he saw the can in the bin and he just waded into me, had me pinned on the floor, kneeling on my face. He was like, "don't touch my food until you pay rent, you're not living for free in this house". I stopped crying in front of him to not give him the satisfaction and just let it out in my room.'

sexual credibility, and excitement: 'it was like a game of cat and mouse.... They knew what I was doing but they couldn't catch me doing it, it was a good buzz.' Joining a street gang, he was initiated into a more violent and organized culture, with an almost para-military structure that enabled drug distribution in the local area. Gang life involved trials of strength and character: being attacked and tested by older members ('toughened up' and 'getting wise'), and having to commit random acts of violence in order to 'earn stripes'. The gang also provided forms of social and emotional support that had been absent from Wilson's family life:

If one [person] got into trouble they'd all look after that person. If you had no money someone would buy you something to eat; if you had no weed someone would split it with you. [...] It was like a family, I'm ready to go all out for you, are you ready to go all out for me, type of thing. They look out for you.

Wilson's ideals and self-image reflected his premature initiation into adulthood and his feelings of social and emotional aliena-tion.[30] Life was about 'going through shit, and not giving a shit, but coming out on top'. He described himself as 'a grafter, a proper hustler, because put me in any situation I can get money. I will not go hungry and I will never sleep on the street.' He expected exceptional levels of loyalty from others, but put little trust in anyone else. His vocabulary of 'feds' (the police), 'beans' (girlfriends) and, 'licking shots' (drug dealing) borrowed directly from the tropes of American gangsta rap, which also provided his heroes. As was also consistent with his 'bad-ass' ideology of cold self-protection, the ethics of drug dealing were dismissed as irrelevant. Wilson recognized that heroin and crack cocaine 'fuck people up'—enough for him never to have tried either—but his approach to his occupation was instrumental and self-serving:

I don't worry about them, that's my money. Some of the girls [who bought drugs from me] I used to say, 'what are you doing? You're a pretty girl, get off this shit. If you weren't on it you could be my wife'. That's their life, I'm only responsible for me. If I weren't here, someone else would be here, and they were on this before I even met them, so it's not like I pushed it on anybody, they had the habit already.

[30] Wilson's early life appeared to be a classic example of premature autonomy: being pushed too early into adulthood, and clashing with those who do not provide the 'respect' or allow the autonomy to which one consequently feels entitled (Toch 1992).

Wilson's mentality was rooted in his emotional history: 'when you get passed from pillar to post you've got no self-worth, you feel like an unwanted dog or some shit like that. It's just, fuck the world, fuck everybody, just do whatever is right for me.' His preoccupation with respect and disrespect likewise reflected the ease with which his self-doubts could surface:

I don't like taking crap from anyone. If I do I feel like a pussy.... I feel like a wimp, like I've got no heart, no backbone, like I'm not strong, I'm just weak and pathetic, and I don't like that feeling.... When someone seriously disses you, it's a pride thing.

Women posed a particular threat to Wilson's self-esteem. He found it especially hard to take 'attitude' from them, and to resolve his desire for emotional nurture with his fears of rejection and betrayal. Thus, it was only with girlfriends that he was able to show his 'soft side', and he was attracted to women who were 'shy and innocent', but he described his current girlfriend as 'the kind of woman I love to hate. [...] She fucking does my head in, the stupid little bitch.' Women were 'dangerous' and emotion was 'not a good thing to have, because when you get emotional that's when people do shit. If you don't care about shit, then nothing can hurt you.'[31] Again, the links to Wilson's childhood were evident:

The more someone knows you, the more they can exploit or seek out a weakness, so it leaves you weak and vulnerable.
Has that happened to you?

---

[31] Wilson described Shakespeare as one of the only things that had interested him in school, and provided a striking and significant explanation of his fascination with Macbeth:

I think I just like the way the man got fucked up, his wife was controlling him, and the power struggles he had going on, he wanted more, he wasn't going to stop. It's the fact that it's a woman fucking him up completely. She's like, 'kill the king, you'll get the crown', so once he's done that he's got to keep on killing to keep what he wanted, whereas if he'd just been patient he would have got what he wanted anyway.
Why did you like the fact the woman encouraged him?
I suppose because people have this tendency to see women as the weaker sex, when to me I think women are dangerous. There are men in here that are in here because of some shit their women did and they went out on a mad one, they lost control. They've gone on a mad one for the love of this woman and that is some dangerous shit. Women are dangerous to me. The witches are quite interesting, that little twist in it, 'not born of woman', so he's thinking, 'I'm invincible', but he wasn't born, his mum was cut open, and he's thinking, 'oh shit', so he knows he's going to die. I think it just shows our lives are twisted.

I think my mum exploited me, because she knows I'll protect her whatever. [But] she's supposed to protect *me*, that's her natural, maternal instinct, but leaving me with a madman, I think that's just fucked up and wrong. All she had to do was pick up the phone and say, 'meet me here, pack a few things, and I'm going to take you away', that's all she had to do, she didn't do it. So if you can't trust your mother, you can't trust no-one'.

Many of these views and preoccupations were relevant to *players*' in-prison behaviour, as coming chapters will detail.

Like *stoics*, *players* were conscious of how power was exerted on them and were acutely aware of the need to act within the terms of institutional discourse. But whereas *stoics* claimed that their prison identities were sincere—that they had to repress their frustrations, but were not acting in ways that were strategically subversive—*players* emphasized the degree to which their public personae were mere performances—'for the paperwork', or for other forms of personal gain. Indeed, these prisoners were acutely aware of the need for self-management and the benefits of doing more than merely following orders.

Players monitored themselves both at work and on the wings, working at double-speed when officers were present, and managing the details of their visible social activity: 'I even think about who I walk round on exercise with and what I have on the walls of my cell, things like that', said Stephen. 'You're being watched all the time', claimed Leon. 'You check who's listening to how you speak to people. You're constantly aware, you've got to [be], so you're seen to be on your best behaviour.' As such efforts implied, prison was consistently described as 'a game', a terrain of tactics and strategy, in which officers were perceived not just as custodians but as active and calculating opponents.[32] For *players*, the tools of the game were wits, guile, and anticipation. 'I'm like a salesman, I talk my way out of trouble', claimed Wilson, 'you've got to have a quick mouth, quick brain, think on the spot'.

The game metaphor that *players* employed was congruous with their perceptions of life outside. Paul described his method as

---

[32] Wilson deliberated as follows: 'I've noticed that when you go for something [e.g. parole] they start fucking with you even more. I don't know why it is, it's just a little game for them. I can't be sure, but I feel certain officers are trying to push my buttons.'

being 'whatever they want you to be in their eyes', a strategy he had employed in various contexts:

Like when you're younger you show one face to your parents and another to your friends. The Police: you show one face to them, another face to your friends. Officers: you show them one face and behind their back you're someone else.

Players accepted that the public roles available to them were 'largely scripted from above' and had to 'reinforce the appearances approved by the dominant' (Scott 1990: 35). 'It's their world—they've got all the power in here', Wilson acknowledged. 'They've got the keys, you want the keys, so you've got to play their game'. Ashley concurred that 'you've got to be adaptable. When you really want something, then you have to learn to eat humble pie'. For *players*, it was not simply that explicit resistance was considered futile, but that to be themselves would also be counter-productive. Instead, they recognized the necessity of frontstage compliance and performed commitment, and the potential for using the system to their advantage:

Like cards, you've got to have bluff. You win if you get out as early as possible. If you're fighting and being messy, you're going nowhere. You've got to get them to believe you're not high risk, not going to re-offend, that you realise your mistake, you're fully rehabilitated, you're never coming back to jail, and they think, 'he's a good lad'—[so] you're going home in two weeks.... I ain't content in the slightest but what choice have I got?... It's their place, at the end of the day. (Wilson)

The way that's useful for me is manipulation.... Being summat you're not, most of the time. Letting them think that you're this good person, and you do this to help other people. It's knowing what to say, when to say it. Playing the system. When I went to sentence planning, and he asked me how I thought about my victims, I knew what he wanted to hear. I says to him, 'I do feel sorry for my victims, and I'd like to have a chance to apologise to them'. But deep down, I didn't give a fuck.... You've got to make sure that you're seen how you want to be seen.... It's an act, I suppose, because I wouldn't say I'm an angel on the landing. [But] that's how I want them to see me. Because it'll all go [well] for me in the end, when it comes to [them] writing reports. (Leon)

As these quotations show, reform and contrition were acted out strategically to accelerate progression through the system. Crucially, this was not the submission to power found among *pragmatists* and *stoics*. By actively deceiving the system and playing the game to their own advantage rather than yielding to institutional dominance, *players* could present themselves as agents rather than objects of power. 'It's their hand, but you play it your way', one prisoner summarized (fieldwork notes). They were not the only prisoners keen to be released as early as possible, nor were they unique in their cynicism about the prison's normative basis. However, their antagonistic orientation towards the prison was such that they perceived release as something that the system sought to deny them, and whose achievement therefore represented a triumph over the institution:

> I don't want to give [officers] or the system the excuse to keep me in longer. That's the reason I don't misbehave. Because I see that as a loss, a defeat, to do an hour longer than [the day of] my release. And until I'm out of the gates and see him on the street, then that's a proper victory. In the prison, it's worthless. I have the last laugh because eventually I'll be going out of the gate. (Stephen)

Players could offset the indignity of their apparent subservience by defining their superficial compliance as a temporary measure that would reap long-term dividends. Isaac recounted the same logic: 'Everything I do in here, I make sure I think: "it's not about in here, it's about outside".' Through such terms, *players* constructed their behaviour as defensively oppositional and resistant: not being 'broken' by prison (Wilson), not becoming 'one of their success stories' (Stephen), doing 'whatever it takes' to survive (Paul). Acts that appeared trivial or conformist were re-symbolized as marks of agency and autonomy. Thus, by closing their cell doors before officers did so for them, *players* could appear compliant to staff while retaining their sense of personal power: 'I am being compliant, but I'm not being told to do something. I won't give them the pleasure of banging me up.' While many prisoners highlighted the prison's overwhelming dominance, *players* emphasized their agency and autonomy:

> I chose to work in that workshop. No-one forced me. I could stay in my cell. Most of the things they say you're forced [to do], well I don't look at it like that, I do it because I want to do it. I could just stay in my cell. If I wanted to rebel and I wanted to prove [something] to everyone I would do. So, yes, there's rules but only if you want to abide by them. You've still got choice. You've got a choice whether you want to take drugs or not, whether you want to eat or not, what you eat—you've still got a choice of menu. (Paul)

Certainly, *players* sought out jobs and activities for strategic reasons. Some took up vocational training to comply with sentence plans, but did so with contrived enthusiasm. Some became Listeners with highly cynical motives, either to appear pro-social or to exploit the trust and freedom that the position involved. Others gained jobs on their wings that allowed the frontstage performance of effort while facilitating backstage trade:

You're cleaning, mopping, sweeping, doing whatever they say. You finish your work, you then start doing what you're doing: double-bubble, selling drugs whatever.[33] You show them that you're willing to do the work and you're polite; whatever else you do in your own time is nothing to do with them. (Paul)

As this explanation implied, *players* were aware of those domains where their behaviour was most under scrutiny. VJ confirmed that, with a little care, it was possible to combine surface compliance with surreptitious illicit activity: 'If you're on a parole sentence, do all the courses they offer you, don't get too mixed up with people. You can [still] do what you're doing, but keep yourself to yourself. And you just go home.' For most *players* though, wing jobs symbolized subservience and had value only in specific circumstances. Thus, after obtaining a good parole report, Paul's efforts at the servery diminished considerably—'they kicked me off because I didn't really care no more'—after which he eventually acquired a post in the work area most suited to drug distribution, alongside several other *players*. As Ashley summarized—with characteristic bravado—'I don't come to jail and work. I sell drugs in prison. I scam and deal.'

Trade was only one of many forms of hidden resistance in which *players* engaged, and which gave them various forms of gratification. Most other prisoners expressed resentment about petty rules, poor treatment, and systemic inefficiency. These frustrations tended to be reactive and, in the face of the prison's overwhelming power, they were generally suppressed. In contrast, *players* held values that placed them in everyday, ideological opposition to the establishment and its staff. Behind façades of conformity and despite their relative powerlessness, they did not seek to contain these values. Where *stoics* were resigned to their own resignation, *players* were dedicated to resistance. To counteract penal power, they worked in its margins, outside its disciplinary gaze, or using its

[33] Double-bubble: lending or borrowing goods at high rates of interest (see Chapter 8)

own mechanisms of control and compliance. This was not just frustration with the system, but often contempt for what it symbolized and an active commitment to defiance: 'I know there's nothing I can do to change my routine each day', said Pierce, 'but give me half the chance to do something I shouldn't and get away with it, and I'll do it'. Stephen expressed similar sentiments of generalized opposition and barely contained hatred: 'I do the bare minimum. All the silly things you have to do here, them daft little rules. But given the opportunity, I would break every rule they'd got.'

In relation to uniformed staff, *players* harboured views that were far more hostile, rigid, and categorical than those of other prisoners. They expressed little sympathy or understanding for officers—'they've got a choice [to] be here, I haven't' (Paul)—and although they disliked some less than others, even these officers were branded 'dumb and stupid—that's why they're in this job' (Ashley). At their most extreme, views towards officers involved violent fantasies of revenge:

Every time an officer gives me an order I want to smash his face in. I just want to push their face into the back of their skull. With a [female officer] I want to kick her fanny up into her brains when they give me an order: 'who the fuck are you talking to?' (Ashley)

Taking orders was a particularly galling dimension of imprisonment for *players*, reflecting not just their anti-authority feelings but also the preoccupation with 'respect' that their life stories emphasized repeatedly. To counteract this resentment, they used a number of symbolic inversions to prove their superiority. Custodial work was portrayed as mindless, subservient, and amoral:

Most of the people in prison are here for trying to get money. [Officers are] here for the same reason, they're no different from us. The only difference is that when we finish our sentence we go home, they come in every day. I wouldn't come here by choice. I know in my heart I'm above them because the job in here that they do is no different to being in prison yourself. They're bored out their skull just like we are. They've got to open our door and shut our door, go on counting: what kind of brains does that take?

Through such denunciations, *players* reduced the moral distance between themselves and their captors while reversing the arrangements of power and status that applied within the prison. On these terms officers were socially beneath them. They were people who, outside prison, *players* disdained and would not mix with.

Male officers were 'bullied at school', and used their power to seek revenge on more powerful, charismatic men. Female officers were portrayed as sexual failures who used their position to punish men or exploit their sexual desperation. Given the scripts of masculine potency that most *players* presented—and since absolute victories over officers were hard to achieve—it was not surprising that *players* advanced such inversions of power, status, and masculinity. 'Out on the road, none of these guys could tell me shit', Wilson declared. 'They would humble themselves if we were on road. It's only because we're in here that they've got the balls of King Kong.' 'I don't class them as men', said Ashley. 'I mean, who wants a job opening doors for arseholes all fucking day long? They're weak. They are weak.' Fantasies of revenge were common: 'I'll smile at them if that's what it takes for me to get through my sentence comfortably', said Ashley. 'But woe betide, if I bump into you outside, because it's your turn to smile. You smile for me now.'

Governors received little less hostility: 'a bunch of wankers' (Wilson); 'they're all arseholes, they ain't got a clue' (Kieran). Ashley described them as 'pricks in suits', worse than officers, 'because they're just not with the real world [yet] they've got this image that they're big and bad and hard.... It galls me to think about it.' Masculine inversions were significant here. Governors were considered naïve frauds, who would struggle in the environs that *players* had mastered and were powerful only in the safe haven of the prison. Some staff were seen as benign—in particular, education staff and some gym officers. On the whole though, *players* bracketed together all prison employees as representatives of the system to which they were opposed and which they considered an appendage of state authority. 'They're all just police', said VJ. For Wilson, psychologists were 'people trying to fuck with your head', drug counsellors could not be trusted, and he was 'no more of a criminal than the government and the police—they have orgies, they're high all the time, smoking spliffs with them posh selves—it's two-faced'.

In contrast to most prisoners, *players* made few distinctions between male and female officers (see also Crewe 2006a). As was consistent with their trenchant, anti-authority views, for *players*, role trumped gender as the primary basis for judgment. They saw 'the uniform before the female' (Stephen), and were the prisoners least likely to express protective or chivalrous views. Female officers who took 'a man's wage', should expect to take a 'man's beating' (Riz) if they overstepped the line of acceptable practice. Wilson explained that he would intervene to stop a female officer from being attacked, 'not for the sake of her; more for my sake—it looks good'. Masculinity was asserted through claims to be impervious to the social and sexual charms of female officers. Whereas some prisoners flirted with female officers to affirm to themselves that they retained sexual charm, *players* were more likely to try to cultivate sexual relationships, not only to satisfy their desires, but as a way of exerting masculine dominance and corrupting staff into aiding illicit trade.

In other respects, the relationships between *players* and officers ranged considerably, from barely concealed hostility to feigned friendship. *Players* were skilled exploiters of officer discretion and manipulated the blurred lines about which other prisoners complained, as Fin recounted:

Getting out of my cell, I'd say: 'well that screw said I could come out', knowing that the screw's not going to be on for another couple of days. Getting extra dinner or extra brew, saying: 'you didn't give me one' when I've already given it to somebody or taken it upstairs to my cell.

Some *players* developed disingenuously friendly relationships with officers to appear pro-social and achieve their ends. 'The more screws on my side the better it is for me', said Wilson. 'I've been caught with a razor and I should get a strike for that, but because I've got a relationship with them they let me off, they just take it away'. He was always careful to apologize when he lost his temper, so that such slips would be seen as 'out of character'. Morgan described how years within state institutions—children's homes, as well as custodial institutions—had educated him in the art of fake charm and manipulation:

If I want something off the officers, I know how to act. I've been playing the system for years.... I just humour them, say 'have a safe journey home' and 'are you alright?'. And then if I need anything I can say 'do this for me, sort this application out for me'—this job [for example]. When they shut me door at night, I'll say 'safe journey home', and just have a joke with them. And if it's hot: 'are you having a barbecue this weekend?' Behind it, I couldn't care less if they had a crash on the way home.

Such strategies of public civility and deference, accompanied by concealed dissent, were reported by a number of prisoners. Isaac explained that: 'if they say the grass is blue, then grass is blue. When you get behind your door, grass is green. That's the way you have to be. [...] You have to give them a bit extra. But I still like to mess about.' 'I've said 'yes sir, no sir, three bags full sir', said Asif. 'But when I've needed to be cunning and conniving, I've had to be.' This was not the resigned compliance of *stoics*. In their frontstage performances, *players* exhibited more commitment and enthusiasm than *stoics* could muster. In their backstage transcripts and transactions, they were more bitter and resistant than *stoics* could care to be or risk. Rather, this was a form of strategic reciprocity—an act of interpersonal respect designed to obtain returns, but committed without normative sincerity.[34]

The returns sought by some *players* were considerably more serious than others. Some merely sought minor perks or positive reports. Others tried to persuade staff to import goods by fashioning the semblance of friendship, and making requests that were initially fairly harmless.

Be friendly with them, have a laugh, but then put a little bit of pressure on them: 'that whisky you've got.'... I got into football with him, and I says 'I'll get you some tickets to go and see Arsenal and you get me some things in, surely you can do that once or twice'. (Leon)

Such requests were soon intensified, and were backed by threats. Here, prisoners used several forms of power normally used against them (threat, reward, and conditioning) to subvert the terms of power (see Chapter 8).

Players struggled to contain their feelings, and to behave docilely and obediently, particularly when they felt provoked or belittled. But unlike *pragmatists*, whose outbursts were uncontrolled and often misdirected, *players* channelled their frustrations to hug the boundaries of lawful conduct. Orders were 'misheard' or 'misunderstood'. Hints were dropped about the pleasures of resistant activity: '[An officer will say] "what do you know about [the false alarm bells]?"—"I don't know nothing, I'm just saying it's keeping you lot busy isn't it, running up and down"' (Paul). Insults were shouted from concealed positions, with unclear targets, or with sufficient ambiguity to be defendable ('you really love this job, don't you?'). Tone and manner were managed carefully:

You put them down in front of everyone. You don't raise your voice, you don't swear at them, you don't do anything they can nick you for. They know you're putting them down and everyone else knows you're putting them down. But if they was to put it on paper they'd make themselves look stupid. (Pierce)

[34] Officers were sometimes aware when they were being manipulated, and sometimes suspected so even when they were not.

While most prisoners followed even those orders whose legitimacy they doubted, a minority of *players* were prepared to stand up for those rights to which they were entitled, even when (and sometimes because) doing so was likely to provoke wing officers. Again though, resistance was constituted with forethought and care:

I will [only] go so far. Like the banging up scenario, I know I'm right. I don't have to be in my cell till half past. I don't care what they say because I know you can't nick me. You can hate me, you can say I'm a trouble-maker, but you can't do me nothing, so I'll take that to the limit. I'll stay out till twenty-nine minutes past then go in my cell and I know you're pissed off and I know if you could nick me you would, but you can't. (Paul)

Other forms of resistance could be committed semi-covertly, or—since *players* tended to be relatively powerful prisoners who could pay others to carry out their wishes—*in absentia*. Fire alarms could be activated by blowing smoke into them; cells could be set on fire or flooded. Such acts aimed to make life difficult for officers, to aggravate them and wear down their morale. They also demonstrated to officers that they should not take co-operation for granted.

Strategies of this kind—the proficient performance of ignorance, borderline provocation, the pushing of rule boundaries, and so on—required levels of bluff, organization, and intelligence that not all prisoners possessed. Furthermore, in being relatively open forms of dissent, they carried considerable risk. *Players* who wanted positive reports adopted more cautious methods to contest staff decisions. Although they could not always bring themselves to act in the ways required to become enhanced prisoners, nor did they break rules or exhibit hostility overtly. Threats to take up issues through legal channels were delivered with sufficient politeness to provide a protective veneer of submission. *Players* also counter-deployed in their favour the tools by which they were censured and regulated:

I write everything down. They say 'the pen is mightier than the sword', and they'll try and damage you with the pen. I've got to use the same weapon. I defend myself with the pen. If I see something, I will challenge it and say: 'if you're going to make an accusation or remark, substantiate your claims and I'll substantiate why your claims are wrong'. (Elliott)

Through such practices, *players* illustrated how, in a system based on documentation, hidden transcripts mattered less than the public simulation of compliance: 'it's how it looks on paper',

Elliott continued. 'It might not be a true reflection of who you are, but if you play the game then they've got no reason on you'. Stephen articulated similar sentiments:

The first thing they put down about me are 'polite' and 'compliant', two important words, and that's what matters. I might walk away and say 'wanker', but as long as they don't hear it, then there's no harm done.... A weapon that staff can use against you is that they'll smile and talk and call you by your first name, and then they'll go into the office and write something bad about you. Once I learned that, I never give them the opportunity to do that to me. Even though they might be sat behind their desk, knowing that I just disabled the windows or whatever.

Other *players* used these arguments in relation to illicit trade. 'They suspect me of many things—being involved in drugs transactions—but without proof, unless you catch me.... That's the whole game of prison' (Paul). Although they walked a risky line, and were unlikely to be given the benefit of doubt in decisions that involved discretion, *players* benefited from the burden of proof that bureaucratic demands for accountability and transparency necessitated. Thus, even public masks could slip a little if prisoners could still maintain documentary transcripts of compliance.

It was because *players* were so preoccupied with interpersonal power that officers were the primary focus of their resistance, and the main targets for their transcripts of resentment. 'However, 'the system' was also a source of frustration. To achieve their ends against it and combat what they saw as systemic stupidity, *Players* applied a number of strategies of manipulation and counter-discourse. First, some *players* capitalized on the prison's attempts to achieve greater legitimacy by exploiting its sensitivity to claims of racial discrimination. One prisoner fought to get soy sauce placed on the prison's canteen list by arguing that it was 'an ethnic product' and that its absence was 'a race issue'. Wilson recounted another incident where he had mobilized race strategically.

He spoke out of turn, so I've gone, 'I'm not going to be talked down to like that. Give me a form and I'll put in a racial complaint in about you right now'. And when I came back later he said, 'sorry about this morning'. He didn't want a report in so he had to humble himself. (Wilson)

Second, some *players*—and some disillusioned *pragmatists*—drew on human rights discourse to dispute orders.

If it's something like banging up, that's just the general rules, which you've been told when you come in. But if an officer asks you to clean up mess which ain't yours, you're in your rights to say 'no, it's not my mess and I don't want to do it'. And they can't make you. (Jordan)

These men were more aware than most prisoners of their rights and were more vocal in demanding institutional answers when the prison did not meet its obligations. As VJ noted, 'I'm entitled to exercise, so I'm entitled to an explanation if it's cancelled'. Grievance procedures could be exploited to turn the prison's rules against it.

A third means of counter-discourse was to exploit the prison's aversion to risk and its duty of care. Prisoners could rid wings of their rivals by hinting to staff that others on the wing were preparing an assault—a strategy that achieved its primary goal while also promoting an image of pro-social concern. Prisoners who did not want to cell-share could claim mental instability or pretend to be violent racists. As one officer noted, 'you'd have to take that threat as being real, and you'd have to work accordingly. You might know it's manipulation, but you can't ignore it.' Here, like staff, *players* sought to resist not by expressing their own voices, but by ventriloquizing their interests through the mouths of others.

The prison's rehabilitative ambitions were also open to manipulation. Fourth then, many prisoners believed that the best way to advance through the system was to show improvement, by 'acting up' at the start of the sentence and then improving one's conduct over time. Some manufactured histories of drug addiction in order to be seen as 'victims' that the prison could then claim to repair. Paul elucidated this logic:

I said that I was a crackhead and I only sold drugs to maintain my habit, which was a lie, but it worked. When you come to prison, you have to have something to blame, something to correct. Their job now is to try and help me address my drug problem. [It] Helps you get parole and stuff. Because [in their eyes] they have rehabilitated me. As far as they were concerned, I was a raving junkie when I came to prison and now I'm not. If I come to prison and say: 'I sell drugs cos I like money' that would never work. You can't stop me from wanting money. If I said: 'I don't take drugs, I don't drink, I haven't got an anger problem, I just sell drugs' they'd say: 'Well how are we going to do this?'

Such strategies subverted the prison's progressive ideals. They also corrupted institutional data in ways that falsely affirmed its priorities.

Offending behaviour programmes were also exploited for unintended yields. Although *players* obliged the prison by attending whatever courses were required, they did so with cynicism and contempt, regarding them as empty lessons that served only to legitimate imprisonment to a wider public. They feigned interest, commitment, and change, parroting the requisite language without inner conviction, and absorbing what they could for oppositional purposes. As Ashley scoffed: '[It's] given me a bit more knowledge, I know a bit more about the system, you've just tooled me up for more bullshit when I get out there.' The prison's rehabilitative aims were either summarily dismissed—'I think they don't really give a shit' (Wilson)—or they were ridiculed as irrelevant to the criminal lifestyles that *players* expected to resume on release. Like Ashley, most *players* could not stomach the tedium or pay of mainstream work—especially when placed in comparison to the lifestyles they could afford through criminal activity. Imprisonment did little to inculcate them with 'pro-social' values, indeed, the opposite was often the case. As Wilson said: 'I hate the system even more now, definitely hate the police more than I did in the first place. I hate authority even more now.'

The establishment's operational imperatives and procedures could also be turned against it. In particular, the prison's need to keep the segregation block as empty as possible was a potential source of leverage. Refusing to bang up, threatening a member of staff, or claiming to fear for one's safety meant being taken to 'the block', at which point one's negotiating power could be considerable. 'They don't like keeping you [there]', said Darren. 'They'll come and offer you jails. And if it's not the one you want you go "no, I'm staying here". You're holding a gun to their heads. They give in, in the end.'

Likewise, the obligation for a governor and medical practitioner to make daily visits to segregated prisoners provided a potential short-cut to influential personnel who were otherwise difficult to see. Indeed, the disdain that *players* had for the power and efficacy of officers and the inefficiency of the application system were such that, to chase up their concerns, they often tried to bypass wing procedures, both formal and informal. As Amar stressed: 'you have to go straight to the head. You have to physically and verbally talk to someone. They can't see a person on paper, they can't see your needs on paper.'

Finding such shortcuts required a certain amount of prison nous. *Players* were adept at such tactics—at working both *around* and *within* official procedures. Those who wanted to get to the prison's reception and distribution centre would make appointments to go to the healthcare centre nearby and make their way from there. Pierce explained a similar method that he had used to jump the queue to see a dentist:

Instead of saying that I wanted to see the dentist, I knew that the dentist comes in every Friday. So on the Thursday when I came back from gym, I said: 'I've got to see the doctor'. And because it's a gym injury, they've got to send you to the doctor. I said: 'I've got a real bad toothache'. And she said: 'Oh, you need a dentist'. So she give me a couple of painkillers for that night, and said: 'I'll put you down for the dentist tomorrow'. So instead of waiting six weeks, I got to see him the next day.

Other *players* took advantage of the goodwill of civilian staff, such as drug counsellors, workshop instructors, and education staff. 'Blagging' them included faking distress to try to gain support for changing wing or simply charming teachers to bring biscuits to their classes. Gaining the support of psychologists demanded special performances:

I get to know them straightaway, I introduce myself. If somebody's got to write a report about you later on, you're best at least communicating with them. It's like juggling. With a psychologist, you might want to come across as being a bit weak and timid. But on the wing, if you come across like that, the screws don't like you very much. If you're in for a violent offence, they expect you to be pretty solid. (Stephen)

There were also means of avoiding, fooling, or escaping mechanisms of compliance and punishment. Some *players* excelled in beating disciplinary charges or complicating adjudication procedures (and in advising others how to do so), for example, by exploiting technicalities, delaying procedures or calling for McKenzie friends.[35] Many boasted of their ability to hoodwink drug tests, by corrupting urine samples, paying other prisoners to claim they had spiked their food with drugs, or substituting someone else's urine for their own. Such methods—the subjects

[35] A McKenzie friend is a prisoner or member of prison staff who can be chosen to assist and advise a prisoner during a disciplinary hearing if he (or she) has no other representation.

of much bravado and one-upmanship—often failed. Nonetheless, *players* had further means of complicating proceedings:

[If the test proves positive] They've got to send it off to be analysed. That takes a week. Then it comes back, I'll send it off again for a second analysis, which takes another week. Then when they send it back, and they say it's still positive, 'I'm not happy with that. I want to send it to my own scientist', so I'll contact my solicitor.... (Ashley)

Again, such approaches required a confident knowledge of prison rules and personal rights. Only some prisoners were sufficiently shrewd and self-assured to adopt them with the appropriate level of assertiveness.

The final, and perhaps the most significant, mode of resistance took the form of illicit trade. This ranged from the minor lending that many other prisoners did to 'get by', to more organized and significant activities such as drug dealing, and stealing from workshops and kitchens. For *players*, such pursuits served a number of purposes that were consistent with their behaviour outside prison. They satisfied the drive to maintain control of the social milieu: 'even though they've took my freedom away, they can't take away my freedom on the fucking landings. I'm still in control of my environment', Ashley boasted. They allowed *players* to maintain the status, self-image, and lifestyle to which they were accustomed outside, albeit in relative terms. Paul explained that:

Even in prison it's all about money. You just live on less in here. Most of the things you need to get by you can afford but it's like in life: it's nice to have a bit more than you need. Like phonecards, you can maybe survive on two but it would be better with eight or ten. It's your aims isn't it, it's how much you want, how much you are willing to settle for, isn't it? You can get by, a lot of people get by and then there's people that don't get by and end up borrowing and I've always rather been the person that [lends] than be a borrower.

The money and power that could be accumulated from prison drug dealing was considerable (see Crewe 2006b). Ashley argued that it enabled him to live 'a lot better than the enhanced prisoner', without having to comply in the manner required to earn this official status. It also meant that he could continue to provide for his children, and could 'keep my brain active', a benefit that several other *players* noted. Such motives flagged up some important psychological functions of *sub rosa* activity. For prisoners with oppositional attitudes, it also represented, in fairly explicit terms, a subversion of institutional dominance and a personal triumph over the apparent supremacy of custodial staff. Paul claimed to flaunt his activities to staff (see Crewe 2006b), knowing that, without proof of his misconduct, the prison had a limited capacity to punish him:

They would always say: 'What are you up to today? What drugs have you got?' I'd say, 'Everything, what do you want?' [Laughs]. They'd say 'we'll get you'—I'd say 'yeah, keep on trying'.

Ashley's testimony offered a similar celebration of illicit activity:

I get my victories by selling drugs. They pay me £11 a week. I live well above that. I can have what I want.... I don't like to just survive. Just surviving is having what the officers say you can have. I like to have plenty. If they say I can have an ounce of burn, I like to have two ounces. The meal that they give me—I've got a guy in the kitchen who's bringing me three times as much food, I can't even eat it all.... And that's enough victory for me. When a screw comes in my pad and sees my pad overflowing with food and tobacco and just everything, that's good enough for me. Just to let them know 'you can't stop me'. No matter how much you say I can spend, I'll have more than that. [And] I like to come into their world and make money underneath their noses. They couldn't come into my world. They wouldn't survive two seconds in my world. Man to man, in a dog's world, they wouldn't survive a second. But I can survive in their environment very well.

Through such terms, *players* presented themselves as above prison staff, unmarked by the prison experience, and undefeated by the ultimate aims of imprisonment.[36] They mocked peers who were subservient to the regime or who were unable to channel their frustrations. As Wilson said: 'They've got caveman syndrome or some shit like that. Their style is so old-school, they need to think and act differently.' As suggested here, some forms of resistance were more suited to the times and context than others.

Discussion

Typologies are always approximations of social life and always present distinctions that are more marked and rigid than the messy realities. As well as to flesh out each prisoner 'type', and illuminate the links between adaptations and biographical narratives,

---

[36] Ashley claimed that the only thing he lacked in prison was regular sex.

one aim of providing case examples has been to demonstrate that these types are more than just caricatures. Nonetheless, as exemplars of each adaptive category, these were not typical of the adaptations that most prisoners made. The majority of prisoners could be clearly identified as one type or another, but not all fell cleanly into a single category and there was some degree of bleeding between each adaptive style.

More significantly, many prisoners had 'changed' identity over the course of their sentence or during their prison career. Life stories often revealed behavioural arcs in which involvement in or seclusion from trade and exploitation deepened at certain stages of the sentence or points in the life-stage (Wheeler 1961). For some prisoners, these shifts were strategic. *Players* in particular were conscious of the need to wean themselves off illicit activity as they neared release; adaptation was thus different—at least in degree—in a Cat-B or maximum-security prison.

These arcs also had institutional determinants. The most instructive prisoners in this respect were the *disengaged*: prisoners whose self-interests were no longer yoked to institutional contraptions. While *retreatists* found purpose in the prison through the desire for self-renewal, prisoners whose engagement had been lost during their sentence experienced a dangerous state of anomie and alienation. In the absence of narrative lifeboats, these men could be drawn towards more resistant forms of behaviour, forms that would provide them with meaning and motives. Other slippages occurred across surprising boundaries. Some *enthusiasts* had initially been *players*. But in finding their artificial compliance rewarded in unanticipated ways, they had been converted by their own performances. Kyle provided a striking example:

I was pretending, and then after pretending for so long I sort of drilled it into my own head. They started throwing more trust towards me, and I thought: 'I'm onto a winner [laugh], this is a good thing'. Before, they'd only give me jobs like in the packing workshop—they started giving me more trustworthy jobs. Before, I'd be like Jekyll and Hyde, two different people. Now I'm just me, I find it better.

The opposite trajectory was also possible. Behind the confident optimism of their proclamations, the identities of *enthusiasts* often appeared fragile and unstable. By committing all their existential eggs to one basket—investing in an unambiguously pro-social identity, which left no room for moral failure—they made themselves highly vulnerable. If they could not live up to their own expectations (for example, by succumbing to drug use), or if they encountered immutable obstacles to their ambitions, the grand edifices on which their identities depended collapsed.[37]

A second possibility for these prisoners was that their fixation on personal integrity could turn them from committed supporters of the regime to its most rabidly censorious critics. When *enthusiasts* perceived staff as corrupt or uncaring or saw the system as deficient, righteous indignation became proof of their virtue. In such circumstances, they embraced the moral legitimacy of their punishment, but fiercely resented the hypocrisies and shortcomings of its execution. These were hyper-censorious prisoners— 'crusaders'—who pledged allegiance to pro-social values and made projects of scrutinizing the prison to ensure it matched the integrity of their beliefs. As Scott (1990: 107) notes, this is a particularly powerful form of dissidence: 'The disillusioned mission boy...is always a graver threat to an established religion than the pagans who were never taken in by its promises.'

Other prisoners were in different kinds of transitions. Both Fin and Alexis had been manipulative and rebellious on previous sentences, but were looking to reform their lifestyles and identities. Both had gained character insight from offending behaviour courses, and talked of 'working on themselves' with the prison's encouragement.[38] At the same time, they lacked the inner conviction and absolute certainty that *enthusiasts* exuded. Fin acknowledged that 'as much as I feel I've changed while I've been in here, there will always be a part of me that's programmed to [have a] criminal side'. Alexis pondered that 'everyone's got good and bad, haven't they?' As with *enthusiasts*, the process of self-questioning

---

[37] At the end of my fieldwork period, rumours emerged that Zack was re-using heroin, something that would have shattered the identity that he had constructed around him. It was interesting too that both Ian and Zack described educational attainment as the kind of 'buzz' that drugs used to provide, suggesting that their addictive tendencies may simply have been transposed from one sphere to another.

[38] Such transitions were effectuated by the prison's character and location. Fin and Alexis had both sought out a place at HMP Wellingborough because they knew it was a 'quiet prison', in which they could avoid being caught up in drug culture, prison politics, and the loyalties which would have dragged them into conflict in prisons closer to their homes (see Chapter 6).

and the constant reiteration of personal change were themselves part of the change process. Yet these prisoners retained some suspicion of the prison's 'hidden agendas' (Alexis), particularly when decisions were delayed or went against them. This ambivalence made their conversions partial and precarious. They wanted the prison to recognize their internal struggles and to support their attempts to bring out their 'good side' through reassurance that they were 'doing the right things'. Without such reinforcement, it was all too easy for them to revert to the more resistant behaviours to which they were accustomed, and which gave them more existential security. Highlighting the predictable outcomes that resistance provided, Fin talked of 'a boundary—and when you step over it, you know you're going to get punished'. Alexis deliberated as follows:

There's a battle going on inside me. I do generally wanna sort myself out. I'm trying to get help, and when I can't get that help it's frustrating. Sometimes I think to myself 'would I be better [off] if I went back to where I was and what I was', but then I think of my family. (Alexis)

For these prisoners, the prison and its staff played a crucial role in steering possible futures.[39] Feedback and the nature of their treatment could channel them down what they called the 'right' or 'wrong' path, and could bring out their 'good side' or 'bad side'.[40] The binary language employed here was striking, suggesting an

---

[39] Officers differentiated prisoners in a number of ways. One senior officer divided them into 'players', who looked to make money in prison, 'cons', who wanted to do their sentence with minimum fuss, and 'wannabe players' or 'nobheads', who lacked the means and maturity to be players. Another officer classified prisoners as 'shitbags' who made 'no effort or contribution' within the prison, 'barrack room lawyers', those involved in drugs, either as dealers, users or intermediaries, and 'alrights', who caused no problems or concerns. Another senior officer explained that:

You make a decision in a matter of minutes of speaking to a prisoner what sort of group he falls into. You get the quiet prisoners who aren't a problem. You get other prisoners who are quiet, weak and inadequate and they have victim written all over their forehead. Then you get what I call 'Jack-the-lads'. And then you get your older, sensible prisoners. And then you get your out-and-out shits, and you do very, very quickly put people into those categories.

In summary, most officers classified prisoners in terms of institutional compliance or resistance ('good lads' or 'trouble-makers'), in terms of strength, weakness, use of power, and ability to cope (bullies and victims, including 'fraggles' and 'muppets'), and according to role and involvement in the prison's informal economy.

[40] Many prisoners talked about 'hanging with the wrong crowd', a term that implied moral censure.

almost schizophrenic sense of self. Whether this derived from the terms of the prison's cognitive behavioural courses or from its language of 'basic' and 'enhanced' was hard to decipher. But it left little room for ambiguity, ambivalence, or the benefit of doubt, and invoked a rather simplistic notion of identity. In a context of risk-aversion and where power could be so unforgiving, prisoners who struggled with change had little margin for error, as Alexis complained:

I am gonna make mistakes. But I'm gonna learn from that. I'm not gonna make the same mistake when I do eventually get out. Why should I be punished for making a mistake, a genuine mistake? I haven't gone out of me way to disrupt anything or get meself in trouble—help me put it right, y'know. [...] What do they expect? That you're gonna get up every morning smiling and happy?

The dangers of penal power

Such comments alert us to some of the dangers and ironies of a system with such profound imbalances of power. The first of these relates to the issue of *agency*. Each prisoner type emphasized the degree to which compliance—however shallow—was ultimately 'for me and my benefit' rather than to gratify the prison. This refrain meant different things for different prisoners: for *enthusiasts*, it spoke of an innate goodness that was not just the outcome of institutional compulsion. For other prisoners, the point was to highlight the pragmatic benefits of compliance. Each type made a different virtue out of the same necessity. Likewise, it was important for prisoners to feel that they were changing themselves rather than having change forced upon them. The majority of prisoners defined 'going straight' as a matter of cognitive transformation, an act of individual will rather than social opportunity.[41] In doing so, they portrayed themselves as agents rather than objects of power. In this respect, the subjectifying tendencies of penal power were in some ways highly effective—allowing prisoners to feel responsible for making choices and resolutions that, in reality, they could barely refuse. But for those prisoners who were aware that their decisions were circumscribed by coercive parameters, to resist prescribed

---

[41] Such a definition was consistent with the rational-choice view of offending that most prisoners propounded and which was emblematic of the almost complete absence among prisoners of more radical, politicized interpretations of crime.

options was a tempting means of exhibiting agency. As penal power increases, this temptation may become more potent, not less.

A second outcome of this power surfeit was that legitimate grievances were frequently suppressed. Many prisoners were scared to raise concerns, even when these related to legal rights, entitlements and reasonable expectations of the system—'you can only push so much', noted Tyler. Yet to be passive—to fail to remind officers of their responsibilities, to allow repeated delays in important decisions, or to let yourself be 'brushed off'—also had harmful consequences, particularly in a context where officers took little initiative. Being suitably assertive was difficult:

If you've got a bad attitude around the wing and you go and scream up, you'll be unlikely to get it, but if you don't, and you only rear up once, they go, 'yeah, he'll be alright tomorrow, he'll be back to normal'. (Alexis)

In effect, resistance was redefined to include some matters that prisoners should not have needed to pursue. At the same time, intended forms of resistance either became less overt or took shape in elaborate texts of dishonesty. The surfeit of power thus caused its own problems. As coming chapters show, these ironic outcomes of managerial power—which led to aggression and abuse taking evasive forms—were also germane to the social world of prisoners.

At the institutional level, the implications were complex. For prison administrators, there was a need for more nuanced measures of consent and dissent. The rigour and rigidity of managerial power pushed resistance into clandestine forms: hostility to officers became 'secret' (Paul), rebellion was driven 'underground' (Ashley), and unlawful activity became more surreptitious. Figures on staff assaults and positive drug tests capture these things in deeply limited ways. They are unreliable indicators of normative consent. Order in Wellingborough was cemented by everyday legitimacy, even if, as in all prisons, it was ultimately buttressed by coercive scaffolding. But the primary bases of compliance were personal morality, instrumental pragmatism and fatalistic resignation.

When compliance is achieved through such mechanisms, and when the armoury by which it is sought is so large, it is easy for the normative dimensions of order to be disregarded. The prison's moral mission may be easily neglected when the imperative for smooth governance is so compelling, and when the official transcript of calm efficiency is so important. Managerialism also undermines its own legitimacy if it appears to operate for its own sake while ignoring real needs, or if it pursues targets as ends in themselves. For prisoners in Wellingborough who were marked down as engaged in constructive activity while playing cards in idle workshops, the fetishism of targets was deeply alienating.

Further, if order is the organizational priority, it may be fulfilled at the expense of sincerity, consent, and legitimacy. An excess of power may be more effective in producing hollow performances of commitment than producing genuine contrition or persuading prisoners of the value of change. 'They have got all the power', stated Pierce, 'so you're always just telling people what they want to hear'. To use Scott's (1990: 3) terms, 'the more menacing the power, the thicker the mask'. Many prisoners were adept at rehearsing those scripts demanded of them, but experienced the insistence on such performances as an affront to personal integrity. Other prisoners were in effect punished for speaking unacceptable honesties or acknowledging human frailties, while skilful actors progressed. This too undermined the legitimacy of the system.

Order forged on this basis should give little grounds for confidence. Even when surface compliance predominates, penal order is always fragile. A simple act of insubordination 'pierces the smooth surface of apparent consent' (Scott 1990: 205) and serves as evidence to others that their resentments are shared. Fatalism may appear a solid basis for social stability, but where prisoners feel powerless to alter their circumstances, it may rapidly transmute into despair or desperate rebellion (see Carrabine 2004). As George described it:

A guy on our wing went on hunger strike he got so frustrated. He knew damn well that, if anything, [it] would just delay the decision, because the lifer division would see it as being blackmailed and would stop the process until he came off it. He knew that. But it's just that feeling of frustration, of powerlessness. You feel you've gotta do something just to show that you're not just a bloody cog in the machine.

This attitude of impotence was not shared by all prisoners. *Players* often rehearsed the sociological cliché that staff relied on the co-operation of prisoners to keep order. On D-wing, although prisoners required no cajoling to comply with the regime, their familiarity with prison regulations and their readiness to use legal channels gave them some sense of power over staff. 'We only have as much control as they let us', noted one officer. 'Anything that involves interpreting the rules, they challenge—"you'll be hearing from my solicitor"'.[42] Yet the vast majority of D-wing prisoners perceived themselves as highly compliant, collectively weak, and socially atomized. This attitude was even more apparent elsewhere in the prison. Compromises and trade-offs were everyday occurrences, but they were not the major corruptions that Sykes (1958) regarded as unavoidable. Officers were confident of their dominance and self-assured in their feelings of control (see also Drake 2007). The majority of prisoners were in no doubt that power lay with staff, even if not directly in the hands of officers. Indeed, although prisoners relied on officers to deliver the regime, the staff responsible for the decisions that affected many of them most significantly were beyond their reach. Like officers and governors above them, they felt that they had few means of defining their conditions and were largely submissive in the face of power. By pulling power to the upper layers of the organization, managerialist control mechanisms exacerbated the tendency for all penal strata to feel that power was elsewhere.

Order and Resistance

Resistance and the social context

The tapestry of dissent is more than a compilation of the individual adaptations that I have detailed above. Resistance is constituted through social interaction and it reconstitutes the potential for further action. Minor forms of opposition are, as Scott argues, more than just 'harmless catharsis' (1990: 187). They test the limits of acceptable practice and have the potential to aggregate. In Wellingborough, when individual prisoners stuck pornographic posters on their cell walls, when they moved their furniture into unauthorized arrangements, and when Muslim prisoners began to pray together on the prison landings, they sought to repaint the lines of permissible conduct in ways that would have collective consequences. Resistance is also kindled and sustained within a social community. Practices of defiance are informed by

---

[42] The examples given here were policies that allowed staff to open prisoners' letters and allowed female officers to conduct rubdown searches. It should be noted that only a minority of prisoners were challenging in these ways, though their persistence could make life very difficult for staff.

ideas that circulate within the prisoner world, and their success relies on mass collusion. While the compliant majority may themselves follow rules, they can at the same time instigate, support and delight in the rule violations committed by their peers. When prisoners brew hooch or pilfer from kitchens, they depend on collective complicity.

The reasons why prisoners allowed such infractions to occur— why they did not 'grass', for example—varied considerably, as Chapter 8 discusses. More significantly for current purposes, it is worth tracing the form of social solidarity that existed among Wellingborough prisoners. The social terms that incite and allow oppositional activity can also inhibit it. Where community support for oppositional practices is weak, prisoners with resistant tendencies are discouraged from the individual acts of resistance that require passive collusion (e.g. drug dealing, escape attempts) and from the collective challenges to power which require active support (such as protests). Prisoners in Wellingborough who proposed protests were met with uncomfortable silences, muted enthusiasm, or frank refusals. Whether made sincerely or out of bravado, these propositions—e.g. to refuse *en masse* to lock up, to have a sit-down protest, or to intervene radically on behalf of one's peers—did not progress beyond verbal machinations or lightweight appeals. Petitions about food quality were polite, unthreatening, and occasional. When potentially inflammatory policies were introduced, such as a new pin-phone system, staff were surprised by how passively prisoners accepted them.[43]

There were a number of reasons for this collective passivity. Most prisoners were aware of the long sentences given for 'prison mutiny', a charge introduced following the 1990 disturbances. Most recognized that situational measures made collective protest difficult. Most also saw 'no just cause' (Alfie) for wholesale resistance, in an era when basic rights such as regular phone calls,

---

[43] This was a transition from a phonecard system, which allowed prisoners to call whomever they wanted, to a pin-phone system that required them to specify the numbers they wanted to use. Prisoners resented the policy for three main reasons: first, because it added an extra layer of scrutiny to their contact with the outside world, which for some prisoners included criminal associates; second, because, under the new system, call recipients would be told that the incoming call was from a prisoner; third, because prisoners feared that the removal of phonecards from the internal economy would reduce currency on the wings and make illicit transactions more difficult.

showers, and visits were assured, and when improvements in the physical environment, shifts in the attitudes of officers, and the introduction of a range of privileges had reduced the depriving and confrontational nature of imprisonment. Wellingborough's location within the prison system was also vital. 'In a B-Cat', noted Nathan, 'the outside world's unreal. Your dream is to get out, but it has an unreal quality to it, it has no substance.' Once prisoners reached the Cat-C estate, however, freedom was tangible. Very few prisoners were prepared to risk their release date for the sake of peer solidarity, as Callum's view illustrated:

If I see a screw jumping on somebody's head, I'm not going to get involved, no way. Because I'd be the only one on the wing that did, and I'd be the only other one getting my head stamped on. You see people getting dragged away from visits all the while, but people don't get involved: 'That's his business. I'm going home in four weeks'. [And] there is no way on earth you're going to get me in a protest about anything. There is no point in me getting [added] days to get something sorted for long after I'm gone for somebody else to benefit.

This attitude of prudent individualism was not universal, as Chapter 7 details, but it was the dominant mindset of the prisoner community and found expression in a number of its daily idioms. Common phrases such as 'do what you're doing' captured its values of self-determination and mutual toleration. Such slogans partly reflect the 'situational moral sensibility' that social theorists have identified throughout late-modern societies (Garland 2001a: 88; see also Bauman 2000). In Wellingborough, they were refined by the proximity of freedom: 'Everybody is just greedy for that date to come', Jacob summarized, 'everybody is just doing their time'. As suggested here, for some prisoners, this ethic represented a culture of selfishness and fear: 'Fear of the system. Fear of losing' (Pete). For others, like Alexis, it was a release from the burden of other people's interests and campaigns: 'nowadays, everyone's getting on with their own sentence, instead of doing someone else's'.

Stephen described the culture of atomized self-interest and self-regulation as follows:

It runs itself. They don't need to control anything. Because we all want a quiet life, we all want to get out. It keeps you under control: getting into getting out. [...] I'd like to think that I'd still speak up, but I might not go as far. I might back down if it came to the crunch—if I was gonna end up in the block. [...] The majority of people have got it in their head: 'I'm going home in a few weeks, I'm not interested'.

The proximity of release inflected the tone by which resistance was conceived. Anger and frustration were offset by thoughts of freedom; victory over the system was redefined by many prisoners as 'getting out on time'—a formulation that assumed that the prison wanted to keep prisoners inside for as long as possible. As *players* illustrated, self-esteem could be derived from notions of status in the outside community, a rationalization that was more difficult higher up the system. As Isaac stated, by the Cat-C stage of the sentence, 'everything's about outside'.

While diluted by the prospect of freedom, solidarity was also splintered by the everyday incentives through which prisoners were addressed. First, everyone had more to lose from collective involvement. Second, the IEP scheme differentiated prisoners' lifestyles so that they were rarely fighting the same battles. In the past, everyone had been entitled to the same goods and treatment, minor and strict though these were. This had resulted in clear demarcations between prisoners and staff, and clear solidarities within the prisoner community:

It was 'them' and 'us'. You had nothing, they gave you nothing, there was nothing to take away. (Darren)

Say the rule was that you could have your radio. Everybody had the same. Nobody got any more, nobody got any less. You couldn't lean against a fucking wall—strange—but *everybody* couldn't lean against a wall. You were all the same. Now we're all individuals. That's what's caved in. (Pete)

For many experienced prisoners, the IEP scheme's ambitions to refashion these antagonisms and affiliations represented an underhand attack on the clarity of the inmate identity and the integrity of the prisoner community. Changes in rules now had uneven consequences and policies had differential significance. For example, prisoners who could supplement their meals with large spending allowances cared less than those without such resources about the quality of prison food. In such respects, prisoners walked 'their own little avenues' (Dave), pursuing their interests as individuals. There were fewer issues around which to unite, and, even for those prisoners who were inclined to protest, the hope of reciprocal support was diminished. Solidarity can form through alienation or affinity, but the IEP scheme led to decreases in both. It reduced the *basis* of collective identification. Meanwhile, by easing the material deficits of imprisonment through formal channels (rather than allowing them to be alleviated through informal arrangements between prisoners) it also reduced the *need* for peer solidarity.[44]

Specific components of the IEP scheme and the regime also altered the dynamics of prisoner social life, hindering the development of collective culture and dissent. As well as providing diversion, televisions and PlayStations encouraged self-isolation. Some experienced prisoners described in-cell entertainment as a kind of pacifier—'visual Mogadon' (Matt)—and attributed the decline of 'the social prison' to its stultifying effects (see Jewkes 2002):

They're basically just sitting in their cell watching telly. Basically doing nothing. That's how it's changed. At one time you would get a group of lads together and they'd be sitting talking about things, having a laugh, playing dominoes, going down to education. I mean education used to be full at night time. Now you're lucky if you get twenty people. (Den)

Many prisoners recognized that having a television discouraged them from cerebral and social activity, and from the kind of discussions that developed group empathy and consciousness. Situational measures such as the end of communal dining and limits on movement between wings also reduced social mixing.

Peer solidarity was also eroded by the culture of hard drug use that had developed across the prison estate from the late 1980s (see Crewe 2005b; and later chapters). As Stephen detailed, heroin encouraged a range of activities that undermined trust, goodwill, and mutual identification:

Smack—that's what's changed things a lot in prisons. People would never steal from people or grass each other up. Now that's just commonplace: grassing and co-operating with staff.... It's lowered general morals in the prison system. Proper heroin addicts have got no morals, y'know, they'd steal from their mum, they can't be trusted with anything.... So there's a kind of general mistrust around the place. The violence levels have gone right up because of drugs as well, over [debt]. It's hardened people's feelings

[44] The Director General of the Prison Service, Phil Wheatley, had been impressed by histories of anti-terrorism in Northern Ireland which argued that the best way of eroding terrorist influence was to tackle the issues (such as housing provision and crime control) around which grievances could unite and unofficial bodies could provide solutions (Wheatley, pers. comm.). The same principles could be applied to the prison, where the aim was to ensure that prisoners could not (or did not need to) organize around collective issues and to prevent power from coalescing around influential individuals.

towards their fellow prisoners.... The heroin culture has destroyed the humanity that was to other prisoners, that's gone now. That's why I think there's more slashings, because people don't look at each other as humans anymore, especially if they're smackheads—that's all they are: they get that label and they're finished.

Non-users were suspicious of the motives of their peers and were unwilling to promote the interests of strangers. Those prisoners who were involved in the drugs economy were more preoccupied with the acquisition and distribution of heroin than with collective interests or identity. As one prisoner explained: 'drugs have killed the morals of the prison. [Heroin's] a hungry drug: your mind, spirit and emotion are owned by the drug' (fieldwork notes). In such circumstances, collective action was less tenable. 'It's not us against *them* anymore, it's us against *us*', one prisoner argued. Another laughed when asked about loyalty between prisoners: 'the only loyalty here is heroin'. These various forces of individualization influenced all aspects of the prisoner social world, as coming chapters will describe.

While keeping collective opposition in check, these conditions also threatened backstage resistance by creating a climate ripe for informing. Prisoners seeking protection to escape drug-related debt were pushed by staff to reveal the names of drug dealers and suppliers; those looking to avenge market exclusion or exploitation, and those seeking to purge rival traders from the market, were also tempted to inform (see below). Men looking to enhance their living standards or advance through the system could improve their chances by leaking the details of *sub rosa* activity. Such betrayals were perpetrated with the knowledge that the same factors that inhibited resistance also meant that many code violations were not severely punished, as Chapter 8 details. This is not to say that backstage opposition or resistance were rare, or that they were always hidden. But the fragile nature of trust between prisoners contributed significantly to the forms in which opposition and resistance were expressed.

Forms of resistance

One of the foremost aims of this chapter has been to illustrate that, contrary to Foucault's vision, the prison does not produce 'homogenous effects' (1977: 202). Prisoners managed and counteracted power in diverse ways, according to the differential experiences of power that their values, needs and expectations engendered. The motives for resistance and compliance ranged enormously, reflecting very different interests and frustrations, and different perceptions of the location and extent of the prison's legitimacy deficits.

Enthusiasts were disinclined to challenge the terms of a system with which they normatively identified. They were censorious about individual officers and institutional failures, but embraced the ends and means of the system. *Pragmatists* accepted rather than supported the goals and techniques of the prison. To them, the techniques of power were invisible or unalterable. They had no conception of strategic resistance and much to gain from toeing the institutional line. They were more liable than *enthusiasts* to criticize the prison in private and quicker to lose their tempers in public. Nonetheless, the extent of their criticisms was limited, focusing on service delivery, interpersonal disrespect and systemic inefficiency rather than the principles and methods of imprisonment.

In contrast, *stoics* were critical of the terms of the system, in particular, psychological power and the policies that officers implemented. However, they were often sympathetic to officers and tolerant of their everyday treatment and conditions. They recognized that the staff on whom their hopes most relied were beyond their grasp. This was a significant frustration. But *stoics* were also well aware that they were the tools of power, and that to resist too visibly—to relinquish self-control—was tantamount to self-punishment. As a result, their compliance was a matter of discontented resignation. *Retreatists* made no conscious effort to resist, although their indifference to the system threatened its logic of active engagement. A very small number of *disengaged* prisoners practised 'passive dissent' more consciously, asking nothing from the system so as not to 'give them the satisfaction of saying no'. *Players* were more active in their resistant activities and more extreme in their censoriousness. They disparaged officers and disputed both the principles and techniques of the system. For these prisoners, resistance was meaningful, desirable, and beneficial. For others, it was unnecessary, unimaginable, pointless or counter-productive. These different perceptions were indicative of the differential significance of legitimacy, fatalism, self-interest, and coercion in securing individual compliance.

These were very significant differences. However, some general comments can be made about the predominant forms of resistance. Within any social domain, the way that forms of power are combined to establish order creates a broad topography of resistance (Wrong 2002). The institutional environment structures the meanings of and motives for resistance. It makes some forms of assertion more likely than others. Nathan summarized these general tendencies as follows:

> The more authoritarian the prison is, the more violent it is. Because in many ways, it's more *directly* frustrating. Now, don't get me wrong, being in a bureaucratic prison is bloody frustrating. But there's more movement, there's more negotiation possible. When you're in a more directly authoritarian place, where everything's 'no', 'NO', and that's right there in your face, that's more directly frustrating, therefore you get more explosions, more outbursts of violence.

No formula can predict the precise form that resistance will take within a particular context of power. But there are clear links between the aims and techniques of power and the means by which it is defended, subverted, and counteracted. In the past, when the system demanded passivity, it was no surprise that resistance often took the form of active confrontation (see, for example, McVicar 1974; Boyle 1977; Parker 1990; Scraton *et al.* 1991). Violence was provoked by the aggression and indifference of the prison and by corrosive cultures of staff hostility. Now that active engagement is the aim of the system, passivity and performance become more salient forms of subversion. Meanwhile, the prison's bureaucratic organization, its reliance on discretion, its increasing use of psychological power, its more positive staff culture and its enhanced baseline of legitimacy invite manipulation, counter-discourse, censoriousness, and legal challenge.

These are not new styles of resistance. Prisoners have always played games, sought out 'angles', acted out improvement and found means of manipulating the system (see Boyle 1977; King and Elliott 1977; King and McDermott 1988). But the primacy of these modes of counter-conduct and their particular forms reflect the nature and organization of contemporary penal power. Resistant attention is directed at 'the system' as much as 'the landings'. Meanwhile, the almost total absence of organized or collective resistance speaks, in part, to the way that power has been designed to individualize prisoners, by addressing their individual interests and differentiating their needs. Prisoners did not resist for different reasons, but almost all had a relatively individualistic attitude —or only limited loyalties (see Chapter 7). Even those with solidary inclinations recognized the futility of attempting organized dissent in such an atomized culture, where support could not be relied upon.

Resistance has been individualized accordingly. The collective tactics of mockery and re-signification used in other penal contexts had little such purpose in Wellingborough (c.f. McEvoy 2001; Buntman 2003). Likewise, when prisoners used the law to pursue their grievances, although their efforts had collective consequences, they were undertaken for personal rather than collective ends. Few prisoners expressed the kinds of political conceptions of status or the shared notions of identity on which collective resistance is normally founded.

Lacking both the options and the motives for collective assertion, prisoners generally pursued their ends through individual staff and individualized strategies.

Everyone is in different circumstances, everybody wants something different, so instead of going to the screws as a whole, saying 'We're changing this and that', you get on friendly-ish terms with one or two of them, you sort of make arrangements. You can't push them as a group, you do it on a personal level. (Callum)

Connections with individual officers were sometimes based on genuine affection or affiliation. But they were also sought out to gain favours and bypass bureaucratic obstacles (e.g. seek job transfers, expedite the passing on of handed-in items). This strategy—cultivating a relationship and 'sticking with [it] until he's got it done' (Jacob)—was encouraged by the nature of staff power. Officers were not a homogenous bloc, united in style and severity. Personalities differed, as did the ways that officers used authority and discretion. Prisoners looked for natural affinities, pursued 'good screws', who could be relied upon to make extra effort, or searched for chinks in staff consistency. For officers, discretionary culture could be a burden, leaving them feeling powerless and compromised, without clear boundaries through which to gauge requests.

When grievances were shared and prisoners were united in their interests, they remained reluctant to work collectively. Instead, as Kyle illustrated, they were more likely to achieve group goals by working as un-coordinated individuals:

Everyone has a little nibble. It's like one member of the lion family will go for the throat, one will go for back leg, one for the stomach—everyone has a limited ability for something. I can't think of one where we've all gone for the same part of the body, I've never seen that happen. They'll all have a little nibble, not at the same time, [and will] run off with the bit they've got.

Resistance and pressure were not the organized and ostentatious assertions of power documented in some studies of prison life (Jacobs 1977; McEvoy 2001). They were unorganized, furtive, disguised: *concealments* of power. Even prisoners who were openly seditious—disputing prison decisions or challenging officers in their use of power—were careful not to be labelled 'ringleaders' or provocateurs. Visible agitators lasted little time in Cat-C conditions. This almost total absence of active rebellion was striking.

The most visible forms of resistance did not come from the prisoners with the most resistant sentiments. They came from those prisoners least capable of either disguising their frustrations or identifying alternative channels through which to resolve them. Very occasional dirty protests were more often acts of despair than concerted strategic decisions (c.f. McEvoy 2001). Other open expressions of dissent—'kicking off' and 'smashing up'— were effective methods of gaining attention and resolving some issues. Ultimately though, they were counter-productive, resulting in long-term costs that outweighed their short-term benefits. In this respect, the losers of the system were the *pragmatists* who were its most vulnerable members. Prisoners with more guile and experience scorned the naivety of unplanned outbursts. As Paul declared, direct confrontation could always be avoided:

To get nicked in this prison you have to go out your way. In most prisons now you have to be an out and out idiot really [to get nicked]. There's ways and means you can go round and do everything you've got to do and not get into a confrontation.

Illicit activity was also heavily disguised. Prisoners involved in prison drug supply could orchestrate activity from a distance and through less powerful peers (see Chapter 8). As Ashley noted, drug users also had to conceal their consumption: 'When there weren't [drug tests], you could walk around the wing stoned out of your face, and they couldn't do nothing. Now you can't afford to—you're losing bad. You've got to be more devious.'

Moreover, with trust between prisoners so low, dissonant practices and opinions were not always exhibited or revealed, even in the absence of staff. Although most prisoners disclosed hostility among their peers, a minority sustained their performances throughout the public spaces of the prison. Self-regulation applied not just in the face of the system, but also in relations with other prisoners.

When this noisy guy moved on, people said 'look, I'll just put up with it. I'll put my headphones on. I'll turn my telly up louder. I don't want to get involved'. Whereas ten years ago, when they were first sentenced, they'd have been in there smashing the guy up. (Stephen)

As coming chapters will detail, most prisoners readily admitted that, with release in their sights, they bit their tongues, unclenched their fists, and restricted their personal loyalties. These forms of self-regulation aggregated into a culture of relative indifference, recursively fuelling feelings of social fatalism. As such, they formed part of the social dynamic of institutional order.

Order and social relations

In the prisons described by Sykes and Irwin, the social world was a domain of relative autonomy. Within a highly authoritarian system, prisoners were left more or less unhindered or were required to collectively self-govern. 'Order was maintained in Southern prisons [in the US] by elevating some prisoners to trusty positions and giving them power to beat and kill other prisoners and enforce discipline' (Irwin, pers comm.). In prisons in the American North, the administration maintained the institution's perimeter but left convicts to 'virtually run the prison', with a system of leaders taking responsibility for encouraging compliance and brokering peace between prisoners (ibid.). In both cases then, prisoners were essential components of institutional government (Irwin 2005). The focus in research of the time on the codes and hierarchies of the inmate world reflected an era when everyday order was accomplished *through* the prisoner social community. Globally, some prison systems continue to operate along these lines, with officers rarely entering residential spaces and prisoners developing extensive, sovereign subcultures with extended hierarchies of informal power (see e.g. King 2007). In the prisons of England and Wales, however, it is not the collective so much as the self that is expected to self-regulate. Power is not ceded to gangs or powerful individuals. Instead, order is contracted-out to the sphere of the individual.

Nonetheless, order in Wellingborough had social dimensions that supplemented the forces of individual self-government. A common way of 'running' wings in the past was to appoint powerful prisoners as wing cleaners and servery workers, and give them perks in return for them ensuring relative peace among prisoners.[45] In the pre-IEP era, when there were few other ways for prisoners to obtain privileges such as better cells or extra time out-of-cell, this arrangement relied on a number of factors: first, the desirability of illicit incentives; second, the willingness and ability of staff to impart these privileges with relative impunity; and, third, the readiness of staff to turn a blind eye to the illicit violence that resulted when they devolved power to the prisoners supposedly in their charge. In UK prisons, this custom—'using them to do our job for us' (King and McDermott 1990: 462)—has been largely superseded by a belief that 'we [should] do the job we're paid to do: we manage prisoners, we don't use other prisoners to manage on our behalf' (governor, HMP Wellingborough).

This shift is the consequence of a number of developments. First, the IEP scheme has institutionalized the provision of perks, giving them an official and more accountable outlet. Incentives can be gained through co-operation rather than corruption. Second, an anti-bullying policy focus has shifted staff perceptions of how power relations among prisoners should be managed. As one senior officer explained, 'the guy [to whom we] used to say "we'll [help] sort you out if you keep the wing quiet", [now] he's a "bully", and we don't tolerate bullies'. Prisoners obtained influence with staff by being friendly and obedient: 'a decent lad who talks civilly; not a screw-boy, just someone sensible' (senior officer).[46] Third, the empowerment of staff in the mid-1990s encouraged and enabled them to take greater control of the landings. Although a small number of Wellingborough officers extolled the model of delegating power to 'number one prisoners' as easy and effective, most took pride that their hold on power had been tightened. Officers emphasized to prisoners that they had the monopoly of legitimate authority, and that prisoners should not

[45] 'You would have what they would call the "number one" on the landing and then a "number one" on the wing, and you would have a definite pecking order, and if there was a guy playing up on the wing you'd go to the number one and have a word. And the guy would [soon] be walking round with a black eye' (governor, HMP Wellingborough).

[46] A 'screw-boy': a prisoner who is close to or sycophantic towards officers.

take it upon themselves to discipline each other:[47] 'Now, we don't let prisoners sort each other out—we say, "come to us"' (senior officer); '[we say] "if you know who's doing it, let us know, don't sort it out, tell us, and we'll get them off the wing"' (wing officer).[48]

There was some evidence, nonetheless, that staff still sometimes enlisted the coercive capacity of powerful prisoners. When officers circulated threats about 'banging up early', or asked prisoners to 'have a quiet word' with one of their peers, they recognized the possibility that their interventions were endorsing violence: 'people understand the threat and that others will be pissed off if they smash windows again'. One principal officer regularly addressed the most influential prisoners on the wing in order to resolve problems, with a clear understanding that persuasive influence often had coercive foundations.

My expectation was that they would go back and spread the word to the prisoners that I was going to lock them down if this did happen, and I knew that the strong ones would take the people who they knew were doing it to one side and say: 'Look, if I lose my association tonight because of you, I'm going to come and get you tomorrow', type of thing.

Officers claimed that, since violence was not tolerated in such situations, it was highly unlikely that it would result: 'they know that if somebody "fell in the shower" the next day, so to speak, with a black eye, that I will straight away go to them and say: "I know one of you has done [this]"' (ibid.). The line between disseminating information and sanctioning violence was in these situations rather fuzzy. The same was the case when a governor advised senior officers that one way to reduce the amount of litter being thrown out of cell windows was to appoint someone with 'clout' to be in charge of clearing debris from the wing perimeters. Elsewhere, the stimulation of violence was barely concealed.

You let it be known that next time they'll be locked up—[you say:] 'you know who's doing it, just have a word with him but don't let me see it'. You say it out loud, as you're walking along a landing. But you don't [directly] target one prisoner to go and hit another.

---

[47] It could be said—in certain prisons in particular—that what officers hold is *control* rather than confident, legitimate authority, but certainly the yielding of authority to prisoners makes it hard to claim any kind of staff legitimacy.

[48] Prisoners corroborated these claims, contrasting current policy with times when staff would unlock prisoners who were involved in disputes during quiet periods and simply allow them to 'sort things out between them'.

Such procedures were not the norm, nor were they the principal means by which control was achieved. Nonetheless, they pointed to the persistent, low-level involvement of illegitimate devolution in the maintenance of everyday order.

Prisoners employed on the wings as cleaners and servery workers (sometimes referred to as 'trusties', and the nearest equivalent of 'red-bands') provided another mechanism of regulation from within the prisoner community. However, their role was not one of enforcement and their status among their peers was mixed. Picked on most wings by informal polling among regular wing staff, these prisoners were generally strong enough to defy intimidation by others, but were not so strong that they might abuse their power or prove difficult to control. Occasionally, prisoners who were suspected drug dealers were placed in trusted positions so that officers could 'keep an eye' on their activities (with limited success). More often, officers chose prisoners who were dependable, obedient, who might 'tip you the occasional wink', and could be relied upon to act as figures of sense.

These prisoners served as conduits for information rather than direct agents of control. Through them, officers spread a range of messages, from information designed to clear rumours (e.g. about prisoners accused of being sex offenders) to details about regime changes and warnings about the consequences of continued misconduct (e.g. newspapers being thrown out of cell windows): expressed at their most forceful, 'tell that prick that unless he calms down I'm going to have to deal with him' (senior officer).

In the other direction, officers regularly received warnings from wing workers about tensions between prisoners (e.g. problems between cell mates and grumblings about food), minor acts of subversion (e.g. prisoners pressing alarm bells, brewing hooch or breaking windows), and sometimes more serious matters, such as drug dealing and incipient violence. In informing about such matters—often trying to avoid 'naming names'—wing workers often hoped that issues could be handled without resort to formal measures. Here, they partly protected their own interests. Any serious trouble could lead to a temporary lock-down of the wing, and this curtailed their freedoms. But they also acted to some degree as collective peacemakers, helping to smooth out problems that would be hard otherwise to resolve, and serving as mouthpieces for feelings of collective frustration.

In return for their goodwill and assistance, wing workers received a number of illicit but minor perks. These included surplus meals and occasional pouches of tobacco or phonecards. They were also given extra assistance to resolve any problems, more positive reports for things like HDC applications, and 'a bit of leeway' (officer interview) to roam the wings and beyond. Such arrangements made wing positions particularly attractive to *pragmatists*, who coveted everyday incentives, and *enthusiasts*, who sought out trusted jobs to demonstrate their integrity. Prisoners involved in informal trade could capitalize on the relative freedom that wing positions allowed, but the trade-off for this was oversight by staff and the need to subordinate oneself to orders. Only a minority of drug dealers felt able to combine wing work with *sub rosa* activity. Experienced prisoners reported that, since the nature of wing jobs had changed, 'the lads' no longer worked on the servery.

As Max explained, reciprocity was built into relationships between wing workers and officers.

> You can use [the relationship] as a bit of leverage. You say to your personal officer: 'I've done you a favour. I've found you this and that, what are you going to do for me? Are you going to have a good word for my Cat-D, are you going to put in for my enhanced?' It's give and take.

Relationships of this kind lent themselves to informing. Indeed, 'grassing' was a natural outcome of systemic pressures. In particular, the desire among prisoners to obtain early release and the difficulty of doing so through formal channels incited prisoners to promote themselves informally to staff. This mechanism served as a further source of prisoner self-regulation.[49] Experienced prisoners claimed that the frequency of grassing had intensified over the years, eroding interpersonal trust. Whether true or not, the widespread suspicion that grasses were ever-present restricted prohibited activity.

Informants were also cultivated in more formal ways. The prison had over ten 'official' informants, each with their own handling officer. These prisoners had mixed motives, ranging from moral objections to drugs and bullying to self-interested

---

[49] Most officers reported having three or four prisoners who provided information to them in return for low-level assistance e.g. in getting jobs or items from reception.

hopes of reward e.g. obtaining transfers. In effect then, it was not so much powerful prisoners within the inmate hierarchy who were employed to curb the activities of their peers, but prisoners on the lower rungs of the social ladder. These were men who struggled to secure privileges through other means or who resented their more powerful peers. As one governor noted: 'If you've got people prepared to rise to the top of the pecking order, they will have made enemies on the way.'

As the chapters that follow will show in more detail, drugs were one of the main sources of power in the prisoner world. It is therefore unsurprising that they played a major role in determining order, disorder, and the structure of informing. In times of shortage, when drug prices were high, it was debt that most often led to grassing. Prisoners who could not repay their arrears had to go to the segregation unit, where pressure was placed on them to reveal the names of drug dealers. When supply was stable, grassing was more likely to be an outcome of resentment about market exclusion: 'a dealer will say "I'm not selling to you because you didn't pay me last time", so the person dobs him in and says "he won't sell it to me so no-one can have it"' (governor). In times of surplus, informing was less common—'because everybody's happy' (governor). At such times, disputes related to turf wars between dealers over market share.

Like all prisoners involved in illicit activity, drug dealers had much to lose from close policing of the wings. For these prisoners, a peaceful wing meant good business. While violence was woven into the everyday fabric of their trade, and served as a form of market regulation, dealers also discouraged disruptive behaviour if it jeopardized their interests. Activities that attracted the attention of officers, e.g. fighting, commotion and conspicuous commercial traffic, were therefore inhibited. In this respect, dealers had much to gain from maintaining a certain form of everyday order.

It was hard to evaluate whether prison staff colluded in the fragile peace that dealers encouraged. Some prisoners suggested that, at the least, officers were aware of who dealers were and their stabilizing influence:

You can see where all the main heads[50] are on the wing. The screws know where they are, what's happening, what they're doin. They know it's not

---

[50] A 'head': a powerful prisoner, a prisoner with reputation or influence.

them that's kickin anything off on the wing. The wing's quiet because people that bring the wing on top[51] will get hurt, because [the heads] don't need it. (Bradley)

Descriptions of some other establishments—mainly local prisons and prisons with traditional cultures—pointed to a more active employment of drug dealers in the achievement of control:

In [prison x], the main people on the servery are drug dealers and the staff know. [Dealers] get turned a blind eye because they keep the wing quiet. They know that they can't fucking *do somebody in* for debt [but]. They'll give them a slap. But they can't do them in. The staff in there will know whether an inmate will comply just to that edge—[so, a dealer on the servery isn't] an out-and-out thug. He's got a brain, basically. He says 'right, this is the game I'm playing now, and I've got to give [something to staff] for them to give [something to] me. I've got to give them a quiet wing' (Fin).

This was not the picture at Wellingborough, where staff recognized that delegating power to drug dealers meant being complicit in intimidation, exploitation, and drug culture. Inasmuch as prison drug dealers contributed to institutional order, they did so alongside, not in league with, official policies and mechanisms.

The rules by which prisoners negotiated everyday frictions also represented a form of collective self-policing. Although frequently breached, nebulously defined, and differentially enforced, norms about noise, boundaries, and exploitation contributed to the precarious harmony of the wings. In some situations, these norms were agreed explicitly. On many spurs, prisoners decided that in-cell stereos should not be played loudly at weekends until a particular time, to allow everyone to sleep late. Everyday culture thus contributed to order in important and unseen ways. In other respects, the prevention of conflict was a result of interpersonal affiliations. As the chapters that follow will show, prisoners curbed aggressions and hostilities to prevent the escalation of conflict, albeit in different ways according to their adaptive patterns and their resulting social loyalties. This was not order through the prisoner *community* as such, but through a series of interlocking and counterbalancing social relationships. But institutional power primarily

---

[51] 'Bring the wing on top': attract staff attention, cause trouble.

addressed the individual rather than the wider social network, and it was individual rather than collective self-government that was the primary source of order.

Conclusion

This chapter has detailed five main adaptations to the terms of a contemporary prison. These can be summarized as: committed compliance born of personal morality (*enthusiasts*); two forms of resigned, pragmatic compliance based on different states of need and powerlessness (*pragmatists* and *stoics*); passive compliance, founded on personal fatalism (*retreatists*); and feigned compliance—or normative opposition—performed alongside (and as a form of) resistance (*players*). Neo-paternalism was experienced by these prisoners in different ways, due to significant differences in penal predicaments, personal resources, backgrounds, and expectations. Its 'soft', neo-liberal core was harnessed by *enthusiasts*, resented by *stoics*, exploited by *players,* and accepted or submitted to by *pragmatists* and *retreatists*. Material inducements raised legitimacy in the eyes of *pragmatists, enthusiasts,* and *retreatists*, but were perceived by some prisoners as a form of manipulation. The distributive power of officers was more potent for poor coping *pragmatists* than for experienced *stoics*. For prisoners on parole sentences, psychologists rather than uniformed staff were the core agents of control.

The de-coupling of wing staff from the wider system also had various consequences. It encouraged greater empathy and intimacy between prisoners and staff, and this contributed in certain respects to the prison's legitimacy. For some prisoners though, it enabled corruption and collusion. *Players* sought to manipulate friendly relations and exploit inconsistencies. For other prisoners, the discretionary buffer created new aggravations, such as uncertain expectations, which complicated demands for compliance and often felt like 'tests'. Put more summarily, shifts in the nature of power created distinctive frustrations, but the differential experience of power meant that these frustrations also varied. In effect, imprisonment entailed different deprivations for different kinds of prisoners (see Toch 1992): for *pragmatists*, the primary concerns related to safety, security, and material goods; for *stoics*, they were issues of autonomy and self-identity; for *players*, imprisonment challenged assumptions of interpersonal power, masculine status, autonomy, and material comfort; for *retreatists* and *enthusiasts*, external experiences of powerlessness and moral degradation meant that the deprivations of imprisonment took on particular kinds of meaning.

Order was accomplished through this *individualization* of experiences and interests, and through multiple strategies of compliance that targeted active, *individual* subjects (Garland 1977). Although aided by currents within the prisoner world, it did not *rely* on enlisting the influence of individual prisoners or social groupings. Indeed, institutional policies fragmented the prisoner community to the degree that there was little collective power available to harness or accommodate. The strength of a subculture depends upon common plight, mutual reliance, relative isolation and a lack of mobility out of the shared predicament (Scott 1991); these are conditions that a modern Cat-C prison does not ordinarily present. Yet the production of order did not bypass 'the social' completely, relying on tough, faceless governance to stabilize the institution and promote rehabilitation (see DiIulio 1987). Staff-prisoner relationships contributed significantly to smooth governance, making order in part a *relational* achievement. These social dimensions of order are more restricted than those reported in the classic studies, but they remain critical to institutional maintenance, and to the prison's tentative legitimacy (Liebling 2004).

The disaggregation of prisoner interests imprinted and constrained prisoners' loyalties and behaviours in significant ways, but did not do so homogenously or in the absence of other social forces. Institutional pressures to comply with organizational goals and limit their social affiliations acted in tension with structural impulses that simultaneously encouraged prisoners to form social allegiances and relationships. The relative pull of these 'vertical' and 'horizontal' influences reflected differences in prisoners' frustrations, needs, and preoccupations, and structured their differential involvement in the prisoner social world. All prisoners engaged in certain forms of social interaction. As Sykes noted, the prisoner world can only be 'an aggregate rather than a social group, a mass of isolates rather than a society' if prisoners are 'locked forever in their cells, shut off from all intercourse with each other' (1958: 5). Once interaction occurs—however cautiously, under whatever conditions—it creates 'the realities of [a] prison social system' (1958: 6). It is to this social system that the book now turns.

6

The Prisoner Hierarchy

Previous chapters have described the nature of power in HMP Wellingborough and the adaptations that were shaped by the practices and principles of contemporary prison governance. They have shown that prisoners' adjustments to the environment were outcomes of interactions between various forms of penal power—implemented within the particular context of HMP Wellingborough—and the different values, expectations, and ambitions that prisoners carried with them into the establishment. The rest of this book provides an analytic description of the social life and culture of HMP Wellingborough, arguing that the form of this social world was also determined by the prison's inherent conditions, its institutional policies and practices, and the attitudes, orientations, and characteristics that prisoners imported into the prison. This chapter turns specifically to the system of power and status between prisoners. Through a framework that incorporates existing theoretical approaches, it describes the prisoner hierarchy and untangles its determinants and consequences.

In studies influenced by 'indigenous' perspectives, power and status were seen as the outcomes of *structural* and *institutional* factors. Certain behaviours were rewarded and reinforced by official incentives or generated kudos among prisoners because they alleviated the deficits and frustrations of imprisonment. Sykes (1958), for example, argued that the most respected prisoners were men who conformed to codes of behaviour that mitigated collective pains. These men were loyal, generous, and tough without being provocative, for example. Other prisoners accrued power by taking advantage of scarcities in information, goods, and services, or exercised power over their peers as a reactive consequence of threats to their masculine status, autonomy, and personal safety. Among other roles, there were 'merchants' who sold desired commodities at profit, and 'toughs' who strong-armed what they wanted from weaker inmates. The institution stimulated relations of domination and exploitation, as well as behaviours that reaped moral admiration.

Recent works by McEvoy (2001) and Buntman (2003) have likewise suggested that prisoner leadership is defined in relation to changes in institutional cultures and strategies, with certain prisoners ascending internal hierarchies when their values are appropriate to the environment (see also Boyle 1977). Such studies endorse a more dynamic, interactional approach to the analysis of hierarchy than earlier work. Power and status are responsive to shifts in the tone and technique of prison administration, and the needs and values they produce. But they are also conditioned by social and cultural tides *outside the prison*. The significance of these factors has been documented in a range of work which has emphasized how social structures in prison are defined by social movements, cultural values, and notions of power and prestige imported from the community. Irwin and Cressey (1962), for example, differentiated between the status held by professional 'thieves' and the influence acquired by 'convicts', and traced these different forms of power within prisons to criminal experiences and identities outside them. Jacobs (1977) described how the power structure in *Stateville* prison directly reproduced gang structures on the streets of Chicago, with leadership automatically transferred to top-ranking gang members on their entry into custody. Other writers (e.g. Newton 1994) have noted the parallels between hierarchies of masculinity outside prison and hierarchies of power within them. Although little consideration has been given to the role of *biographical experiences* in shaping the terms of status and stigma, these factors also merit attention.

Some comments about definitions should be offered, for, in some studies, little attempt is made to distinguish between power (influence, or the capacity to achieve things) and status (social standing or prestige), or between different forms of 'respect'. In their research on inmate culture, for example, Winfree *et al.* (2002) asked participants to rate offender types 'according to how much respect you would give them', without clarifying what this 'respect' might entail. Clarity is crucial here because the term 'respect' is used in prison in a number of ways. In its first use, it conforms to the Kantian notion that all persons are worthy of respect as a virtue of being human. Respect here is a moral right. It involves an obligation not to treat others as means or with contempt, not to ridicule them, and so on. In Darwall's (1992) schema, this ethic is defined as 'recognition respect', the disposition to take something or someone into account in one's deliberations and regulate one's behaviour accordingly. When prisoners talk of 'treating everyone with respect', they are acknowledging this basic right of others to be taken into due consideration.

Darwall argues that recognition respect is 'essentially a *moral* attitude' (1992: 40, italics added). However, he notes—without much elaboration—that, when 'a boxer talks of having respect for his opponent's left hook and an adventurer of respecting the rapids of the Colorado' (1992: 40), their concerns are primarily *prudential*. The term 'respect' is very often used in this way in prison. It conveys an obligation to restrict one's behaviour towards someone that is based not on moral consideration but rather fear, awe, and other such sentiments. 'Respect' of this kind is offered for the sake of self-protection. When prisoners say that 'you *have* to respect someone', because of their physical potential or social influence, they convey the instrumental nature of this requirement.

A third form of respect is what is commonly thought of as admiration, regard, esteem, or veneration. Darwall calls this 'appraisal respect', and distinguishes it from recognition respect by noting that it involves the positive appraisal of a person's personal qualities or character, not just the recognition of their right to respect as a member of humanity. This kind of respect has normative dimensions, although, as Darwall highlights, it is possible to have appraisal respect for someone's ability (e.g. as a sports player) without having any moral regard for them. In prison, as this chapter explores, the admiration among some prisoners for behaviours that induced fear in effect conflated appraisal and instrumental respect. Nonetheless, this chapter seeks to distinguish conceptually between what could be called recognition respect, instrumental respect, and appraisal respect.

Structural Components of the Prisoner Hierarchy

A number of dimensions of the prisoner hierarchy in Wellingborough related to the intrinsic conditions of prison life. As seemed appropriate in an environment of physical and social compression, appraisal respect was given to men who showed loyalty, sincerity, and respect for personal space and property, who dealt skilfully with prison staff, did not create problems for others, exhibited stoicism in the face of provocation, and upheld high levels of personal hygiene (see Kaminski 2004). As would be expected at this structural level of analysis, the list of respected traits is redolent of Sykes's (1958) description of admired characteristics. These are qualities that have been repeatedly identified as the basis of prison prestige (see, for example, King and Elliott 1977; Winfree *et al.* 2002). As Cameron summarized, the backbone of respectability was to be someone who 'don't cause trouble, keeps his mouth shut, if a problem comes to him, he deals with the matter, [and is] never in need of anything'. In the terms of another prisoner, 'lads are proper, clean, have an aura, know how to have a conversation, and don't get in debt' (fieldwork notes).

Stigma was also structured by intrinsic conditions. The main terms of abuse and derision were reserved for prisoners who struggled to cope with environmental necessities or did not respect the imperatives of collective living. The primary pariahs of the mainstream prisoner community (i.e. where sex-offenders were not openly identified) were 'grasses'. As Chapter 8 details, definitions of grassing were heterogeneous. Despite this variance, to be labelled a grass was to be branded almost indelibly as treacherous and untrustworthy. Grasses could not be trusted to keep the silences required for the prisoner community to sustain its hidden activities. 'Pad-thieves'—prisoners who stole from cells—were denounced for similar reasons. While stealing in the outside community or from the prison could be justified, a prisoner who stole from his peers transgressed a fundamental rule of the prisoner community.

Among the mainstream population, 'fraggle' and 'muppet' were the most common labels of disrespect. Although the terms were often used interchangeably, the former carried an implication of mental fragility or instability: prisoners who 'don't know where they are [or] what they're doing' (Den), who 'ain't got a clue...and don't really learn' (Callum), or who simply 'can't do their bird' (Zack). Prisoners often appreciated that some 'fraggles' simply did not comprehend the boundaries of appropriate social action. They over-reacted to banter and provoked conflict; they discussed trade and conflict with insufficient caution; or they struggled to keep themselves and their cells clean and hygienic. Those who scavenged for tobacco and begged for goods advertised their vulnerability, both in their inability to fend for themselves and their failure to disguise these acts of desperation.

To be a 'muppet' (alternative terms included 'donut', 'numpty' or 'idiot') denoted a range of behaviours. These included 'messing around', having needless 'attitude', moaning excessively, and causing unnecessary trouble e.g. by setting off fire alarms or throwing newspapers out of cell windows. These were acts that had collective consequences, causing general irritation, collective punishment, or 'bringing heat' from staff. The term was also used to characterize prisoners who exaggerated their wealth or criminal credentials. When untrue, such claims were easily falsified by information flows from outside the prison or through narrative flaws that were easily exposed in the prison's compact informational environment. Stories were told with insufficient knowledge, in incompatible ways—'he told one man he done this armed robbery and got a hundred grand, and [he told] the next geezer fifty grand!' (Bradley)—or they were inconsistent with behaviour—'they say "I've got this, I've got that, I've got a Lexus", and then ask you for some burn...' (prisoner, fieldwork notes). To lie in such ways was seen as unnecessary, although such boasts were promoted by the association of affluence with moral status. It was also considered a breach of honesty in a world where identity cues were limited and trust relied on truthfulness. As Bradley noted, 'if they're going to lie to you, what else are they going to do to you?'

Prisoners deemed physically defenceless or lacking in emotional fortitude were also labelled fraggles or muppets. Some prisoners despised weakness as a thing in itself, punishing others for representing the fears that they fought to suppress. These prisoners held the vulnerable responsible for their own persecution. Jordan argued that: 'a victim is someone who *allows* themselves to become a victim. Anybody can be a victim, but anybody can choose not to be as well.' Having 'guts' was inherently admirable, whatever the outcome of their display, as one exchange with Cameron illustrated:

If you was a fraggle, and I was slapping you round the face and you retaliated, I'd respect you a lot more.

You might hit me again.

Yeah, yeah, possibly. But you'd be taught something about hitting, wouldn't you? And I'd respect you a lot more for it. And you'd get respect off loads of other people.

Prisoners repeatedly testified that 'standing up for yourself' was admired whether a fight was won or lost, whereas 'backing down' led to an instant loss of credibility (see Chapter 8). Such views reproduced notions of masculine credibility imported from the streets. These gendered imperatives carried particular intensity in prison, where the social stage was restricted and opportunities to be 'tested' were manifold (Sykes 1958). Weakness was also associated with grassing. Prisoners who lacked courage in their dealings with their peers were assumed to be less resilient to staff pressures to expose illicit activity. If accused of grassing, to put oneself 'on protection' (by asking to be segregated from other prisoners) was deemed an acknowledgement of guilt, whereas to stand up to allegations was to refute them: 'If you come out and stand your ground, then I'll look at you and think "my man can't be an informer, it can't be him". Because he's come out for his beating and he's still there' (VJ). Grassing and weakness were thus mutually associated.

A third source of stigma was heroin use. The majority of prisoners were from communities that had been ravaged by hard drugs. Many had lost family members to drug abuse, had experienced drug-related crime within their families, or had themselves suffered the degradations of addiction. Heroin was seen as a particularly 'dirty' drug that reaped social devastation, and brought out ruthlessness and moral squalor in its users. Zack's description was typical. A heroin addict would 'take the gold teeth out of his dying fucking grandmother's jaw; they're just conniving, manipulative bastards, who'll try and get anything out of anyone just for a fix'. Inside prison, users were repositories for the resentments that prisoners harboured about these activities in the outside world, and, often, for the feelings of shame that they carried about their own past acts while on drugs.

In addition to this, as Chapter 5 noted, heroin was blamed for having 'fucked jail up' (Carlton), dissolving whatever bonds of trust and mutual toleration had pre-dated its widespread appearance in UK prisons from the late 1980s (Atherton and Lloyd 1995; Bond *et al.* 1995; Walker 1995; Duke 2003; Crewe 2005b). 'It's hugely, hugely eroded the relationship between inmates, hugely', said Nathan. 'People on heroin become very, very desperate. Literally the level of grassing, the level of thieving's gone up, the level of bullying has gone up.' The solidary nature of the prisoner community prior to this influx may have been exaggerated. There was no doubt though that, in maintaining their habits, 'smackheads' breached a range of norms that helped lessen the everyday frustrations of imprisonment.

Some such breaches were major violations of ethical codes. In order to get items with which to buy heroin, users stole from cells, 'ripped off' other prisoners in deals, or intimidated weaker men into handing over goods: '[They'll] just go to a geezer and basically put it on him: "you're giving me something or we're fighting". As soon as there's drugs involved, people just lose all their morals' (Connor). Once in debt, users often revealed the names of drug dealers to staff in order to secure transfers to other establishments, thus breaching norms about grassing. Many drug users put pressure on their families to send in money to repay debts or obtain more drugs, often lying in the process of persuasion. As Matt summarized, 'a smackhead resorts to any dubious moral practices to get the gear—stealing from people, grassing, [he] doesn't give a fuck'.

Many violations exacerbated the mundane frictions of the prison experience and polluted its everyday culture. Heroin users begged and borrowed in order to replace goods (such as tobacco) that they had already traded for drugs. These requests put pressure on other prisoners to eat into their own supplies or risk generating confrontation by refusing to do so. Drug users also cultivated friendships with cynical motives, making others wary of extending trust. Their moods were volatile and unpredictable. In conversation, they were fixated on individual needs at the expense of collective issues. In these respects, they ignored and infringed the physical and social boundaries that reduced interpersonal tension.

Disdain for heroin users also had symbolic dimensions. The much-used term 'dirty smackhead' implied contamination and moral decay. Some prisoners considered 'smackheads' an affront to collective dignity and an insult to more heroic versions of the prisoner identity:

My attitude has been, and I've actually said it to people, 'where's your self-respect gone?' Staff that come in, and go out at night to the pub, those people are gonna go out tomorrow and tell all the pub that you're selling your arse or your shoes or whatever you're selling, and then that society thinks that all of us are like that, all prisoners are like that. (Stephen)

Almost all forms of prison heroin use were stigmatized. The taint of usage was such that prisoners who confessed in private to being 'occasional users' nonetheless condemned heroin when in public arenas. Any suggestion that a prisoner was a habitual consumer or that his life revolved around drugs was fiercely resisted. The distinction mattered in practice and took form in everyday language. Terms such as 'bag-rat', 'bag-head', and 'smack-rat' denoted men whose behaviours and identities were dominated by the search for their next fix:

There is a difference between a heroin user and a baghead. A baghead is the kind of person that will go all out to get a little touch [of heroin], the kind of bloke who would rob his mum and all that shit. That's why nobody likes being called it because they know what it suggests. (Callum)

Terms of this kind carried a moral insinuation. Sometimes, they were used to describe prisoners who had shed their physical addiction but retained the mentality of petty hustling, or those, like Alfie, who recognized that they were far from purging their desire for drugs. Heroin users who could control their habits or afford them without cost to others were more likely to be tolerated:

It depends on what type of smackhead you are. [Some are] just open about it, you can't fault them, as long as they keep themselves locked in their pad and pay their debts. Then you've got the ones who spend all their canteen buying brown, and then they ain't got shit, so they're begging and they try and bullshit you: dirty smackheads who don't give a fuck, they just want their smack. (Wilson)

Heroin users whose use caused no secondary effects could avoid the 'smackhead' label and its moral censure. Some cachet could also be derived from being an occasional user with sufficient will to resist addiction or dependence, from knowing where to find drugs, or from hustling successfully in order to obtain them.[1]

The same conditions were applied in relation to prisoners who self-harmed. Any activity of this kind connoted weakness and an inability to cope. Self-harm was also a visceral reminder of pain— one that many prisoners did not want to be confronted with. Prisoners who self-harmed repeatedly were labelled 'fraggles' and 'attention-seekers' and were aware of being objects of both fascination and disgust (although they were also given sympathy from

---

[1] No such stigma was attached to the use of medicinal drugs. Men whose behaviour was psychologically 'off-key' were considered 'fraggles', but those whose use of psychotropic drugs rendered them stable were not disparaged. Indeed, prisoners talked very openly about medical and psychological conditions, even when their descriptions drew attention to mental health issues such as personality disorders or problems such as dyslexia.

some quarters).[2] Those who 'managed' their self-harm without seeking pity or monopolizing staff resources lost far less credibility. The need to meet the requirements of the environment was also signalled in less common terms of stigma. Thus, a 'stresshead' was a prisoner who could not handle everyday frustrations, while a 'debthead' was someone perpetually in arrears and incapable of managing his money.

Institutional Components of the Prisoner Hierarchy

Sykes (1956, 1958) argued that the inmate hierarchy was structured by institutional characteristics. Power and honour accrued to those prisoners who helped assuage the pains and scarcities of prison life through trade and cultural leadership. These pains also created 'alienative' responses. Some prisoners compensated for deficits in power and autonomy through interpersonal exploitation. If the prison could diminish the burdens of imprisonment, Sykes speculated (1956), patterns of coercion, fraud, and 'chicanery' could be altered or reduced.

In the UK, institutional policies have been refigured with such social consequences in mind. The IEP scheme in particular was conceived as a means of altering the prison's social dynamics by tying rewards and privileges to individual compliance, and by easing some of the material and psychological deficits that would otherwise be alleviated through the prisoner subculture. The consequences in Wellingborough were twofold. First, the institution appropriated some of the power that would previously have been attained by individual prisoners. For a prisoner to improve his lot, he could turn to the institution's formal structures as well as to members of his peer community. The possibility of raising one's living standards through legitimate means also decreased the need to exploit or manipulate others. Second, there was more to lose from being involved in the informal economy, and from efforts to obtain power or status through strategies of extortion

---

[2] Although this was not a topic covered by the interview schedule, four of my seventy interviewees discussed having self-harmed. Three were relatively powerful prisoners, who had tried to disguise their behaviour from other prisoners. Stephen explained: 'I was weak, I was weak. It's an embarrassment now, a part of my life that I don't want people to know about. I don't want people to know that I was weak and felt inadequate.'

and deception. In a Cat-C prison, prisoners were all the more reluctant to accrue power conspicuously, in case it jeopardized their release. Power in prison is always somewhat provisional: to assert it too openly risks inviting challenges from men more determined to obtain it. In Stephen's words, 'there's always someone in the system who's badder'. With freedom so proximate, it was hazardous to risk such battles. Moreover, at this 'shallow' end of the system, the impulsion to counteract feelings of powerlessness was not as strong as in higher-security establishments, where the deprivations were more potent (Wheeler 1961).

In the culture that resulted, most prisoners sought to avoid being labelled 'trouble-makers', bullies or 'subversives'[3] and stressed the significance of having social status in the outside community as well as in the prison. Riz stated his views as follows:

[Prisoners] who don't know me, they probably think I'm some dumb Indian. And I'm quite happy with that. It doesn't bother me. Status doesn't really bother me within prison. The ones that know me, they know what I'm about—that I can look after myself, that I know a lot of people out there what are dealing drugs in large quantities. The ones who don't, I don't really care.

In such ways, the prison's Cat-C status directed the gaze of many prisoners outside the institution.

Veteran prisoners and those with significant criminal experience often observed that influence would be easy to seize in Wellingborough. Officers were diffident in their use of authority and there were few organized groups of prisoners, leaving power relatively open to amass. Only one prisoner did this visibly during the period of fieldwork, using his notoriety and charisma to build around him a small following of acolytes. In general though, men with criminal reputations had neither the desire nor the need to assert themselves overtly, and instead kept low profiles. For them, recognition respect and instrumental respect were guaranteed, while the appraisal respect of Cat-C prisoners was barely worth having. Since the prison did not cede power to influential prisoners, there was little to gain from the institution in ascending the prisoner hierarchy.

---

[3] Some prisoners noted the decline of an institutional terminology of 'subversion' and its replacement by a language of 'non-compliance'. The shift seemed emblematic of the change in penal ends from containment to engagement.

The overall outcome was a flattening of the top end of the social hierarchy. Most prisoners could identify men with *less* power than the norm—largely, those described above—but dismissed the notion that there were men with significantly *more*. Nobody 'ran' the wings. Weakness was more identifiable than strength, as staff also noted. 'You can spot the victims quicker than you spot the major players', said one senior officer: 'You can normally spot somebody the minute they walk in that's going to be a victim.' Prison terminology reflected this state. There were fewer shared terms for prisoners who were powerful or respected than for those who were the opposite. To be in the former category carried fewer consequences. As Callum noted, 'if you're sound [i.e. alright], everybody [just] knows you're sound'.

As most prisoners saw it, the main social division on the wings was a relatively simple split between prisoners to whom you gave some leeway and 'wouldn't mess with', and those whose status was more questionable. While the former garnered instrumental and recognition respect, the latter were guaranteed neither. Prisoners expressed this division in various ways, and some identified further tiers, but there was near consensus about some basic distinctions:

We're virtually all equal, but you've got people who are *on* the line, then you've got a certain amount of people who go *above* the line. You get the people who sit in their cell on their own, don't really associate with anyone, they'll be bottom.... Half of the wing to two-thirds of the wing are normal, then you've got the top-tier people, about ten. (Ewan)

There's people that are one of the lads. They're somebody who's not a fucking idiot, but he's decent. Then you've just got the normal people on the wing. Just normal people who you wouldn't have a conversation with but you'd have a laugh and a joke with. All the people that sit in their cells. (Fin)

As far as I'm concerned there's only three labels: you're either an idiot (a muppet, div, whatever); you've got nutters, which are not right in the head; and you've got the lads. (Danny)

There's always that one person you don't fuck with, on every wing. There's the fraggles and the normal people, [i.e.] the staunch people. (Zack)

The variance in such descriptions partly reflected the different locations from which prisoners viewed the hierarchy. It also indicated the relatively unfixed and unclear nature of the 'pecking order'. Unlike in some penal jurisdictions, the power structure was not rigid or highly prominent; nor was it determined by formal, organizational status (such as paramilitary or gang ranking) or set through ritual practices (c.f. Jacobs 1977; McEvoy 2001; Kaminski 2004). Rather, the division between the more and less respected denoted several interrelated distinctions, each of which was emblematic of certain deficits in prison life. The first related to economic resources and activity. As Alfie suggested—albeit at a stretch, in his own case—a certain form of status was assured by the ability to 'make do' materially:

It's the 'haves' and the 'have nots'. I would classify myself as a 'have'. I'm a have through my personal choice. I smoke a brand of tobacco that's cheaper, and that's how I started off, I just bought a shitload of that and forced myself to smoke it.

Are there people who would say, 'Alfie's only smoking shit tobacco'?

Yeah, but Alfie's got a jar of mayonnaise in his cupboard and a jar of coffee and fresh milk every week! And noodles whenever I want it, and peanut butter and jam and pork scratchings.

Prisoners who avoided debt and managed personal resources with skill thus derived some basic credibility. One prisoner characterized the hierarchy in terms of those prisoners who had to buy 'double-bubble' and those with enough goods not to require such transactions. Organized involvement in trade derived further status: 'the respect comes from what you do. If you shop things— phone cards and burn and drugs, you're respected, because you're offering your service' (Cameron).

On the prison's induction wing, where there was a constant turnover of prisoners, the informal economy was dominated by a handful of cleaners and servery workers, whose relative permanence on the wing gave them a foothold to establish themselves as intermediaries in trade and information:

There's a certain few of us who are the ones to go to if you want burn, or to see if you can get bits and bobs. Cleaners. We're out all the time, so when people come on they [ask us] 'what's it like on here?' or if they've got things to sell, they come and see us. So we've got more respect in that way than every other con. And we get away with more things with the screws. (Leon)

Elsewhere in the prison, trade was dispersed more widely. As suggested above though, workers on all wings held some influence through the amount of time they spent unlocked and the relationships they developed with staff: 'they find out what's going on on the wing before anybody else, so it's usually them that know things [and] if they go to the office and say something, the screws would listen to them more because they are trusted more' (Ronan). Deficits in information thus gave some power to prisoners in high-trust positions.

A prisoner's material subsistence and his potential to trade were assisted greatly by his integration into social networks. To be part of a social group enabled a prisoner to borrow small quantities of goods from his peers without charge. Prisoners who were socially isolated relied on more formal transactions to get by. Further, men with 'things on offer' tended to socialize together, whereas those without were more often loners, either by nature or precisely because they were perceived as drains on the goodwill of others. Sociability and trade—social and economic capital—were mutually reinforcing. Each advanced the other, and both symbolized and consolidated status. Group membership was thus a further marker of credibility, with 'lads' often described simply as men who 'know a lot of people' or 'mix with everyone'. To socialize widely was a sign that one was a 'good lad', worthy of trust, and wise to the prerogatives of prison life.

Social networks provided the kind of physical capital that placed a prisoner beyond the realms of victimization. But 'lads' were also defined to some degree by their *personal* capacity for violence, their willingness to defend themselves without help from others. Connor described the key line of distinction as 'people who you know not to say certain things to, because you'd end up fighting with them [and] people who you can say what you want to, and they're not going to go for you no matter what'. Danny divided prisoners likewise: 'people know whether, if they tried to take a liberty with you, you're gonna accept it or whether you're gonna fight back'.[4] Prisoners who did allow themselves to be 'mugged off' or 'took for a dickhead' (Cameron) risked widespread and daily exploitation (Edgar *et al.* 2003; and see below). 'Prison is hard if you're weak— you get asked for tobacco every day', one prisoner commented (fieldwork notes). When prisoners talked of some men being 'above the line' and others 'below it', it was this possibility of routine victimization that their terms delimited. 'It's not about

---

[4] To 'take a liberty': to do something unacceptable.

power', said one prisoner. 'It's about not getting fucked with' (fieldwork notes).

Accordingly, 'respect' was sought out by most prisoners not as a way of accumulating power, but as a means of carving out relative autonomy (see Sparks *et al.* 1996). Defined in this way, respect was something that you 'had to have'. As on the streets (Anderson 1999), to be at the top of the hierarchy was to be assured of being 'left alone', to be free to go about one's affairs without external interference: 'there's some people you don't mess around with, you don't play games with them' (Dave). This power was frequently expressed in terms of what could or could not be 'said' to another prisoner without sparking confrontation. 'No-one can say nothing to me', Paul boasted, explaining that he played his music at high volume even though he knew this was an irritation to others and a breach of normal practices. In similar terms, Martin claimed that no one could 'tell me nothing'. These anodyne phrases spoke of the daily injuries of social subordination, of having been told what to do throughout one's existence (see Charlesworth 1999). They also highlighted the importance of autonomy in some versions of masculine pride (Jewkes 2002).

In queues for phones or meals, powerful prisoners could push in line with little risk of challenge. Other men recognized that to do so, or take more than their share of time or resources, would meet resistance. 'If I go on [the phone], I'll only take five minutes', said Callum, 'some people don't give a shit'. Power and status were thus acknowledged in silences and unstated allowances. Indeed, they were continually expressed and reinforced through space and symbolism—the volume of one's music, the quality of one's trainers (Jewkes 2005a)—and fought out in micro-interactions around scarce resources. High-status prisoners were the first to choose sports equipment in the gym; they asserted themselves confidently and vocally around pool tables and on the landings; and they consumed more space than other prisoners as they walked down corridors. In these ways, the capacity for violence was communicated without the need for its actual assertion (see Gambetta 2005). Prisoners drew conclusions about violent aptitude and other aspects of identity from what Bourdieu (1984) refers to as *hexis*: gait, posture, and the minor but multiple ways that the body's potential is expressed. Prisoners maintained that you could 'spot a lad or a donut straightaway', through 'gut instinct' (Tyler). Confidence, physical prowess, and the determination to impose one's will—the essence of machismo—were shown immediately in 'the way you carry yourself' (Danny), 'your attitude, how you deal with people—and at the end of the day you don't have to fight' (Paul).[5] Stigmatizing labels were also allocated on the basis of unusual appearance or demeanour. Prisoners who carried themselves without confidence or simply looked 'a bit different' were especially liable to be labelled 'shady characters' or sex-offenders.[6]

A prisoner's physical capacity and appearance, his integration into social networks and his involvement in trade all, therefore, contributed to his social power. In practice, as Danny explained, physical, social, and economic capital were interlinked:

It all goes hand in hand, the dealers, the barons and that.[7] They wouldn't be able to do that if there were [physically] light. And they've got some respect—you couldn't take the piss with em. So they're all what I would call 'the lads', they're the ones with the influence, the main players. People that you can't take liberties with and that have got back-up, if needs be.

All such prisoners were unlikely to 'get trouble' unless they courted it, but they did not necessarily seek out power as such. On all wings, however, there were a handful of prisoners (between five and ten) who did covet influence and were more powerful than the wider cohort of 'normal lads'. Described variously as 'proper lads', 'heads' or 'faces', these tended to be prisoners with reputations outside prison: 'a geezer who does pretty heavy things. He could have shot a couple of people, robbed a few drug dealers, and got away with [it]' (Tyler); 'in a [certain] family, with a slight bit of menace behind them, and you know that they're a competent person in their line of business' (Ewan). These reputations preceded or accompanied prisoners as they entered custody, enabling them to establish social and economic clout as leaders of primary groups.

---

[5] This was more than a question of size or muscularity. Prisoners who were disposed to use weapons (in particular, knives forged from toothbrushes or toilet brushes and razor blades) needed little physical strength. Those who talked a sufficiently convincing game, or successfully conveyed threat, volatility or ruthlessness, could also avoid confrontation through display alone.

[6] Listeners—prisoners trained by the Samaritans—reported that one of the most common problems that prisoners expressed was being mocked or rejected by their peers, or by staff, for 'being ugly, not fitting in' (fieldwork notes).

[7] A 'baron': an old-fashioned prison term for a tobacco dealer.

The nature of power

Ashley was a prime example of this kind of prisoner. A well known pimp and robber in his home city, his criminal experience, propensity to use violence, and ability to make connections with other influential prisoners placed him by common consensus among the most powerful men in the prison. From his perspective, 'normal lads' were merely 'neutral—they're not from a city that's recognized, but they are good lads'. Paul expressed a similar form of snobbery:

I'll say hello to most people but I don't talk to everybody. I ain't got a problem with no-one on the wing but I've got a set of friends and that's it, people I talk to, who can come in my cell and sit down and talk and I'll talk to them. The rest I have nothing to do with.... There's other people that do double-bubble or drugs or they just carry themselves in a way that people know they're alright. I only talk to people that are like that. I don't talk to idiots.

Such dismissals were characteristic of these men. They were not necessarily given appraisal respect, but they had significant influence through their economic activity and the physical and social capital that accompanied such dealings. Paul clarified the nature of this influence as follows:

Are you one of the people on the wing that's influential?

Yeah but—how can I put it—in my own little circle. I'm influential to people that need to know. If you want burn you can get it [through me], double-bubble. Maybe drugs, and if I haven't got it I might know where it is. If you're getting bullied. Anything like that, I'm influential in that way.

Your influence is from what you can get people, is that what you mean?

Yeah and the people around me who are my friends who I get on with.... There's a clique of us that the officers don't like because we seem to have influence. If I'm upset everyone could be upset. It's influence.

To some degree, power was limited in scope to those who 'needed things' or were involved in certain activities. Certainly, it was only activated in some situations. The most powerful heads sometimes arbitrated conflict between factions, and men like Paul and Ashley were consulted by less powerful prisoners on whether to settle disputes through violence. However, they exerted little direct influence over prisoners who were not involved in prison trade and politics. To be powerful was, to a large degree, to have things that other people wanted. It was for this reason that a number of prisoners (particularly lifers, who were generally more self-sufficient than other prisoners) claimed not to be able to identify a hierarchy at all. Claims that 'I'm not interested in it' (Derek) or 'don't see it' (George) evidenced the degree to which power could be invisible from certain social angles and was normally held in reserve. As Rhys noted, 'you don't have to be part of the power scene'.

Whatever power one individual held over others, there was no person or grouping that 'called the shots' across the prisoner community. 'No one clique is going to be big enough to take the whole wing on', Alfie commented. Noah concurred that: 'you might run things in two or three cells, and you might be running one thing, but you can't run everything'. As the next chapter describes, on most wings there were a number of cliques whose influence was limited by the weight of other groupings. The scope of power was often a matter of peer group influence, with 'heads' generally the leaders of these co-existing factions, formed around shared hometowns or ethnicities.

Institutional policies were significant in delimiting the shape and reach of power. First, any grouping that became too large was highly conspicuous to the authorities and tended to result in certain prisoners being 'shipped out' or moved to other wings. As a consequence, power was widely distributed, not concentrated in the hands of groups operating with the tacit approval of staff. Second, since interpersonal dominance among prisoners was officially discouraged, powerful prisoners recognized the importance of disguising their activities from the authorities:[8]

It's not good to be too noticed. You've got this anti-bullying campaign. You could get away with it before, but not now. They'd be on you like a rash. You have to become more devious, more underground. Nowadays, you won't find the real bullies. You'll notice the weaker people more. Because the bully's in the background. He doesn't really need to leave his cell. He's got ten lads on the wing doing what he wants.... They're getting

[8] Some prisoners complained that their influence within their peer group was conflated with 'leadership'. To be identified as a leader was not desirable, as Mohammed suggested:

Every time, when [we] pray [on the landings], they come straight to me and they will speak to me. But I would say to them, 'don't speak to me, speak to everyone'. Because everyone else wants to pray, it's not just me. But they would really straight first come to me. They would think I'm a leader, but I'm not really leading anything.

noticed. So the screws will look at them and not him. Whereas before the bully could be upfront.... A top dog doesn't want to be spotted. You might not notice him at all.

Powerful prisoners rarely caused problems for staff directly. Staff often commented that they were normally 'chatty and friendly to staff, and very polite' (senior officer). Often, they were enhanced prisoners—*players* who subverted the system without appearing disobedient. Influence was exerted by building 'links' and orchestrating the activities of other prisoners rather than employing direct physical coercion.

Drugs and power

Drugs, in particular heroin, provided the hidden dynamic of interpersonal power. Prisoners testified with almost universal consistency that they were the primary source of power and influence:

If you've got powder in jail, you are a fucking powerful man. If you've got enough smack in jail you could get someone killed, no problem. If you want someone to wipe your arse for you, the geezer will wipe your arse for a bag. You ain't got to do a thing. You ain't got to lift a finger. That geezer will put a roll-up to your mouth and pull it away from your mouth. (Bradley)

What are the sorts of things that give people power?

Power? Power's drugs. Drugs is power. (Alfie)

All you need in this place to have respect is a pocketful of drugs. (Ronan)

The nature of the power bestowed by drugs was complex. It held particular sway over those prisoners dependent on its supply, allowing dealers to buy other prisoners to 'do their dirty work for them' (Kai). Often, it was only by carrying out tasks for their dealers that drug users could settle their debts. These tasks might involve duties such as ironing or storing goods (e.g. phonecards). They also included acts of robbery, revenge, and intimidation undertaken on behalf of creditors. Paul described such transactions as follows:

At the end of the day, people owe you. [So if] you don't get on with someone and you want their cell burnt out: 'you owe me ten items: burn his cell out'; or 'my mate's just come in, he ain't got a radio—you've got a radio, you owe me items, you're going to give me your radio and [I'll] forget the items'.

In this way, influence could be exerted beyond the immediate pool of drug users. Although dealers had no direct hold over those prisoners who did not require their supplies, they had abundant means to terrorize them in the event of conflict. Heroin was also the currency on which the rest of the informal economy depended (Crewe 2006b)—'without drugs, tobacco and phonecards don't work' (Paul). This meant that anyone who borrowed other goods (or who associated closely with someone who did) could be drawn into the wider politics of the heroin economy. Non-users could avoid drug culture, and were not hassled to become consumers, but the power accumulated through the drug trade could skew and stain social relationships beyond its primary markets. In these respects, although heroin's influence was to some degree circumscribed, its potential meant that dealers were given enormous levels of instrumental respect.

To be a prison drug dealer also generated appraisal respect among certain prisoners. Dealing was a high-risk activity that required nerve, contacts, organization, and a level of entrepreneurialism that many prisoners admired. As Kai noted, 'they must be big people if they can get drugs into jail, big quantities of drugs. Just like people who get mobile phones—"god, he's got a mobile phone, how the fuck did he get that?"' Alfie expressed similar sentiments of awe and incredulity:

I was just standing back, admiring the way they done it, because they had everything under wraps; they just went on a power trip. Started treating everybody with total disrespect, started leading a very laid-back lifestyle. I admired the way they done it. They got the whole wing under wraps, under control. They could have lifted a pinkie and got somebody wiped out, just through sheer power.... They had everything: boxes and boxes under their beds, chocolate bars, boxes of brand new trainers and tracksuits all hanging up.

Such terms partly highlighted heroin's immense profitability. Heroin was not only valuable in itself; it could reproduce its value exponentially through the other goods it could purchase, which were then lent out for further income. This capacity, and the need for some users to sell their clothing or possessions to fund their consumption, meant that dealers did not want for material goods—'if you've got drugs, you can get anything' (Howard). The display and possession of consumer items was a further source of symbolic prestige. Drugs, goods, and the status they provided were then magnets for social allegiance: dealers could always 'get aggressive people around them' (prisoner, fieldwork notes).

Yet many prisoners distinguished between appraisal respect and instrumental respect, and drug dealers were sources of resentment as well as awe. One reason for this was that the power relationship between supplier and consumer was so easy to exploit. The term 'powder power' captured the tendency for some dealers to flaunt their power or abuse their grip over users by holding out for gratuitously exploitative deals or delaying transactions repeatedly. It also signalled the transient nature of the power that heroin imparted. As the term suggested, dealers held power and popularity due not to personal qualities, but what they held in their possession. While a prisoner had drugs to offer, his public status appeared high and he attracted popular attention—'like flies around shit', Ian remarked. Once supplies ran out, influence, and popularity also dissipated. 'It's what I call "king for the day"', said Gerry. 'He's suddenly promoted to the top rung of the ladder until his parcel's gone. And the minute his parcel's gone, he's back down again. It's not respect. It's false. It's artificial'. A prisoner with access to drugs was therefore a 'top dog' in certain respects: someone with influence. However, as Tyler noted, that 'doesn't make him a leader', someone whose views were respected.

Much of the antipathy directed against drug dealers reflected these perceptions that their power was unmerited and their social allure artificial. 'Powder power is thinking you're the man because you've got drugs, but not really being anybody' one prisoner commented. Others complained that heroin distorted established patterns of status and corrupted social affiliations. 'Powder power means you can have a twenty-three year old selling to a grown man, who's licking their arse', one prisoner protested. Pete lamented heroin's ability to suppress traditional sources of stigma:

Whoever brings in the most drugs is the hierarchy now. If you can get drugs in, you're somebody. You can be the biggest rapist on fucking earth, but as long as you're bringing smack in, it doesn't matter a fucking toss what you've done. The hierarchy now is definitely drugs.

Despite its hyperbole, Pete's statement succinctly described the way that heroin could inflate a prisoner's social credibility. However, claims that heroin conferred power on men who were otherwise powerless were overstated. Heroin amplified a prisoner's influence and kudos, but it was insufficient on its own to secure them, certainly beyond the short-term. Weak prisoners who meddled in the drugs trade were quickly relieved of their stocks. 'If you're not a face and you're selling drugs, you're going to get robbed' said Zack. In this respect, the potency of drugs made them risky business: '[they can] set you up for a big fall— you could start thinking you're a lot more powerful than you are, and then people come and rob you, take your things [and] you lose respect' (Martin). In fact, drug dealers were generally prisoners who already had some degree of social or physical clout— extended networks, violent potential, or interpersonal confidence. Drugs did not simply 'create' power. Rather, 'powerful people end up in control of drugs' (Callum). In summary, heroin expanded the amount of power available to prisoners who were already relatively strong or secure within the prisoner community. When drugs were not available, the hierarchy was considerably less extended: 'there isn't really no top dog no more, [because] there isn't really no drugs' (Paul).

For prisoners who had access to drug supplies but lacked other forms of power, one solution was to establish mutually beneficial relationships with prisoners who could offer trade networks or protection: '[Heroin] don't make you a head, but it means you've got the back-up. You go to one of the heads', Fin explained. Drugs provided the purchasing power to build alliances with prisoners who held physical and social capital. Several prisoners argued that Asian prisoners involved in the drugs trade had made up for their relatively low physical capital by purchasing security. There was little other evidence that the hierarchy was structured by race or ethnicity.

While the supply of drugs led to social elevation, their use promoted the opposite trajectory, undermining the status claims of prisoners who would otherwise have been respected:

Before the introduction of heroin, you would have had people who would have become strong within the prison system, who would have been higher up the hierarchy, [but] because they're heroin users, they may be strong physically, they may be strong willed, they may be a bit of a bully, but because they're on the brown, people will frown on them. (Nathan)

Prisoners often made reference to former friends or criminal associates whose use of heroin had transformed them from men of strength and honour to men of weakness and dependence. 'He's a smackhead now' was a term used ruefully and frequently. To become a heroin addict was to be marked permanently by associations of immorality and unreliability, and therefore to lose the essential credentials of criminal culture. Established patterns of status and power were thus skewed.

Heroin's central role in the power structure merits one further observation, for it appeared almost perfectly adapted to the official techniques of penal power. As the excerpts above have described, suppliers could pay other prisoners to store their products and proceeds. They had no need for personal involvement in the handling or distribution of drugs, or the enforcement of debts. Crucially then, heroin allowed power to be exercised covertly, inconspicuously, and at distance. Despite their use of network-mapping software, officials were often unaware of who drug dealers were. When they had suspicions—either through observations of wealth or, more often, information from others prisoners—these were often too weak a basis for formal action. Dealers could move through their sentences with minimal visibility or maintain unblemished official records even when under suspicion. Significantly too, unlike other goods or services that alleviated everyday frustrations, heroin could not be integrated into the IEP scheme. As one of the few things that prisoners desired that could not be provided by the institution, it offered an ideal basis for the accumulation of power.

Institutional Culture and the Prisoner Hierarchy

Systemic policies and institutional characteristics set the terms for the structure of Wellingborough's hierarchy, but status was also shaped by the particular culture of the establishment. General and local factors interacted most clearly in relation to the role of violence, whose currency throughout the prison system had apparently diminished in recent decades:

You can't show violence now. Violence does not rule no more in prison. [In the past] if you could look after yourself, it got you the respect you wanted. But the system's changed where violence is not viewed by you, the system, [or] the [world] outside as an 'in' thing. (Pete)

Subtly, it's changed. If you don't agree with what people say, then you're not in the clique. In the old days you didn't have to agree. If you were rough and ready, you'd be in the clique. Your status was more important than what you agreed with.

What did your status come from?

Violence. Or the potential of your violence.... Physical status was every-thing, because in those days there was real violence. Nothing like today.

And what is it now that matters?

Opinions. Whether they can relate to your opinion or not. Whether you'll conform to their opinion. Timidness is only to do with how you present your own opinion. If you're strong in your opinion, then you can hold your own. [It's about] what you believe, or what you're willing to accept. Opinion is a must now, where years ago it used to be 'I like him because he's aggressive, he can kick off in violence. I'm in that pack'. [There's] a certain amount of underlying [violence]. But violence in prison is a last resort now. (Gerry)

There were a number of reasons why violence had been deval-ued. First, it was no longer tolerated by the institution. For rea-sons already outlined, staff were less inclined to turn a blind eye to exploitative behaviour, and prisoners were aware that overt aggression was imprudent. Second, violence was less likely to be incited by everyday antagonism or institutional violence (c.f. Scraton *et al.* 1991; Sim 1994a). Prisoners took their behavioural cues from uniformed staff—'if prison officers are aggressive to-wards you, you know you're in an aggressive environment. You know it's on top if you step out of line. So when you go on the wing and somebody steps over that line, you know what to do—you deck him' (Gerry). Since staff did not resort to violence too eagerly, prisoners responded in corresponding style. Violence against offic-ers was less often merited than in the past. Meanwhile, in their interactions with each other, prisoners were less prone to the kinds of aggressive outbursts that in earlier times had been inflamed by poor access to phones, limited visits, and degrading physical con-ditions. Many prisoners felt powerless but not completely without autonomy. Feelings of subordination were not so profound that interpersonal domination was the only means of recouping a sense of agency or control (cf. Hassine 1999).

Wellingborough's culture built upon these tendencies. As pre-vious chapters have described, it was generally considered 'a laid-back jail, nice and slow' (Callum), where control was exerted with little aggression and prisoners were not constantly on edge. 'It's not a fronting prison', VJ noted, 'you don't need to front nothing'. For the prisoner hierarchy, this ethos had significant consequences:

This jail's soft, man. In some prisons, if you push it too far, you expect to get done in. If you've done a lot of bird and you've been to places like

Stafford or Winson Green, it's what you expect: if you push it too far, you expect to get done in. If you're a lad, or if you want to be known as a lad, it's standard. You fuck about with them, you expect to get hurt. When you want to be a boss or a lad, you're pushing all the time, and when you step over the line, you expect to be done in. (Fin)

By resisting the over-use of coercive measures in response to defiant behaviour, Wellingborough avoided reinforcing the status of prisoners whose identities were built on direct confrontation with the system. A more measured institutional reaction meant that prisoners did not gain rebellious credit through the acts of deliberate provocation that Fin described. Having a credible threat of violence certainly served as a means of self-protection and marked someone out as 'above the line'. But the institutional ethos contributed to a culture in which violence did not lead to perverse forms of credibility. Prisoners saw little heroic quality in attacking an officer who did not deserve it, or little bravery in acts whose consequences were to be walked calmly rather than dragged violently to the segregation unit. As Stephen explained, violence was not therefore the key component in the pecking order:

In more violent prisons, obviously the more violent person rises to the top, whether they're likeable or not. But in these more mellow places like our wing, you respect people for different reasons.... If you're clever, it doesn't matter how [little] money you've got, people will still want to know your opinion. Whereas you might meet someone who you can tell within moments of speaking to them is a div.[9] (Stephen)

Indeed, because everyday treatment was not brutal or antagonistic, and since being released as soon as possible was an almost universal ambition, overt resistance was seen as naïve, unnecessary, and outdated. For a high proportion of prisoners, the battle worth fighting was the pursuit of liberty. Respect was reserved for men who were: 'doing whatever they can to get out. [Because] this ain't where it's at, it's all about outside' (Isaac). Even prisoners who were relatively resistant appreciated the benefits of caution and recognized the value of mental as well as physical competence. 'Being staunch is being wise', Ashley commented, providing a significant twist on traditional norms. Paul agreed: 'If you get into a confrontation you're an idiot in this day and age. There's ways of being passive but still assertive. I stand up for my rights,

[9] A 'div': an idiot.

but I'm careful how I do it'. Appraisal respect was thus related to shrewdness and stealth, manipulating the system effectively and inconspicuously.

Agency was an important factor here. Although acquiescence to the regime was given little credibility, a prisoner's status was not diminished if he could present his compliance as a form of self-improvement rather than an attempt to satisfy the system. In this respect, by linking progression through the system to self-management, and by providing educational and vocational opportunities, the Prison Service had restructured the status system so that prisoner values and the ideals of the system were not in direct opposition. 'We're a jail full of silver back gorillas', said Kyle, '[but] the game is not to try and be "the daddy" all the time, it's to try and work alongside the zoo-keeper'. A 'model prisoner', in institutional terms, could be admired by his peers. Jobs that appeared subservient were often taken up by prisoners of fairly high status. As Pierce observed: 'The best way to get what you want is to be a screw-boy [and] half the time it's the lads [who are]!'

Intelligent prisoners and those who understood the intricacies of the system were also given some appraisal respect by their peers. This was particularly the case if they were willing to help other prisoners or could play the system in ways that officers could not challenge. Prisoners who offered advice on legal issues and prison rules or who assisted their peers in writing applications for early release were considered 'decent' and 'staunch'. Those who helped others beat adjudication charges on technicalities were likewise celebrated. For Stephen, opportunities to draft other people's requests and complaints allowed a kind of surrogate resistance, one which could not be held against him: 'I can get my grievances with the system, and put their name on it!' Prisoners who required such assistance were among the new losers of the system. As Stephen commented:

It's all very well having different ways of complaining, [but] if [someone] doesn't know how to express himself, it's not going to do any good. I've seen people tearing up complaint forms because they can't write down what their complaint is.

Men who were not skilled in using bureaucratic avenues were not disparaged by other prisoners, but they were unlikely to reach the zenith of the hierarchy.

Some prisoners suggested that a growing respect for intelligence was partly an outcome of increased access to the kinds of materials that stimulated serious discussion: current affairs programmes on television, improved library facilities, opportunities to do Open University degrees. But personal views and attitudes were also easier to express in an institutional culture that eschewed the routine use of violence. Relative to other prisons, and earlier times, Wellingborough did not put prisoners constantly on edge or demand public performances of taut machismo. Space was therefore opened up for social roles and credibility to be linked to non-coercive traits.[10]

The Hierarchy of Crime

Some criminal offences have traditionally carried more esteem than others. Both within criminal culture and in most prisons, organized crime and certain kinds of murder have occupied the apex of the hierarchy of kudos, with petty crimes and sexual offences at its base (Winfree *et al.* 2002; Sapp and Vaughn 1989; Jewkes 2005a). This hierarchy featured in discussions of crime and credibility among Wellingborough prisoners. Men convicted of burglary understood the shame and dishonour attached to their crimes and tended not to advertise their index offence. Breaking into another person's house was seen as an intimate intrusion, and as 'stealing from your own': destroying the lifetime material accretion of an ordinary working family.[11] Generally therefore, burglars tried to convince other prisoners that their targets were commercial rather than domestic—the former being considered victimless.[12] Robberies were evaluated according to similar factors, based largely on the status of the victim. To mug a woman or a pensioner—'some poor old lady, somebody's mum, who can't defend herself' (Den)—was considered an act of cowardice. However, it was more acceptable to rob a man of normal age: someone deemed able to resist and recover from assault. Taking

[10] The use of the term 'head' as a suffix to many labels (e.g. 'stresshead', 'smackhead', 'debthead') was suggestive of the significance of character and inclination in defining social roles.

[11] Burgling from the wealthy was seen slightly less negatively.

[12] Prisoners generally argued that, since companies could claim back their losses through insurance policies, there were no real losers from commercial burglaries.

the proceeds of a rival drug dealer was considered a crime of courage and intelligence, a contemporary counterpart to the traditionally admired crime of armed robbery.[13]

The respect accorded to bank robbery reflected a number of factors: the organization required to target a secure building, the confidence needed for 'face-to-face' crime, the dangers of an armed response, the corporate victim, and the potentially enormous spoils. The amount of money that could be gained through crime was an important source of respect (professional fraudsters were highly admired, for example). Offences such as armed robbery were also signifiers of certain forms of masculine bravado. The language of 'balls', 'bollocks', and 'guts' used in descriptions of such acts was indicative of these notions of machismo, based particularly around the imposition of personal will onto a situation (see McVicar 1974). Terrorists were admired for similar reasons, although more for their internal self-assurance and unyielding determination than for the outward bravado of the armed robber. Burglary, car theft, and petty fraud also served as shorthand descriptions of identity and attitude, with their perpetrators assumed to be of '[lower] calibre—more furtive, more petty in their views and the way they conduct themselves' (Nathan).

These discourses of agency, ambition and masculine esteem were more potent sources of status than criminal acts *per se*. It was far more prestigious to be involved in a pre-meditated robbery of a large bank than an unplanned hold-up of a rural post-office, undertaken to feed a drug habit. Not least, the latter was a crime of dependence, and addiction was a mark of passivity, physical degeneracy, and moral deficiency. Prisoners who dealt drugs outside prison were highly reproachful of the clients who bought their goods. They condemned their customers for the crimes that they tended to commit (e.g. domestic burglary, shoplifting) and looked down on their socio-economic subordination. As Paul described: 'if you're a person that takes drugs, you're a loser, and you've got to pay. If you're a seller, you're receiving it. A person who takes drugs will be forever selling his things, so [they'll] always be below you.'

---

[13] Robbing someone else involved in criminal activity was also considered astute, since victims in such cases were very unlikely to turn to the police (see also O'Donnell and Edgar 1998).

These external hierarchies were reconstituted within the prison in complex ways. Some crimes were judged to sit outside normal considerations of prison status. White collar criminals convicted of company fraud or drink driving, and 'ordinary blokes' who had been involved in pub fights, were largely seen as unlucky and out of place. In effect, these men were exempted from judgment. Crimes of passion were likewise relatively 'neutral', seen as unplanned acts of anger.

Life-sentence prisoners generated instrumental and appraisal respect as much because of their sentence lengths as their crimes.[14] Category-C prisoners with shorter terms were often awestruck by the sheer amount of time that lifers had already served. Many were fascinated by tales of 'heavy-duty' jails, and impressed by the dignity, stoicism, and intelligent cynicism that most lifers exhibited. More experienced prisoners deferred to the needs of those on very long sentences, recognizing that the anxieties and difficulties faced by lifers were more profound than their own. Those with less experience acceded out of fear as well as respect. These men believed that lifers were, by definition, dangerous and had 'nothing to lose' given their distance from release. Since most lifers in fact conducted themselves with incredible caution, such perceptions were generally misguided.

The clearest offence distinction among prisoners was between those who saw themselves as accumulative career criminals, many of whom were drug dealers outside prison, and those convicted of petty acquisitive crimes, most of whom were drug addicts on the streets. Experienced prisoners bemoaned the influx of 'non-criminal types' into prisons—men who were drawn into the carceral net mainly because of drug addiction and neither looked nor acted like professional criminals:

Ten years ago, you had a lot of hard men. Everyone was a big bloke. Now it's so much more mixed. You've got little weedy guys running around the wing. Anyone can be a criminal nowadays, because there's so much more of it. (Den)

Prisoners like Den were nostalgic for an era when crime was (putatively) the preserve of organized gangs and was conducted

---

[14] Some lifers also claimed that staff treated them differently—both more cautiously and more respectfully—once they knew that they were serving long sentences.

with flair, pride, and expertise: 'it was more of an art—nowadays, it's just gung-ho, charge in, wreck people's homes.' According to these prisoners, prison was 'no longer prison', its culture diluted by men with no concept of appropriate behaviour. The honourable—perhaps apocryphal—identities of the old-fashioned criminal and the dignified prisoner were thus threatened. No doubt such memories were romanticized to some degree. However, there was certainly a cultural split between prisoners who perceived themselves as criminal *agents*, for whom crime was a commitment, and narcotic *subjects* whose crimes were a direct outcome of addiction. This division overlapped considerably with in-prison categories of 'haves' and 'have nots', and 'lads' and 'idiots'.

Convicted drug dealers continued to perceive their former consumers as weak, inferior, and untrustworthy (see Jewkes 2005a). However, within prison, such judgments were to some degree suspended. In terms of everyday social interaction, established hierarchies were compressed considerably:

You get more respect if you're an armed robber than if you were a house burglar, of course you would. But nobody's gonna pick on you because you're a house burglar. Everybody mingles, you have to mingle in prison. I'd have no problem talking to a housebreaker inside, I would have no problem classing him as a friend inside. But I wouldn't associate with a house burglar outside, in case it rubbed off on me. That's a lowlife crime.... If you're out there dealing, then you look down on them sort of people. You think, 'you fucking smackhead'. The chances are they're burgling houses, they're robbing off friends, they're robbing off family, they're scum. (Danny)

A senior, heavy, millionaire drug dealer—he will be polite and have polite conversation with a house burglar, whereas outside he wouldn't be seen dead talking to that person. (Stephen)

As these quotations suggest, it was not only hierarchies organized around drugs that were flattened by the terms of imprisonment. Many prisoners felt that their shared predicament should overwrite disparities in status and that no-one was entitled to assert social superiority on the basis of imported characteristics alone. 'I don't see anyone higher or lower', said Ross. 'It's just a group of blokes doing time.' Asif argued that: 'in jail, it doesn't matter who you are, where you come from, or what you are out there. You're all the same. No-one's better than no-one else.' Jacob put things in more self-effacing terms: 'we're all as stupid as one another for being here in the first place'. In recognition that the struggles of surviving imprisonment trumped personal conflicts, enmity from the streets was often set aside:

Somebody can come in that I've got problems with on the street and I'll probably speak to him, and he'd probably speak to me. What goes on out there isn't brought in here. You've got enough problems in here anyway (Danny)

For the same reasons, the majority of prisoners were more socially tolerant in prison than in the community:

Ninety-five per cent of the wing, I wouldn't give the time of day on the out. They're not in my league out there. In jail, you've got to live with everyone, so I show them the respect they show me. For instance, there's a lad opposite me, he must be about four stone. Every day he comes to my pad: 'can I have a look at your telly guide?' or 'have you got a bit of sugar?' or a tea bag. And I'll give it him. I wouldn't give him the time of day out there. (Kieran)

Most prisoners, like Kieran, claimed to give recognition respect to anyone who reciprocated, 'regardless if they're the biggest smackhead or the biggest drug dealer'. Imprisonment thus functioned in some respects as an equalizing force. For a small proportion of prisoners, it was not common circumstances that levelled the social surface so much as the prison's despoiling effects. Incarceration stripped away accessories of wealth, such as cars and consumer goods, and guarantors of power, particularly guns. As Leon said: '[People] can have a big reputation out there because they're not afraid of using a shooter. But anyone can pull a trigger, it don't mean you're handy with your fists.' Prison thus became a site where the importance of many past credentials was expunged, while new spurs had to be earned, with few external props.

The exception to this relative flattening of external hierarchies was in relation to sexual offences. The anonymous integration of sex offenders into the mainstream prison population was a source of febrile outrage among Wellingborough's prisoners (the majority of whom supported capital punishment for serious sexual crimes). Fears of being contaminated by the presence of 'nonces' were voiced constantly and with neurotic concern. Some prisoners were so preoccupied by the spectre of paedophilia that they did not display photos of their own children on their cell walls, for fear that 'some nonce might perv over them' (prisoner, fieldwork notes). Sex-offenders undoubtedly served a symbolic function within the prisoner world, as the cultural bogey-men in relation to whom anyone could claim moral superiority.[15] But the opprobrium directed at these offenders was sincere, often based on a view that victims of sexual offences were 'scarred for life' (Darren) and that there was a moral distinction between 'doing something to survive and doing things for gratification. People who rob, steal, sell drugs, kill people—it might sound stupid, but they've got morals' (prisoner, fieldwork notes).[16]

In summary, a prisoner's index offence could virtually guarantee contempt but could not ensure credibility (Morris and Morris 1963). Certain crimes (and their connotations) incurred more kudos than others, and behaviour inside the prison often reproduced aspects of criminal choice and behaviour outside. Yet imprisonment compressed many status distinctions outside prison, and there was no necessary overlap between offence type and the traits that generated status and regard within the institution. As Tyler summarized: 'just being in for an armed robbery and being a hard cunt doesn't mean you're a good, decent lad. People can be an armed robber and be a right knob.'

Consumer Masculinity

Another significant source of status, with both indigenous and imported components, was consumer possessions. To wear branded-clothing and bright white trainers,[17] and to have a large number of toiletries, was in part a display of wealth and power outside

---

[15] Sex offenders have their own hierarchies, with child rapists at the base of the substructure and those who rape adult women sometimes able to defend their actions to their peers e.g. if the victim can be presented as having in effect consented.

[16] This aspect of the prisoner hierarchy was often reproduced by uniformed staff, as were denunciations of 'granny-bashing'. In discussion with prisoners, one senior officer pointed out that 'there would be more room in the system if we shot all the nonces' (fieldwork notes). At the same time, in challenging definitions of sexual offending, he reinforced a deeply regressive form of masculinity: 'we've all been there…who hasn't carried on when a woman's said "no"?'

[17] It is notable that white trainers, the footwear of choice in prison, are the goods most capable of displaying newness and therefore indicating income. This may be particularly important in those prisons where shoes are the only items of their own that prisoners are allowed to wear.

prison.[18] 'It's like the peacock effect', Tyler explained. 'Everybody wants to fan their tail out, show you what they are. Jail's a very materialistic society.' Prisoners entering Wellingborough, especially those who were young, were often fixated on issues relating to clothing: what could be handed in or worn on visits, for example. One new entrant to the prison was more concerned that his spare trainers had gone missing in transit than that his phonecards had also been lost. Prisoners were judged to some degree on the amount of money they earned through crime, and a prisoner with 'the best trainers, the best clothes on' was generally assumed to be 'hiding money out there, a drug dealer or something' (Morgan). Expensive jewellery or top-end designer clothing therefore operated as forms of decorative violence, communicating a prisoner's criminal success and experience. Possessions and appearances were also equated with personal ethics and social standing:

His cell—that plays a good part in [defining status]: what he's got in it, what clothes he wears, what trainers he's got on, if he's got a bit of dough or not. If he's got scruffy clothes on, [and] fucking stubble round his face, a trampy-tramp, you think 'fucking hell'; and if you see a man next to him smart as you like—nice jumper, nice pair of jeans, bad-boy pair of trainers, looking all fresh and sharp and that—you think 'they respect this, they've got morals'. The other guy obviously hasn't. (Cameron)

[If] you can afford things obviously you know the way to work the system, like how to do double-bubble, how to always never go short, how to get extra things and live a better life.... If someone comes into your cell and they see you've got everything in your cell, and your cell looks nice, they're going to think 'well obviously this guy's got something'. You'll go into someone else's cell and he's got nothing in there, he might be hard but he's got nothing—he don't know how to get things, he don't know how to sort himself. That's just the mentality of how people think.... They'll look at you and think: 'he's got nothing so he must be a nobody'. (Aaron)

The association of goods and clothing with status and morality had several dimensions. In part, it reflected a common belief that men who dressed in prison clothing were social and criminal failures, with few friends or resources on which

---

[18] The possession of toiletries was particularly important to younger prisoners, especially those who had come from YOIs, where toiletries were ostentatiously displayed in cells to demonstrate status, and personal appearance carried huge significance. The same values were applied to prison staff. One governor was particularly admired for his choice of designer shirts.

to draw.[19] Most prisoners questioned the moral credibility of anyone without such support. Indeed, a lack of external contact was often interpreted as a signal of disloyalty and depravity:

The way I look at it, if you've got friends outside that are in contact with you, that are sending you money and doing things for you and you've got family that are sending you money and doing things for you, then you must be a half decent person outside. [If they] don't have private cash, don't have friends writing or visiting, they must be a shitbag out there, they must be robbing friends or family, they can't be much of a person if they've got no contact with anybody. (Danny)

Cameron's quotation (above) also illustrated a perception that low self-respect was a manifestation of a lack of respect for others. Accordingly, prisoners who were drug users outside prison but sought to distance themselves from stereotypes of addiction often emphasized that they had always preserved personal pride, cleanliness, and visual respectability. Kieran asserted that, even when on crack: 'I've always maintained my personal hygiene...and I always dress good. That don't change. I never let my appearance go AWOL.' Aaron's statement highlighted the general materialism of prison culture. It also illustrated the alignment of personal possessions with prison wherewithal. A prisoner who could accumulate goods in a world of deficit transmitted intelligence, self-discipline, and an awareness of how to work the system. Conversely, to live in scarcity was to be marked out as a debtor, drug user, or poor coper. Here, the indigenous terms of imprisonment supplemented consumerist judgments imported from the wider community.[20]

Biographical Factors

Culture cannot be reduced to individual psychology. However, prisoners regularly referred to life events when expanding on views of status, and the links between moral attitudes and personal experiences were often plain. These connections inflected four

[19] There were some exceptions here. It was possible to generate kudos through an identity of ascetic purity: doing prison 'the hard way', without luxuries such as in-cell television or mattresses. This strategy was extremely uncommon, expressed in claims more than action.

[20] Disputes between prisoners and staff about cell hygiene and tidiness had different causes. These skirmishes represented wider struggles about power and control, particularly in the light of the escapes of the mid-1990s, when prison officers had been conditioned not to enter or interfere with prisoners' private spaces.

main areas: views on grassing, violence against women, sexual offences, and bullying and victimization.

A large number of prisoners blamed their predicament on having been grassed on, often by criminal associates or former friends. This attribution contributed to an intense resentment against forms of perceived treachery. For many prisoners, norms against grassing had been inculcated from an early age and were reinforced by experiences of emotional rejection by parents or girl-friends, creating acute sensitivities about disloyalty and breaches of personal trust. The contempt expressed for grasses was in part symptomatic of these deeper-seated feelings of betrayal.

Hostility to the physical and psychological abuse of women had its roots in widespread experiences of being raised in abusive house-holds or by single mothers. Protective discourses about female offic-ers were grounded in codes of honour that had often developed from witnessing domestic violence and being powerless to inter-vene, or from associating the difficulties of being a female worker in a male environment with the daily struggles of single motherhood. 'I've seen my mum get beaten long enough', Zack commented. 'No woman deserves a fucking beating. They weren't put on this fucking earth to be battered by blokes.' Many prisoners considered anyone who threatened to assault a female officer and anyone convicted of an offence against women as morally reprobate.

Life events had most significance in relation to sexual offences, bullying, and victimization. A large proportion of prisoners had been sexually and physically abused as children. These men strug-gled to contain their personal anger when discussing sex offenders or convictions relating to child abuse. Likewise, many prisoners had been bullied as children. When talking about prison victimiza-tion, they expressed their contempt for perpetrators with a searing sense of their own experiences (see Crewe and Maruna 2006).

Just because somebody's weaker, doesn't mean they're wrong. I don't like it, I don't like hearing about it. Because I was bullied when I was at school. And I won't sit around and watch people do it. (Carlton)

If anyone goes near [a vulnerable prisoner], the person that gives him grief will be in hospital. He's been bullied the whole of his life. I was bullied by my dad up to the age of eighteen so I know what being bullied is like. Anyone touches him, then the person who it is will be carted off the wing on a stretcher because I can't see that geezer get bullied. He's so vulner-able and he's suicidal with it. . . . I hate people that pick on the weak in jail, I really do detest bullies in jail. (Bradley)

Prisoners often insisted that there was no toleration for 'outright bullying' and that perpetrators were 'dealt with' on the wings. Although such claims were somewhat overblown, and prisoners defined bullying rather narrowly, interventions did sometimes occur. On E-wing, servery workers collectively confronted a prisoner discovered to have been bullying a foreign national who had few friends and a poor grasp of English. In a prison workshop one morning, Danny challenged a large, aggressive prisoner who had been berating an older, mentally vulnerable man for his lack of personal hygiene. Discussing the incident in an interview some weeks later, Danny explained his actions:

I can't abide a bully, I won't see it, because I know from my own personal experience what it's like. . . . Bad as I am, I've got a heart, and when I see that I feel sorry for that geezer [and] there's a big rising anger in me for the bully. . . . I've nearly been in a few fights over that guy. . . . I understand that he smells and all the rest of it, but you don't have to start shouting your mouth off and making him feel bad. I just can't understand how people can be so insensitive. I dunno whether that's because of what happened to me when I was at the kid's home, but I've always been the same. If I see somebody's scared, I won't let it happen.

The compassion conveyed in these quotations was not unique to those prisoners who had personal experience of victimization. In this respect, it is important to emphasize the ethical codes that exempted certain prisoners from normal judgments and placed limits on the consequences of weakness.

The Consequences of Weakness and Stigma

Sympathy for the vulnerable, weak, and drug-dependent was limited by two main factors. The first was a widespread ideology of personal responsibility that held individuals accountable for their own outcomes. 'I don't feel sorry for them because I've told them not to do it, or someone else has, but they've completely not listened, and now they've fucked themselves up. That's their fault' (Chris). Debt and addiction were widely seen as self-inflicted matters:

I feel sorry for anybody that's in a bad way, but at the end of the day, you normally find with those characters, bad smackheads, they quickly burn that [sympathy] off, y'know, you lose that very quickly, because it's self-afflicted. They've got themselves into that position. They never learn. (Stephen)

As implied here, the second limitation was the fact that, in the context of the prison, sympathy was quickly diminished and easily exploited (see Chapter 7).

Displays of emotional vulnerability were considered acceptable only in exceptional circumstances. These would include the death of a close family member, but not necessarily the break-up of a relationship, 'unless people knew that you'd been with your missus for say fifteen years and you was married and had kids' (Martin). As Danny noted, in general, the prison environment made emotional control crucial:

I've seen him on the phone crying, so I take it he must have family problems, but if you come to prison, you've got to know how to deal with it. Outside it's the same, it's just more intense in here. If you're weak, there's always gonna be somebody there to exploit you.

Most prisoners considered emotional expression a mark of weakness and a trigger for derision outside prison as well as inside. Masculinity was associated with emotional fortitude. The majority of prisoners came from socially dense communities, where reputation could be corroded by signs of frailty. In prison, where personal repute was even more essential and masculine identity was under greater threat (Sykes 1958; Newton 1994; Sim 1994a; Jewkes 2002), it was all the more important to suppress displays of emotional fragility.

Prisoners who could not 'handle themselves' or 'deal with their bird' were generally scorned. Verbal abuse was used to isolate prisoners from social support (O'Donnell and Edgar 1998), and men who succumbed to intimidation or failed to stand up for themselves were vulnerable to more intense forms of victimization:

In the majority of prisons you're not allowed to show any weakness at all. On my first sentence, I noticed then that people weren't allowed to show any weakness, because if they did they were targeted. People beat people up with words in prison; they'll find out who is the weakest by beating them up with words first and then spread the word, so then people will move in for the kill. (Jordan)

If anybody sees a weakness in you in jail, they'll prey on that weakness and they'll keep picking away at it. I'd prefer to have my face punched everywhere than let somebody take a liberty with me. I don't like violence. But I wouldn't let anybody take liberties with me. Because you back down to them once, you're going to back down to them all the time. And they're going to prey on that all the time. (Darren)

Concerns about appearing weak pervaded social interaction. Great significance was attached to seemingly trivial incidents, and apparently minor exchanges served as tests of nerve and character (Morris and Morris 1963; Toch 1992). These tests took several forms. When new on wings, prisoners who appeared weak or naïve were subjected to requests for tobacco or phone credit that ranged from outright intimidation—'I'm taking this off you'—to pressure—'you got some burn for me?'—or manipulation: 'can you lend me some burn, my private cash hasn't arrived; I'll give it you back'. Such situations demanded social skill. Refusal required an ability to say 'no' with enough assertion to be taken seriously but with suitable courtesy not to cause offence. Agreement required a capacity to say 'yes' without betraying fear and opening oneself up to more taxing demands. Men who responded naively or submissively risked further exploitation: 'you give them some burn, the next day they come back, and the next day—"oi, gimme some burn". Because I've given them it in the first place, they're taking kindness as weakness' (Leon); 'you ask for it [back], and they say: "listen, fuck off". You do get took advantage of' (Ross). Individual persecutors could intensify their level of victimization—'once they start taking the piss they think they've got one over you and they think, "I'm borrowing that" . . . ' (Max)—or exploitation could snowball and proliferate: 'if one person takes you for a pussy, there's going to be another twenty that will take you for a pussy' (Rhys).

Tests were built into the everyday social architecture, in particular, around the servery, phones, and pool tables, where confidence and assertiveness were routinely challenged.

People try and jump on the pool table. If you say, 'next', and some guy comes along and says, 'hold on, I'm next', and you say, 'hold on, you weren't here', then that's it: the chest comes out, the neck gets put forward, and one of you has got to back down. (Kyle)

If you're waiting for the phone or the pool table and a group of four lads come over, and say 'no, we've booked it', and you know quite well they haven't, you've got to say 'no you're not. I've been waiting ages. I'm next'. And just show them that you can't be walked over, basically. (Wilson)

These disputes were trivial in their immediate outcomes, as prisoners often recognized, but not in their wider consequences. To take a small amount of sugar from someone's cell or use complicated language in front of someone could be interpreted as an attempt to 'take liberties' or 'mug them off'. Allowing such things to occur put one's public credibility at risk.

For some prisoners, the possibility of being 'disrespected' was more than a matter of practical consequence. Morgan, for example, had contemplated attacking a prisoner with an improvized weapon simply for having sat in a seat normally used by his hometown associates and refusing to move when challenged. The event had 'really done my nut in', and left him feeling 'humiliated'. Other prisoners used similarly emotional language when they felt someone had 'taken the piss'.[21] These prisoners were paranoid about social reputation and hypersensitive to perceived slights, which they interpreted as slurs upon their entire character. Johnson (1987) argues that such reactions are typical of 'state-raised' prisoners (see Irwin 1970), who feel a kind of 'impotent rage' towards a world that has rejected them and precluded their emotional development. These men present menacing façades of cold masculinity, and are easily provoked to violence, but these psychic defences conceal brittle self-identities. Other authors have argued that the anxieties provoked by perceptions of being 'disrespected' often reflect childhood experiences of abandonment and residual feelings of shame (Gilligan 1996; Butler 2006). Certainly, for these prisoners, minor threats appeared to resonate with deep-rooted concerns about masculine status. To be 'above the line' of victimization was thus a psychological as well as a physical concern—protection from feelings of self-doubt and inadequacy.

---

[21] Interactions with staff were imbued with similar significance, as Fin's tale illustrated:

I said 'Miss, is there any chance you could possibly open my cell door for me?' She said 'no, no chance' [and] turned away and carried on talking. I put it across exactly that way. And the other lad ripped the piss out of me basically, for how nice I was. Now all the staff on the wing, even the ones that I particularly don't like, I'm always really polite with them. So straightaway my back was up. So I went downstairs, got a senior officer to open my door, [then] went in the shower. And I'm having a shower and I'm thinking 'how the fuck does she think she can talk to me like that? I've been nothing but courteous and nice to her'. And I thought 'no, I'm not having it'. If I didn't get it off my chest it would wind me up all night. So I've come out of the shower and I was rude. I went up to her and I said 'listen miss, it's obvious you didn't get this job for your looks'—another way of saying 'you ugly cunt'—'so I know you're not bone idle. So next time, when I speak to you nicely and ask you politely, don't think you can talk to me like I'm a prick, because I'm not a prick'. And I did go back afterwards and apologise to her, but it worked. Because it got my frustrations out. I went back and I said 'listen miss. I did go a bit ballistic at you but I just wanted to know that you did really offend me. I talked to you with nothing but courtesy. And talking to me like that especially when there's another inmate in earshot round you, I'm not having that. I'm not having you treating me like a cunt. Because I'm not a cunt and you can't treat me that way.'

For sex-offenders and informers, it was critical to maintain anonymity. Prisoners discovered as either risked hostile ostracism at best and organized violence at worst. Since there was much to lose in attacking another prisoner, exposure did not always lead to direct confrontation (see Chapter 8). A more common strategy was to leave a note under a prisoner's door advising him to put himself on protection or face the consequences. An alternative tactic was to set fire to a prisoner's cell. This was a form of retribution that could be enacted without a face-to-face encounter and was therefore less hazardous than a direct assault.

Similar reasons meant that 'muppets' and 'fraggles' were not always subjected to direct victimization. Outright harassment and physical terrorism were uncommon, and stronger prisoners often looked out for their weaker peers. Instead, bullying took forms that were softer, subtler, and less direct. Verbal derision and social exclusion were commonplace. Men considered 'bullshitters' were mocked and disregarded. Those who were particularly impressionable were used as entertainment ('stress toys')—wound up, misled, and manipulated. For example, one prisoner who had clear mental health deficits was persuaded that he should propose marriage to a female officer on the wing. Prisoners who were mentally slow or who struggled to make ends meet were easily exploited—paid to store goods or carry out acts of violence. Often, these prisoners did not recognize that they were being taken advantage of and were mocked all the more for the gratitude they showed when carrying out tasks that actually placed them at risk. To use Irwin's (1970: 79) term, these men were 'human putty' in the social world of the prison.

Yet it was rare for prisoners who were particularly weak, or whose agency was deemed defective, to be exploited ceaselessly or ruthlessly.[22] Little status could be derived from proving one's strength over prisoners who were old, defenceless, 'not made for prison' or 'not the full shilling' (prisoner, fieldwork

---

[22] It should also be noted that the hierarchy was not expressed through sexual exploitation. There were no specific terms for forms of interpersonal sexual activity or coercion, and no indication that they occurred at any time during my fieldwork. No doubt they do (O'Donnell 2004), but they are not central parts of the prison experience for the majority of UK prisoners.

notes). Prisoners often extended sympathy to white-collar criminals—although there were few—arguing that it was harsh to place them in an environment that was so alien to their experience.[23] Many also expressed a view that men who were 'just not fighters' should not be forced into physical confrontations. These exclusions were gendered: being either weak or effeminate meant being exempted from attack because both signified an acceptance of being subordinate in a hierarchy of masculinity.

Prisoners who had manifest mental health problems were also exempted from customary judgments. One such prisoner—who smoked cigarette butts discarded by other prisoners onto the wing floors, and begged for basic goods—was deemed too damaged to be held responsible for his own actions, even when these violated normal protocols:

He don't realise certain things. He owed me burn, and he was shouting downstairs, 'I'll pay you back next week!'. You can't do that in front of the screws because that's what brings it on top. I don't want to be seen as bullying—and he did it about four or five times. He's slow, it's too much work to make him understand (Wilson)

Seb also expressed a widely held sympathy for mentally ill prisoners for whom incarceration was patently inappropriate:

There's one kid I was padded up with, he can't read and write, he don't know the meaning of time, he don't know what a week is. I tried to explain it to him. He can't grasp it. I've helped him read and write his letters. He's had a bit of stick, been thumped a couple of times, because he's slow and he's trying to fit in. He's completely and utterly on his own. He don't know the difference between right and wrong, you know. I just think why on earth is something like that in here?

Compassionate sentiments were by no means universal. Nonetheless, to exploit vulnerability was to breach shared values, and carried penalties (at least in principle): 'If you do pick on somebody who everybody knows is weak, other heads will do you in' (Fin). Prisoners at the extremity of the hierarchy were often therefore protected, as well as sometimes abused. Men who

---

[23] Explaining that one prisoner did not 'suit prison', Danny observed as follows:

I'm not being funny or anything, but he's more like you than what he is us.
What, straight?
Straight, yeah.

were considered capable of looking after themselves or who had no obvious handicaps were afforded no such latitude:

If you're 'alright'—one of the lads, not an idiot—and someone's giving you a hard time, the chances are—depending on who's bullying you, what social status they've got, how aggressive they are, how game they are to have a straightener[24]—you've got to sort it out. If somebody's bullying somebody but you think they're roughly the same [in terms of ability to fight] people will leave it, unless it was the main geezer on the wing [or] somebody was directly taking a fucking liberty. (Fin)

If you're quiet on the wing and you're not doing no business, only a bully is gonna put it on your toes.[25] And then a couple of lads on the wing would probably do something about that. But if you was a loud character, a bit boisterous and someone puts it on your toes, for you to back down, you will probably have a couple of people say to you: 'I wouldn't have had that, I wouldn't have done that'. (Martin)

Prisoners who had already established their authority were allowed to display forms of kindness or vulnerability that other prisoners were wary of exhibiting: 'If you're a big, massive lad, if you've got muscles coming out of your neck, you can show as much weakness as you like and no one is going to say a peep to you' (Jordan). At the same time, a prisoner who was physically large but was witless or unwilling to fight was open to ridicule: 'If you're big and you're an [idiot], then people are going to slag you more. People are going to single you out in front of other people more' (Fin). Powerful prisoners who betrayed others or failed to support their claims to status were regarded with particular contempt:

If you're supposed to be a head, and you don't back it, you're a fucking faggot, and you're even worse than a faggot. Because you're trying to back it. You're trying to make out you're a head, but you're not. People will target you even more, it irritates [them] even more. Because you're trying to be something you're not. You're trying to rise up in the ranks and you ain't got it. And if you ain't got it, you're going to get punished. And people will go out of their way to do you in, because it's almost justified…. Like a weak person, a very weak person grassing on somebody: it happens. But, if you're a head, you're getting done in [if you grass]. (Fin)

[24] 'A straightener': a one-to-one fight, often informally arranged, which takes place without the use of weapons.

[25] To 'put it on someone's toes': to confront someone, forcing them to act or explain themselves.

To be powerful or to engage in status games carried certain expectations and responsibilities. Prisoners who pushed in queues had to be 'prepared to brazen it out' (Callum); those who got involved in trade had to be 'willing to take the consequences. [If] you're not willing to stand up for yourself and fight, then you're in big trouble' (Ashley).

Such consequences formed an oppressive social obligation. For some prisoners, gaining enough respect to avoid victimization meant embellishing tales of personal prowess and presenting a façade of fearlessness. Yet be found out as inauthentic, to be unable to 'back' one's claims, or to over-assert power were violations of the value system, and could justify retribution. Prisoners were therefore at risk if they showed weakness *or* if they faked strength. If strength was not naturally conveyed through a prisoner's aura, he walked a narrow path between deficient grit and excessive bluff. Admiration respect was greatest for prisoners who naturally *embodied* the prisoner code. These prisoners stood up for themselves when required and fulfilled the obligations of power without abusing their strength or imposing themselves without reason.

I think Bert is quite respected, because he doesn't go pushing his weight around just because he has got a lot of tobacco and if people don't pay up he don't go off his head, he says 'if you can't afford to pay me, tell me now, don't tell me when it comes to pay-day and you can't pay me'. He's that kind of person. He's not going to say he's better than anybody else. (Ian)

There's a few inmates on the wing who I have got genuine respect for because I like the way they carry themselves. They *could* be right intimidating bastards and they're not. They know what they're capable of and they don't flaunt it about. They don't abuse their power. There's a certain inmate on my wing, and he is one seriously fucking hard nut [but] he doesn't chuck his weight about [and] he will not tolerate bullying. (Zack)

The parallels with Sykes's (1958) analysis are striking. Admiration respect was strongest for prisoners who personified shared values while mitigating collective pains—showing generosity, consideration, and concern for others. Other prisoners carved out admiration through skills and talents (in sport, music or arts, for example), but these were seen as natural abilities rather than character *per se*, and they benefited the individuals who held them rather than the prisoner community as a whole.

The Experience of Stigma

Prisoner autobiographies have tended to be written either by high-status, relatively violent prisoners (McVicar 1974; Boyle 1977; Smith 2004) or by middle-class prisoners whose experiences have been conditioned by their social and cultural capital (e.g. Caird 1974; Peckham 1985; Archer 2002; Aitken 2003). The former are 'insider' perspectives, written from the vantage point of power. The latter are 'outsider' observations, whose narratives document a 'loss of innocence' about the system that is predicated on imprisonment being 'an aberration which has no coherent links to a past' (Morgan 1999: 335). Much less is known about prisoners for whom imprisonment and stigma are customary experiences. Although few interviewees characterized themselves as low-status prisoners, those who did exposed the particular pains that this burden engendered. Max, a prisoner trying to escape a reputation for grassing, reported feeling 'under stress, under pressure', and a 'niggling thought every time a new set of lads come [into the prison]' that they might know his history. Sid, who had placed himself in the segregation unit when other prisoners discovered the nature of his offence, described his situation thus.

Very stressful, very depressing, I sit in my cell and break down and have a little cry to myself, but there is nothing I can do about it, I've just got to hold strong.... Deep in my own heart and soul, I feel very vulnerable, I feel at risk, I don't know which way to turn, who to talk to, just in case they say, 'my mate knows you're...' whatever. I do get a bit scared, I can't deny that. [And] I've got to go back to the same area.... God knows what will happen.

How much of your time do you spend fearing this stuff?

Every day and every night and every second. I put a mask on, to hide the pain, so I try to have a laugh to bury that pain, and when I'm back in my cell I take that mask off and the pain is there again. It's been very painful.

Another prisoner in the segregation unit commented ruefully that, by placing himself in protection, his 'pride [had] gone'. If people from his home community were to find out, he said, his name would be permanently tarnished. To go on protection for reasons of debt or severe emotional vulnerability was not to be stained irrevocably, but it certainly tainted any claim to status.[26] Flows of information from the prison both to the outside world and to other prisons meant that bad reputations were easy to gain and much harder to discard.

Prisoners who struggled to cope materially expressed deep embarrassment about the lengths they went to in order to subsist. Lacking private resources and unemployed, Colin resorted to loaning out his television (in return for enough tobacco to make three roll-up cigarettes) and selling his food in order to get by. Explaining how this affected his self-esteem, he highlighted how personal dispossession reinforced shame and stigma:

I just feel bad that I have to do it. I suppose I feel bad that I've only got one pair of trainers in prison. And I don't have nice clothes. I feel that bad basically, when I look around.

What does 'bad' mean, when you say 'bad'?

Low, I just feel low, low in myself.

Ronan expressed similar sentiments:

I ended up selling loads of my stuff to get heroin. I had a brand new Ben Sherman watch, ended up selling that, I had a brand new Nike jacket that cost a hundred and forty quid, ended up selling that, I've sold a brand new Reebok tracksuit to get a bag of heroin for a tenner. And now I'm walking around with jeans that have got holes in. It don't make sense. I wish I had all them things back.

Weakness and stigma were mutually compounding. 'Smackheads' were disparaged in part because they were forced to sell goods in order to fund their habits. Prisoners who got themselves into debt were considered weak both for allowing themselves to sink into arrears and for the roles they were obliged to take on as a consequence.

Other prisoners were aware that they had little status among other prisoners, but professed little concern at this position. Ian, for example, knew that he was 'at the bottom', but declared that: 'it's where I want to be, I don't want to be part of the clique. Right at the bottom: that suits me fine. If I'm a fraggle I'm not bothered.'

---

[26] Any prisoner who had sought protection struggled to salvage his reputation (against suspicions of grassing and general mistrust), but this barrier was not absolute. Some interviewees were sympathetic to certain causes of self-segregation:

If they've shown vulnerability in the past, it might have been a stressful time, they split up with their wife, not getting any money sent in, having to borrow things, buy tobacco on the wing for double back and stuff and got themselves into debt and then had to protect themselves. I can show a bit of sympathy there and understand. (Alfie)

Claims of this kind were plausible because a prisoner did not need to seek status as long as he was above the line of potential exploitation. They also signalled important differences in views about status and stigma.

Status, Stigma, and the Prisoner Typology

The analysis up to this point has provided a broad picture of the prisoner hierarchy. The aim has been to provide as much detail as possible without underplaying the complexity of the status system or eliding the differences that cut across the general portrait. Given the significant differences between prisoners that were outlined in Chapter 5, it follows that there were important variations in what prisoners feared, admired, and denounced.

Focused on personal missions, *enthusiasts* avoided prison politics and struggled to comment on the details of the status system. Although they recognized that a hierarchy existed and that they were not its heroes, they inverted its normal co-ordinates. They condemned terms like 'fraggle' and 'muppet' as disrespectful; they were disdainful of prisoners who rocked the system; and they were openly apprehensive of the 'very, very dangerous' people (Luke) who inhabited many of the cells around them. Indeed, they sought symbolic distance from these men, differentiating the scope and morality of their offences from people who wilfully caused hurt or destruction. While they gave instrumental respect to armed robbers, murderers, and drug dealers, they granted them no appraisal respect, considering them immoral, irresponsible, and anti-social. They admired other *enthusiasts*—men who were trying to improve themselves and give something back to society. To illustrate their social munificence, they offered recognition respect fairly freely—certainly, to anyone prepared to reciprocate it. In terms of the respect they sought for themselves, they craved only certain forms of validation. Both Zack and Ian believed they were respected for their decency and sincerity: 'Because I am what I am, you know, the way I act, I don't put any [masks] on' (Ian). Luke sought respect only from his 'mature friends', 'for the fact that I keep myself clean and carry myself well'. Power over others was of no interest.

Retreatists expressed similar sentiments, although they were less inclined to judge other prisoners and more capable of acknowledging their own low status. 'I'm just a petty criminal really', Rhys mused, 'they look on me as nothing'. Alfie's shame about his own history meant he tried not to evaluate others on the basis of past behaviour: '[I] judge them face value, what they mean to me [and] their conversation.' Both Noah and Alfie acknowledged that they mixed in relatively low-status cliques: 'they wouldn't be looked at as cool characters on the landing. Mine's a bit of a mix-up, odd-job sort of mob' (Noah). Like *enthusiasts*, they were wary of, rather than impressed by, serious, violent criminals, and dismissive of the 'belligerent' behaviour of younger, more boisterous prisoners. In general though, their withdrawn mentality meant that they were more ambivalent than *enthusiasts* about matters of respect, and about their own moral value being recognized overtly. Whereas *enthusiasts* took care of their appearances in order to exhibit their pride and spiritual rebirth, for *retreatists*, it was unimportant to display these sentiments to others. Neatly worn prison clothing was adequate in order to signal self-esteem. At most, *retreatists* wanted to be acknowledged by others as worthy of basic respect and civility, and then left to their own devices. Reflecting their hopes to be treated with recognition respect despite their past transgressions, they offered respect to others as a matter of course.

Different kinds of *pragmatist* held quite different attitudes about power, status, and stigma. Some claimed indifference to such matters, recognizing that they were ordinary, somewhat invisible, prisoners with little claim to status and little interest in its accumulation. Younger *pragmatists* were the men most likely to lack compassion for weaker prisoners, often reflecting the culture of ruthless and endemic bullying that existed in the Young Offenders Institutions from which they had graduated. They expressed little sense of automatic allegiance to other prisoners and considered some men almost unworthy of recognition respect. Cameron used a pitiless language of 'fraggles', 'saps', 'tramps', 'dickheads', and 'out and out fools', for whom he disclosed little sense of empathy or compassion.[27] He also admitted that he used his size to his advantage against prisoners with less bulk and confidence:

I stamp my authority a little bit too much sometimes. I'll pick on a weak person, for some reason. I don't know why, I just will. Probably just to

---

[27] The term 'disclosed' is used here because it seems likely that he felt compassion even if he did not express it. The life stories of prisoners like Cameron were awash with contradictions. They frequently veered between heartlessness and vulnerability in ways that betrayed their overt appearances of callousness and instead suggested that any admission of softer feelings provoked considerable anxiety.

get a bit of confidence for myself. [Or] just to get on the phone first, or something like that.

Bullying served in part to boost low self-esteem and to ensure being classified as 'above the line'. Cameron employed an analogy of 'managers and employees' to characterize what he saw as the key division on the wings. He was desperate to belong among the former. This distinction also marked a particular admiration among younger *pragmatists* for prisoners with 'things to offer'—goods, services, and wisdom about the prison experience. Cameron disapproved of drug users, but he revered the men in prison who supplied them. Pragmatists thought highly of prison drug dealers (mainly *players*), while lacking the contacts, confidence, or resources to emulate them. Callum, for example, noted that, 'because I'm a loner, I'm just not in a position to do it'. He was also candid about the power differential between himself and more dominant characters on the wing:

Certain people you don't fuck with. I'll walk in the front [of the dinner queue] and there will be at least five people going, 'fuck off, what are you doing, man', and then somebody else will walk in and it's 'alright mate'.... Nobody will argue with them and say no.

For these *pragmatists*, the ability to defend oneself and 'keep quiet' were characteristics that were considered both admirable and prudent. The conflation of these traits—of instrumental and appraisal respect—was significant. It indicated the socialization of these prisoners within a range of environs where such behaviours were essential both for respect and for survival: urban ghettos, children's homes, juvenile detention centres, and YOIs (see Irwin and Cressey 1962; Irwin 1980). For these men, status within the prison was both a means to an end and an end in itself.

More vulnerable *pragmatists* professed slightly different values. They were aware of their lowly status and their relative insignificance in the eyes of others, although they often claimed that the terms by which they were labelled were used widely or in jest. 'Everybody gets called a muppet', said Dom, 'I mean I have a few times, as a joke, but I just laugh at it'. These claims were the protective techniques of the disrespected, prisoners who strived to claim status but often did not receive it. Accordingly, they resented prisoners who they knew looked down on them: men who 'think [they] rule the wing' (Declan) and 'like to think they're bigger than others' (Joey). These men they branded as bullies or 'cowards [that] hide behind other people's muscles' (Chris). The prisoners they most admired were the older, more mature men who coped with imprisonment in ways that they could not, and who often provided them with guidance, advice, and pledges of protection. Lifers and *players* were to some degree feared and were certainly seen as a different category of 'more serious' prisoner. As low-status prisoners, often having committed petty offences, there were few peers on whom these *pragmatists* could look down.

Stoics tended to avoid prison politics. Many of them were willfully oblivious to the dynamics of wing affairs. George, for example, had stopped playing pool on the wing in order to escape status games and competitive bravado.[28] Since their primary purpose was the avoidance of trouble, *stoics* did not actively seek to be respected so much as ensure that they were not *dis*respected. As Nathan put it:

I don't wanna be put on a pedestal by anything or anyone. But also I don't want the reverse of that. That's what it's all about you know, you don't want to be labelled, to get a negative label, because it can cause problems and the whole purpose of going through jail, from my point of view, is to avoid those problems:... grass, nonce, they're the two extremes [labels], but then you've got debt-heads, hypocrite, two-faced, shit-stirrer, bully— they may cause you hassles.

Given the sentence lengths that most *stoics* were serving, and the awe this yielded among many prisoners, the ambition to avoid being tested or troubled was achieved almost automatically. From their perspective (and compared to the higher-security establishments they had experienced), the hierarchy in Wellingborough was relatively shallow and insignificant. Labels carried 'less weight' (Tommy). These included some categories that they privately felt were significant—in particular, the label 'wrong 'un', when applied to domestic burglars and those who robbed the vulnerable. 'I wouldn't piss on these granny-bashers if they were on fire', one lifer claimed (fieldwork notes). Many expressed nostalgia for a more dignified era of imprisonment and looked down both

---

[28] Many prisoners also talked about the petty dangers of the gym, where the amount of weight one lifted could be the basis for macho brinkmanship:

If I go to the gym I would just like to go and just do my little bit and keep my muscles flexed and tight but some guys...their mentality, they'll be in the gym and they'll be watching you and because they're probably pushing more weights they think 'oh he's a wimp'. They're just waiting for a little raindrop to just drop and catch them before they blow it into a big argument and then before you know it you have to end up trying to push your weight. (Jacob)

on drug addicts and drug dealers, who they felt had sullied the prison environment. Likewise, they despaired of the immaturity of many younger prisoners, who they felt were excessively noisy, inappropriately fussy, insufficiently stoical, and too easily mollified by the prison's material incentives. *Stoics* were judgmental in these respects, and often rather snobbish about petty criminals, but they also dismissed the notion that more serious crimes were 'impressive'. Years of prison experience meant that there were few prisoners whom they feared, particularly in the Cat-C estate. Their default position was to give recognition respect routinely, on the basis of shared predicament. Often too, they reserved judgment about the particulars of other people's cases and behaviour: 'he's got his own burden to bear, y'know, who am I to judge him?' George asked rhetorically. Admiration respect was granted primarily on the basis of prison behaviour, to men who were self-contained, honourable, and sensitive to the imperatives of institutional living.

Players were considerably more judgmental and were less inclined to respect other prisoners on principle. As signalled in the terms they employed to describe the prison's pecking order, they perceived the hierarchy as steep and clear-cut. There were 'leaders and followers...those who give and those who take' (Paul), 'head men and soldiers' (VJ). Prisoners in the subordinate categories were viewed as socially inferior: 'thick, stupid, immature...not on my level' (Wilson), 'nobodies' (Paul). These included 'screw-boys', drug users, 'punks, who talk shit' (VJ) and 'plastic gangsters who think they're the main man' (Pierce). Whereas *enthusiasts* distinguished between 'sensible lads' and 'jack-the-lads', *players* divided prisoners into 'lads' and 'idiots', while often casting young *pragmatists* as pathetically aspirational 'wannabes'. More powerful *players* exploited men who were weak and pliable, and felt little concern about the humiliations that they imposed on others.

In contrast, their veneration of power meant that more powerful *players* had admiration respect for other prison leaders, even when these men were from rival cities or factions. Throughout his life story, Ashley described his regard for other powerful men and detailed his realization that he could bolster himself by establishing connections with other 'heads' and 'faces'. His declared strategy in prison was similar: to 'get to know the top boy in each job' and reinforce his influence through social links across the establishment. One prison work area had become a magnet for a number of heads, who had recognized each other's social prominence. These more powerful *players* admired other men who were at the centre of prison trade and politics. Although other *players* (and some *pragmatists*) had little lust for power, they still granted esteem to men of influence:

Ashley's a well-known and feared man in Nottingham. Very well known and very, very, very feared. He's dangerous. He's known to switch on people, and he'll beat them and humiliate them. But at the same time he's the most lovable guy you can meet. He's a really nice guy.... He was a bad boy, but he would talk to anyone. And he would talk to anyone with respect. [If] you're vulnerable, he wouldn't see that and try and take advantage. I think a lot of people respected that. Because he could have took liberties on there with people and he didn't. (Kieran)

Ashley got on with everybody. Grew up in the slums, but nice as pie. Could talk properly, could act properly. Very smart, really. And he had a lot of respect for the way he was. Because he wasn't a cunt. But at the same time, he were an evil cunt. He can be an evil cunt, but he weren't an evil cunt. (Fin)

For these *players*, the fusion of ruthlessness and beneficence was admirable. Power was a thing respected in itself, and to be respected through fear was as good a reason as any. *Players* policed their reputations fastidiously, drawing clear lines around the behaviours they would tolerate from others, and reacting aggressively if anyone tried to label them pejoratively.[29] They almost never expressed any fear of others; rather (as above), they redefined their fear as admiration. Appraisal respect and instrumental respect were in this way conjoined.

Players cared more than other prisoners about the geographic origins of their peers, distinguishing between major conurbations and what Wilson branded 'faggot towns'. Kudos was attached to big-city criminality. They also made more categorical judgments than most prisoners about the offences for which other men were convicted. Paul evaluated prisoners according to whether they were in prison

---

[29] Paul was shocked to see a man allow other prisoners to shave off his eyebrows, dunk him in the showers, and cover him in custard as part of his pre-release celebrations:

I wouldn't have that, no way. No-one could shave my eyebrows. I'd say: 'whoever does it, do it—but I'll do them', and I would, that's it, end. I wouldn't take it. I've been involved when people go home. I'll chuck water on them, I might give them the odd little [punch], [but] that's the end of it. And that's all I expect. If anything goes further than that then I'm not having it, and most people know. Most of the dickheads that do [that] rubbish, I don't [mix] with them so if they join in they ain't got no right to.

for selling drugs or for using drugs. In direct contrast to *enthusiasts*, *players* saw 'blatant', violent crime as morally superior to minor, acquisitive offences—less 'shady' or 'dirty', more honest, upfront, and masculine. They judged others on the basis of their backgrounds, but they also saw prison as a key site of authenticity—a place where 'true colours' were exhibited and 'real men' made their marks afresh.

The relationship between adaptive mode and status was not straightforward. No prisoners were universally respected. In Noah's words, 'some kids are top dogs just because they are the muscle and nobody can beat them. [But] what some people's top dog [is] to me might be top mug. To me, he's top plonker.' *Players* tended to be relatively powerful prisoners, and more credibility was granted to men who manipulated the system than those who complied with it. But even *players* acknowledged that there were benefits in having positive relationships with staff and in certain forms of compliance. 'Even the baddest man talks about his parole', Isaac commented. For some *players*, there were limits to the steps that might be taken to appear submissive: Stephen was adamant that he would never become part of the 'toilet cleaning gang' (i.e. wing cleaners). Others dismissed the possibility of applying to be on the voluntary testing unit because it meant being subjected to a more demanding, and therefore humiliating, regime. Yet many prisoners with powerful reputations were unashamed to make compromises if these accelerated their progression or allowed them to continue their illicit activities. They, as much as others, considered being released as quickly as possible the primary objective. Obedience could therefore be presented as an enlightened form of wisdom.

Enthusiasts who complied without cynicism, or aligned their aims to those of the system, were rarely accorded high status. In the eyes of many *players*, these men were 'mugs' and 'suckers'. Yet they were often influential among other *enthusiasts* and among those *pragmatists* who saw self-improvement as an admirable objective. When pursued with caution, without yielding too fully to institutional objectives or without an explicit discourse of moral 'goodness', self-improvement was certainly not looked down upon. This path was steered by most *stoics*, whose status was more or less guaranteed by their prison experience. *Pragmatists* occupied various points in the status system. Some were the prison's most vulnerable inhabitants, and sat on the lowest rungs of the social ladder. Others were more neutral, or were the mobile young tearaways whose future trajectories were as yet unclear.

Conclusion

The sociology of American prisons tells a story of the gradual dovetailing of appraisal and instrumental respect. In the Big House prison, while 'toughs' who exercised coercive power in exploitative ways were both feared and envied, it was 'real men', whose behaviour was co-operative, who were admired (Sykes 1958; and see Irwin 2005). By the 1970s, changes in the prison's population and administration had transformed its normative system and social structure. As racial and ethnic conflict outside the prison seeped into the institution, the prisoner society fragmented into mutually antagonistic groups. Violent street gangs began to dominate the prisoner world, and rejected the informal incentives that until then had structured the inmate hierarchy and been the basis of institutional order. Gang membership became the most effective way of alleviating the pains of imprisonment. Codes of allegiance and equality applied only within these secondary groups. Other norms encouraged the exploitation of out-group prisoners (Jacobs 1977, 1983; Irwin 1980, 2005; Johnson 1987; Hassine 1999). The collective ideals of toughness and machismo that had previously helped to diminish the frustrations of imprisonment became sources of exploitation. Aggression supplanted fortitude as the basis of admiration. In many institutions, the administration accommodated gang leaders in the interests of stability, reinforcing their power over other prisoners (Jacobs 1977). More recently, this stratum of violent and gang-affiliated prisoners has been amputated from the mainstream prison population through super-max segregation. These ultra-coercive environments have produced behaviours that are ever-more violent and desperate (Rhodes 2004).

In the UK, the prison's social structure has been defined by very different interactions between the institution and the external environment. Most European societies have not had the kinds of organized gangs or profound racial cleavages whose importation into prison have led to so many problems in the US (Morgan 2002). Mathieson (1965) accounted for the much flatter hierarchy within a Norwegian therapeutic prison in part by pointing to the country's much less developed criminal culture. Yet the similarities between some aspects of Wellingborough's prisoner hierarchy and those described in the international literature show the significance of structural factors in defining prisoner prestige. Attributes such as bravery, stoicism, criminal maturity, intelligence, honesty, and generosity have been repeatedly identified as sources of respect, while stupidity, naivety, cowardliness, disloyalty, and instability have been consistently associated with stigma and dishonour (e.g. Clemmer 1940/1958: King and Elliott 1977; Winfree *et al.* 2002; Irwin 2005). Such factors reflect the inherent properties of the prison: its compressed social environment, and its deficits in personal space, safety, trust, information, and material wellbeing. Prisoners who conform to collective imperatives acquire appraisal respect. Those who breach them—in changing ways, for example, through drug use—are degraded and devalued.

Instrumental respect and influence can be achieved through the exploitation of the prison's deficits and the provision of services that mitigate its pains. In Wellingborough, the primary source of power—heroin—was notable in that its provision could not be integrated into the official reward system, and its influence could be exercised indirectly and inconspicuously. Drugs fulfilled an important need, and the service that dealers offered gave them considerable power, if not necessarily admiration. Physical and social capital were likewise useful resources within the environment, allowing prisoners to forge some degree of social autonomy. But violent potential was not the primary basis of prestige, reflecting an institutional culture that eschewed authoritarian means. Violence against the regime was difficult to justify and was not stoked or rewarded by institutional reactions. The prison was not defined by an all-pervasive culture of violent masculinity (c.f. Sim 1994a). The traits that reaped benefits and elicited appraisal respect were more often shrewdness and stealth than unrefined aggression.

Institutional factors were thus significant in shaping the terms of power. As previous chapters have explained, there was much to lose in explicitly asserting power or engaging in many of the illicit activities that could lessen the pains of imprisonment. Meanwhile, the institution relinquished little power to influential prisoners or factions in the interests of accommodation (c.f. Carroll 1974; Jacobs 1977). The main frustrations of prison life could be resolved more effectively through institutional compliance than through other prisoners. The degree to which individuals sought to amass power and exert interpersonal influence was thereby diminished. There were no 'king-pins' directing affairs between prisoners or pulling strings across the establishment with tacit institutional approval. Category-C conditions, where status could be forecast into external spheres, meant that prisoners were less inclined to try to acquire visible influence or dominate their peers: for most prisoners, the battle was 'getting outside'.

At its apex, the social hierarchy was therefore relatively flat. For the majority of prisoners, the most important thing was to be left alone—'above the line'. Prisoners who actively sought power did so within limits, and through relatively surreptitious means. Influence was generally restricted to cliques or trade circles. In general, its scope was cellular rather than linear, creating pockets of interpersonal power. There was almost no 'leadership' to speak of, and—as Sparks *et al.* (1996) also reported—no 'ruling class' as such. Where leadership did exist, it was fluid and informal. Unlike in some jurisdictions (see, for example, Kaminski 2004), the hierarchy was not highly rigid or steeply stratified. Most prisoners knew their approximate location within the hierarchy, but these were not formalized rankings or well-defined positions so much as vague categorizations. There were no ritual procedures for vertical mobility and few barriers to contact between prisoners of different status. Inasmuch as some prisoners did not mingle across social strata, they did so electively—often because of their general orientation to the sentence rather than because of being actively excluded. These distinctions in adaptation and attitude also meant that there was not a universal consensus about what crimes and activities were worthy of awe, admiration, and fear.

Structures of power from outside prison were not reproduced or translated inside prison in a simple manner. Certainly, criminal experience and wealth, and a range of attitudes about issues such as masculinity and drug use, were relevant in the allocation of status and stigma. But status could not be guaranteed by offence category alone, and there was no simple equation between crime-type and social prestige (Morgan 2002). In many respects, imprisonment compressed criminal hierarchies from the streets, inciting prisoners to mix more broadly than outside, stripping away many identity props, and exposing prisoners to conditions that could revise and transform existing reputations. Judgments and perceptions inside the prison were also mitigated by notions of strength and weakness, with prisoners at the extremes of the hierarchy held to account in different ways for their actions and behaviour. Power meant obligation, while extreme vulnerability did not lead to brutal or universal exploitation. The hierarchy was shaped by moral considerations as well as structural deficits, institutional imperatives, and views imported from the community.

7

Friendship and Social Relations

It might be expected that the conditions of imprisonment would give rise to close friendships and strong bonds of solidarity. With the exception of super-max establishments, where social life is all but obliterated, prisons impel their inhabitants to form social relationships, throwing strangers into shared residential spaces and encouraging alliances that help mitigate deprivations in physical safety, material provision, and social support.[1] In some carceral conditions, the sense of common purpose and shared circumstances leads to what might be called 'structural solidarity'. Yet, at the same time that the prison incites affiliation, it also circumscribes the forms that these relationships can take. As Sykes (1958) highlighted, the common experience of captivity can create social bonds, but prisoners are acutely aware that their peers have committed some form of social transgression. In an enclosed social space, this can create defensiveness and suspicion. As this book has emphasized, prisoners range considerably in their backgrounds and values, and they may feel bonded neither by their current situation nor by their future expectations.

In Wellingborough, 'you don't make friends in prison' was a recurrent assertion, yet its meaning was complex and not all men agreed with its claim. Almost all prisoners described an environment that was low in trust and emotionally alienating, where the risks of personal disclosure and the obstacles to friendship formation were significant, and where alliances were shaped by complex continuities and disconnections between the prison and

---

[1] The closest equivalent in the UK of a super-max facility is the close supervision centre at HMP Woodhill. Around thirty prisoners are kept in conditions ranging from total solitude to very limited social mixing. But even for those on total segregation, some form of social life is possible: prisoners can communicate with each other by shouting through windows or under doors, by talking via ventilation systems, heating pipes, or toilet cisterns, or by sending letters to each other—even though these have to go outside the prison system before coming back in.

the outside community. However, these conditions set the terms for a variety of social outcomes, enabling as well as constraining the formation of social relationships according to differences in personal history and future aspirations. Often rooted in the outside world or in common social experiences, relationships carried complex obligations, were subject to particular limits, and were entered into with various degrees of commitment and motivation. It is these aspects of interpersonal relations in prison— their roots, terms, and implications—that the chapter aims to document.

The chapter begins by describing the structure of primary social relationships and by highlighting the structural, institutional, and imported factors that encouraged and obstructed their formation. It accounts for exceptions to general trends, explains the bases and nature of prison friendships, and the social inclinations and expectations of different prisoners. It goes on to explain the organization and character of primary and secondary social groups, and the relationships between these groups, focusing in particular on ethnic and race relations within the prison.

The Structural Determinants of Prisoner Relationships

Structural inducements

Like all institutions, but particularly those that are more or less 'total', prisons are places of enforced interaction and civility. As a result, there is a ritual quality to many social exchanges, one which is found in the outside world, but is all the more vital in a domain that is so volatile and compressed.[2] In Wellingborough, it was essential to find a *modus vivendi* with cellmates and co-workers that was neither too indifferent nor too familiar. Prison etiquette demanded that a prisoner did not ask too many questions about someone else's crime—although to reveal one's own was expected—nor disclose too readily the details of his own personal life. At the same time, suspicion was cast on the taciturn and the socially reticent. On a prison corridor or waiting for a gate to be opened, sustained, direct eye contact could be taken as

---

[2] The ritualized nature of the environment meant that the nature of prisoner social relations was somewhat inscrutable on the basis of observation alone. A handshake, a joke, or the sharing of a cigarette could represent anything from a trade relationship to deep friendship. These distinctions became more apparent only through interviews.

a challenge, but bowing one's head or averting one's gaze could be interpreted as a sign of weakness. Nods and perfunctory greetings had to be exchanged, while accidental physical contact was to be avoided. Despite the underlying tensions and violent punctuations of prison life, these rituals helped maintain a generally smooth façade and contributed to the daily reproduction of social order (Goffman 1961; Sparks *et al.* 1996).

Social contact was hard to avoid. A small number of prisoners enjoyed relative solitude and remained in their cells throughout association periods, working on personal projects such as university assignments or artwork. However, some interaction was inevitable, not only when using showers or telephones, or when in work or education, but also because there was no such thing as private territory (see Cohen and Taylor 1972). Noah described this deprivation as follows:

On the outside, once you've come into your own house, you shut your door, you've got your privacy. And that's what prison takes away from you. My door cannot close. When it's time for association, anybody can walk through that door. So you're permanently meeting people.... You have to tolerate it. Some days, I get back from work, it'll just be people, people, people, everybody there. You want to get away, but there's nowhere to get away to.

There were other pressures to socialize. Although many prisoners found association periods tedious (and dreaded weekends, when these periods were extended), even these prisoners described a powerful compulsion to leave their cells:

It's boring. [Association] every day is too much, it really is. You can stay in your cell. But when your door's open, if you're banged up for x amount of hours in the day, once that door gets opened it's human instinct to get out. Lock an animal in a cage, open the door, it's going to walk out. You can bang your own door up but you don't want to do that. (Ross)

It drags. The amount of people that say, 'I just wish you could get your dinner and then get behind the door'.

Why not just close your door?

Because you know it's open. I think. Because you know it's open [and] you can just walk out. (Joey)

These comments signalled the social impetus produced by the deprivation of liberty. Furthermore, men who kept to themselves were suspected of having 'something to hide' and risked stigmatization. There were also institutional requirements to be sociable: 'I'm more of my own company person', said Jordan, 'but I will socialize because it's expected of me. They say it's not good to build up an antisocial attitude'. Prisoners did not necessarily want to socialize but nor did they want to self-confine. Many were induced into a state of social purgatory that lay between seclusion and sociability, with the advantages of neither.

While these conditions impelled only shallow social contact, and it was possible to engage on this level alone, structural imperatives encouraged the formation of more durable social ties. Mutual alliances countered three intrinsic threats (Sykes 1958). The first was social isolation. As Danny explained, social relationships were vital in providing company and conversation:

If people say 'you've got to be loyal to yourself', that's not true. You might think of yourself first, like you make sure you've got your own burn before you buy burn for him, but it definitely goes more than just yourself: you gotta think of your group.... I pick friends because I need people to talk to, people I can relate to, that are on the same level as me. It helps me get through my bird.

The second threat was material hardship. Group membership enabled prisoners to borrow goods and combine resources. It gave them confidence that their basic needs would be met in times of adversity. When a prisoner lost his job or was denied private spending as a punishment for rule violation, it was common to see his friends purchasing tobacco on his behalf and providing him with phone credit. Third, social groups provided physical support, mitigating deficits in personal safety. Being associated with a larger social body reduced the risk of being attacked or exploited. As the following quotation indicates, when assaults on individuals were weighed up, they took into consideration wider social affiliations:

I don't think it would come to [an attack] because they know that the four of us are close. They can look at us and we're all a half decent size and they know we've always got burn, we've always got food, we've always got everything, so they know that we're not nobodies, so they're going to think twice. (Aaron)

For the majority of prisoners, relationships of some kind were therefore a social necessity. Group development was partly an outcome of the risks of the environment. Structural conditions also shaped the nature of relationships, limiting their depth and making 'friendships' possible only in certain circumstances. As the following sections detail, most prisoners differentiated between 'proper friendships' and the more pragmatic relationships that imprisonment generally enabled.

The structure of primary relationships

Friendship patterns varied, but there were consistencies in the ways that prisoners characterized different kinds of social relationship. 'Proper friends' or 'real mates' were uppermost in the hierarchy of affiliation. Most prisoners reported having between one and three friends of this kind in the prison, although some had none. Generally, these were men known prior to imprisonment: relatives, co-defendants or close friends from the community. Loyalties between proper friends were deep and powerful. In terms of physical and emotional support, most prisoners claimed that they would 'go to the end of the earth [for them], even if they were wrong' (Brian), 'be there, whether they need it or not' (Martin). Trust was high: 'if I say something to them I know it won't go no further. There is honour there, they ain't going to say anything to anyone else' (Bradley).

For the majority of Wellingborough prisoners, prison was a place where establishing these proper friendships from scratch was impossible or imprudent (see Morris and Morris 1963; Jewkes 2005b). Relationships between prisoners who had met only while imprisoned were instead categorized as 'prison friendships'. Prison friends were men to whom you would lend goods without interest or offer tobacco in times of need. They were prisoners whose circumstances and release you cared about, and who 'you could go to if you got a [bad] letter'. A prison friend could 'go in your cell without telling you', and be trusted not to steal anything or read personal letters. Rhys described these friends as 'lads who I could meet up [with] on the out, and go for a few drinks'. However, the conditional tense was significant here, since contact on release was unlikely. On the whole, these were wary, situational friendships that involved less commitment than proper friendship, as Callum detailed:

I'd get involved [for a prison friend] but not as far as I would for someone in my own firm. I'd split up a fight, I might throw in a couple of jabs, I'd pull somebody off him if he was getting his head stamped on, but I wouldn't go in fighting like [I would] for a co-D or if my brother was in here.[3] [For them] I'd go fucking sick on the bastards.

---

[3] · 'Co-D': co-defendant.

With prison friends, rather than proper friends, trust was also limited: 'I wouldn't let them into personal details and things like that', said Connor. 'You don't really go deep, you don't really talk about family and stuff', Pierce explained. Very few prisoners gave family details or addresses to men they did not know prior to custody. The limitations of these relationships were widely and openly acknowledged. Prisoners talked in front of each other about their shallow and transitory nature: 'it's just prison friendship isn't it, it won't last'. Many prisoners saw 'friend' as too intimate a term for men in this bracket, preferring to describe them as 'very good acquaintances' (Joey).

'Associates'—the third tier of prison affiliation—were sources of routine company and conversation. Often, they were drawn from beyond the wings—from workplaces and areas such as the gym.[4] Parallels were often drawn between prison associates and work colleagues in the community: people for whom one did not have strong emotional attachments but would not want to see in trouble and would support in certain situations: 'say you went out for a drink with your colleagues, and one of them got into a fight, you'd probably either try and split the fight up, or you might back them up a bit' (Pierce). Most prisoners had several associates and a larger number of casual acquaintances—'people I say hello to or who I work with' (Rhys). Some prisoners classified anyone who was courteous to them as an associate of sorts, although, as Carlton noted, these relationships were rudimentary and somewhat superficial: 'anyone can treat you with respect, and that's reciprocated, but it's not the same as *trust*'. Trust was the resource whose absence was the main hindrance to friendship formation.

Structural impediments

The scarcity, dangers, and limitations of trust were crucial impediments to the development of close social relationships. Trust is particularly important in situations of 'ignorance or uncertainty with respect to unknown or unknowable actions of others' (Gambetta 1988: 218, cited in Sztompka 1999: 25). Paradoxically though, it is in such contexts that trust may be hardest to achieve, for placing trust requires that one has true information about the

---

[4] Precise definitions varied considerably. Some prisoners distinguished only between 'proper friends' and 'associates', and characterized the latter in ways that were closer to my definition of 'prison friendship'.

trustee. In particular, it requires accurate knowledge about their past and present conduct: 'Without such knowledge trust is blind and the chances of breach of trust are high' (Sztompka 1999: 70). In Wellingborough, the difficulty of making reliable judgments about personal character and credentials placed significant limits on the granting of trust. As the following quotations indicate, the prison was considered a highly partial and inauthentic social setting:

People tell you what they're in for, but you don't know what they're in for.... Because people front. Sometimes in jail you don't see the real person. People claim they're driving this car or that car and they're doing this and they're doing that, and really they've got a Metro and they're not doing fuck all.... People can chat shit outside, but you can see. (Isaac)

Outside, you see the real side of people more. By the things they do, and how they go on out there. Because when you're in prison, everyone's got a sort of barrier.... Outside, you can see how someone really lives, what they get up to. There's just more leeway on the outside, basically. Inside, people have certain barriers up.... You don't see their bad side as much, their bad habits. They're not going to start telling you all the bad and horrible things they've done out there. Basically, if you meet someone in jail, you tell them what you want them to know. (Connor)

Imprisonment limited the potential for evaluating others in four main ways: it inhibited opportunities to gauge personality and sincerity; it encouraged artificial behaviour; it effaced information about past behaviour and social credentials; and it provided limited guidance to future conduct.

First then, although imprisonment provided sustained opportunities to observe others, it restricted the range of situations in which character could be evaluated. As Gavin outlined, outside prison, 'I know what my mates are like at the pub. I know what they're like drunk. I know what they're like on holiday. I know what they're like in front of women.' Kieran explained that: 'you've done more things with your friends on the out. [In jail] you ain't gone on the pull together, you ain't gone raving. There's millions of things you ain't done.' The basis on which identity could be judged was highly restricted.

Second, prisoners were sceptical that public behaviour in prison was a true reflection of character. Life on the prison landings is more *omni*-optical than 'panoptical' (Cohen and Taylor 1972; c.f. Foucault 1977). Surveillance is conducted not by the minority but the masses. Since there is little escape from public judgment, the consequences of social interaction are amplified. As Chapter 6 noted, stigma was highly adhesive and status could easily be lost. This culture of hypervisibility could in theory serve as an aid to trust, heightening 'accountability' (Sztompka 1999). Instead, by producing a culture where self-presentations were defensive, it mitigated against the tendering of trust. Most prisoners recognized that distorting one's character was a common coping mechanism, and assumed in others the same strategies, performances, and social masks that they themselves employed to avoid negative social labels: 'I'm fully aware that people exist from behind a mask. I know I'm not getting to know that person fully. There's going to be a certain thickness of barrier there' (Nathan). Social identities in prison were thus generally assumed to be artificial and unreliable.

A further obstacle to trust was caused by the prison's dislocation of prisoners from their pasts. Much of the anxiety felt towards strangers centred on the potential for them to lie about their criminal history and moral credentials. In particular, the widespread assertion that 'you don't know what someone's in for' was indicative of the anxiety that apparently respectable associates might turn out to have committed morally questionable acts. Gavin's comments illustrated the extent of these suspicions:

You don't know what they're like out there. Because I mean some people have got two sides to them. [Some] Governor got arrested for noncing a couple of months ago. That police officer was arrested for paedophile stuff. You don't know what people are like. I know my friends out there. I know what they do. (Gavin)

Some prisoners had reservations about being around particular kinds of criminals: 'dirty smackheads' and petty offenders. A more common sentiment was to be mistrustful generally of other prisoners. The most reliable assumption was that everyone inside had breached social norms in one respect or another. 'Most of us who are in jail are thieves. So I can't trust no-one', said Declan. In explaining his lack of trust in others, Charlie flagged up the ironies of mutual suspicion: 'I'm a hypocrite really. But they'll rob you man, they'll rob you'. Matt labelled all prisoners 'self-serving bastards. I don't believe in loyalty amongst prisoners. Enough people stab you in the back. If it's not to their advantage they're gonna do it.' Without evidence of integrity, the default attitude was wariness and suspicion.

Distrust in the integrity of others and scepticism about the value of establishing friendships were also future-oriented. Drug use was particularly salient in this regard. Many prisoners were cynical about the lifestyles that potential friends were likely to resume or adopt once released. 'People are different when they're in prison from what they are on the out. It's the drugs mainly', Billy summarized. Tyler explained the relevance of drug addiction to the transience of prison friendship:

I've got a few people I would consider good friends. But it's jail where I've made that friend. I'd like to think that I could call on them if something happened, whether good or bad. But if we were on the outside world, it's a whole different ball game. The same people I know in here who are shit-hot with me, might be a crackhead on the out, might be a brownhead on the out, might just be a violent person on the out.

Scepticism about the durability of prison friendships was normally the outcome of past experiences. Most men had been promised money, visits, or letters by prisoners about to be released, only to hear and receive nothing.[5] Pete explained that prisoners would 'swear on [their] baby's grave, on [their] nan's grave' that they would visit or send money, but that none met their promises: 'as soon as they get out, that's it, they're not interested'. Such pledges were generally made with sincerity, but went unfulfilled either because prisoners returned to chaotic lifestyles of drugs and crime, or because they tried to put prison out of their minds as soon as possible on release.[6] As the following excerpt suggests, this was partly an involuntary psychological adjustment, partly the need to get on with life on release, and partly a matter of prudent self-protection:

Lads say when they get out: 'I'll keep in touch'. It just doesn't happen. When you get out of jail you forget about the jail. You forget all about the

---

[5] Prisoners were surprised when they did receive letters from people they had known in prison. As well as providing a psychological boost, such gestures cemented relationships, often transforming them from undefined and tentative associations into more solid, ongoing friendships:

Funnily enough, I got a letter come through the door about six weeks ago. He got out of prison and said he'd keep in contact because he comes from nearby. And I got a letter from him: 'out, alive! Sorry I haven't written to you for six months, I know I should have contacted you, here's my phone number, ring me up'. So I'll see him when I get out. He thought about me while he was out there, to sit down and write a letter and send it to me in here. So I know that my instinct was right, that he's a genuine fellow, he's alright, he's a good friend, he's a nice person. (Luke)

[6] 'What I say is, "if I've got the money, I'll sort it. But I'll tell you now, if I'm smoking [crack], you've got no chance"' (Pete).

bad times. You forget all about how long a day in a cell is, about having no sugar or whatever. You forget about the lads inside. When I get out, I'll be thinking about myself. If I stay in touch with people and they carry on doing crime, it's going to make me carry on. I don't want that. So that's how I was seeing it: I don't keep the friendships past the gate. (Ross)

Considerations of the future figured significantly in assessments of whether (and which) friendships were worth forming and maintaining. These decisions were determined significantly by prisoners' future aspirations and by calculations about the likelihood of future contact. First-time prisoners who wanted 'to get back to normal' (Joey) and those determined to avoid drug use and crime either eschewed friendships altogether, mixed only with prisoners who held similar aspirations, or defined and developed relationships in narrow terms: 'people who are helping me get through my sentence the easier' (Ross). For other prisoners, friendships were worthless or temporary because of the *practical* difficulties of maintaining them on release. 'I'm not gonna see any of these when I go home, so why build up a friendship with something that's gonna end any day?' Alexis reasoned. Locality was crucial in determining the value and outcome of prison relationships:

The lads I knock around on the wing with, they're only jail acquaintances. I don't know them from Adam, I've never knocked around on the street with them, they're not from my area. We'd probably get on famously. One's from Coventry, two are from Northampton, I'm from Leicester. I mean come on, there's four unlikely areas to have all together as one. Anywhere else, if there was fucking four Coventry lads and one Nottingham lad, I'd probably find it a bit hard to get in with them you know. (Tyler)

My friends in prison will be from Corby or Northampton or somewhere close. Because I go to them places, so I'm likely to see them again. Someone who lives in Leicester, the chances of me bumping into them are slim. (Aaron)

Prisoners not only expected to bond more successfully with men from their hometowns, but had more motivation to do so given their limited geographical mobility. The majority had neither the financial means nor the inclination to travel even relatively short distances in order to sustain friendships after release.

In a variety of ways, therefore, friendships in prison were constrained by concerns about the reputation and credibility of others. They were also inhibited because the prison environment heightened the risks inherent in personal disclosure. The divulgence of personal information was perceived in itself as 'a sign of weakness' (Seb), or 'ammunition used against you in the long-run' (Tyler). Admissions of self-doubt, fear, confusion, or anxiety could be used as leverage by other prisoners. The revelation of intimate details could also lead to ridicule and disrespect: 'That's when they can start calling names and things. I've got to put up [that barrier] because I don't want to get hurt' (Ellis). The difficulty of shedding pejorative labels without taking serious action (e.g. by fighting) meant that most prisoners chose to keep 'a certain reserve' in almost all interpersonal relationships, and assumed such strategies in others. This perception that other people were inauthentic reduced one's own inclination to open up and proffer trust.

Fears of emotional vulnerability and disappointment also influenced the reluctance of some prisoners to form strong bonds (Cohen and Taylor 1972). Several men described the sadness that had resulted when friends had been released or transferred:

This guy who was released last year, I was very pleased for him, that he was gettin out, but there was a bit of a gap for a while, in the class, cos he weren't here anymore. Cos he was a valuable member of the class, but also I enjoyed his company. (George)

[Friendship] can be a burden. You could be in here now and you know somebody who you can really trust and talk to…and all of a sudden that person who you trust gets moved to another prison, you know, shatters all your…whatever, you know what I mean, so you're back to square one, so you can't put all your eggs in one basket. (Amar)

Overtly emotional terms rarely featured in accounts of prison friendship. However, when prisoners talked of missing prison friends or being 'wounded' when they lost contact with them (Ian), they leaked stronger sentiments of intimacy and dependence. The common decision, when sentenced, to break off relationships with girlfriends was an outcome of the same desire to avoid feelings of emotional powerlessness, as well as to preclude anxieties about sexual betrayal. Prison was a difficult place to handle feelings of vulnerability or other strong emotions, as Matt—who disclosed that he was gay during our interview—conveyed.

Do you not develop forms of very strong emotion towards people?

Yeah, I have them, but I've started to cut meself off from that sort of thing; it's just difficult ain't it. It's just a bad place to go through those sorts of emotions, jail is. You've gotta try and cut them off. It doesn't always work like that. You know sometimes you still get it. I've been there in the past.

Can you give me an example?

...yeah, falling in love with people. That's what I'm saying. It's not permanent is it. So, it's not going to be a permanent thing for either of you. The emotions and the feelings are real and all that, [but] it's just a pointless exercise ain't it.

Matt's experiences highlighted the particular (and relatively unusual) frustrations involved in managing love within a place of constraint. Emotions of this kind could be hazardous to reveal and they were unlikely to be reciprocated. Whether expressed or suppressed, they inflamed troubling feelings that life was beyond one's control. Imprisonment provided few outlets for such feelings to be discharged (not least because of the absence of 'neutral' figures to whom disclosure was possible) and for mundane frustrations to be released. The conditions of confinement—in particular, the lack of autonomy that it engendered—meant that emotional difficulties of all kinds were likely to be exacerbated. The inability to influence events beyond the prison, especially those concerning family members, was one of the key pains of imprisonment (see Chapter 8).

In dealing with these burdens, prisoners faced significant prohibitions. Even when prepared to share problems, they generally assumed that others were reluctant to take on their concerns. Prisoners recognized that, despite the untroubled façades that their peers generally presented, most were wrestling with their own frustrations. As Nathan described, the tolerance for emotional imposition was limited:

You can't go unburdening yourself emotionally over and over and over again. [If] I say 'look, what's up?' and he comes to me and out pours, that's alright once. If it happens again, *hmm*, if it happens again, *hmm*, if it happens everyday, [you think] 'Fuck off mate I don't need it'.

Personal disclosure was therefore culturally discouraged as well as being potentially hazardous. Moreover, many prisoners struggled to disclose their emotions to other males. While most claimed to assume more trust in friends outside prison than inside, many noted that emotions featured minimally in all their relationships with men. To 'open up' was unmasculine and invited ridicule. Outside prison, lives were generally dominated by male peer groups. Yet the majority of prisoners claimed to feel more comfortable in female company, and women were frequently depicted as the sole catalysts for emotional release and authenticity. In this way, imported codes of masculinity contributed to the silences and barriers that characterized prison friendships.

Imported factors were significant in another respect. Trust is partly a function of biography, and for a significant proportion of prisoners the disinclination to place trust in other people was informed by events that preceded incarceration. For some, this related to a general distrust of 'The System': state institutions such as children's homes, social services, and the wider penal complex, where many prisoners had experienced such abusive treatment that their basic capacity for trust had been damaged. More often, it reflected betrayals by family members and intimate partners that left equally profound emotional wounds:

To me, emotion is not a good thing to have, because when you get emotional that's when people do shit. If you don't care about shit then nothing can hurt you, and that's how I see things.... At the end of the day, I don't like being dependent on people, because if you get too dependent on them they let you down or they leave you, you're fucked. If you're too nice to people they take the piss. (Wilson)

I've not trusted people for a long time. I find it hard to trust anyone. I think I always have. But a lot more, since getting that first sentence. Because I trusted Helen, I trusted her with my life, and she shit on me from a great height. If you trust anyone you're going to get hurt. So I was wary of people. I thought, 'you can't trust no-one here'. (Ross)

These were extreme cases, but by no means exceptional. Experiences of abuse and betrayal powerfully impeded the enthusiasm and capacity of many men to form meaningful relationships. In aggregate, this contributed to a culture of widespread emotional suppression. For almost all prisoners, therefore, while the prison provided company in abundance, it offered little emotional sustenance:

When you're in prison, no matter how many friends you've got, you are a lonely person. No matter how many friends you've got around you, you are on your own. When that door shuts you are on your own, and they can do anything they want. (Danny)

[It] can be a lonely place. It is a lonely place. I think it's one of the loneliest places you can ever be, a prison, cos you're not free, you have a lot of people around you, people who you don't know and people who you don't probably feel you can be relaxed to all the time.

Why can't you be relaxed?

Well, because it's prison, you don't wanna show that you're too weak or too soft or whatever. You don't have to be too tough; you just don't feel like you would do at home, y'know. Cos people are trying to judge you, cos they've just met you, they're trying to judge you all the time, they're trying to see who you are. (Colin)

Such quotations illustrated the distinct emotional texture of an environment where social interactions were essential and unavoidable, yet lacked the conditions that enabled them to flourish. In particular—and to summarize this chapter so far—the prison's combination of enforced interaction and social scepticism generated a culture of reserved and pragmatic social exchange. Instrumental loyalties were encouraged, but relationships of trust were largely prohibited.

Institutional Factors

Medium-security conditions did not lend themselves to deep, enduring friendships. Relative to higher-security prisons, turnover was rapid and prisoners had few outlets for co-operative activities such as cooking that enabled friendship formation. More importantly, in Cat-C conditions, prisoners had less inclination to develop stable social groups. The atmosphere was less 'edgy' than in high-security establishments, where issues of personal safety were stronger drivers of social allegiance. Wellingborough's relatively relaxed social dynamics meant that being constantly 'on guard' was less necessary than in some Cat-Cs. Prisoners were also less isolated from the outside community, with less need to develop an alternative social community:

If I was in Whitemoor [high-security prison] now, I would be moving around creating a little gang-group, because you think 'yeah we cook together, we'll make our drink together, we smoke together', so you move around that way. But not here, not in this jail. I just want to do this sentence and get out there and be with my family. I [don't] link with too many people. (Jacob)

For prisoners coming from longer-term prisons, Cat-C conditions focused the mind on the world outside the prison, weakening the grip of prison loyalties. Those who came in from local prisons often saw little advantage in developing strong ties beyond limited circles, as Colin noted:

Loyalty goes as far as an individual group of inmates. [Beyond that] it wouldn't be in my interest at all. When you're in a C-cat, you come as an individual, and you try and get along, and try and get each other to get along together.

As Colin's comments suggested, in medium-security conditions, both individual and collective interests were best served by a form of prudent individualism. Not all prisoners prioritized personal over collective interests. But the prospect of release was a pervasive concern with considerable social potency. Most prisoners declared that their primary loyalties were 'to myself'. As Isaac summarized, solidarity existed 'in a way, but not when it comes to the crunch'.

Prisoners commonly asserted a view that, at its core, custody was an individual experience:

I'm there for myself, I've not been put in prison for anybody else, I'm not here for anybody else's amusement or to help anybody else, I've got my own problems, my own things to do. (Jordan)

So who are your allegiances to in the prison?

Me. Because I came in this jail on my own. [If] you've got a bit of trouble and I'm knocking around with you then I've got your back. I'm not going to stand there and let somebody do something to you if you're losing. I'm not saying I'm gonna smash the geezer's head in, but I'll pull him off and say 'piss off mate'. [But] You've got to look out for number one at the end of the day. Regardless of anything. (Tyler)

This discourse of individualism had several dimensions: the belief that responsibility for imprisonment lay only with oneself; a more protective sentiment that recognized that the physical and psychological vulnerabilities entailed by imprisonment necessitated a defensive social attitude; and a mournful focus on personal problems, missed opportunities, and potential solutions (Goffman 1961). These tendencies constrained the logic and energy for extending significant loyalties elsewhere.

General Exceptions

There were exceptions to the tenet that establishing enduring, emotional relationships in prison was impossible, undesirable, or unlikely. Some were specific to particular adaptive dispositions, while others cut across typological distinctions. These exceptions provided significant countertrends to normal patterns, although their terms evidenced the same factors that generally hindered friendship formation.

The sharing of social space

Friendships of a kind were often the outcomes of cell-sharing. Proximity forced upon 'pad-mates' unusual forms of intimacy: everyday rituals of washing and using the toilet, sleeping and waking in bunkbeds, and the sharing of cigarettes and newspapers.[7] Extended periods of cohabitation also gave prisoners scope to exchange life stories, aspirations, and wistful reminiscences, and to recognize common goals and values. 'You know them better than what they know their self, you're with them that much', Pierce noted. Cell-sharing was in this respect a humanizing process. As a result, prisoners with little in common sometimes developed bonds of loyalty and mutual compassion. Seb described his sympathies for a former cellmate: 'I shouldn't really care but, you know ... I'm probably the only person that knows him'. Several other prisoners described incidents when, in uncharacteristic ways (by their own admission), they had protected vulnerable cellmates or provided emotional support without expectations of reciprocity. Such tales were unverifiable. Nonetheless, it was apparent that the sharing of physical space was often sufficient to generate certain kinds of loyalty. Despite the common assertion that 'in prison, kindness gets taken for weakness', behind closed doors, acts of selflessness, warmth, and empathy were common (see Harvey 2007).[8]

Just as sharing cellspace was one basis of affiliation, prisoners often bonded during transfer from one prison to another, or on the basis of having been in the same prison prior to their current establishment. For a prisoner to have known someone in another context added to his sense of their authenticity and trustworthiness, even though this context was another prison—and thus another site of inauthenticity. Prisoners who had met on previous sentences or at earlier stages of their current sentence often greeted each other warmly, reminiscing about people and events they had known years before. Erwin James (2003: 150) has compared such

---

[7] One prisoner shaved his cellmate every week because he was too physically and mentally infirm to shave himself.

[8] The following quotation continues to describe Seb's stance towards his former cellmate:

I read his letters for him.... I've had to lie to him. He got a letter off one of his wife's mates, saying 'I don't know how to tell you this, but she's been sleeping with another geezer'. So I'm reading the letter through and I don't know why but I just skipped that.... He hasn't got nothing, and to hear that your missus is shagging someone else—to have the only thing that he's got...the only thing he gets is letters from her...

warmth to 'the way that marathon runners who begin the course as strangers greet each other like comrades once past the finishing line'. Certainly, these greetings conveyed a sense of having travelled some way, over 'demanding terrain... to a place of relative safety' (ibid.). They were also ways of revalidating reputation.

In similar fashion, a common starting point for a new relationship was to be introduced by a mutual friend as 'a good lad', 'solid', or, for example, 'my mate's ex-padmate'.[9] To be vouched for in this apparently minor way was a shortcut to credibility, proof of provenance and reliability. Early conversations on a wing often focused on hometown connections ('so you must know Stevie Smith...?'). As well as being ice-breakers for initial conversation, these questions helped to evaluate credentials—testing whether a prisoner's friends outside were 'sound lads'. 'The first things you ask someone new are where they're from, which jail they've come from, and what they're in for. Then you drop some names, and if they know them they're alright' (prisoner, fieldwork notes). A new prisoner's character, his professed offence, and his claims of friendship or influence could be verified through phone calls and letters to contacts elsewhere in the prison system and in the outside community. These information flows across the physical boundaries of the prison made it highly risky to lie about one's background.

Locality, identity, and trust

Reputation networks within the prison system were in part products of the dense social systems of the housing estates from which the majority of prisoners originated. These roots merit further elaboration because their role in prisoner social relations was of such significance. The typical prisoner life story depicted a tight community where 'everyone knows everyone' (Morgan), and the units of social life were not individual households but peer groups and extended families. Most prisoners described friendship groups that had existed since infancy and had shared key episodes of adolescence and adulthood: drug-taking, intimate relationships, deaths, and crime. Indeed, for many prisoners, these peer groups

[9] One interviewee, with whom I maintained contact after his release, described how it had taken him some time to realize that his difficulty meeting new people outside prison was partly due to his expectation that they should be introduced to him by a third party. In over a decade of imprisonment, he had very rarely initiated a friendly conversation with a total stranger.

functioned as surrogate families, proving more empathy, support, and emotional consistency than biological parents. The following descriptions were typical:

From the age of thirteen to about twenty-one, my friends meant everything. They was my life. I'd be with them twenty-four hours a day. [I'd] Come to jail and be with all my friends. Family, I didn't really have much for. (Morgan)

The people who I hang around with when I'm out, from my estate, we've all known each other since we were kids. We've grown up together. And basically I treat them all like brothers. (Pierce)

These friendships were often characterized by high levels of trust and emotional sincerity, certainly in relation to the prison relationships with which they were contrasted. One prisoner summarized the comparison as being the difference between someone you know 'inside out' and 'someone on the street who you pass every day— that's a relationship, but it's not a friendship' (fieldwork notes).

External peer groups took extended forms. Often, they were dominated by a set of 'older lads' who defined public life within the estate and served as primary masculine role models in the absence of interested fathers. These were highly bounded communities, defined by local characters, influential families, and specific locales such as pubs and playing fields. Rivalries with nearby estates reinforced pride in the territory of the community and in the masculinities of those who defended it (Tolson 1977). Attachments to these places were profound, as Kieran illustrated:

I've been in secure units, in kids' homes, in Wales, Birmingham, London, Liverpool, Manchester, all over the country. And every single opportunity I got to get on my toes, I'm back to Nottingham.

What did you miss about it?

Just the—it's just my area, where I grew up. I know everyone there. I just love [the area]. To this day I just love it. It's bad for me. I know it's bad for me.... I just get in trouble and all sorts. But I just love it. I just love it.

...So what are the general frustrations for you here?

For me here? Just being away from Nottingham. Just not being around my own people.

This nostalgia not just for 'home' or for particular individuals but for a particular spatial location was widespread (see also Medlicott 2001). These were deeply emotional, and often ambivalent, identifications. Experiences of place were engrained in self-identity (Proshansky *et al.* 1983). Communities and housing estates offered the embrace of being known and being 'someone', even while they were also portrayed as places of boredom, violence, and criminal temptation.

The significance of regional identity was apparent throughout prisoner culture. During induction processes, prisoners asked about the possibility of subscribing to their local newspapers. Staff and prisoners dispensed generic nicknames on the basis of hometown or accent: 'Scouser' for a Liverpudlian, 'Jock' for a Scot, and 'Taffy' for a Welshman. Some prisoners argued that different cities had distinct values and terminology: one insisted that Nottingham was a particularly homophobic city, for example. Certain phrases were more or less indigenous to local areas. Credibility was assigned in part on the basis of the size of one's home city. Place was not just an abstract entity. Prisoners were buffeted by the forces of late-modernity, but their lives were highly immobile and deeply rooted in specific geographical locations: more 'pre-modern' than 'late-modern' (Giddens 1991).[10]

Within the prison, locality was highly significant in defining social norms and cementing affiliations. To come from the same area enabled conversation about people and places in common: 'you talk about prison a bit, but it's mostly outside you talk about. Good places to go, just things like that' (Connor). To 'come from the same place' also had wider meaning:

There's one lad [from my hometown]. We know all the same working girls. We know all the same dealers. I've heard about him, he's heard about me. But we'd never bumped up [i.e. met] before. We were the only people that were alike in this jail, because we're from the same place. I don't mean the same place as in area, I mean the same place as in what we expect, our attitudes. Every area's got different cultures, different morals, different levels of drug use. I'm from the ghetto. [There,] you're all fighting the same battles, you're all doing the same sort of crime, you're all earning in the same sorts of ways. The level of violence you have to use is virtually the same.... Everybody's pissing against the wind. (Fin)

As this excerpt indicates, a shared regional background promoted a sense of shared ethics and disposition. Prisoners who derived from the same towns or cities—who had occupied the same social and spatial locations—not only had shared reference points, but

---

[10] Bauman has argued that this lack of mobility is a vital component of social exclusion. Speed of movement has become a 'major, perhaps the paramount factor of social stratification and the hierarchy of domination' (Bauman 2000: 151).

also a common perceptual apparatus or 'habitus' (Bourdieu 1984). 'You aspire to the same people, you have the same moral values' (prisoner, fieldwork notes). Prisoners from large urban conurbations were considered mutually familiar with a higher pace of social activity, and more sophisticated criminal cultures. London, in particular, was perceived as 'a bit faster' than other cities (Max): more ruthless and frenetic. Prisoners who recognized in each other these instinctive mentalities of place and culture bonded more readily, rapidly, and deeply than those who lacked this embedded social adhesive. Shared hometown origins provided the primary and most reliable basis of prison loyalty and affiliation.

On arrival in prison, prisoners quickly found friends and acquaintances from their home communities, or built connections by discovering people and places in common. As Jacobs (1977) highlighted, for many prisoners, entry into custody was not characterized by the complete severance of ties to the external community (cf. Goffman 1961). Rather, it entailed partial disconnection alongside selective re-acquaintance. However, external relationships were not transplanted into the prison in a wholesale or consistent manner. Prisoners from the same area often put aside personal quarrels if they were located in a prison where it was prudent to stick together. Those who, in a local prison, would have 'represented' different towns or gangs, united if they found themselves in an establishment where they were a minority, as Phillips (2008) has also reported. As Cameron explained, somewhat dramatically, 'Say two Manchester lads go down to Birmingham, we're foreigners. And if we don't stick together, we're going to fucking die. Well, we're going to fucking die anyway but we'll last a little bit longer.' Another prisoner simply commented that 'all southerners are foreign in a northern jail' (fieldwork notes).

Mutual identification was not the only factor that made shared regional origins such a binding force. The structural conditions that impeded the formation of new friendships among strangers applied much less to prisoners from the same communities. In particular, links to external networks meant that imprisonment did not involve the same disconnection from past identities. Claims about actions and reputations prior to imprisonment could easily be verified, as Morgan described:

I don't want to be hanging round with someone and then find out later that person's a rapist or that person's a nonce, or something like that. At least if I know the person's from Leicester, I'll feel comfortable and I can find out if that person's all right. And if I hear through another friend that he's all right, I'll knock around with him. It's quite easy. Leicester is a small city, a close city, everyone knows everyone. Most estates in Leicester, I know someone from.

Access to such information did not mean that prisoners from the same hometowns always developed strong friendships. Reliable knowledge of someone's past character provided a sound basis to dislike or dismiss them, as well as the basis for enhanced levels of trust.

Except in cases of real antipathy, shared provenance guaranteed low-level forms of reciprocal support and provision. The anticipation of returning to the same extended community was significant here. Shared destinations meant that prison friendships were not merely fleeting. When relationships could be continued on release, they were worthy of greater emotional investment. They also provided possibilities for economic and criminal transactions in the future. Dave noted that loyalty was one way of 'covering your interest. Because, if I stick up for him in here, in the long term, no doubt he will see me when I'm out on the street again, and I might have something for sale; and he might give me a better offer for it.' If prisoners were returning to the same community, the nature of their relationship in the prison also had implications for personal reputation. Acting with insufficient loyalty or breaching trust put status at risk both within the institution and in the future, as Danny explained:

Would you be able to say, 'Listen lads, I really don't wanna get involved, I'm out in four weeks'?

Four weeks. They'd probably accept that, yeah, but if it was Derby lads, I wouldn't say that. I would get involved because if I ever come back to prison and something happened, people might remember that, and they might not be so quick to jump in and help.

Can it affect your reputation on the out?

Yeah, of course it can, yeah. Something can happen on a Tuesday, and by Wednesday afternoon it's all round Derby, everybody knows.

Information flowed through the prison walls with speed and serious consequences. Prisoners were well aware that their actions reverberated beyond the institution, not only in their local communities, but in other prisons they might enter in the future. In this respect, local loyalty was partly a function of the fear of appearing disloyal: 'If they grass you up you're going to see them outside, aren't you' (Bradley). In some situations, the 'accountability' provided by future contact hemmed prisoners into obligations that they would rather have avoided. In others, by reducing the likelihood of inauthenticity, it was an important enabler of trust.

Drug addiction, identity, and authenticity

For the majority of prisoners, the prison was a site of inauthenticity and a place where social conditions inhibited the formation of friendship. For some former drug and alcohol addicts, however, the opposite was the case. Unlike most prisoners, these men saw themselves as more 'real' inside the prison than when dependent on drink or drugs in the community. In disavowing their pasts and seeking to rebuild their lives while inside, they had distinct motivations for forging new social ties. Normal perceptions of trust and authenticity were inverted, as Stephen's comments highlighted:

People outside, you only ever meet them in the pub, or when you're doing some sort of crime, or when you're on drugs, or in that sort of situation. Whereas here, you're pretty clear-headed, so I get to know the real people here, in prison.... I've got mates I've known for twenty years outside, but I've only ever met them in a pub, or back at their house after the night out. [They] don't really know the real me.... Whereas the couple of guys I've met on this sentence, I've seen every day for two years solid, they're gonna know me better than those people.... They've seen the real me, what I'm like when I'm depressed, what I'm like when I'm happy, not through drink and drugs.... The guy I left in my last jail, he's the closest friend I've ever had. Because we spent all our days together, we worked together, we hung around together, we ate together for two years, now that's a long time to be together.... Outside people are false. I think this is the real world. There's some people who'll go back outside and get on the drink and drugs again, and then that's not the real them is it.... But if that person doesn't do that, you're meeting the genuine person.... They're the same in here as they are outside. [And] this is the real you.

For these prisoners, it was life in the community rather than in prison that was limited and inauthentic. Addiction masked true identity, confined personality, and placed limits on social interaction, while imprisonment compelled social and emotional exposure. In Alfie's terms: 'I come in prison and this is as near as the real me. Outside I'm totally false, lying, cheating, robbing, it's a chemical lifestyle I lead, my whole character changes. I turn into a horrible person.'

These prisoners—from all parts of the typology—also perceived their personal judgments to be more finely tuned in prison than when on drugs outside. As a consequence, they trusted their ability to evaluate their peers and build genuine relationships. Coming off drugs made them confessional and optimistic, encouraging the kind of candour and sociability that helped cement new relationships. Feelings of authenticity also made them more receptive to friendly approaches from other prisoners, particularly those with similar histories who they assumed, like them, had been liberated from addiction into states of relatively unguarded sincerity. Mutual disclosure evidenced empathy and it bound both parties into relations of trust:

Mick, he used to tell me everything. He said when he was my age, he used to drink a lot as well, and piss the bed. Something like that, I could tell Mick. Because I'm an alcoholic, [and] one time I got that paralytic I pissed the bed. I could tell Mick, but not other people.... Because I don't trust them. They might go around and tell everybody else.

Ex-addicts also re-evaluated their pre-carceral relationships. Often, they reported regret at having pushed away 'proper friends' in favour of other users—drinking companions, partners in drug acquisition, and colleagues in associated criminal activities. Once inside prison, they disowned these associates, who they regarded as having encouraged their addictions, polluted their characters, and 'used' them to help feed their own habits. 'The only thing you've really got in common is drugs and stealing', Rhys noted, highlighting the highly instrumental nature of these past relationships. Having been reconceived as selfish and exploitative, these former associates confirmed these depictions by failing to visit or maintain contact.[11] It was these relationships, rather than those inside the establishment, which were characterized as transient and superficial. They were also hazards for the future. As Aaron summarized, 'I can't class them as friends if I want to stay off drugs.'

The potential for developing friendships within prison was greatly enhanced by the belief that other prisoners had sincere motives for establishing relationships. Contrasts with the past

---

[11] Many prisoners stated a view that, in prison, 'you find out who your friends are' (Pierce).

were important here. Outside prison, these men believed, it was the allure of alcohol, drugs, or money that had attracted others to their company. Imprisonment stripped away these appeals. Normally, these were fairly low status prisoners, with little accumulated wealth. They received little private income, normally because relationships with family and friends were highly frayed; and they tended to avoid *sub rosa* activity within the prison. As a result, and by default, other prisoners could have few ulterior motives for friendship:

I'd say I'm more friends now with people in here than on the outside. Most of my mates out there were because I was drinking, because I had the money at the time to take them out drinking. Because I'm not drinking now, I can see that if someone likes me it's because of who I am, not because I'm a good laugh or someone to laugh at. (Jordan)

They don't want fuck all from me cos they know I ain't got fuck all. Cos there's nothing in here. I'm in the same fucking clothes pretty much all the time. Two or three sets of clothes and that's it. You've got fuck all else. On the out you've got a lot more you can do for yourself. [In prison] you've got very little for them to go on. (Tyler)

Not all former addicts sought to develop new friendships in prison. Few expected these relationships to endure. All were aware of the hazards of extending trust. Certainly though, by looking to 'make a new start', some prisoners were inclined to see imprisonment as an opportunity to forge meaningful, sincere relationships. When these friendships survived, their origins in prison and their resilience to the destructive social pressures of imprisonment meant that they were highly prized.

The Bases and Conditions of Prisoner Social Relationships

The following section specifies the nature of prisoner social relationships, including their conditions, obligations, and implications, and the main bases on which they were established.

Locality

Local loyalties trumped most other affiliations and were the most evident basis of social identification. Prisoners reported that, in the event of an existing friend entering an establishment, this relationship would displace a friendship formed only while inside.

Even men from a prisoner's hometown who were not directly known to him could expect to receive a certain level of support in times of conflict, as Cameron suggested:

If someone was to have any grief with any of the Leicester lads, I'd have his back. It doesn't matter what he looks like, he's still from Leicester. [Even] If you don't know them, and you're from Leicester, you automatically connect. If it was to go off [between] a Leicester lad and some other lad who I didn't know, I'd back your Leicester man.

What if it went off between a Leicester lad you didn't know and someone that you knew quite well?

I'd split it up. Because I like [the first] man there, I respect [him]. And [the other's] from Leicester and I respect him as well. [Or] If it looked equal and fair to me, I'd let them carry on.

Weighing up competing loyalties was a complex act and a matter of subtle distinction. Local allegiances were always in balance with other commitments, including trade networks, and ethnic and religious alignments. Callum described how, all things being equal, he would always form trade links with men from his home city, but he would not sacrifice prison connections for men from his city if he did not already know them. Ashley explained that, despite his primary loyalties to prisoners from his home city, he had intervened to prevent them attacking a fellow black prisoner with whom he traded drugs. In such situations, current priorities supplanted abstract hometown loyalties. In others, when the stakes were high or when external connections were more intimate, prisoners valued future credibility over present concerns:

I'd have to stick up for the Northampton lads or be on their side, even though I have to live with and I'm maybe working with this other lad. I suppose that boils down to reputation as well. I can't be seen to be siding with him [or] my lads will go outside and say 'He stuck up for someone he don't know over me'. (Leon)

To stick up for someone from one's town was to maintain both personal and collective reputation. In asserting that men from one's own area were particularly loyal—'one Coventry lad's worth five from Birmingham'—or that men from other cities were notoriously fickle, prisoners expounded mythologies of place that gave them a sense of dignity and exclusivity. 'Place' was a source of symbolic status as well as material support.

However, relationships founded on shared roots could involve unwanted obligations as well as guarantees of aid, support, and protection. Prisoners consistently reported that the mutual binds of regional loyalty could push them into acts and activities they would rather avoid. Dom, for example, had been put under pressure by his hometown peers to store hooch, and to bring drugs back from his visits: 'I didn't want to do it, but sometimes you had to; if you didn't, you'd just get grief. It does make it easier if you know people, but it causes hassle as well.' Other accounts corroborated this view that local allegiances were double-edged:

It's good in a way [to have friends from outside around]—you can't really get in no drama. Because you've got a big gang there, and everyone will always defend where they're from. But in a way it's worse, because if you want to keep your head down and not get into any trouble, then if there are mans from your area, you're put in a situation where you have to do certain things you don't really want to do. Say I'm in my local jail. If I hear that one of my friends on a different wing just got beat up, all the mans there have to link up and go and deal with this. You might not really want to. But because everyone else is, peer pressure's got you and the next thing you know, you're involved in something you don't really want to be involved in. If you try and say 'no, listen, I'm not involved', you've got a whole heap of people looking at you like, 'what?!'. People would lose a lot of respect for you. (Isaac)

If you're on a wing and there's people you know from your manor, you've got a lot more freedom to do or say whatever you want. People think 'Well, I ain't going to fight him, because they'd get repercussions afterwards. Even if I grass him up and send him down the block, I've still got the rest to deal with'. [But] my last sentence, I was down the block every two weeks: nickings, threatening use of words and behaviour, fighting, the lot. Because you have to back up your mates as well. (Fin)

To be in a prison with an extensive regional peer group ensured freedom from certain forms of exploitation, provided social confidence, and offered access to trade networks. At the same time, it limited a prisoner's ability to control his own fate, putting him at the mercy of other people's behaviour. Friends could escalate a prisoner's problems by involving themselves whether asked to or not: 'If they turned round and said "no", they know I'm still going to do it' (Bradley). Being in one's local prison thus brought disadvantages. Several prisoners expressed relief that, in being in an establishment some distance from their home city, their relative anonymity allowed them to withdraw from the trials and temptations of prison politics: 'This is easy bird for me', Fin noted: 'I know I have no back-up—well not as much—so I get in less trouble.' Danny explained that, in a prison where he knew few people, he could negotiate himself out of any trouble by emphasizing his impending release. In contrast:

If I was in a prison where everybody knew me and somebody put it on me...I'd have to go for it, because I know if I don't, I'm gonna get slated out there. I'm gonna come out and they're gonna say, 'What happened Danny, did you lose your bottle?'

Isolation from a local peer group had likewise opened up the possibility for Stephen to resist peer incitement:

I just had to say: 'I don't wanna know'. Which I didn't like doing at the time, but I had to balance that up—whether I got some extra charges, loads more years in jail, or just took the bit of embarrassment that I felt at the time and moved on.... That's what I've been doing lately, to get through those sorts of situations: I say 'Look, I don't know these people, they're never gonna meet me outside, they're not from my town, so it doesn't matter what they think of me, what matters is that I get out'.

Situational factors such as a prison's location could thus influence not just a particular stance, but the general adaptive position that a prisoner could take up.[12]

Race and ethnicity

A second key basis of identification and association was race or ethnicity.[13] Both provided visible and immediate grounds for first contact, the kind that was of particular importance in prison. Isaac had been raised always to say hello to other black people and suggested that this served as social glue between Afro-Caribbean prisoners. The same was true for Asian prisoners, while Muslims (some of whom were black or white converts) met in the prison mosque and were bonded by rituals around praying, eating, and religious festivals. In the prison's public spaces, particularly along the main thoroughfare, black and Asian prisoners expressed their fraternalism visibly and vocally as they exchanged greetings.

---

[12] In a less overcrowded system, this finding would be more significant, in that it suggests the value of asking prisoners whether they would prefer to be located near their home towns (as the majority do, in order to receive regular visits) or in a prison that would allow a degree of social isolation.

[13] Race is a term that describes biological descent, while ethnicity refers to cultural heritage: shared history, identity, customs, or geographical roots.

Minority ethnic prisoners were keen to emphasize that their preference for socializing with men of the same race or ethnicity was 'a bonding thing, not a segregation thing' (prisoner, fieldwork notes); 'it's about culture and music and stuff...it's not really a big [race] thing' (ibid.); 'we act a different way and speak a different way' (ibid.). Mohammed noted that Muslim prisoners socialized together through prayer, but then 'We go about our business', mixing with prisoners from other ethnic and racial groups. In most cases, affiliations were predicated not on a political sense of identity and difference, but on assumptions about shared experiences of family life and youth—what Genders and Player (1989) identified as commonalities of experience (see Phillips 2008).

Most of us have been through the same thing kind of thing. Like, when we were talking about parents and joking about who used to get beaten, and things like that. We understand each other. It ain't like, 'we're black and we should stay together for the revolution' or something. (Isaac)

This was not to say that identification was guaranteed by shared ethnic roots. There were fissures within ethnic constituencies, not least on the basis of personality. Isaac declared the limits of ethnic identification in the following way: 'I'm not going to go and sit and talk to them *just* because they're black. You get black idiots, white idiots, Asian idiots, [and] you get all types of good people.' There were points of conflict within as well as between racial-ethnic groups. Connections between Black Africans and Black Caribbeans, and between UK-born Afro-Caribbeans and black foreign nationals, were not always strong. Few prisoners mixed only within ethnic categories.

Muslim prisoners were the most collectivist in outlook, and had a highly cohesive group identity (see Phillips 2008). Most placed religion above all else in their hierarchy of allegiance. Mohammed, a devout believer, declared that his loyalties were to 'every Muslim' and claimed that 'if one of the Muslims needed something, all of them would want to give it to him'. The social unity among Muslim prisoners was informed and bolstered by a religious-political interpretation of global politics and social issues. Whereas the majority of prisoners were politically docile or indifferent, Muslims often railed against the role of British government in world affairs. They were more likely than other prisoners to explain crime in terms of poverty and alienation. They were also more challenging towards the prison administration than other prisoners, generally over issues relating to religious practice rather than in opposition to the institution *per se*.

Although most Muslims interacted with other prisoners, and refuted any suggestion that they experienced imprisonment differently, Islam was the social axle around which they did their time:

A lot of the Asian guys, Muslim guys, I've noticed, their time revolves around their religion. They pray a lot, they spend a lot of time talking about their religion and following that lifestyle. They use religion to get through it. Where I might use a book, they go to the Mosque. (Stephen)

White prisoners often conflated Islamic faith and Asian identity. From the outside, the distinction was hard to identify and was one that not all Muslims or Asians considered significant. Riz prioritized cultural identity over faith in determining his associates: 'when you're Asian, you all stick together. I think it's something about [being] in prison. On the out it's different.' More committed believers were less interested in mixing with 'Asians' simply on the basis of skin colour or ethnic roots. As a result, the relationship between Muslim and Sikh prisoners was complex, with the latter normally associating with the former without being fully accepted into their fold.

Two other ethnic groups were known for their cohesion. These were black Jamaicans, often referred to as 'Yardies', and Travellers, who were generally Irish in nationality or origin. Both came from very different social backgrounds from those of most prisoners, and formed instant and powerful connections with others like them. 'If you fuck with one, you fuck with them all', one officer noted. 'They might be from rival clans and kill each other on the out, but when they're in they stick together.' Prisoners used identical terms: 'if you fuck with them, you're fucking with them all' (prisoner, fieldwork notes).

Other bases

Other bases of social relationships were harder to classify. In describing prison friendships, prisoners cited being 'on the same wavelength', 'on a level', 'clicking', or 'relating' as the foundations of social bonding. These terms stood for several interrelated factors. The first was an issue of social background. Just as coming from the same hometown provided a shared sense of personal experience, so too did occupying similar social positions within comparable cities. Ashley explained that the people with whom he found things in common were those who had experienced 'the same kind of upbringing as me—lived in a ghetto, robbing and stealing'. The sharing of social narratives and trajectories also provided a basis of identification: 'A lot of us have shared the same experiences; we've come through crime, been to the same places, been in the same world' (prisoner, fieldwork notes). For Olly, connections were made with prisoners who had 'been through the same kind of struggle as me, the same areas, the same music'. The inscription of such experiences on the body (Bourdieu 1984) meant that prisoners could often identify men with common histories of poverty and addiction from their carriage and movements alone.

The second basis of social identification was criminal experience (a quality that long-serving prisoners reported had been a more significant source of affiliation in the past[14]). As the preceding chapter detailed, criminal background distilled various aspects of identity and orientation. Prisoners were drawn to others who understood the cultures, characters, and criminal transactions with which they were familiar. In general, 'straight' prisoners identified with other 'hardworking lads—not addicts—who have got into trouble through no fault of their own' (prisoner, fieldwork notes). Convicted drug dealers tended to judge others according to personal wealth and clothing, and found common ground in an antipathy towards authority, a rigid equation of masculinity with strength, a worship of material goods, and a sense of their social superiority.

Drugs provided a third basis for social mixing, often across lines of criminal identity:

You can have a senior heavy armed robber type character who'll be hanging around with a house burglar, simply because they both take smack, whereas in the old days you wouldn't get that. People were drawn to each other because of what they were in for. Now, it's still to an extent to do with what you're in for, but drugs has made a big influence on that. (Stephen)

Many prisoners attributed a process of social equalization and destabilization to the presence of heroin (see Crewe 2005b). When

---

[14] Such assertions may have reflected the more stratified social worlds of higher-security institutions rather than shifts over time.

drugs were available on the wings, non-users distanced themselves from users with whom they previously associated in order to avoid being exploited. Meanwhile, users with little otherwise in common were drawn to each other, developing loose, shallow, and highly functional relationships which trumped other bases of identification (see Preble and Casey 1969; Irwin 1970). 'Asian guys who are smackheads just associate with the other smackheads, whatever their Asian background', Stephen noted. Drug users trusted each other no more than non-users trusted them. They were loyal only 'to each other's company' (Larner and Tefferteller 1964: 14), and stuck together mainly insofar as doing so aided the procurement and consumption of drugs. As Alfie summarized: 'It's not loyalty, it's "co-operative finding". You find the knowledge of where the [dealer] is, and once you know, it's every man for himself. [Once] the smack appears, loyalty goes out the window.' Certainly, these prisoners showed little inclination to maintain their relationships when drugs were no longer available. Groupings based on drug use were soluble and unstable.

Attitudes towards 'doing time' and the future (which were themselves shaped by criminal and personal histories) also provided the foundations for social relationships. In-prison activities—such as going to the gym or the prison chapel[15]—provided starting points for conversation. Wing cleaners and servery workers often formed friendships of a kind due simply to the amount of time they spent together. Interests in music, sport, books, or culture likewise facilitated deeper acquaintance:

It's just people you hit it off with. I've just got mates with a guy because we're into the same sorts of things. I'm interested in art; he's quite useful to know about that. And conversation, we just kind of...y'know, how do you meet people in the real world? It's the same thing. You might

[15] Many prisoners who used the chapel did so because it provided an opportunity to 'get off the wing' and was a more normalized environment than most other places in the establishment. Repeated visits to the chapel did sometimes lead to the development of faith, but many church-attending prisoners had no intention of maintaining their interest after release. Likewise, the majority of prisoners who used the prison gym had little expectation of maintaining the habit once in the community. Common motivations for gym use were to relieve frustration (see Chapter 8), to 'get back in shape' after years of drug abuse, to put on muscle as a defence against potential victimization, and to improve physical appearance in anticipation of release: 'Outside, the girls love it, broad shoulders, large chest, it's a tribal-type thing' (Wilson).

seem like totally chalk and cheese, but once you get to talk, you might be interested in a football game or art or a certain way of life, you've shared experiences. (Stephen)

Other prisoners likewise emphasized the primacy of past lifestyles or current orientations above factors such as criminal history and ethnicity.

People just seem to connect with you. You just keep chatting at work, and you think, 'You're the same kind of person, you've lived the same kind of life'. Not just drugs, but the same kind of lifestyle. I've probably got more in common with someone who was on drugs or somebody who was selling drugs or people who lived that kind of lifestyle.... You get into a more serious side of things. Like, 'I'm dreading getting out' or 'I've got to stay off [drugs] this time when I get out', or 'isn't it horrible waking up in the morning needing the gear?'...Definitely, people who have been using drugs out there, I do believe they can relate more. They're on the same level, they know what it's like. (Connor)

He's not necessarily the best lad, but [he's] more on my level than anyone else. We haven't really got a lot in common. He's a smackhead, I'm not; I'm a thief, he's not. It's not so much your lifestyle, it's the way you think. He doesn't want no trouble, he's just doing his bird, same as me, he wants to get out, same as me, he's looking to do something for himself when he gets out, leave all the jobs and that behind, same as me. He's just a good lad, I like him, simple as that. (Callum)

To think in the same way as another prisoner made him more predictable and therefore more worthy of trust (Sztompka 1999).

Other characteristics of prison friendships

Some other general features of prison friendships can be outlined. First, despite their limitations, most prison friendships had some emotional dimension, however, sublimated. At the same time as they routinely denied caring about those around them, in describing their relationships, prisoners often revealed warmth, attachment, and intimacy. One frequently expressed concern was that friends would return to crime and prison:

I always said to him when he was here, 'You're not going to come back, are you?' and he says 'No, no', and just before he got out I said to him, 'You're not going to come back are you?', and he hesitated and said: 'I don't know, I don't know what I'm going to do when I get out', sort of like admitted defeat before he's ever got out, so, that's why I think he's going to come back. If he's done well and he's doing alright then I'm buzzing for him. (Ian)

Ian's description illustrated the investments that sustained interaction encouraged. Prisoners who passed time together developed
emotionally comforting routines and soon became attuned to
each others' moods and emotional rhythms:

With Mark, I talk with him, I can have a laugh with him. We don't talk
about the same things over and over again. We watch the news, we talk
about the world, we've got the same sort of interests. He likes sculpturing,
I like drawing. He's got a good imaginative brain on him. I buy a lot of
things like coffee and food: cakes and sweeties and stuff like that. And
Mark doesn't have much. So I share what I have with him. If he needs
something, he'll come and ask, but he won't keep coming and keep coming and asking and asking. (Den)

We all sit there in a cell, having a cup of coffee and you can tell if one of
us is upset because they'll be not their usual self. We'll say 'What's the
matter?' and they'll go 'Oh it don't matter'; 'Come on, you can tell us'.
(Aaron)

Second then, by nature of their context, prison relationships
had domestic qualities, playing themselves out over the provision of food, drink, and hospitality. Prisoners pooled their canteen money to maximize their comforts— 'I'll get the coffee, he'll
get the sugar' (Jordan)—and developed teaboat routines that
had familial overtones. Gym partners often displayed an intensity of support that was clearly suffused with affective meaning.
Yet prisoners frequently dismissed suggestions of closeness, often
refuting in front of each other any notion that their relationships
had emotional substance. These pantomimes of denial, alongside
constant jokes about homosexuality (both pretences to be gay
and accusations of irregular sexuality) served to tame and regulate the strong feelings of intimacy that were bound to develop in
what was a profoundly homosocial environment. Prisoners teased
each other about fidelity and about who was more dependent on
whom. Banter of this kind provided glimpses of the suppressed
emotions that infused male relationships and transcended normal
friendships in the absence of female company. These were also
relationships of humour and enthusiasm. Alfie reported having
sat down four friends in his cell and read them a speech from a
Shakespeare play 'with that much passion I think I scared them'.
Morgan admitted that he had 'had some great laughs in prison',
sitting around with friends, drinking prison hooch: 'It wasn't like
I was in prison. It was like I was outside in the house having a
drink, having a smoke with some lads, some good lads. It was

alright'. The prison was a place of mirth and warmth as well as misery.

Third, among most prisoners, the terms and expectations of friendship were negotiated in ways that reduced interpersonal disorder. Prisoners often took pre-emptive action to defuse and de-escalate potential conflicts, reminding their friends of the risks of petty squabbles. 'I just pull the guy away', said Isaac. '[I] say "Listen, what are you fighting over? Is it really worth doing another year in jail, just for that?"'. As well as saving others from trouble, such mediations were self-protecting. Most prisoners had no desire to lose days 'for someone else's fight' (Aaron). These interventions also provided a counterbalance to those tendencies within prison subculture that incited violence—in particular, concerns about public pride and reputation.

Fourth, while there was little active solidarity between prisoners, emotional empathy and sympathy for the plight of others were more common. Many prisoners expressed a view that all they shared was 'being in here', but this did allow for low-level solidarity and limited kinds of emotional identification:

A guy I roll with, his kids have been taken away from him, so he totally knows how I feel. He understands what we're going through, because we're both in jail. [And] if someone talks to me because they're paranoid because their girlfriend goes out certain weekends, obviously I know what it's like. (Isaac)

Prisoners commiserated over parole refusals and raised injustices on behalf of others. Some kept an eye out for the vulnerable and helped out wing pariahs.[16] Others broke up fights before officers arrived to prevent those involved having time added to their sentences. These were passive, minor, or furtive forms of solidarity, which required little personal sacrifice and were sometimes predicated on antipathy to the system as much as warmth towards others. When Paul claimed that, in the event of conflict, he would 'normally stick by the prisoner, unless [he's] a total twat and has gone out of his way to make it hard for everybody else', this support rarely meant more than providing passive, silent support. Nonetheless, these claims evidenced some sense

---

[16] Ronan, for example, was more or less adopted by a couple of older prisoners, who recognized his vulnerability, made their presence felt around him, and tried to advise him against selling his possessions to buy drugs.

of shared status and humanity, whose expression was restricted by institutional imperatives as much as moral indifference.

Fifth, patterns of loyalty and solidarity varied within the prison. On the VTU, prisoners were more likely to self-isolate—'working their own ticket in their own way' (Harvey)—and were less inclined to intervene on behalf of others. On D-wing, where long-term prisoners were located, there was a culture of broad but shallow social respect. Cell theft was rare (except in the period when there was a large amount of heroin in the prison), noise was kept to a minimum, and goods were lent more readily than elsewhere in the prison, without any expectation of interest payments.[17] Friendships were somewhat weak and conditional compared to other wings, but courtesy towards strangers was routine. Although socially atomized, long-termers thereby constructed an environment of mutual consideration and social distance that alleviated everyday deficits, discouraged conflict, and limited the social obligations that could jeopardize progress. Elsewhere in the prison, the expectations of friendship were more demanding, while consideration towards strangers was weaker.

Sixth, many prisoners were highly self-aware—undoubtedly *agents*—in their social choices. Most men coming to the ends of their sentences gradually relinquished interpersonal responsibilities, withdrew from trade networks and retired from prison politics. This was a 'U-curve' of social involvement—i.e. at its highest during the mid-point of the sentence (Wheeler 1961)—based on conscious decision-making and forethought. Friends were picked strategically, to aid the everyday experience, and carefully, to minimize risks:

I realised when I was coming out of the drugs scene that I had to break away from the drugtakers. Same with troublemakers. If you wanna stay out of trouble, you have to avoid them circles, the ones who are always trying to agitate. (Stephen)

Many prisoners sought out men throughout their sentences with similar orientations to doing time. In describing his social circle, Isaac, for example, noted that most of his friends were

---

[17] Staff on D-wing allowed prisoners more leeway in terms of in-cell possessions and borrowing goods. This was partly because they recognized the extra burdens of long-term imprisonment, and partly because lifers were more assertive about their rights.

on parole sentences, like him: 'They know they've got to keep their head down if they want to get out, kind of thing. So that's another reason why I roll with them as well, because we're all after the same thing.' Social relationships were not reducible to the typology outlined in Chapter 5, but they were strongly conditioned by adaptive modes. Most prisoners looked to mix with men who shared their ambition to self-improve, their desire to 'do time with no hassle' or their inclination to 'get involved'. These styles reflected differences in social needs and expectations, and shaped notions of loyalty, solidarity, and obligation.

Social Relationships and the Prisoner Typology

The majority of *enthusiasts* loosely fitted the profile of recovering addiction that is described directly above. For these men, prison wiped clean the social slate and offered a fresh surface on which social identity could be inscribed. In their personal remodelling, *enthusiasts* gravitated towards other former addicts looking to reform, connecting over shared experiences of dependence and degradation, and offering mutual support for pledges of personal transformation. They also mixed with prisoners who shared their orientation to the sentence or their future aspirations: 'good, genuine people' (Ian), men who were 'more intelligent, more mature' and did not hold a 'purely criminal mindset' (Luke).

Although some were classified as 'genuine friendships', these relationships were not necessarily highly trusting or loyal. Confident, self-motivated and oriented to audiences outside the prison, most *enthusiasts* were relatively self-sufficient in psychological terms. Their single-mindedness detached them somewhat from the bustle of the wings. By avoiding involvement in the informal economy and mixing in fairly limited social circles, they also restricted their exposure to the hazards of prison politics. In this respect, for *enthusiasts*, the primary purpose of prison friendship was neither emotional support nor physical protection. Its main function was to provide risk-free social company—'a cup of tea at dinner time [and] a good laugh' (Ian)—and to affirm pro-social self-perceptions. Friendships provided sounding boards for plans and an audience for pronouncements of progress. They also confirmed to *enthusiasts* their integrity by illustrating the quality of prisoner who was prepared to befriend them. Informal 'mentoring' relationships with younger prisoners served similar purposes, demonstrating (to an unspecified audience and to themselves) a commitment to helping others.

Asked about their social loyalties, *enthusiasts* cited themselves and their families above their peers. 'There's one or two prisoners I've got admiration for and loyalty', said Zack. 'Other than that, I come to jail on my own, and I'm going home on my own.' Where *enthusiasts* did express loyalties to other prisoners, these were defined by their commitments to being on the right side of the moral divide and staying out of trouble. Luke claimed that he would intervene if a younger prisoner came to him for help with being bullied, but would do so 'carefully, so I wouldn't get myself into trouble'—ideally, through polite approaches to the perpetrator, but, if necessary, by informing staff. Zack had given up 'doing other people's sentences for them', and operated with loyalties that were highly restricted:

because somebody might want to kick off or something and you might be associated with them. And they're going to expect you to get involved. When I keep myself to myself, they can't come and ask me to get involved. I do not get involved unless I want to get involved.

There was little sense of general solidarity. As with Luke, though, the exception was in relation to vulnerability and bullying. 'I won't tolerate it', said Zack. Luke agreed that 'It was 'wrong...a bad thing.' To confront it—or pay lip service to doing so— reinforced the sense of one's own moral honour. Likewise, in explaining his hope to become a prison Listener, Zack noted both the benefits to himself and his feelings for those in need: 'He's a vulnerable guy and he shouldn't be in jail. He should be in another place, a special place for these sort of people.'

Enthusiasts felt some allegiance to anyone who treated them respectfully, regardless of their institutional position. Often, they trusted members of staff—such as nurses, chaplains, and drug workers—more than other prisoners. Luke declared that, if he needed advice, 'it wouldn't matter whether it was staff or inmate' (but could only be a certain kind of prisoner, someone 'educated...a grown man'). Max—a prisoner caught between enthusiasm, play, and pragmatism—expressed a similar attitude:

I wouldn't want to see anybody get hurt: [the other] cleaners, staff, anybody, but to be honest with you, I get on with staff safer than I do with cons, because the screws ain't going to hurt me, they can't come in my cell and do me in. I wouldn't trust no one, not a con. I'd rather talk to a screw than a con, definitely. Because I know if I tell them something in confidence it's staying in confidence.

For more vulnerable *enthusiasts*, trust in officers was not abundant, but staff posed fewer threats to personal and psychological safety than other prisoners.

Retreatists were less concerned than *enthusiasts* about mixing with prisoners who shared their aspirations for the future or reinforced their social identities. Their priority was everyday company, prisoners with whom they could share 'a laugh and a cup of tea' (Noah), or 'have a conversation, talk about books and stuff.... Conversation to me is the most valuable thing' (Alfie). Most could relate to one or two friends, with whom they were comfortable opening up about their lives and providing reciprocal advice. These were companionable and affectionate relationships. Noah was a sage and sympathetic listener for a number of men on his wing. Alfie was familiar with the intimate details of his friends' lives and offered them measured guidance on how to interpret letters and get their lives back on track.[18]

Despite their affective qualities, these relationships were also rather pragmatic. *Retreatists* characterized most prisoners with whom they socialized as associates. Relations were convenient and impermanent, involving mutual support and protection without enduring commitment:

When it's time to go, it's time to go. Don't get it wrong, I wouldn't like to see [anything] happen to them. If I thought they'd been bullied, it's back to the old 'in numbers is strength'. We just help each other along the best way we can, through the day. (Noah)

Neither Alfie nor Noah expressed loyalties to the prisoner community as a whole. Both said that they would not get involved in the problems of prisoners they did not know. With those they did, their interventions were cautious and negotiated. Noah explained that he would offer help initially if a friend were getting in debt, but would quickly resort to concerned advice alone: 'get yourself

---

[18] 'I want to see the back of Richard. I want him to get out and do something decent with himself. I know he's a better person than he portrays. I know he's got the potential to be a better person, and I want him to get out. He's got a son out there, his son's eight. Richard's only twenty-six and I want him to make a life for himself. I can't see it happening, but I'd like to see it happen. I don't wanna get a letter from [him from] his Local Prison telling me he's been breached for his licence or something. I like seeing people get out, it gives me a buzz' (Alfie).

down that block, and get yourself cleaned up, because you've got a habit coming on'. Alfie's mediations would also be careful:

If somebody tried to bully Kelvin, I think I would step in and say something. I wouldn't turn violent, I would be hoping that I could avoid violence, perhaps talk sense into the guy who was bullying.

Future contact was unlikely not because of deficits in the friendship as such, but because of the vicissitudes of life on release and the need to prioritize self-regeneration over social ties.

When they get out I'll still be here and then meet more friends and they'll get out and I'll still be here.... I can make mates wherever I go [or] acquaintances. I can converse with the best of them and the worst of them. I'm quite happy if it came to the crunch, and I was left to my own devices, I'd be quite happy with my own company. (Alfie)

My loyalties are to myself, aren't they? My main priority is to try and get through this and just get out the best I can. I'm not here to hurt anybody, I'm not interested in what anybody else is doing.... People come to my pad. But personally, if they didn't come there, I could live without them. (Noah)

In such terms, *retreatists* partly conveyed their self-sufficiency and the modesty of their ambitions. They also expressed a fatalism that was consistent with their general orientation to life: a resigned acceptance that other prisoners were likely to change or 'get on with their own lives.... I've met a lot of people, once they're released and I'm released, I've kept in touch with a couple of letters and then we lose touch. If they don't write back, I just close them off' (Alfie).

When other prisoners did return letters, *retreatists* were able to develop relationships of personal value in a form that was highly unusual. Pessimistic about refraining from crime, they recognized that relationships formed in prison might be resurrected during future sentences, as Alfie explained:

It's not as though when you get out the friendship ends, it could be reignited at any time, you could end up in prison again.... One guy got out last Christmas, Steve from Manchester, he was in Nottingham in 1999, on remand for six months, he went to Stafford, I went to Ranby, he got out, kept in touch through the whole time he was out, then I get out the following May and then I was back in the following year and we met again in Lincoln jail, January 2001, and I just heard that he's got a four year sentence. As soon as I got out, [I was] back in, in June, six week remand, and I've wrote to him, then I got out again in July, we've lost touch and I told him my address, but I was only out in August and back in, in September and I wrote to him again and kept in touch. I was in for three and a half months that time, then I got out in December, kept in touch with him up until then. The correspondence stopped, and then I came back in, in March, and the first person I wrote to in prison was him—got a letter straight back. That's the sort of friendship I cherish, that's what I'm looking for, just a letter.

As indicated here, *retreatists* had minimal expectations of friendship. Asked if he counted his prison friends as 'proper friendships', Alfie responded that 'They're as close to friends as you'll get. I tell some of them, "we're going to keep in touch", the majority will get out and get on with their own lives. I've probably done it myself.' Again, such terms signified the sense of resigned fatalism that defined the lives of these prisoners.

Despite being the prisoners who had spent longest in prison, *stoics* were the prisoners who were least likely to report having any proper friendships. This was not because they were self-serving, disloyal, or untrustworthy; indeed, they were often the prisoners most willing to give guidance on applications or provide small quantities of tobacco to those in need. In these respects, they acted in more solidary ways towards casual associates than the vast majority of their peers. However, in terms of sustained and binding relationships, their commitments were highly limited. George described his loyalties as being 'fundamentally, to myself' and could see no circumstances where he would intervene on another prisoner's behalf if it might put his own progress at risk. Asked if he would step in to stop another prisoner being bullied, Nathan also expressed reluctance: 'I was going to say I'd intervene but I'm not sure if I would now. A few years ago I definitely would have. [Now] I'm far more cynical.' Instead, social relationships were seen as matters of expedience—'because you're in the same confined spaces.... You've gotta be sociable, just to get on with people' (George)—or as functionally casual attachments:

We'll get on with each other great, but I'll always keep at a distance. I won't let them come too close, too personal.... It's just what they call a 'prison friendship'. You help each other on while you're in prison, then once you leave, you're out of their life. (Tommy)

You can get to know people and you can get to like them, but you know at the back of your mind that you're gonna be transferred, you're never gonna see them again, so there's not much point in investing too much emotional energy in a friendship that ain't gonna last.... There's no future in it, and as far as I'm concerned, prison's just about getting through it, y'know. Even when you get out you can't really arrange to carry on a friendship because you wouldn't be allowed to, it would be frowned upon. (George)

Relative to most other prisoners, *stoics* were particularly guarded with their emotions and careful to keep other people at a certain distance.

As George suggested, the constraints placed upon friendship formation were in part a consequence of institutional proscriptions. Life-sentence prisoners frequently noted the paradox of being expected to show healthy adaptation to imprisonment and suitability for release, while in effect being discouraged from forming the kinds of relationships that might help them meet such expectations:

It's hard to develop a genuine friendship in prison. Because technically I'm not allowed to associate with them when I get out.... I had a really good friend [in prison X], someone I knew on the out. The minute he left prison, I was encouraged to terminate the relationship: it was 'associating with a known criminal', and it would cause me problems.... I could see what they were getting at: that it didn't do me any favours having known criminals as friends. But these are the only people I do know. (Tommy)

Friendships of intimacy and commitment were considered imprudent as well as impractical. *Stoics* spoke of the same limits to trust as other prisoners, but many had experienced trusting relationships earlier in their sentences, particularly in lifer centres where the prison population was more stable. In Cat-C conditions, they were more cautious, and avoided developing close social relationships in order to minimize obligations, maximize control over their lives, and ensure uneventful progress towards release. Burned in the past by misplaced loyalties and poor judgment, they picked social company with care. Tommy described himself as having been 'a bad judge of character' in the past—'it taught me a lesson: they're going home, but I'm still in prison'—and characterized his friends as 'the sensible element. They're not rocking the boat every two minutes.'

Other *stoics* were even more socially isolated. Having learned self-reliance during lengthy sentences and been bruised by past experiences of emotional betrayal, dependence, and loss, they either chose to be self-sufficient or considered emotional solitude a natural outcome of the environment (see Cohen and Taylor 1972):

I've seen so many people come and go. You get close to people and the next thing you know they're not there, and then you've gotta start all over again somewhere else. I'd rather just stand on me own. And that way, I'm never gonna leave myself. (Alexis)

Are there people that you would count as friends?

Friends? In prison? To trust within prison itself, no, it's very hard. Because you're so volatile in the sense of what you want outside that wall. And a lot of people will sell up their soul to get outside that wall.

What about emotional trust?

None at all. None at all. None whatsoever.

Does that mean in fifteen years, you've not had that kind of relationship with anyone?

No. No. No emotions, no. There's no love in these bricks. No love in these bricks at all. (Pete)

Pete's comments were sobering, but not unique. Several lifers described having had no meaningful friendships within prison during sentences that had spanned decades. Most men on long sentences were loners or mixed in very limited circles. George estimated having had 'only three or four people over the years who I would call a friend and I would want to meet again outside.... But I don't think I've got any friends here, not genuine friends anyway.' Despite sometimes having been imprisoned for over half their lives, they still perceived the prison as somewhere socially impermanent and unreal.[19]

Prisoners exposed over many years to this context of emotional retrenchment and mistrust feared permanent damage to their capacity to relate to others (see Jamieson and Grounds 2005; Cohen and Taylor 1972). George was resigned to the likelihood of

[19] Perhaps the most telling illustration of this was that, when asked to tell their life stories, almost all long-term prisoners stopped at the point when they were sentenced to prison, even if this meant effacing two decades of their existence. In this respect, the metaphor of prison as a 'deep-freeze' normally associated with quantitative analysis of 'prison effects' (Zamble and Porporino 1988) clearly has some merit for understanding the existential experience of long-term imprisonment (see Cohen and Taylor 1971). This should by no means suggest that extended sentences have no social, psychological, or physical consequences (nor is this necessarily what deep-freeze studies imply). It is highly consequential that life in prison is experienced as deeply artificial or, to some degree, 'on hold' (see also Jamieson and Grounds 2005).

never having an intimate relationship once released, and talked at length about the annihilation of his emotional identity:

This has been my life for so long. I spent three years at [high-security prison X], and I spent two years at [category B prison Y] and for those five years I was totally locked up [emotionally]. I had to be, just for survival. Everybody did, because of the nature of where we were living. Keeping people at arm's length, because that was the safest thing to do.... It's in reports about me that I am locked up and controlled emotionally, so a large part of Cat-D for me isn't simply gonna be about getting used to being out there again, it's putting myself forward a bit more.... Just the length of time, y'know, it can wear you down. There are other people who've done longer than me [and] seem to be on top of the world. Maybe they get visits every month from a loving wife and a few bouncy children, so, y'know, that gives em a sense of belonging and a sense of worth, a huge part of their identity.... I haven't had visits for years.

Interviewees of all kinds reported that prison instilled 'a certain amount of paranoia' (Luke) or made them 'stand-offish' when meeting new people on the outside (Brian). For prisoners on longer sentences, the impact was more profound. Trust and intimacy became increasingly alien sentiments. Lost time could not be recaptured (Jamieson and Grounds 2005).

In contrast to *stoics*, many *players* expressed negligible emotional solidarity with other prisoners, and were indifferent to the struggles of strangers, but were highly loyal to their immediate peers. Ashley declared that he had: 'solidarity for me and my closest mates. And it ends right there. If he ain't no mate of mine, I could see ten officers kicking him to death [laughs]. It means nothing to me.' Although *players* instinctively sided with other prisoners in disputes against staff, they did so more because of antipathy to the system than peer allegiance. In relation to friends, however, their stated loyalties were almost absolute. VJ and Bradley described allegiances to prison allies that assumed personal sacrifice and considerable commitment:

I could be going home tomorrow, and you could have a beef tonight and I'd be there the next day.[20] I'm still there for you. Because it's a loyalty thing.

Even though it puts you at risk?

Yeah, you'd do it for me, why shouldn't I do it for you? If you're going to stick your neck out for me, I'll stick my neck out for you. It's a loyalty thing.

[20] 'Beef': an issue, argument, or problem.

So what if it was the other way round and you came to me, and said 'Ben, watch my back', and I said to you 'Listen, I'm out tomorrow...'.

I'd call you a pussy-hole. You'd better not talk to me again. We're not friends no more. You're nothing. Don't even look at me. Don't even talk to me. We're supposed to be tight. You get me? It's a B[rethren] thing and we're all there. It's a family affair. (VJ)

It wouldn't bother me if it was the day before I was getting out: [if] one of me mates got in some trouble and he needed some help, I'd help him. If it was the morning I was getting out, I wouldn't turn me back on him. If they turned their back on me then it would do me head in, because I would back them up a hundred per cent no matter what the consequences were. (Bradley)

For these *players*, mutual obligations trumped individual interests. Loyalty was a mark of masculinity and an inviolable pledge. Threats to friends were interpreted almost as personal insults: 'I'd take offence if anyone hurt them [or] hurt their family' (Ashley).

Players were no more trusting than other prisoners. Indeed, their involvement in the informal economy made them highly wary of the motives of their peers. Social life was inauthentic because the stakes involved with trade made it almost hyperreal. But while the threshold of acceptance into inner circles was high, once inside, the trust required by illicit activity made it a powerful source of loyalty. *Players* involved in prison trade expected their partners to 'take the rap' if caught with forbidden items and presumed they would remain silent when questioned by prison staff. Prisoners who fulfilled such obligations, or were willing to share the risks inherent in prison drug dealing, earned considerable fidelity in return.

Trade was both the root of and the route to certain kinds of friendships and affiliations. Ashley described how prisoners like him bonded over 'little things—you might get a shipment [of drugs] come in, and it's just between you two'. Some *players* sought out alliances in order to facilitate prison trade. 'You make friends with people to help with business' (prisoner, fieldwork notes). Ashley declared that he was 'constantly searching for good men, the loyalist people I can find. You can never have enough loyalty'. Those who were committed to illegal activity on release sought out relationships that could aid their future interests. Darren had 'made lots of money through people I've met in jail. I've done business with them out there. And I class them as friends, some of them.' VJ said he could depend on 'at least five men on each wing in the jail', most of whom he had met on previous sentences. He explained how relationships established in prison were actively pursued on release:

Some people say you don't make friends in prison.

No. You make links.

So they're not friends?

Well they are friends, but you've met them in prison. If I meet you in prison and me and you are tight [i.e. close, trusting] with minding [e.g. drugs, phonecards] and things, when I get out, I'll phone you: 'What's happening Ben, I'm on my way now to link you'.... All we talk about [in prison] is: 'Yeah, I can get this and I can get that' [i.e. drugs, stolen goods], that's mostly talk. Until you actually link them then you don't know what they're about. Just say us two are mates in prison. And you're saying to me: 'Yeah, I can get x amount of stuff at this price', and I'm thinking: 'That's a good price, you know', so [when] we're both out, and I come to link you, I come to see what you're really about.

It was only on release that the authenticity of a prison relationship could be verified. Only then might it develop into something more than an instrumental business connection. Because of their involvement in relatively organized crime, *players* were more willing than most prisoners to travel beyond their hometowns in order to pursue useful contacts. Prison was thus a springboard for relationships of depth and emotional trust, rather than a site of trust and commitment in itself.

Some *players* sought little more from their relationships than the loyalties demanded by trade. For reasons already documented, Wilson kept emotional relationships at a distance ('I don't really let nobody in.... Emotions will just fuck you up'), and described his closest social partner as 'a bit stronger than an associate, but I don't consider him a friend. We're [just] in business together.' There were no associates for whom he would put himself at risk. Other *players* expressed powerful loyalties independently of trade, loyalties that were stronger than those expressed by other prisoners. For example, Darren, Pierce, and Morgan all spoke of the importance of loyalty—'the most precious thing anybody can have' (Darren)—and described relationships of unmitigated, mutual support with one or two close friends: 'If somebody starts a fight with him, no matter who they were, I'd stick up for him', Pierce asserted. Darren declared that: 'if anything happened to them which was wrong, I'd back them up and they'd do the same

for me. And I'd go one hundred per cent, whatever their decision would be.' Asked if his loyalties inside prison conflicted with
those outside, he said: 'all I can concentrate on at the moment is
people in prison because these are the people that I'm living with.
People outside, we're in different worlds at the moment.'

Despite their strength, these were negotiated loyalties that took
some account of personal circumstances. *Players* of this kind
reported consistently that although they would not refuse help
to close friends if asked, friends were unlikely to ask for forms of
support that might put their progress in jeopardy. 'Even my Co-D,
if he knew that I really wanted my parole, he wouldn't even come
up and ask me' (Pierce). This kind of pre-emptive consideration
was an important component of interpersonal relations.

Social relationships among *pragmatists* were varied. These were
the prisoners most likely to differentiate between 'prison friends'
or associates and 'proper friendships'. Some *pragmatists* were
self-described 'loners', who socialized only as much as their needs
required. Others were more socially involved, mixing widely but
in terms that were relatively shallow. In general, they were less
self-sufficient than *stoics*, and expressed little social or emotional
solidarity beyond immediate circles. Within these circles, loyalties
were firm but somewhat negotiable.

A small number of *pragmatists* developed what Cohen and
Taylor (1972: 82) called 'intimate dyadic relationships' with more
mature and experienced prisoners. Gavin had been taken under
wing by a group of older men who recognized his vulnerability
and advised him on how to avoid being exploited. Cameron had
developed an intense bilateral friendship (with Darren), whose
trust, generosity, and emotional warmth distinguished it from the
majority of prison relationships:

You've got mates and that, but Darren is a real friend. I bought him
shampoo last week, knowing he's got no hair just as a joke, and we had
a laugh about that. He got me a shirt for Christmas, and I give him some
phonecards and one of my toiletries. There's not many people who'd do
that in jail, who'll say 'Here you are son, here's your Christmas present'.
We ain't got no things to give, but I'd give Darren fucking anything mate.
I can always go to him for advice. I fully trust him a hundred per cent.
(Cameron)

Relationships of this kind had paternal overtones and were
founded on deep identification. When asked how he had formed
his friendship with Darren, given the age difference between them,

Cameron replied that 'he looks at me as his son'. Interviewed separately, Darren explained that 'he reminds me of myself when I was that age, when I was twenty-one'.

A small number of 'loners' mixed with other prisoners only superficially. 'I keep myself to myself pretty much', said Harvey. 'I don't really associate with the other people, I like to just keep myself to myself'. More commonly, *pragmatists* developed prison friendships for reasons that were largely instrumental. Some admitted that they cultivated friendships to obtain low-level quantities of drugs, food, or money:

Sometimes you'll go out of your way to get on with certain people because it can make your style of life in the prison better. Maybe they're in a better position the way they're living, maybe they've more money than you, more private cash. You might even get some cannabis. Things that alleviate the stress, the boredom, the monotony. (Tyler)

Other *pragmatists* were strategic for defensive purposes, deliberately socializing with men who had physical clout:

If you're going to hang around with the fraggles, then you're going to get tarred with the same brush. If you go around with people who are moderately handy,[21] most people won't touch you. I didn't outrightly clique on to them because they are handy, but I always make sure that I go around with the right kind of person. (Ewan)

For most *pragmatists*, relationships were primarily protective and resembled defensive contracts. Ross noted that it was 'always better to have a few people round you. Not just for company but if anything goes off, I know they've got my back.' 'You've got to look after your own', said Kieran. 'And hopefully, if the shit hits the fan with me, they'll have *my* back.' Ewan described how 'If anyone tries anything with them then I stand by them. Same goes for them. If anyone tries anything with me, they'll stand by me'.

Social groupings among all types of prisoner had the kinds of protective functions described here. For *pragmatists* though, physical, informational, and economic assistance were generally their primary purpose. This was particularly the case for vulnerable prisoners, like Colin, who needed social support for basic psychological sustenance. Resources could be pooled, goods shared, and predicaments discussed, but there was little emotional content or

---

[21] 'handy': good at fighting, capable of looking after oneself.

trust in such relationships. Some *pragmatists* were prepared to take the rap for other prisoners who had more to lose from disciplinary infractions, so long as they received something in return. Thus Callum falsely admitted to staff that he had planted hooch in another prisoner's cell, in return for a share of the prisoner's canteen.

For the majority of *pragmatists*, sentiments of solidarity extended little beyond these groupings. Whereas *stoics* regretted their social isolationism and often conveyed empathy for strangers, *pragmatists* expressed a more hardened ideology of prudential individualism. 'If I don't know them, it's not my business', Cameron stated. Howard explained his view that 'if you can help somebody else, then help them, [but] you have to look after yourself'.

Within their social networks, *pragmatists* distinguished between proper friends, known prior to incarceration, for whom it would be unthinkable to 'stand by and let them take a kicking' (prisoner, fieldwork notes), and loose affiliates, with whom one might share social space without feelings of obligation:

> Associates are just someone I'll speak to, hang around with. If someone was having a go at them and a fight was going to kick off, I wouldn't be behind their back because I know they wouldn't be behind mine. A good friend, I'd be right behind their back, ready to help them out. Associates, you wouldn't get involved, you'd try and give the other person a little word, but if they weren't having it, you'd say, 'Fair enough, you'll have to sort it out between you both'. (Jordan)

These were subtle gradations of loyalty, whose terms were to some degree negotiable. Young *pragmatists* on short sentences and without family responsibilities often resembled *players* in declaring absolute commitment to their friends, regardless of consequences. For these men, like Cameron, the prison was the primary source of status and identity. Social horizons did not extend beyond its walls (see Irwin's (1970) 'state-raised youth'). As Marcus said: 'You can't turn a mate down. It's loyalty, and you've got no one in here except yourself and the people around you.' For most *pragmatists* though—as for most other prisoners—social support was conditional. Callum and Joey sketched out the parameters of obligation:

> You don't have to do fuck all for anybody, it's just whether you feel you should in them circumstances. If a weak man is getting grief off somebody you know, you can go to the lad that's giving him grief and say, 'Be cool

man, he runs with my cousin' or whatever. If he says 'no', well, do what you're doing [i.e. stay out of it]. If they end up scrapping and one of them is getting a kicking you split it up, like, 'He's had enough'. (Callum)

Here, the conditions of appropriate action were delimited by the pragmatics of life within the prison. The same template was applied when looking beyond the prison gates. Typically, among *pragmatists*, the boundary for active support was the point at which intervention might jeopardize progression towards freedom. Ross explained that 'I'd be there if they needed me. [But] the limits would be where it meant me getting any more time.' Ronan had similar personal guidelines, admitting that he would try to split up a fight if a prison friend was involved, but 'that's about as far as it would go'. For Joey, an impending parole hearing meant that he would intervene if a friend was 'getting a good hiding', but would let a 'fair fight' go ahead or would intervene only with extreme caution. Involvement in someone else's business was dangerous: 'You do as much as you can to help without putting yourself on the line.' Asked if there were circumstances in which he would refuse to get involved on behalf of a friend, Chris was clear that he would not sacrifice his home leave, nor expect anyone else to: 'Messing up everything to see his own wife and child? I'd disrespect him for that.'

Pragmatists also generally recognized that there were limits to what could be legitimately expected from others. Those whose main focus was being released without incident were particularly aware that they should not make demands on the people around them that they would not want made on themselves. As illustrated here, and in contrast to *players*, a prisoner's commitment to his primary group was not beyond negotiation:

[A friend] was getting a bit of hassle off somebody else. And my mate was worried about it. And he says: 'What's going to happen?'. And I said 'You know I'm your friend...' but I mentioned that I'd got home leave soon, and I says: 'Don't expect me to be fighting, because I'm not losing nothing for no-one.' And he said 'No, I wouldn't want you to do that'. The lads who I'm with know I wouldn't jeopardise anything—they know I wouldn't jeopardise another day in this shit-hole for anyone. (Ross)

For *pragmatists* with family commitments, the outside world could not be disregarded when decisions were made about everyday behaviour. Like *enthusiasts*, such men frequently described their loyalties as being located outside the prison: to wives, girlfriends, and children, and the prospect of a better life outside, rather than to any cause or person within the institution. For these *pragmatists*, the risks of not seeing their families outweighed the risks of losing status within the prison. Indeed, most prisoners struggled to balance conflicting loyalties inside and outside prison. These conflicts were particularly difficult for prisoners who were surrounded by men from their hometowns and cities, for whom divisions between the prison and the outside world could not be maintained so easily.

Everyday Social Relations: Primary and Secondary Groups

This chapter has so far focused on relationships and loyalties between individual prisoners. The following section describes the nature of primary, semi-primary, and secondary groups in Wellingborough, and the relationships between these groups.

The basic unit of social life was the 'clique'. On most wings, there were a number of solitary men (at least one-fifth of prisoners), who did not fit into stable social groups. However, most prisoners worked themselves into small cliques, consisting of between four and ten people, including men who counted as friends and others as associates. These cliques were often made up of prisoners who shared orientations to the sentence, but were also built around regional networks, religion, ethnic identification, age, drug use, and interests within the prison. 'Everyone has got their own group they fit into and no one bothers anyone really, they just do their own thing', Ronan summarized.

As this chapter has detailed, it was within these cliques that goods were shared and physical support was provided. In this respect, wing life was cellular in structure—a series of discrete primary groups that were in many ways self-contained, while allowing considerable external association. Men were rarely members of more than one primary group, but few mixed solely within their 'inner circle', creating some fluidity and overlap between these basic units. 'There are little cliques, they still break off and communicate with other people, but most of the time they stick together', said Ian. Paul noted that: 'You'll find a couple in a clique that will talk to other people and you get the others that will stick by themselves. Most people get on.' Most prisoners had associates at work or from the gym who were from other wings; those involved in trade or with particular hobbies had prison friends outside their principal groups. Many men had multiple and stratified loyalties to other individuals and secondary groups. A Sikh prisoner outlined his own order of commitment as follows: first, to anyone he knew before entering prison, then to fellow Sikhs, followed by prisoners from his hometown, other prisoners with Asian origins, and casual friendships based upon his prison activities.

It was difficult and unusual for outsiders to break into regional or ethnic groups of which they were not natural members. However, to associate casually with prisoners from other groups was a normal part of social life. Indeed, the most *visible* units on the wings were semi-primary groups that comprised prisoners from a number of smaller cliques who came together in order to socialize. Sociability and social activity was the basis by which the majority of prisoners identified wing groupings:

You've got people who play pool, they always associate with each other because they're always there. People are always in the table tennis room. Then you've got like two sets of different lots of black geezers. They just stand around and listen to reggae and whatnot, then you've got the other ones who are listening to ragga and whatnot. Then you've got a few quiet people who are just in their cells just minding their own business doing nothing. Then you've got the rest all running around the wing looking for gear and how they're going to get some gear. That's about it really. (Aaron)

[You've got] people who walk about with their arse hanging out, one leg of their trousers rolled up, or something.[22] Then there's just lads who want to get on with their sentence. They seem to knock about with each other. They'll all be down playing pool or having a game of cards. Then there's the gym-heads: people who go to the gym, pushing weights, 'I'm big and I'm hard and all this lot'. Then there's the blacks. They normally stick together. That's normally the three groups. (Ross)

There is my kind, [who have a] laugh and a joke. More time we're in a pad chilling, listening to music and having a conversation, so we just keep ourselves to ourselves. Then you got the ones that are loners, don't really chat to no one. Then you've got the bunch who are like, 'I don't give a fuck, fuck these screws', they're kind of rowdy. There are those who spend all their time playing pool and table tennis during association. Then you've got your bunch of smackheads. (Wilson)

---

[22] Wearing trousers in a low-slung style and with one leg rolled up was a common style among Afro-Caribbean prisoners.

Players often saw the wings as stratified according to involvement in the drugs economy—'people that sell drugs...people that will hold items for you, [and] then you've just got little idiots that just do what they've got to do, you don't really see them' (Paul). Certainly, drug users were one of the most obvious groupings on all wings, and were themselves divided into a number of categories: those who liked cannabis as opposed to heroin, and those whose consumption was heavy or casual: 'your hardcore ones who are out every day looking for smack or whatever, and then the ones who just have it now and again' (Stephen). The divide between users and non-users was one of the most evident splits within the prisoner community (although one which was less clear in reality than theory):

You get people that are interested in drugs and those that aren't. [And] some people just stay away from drug users. You get that dividedness. Even though they still talk to each other as in 'Alright mate, how you doing', they still get on that way but they're not people that you would sit down and associate with. (Den)

Drug users were widely rejected by non-users as sources of social company. They could not be trusted in cells and their activities were, at best, a dull irritation. The protracted requirements of drug acquisition and the rituals of consumption were of no interest to those who were not involved. When seeking to obtain drugs, users abandoned friends who were of no material use to them in favour of instrumental associates. As Aaron noted, addicts were: 'Always looking for who's got something they can put together to get drugs'. In general, their habits were considered a cause of disloyalty and social instability.

In general though, semi-primary social groups, like more intimate cliques, were relatively stable and consistent. The same prisoners tended to play pool or table tennis every evening, while other men were known as 'gym-heads', church-goers, card-players or 'weekend drinkers' because these labels conveyed their regular social activities. To be outside these groups was not necessarily to be actively excluded so much as to have different interests:

Certain people who will play pool all the time, and other boys who will be in the gym all the time. They won't go down and play pool with the other lads because it's not their circle. It's not that they're not friends with the people, it's just that that is not their activity, so they won't do it. (Den)

Race, religion, ethnicity, and region could form the basis both of primary and secondary groupings. Many prisoners associated in ethnically homogeneous primary groups. Others—at least half—made no distinctions on the basis of race or colour and associated in ethnically diverse cliques. Generally, these were men who had been raised in ethnically integrated inner-city areas and had friends from a diverse range of backgrounds in the community as well as in prison. In both contexts, they were essentially colour-blind in their social interactions. Many came from mixed-race families or had half-siblings, children or other relatives of different ethnicities to their own.

For these prisoners, race, religion, and ethnicity were secondary identities. In general, these identities were more salient for minority groups than for the white majority. As Callum noted, white prisoners did not develop the same natural associations with other whites as prisoners from minority ethnic groups did with each other: 'The black inmates, wherever you go, will stop and talk to all the black inmates, whereas if I'm in jail and I see a white guy I don't go "how you doing?".' For minority ethnic prisoners, affiliations based around race provided a secondary layer of support in times of need or solace (see Wilson 2003). The same was the case for prisoners who could count on support from hometown associates who were not in their principal friendship groups. Indeed, it was in times of conflict that membership of primary, semi-primary, and secondary groups was most evident: 'If a beef happens, that's when you'll see the units' (Ashley).

The nature and dynamics of such skirmishes will be discussed in the chapter that follows. In general, groups co-existed without significant problems. Prisoners were aware of how easily conflicts could escalate, dragging in increasing numbers of interested parties. Indeed, different groups formed counter-weights to each other, preventing any one faction from dominating most wings and limiting as well as inflaming hostilities in what was a complex dynamic. Institutional monitoring sought to ensure that wings were ethnically balanced. Connections between different social and ethnic groups also aided institutional stability. There were black prisoners who were Muslims, links between *players* from different cities, and established relationships between ethnic groups who came from similar areas of big cities.

Race Relations

Relationships between black and other prisoners

Relations between black prisoners and other groups were neither tense nor entirely harmonious, as Rhys described:

> It's not like there's a black and white divide or anything. There are some people don't like blacks, just like in normal life. They stay away from them. But I think in general people seem to mix quite well. I wouldn't say it's like 'Wahey, we're best mates', but everyone seems to get on.

Much of the time, prisoners operated with a benign indifference towards the views and activities of other ethnic groups. As Phillips (2008) has argued, the prevailing discourse was one of harmony, unity, and tolerance, and outward appearances suggested a culture of 'constrained conviviality'. At the same time, many prisoners harboured private views that were more hostile. The result was a state of fragile calm. On one wing, for example, a number of prisoners began to express far-right political sympathies, bringing conflict closer to the social surface without precipitating it directly. 'It's more of a stay out our way and we'll stay out of your way sort of thing. But it would only take one silly incident and you could have quite a situation on your hands' (Brian). Many white prisoners overstated the level of tension and antipathy, using a hyperbolic language of 'race wars' to describe how wings could fracture along ethnic lines in the event of interpersonal conflict between men from different ethnic or racial groups.[23] Most believed that non-white prisoners were quick to racialize issues and leap to the defence of their ethnic peers: 'if a white man gets beat up, he gets beat up. If you attack a black man, chances are you've got the other blacks to cope with' (Charlie); 'There is always an undercurrent of racism in prison. If a black guy and a white guy would fight, straightaway the black guys on the wing assume, sometimes rightly, that it is a racial thing' (Stephen).

Black prisoners were less likely to portray the prisoner community as being ethnically divided, and emphasized the concerns and experiences they shared with all other prisoners (Sparks *et al.*

---

[23] Such claims and predictions were redolent of what Genders and Player (1989: 103) described as 'virtual racial warfare' (and see Sparks *et al.* 1996; Edgar *et al.* 2003).

1996). If anything, they underestimated the level of underground racism, claiming that there was little ethnic tension or hostility. While they acknowledged that ethnic fissures could develop when disputes were explicitly related to race (see Owen 1998), they insisted that such splits were by no means inevitable. Olly, for example, argued that black prisoners did not automatically stick together:

unless it was a racist war, and if it was a racist war, that doesn't mean the black guy is going to fall out with the white geezer's friends. I wouldn't and my friends wouldn't either.... I've seen it a few times in prison where a white person has knocked out a black geezer and everyone has just stood there and looked. It's just nothing to do with you, why get involved. Unless it's directly to you, it's none of your business [or] unless it's a racist thing.

So, there might be a fight between a black guy and a white guy that's not to do with race, it could be to do with drugs...

...that's different.

That's different from if they made a racist comment?

Yes, that's completely different, you're not just talking to him, you're talking to all the blacks or all the whites. (Olly)

In conflict situations, the spectre of race heightened the anticipation of violence (see Edgar *et al.* 2003). Some prisoners reported being encouraged to escalate skirmishes when race was involved. In general though, all groups had an interest in the avoidance of collective conflict ('everybody needs to get on with each other', Callum summarized). After an incident on D-wing between one black and one white prisoner, prisoners reported a 'really weird...lovey-dovey' atmosphere on the wing (Stephen)—a collective attempt to cool any simmering tensions. On the whole, racist views were expressed within the safety of cliques or in covert forms, through anonymous graffiti or disguised shouts out of cell windows.

Some prisoners were undoubtedly prejudiced (Genders and Player 1989), while others were explicitly racist, expressing contempt for minority ethnic groups. Bradley was 'all down for white purification', although he did not 'go round broadcasting it', and said he was prepared to 'stand and talk to the Indians and the Pakis—they've done nothing wrong to me'. Others maintained that their attitudes were 'more of a nationalist thing', presenting arguments informed by the British National Party about immigration and the welfare system: 'I don't see how people will come to this county from another country and get priority over people born in England. It's not a race thing. Well, it is race, I suppose, but it's more' (Brian). Fear and ignorance about such issues was rife. As Phillips (2008) has argued, white prisoners were defensive and confused about their own ethnic identities.

White prisoners who expressed critical views about black prisoners were generally insistent that these were about 'attitude' rather than race *per se*. Many considered black prisoners overbearing, belligerent, and aggrieved excessively by historical racism.

The blacks seem to have a more aggressive nature about them. They're more arrogant. They want things their way. They've got a chip on their shoulder. They're nice as pie, as long as they're getting what they want.... They're kind of arrogant and they don't just get on with their time. (Ewan)

They really mean it, like they've still got shackles on their fucking left ankles or something you know, still picking cotton.[24] Them times are long gone you know, and they're still living in the past. They get brought up with all this fucking slave history bullshit piped up em. If you're gonna walk round with a chip on your shoulder at least be blatantly obvious about it you know. Don't turn round and say 'is it because I'm black?'. Say 'do you think I'm a fucking knob?', you know, '...it's got fuck all to do with your colour mate I just [think] you're a twat'. (Tyler)[25]

One aspect of such criticisms was the belief that many black prisoners did not conduct themselves with sufficient nobility or consideration for others. When men like Alfie asserted that black prisoners were 'always complaining' and were always late to lock up at the end of evening association, the implication was that they could not handle their sentences: 'At ten past you hear them out on the landing. I think they just don't like being banged up, they've got to hear their own voice to reassure themselves, stupid nonsensical stuff. I don't think they can do their time.' Volume was also a significant source of mundane irritation. Black prisoners were often perceived as 'brash and loud' (Alfie), more prone than other prisoners to material boasts and facile complaints, and

---

[24] Some Afro-Caribbean prisoners walked with a limping style.

[25] There was also considerable dislike for white prisoners who were seen as acting as if they were black (see Phillips 2008): 'they suck their teeth and bounce around, they'll try and talk how black people talk' (Dom).

more obstinate in conversation. Jacob, himself a black Jamaican, complained that: 'If [a group] is pure black, everybody think that you can't tell them nothing, like they all know it already. Nobody wants to listen or ask questions, it's just shout, shout, shout.'

Indeed, this condemnation was often voiced within the black population. Older black prisoners often castigated younger black men for their 'mentality', while many second- and third-generation Afro-Caribbeans distanced themselves from more recent immigrants, in particular Jamaican prisoners, who they perceived as arrogant, aggressive, and discourteous:

They've got too much attitude, they're loud and chat shit: 'I'm the baddest man'. Yardies beg for everything, if you've got a pen they say 'give me the pen', beg for your jeans, shoes, top because they think English people are rich. (Wilson)

Being a black guy myself, I'm proud of my colour.... But there is a lot of guys of Jamaican origin that have got bad attitudes. And I'm not in that bollocks, I'm not into the bullshit. Bravado. Bad attitudes. Ignorant. Full of themselves. I can understand the mentality behind them. It's hard over there. You come over to a country of this nature, it's like rich pickings to them. So they think because it's rich pickings they can go and just take what they want to take, and they treat everybody on that sort of principle. (Carlton)

A second complaint was that black prisoners mistakenly or dishonestly attributed actions that they disliked to racism.

It's always their flip card. If they don't get their way, it's racist, you're racist. (Ewan)

I see people who claim racism, they say 'Racist fuckers, they're doing this because I'm black', and I [think] no, it's not cos you're black, it's because of your attitude, because the person you're arguing against has no choice because that's the prison rules, or there may be some other motivation. A lot of people of colour, specifically black, take it as a personal affront and therefore call it racism where it may not necessarily be. (Nathan)

When anything goes wrong now, it's a 'racist' thing. And it's just spoiling everything for everyone. (Tommy)

In particular, white prisoners resented what they saw as attempts by black prisoners to turn disputes between individuals into 'racial' issues. As Phillips (2008: 322) notes, the negotiation of race was 'difficult terrain', and many white prisoners felt that their language and behaviour was subject to unfair scrutiny. 'If they get into a fight they'll say "it's because I'm black", and they'll try and get all the blacks behind them', Kieran claimed. Since there was almost total consensus among prisoners that racism was wrong, to be labelled a racist was a serious thing. Anti-racism and acceptance of ethnic difference were parts of the prisoner code (see Phillips 2008). If an incident gained public definition as having a racial dimension, this transformed the distribution of moral righteousness and censure. Stephen's description of a fight on D-wing illustrated how blame shifted when racism was involved:

Originally, the black guy who went to his cell to cause trouble was in the wrong. But because [the white guy] said, 'you black bastard', that makes him in the wrong. If he hadn't said that one expression then we would have said: 'Oh, that black guy's out of order'. [But] He's in the wrong morally because he brought black and white into it. (Stephen)

For many white prisoners, racism was to be condemned, but accusations of racism were not to be thrown around casually.

A third accusation made by a number of white prisoners was that some black prisoners were themselves racist or were hypocritical in their expectations of treatment. Many argued that black prisoners did not extend to them the respect and courtesy that they expected for themselves. Den claimed that: 'A few of the black guys on the wing won't give you the time of day.' Other white prisoners maintained that the racial politics of the prison were deeply inconsistent.[26]

A lot of blacks don't like white people. But it's [supposedly] different. They see it as 'but we're allowed to be. The white man's been trampling on us for years'. [They think] it isn't wrong for a black person not to want to be around a white person, that's not wrong. But if a white person doesn't want nothing to do with a black person, then all of a sudden, you're a racist. It's double standards. (Ewan)

If you've got ten lads playing football, and one's a black guy and he says 'let me have my mate come in', his mate comes in, no problem with that. Then the two of them want another mate come in, then before you know it the majority of the team's black lads. They'd rather have one of their mates, another black guy, than a white lad. Yet I couldn't turn around and say 'what's this? Is this a fucking white thing?' cos then I'm an automatic racist. (Tyler)

---

[26] Wyn complained that being nicknamed 'Taff', by black prisoners, was 'a racist thing.... How would they black lads feel if I called every one of them Winston? I don't like people classing me along with every other Welshman that ever existed.'

The point here is neither to corroborate nor dispute these observations and accusations. Certainly, there were some white prisoners whose views were racist, some whose attitudes were defensive, and others who merely disliked certain forms of behaviour that some black prisoners exhibited. Certainly too, there were some black prisoners whose demeanours appeared aggressive, and some with acute sensitivities to racist treatment based on structural discrimination outside prison.

Relations between Asian and Muslim prisoners, and other prisoners

Relations between Asian and non-Asian prisoners were complex. Forming a highly cohesive group, Asians elicited jealousy and resentment in equal and related quantities. Most non-Asians respected their closeness and solidarity, noting their readiness to intervene on behalf of each other and the unity of their conduct: 'They tend to stick together more than the average inmate' (Callum). One white prisoner explained that Asian prisoners more often pooled resources: 'Like we might have fifteen items between us to get draw at Christmas. They'll do that regularly: split an eight [of cannabis] and then share the profits' (fieldwork notes). Another common observation was that a confrontation with one Asian prisoner would automatically bring others into the fray. Prisoners who were not the recipients of such allegiances considered them to be highly exclusionary. These sentiments were aggravated by a lack of familiarity with Asian culture. Whereas 'black culture' permeated the lives of most prisoners, in the forms of dance music, fashion, and urban slang (and 'blackness' itself carried social cachet), the tropes of Asian culture and the rituals of Islam were more alien to most prisoners. And while their deviations from mainstream prison culture were perceived as threatening, by displaying their relative wealth through clothing and jewellery, Asian prisoners exhibited an ability to compete successfully *within* the terms of dominant culture.

This dual location, both within and outside prevailing culture, caused other tensions. A number of prisoners complained that Muslims inside and outside prison were quick to denounce British society but keen to enjoy its freedoms. 'They hate the West', Martin argued, 'but they're quick enough to come to our country and take our things. I haven't got nothing against certain

[Muslim] lads, but that religion I hate.' Den resented that they were 'trying to dictate our law'. Certainly, although Muslim prisoners were 'not running around talking about how [Christians] should get killed' (Callum), some asserted their political-religious identity fairly forcefully and proselytized an interpretation of The West as global oppressors. These terms caused some annoyance among non-Muslims, who either disputed their reading of politics (much of which was highly anti-Semitic), mocked their predictions of global insurrection, or disliked what they perceived as an aggressive form of social preaching. For many prisoners, the complex terminology used in such pronouncements was itself threatening: its use was taken as a claim to intellectual superiority, and its militant tone was perceived as hectoring and overbearing. Others—although a small minority—were attracted to the moral certainties of Islam, and the narrative salvation that, like other religious systems, it could offer.

Just as their solidarity provoked emotions of jealousy, the role of Asian and Muslim prisoners within Wellingborough's drugs economy also produced considerable social envy. Claims of piety alongside involvement in drug supply generated accusations of hypocrisy. Many non-Muslims also believed that it was somewhat too expedient for Muslims to declare commitment to the strictures of Islam only once incarcerated, having breached them previously without compunction. More significant was the manner in which Asian and Muslim prisoners participated in the drugs trade. According to a number of interviewees, they were often sources of heroin supply, but employed other prisoners to conduct their trade while they themselves maintained low visibility:

They're very undercover yeah? They're up there, but they just don't want to be known to be up there. In the hierarchy of drugs, they do their fair share but the difference between them and me is that I will blatantly say 'yeah it's me', [whereas] they will never because they feel that if they say [that] they'll be eaten [by] other people that feel they're above them or maybe even below them and know that they can maybe beat them or rush them for their things. They'd rather go through me or someone else. (Paul)

Believe it or not, the Indians bring most of the drugs in. Indians have got lots of money. [But] they're not powerful people. They're powerful with money, whereas the black male is powerful with money and powerful with violence. The Indians don't have the violence. They'll get a parcel of heroin, and they'll find a black lad among the top lads, and they buy people, basically.

So are they pulling strings or are their strings being pulled by other people?

They're pulling strings but the strings are nylon, it's thin. That Indian will pay that person not to rob them. . . . They're only not being robbed because of that black guy. If that black guy weren't there, the white boys would rob his little house. . . . But you've also got to remember the person who can rob this Asian, he knows it's to his benefit to befriend him because he's got lots of money and he's always got drugs.

So who then deals with the selling?

The black guy. And the odd white guy.

And the Asian prisoner?

He just kicks back in his cell, basically. Very comfortable. They want for nothing.

Both excerpts suggest that, lacking confidence in their collective physical capacity, Asian prisoners traded their economic power for protection and assistance. Whether this was the case was hard to verify, not least because Asian prisoners disclosed nothing to me of their activities in the prison's drug trade. Men like Paul and Ashley had their own interest in depicting themselves as part of a more powerful social and ethnic constituency. But the portrayal of Asian and Muslim prisoners as a group who held their power in reserve was corroborated by other interviewees and by their restrained yet notable presence in the prison's public spaces.

Such representations undoubtedly signalled the perceived location of Asians and Muslims below black men in a masculine hierarchy that valued both physical and economic capital. Ashley labelled Asians as 'pathetic...cowards' who 'want to be black guys'. Another prisoner distinguished the forms of power that they wielded as follows: 'They're not powerful *people*—they're like matchsticks—but they have power through the drugs they bring in' (prisoner, fieldwork notes). Many prisoners who had been accustomed to Asian prisoners being a smaller, more submissive, and less influential body within the prisoner community resented them 'getting ideas above their station' i.e. making claims for social space and recognition. Indeed, it could be argued that much of the resentment expressed by white prisoners against both blacks and Asians reflected the relative dominance of minority ethnic groups in the prison's public spaces. Certainly, when Muslim prisoners on one wing began to pray collectively on the landings, many white and black prisoners interpreted it as an attempt to assert social superiority. For other prisoners, objections were more mundane: 'People don't mind them praying, but do mind that they shave their body hair in the showers and don't clear it up' (Dom).

Relationships between minority ethnic groups and staff

Most black prisoners shared a belief that officers did not understand certain elements of their culture, in particular, their vociferousness and a kind of performed aggression that staff often interpreted as belligerence:

> They tend to think that a lot of black guys are trouble, because a lot of black people are loud, they don't mean to be like it, but they're just loud people, expressive people. [When they play dominoes] it seems aggressive, it seems like they want to fight each other, but that's just how it is. And [officers] are generally wary of it. (Isaac)

> Most black people are loud, and some people look on that in a bad way, but it's just the way we are and some people find that intimidating, like officers. Say we're talking, some of us talk loud and laugh and joke loud. The size of us don't help either. We stand out more. When black guys do something they notice it straight away, not like white guys, and they get nicked for it straightaway. (Olly)

There were few claims that officers were blatantly racist, either in their language or their more overt practices. Rather, some black prisoners maintained that they faced what Edgar and Martin (2004) have called 'informal partiality'. In describing this tacit discrimination, black prisoners argued that they were rarely given trusted jobs and were more harshly penalized for minor rule infringements than white prisoners. Younger black prisoners routinely attributed refusals over job requests or wing moves to racism. More experienced black prisoners more often complained about officers using inappropriate language, especially in their attempts to create 'banter'.

Muslim and Asian prisoners made similar accusations, although their attributions were quite different. Some Muslims argued that the prison made insufficient effort to encourage Islamic worship and did not provide enough access to the Mosque. Those whose religious commitment was most explicit—for example, through the growth of beards and the possession of religious texts—believed they were suspected of fundamentalism in a context where this had become increasingly analogous with acts of violent terrorism. Again, the emphasis here was not on blatant 'racism' based on colour so much as cultural stereotyping and discrimination.

Many officers were clumsy in the assumptions that they made about ethnicity and its implications. A minority of staff drew hasty conclusions about individual prisoners based upon spurious, actuarial assumptions—for example, associating drug dealing with a certain kind of black or Asian identity. Asian prisoners were also identified as generally 'easier to handle' than black prisoners in terms of their everyday behaviour, although Muslims were at the same time considered vociferous and disruptive, particularly on issues relating to diet, religious expression, and 'not being recognized by staff as a superior race type thing' (officer, fieldwork notes). Staff on one wing were especially concerned by what they considered to be Muslim prisoners 'testing the water' by trying to pray on the landings. 'There was a bit of resistance, questioning—"we can do what we like". And I said "No, you cannot do what you like". They were challenging staff' (principal officer). Ethnicity was in these ways used as a means of questioning the terms of institutional control (Bosworth 1999). Certainly, Asian and Muslims were not perceived as 'model prisoners' (cf. Genders and Player 1989; King and McDermott 1990; Sparks *et al.* 1996)—passive, unobtrusive, and compliant.

Meanwhile, among officers, talk of prisoners playing 'the race card' was widespread. Some officers were sceptical about almost any complaint that involved race or ethnicity. Much of this cynicism was aggravated by the wider climate of racial politics. Labels of 'institutional racism' were being widely applied within the domain of the CJS, and racist incidents had recently been redefined as 'any incident which is perceived to be racist by the victim or any other person' (MacPherson 1999). Many officers felt that these terms were vague and offensively critical. These were complex definitions, which were not well understood by most staff. In practice, most officers recognized the moral importance of the race relations agenda and strove to be sensitive to issues around race and ethnicity. But many felt stifled by a pervasive anxiety about causing offence and being accused of racism. Some were bitter about institutional attempts to promote minority ethnic festivals and holidays. One senior officer claimed that 'Muslim' was 'the biggest bogeyword in the Prison Service. They [senior managers] are terrified of it. When *we* have a religious festival, fuck all gets done. When [Muslims] do, we bend over backwards.' Prisoners often commented that officers were wary in their interactions with minority ethnic prisoners—'very tippy toey about cell spinning, doing bolts and bars' (Tyler)—a bearing that felt like mistrust to those who were subjected to it and like preferential treatment to those who were not. In a context of scarcity, it was unsurprising that there were contradictory claims from different prisoners about whether minority ethnic prisoners were treated unfairly or excessively favoured.

Conclusion

Accounts of the social systems of men's prisons have documented patterns of social relationships in two main ways. Some studies have described exceptional levels of in-group loyalty and cohesion, in contexts where relations between prisoner subgroups, and between prisoners and the institution, have been deeply hostile (e.g. Jacobs 1977; McEvoy 2001). Other studies have portrayed more disorganized worlds of social caution and mistrust. Clemmer (1958) described prison friendships as, on the whole, tense, fragile, and defensive (see also Morris and Morris 1963), based on the need to prevent exploitation rather than on admiration or affection. Only a minority of (high-status) prisoners socialized and co-operated within cliques and semi-primary groups, and even these groups lacked 'basic cohesion' (Clemmer 1958: 129; see also Mathieson 1965). Most prisoners were 'ungrouped', or had only superficial relationships with their peers. Examples of loyalty, sacrifice, and kindness could be found (Clemmer 1958). In general though, the prisoner community was characterized more by 'trickery and dishonesty' than 'sympathy and cooperation' (ibid.: 297).

Both kinds of accounts point to some of the structural determinants of prisoner relationships. The terms of imprisonment in Wellingborough both inhibited and promoted forms of loyalty and affiliation. Concerns about material resources, loneliness, and safety pushed prisoners into social associations that buffered them from insecurities and hardships. At the same time, the risks of intimacy, the difficulties of trust, and the transitory nature of the environment placed limits on the terms and possibilities of friendship. This chapter has outlined these compulsions and restrictions in the context of the medium-security institution, where social loyalties were compromised by the proximity of release and generic solidarity was extremely limited. By interrogating in some detail the impediments to and imperatives for relationship formation, the chapter has also explained deviations from these general patterns of mutual mistrust. The same environment that was seen by most prisoners—even those on lengthy sentences—as temporary, unreal, and artificial was regarded by others as a site of sincerity and authenticity. The conditions that made the development of new friendships problematic were what enabled and determined relationships of reciprocal support and provision between men from the same areas outside prison. And, within the same setting, the different values, needs, and plans of different kinds of prisoners produced considerable variation in the aims and obligations of social life.

The chapter has also elaborated the overall pattern of Wellingborough's social relationships. As previous studies have suggested (e.g. Clemmer 1940; Morris and Morris 1963)—indeed, in terms that are strikingly similar— most prisoners differentiated between a small number of trusted friends (often known prior to imprisonment), prison friends, and more casual associates. Social life was cellular, based on loosely structured, interlocking groups formed around factors such as locality, religion, age, lifestyle, and criminal identity (Irwin 2005; Crewe 2005a). Such groups generally offered material, social, and physical support, while also providing networks for trade and avenues for the settlement of disputes. Unlike in the US, where race and ethnicity define the prison social system (certainly in men's establishments) (Jacobs 1983; Wacquant 2000; Irwin 2005), racial, religious, and ethnic identities were 'subtexts' (Owen 1988: 151) rather than organizing features of the prisoner social world (see also Sparks et al. 1996; Genders and Player 1989). Likewise, these were not the highly developed social groups described in some work (e.g. Jacobs 1977; McEvoy 2000), which shielded their members from the pains of imprisonment while creating deep internecine conflict. There was little sense of communal objectives, but nor were there deep divisions between groups or major battles for collective power.

8

Everyday Social Life and Culture

Writing about the eclipse of prison ethnography, in the US in particular, Loïc Wacquant has recently argued that the social netherworld of the prison has become increasingly obscure:

With the jettisoning of the philosophy of rehabilitation...and the turn-around towards the criminalization of poverty as a queer form of social policy aimed at containment of the lower classes and stigmatized ethnic groups, the doors of penitentiaries were gradually closed to social research-ers and severe restrictions were imposed on the diffusion of inmate writings.... observational studies depicting the everyday world of inmates all but vanished. (Wacquant 2002: 384)

Much of the early interest in the daily culture of the prison was concerned with questions of how it might aid or hinder rehabili-tation. Clemmer, for example, characterized 'prisonization' as the taking up of criminalistic ideologies alongside particular patterns of speech, dress, and eating. The assumption was that men who were socialized 'to any appreciable extent' into the dogmas of the prisoner world were unlikely to be 'salvaged' by institutional pre-tensions to reform (Clemmer 1958: 313). 'Rehabilitation happens *in spite of* the harmful influences of prison culture, and this tends to be men who should never have been imprisoned in the first place and who are only slightly engulfed by prison culture' (ibid.; emphasis added). Later studies demonstrated that prisonization was not a linear process (e.g. Wheeler 1961). Prisoners did not become ever more socialized into prison culture over time. Commitment to inmate values was strongest at the 'deepest' point of imprisonment, when the free world was especially distant and prisoners were most reliant on the prisoner community for aid, status, and identity. As release became imminent, it was argued, prisoners re-assumed the norms they had held when they entered the prison.

These findings supported Sykes's attempt to theorize the ori-gins and function of the inmate code. Sykes argued that the ide-alized behaviours and public values of the prisoner world were cultural mechanisms for alleviating the pains and deprivations of imprisonment (see Sykes and Messinger 1960; Sykes 1956, 1958; and Cloward *et al.* 1960). The informal economy arose as a response to material scarcities. Norms that proscribed informing, promoted anti-institutional attitudes, and emphasized the need for 'manly conduct' derived from the indignities, dispossessions, and threats to identity that imprisonment entailed: 'A cohesive inmate society provides the prisoner with a meaningful social group with which he can identify himself and which will support him in his struggles against his condemners' (Sykes and Messinger 1960: 16). Solidarity, tolerance, generosity, and masculine courage likewise worked to counteract the dangers, degradations, and deficiencies of prison life. If these were seen as inherent properties of incarceration, the prospects for altering the norms of the prison were poor. If they could be diminished by the institution itself, there were possibilities for moulding alternative cultures.

Importation theories (e.g. Irwin and Cressey 1962; Irwin 1970, 1980; Jacobs 1977) concurred with 'deprivation perspectives' to the extent that they saw 'the total set of relationships called "inmate society" [as] a response to problems of imprisonment' (Irwin and Cressey 1962: 145). However— revisiting Clemmer's formulation—they also pointed to the similarities between prisoner values and cultures that existed outside prisons, be these criminal codes, the values of the street, or the norms of masculine fratriarchies. The rules and ideals of the prisoner world, they argued, stemmed principally from these external cultures and from latent behavioural patterns rather than the prison's structural conditions. Since prison subculture originated outside the prison, exposure to it was unlikely to impact significantly on rates of recidivism (Irwin and Cressey 1962).

As befitted 'conflict theories' of the period, an important point of emphasis in such studies was that the prisoner world could not be characterized as a single normative community. Clemmer and Sykes had both been clear that there were glaring discrepancies between prisoners' public standards, their actual practices, and the views they held in private. Yet both implied that there was a dominant value system that all prisoners recognized, and which had force in sanctioning behaviour and forming the basis of public judgment. By the 1970s, this portrayal of a unitary culture no longer captured the social disaggregation of the American prison (Irwin 1970; Carroll 1974; Jacobs 1977). The prisoner world comprised a number of belief systems that clashed and overlapped. As a sense of common purpose and a code of mutual aid were superseded by ideals of mercilessness, exploit-ation, and intergroup hostility, prisoner subculture became the principal source of the pains of imprisonment, rather than a collective means by which they were resolved. The power that prisoners exerted on each other was at least as destructive and fear-inducing as the power exercised on them by the institution.

Theoretical debate has advanced rather little since this time. In the US, the most pressing questions no longer relate to the impact of prison subculture on individual prisoners, but the impact of 'mass incarceration' on children, communities, and the wider polit-ical system: the 'collateral consequences' of endemic imprisonment (Garland 2001b). Researchers accept that prison culture combines imported and institutional variables. What is less clear is how they combine *in practice* and what world of norms and practices they actually create. In the UK, the ordinary life of the prison has not entirely disappeared from view. As in the US, prisoners have pro-vided their own perspicacious accounts of its tone, texture, and temperature (e.g. Wyner 2003; James 2003). Details of the mun-dane norms, routines, and practices of the prisoner society can also be gleaned from some academic studies of particular dimen-sions of imprisonment, such as violence (Edgar *et al.* 2003), the use of media (Jewkes 2002), and prison work (Crawley 2004a).

This chapter focuses specifically on Wellingborough's everyday culture and social practices. It details the normative framework that legitimated prisoner behaviour. It explains deviations in belief and action, and the consequences of violating codes of acceptable practice. It shows the dynamics of everyday behaviour—how 'ways of doing things' were asserted and negotiated, and how norms were manifested in the daily politics of the prisoner world. It documents prisoners' public attitudes on a range of everyday issues, and explores the gaps and inconsistencies between public performances and private sentiments. First, it describes the func-tions, logistics, and appeals of the prison's informal economy.

The Drugs Trade and the Informal Economy

Wellingborough's informal economy was vibrant but relatively limited. Prisoners could obtain many essential goods through legitimate means and most were prepared to forego the kinds of commodities that they might search out if facing longer periods inside. Higher-security prisons, where deprivations were stronger and prisoners had greater access to facilities for cooking and cleaning, had more extensive trade networks—'like a little town' (Darren); 'every man has got a little role' (Jacob). Nonetheless, deficits in goods, services, and interpersonal power promoted illicit trade, on the basis of need, profit, and the desire for personal reputation.

In Wellingborough, no prisoners were able to obtain all goods that others might desire. However, certain men had reputations as traders and fixers, and there was some cachet in being 'in the know'. VJ considered himself a hub in networks of trade and distribution:

If I can't help them, I might know a next man that can help them.... My mate might have some. I'll go and see him for you. And as we're walking round I'll point him out—I'll say 'See my man there in the red cap. Go check him, he's got it'. And you'll go to him and he'll hook you up.

The role of drugs in prison social life and culture would be hard to overstate. They were a keystone of public discourse and were repeatedly spotlighted as the engine of social dynamics throughout the prison system: 'Seventy per cent of things in jail are about drugs', one prisoner asserted (fieldwork notes). Drugs were accepted by staff and prisoners both as a banal, unremarkable feature of everyday life, and as a constant preoccupation both for those who used them in prison and those who did not. Drugs, in particular, heroin, exercised a 'very, very, very powerful effect' (Colin); 'People do go mental for it.... It's worth more than gold' (Callum).

The prison drugs trade

Interviewees described five main methods of acquiring drugs (see Crewe 2006b). The first and most limited method was through the post. Drugs could be fixed beneath stamps or placed between a folded-over sheet of writing paper. The second was through town visits, home leave, or other forms of temporary release. Prisoners granted temporary leave were offered sums of up to £1000 or a share of profits to bring drugs delivered to their homes into the prison, by plugging them in anal cavities or swallowing them and emitting them at a later time.

The third method was through visits, where drugs could be passed to prisoners in various ways by skilled and willing visitors.

Small packages could be stored in bras or baby clothing, or in the throat or vagina, in order to get past searches. Once retrieved during a trip to the visits shop or toilet, they could then be dropped into cans of drink, cups of coffee or crisp packets, or passed directly under the cover of a tray or into the mouth through a kiss. Packages were then swallowed or 'plugged' by prisoners.[1] Men who regularly obtained drugs through these channels could strike deals with other prisoners to bring in their produce, with profits split between the two parties. Invariably, dealers were the prime beneficiaries, taking little direct risk. '[He's] never directly involved, he's never going to fail the piss test because he doesn't do it himself, but he's reaping the benefit, getting all the money sent to his house. It's his drugs coming in' (Callum).

The fourth strategy involved the corruption or collusion of staff. This was the most fruitful route, for, if successful, it enabled the smuggling of far larger quantities than other means. Prisoners sometimes knew staff members from outside prison, and either made arrangements with them directly or organized deliveries through friends with connections to external drug markets. Payments (between £500 and £1000 per month) were then made for staff to bring in packages whose contents they did not always know—often including heroin, cannabis, steroids, mobile phones, alcohol, and pornographic films (which could be played through PlayStation consoles).

The alternative was for a dealer to approach a prisoner who had a particularly good relationship with a member of staff, and ask him if he thought there was potential for corruption and if he was interested in brokering a deal. The opposite also occurred, with prisoners who had developed strong relationships with staff approaching known dealers to seek out their interest. Once identified, a target could then be manipulated, bribed, or blackmailed. Ashley's starting point was to reel in members of staff by

---

[1] 'You don't get seen. You're sat there having your conversation, everybody needs to go to the toilet at some point in your visit, you're there for two and a half hours. She transfers it from internally, sticks it in [her] mouth, and sits down carry on talking, and at some point you reach over and just have a little kiss. You've got to be really unlucky to get caught doing it, or really stupid. [But] the stakes are high, it's four or five years if you get caught doing it. Nine times at out of ten it's your babymother, and you don't want your babymother doing five years for you because then your kids go into care and you've got nothing else happening. It's whether you're prepared to put somebody in that situation'. (Callum)

extracting 'little snippets' of intimate information. The goal was to build up trust, and discover material or emotional vulnerabilities that could then be exploited:

You can start off: 'Bring me summat to eat, bring us a cake or something, miss'. You're with that person every day: 'Bring this for me', and they'll bring it. And things start getting bigger and bigger. And at the same time you're hearing their problems. They're human.... they'll start telling you about their bills and 'I've got to do this, and I've got to do that', and you [say]: 'I can make that easier for you' and then you don't mention it again. Let them suffer for a few more months. Then you show them bits more.

The initial aim of such strategies was to lure the staff member into bringing in relatively harmless goods, but gradually to escalate requests beyond the point at which they would be legally defendable.[2] At this stage, a prisoner could make a more serious approach, framed by the threat that, if refused, he would inform the establishment of infractions that had already been committed. Charm and persuasion were thus succeeded by threat. Once a transaction was made outside the prison, the staff member was 'finished, because any smart person, when you're outside dropping off the money, you'll have a car behind or someone across the road taking a picture' (Ashley). Projecting his own drives, Paul described the process as one of relative simplicity:

Everyone comes here for money, yeah? I'm here because of money, you're here because of money, it's all the love of money and more money. Everyone would like a little bit more and whilst there's people that want a little bit more money and criminals that want a bit more money, it just takes two of them to link and that's it.

The fifth method of importing drugs involved arranging for goods to be thrown over the prison's fence, normally through mobile phone calls to peers outside the prison. Parcels were flung in socks, tennis balls, or taped-up cigarette packets, and were collected by prisoners who worked as external cleaners or garden workers. These men were paid around a quarter of the parcel's value to pick it up and pass it back to the wings. Kai claimed that packages could sometimes be hauled in directly from cell windows using mop handles tied together with a makeshift hook on the end: 'You just pull it out, hook the parcel up and pull it

---

[2] Prison staff were often aware of attempts to 'condition' them and received training on the matter.

in. It's all easy.' These packages usually contained a mixture of contraband—normally some cannabis and heroin, and sometimes steroids or crack cocaine.

Once in the establishment, high-level dealers had minimal contact with their goods. Some sold them on immediately, halving profits with middle-range dealers or accepting one-off payments to outside bank accounts. Others kept hold of some supplies which they split into portions and paid trusted associates to store, selling them on gradually while ensuring that they were never in personal possession of their stock. Such techniques ensured that, even when under suspicion, dealers could avoid their activities being exposed or proven. Most also sought to minimize the chances of being identified and informed upon. Those men who saw drug dealing as a way of 'getting by' or accumulating savings, rather than a route to status, tried to disguise their involvement from most other prisoners. For prisoners concerned about recategorization, parole, or avoiding transfer, dealing was a risky activity that was publicized only in limited circles. 'In jail, there's a lot more risks you're taking', VJ reported, noting that years could be added to your sentence if you were caught dealing drugs. Charlie described putting a halt to his activities as soon as they were discovered by his cellmate: 'He'd have told everyone. Then they'd have all been telling people. And then you'll get in trouble, days on your sentence. So I stopped.' Ironically then, drug dealers did not always want other prisoners to know about their activities. Many traded only within tight and trusted networks of friends and associates. From the perspective of low status, untrusted prisoners like Colin, the drugs world was therefore 'very hush hush', a venture from which he was excluded: 'Nobody lets me know what's going on. Things are happening, but I'm like Mr Magoo[3] at the moment.' As he also suggested, the increasingly close policing of the drugs economy had made some forms of social generosity less common: 'It's not like before. People used to go: "Go on have a spliff". [But] The more tighter the system gets, the more tighter the individual will get.'

Men like Paul and Ashley, whose motives related to power, mastery, and the relief of boredom, were less secretive in their affairs.[4]

---

[3] Mr Magoo: a cartoon character with very poor eyesight.
[4] 'If prison was a place where you came and there was nothing going on it would be very boring. You've got to do something to liven it up. It gives you something to do, it keeps your brain working and also there's a bit of excitement in it.' (Paul)

They did not advertise the mechanics of their activities beyond inner circles, and were circumspect when drugs were scarce and demand rose to precipitous heights. At the same time, they revelled in the knowledge that their involvement could not be proven and took pleasure in the psychological machismo of the contest that ensued:

They've caught drugs on other people and they know it's mine. They say: 'oh we got your stash today'. I'd say: 'I don't know what you're talking about' but they know and I know. They caught Griffiths, yeah, with sixty-two phone cards, twelve packets of burn and a mobile phone and when they got that from him they came to me and said: 'We've got your stuff'. I said: 'What are you talking about?.... Look I've got another friend, so what—you got one, you ain't got the other one and you won't get it', and that's it. I said: 'Sixty-two phone cards, twelve burn, that's nothing! I've got that and more'. (Paul)

In line with their ambitions, these dealers countered the threat of being 'grassed up' not by hiding their operations from other prisoners, but by spreading the benefits of their trade across the wings. In doing so, they maximized the number of prisoners who had an interest in their activities. Ashley declared that 'it's not good to be mean in prison', and that people who abused their powder power were invariably informed upon because they generated resentment. 'Everyone wants [drugs], but not everybody can have them', Howard summarized. Paul explained his strategy in some detail, highlighting the dangers of trading selectively:

I just give each of the cliques something:...drugs to sell, or items. If I've got too many items I'll give—'Yeah you do some double-bubble or hold them for me'. [If] there's a phone about, you don't just keep it to yourself, you pass it about so everyone gets a little taste of it so no-one wants it caught.... If everyone is gaining by it then there's less chance of the screws ever finding out. If you're not generous there'll be some dickhead that will blow you out. When I came to prison no-one [grassed] on me and said I sold them any drugs because I was alright with people. I was the person that would be willing to give anyone the benefit of the doubt.... If you're a person that hoards everything to yourself and don't share with no-one, everyone is jealous of you so you'll never get anywhere.

To mitigate the danger of being informed upon and the threat of being robbed, benefaction was built into the system. Prisoners perceived as dangerous were often 'kept sweet' with small quantities of drugs. Less powerful or savvy prisoners who had regular supplies had little choice but to co-opt more influential and experienced men into their activities:

You go to one of the heads on the wing, and say: 'Listen, I've got things coming in, I'll give you 50 bags, sell 35 for me and have 15 yourself'. Or: 'Watch my back, and I'll make sure I give you something every day, make sure you've got items, canteen, toiletries. You don't have to want for nothing, you've just got to watch [out for] me'. (Fin)

As well as purchasing protection, the power and profits generated by drugs were used 'wisely' to build up favours and 'respect' over the long-term:

If I get drugs, I give everybody a bit. All the smokers, everybody.... Because hands wash hands....I don't expect nothing, until it arises.... I like looking after the poor people because you get more benefits from them. It's not that I'll directly go to use them, but I may need one of them...to hold this for me, or I may need them to take [drugs] somewhere I can't go. (Ashley)

Such actions were highly self-interested, and illustrated the strategic intelligence with which dealers operated. For these men, trade was serious business that required considerable intelligence and organization. Accordingly, the drugs economy was characterized by oligopolistic co-operation as well as competition. Dealers on different wings sometimes borrowed small quantities of drugs from each other to make up temporary shortfalls in supply. Those on the same wings routinely shared information about debtors and took turns to handle canteen day, trying to ensure that men in arrears could not play dealers off against each other.

The cost of a tiny bag of heroin—enough for a night's personal use—was around £8–10 (three or four times its street value), while a cannabis joint cost around £4. Without a cash economy, the main forms of currency ('items') were tobacco and phone-cards, as well as foodstuffs and toiletries. Prisoners making larger purchases had to involve outside parties in their transactions, using phone calls to relay to wives, friends, or family members the details of bank accounts or addresses to which they should deposit money. Once a dealer had checked with his outside contact that a payment had 'landed', he would deliver the appropriate quantity of drugs to the cell of the customer. 'Like ordering a pizza', one prisoner summarized (fieldwork notes).

The appeal and effects of drugs in prison

[Heroin] takes away all your worries. It takes you out of the prison system. It's the best prison drug. It could have been invented for prison. (Stephen)

The appeal of heroin and cannabis in prison needs to be understood in relation to the conditions of incarceration. Drugs were used for recreational purposes and to counteract boredom. They also provided a means of coping with insomnia and frustration in the absence of institutional devices that could fully offset these states. Stimulants such as cocaine and ecstasy were also reported to be available in Wellingborough. However, in a milieu that was intrinsically constraining, few prisoners sought out drugs that induced energy and enthusiasm. In contrast, the abilities of cannabis and heroin to alleviate stress and aid relaxation suited an environment of pervasive anxiety:

[Cannabis] calms people down. You're not worrying about your people too much. Things come into a bit more perspective. You don't make assumptions. It's easy to go on the phone and make assumptions, because you ain't heard off your missus for a couple of days. Your mind gets overworked in here. You're constantly thinking, so there's got to be something to slow you down. (Den)

Many prisoners preferred the less intense and addictive effects of cannabis to heroin.[5] These men resented the measures that they believed had led to the displacement of cannabinoids by opiates as the drug of choice in prison. For other prisoners, cannabis was insufficiently powerful for the mental diversion they desired and merely enhanced feelings of paranoia.

Heroin's greater attraction lay in its more potent capacity to 'kill time' and enable a temporary respite from reality (Larner and Tefferteller 1964; Dorn and South 1987; Pearson 1987). In describing the impact and appeal of heroin, prisoners repeatedly drew on discourses of sanctuary, relief, and escape. Two particular themes predominated. The first related to the pseudo-physical effects of heroin, specifically its ability to provide feelings of warmth, comfort, and psychological security, and its corresponding inducement to sleep. Here, the recurrent phrase was that heroin 'wraps you up in cotton wool', serving as a narcotic

---

[5] Afro-Caribbean prisoners often claimed that heroin had been seen as 'not a black drug' until relatively recently (see Pearson 1987).

blanket.[6] The second theme was captured in repeated assertions that heroin 'takes the walls away'. Here, the psychological dimensions of heroin use were clearly conveyed:

It just blocks everything out. When you've got problems and you want to take your mind off them it just used to like chill you out and like wrap you up. I used to forget all about my problems, it were like they never mattered.... Nothing can hurt you, nothing bothers you if you've got problems. When you get banged up at night in your cell you forget you're in jail because it tires you out and you fall half asleep so it doesn't really bother you about being in jail. If you've got problems it blanks them out for you. (Dom)

It just made jail that bit easier, it used to bring the walls down, used to feel like you weren't in prison, didn't really used to seem that you had no cares in the world.... You're kind of here but you're not sort of thing, you reminisce about all the good times. [But as] soon as it starts wearing off, all the bad things come back, not like they were before but three times worse cos you're over-analysing. (Tyler)

The excerpts suggest two more general themes. First, many prisoners expressed profoundly ambivalent views about their relationship with heroin, recognizing that it suppressed anxiety only temporarily, and that 'problems come back tenfold' (Fin) once its effects subsided. More fundamentally, the surrendering of self that could provide relief was in other respects a source of deep discomfort. Tyler provided a powerful description of the overpowering mental hold that heroin could exercise:

Heroin's like a woman you know. The woman could be the best fuck you've had in your life, but I tell you what, the earache and the head-ache you can get out of it at the end of the day just ain't worth the shag so you can't be together, you know. You might love her with all your heart but you can't be together. Heroin to a degree was the love of my life.... I loved heroin, it fucking took over my life.... We might both love each other to death, but that's what it is, to death. You know, I love heroin to death, and that's what it'll do to me in the end, same as a woman will. She'll drive you that fucking nuts that I'll end up killing myself or killing her. So we just can't be together you know.

Such comments also implied a connection between addiction, intimacy, death, and desire. The feeling of heroin has been described elsewhere as 'almost sexually orgasmic' (Stephens 1991: 8), 'like the

---

[6] Ian suggested that heroin provided a kind of narcotic hug, making you feel 'wrapped up in your own arms'.

rush of orgasm after a long, slow build-up' (Larner and Tefferteller 1964: 16). Prisoners rarely used such metaphors, but comments that heroin was 'like being back in the womb' (Ian) and that it could make a person into the 'walking dead' (Carlton) highlighted its elemental power.

Drugs were central in the life stories of most prisoners and coursed through narratives of family life, love, and decline. When former addicts detailed the emotional peaks and 'fateful moments' (Giddens 1991: 113) of their biographies, drugs were the chief protagonists. Many interviewees identified the start of their drug use as their biggest regret in life—'because since that my life's just gone downhill' (Kieran)—and struggled to identify good moments in their lives since the onset of addiction: 'I've been smoking crack for eleven, twelve years. There isn't a high point in that' (ibid.). Most were uncensored in condemning their addicted selves, for example:

[On drugs I'm] an absolute shit bag who doesn't give a fuck, who becomes ruthless and moral-less. I'll tell you anything to get it. Beat people up, rob people of their canteen, so I can go and buy more. Lie to people, saying that I've got money that I haven't, tell them that money's being sent when it isn't. (Tyler)

Often, life chapters were divided according to drug use, with transformations in character, behaviour, and morality attributed to addiction. This view was expressed most forcefully by *enthusiasts*, but it was shared by many other prisoners:

It completely changed who I was. It completely changed the way I thought. The way I acted. Robbing people. Stealing off my missus. Selling drugs to people. The way I treated people—aggressively, with malice.... Getting a five-year sentence was the best thing that could happen.... Because I am completely the opposite of the person I was when I came in. (Carlton)

Carlton's comments on the transformational benefits of imprisonment were striking, and were not unusual. An arresting proportion of prisoners with histories of addiction presented their incarceration as a lifeline from ruthless individualism, self-absorption, and death:

I never thought I'd say it, that coming to jail would actually help me. But I think it really has. Definitely.... I feel a lot better.... I don't mean better as in I'm happy to be in jail. But I'm living a better life in jail than I would do on the out. Because I'm not on drugs. I'm working, I'm getting money.

I'm standing on my own two feet, in a way.... I feel like a better person. A different person. (Rhys)

Being locked up is not nice, I don't like being locked up and being away from my family. But as time goes on I'm thinking to myself: 'Well at least I'm not on the street letting people see me the way I was on the shit', you know? ... Once you start to smoke crack people don't respect you again because it's a drug that takes away your morals. People will try to avoid you as soon as they see you, because they know that you're just on a mission to get your next money to go and buy crack. People don't want to know.... If a person is on crack, prison is not a bad place for him to sort himself out, because once crack takes hold of you and takes over it's hard to let go unless you've got a strong head and you can lock yourself away and say: 'I've had enough'. I think if I didn't come to prison this time, the rate that I was going I probably would do some serious damage to somebody, or somebody would do some serious damage to me. (Jacob)

Normal distinctions between liberty and captivity thus disintegrated. The experience of addiction outside prison did not make incarceration enjoyable, nor did it preclude criticisms of treatment. But it altered the interpretive prism through which the relationship between imprisonment and the lifecourse was understood. Prison was perceived as a form of liberation: the 'only way to get off drugs' (Ellis) and an opportunity to 'appreciate life again' (Jacob). Addiction was portrayed as a form of incarceration, a system of total control. Prisoners used metaphors of imprisonment and liberty, and comfort and intoxication, in startling ways:

When you're on drugs, you're not locked in a jail or in a box, but it just runs your life. Everything you do is just down to drugs. It controls you. You have to get them drugs, or you feel like crap. So it runs your life.... In here, I'm locked up in jail, but I'm not on drugs. Drugs don't control me any more. I feel quite free.... I've starting to get back to my old self, how I used to be. (Rhys)

I'm sorted when I'm in jail. I'm wrapped up in cotton wool when I'm in jail. It's a lot easier to say no in here. Because there's more for you to lose in here. I could lose my chance of getting out earlier. I could lose my home leave. I could lose my privileges in here. I could lose all that hard work that I've done.

It's interesting that you say that you're wrapped up in cotton wool in here. Because some people use the same phrase to talk about why they take drugs in prison.

... I find that here, you're wrapped up in cotton wool. Everything's done for you. Whereas on the out.... There's a lot more drugs on the out, obviously. (Ross)

Heroin's capacity to make worries disappear meant it was also capable of destroying emotions altogether (Pearson 1987). Prisoners who had 'got clean' in prison reported the flourishing of their physical and emotional health. Those who used the gym associated corporal growth with spiritual reconstruction. Muscularity served as a beacon of rebirth: 'It gives you a good feeling—more of a natural buzz rather than a drug-induced buzz' (Rhys). Others reported the return of their capacity to feel: 'Love, hurt, affection, you just get all of them back. Strange feelings, because I've not felt them for so long' (Ross).

At the same time, and despite the boundless confidence of some former addicts, shards of doubt constantly threatened pretentions of resilience and recovery. The knowledge that drugs were available in the prison but were being resisted underpinned claims of strength. At the same time, ex-addicts acknowledged the difficulties of resisting temptation and the grip that drugs continued to exert on their everyday thoughts:

You're sitting there thinking 'if only I could get one now', and then the next minute you're saying: 'No, you don't want to go back to this shit when you get out, because you won't have no money, nobody will respect you, and sooner or later somebody will kill you or you'll end up doing a life sentence because you'll end up doing somebody something bad'. The next minute the craving will come over you again. It's like I'm fighting with it in myself now.... Your body is telling you, you miss the drugs, but my mind, my spirit is telling me I don't. (Jacob)

This profound ambivalence about drugs was collectively replicated in prisoner culture. There were pressures to get involved in the drugs economy (particularly on prisoners with jobs in the prison's grounds or other 'public' areas), but also to condemn its impact. There was public contempt for heroin, alongside recognition that use was widespread.[7] Drug dealers were both bitterly reviled and 'respected'. Dealers commented that they frequently sold goods to some of the most vehement critics of heroin use.[8] Few prisoners admitted routine involvement. Even in private, men who admitted to using drugs asserted that their habits were casual, controlled, and did not define their overall mentality: 'I do

---

[7] Prisoners estimated that up to 70 per cent were involved in the heroin economy at certain points.

[8] Drugs were forbidden under the terms of Islam, yet many practising Muslims were involved in the drugs economy.

smack but I'm no smackhead' was a common refrain. This discrepancy between public claims and backstage activity was the basis of considerable commentary among prisoners. Men who denied their usage, or who lapsed into drug use after pledging their desistance, were derided.

'Double-bubble' and debt

Drugs sat at the apex of a sprawling and highly stratified economic system. The cap placed on the number of items that prisoners could hold in their possession meant that the profits of drug dealing had to be spread among others on the wing. These items were then lent out by middlemen at interest rates of up to 100 per cent—hence the label 'double-bubble'—with profits shared with the original dealers. Drug users often repeatedly reborrowed the same items, as they tried to finance their habits with money they did not have. Alfie described how this economy could develop rather like a pyramid scheme, with high-level dealers the main beneficiaries, and lower-level lenders deriving less sizeable profits:

The dealers ended up with all the phonecards—they had about five hundred or six hundred phonecards at their disposal, which they distributed to certain individuals on the wing.... And these distributors are lending the same cards out that the junkies have gave to the dealers initially, for them to buy more smack off the same dealers.... What happens is, say somebody owed me [a distributor] ten cards—they'll come up to me one week and say: 'There's three cards'. And I'll say: 'Right, the seven you owe me, I'm adding another three onto them, so it's ten again the next week'. They come up to me the following week and give me six. I say: 'Right, so you still owe me four. I want six for the four'. They'll come up the following week and give me three. I'll say: 'Right, that three, I'm doubling it up to six. I'm not taking any more shit, I'm doubling it, so that's six again next week'. The following week they come up with four. So I've got about fifteen cards already, and they still owe me five or six cards.... The initial deal between me and the dealer is: 'Right, there's ten cards. You can put the ten out: for the twenty that you get back, five of them's yours'.... So I can sell these ten cards, and I'm getting twenty back the following week. Five of them that's coming back's mine; fifteen's going back to the dealer. But the dealer'll just say: 'Gimme ten, and put another ten out'.

So it just becomes an ever-expanding economy, an ever-expanding debt economy?

Yeah, everybody earns off it. If it can keep going for maybe five or six months, a lot of people stand to make a very, very reasonable living in jail.... Every week, every Friday, there's more cards getting put into that economy. And it ended up on the wing, it was just one big massive store of six hundred cards. And the screws got em, and it was, *bop*, the bubble burst.

Spiralling levels of debt placed limits on the lifetime of these markets. Prisoners who could not pay back what they owed either had to request money from outside parties or, more often, segregate themselves for their own protection. Once the names of dealers were disclosed, they were normally shipped out of the prison, thereby collapsing the market.

The practices and charges of double-bubble varied according to motives and social relationships. Some lenders had differentiated rates for friends and strangers, or offered discounts for 'local lads' and people who might return favours. Others took into account a prisoner's capacity to pay or the loyalty of his custom. Wilson modelled his business ('the best shop on the wing') on large supermarkets, offering 'loyalty points' to regular patrons in the form of lower interest rates. Low-level dealers seeking mainly to maximize comforts rather than profits tended to charge less than more serious traders. Aaron asked for 50 per cent interest, and reduced this rate or withheld lending entirely if he feared that customers were building up large debts. The aim was to protect his interests, particularly when drugs were on the wing and he knew that customers would soon be out of their depths:

At the end of the day I don't want them getting in debt with me because it's only going to bring hassle to me, because I've got to go and moan at them for it, yeah? I don't want to have to do that, I'd rather them not be in debt with me.... So I just say: 'No, just give me that amount'. If they can't afford it one week I'll say: 'Alright, get me two that week and just get me two the following week'.

Other dealers had no such compunction, and were more exacting both in their terms of trade and their pursuit of debt. Paul— whose logic showed the skilled, strategic nature of this 'outlaw capitalism'—explained the rationale of charging at a much higher rate than other prisoners:

People were doing quarter, [where] you give half an ounce [and] get a quarter back [in addition]. I've never done that. If you take half an ounce, I want an ounce back. So when I first come on [the wing], a lot of people obviously didn't bother coming to me because they could get it from someone else for a quarter. But when [that dealer] runs out they've got to come to me, and that's how I established myself. They have to [run out] at some point.... If you're lending for a quarter back you would think that people would pay easier, but it doesn't work like that. People tend to look at you maybe as a soft touch.... It don't make sense doing quarters to me, you don't make nothing, it's a waste of time. People do it but they run out quick. If two people run off and you' still got two people paying you double you're still in the game. With quarters you're not.

Weaker prisoners assumed that if they could not repay debts, they would 'get a kicking' (Rhys), and this was sometimes the case. Colin reported that his size did not prevent him from repercussions: 'It just means more people to come and kick me in.' Violent retribution was the ultimate means of enforcement and the informal economy relied on its potential. For small-scale lenders, this was one reason why debts were ideally avoided. To let them slide was to be exposed as a soft operator, but to demand them meant having to be prepared to resort to violence. Both were undesirable options for prisoners seeking a quiet life. Powerful prisoners understood the value of brinkmanship and some 'fronted out' debts rather than repaying them in the knowledge that traders might not risk confrontation. For those aiming to stay out of trouble, this raising of stakes was a dangerous outcome. The consequences of debt were dependent on the relative nerve and strength of both debtor and creditor.

For other dealers, even small debts were worth chasing because of what was at stake in terms of authority and reputation. As Alfie described, the unwavering pursuit of arrears sent out a clear statement of will and intent: '[It] let[s] the guy know: "If I want what you owe me, I'll get it", [and it's] putting the message out: "I've got the means to pay somebody".' Often, it was other debtors—usually heroin users—who were prepared to take relatively small payments to enforce debts, through whatever means were required.[9]

Yet violence was an unrefined strategy, and it signified a failure of more discreet means of debt enforcement. It disrupted the smooth flow of business (Pearson and Hobbs 2001), attracted un-

[9] Debts owed by dealers were less often honoured. When drugs were intercepted or supply lines shut down, dealers felt little obligation to reimburse payments that had already been made for goods that would not transpire: 'I ain't digging in my fucking pocket', said Ashley. 'That's lost, mate. That's part of prison.'

wanted attention, and raised the chances of being informed upon. Certain forms of lenience were therefore built into the market:

> If I gave you things and you lost it and I said to you: 'You owe me a hundred pound', and I pressure you, the easiest way out is to call my name [i.e. grass]. But if I say to you: 'Look, forget it, we'll work something out', you think to yourself 'yeah' and that's it. (Paul)

Although threats were therefore pervasively implied, violence itself was a heavy-handed and hazardous strategy. It was both the mainstay of the economy and the means of last resort. Loaners often reasoned that the hassles of chasing up arrears were not worth the benefits, particularly where debts were small or customers had provided long-term profit. A more common penalty was to write off what a debtor owed but to exclude him from further trade and insist on small weekly reparations. For weaker prisoners, who relied on borrowing to get through their sentences, to be branded as a defaulter and 'frozen out' of trade was a threat of some potency.

Involvement in the informal economy was always accompanied by risk. Whether as a debtor or a creditor, it meant being prepared to deal with the consequences of debt, obligation, or extending trust. For those prisoners driven by need, it alleviated scarcities and shortages, but it could easily add to the stresses of imprisonment.

Views on double-bubble

Clemmer (1940/1958) noted that views towards the lending of goods with interest varied: 'In some groups [it] is considered shrewd, and in other groups it is not right at all' (1958: 155). The same was true in Wellingborough. Prisoners who self-identified as 'old-school'—mainly but not exclusively *stoics*—perceived double-bubble as a form of exploitation:

> Personally, I get angry about prisoners who live off other prisoners. I've always been against that.... I have borrowed and had to pay back double, but I make sure they know what I think of them when I pay them back. [I] make a point of letting them know that they're out of order, profiting off of other people: '...there's your blood money'. (Stephen)

For these prisoners, lenders who charged interest were 'scumbags' (Bradley), bullies, or 'parasites' (Tommy) with no regard for the shared condition of the prisoner community and the poverty of many of its members. 'I couldn't take off the next man what he hasn't got', said Tommy. 'No-one in these places has got anything. And if a man's struggling, I'd rather help him than make his life harder. Everyone's got enough problems.' Charging interest was considered a violation of moral codes in a culture of material scarcity. For committed Muslims, it also violated religious strictures.

For other men, double-bubble was considered legitimate within certain limits. Nathan argued that, so long as they were entered into consensually, there was nothing wrong with loan agreements that might appear unbalanced. Arrangements should be seen as contracts, and while the repeated doubling of debts was 'taking the piss', not to repay agreed rates was a 'reverse kind of bullying'. Harvey described the charging of interest in more ambivalent terms: 'a bit of a liberty.... It is business but it's exploiting people' (Harvey).

Pragmatists and *players* were more approving of double-bubble, either accepting it as 'just part of prison life' (Leon) or defending its functional utility. Pierce described it as: 'Business: if you don't want it, don't buy it.' Leon argued that it should be seen as a service: 'You're helping them plus you're gaining. I don't really see that there's anything wrong with it.' Ashley's defence was more strident and was consistent with his general cynicism. Double-bubble was analogous with practices deemed legitimate outside prison ('everything's taxed [and] everyone pays taxes, innit?') and debtors were responsible for whatever they agreed to: 'You've still got the choice to say yes or no. I'm not forcing it upon you. It just depends how bad you need a smoke.' For prisoners such as Colin, though, there were few options but to enter into loan agreements and to try to juggle scarce resources.

Other aspects of informal trade and illicit activity

Drugs were the engine of the informal economy, but other goods and services were also significant. Prisoners keen for the taste of alcohol could contribute to the brewing of 'hooch'. Its production was normally a collective effort, requiring multiple ingredients accumulated from meals, stolen from the kitchens or ordered through the canteen in ways that would not arouse suspicion. These ingredients included fruit or fruit juice, yeast (normally in the form of Marmite), and bags of sugar. These components were mixed with water in large plastic containers that had previously held cleaning fluids, and had to be flattened, smuggled back to wings, and then cleaned out before brewing could begin. Usually, a single brew was decanted into several bottles, which were placed next to the radiators of the main contributors or anyone willing to take the risks of storage in return for a small portion of the results. The majority of the produce was split between the main investors. Generally, these were pragmatic associations formed for the sake of a drink rather than arrangements between friends. The final product ('Wellingborough Chablis') was of variable quality: 'It tastes horrible, but it gets you steaming', Callum admitted. Alfie, a self-proclaimed 'master-brewer', boasted that his produce was just like vodka and orange, and described the process as a form of 'alchemy...there is an art to doing it.... You've got to have the conditions and put them in the right order, treat it like a baby, even have pet names for the bottles.' The gains were small: for Callum, a profit of six pounds for five litres; for Alfie, a sense of pride and status.

Alongside drugs and alcohol, mobile phones were the primary target of the prison's security team. Like drugs, they were thrown over the fence or brought in by corrupt staff. Stored in places such as toiletry bags or in the false bottoms of food tins, they were used for various purposes. Once topped up through vouchers purchased outside prison, they could be used to contact girlfriends and family members, or to call sex lines: 'Dirty sluts out of the wank mags, it's just something to do in jail, just kills time' (Kai). Prisoners sometimes rented out their phones for profit. More often, they used them to arrange for drugs to be thrown from the car park at specific times into designated places, where they were soon collected by outside cleaners and passed through windows onto the wing: 'It's gone then, screws can't find nothing' (VJ).

Illicit activity was built into the everyday fabric of prison life. Most jobs carried benefits of some kind, and many prisoners specifically sought out positions that allowed them to supplement their income or enhance their everyday comforts. Workers in the prison laundry could charge for extra washing, and its position along the main thoroughfare was ideal for those involved in illicit trade. Outside gardening jobs were coveted by some prisoners for the fresh air, free strawberries, or opportunities to gather drugs in return for payment. Orderly jobs in the prison stores, education department, and healthcare centre were attractive for the trust and responsibility that they offered, and were often therefore filled by *enthusiasts*. They were also attractive to prisoners keen to exploit the opportunities provided by relative autonomy and access to goods. Positions on the wings meant more time out of cell, potentially useful contact with officers, and minor material perks. Almost all cleaners and servery workers took some advantage of these conditions. Staff tacitly approved some such bonuses, leaving leftover food to servery workers after mealtimes. Much of this was then traded on the wings for other goods. A common arrangement was for servery workers to exchange spare meals or extra sandwiches, fruit, or biscuits for half an ounce of tobacco per week. Some cleaners stole kettles and toasters from wing offices—'What are you supposed to do? I'm a thief. So I stole them!' (Darren)—passing them temporarily to neighbours if they feared their cells being searched.

Kitchen workers were able to eat extra food while on the job and could charge other prisoners for smuggling tuna, pies, or cheese onto the wings in the waistbands of their trousers (the elasticity of tracksuits was particularly handy in this respect). Half a pound of ham or a bag of cheese could raise a phonecard. Larger extractions required more complex arrangements:

Say we're having cheese flan today, and there are a couple of pasties in the freezer next to the flan, so I whip a couple of pasties out first and put them underneath the cheese flan, take them under the trolley back to the wing. There are five extra pasties: you give one to the kitchen worker, two to the servery for sorting you out—for holding them back for you and keeping them out of the screw's way. So then you get your free pasties. (Callum)

To steal food in this manner was seen as taking from the prison rather than from other prisoners. The prison's responsibility to feed everyone meant that no-one would go hungry as a result of this theft. To steal from the servery before all prisoners had been served their meals was less acceptable, because other men might then be deprived of their food choices. Other jobs provided few perks other than decent pay and minor opportunities to make something from nothing: a makeshift clock from a toy watch or a soft toy.

There were other ways to make money. Many prisoners gambled over football matches or card games (particularly Kaluki) using Mars Bars or tobacco as their stakes. Prisoners with little independent means eked out what they could from sparse personal resources and minor opportunities. Those in most need let other prisoners use their private spending allowances in return for small payments or engaged in what Colin called 'very, very low-key trade' in order to subsist, acting as go-betweens for lenders and buyers, offering to store hooch or phonecards, or, where desperate, doing laundry for other prisoners or selling their own food. These humiliations of economic subordination illustrated in stark terms the inequalities within the prisoner population and the inadequacies of institutional wages for men who were vulnerable and unemployed.

Prisoners with more nerve and nous dabbled at the bottom-end of the drugs trade. Two cannabis joints could be refashioned into three; heroin could be adulterated with paracetemol or finely sanded brick-dust. Men with creative skills traded poems, portraits, pottery, to be given out to partners or children on visits. For use within the prison, prisoners could buy pornographic magazines, sticks of incense, and other goods.[10] Tattoos could cost up to £100, portraits between £5 and £20, depending on size and materials, personalized cups around an ounce of tobacco, and personalized writing paper around a quarter ounce for fifty sheets. In prisons where uniforms were obligatory, there were markets in customized clothing e.g. shirts with pockets or turned-up sleeves.

There were a number of other scams and shortcuts. Before the introduction of the pin-phone system, prisoners worked out ways of shaving off the edges of phonecards to stop the depletion of credits. Extra credits could be added using external top-up cards. Makeshift boiling devices could be made by fitting wires into the lead-holes of stereo cords and placing them into cups of water. TV aerials could be fashioned out of coat hangers, and tattoo guns out of motors from tape recorders, biro pens, and sterilized needles smuggled from the healthcare centre. The ingenuity of these means was consistent with accounts of the creativity and resourcefulness of coping and communication strategies among prisoners (e.g. Koestler 1940; Stockdale and Stockdale 1984; Irwin 2005).

Equal creativity was used to deceive institutional instruments of compliance. Darren had convinced medical staff that he had urine retention problems, having noted that this was one possible

---

[10] Jordan pretended to be Buddhist because this entitled him to free incense sticks, which he sold on in packs of twenty for a quarter ounce of tobacco.

side-effect of his prescribed medication.[11] As a result, he was given a day and a half's notice before any drug test, enough time for him to wash traces of cannabis out of his system by drinking copious quantities of water. Other prisoners claimed that they could evade detection by only taking heroin on a Friday evening, in the knowledge that tests were unlikely to occur until the following Monday, or by buying clean urine from other prisoners and delivering it from fingers cut from latex servery gloves. Although tales of fooling MDTs were probably embellished, past research has suggested that almost a third of prisoners are successful in avoiding positive tests (Edgar and O'Donnell 1998).

Involvement in the informal economy

Involvement with drugs and other aspects of the informal economy were patterned in predictable ways. As is consistent with the literature (Sykes 1958; Wheeler 1961), and with a thread throughout this book, prisoners withdrew from the subcultural involvement as they approached release—although they did so not simply because they were less dependent on the prison's inner world at this point, but because they were more concerned about the consequences of detection. Thus, both Paul and Ashley explained that their interest in the drugs economy declined as their sentences came to an end, while other prisoners, such as Martin, expressed their hopes not even to 'see heroin' as liberty approached. Danny elucidated the logic of disengagement:

If you're just starting a four year prison sentence, you're gonna do drugs, you don't care if you get caught on a piss test because you've got all that time to get that remission back—when you lose remission, you go six months without nicking and you can claim it back. But now I'm coming to going home, I don't take anything now, nothing at all, because I don't wanna be given a piss test and be caught out on that and end up having more time. [If] I'm having a confrontation with somebody, I'll have it in my mind: 'If you end up fighting, you're gonna lose days', so I try and cut it out. If I just started my sentence, I wouldn't think twice, I'll just take your head off, regardless of what happens to me because I've got plenty

---

[11] I kept going to the doctor's before I was getting piss tested, and saying: 'Listen, I'm not pissing, doctor, I'm only pissing once a day'. And he said: 'Well, it could be the medication'. And I looked shocked, I said: 'Could it?', you know, waiting for him to say that. So now it's down on my medical file: 'This man needs notice before having a urine test' (Darren).

of time to get that time back. I'm going nowhere and I'm not losing face, *bumpf* I'll get into it. (Danny)

Some prisoners nearing discharge also sought to reduce their use of heroin to avoid having a 'taste' for it when they hit the streets, where its strength was often greater and its addictive traction harder to resist. For other prisoners, drug use and trade were less matters of choice and more issues of need, pain, dependence, and subsistence.

Staff and the informal economy

As Chapter 5 described, drug dealers played an unexpected role in regulating certain forms of wing behaviour, and some prisoners claimed that the wings were calmer when drug supplies were plentiful and markets ran smoothly. However, such descriptions were partial. It may have been the case that the wings were particularly volatile when markets collapsed, dealers called in debts, and supplies ran dry—'people start getting cantankerous, because they haven't got the smack' (Alfie). However, even when supplies were plentiful, canteen days were tense, as debtors struggled to balance repayments and new loans, or tried to avoid having to put themselves in segregation. In fact, the level of supply caused different kinds of conflicts among different kinds of prisoners. When drugs were abundant, violence resulted from competition between dealers over market share. When they were limited, conflict (and informing) came from debts being prosecuted, prisoners resenting being excluded from markets, and competition over increasingly scant produce. As one governor explained:

When drugs are scarce [there's] squabbling over the scarce amount of deals that are going on, and that's when we get to hear about them, because dealer B will say: 'Oh no, I'm not selling to you because you didn't pay me the last time'. So this person dobs him in and says: 'He won't sell it to me so no one can have it'. And we see a rise in information when there's scarce amounts. When there's more, we don't seem to hear about it as much because everyone's happy, but [there are more] turf wars and fights and whatever.

For staff, drugs therefore caused different problems at different times. More importantly, the presence of drugs was a symbolic challenge to staff control and authority. Drug dealers were the paragons of anti-authoritarianism, and were considered ruthless and amoral. Officers resented both the nerve of dealers and their ability to operate in 'their' domain. Some enjoyed the cat-and-mouse element of preventing drug supply and distribution. For most, though, the consequences of drugs for their working lives were fights and frictions. Drug finds and prosecutions were celebrated as practical and symbolic victories. When three members of staff were arrested for their involvement in smuggling drugs into the establishment, the buzz among uniformed staff was palpable. Like prisoners, staff shared a code of loyalty, but they consistently stated that they would inform management without hesitation if they were to discover staff corruption.

It was not difficult to spot prisoners congregating after visits, scrabbling to get items, converging in cells, or 'pinned up' on the wings.[12] Some prisoners interpreted the apparent tolerance of such signs as staff indifference to drug use. Some staff were fatalistic—or resentfully pragmatic—about drug use. Most accepted that major dealers were very hard to catch and that the presence of drugs could not be prevented without draconian preventive measures (higher fences, closed visits for all prisoners, and so on). Often, however, mandatory drug testing and other impersonal means were more effective than direct challenges in the frontline battle against drug use. Proving use through other means was difficult. It was easier and less dangerous to nominate prisoners for suspicion tests or pad-spins than to raid cells oneself or catch prisoners in the act of consumption.

The attitudes of uniformed staff towards heroin users were relatively unsympathetic. 'Druggies', as staff termed them, were generally viewed with derision and considered emblematic of the selfishness, weakness, and immorality of the prisoner population. However, some officers recognized that drugs were a coping mechanism and showed compassion towards prisoners whose vulnerabilities and dependencies were most apparent. Some also expressed regret that heroin had become the dominant means of alleviating frustrations. Prisoners persistently claimed that cannabis use had been to some degree tolerated before the introduction of drug testing, and many staff acknowledged that this was the case. Hooch was a similar matter. Prisoners maintained that most officers would 'turn a blind eye' to occasional alcohol use so long as drinkers were 'sensible lads' who did not cause problems through their inebriation. Likewise, prisoners caught brewing

[12] To be 'pinned up': to have pin-prick pupils as a result of smoking heroin.

hooch in their cells often described being told simply to pour it down sinks or toilets, rather than being formally disciplined. In their own lives, alcohol consumption was more familiar to officers than drug use and this may have contributed to their greater lenience.

Interpersonal Dynamics and the Prisoner Value System

Accounts of prisoner values in custodial establishments for men have consistently emphasized two central and related norms (*inter alia*, Ohlin 1956; Sykes and Messinger 1960; Garabedian 1963; Mathieson 1965; Welford 1967; Irwin 1970, 1985; Thomas 1977; Garofalo and Clark 1985; Einat and Einat 2000; Winfree *et al.* 2002; Einat 2004). The first is the stipulation not to inform on or betray other prisoners. The second relates to interactions with prison representatives, and tends to involve the promotion of anti-authority views and the discouragement of fraternization with custodial staff other than for 'absolutely necessary reasons' (Clemmer 1940/1958: 153). Sykes and Messinger (1960) identified rules that forbade giving respect or prestige to officers or siding with them over prisoners. Attitudes of submission or commitment to authority were prohibited. Irwin (1985: 88) described the mentality of the jail as one of defiance to state agents and an 'all pervasive wariness of "the man"'. Many studies have documented cultures of outright hostility to prison staff (e.g. Jacobs 1977). However, oppositional cultures are not inevitable (see, for example, Mathieson 1965; Akers *et al.* 1977), and almost all accounts of prison life have identified private deviations from these norms of antipathy and mistrust. This relationship and discrepancy between public and private values forms the basis for much of the discussion that follows.

Relationships with staff

As Chapter 5 described, while some prisoners maintained an unwavering hostility to officers, orientations to staff were highly varied. Certainly, Wellingborough's culture was not characterized by the outright contempt that has often been reported (Sykes 1958; Jacobs 1977; Irwin 1985; McEvoy 2001). Institutional policies compelled interaction with staff, and because Wellingborough's officers were perceived as relatively amenable, talking to them did not in itself generate enmity (see Chapter 4 and Crewe 2005a). Prisoners acknowledged the vestiges of an ideal that officers should be shunned and disparaged. In practice though, they could openly interact with staff without their status being threatened. The majority were unjudgmental about how other prisoners related to staff:

There's a lot of people that talk to officers and get on with officers and that, screw boys, whatever, I'm not bothered about that. If that's how you want to do your time you do it like that. (Martin)

Experienced prisoners contrasted this with a bygone culture when to speak in friendly ways with uniformed staff was to cross a key symbolic boundary: 'It was, literally, them and us', Noah noted.

This softening of attitudes applied beyond private sentiments, where the expression of warmth, respect, and sympathy for officers was not unusual. In public culture, prisoners rarely sided with officers against other prisoners. However, in informal conversations between prisoners, blanket disdain for officers was uncommon and crude criticisms rarely went unchallenged. There were always 'some good officers', and always some prisoners prepared to dispute reflex statements that prisoners and staff were in a state of mutual opposition. Many prisoners were bemused by sentiments suggesting that officers should be seen as 'the enemy'.

There were, of course, limits to the intimacies and relationships that could be safely established with uniformed staff. Prisoners who talked intimately with officers—often those with jobs on the wings—were looked upon somewhat warily. Martin had misgivings about Dom, whom he had seen whispering to a female officer: 'If it was a personal matter then it would be probably dealt with in the office, so other than that I don't think you should have anything to tell the screws that other inmates shouldn't hear'. VJ questioned the integrity of prisoners who shared cups of tea or cigarettes with officers in their cells: 'For me, that's informer business. You're telling the screw things that you shouldn't.' Suspicion was also an outcome of staff discretion. Prisoners who were unexpectedly awarded parole or who received comparatively low punishments for rule violations aroused distrust. Prisoners paid close attention to decision-making processes (Mathiesen 1965) and drew inferences from apparently inconsistent awards:

Something just told me that that Dom was a grass. One of my mates got caught with a bit of hooch, it was like a quarter of a one litre bottle—[he got] three weeks loss of TV, three weeks loss of everything. Dom got caught with a five litre container full of hooch—[he only got] seven days loss of TV, seven days loss of canteen. How do you figure that? (Martin)

There's a lot of suspicious minds in prison. You know, a geezer might get his D-Cat. He might be a bit like me, so why has he got his D-cat [but I haven't]? Has he been up to something wrong? Suspicious minds. A lot of that in prison. (Tyler)

The view among prisoners that informers were pervasive was partly an outcome of the complex relationships between prisoners and staff. Since there were good reasons to interact with officers, closeness to staff did not necessarily mean that a prisoner was untrustworthy. But this also made it difficult to distinguish the reliable from the unreliable. Because many prisoners did not disclose their adaptive strategies even to each other, it was hard to differentiate real from phoney intimacy. As a result, the net of suspicion was widely cast.

Grassing

The injunction against grassing, or informing, has been repeatedly described as the cornerstone of the prisoner value system. Clemmer (1958: 152) characterized the norm that prisoners 'should never give [officials] information of any kind, and especially the kind which may work harm to a fellow prisoner' as 'the fundamental principle of the code'. Sykes and Messinger (1960: 7) claimed that: 'in general, no mitigating circumstance is recognized' against such a rule. Both authors were clear, however, that orientations to this rule varied and breaches were widespread. Explaining this discrepancy between words and behaviour, Sykes and Messinger observed that 'all inmates have an interest in maintaining cohesive behaviour on the part of others, *regardless of the role they play themselves,* and vehement vocal support of the inmate code is a potent means to this end' (1960: 18). Some prisoners truly believed in inmate cohesion. Others—'believers without passion'—encouraged it for instrumental purposes, 'because in its absence they would be likely to become chronic victims' (ibid.). A third group preached cohesion while actively violating their own assertions. Similarly, Akers *et al.* (1977) noted that, as with all value systems, there are 'core participants', 'followers', and 'isolates'.

In Wellingborough, there were important differences in definitions, rationalizations, and inclinations in relation to informing.

These were rarely discussed in public, where the prevailing view was that grassing was simply and uniformly wrong. Both publicly and privately, however, there was some consensus about the forms of grassing that were more and less acceptable. The most contemptible form was to grass on another prisoner purely for personal benefit—to gain favour with officers or aid one's progression at someone else's expense. For a prisoner to inform staff about activities that did not affect him directly was deemed malicious: 'You're using somebody as a stepping stone', said Noah. 'You're benefiting really from something that's none of your business.' Acts such as gambling, smoking cannabis, brewing hooch, and stealing from the prison were considered personal activities, irrelevant to the welfare of others, and therefore outside the range of public concern. To grass about such issues was to do staff work on their behalf, and was a form of interference in another prisoner's private practices. Most importantly, it undermined trust between prisoners, and disturbed valued forms of comfort and autonomy. As Brian noted, 'You trust those in your clique and others you know well. Other than that, anyone could be a grass'. Indeed, the idea that informants were increasingly ubiquitous in prison was stated with almost neurotic certainty. Prisoners argued that there were 'a lot more vulnerable people that can be manipulated by officers' (Ian) and believed that managers had deliberately sought to infiltrate and undermine the prisoner community by dispersing informers among them and granting them protection if discovered.

Informing behind closed doors was disparaged partly because it was seen as furtive and unmanly. Clive distinguished between this and what he called 'sweet grassing': dropping public hints to officers about peer activity:

If I'm on the wing and there's a junkie and I know he's smoking heroin and he's trying to give me a hard time I could just walk round the landing or the stairs and shout 'oh fuck off you fucking smackhead' or something like that: 'You live for smack', or 'You're a junkie' and you shout it out loud. And then the screw might think: 'Well, what's going on here?' [The prisoner] might turn round and say: 'You grassed me up saying I'm a smackhead', but you don't really feel too bad about it because everybody knows and everybody can see. Talking to officers on the sly, that's when you look like a proper grass.

One defence in such situations was to pretend not to have realized that officers would overhear one's comments. Another was to 'front' the accusation through an appeal to the candour of one's actions. At a stretch, such acts could be classified as open displays of cunning and power. 'You still wouldn't want an inmate to know that you've said something but he's probably looking at you as the clever one. [You] didn't go and stab him or throw water over him but he's out the prison. He's probably looking at you like a fucking witch or a man who can work voodoo' (Clive).

There was little tolerance either for prisoners who informed staff in order to extricate themselves from social or material agreements that they had entered voluntarily. To grass in order to escape debts was indefensible unless a prisoner had been subjected to extortionate interest rates or was unfamiliar with the terms of prison lending. Similarly, while some prisoners would pardon a victim of unprovoked violence if he took formal proceedings against his attacker, there was no justification for informing staff if one had lost a fair fight or an organized contest: 'If there was a fight between two guys, same height, same build and they've gone at it and the other one's grassed him up, that would be personal, you don't do that' (Kyle). Grassing in this way was a violation of the informal norms by which trust was fortified in the absence of formalized mechanisms of contract enforcement (what Sztompka (1999: 116) calls 'a functionally equivalent strategy').

Grey areas emerged when prisoners engaged in activities that could affect others indirectly by stealth or over time. Escape attempts, for example, were ostensibly private acts, but their outcomes could affect the entire prison. If wings were locked-down or security tightened, the effects on gym time, visits, and the smooth flow of daily life had widespread impact. A more complex example was drug dealing, an activity that provided unwanted temptation, infringed some prisoners' moral sensibilities, and could threaten the tone of a wing. It was significant that experienced prisoners reported a shift in norms about prison drug dealing, an activity that had initially been seen as socially corrosive and had often provoked collective retribution, but was now an accepted part of prison life. 'A big part of the code was not bringing heroin in', said one prisoner. 'Now it's almost the opposite: you can get a kicking for *not* bringing it in' (fieldwork notes). Codes of acceptable conduct altered with the times and were the outcomes of unseen ideological battles about prisoners' collective interests.

Where acts could be defined as assaults on the collective character of the prisoner community, they were more likely to vindicate grassing. If someone represented a nuisance to the wing, by repeatedly bullying other men, for example, some prisoners felt justified in sending delegations to staff warning them that he would 'get seriously hurt' unless removed from the prison (Den). Individuals also felt entitled to point staff in the direction of recognized troublemakers, although they did so with caution:

> If somebody is on the wing and they're making things a bit difficult for everybody like pressing the bell, breaking the windows, and I've had enough of it because it's getting you early lock up, I might just chip past that officer and go: 'Listen, he's the one that pressed the fucking bell'. You're not actually going to [the officer] and saying: 'Guess what, he is selling drugs or he has got drugs'. You use one stone and kill two birds. Instead of going and beating him or burning him out, you just look at the officer and just put him in the picture.... You don't really look at it as grassing, you just look at it as 'Yeah, well everybody could see he was causing trouble anyway'. (Clive)

There were certain scenarios in which informing staff about other prisoners was considered more excusable. Prisoners felt little compunction about telling officers if they believed that someone was suicidal. Matters of life and death also gave a pretext for intervention. Many prisoners said that they would inform staff in the event of—or to prevent—a rape or a serious assault (on staff, especially female staff, as well as prisoners).[13] Interventions that prevented conflicts from getting out of hand, or came to the aid of someone grossly in debt, were justifiable. Indeed, to intercede on behalf of another prisoner, particularly someone defenceless, could be presented as an act of bravery, integrity, and moral fortitude. There was consensus that the ideal action for halting victimization was to step in oneself (the 'protector' identity held widespread credibility).[14] Involving staff was more contentious. Within public discourse, this form of intervention remained somewhat illegitimate, but many prisoners considered it to lie within a sphere of acceptable practices: 'If you tell the screws then you get

---

[13] Offending behaviour course facilitators reported that after discussions involving grassing, one or two prisoners always remained after the class to say that they would inform staff about issues such as paedophilia outside prison or drug dealing within in.

[14] Life history interviews revealed a common pattern whereby prisoners had moved over a number of years from being bullied to being bullies to being protectors.

called a grass, but if somebody else has [grassed] because they've seen it happening, then, yes, I'd say that's quite acceptable to an extent' (Ian).

Likewise, almost all prisoners recognized a distinction between grassing for personal gain and for self-protection, even those whose views on informing were otherwise rigid:

If there is no reason behind anything, if it's just telling the screws for the sake of it, you deserve to die, as far as I'm concerned. If you're getting bullied hard and you can't handle it, if you've got problems at home and everything is coming to a head, you need to get out of there, I wouldn't do it myself but I could understand why you would do it if you were being beat up. (Callum)

I don't think it's wrong, in some situations. It depends what you're grassing em on, who you're grassing on and what the reasons for. If it's stupidness, it's pettiness and it ain't harmed you and it ain't harmed nobody else, then grassing is wrong, but I don't disagree with grassing for bullying in jail. (Martin)

Many prisoners did not even classify such acts as grassing, recognizing that these were essentially defensive acts that reaped no benefits at the expense of others. Informing in these circumstances presented a special case. Most prisoners considered bullying a more significant breach of norms than informing in order to prevent it. It was agreed that the ideal response was to deal with problems oneself, or with the help of others. However, most prisoners were sympathetic to the plight of men who could not defend themselves and faced either living in fear or addressing their situation through staff:

If you're getting bullied, and it's hurting you, you've got to tell somebody, because you could end up suicidal. If somebody did go in the office saying 'He's bullying me', I think they're in their rights. Usually people who are getting bullied are too scared to go and tell the person. (Derek)

I'd understand that, man. I don't go and talk to them, like: 'What did you do that for?' Because if you're in this state where you don't feel like you've got anybody, no-one can sort it out, know what I mean? They wouldn't have to go to an officer, they could go to someone on the wing and say: 'Listen, that guy's bullying me, talk to him for me please'. But they can't, because they haven't got it in them to go and talk to them. (Isaac)

He wouldn't get any aggro over it. Probably people would say, 'You shouldn't have went to the screws, you should have asked us', but he wouldn't get no beating for that if he was getting bullied. (Ross)

Prisoners who were more critical of grassing—primarily *players*, more powerful *pragmatists* and 'old-school' lifers—expressed harsher views, despite some sympathies. They shared with other prisoners a view that it was wrong for people to be exploited or terrorized, especially men who were 'unsuited' to prison or incapable of fighting. Bullying was condemned as an abuse of power and an act of cowardice, and drew powerful emotions of contempt, often expressed in gendered terms. As VJ asserted, bullies were: 'Dickheads, basically. Faggots. They'd rather pick on a man they know is weaker than them than move to a bad man.' Nonetheless, these prisoners argued that there were always alternatives to grassing:

If they're not willing to stand up for themselves, then it's their own lookout. I know it sounds a bit callous, but at the end of the day we're all in here to do our own thing. If someone's getting bullied and they're not standing up for [their self]—not that bullying's right, I don't abide by that at all—but if they ain't strong enough to stand up to it, then they've got to [get] out of the occupation they've got into. Because when you're into crime, you're going to come to jail at least once or twice, so if you're not strong enough to handle it.... If you're getting beaten up every day, you just get a chiv and stab them. That would soon stop them bullying you. (Ewan)

As suggested here, *players* were not pitiless in their views about victimization, so much as tough in judging how it should be tackled. Callum's argument that grassing was 'never acceptable, but at some point it can be understood' encapsulated this view of mild disapproval. It was evidenced too in comments about the likely consequences of informing staff about bullying. On the one hand, prisoners who grassed under such circumstances 'would always be frowned upon' (Den), and risked some level of ostracism. Having shown an inclination to fold under pressure, they were also unlikely to be trusted with privileged information about drugs or other illicit acts. At the same time, they were not likely to face active persecution:

[If] I was selling weed and I knew you'd grassed somebody up, and you come to me: 'Oh, have you got any?' I'd say: 'No, I don't sell weed'. So I wouldn't trust you in that sense. But I wouldn't say: 'Fucking watch him, he's a grass', or try to make your life any harder. (Matt)

I wouldn't go out of my way to be horrible to him. But I wouldn't talk to him or give him the time of day. (Kieran)

The consequences of code violation

Given the vehemence with which the code was publicly espoused, the consequences of violation were surprisingly insipid. The majority of prisoners were very reluctant to act against supposed breaches. Many had learnt from personal experience the dangers of taking rumours as facts, and the ease with which accusations could be manipulated to serve personal interests. Alexis, for example, had seen other people 'bashed up, not because he's a grass, but because [someone] don't like him and they haven't got the bottle to do it themselves'. Reluctant to rush into 'traps' in which he was used for other's people's gains, his preference was for caution and avoidance: 'If there's a rumour about somebody [being a grass], I'm just not gonna let him know anything I don't want him to know.'

Prisoners without such experience were less questioning of the hearsay that circulated in the prison. Their reluctance to act upon rumours was primarily related to concerns about what they might lose rather than doubts about the veracity of accusations. Even when certain that a normative infringement had occurred, many prisoners were disinclined to take action: 'I'd like to do something, but I'd have more to lose than gain', said one prisoner, incensed that someone had slashed the pool table with a razor, but striving for parole. 'In a B-cat, that wouldn't happen—you'd get done in the next day' (prisoner, fieldwork notes). Kieran complained that 'you've got nonces serving your food' and that 'no-one cares anymore about nonces', but he himself took no steps to confront prisoners who he said were known sex offenders.

It took clear evidence and an unusual boldness for prisoners to mobilize against supposed informers. More often, although despised, these prisoners were simply shunned or grudgingly endured. Some suspected grasses had graffiti scrawled on their cells or urine thrown under their doors, or faced verbal or written threats. These were substitutes for direct retribution, aimed at intimidating prisoners into segregating themselves. Sex offenders were less likely to be tolerated and faced more aggressive forms of threat—'burnouts' or furtive attacks. However, most prisoners were reluctant to act against infractions that did not affect them directly. The following sentiments were typical:

I don't like nonces, and I don't really want to associate with them. But it's not my business to go and do anything. As long as they don't bother talking to me or associate with me, I've not got a problem.

I need to do my own bird. I do crime for me. I come to prison to do my own thing and just not to do anyone else's. And if someone causes trouble with me, then I'll have to deal with that myself. But yeah I don't go looking for other people's trouble as well. You'd be there all the time. (Zack) (Fieldwork notes)

This attitude of apathetic individualism was widespread, and was reflected in a number of mundane phrases, as Chapter 5 also noted. 'It don't bother me, I'm going soon', and 'I don't want trouble, and he ain't causing me no trouble' were typical of such refrains. Statements that 'it's not my place to judge', that others should 'do what they're doing' and that life was 'each to their own' (Isaac) were applied to a range of situations. Other people's interpersonal disputes were 'between that person and that person' (Isaac), 'none of my business. It's not for me to go and tell somebody else' (Rhys). In relation to other people turning to staff or informing on other prisoners, it might 'matter a lot' if the victim were a good friend, but 'not if it's someone you don't know— then it's none of your business' (prisoner, fieldwork notes). 'I ain't gonna have a go at you for your view. You've got to live with your actions' (Matt). Direct slights, smears, or betrayals were different matters. These discourses of individualism, toleration, and self-determination were encouraged by institutional policies, and the prison's Cat-C status. Traditional values of 'inmate loyalty' thus competed with forces that promoted the privatization of values and a process of social atomization.

Grassing and the prisoner typology

Enthusiasts were the prisoners most liable to inform staff about the affairs of their peers, and did so on two main bases. The first was normative objection—the belief that certain activities were simply wrong. As the quotation below illustrates, they defended their right to intervene by invoking discourses of moral integrity and by distinguishing between grassing for selfish or spiteful purposes, and doing so for reasons that were selfless or ethically defensible:

If you was sitting in the cell smoking a bit of dope, who'd care? You're not bothering me, not bothering anybody else. If you were sitting in a cell gambling, you're not allowed to gamble. But you're not bothering me, you're not harming anybody else. But if you're got a big fellow bullying a little kid then it is something to do with me because it's wrong. It's wrong in outside society and it's wrong in here.

So how do you then mention that to staff without getting in shit?
I tell them. I just go up to them and just tell them: 'Listen, that bloke's getting bullied'.... If you was in prison and you see a little kid getting bullied by a big fellow, you know you couldn't do anything about it. You'd have to help them some way wouldn't you? You couldn't stand and watch it carry on, could you? (Luke)

The appeal to my own moral judgment was significant here, and showed the force that the code exerted even against prisoners who distanced themselves from mainstream prison values. Seeking absolution for their contraventions, *enthusiasts* presented grassing in such circumstances as a moral obligation of which anyone 'respectable' person would approve. Reflecting on his inclination to tell staff about certain incidents, Max asked 'what would *you* do?' if I were to witness a serious crime outside prison. Moral justifications reinforced the scripts of integrity and redemption that were outlined in Chapter 5. Zack, for example, claimed that informing in some circumstances was consistent with his moral history: 'I've *always* looked after vulnerable people. I've always looked out for the weak.'

In similar fashion, many *enthusiasts* argued that drug dealing was within the ambit of their concerns because it could tempt vulnerable prisoners into addiction. Zack made little secret of his disapproval of drugs and his proclivity to identify dealers to staff in order to have them removed from the wing. Notions of moral righteousness and protective citizenship were used to defend his actions: 'Because a respectable person and a responsible person would not let a kid do smack. I don't wish it on no-one.'

More self-serving motives were less often advertised, but they clearly played some motivating role. Max reflected that he was 'getting older now, I've got to make it easier for myself.... I wouldn't have done it in the past, but because I'm getting a bit more trust now, I'm willing to help more.' Luke explained his reasoning as follows:

There's more than one way to skin a cat in prison. And if someone's done something bad or wrong to me, or abused my good nature, I'll not bother going to attack them. I'll just wait until they do something and I'll tuck them up.[15] Because it's easier for me to do that than to go and put myself

---

[15] To 'tuck someone up': to inform on someone.

in jeopardy [by] being violent towards them, or whatever, because they've upset me.... But I'm not just going to run down the wing and say: 'Oh, officer, officer, this person's doing this', just for the sake of it.

Again, the effort to distinguish between acts that were gratuitous and those that were morally valid was germane here.

Pragmatists and *retreatists* were more instrumental in their thinking about this issue. In discussing the injunction not to grass, they consistently reached for prudential rather than normative explanations, noting that the risks of informing outweighed the benefits. It could 'make things worse' (Seb), 'you [could] get a good hiding' (Charlie), 'it just gets you into more trouble, [and] it's a waste of time, because the cons will find out some way or another, you're just going to get beat up in the end' (Declan). The sense was that informing to staff was perilous and self-defeating as much as it was wrong. Seb advised keeping quiet if bullied rather than involving staff: 'You'd probably be better to take a kicking.... It would be a stupid move to get the label [of being a grass]. You're going to spend the rest of your life on protection.' Olly recommended caution: 'If you're going to do it, be smart about it. Write it on a piece of paper, put it in a box or something. You do it blatantly, people are going to find out and you're going to suffer'.

Dom's reasoning was both instrumental and prudential. It was not his role, nor in his benefit, to provide assistance to the staff.

[Officers] drop in little questions and I just laugh: 'I'm not telling you even if I knew'. It's not worth it at the end of the day. If they want to find [the hooch] it's their job to find it, I'm not going to make it easier for them.... At the end of the day it's a risk. [The officer] probably wouldn't say nothing to nobody but there's still a chance that someone else will find out and then you get called a grass so it's not worth it at the end of the day because it'll just cause more trouble than it's worth.... They're not going to give you anything for letting them know so what's the point? It's their job to find it, they get paid enough so why should you help them? You don't get nothing out of it so why should you help them? (Dom)

Cameron's attitude was equally individualistic, exhibiting a belief in self-reliance and an indifference to the activities of others:

It's not my business giving chat to another man's business. But if anyone wants to do that, let them carry on. That's his business at the end of the day, I've got no qualms with it.... It won't affect me. Because if it affected me I'd do something about it myself. I wouldn't go running to a fucking officer.... But if it affected other people, I can't do nothing about it can I?

This outlook applied both to Cameron's reluctance to intervene on behalf of others and his stance towards less altruistic forms of grassing. Claiming that he knew there was an informer on the wing and had been told to 'give him a beating', Cameron explained that he had chosen not to because 'I wouldn't gain anything out of it. Only a fucking nicking or a ship-out'.

This attitude of protective self-interest was not unique to *pragmatists*. However, they were more inclined than most prisoners to excuse themselves from class action by classifying other prisoners' affairs as beyond their scope of concern. At most, their objections to grassing were a form of collective pragmatism: a desire to reduce the burdens of imprisonment, inject some loyalty into the environment, and make the most of a shared predicament: 'We're all in together, we've got to make lives better for ourselves' (Ewan); 'If you can't trust the people you're living with, then who can you trust? ... You've got to live with people' (Harvey).

Players expressed similar sentiments in stronger terms, emphasizing notions of honour and the integrity of criminal identity. Grassing was a breach of the collective loyalty that crime and imprisonment engendered:

You're all in the same boat right? You all do the same things, you all commit crime—why would you want to grass on another criminal? If you look at it, the criminal activity is like a family. Why would you want someone to come in and burst a bubble? (Bradley)

For *players*, the code was an essential part of criminal culture. Among 'professional' criminals, reputation relied on an ability to keep one's mouth shut (see Parker 1990). To be involved in crime was to accept the norms of the subculture and forfeit the right to most forms of moral censure, particularly those with pretensions of conventional respectability: 'If you're a criminal, there's laws you abide by', said Pierce. 'It's just something that you don't do'. Grassing was for 'straight-heads' and was the reason why most people were in prison (Clemmer 1940; Morrison and O'Donnell 1994).

Players therefore held to the widest and most stringent definitions of grassing, and were the prisoners least likely to view it as a defensible act. Martin classified 'anything you say to the screws about someone else' as informing, offering as an example an occasion when a servery worker had objected in front of staff to a prisoner taking extra food from behind the serving counter.

In such situations, he argued, the appropriate response was to let the event pass and confront the prisoner in private at a later point. The recourse to staff was considered a sign of cowardice as well as a form of betrayal:

If someone is playing loud music and someone else pressed their buzzer, he's now a grass. You can't be seen to be dealing with the officers to do your mess. You wait till the morning, you go to the person, you say: 'Look your music was a bit loud last night, sort it out'. As soon as you press that buzzer you're a grass. You don't use the officers, you do it yourself. (Paul)

To turn to staff was to 'pick the screws over inmates', arousing wider suspicion about loyalty and moral calibre: 'Why would you rather talk to them than us? Are you better than us? You're a grass. Are you a kiddy-fiddler?' (Fin). Expressed in a more extreme form, aiding staff in any way was a violation of symbolic boundaries and a form of collaboration with the enemy: 'It's like selling yourself to the devil', said Wilson. '[It's] getting another one of us in trouble and it's an us against them type of thing.' Such views were less to do with honour or solidarity *per se* than with an ideology of opposition to authority.

Like *pragmatists*, *players* were unlikely to see altruistic interventions as their business: 'It's not down for me to run to the screws and say: "I think my man's being bullied by such and such". It's not down to me to say that' (VJ). At most, *players* argued, it was acceptable for victims to tell staff they were being intimidated and ask to be moved, but without providing the name of their aggressor. Even this was an indication of personal weakness. Prisoners who were bullied should defend themselves, 'take it like a man' (Wilson), and assume responsibility for their criminal choices and carceral outcomes.

Stoics considered such attitudes somewhat callous. They were staunch adherents of the code, and insisted that there were almost no circumstances when they themselves would inform on others. Grassing for reasons of self-interest was seen as deplorable, a normative offence. At the same time, these prisoners recognized the legitimacy of others turning to staff in certain situations:

If a man's bullying someone, me personally, if that [victim] goes and tells an officer, I haven't got a problem with that.... Technically, he's broken an unwritten law. But personally speaking, I wouldn't persecute him or anything. [And] I think the majority of long-termers wouldn't. (Tommy)

Grassing for the reasons above was considered a regrettable but understandable expression of vulnerability. When a prisoner was the victim of a code violation, it was more pardonable for him in turn to infringe normative codes by informing staff. *Stoics* were reluctant to get involved in wing politics, but felt that the expectation that prisoners should deal with such issues on their own was 'daft'. In certain situations, tip-offs to staff could be justified, although they were done carefully. 'A guy's cell was burnt out, and someone nicked his stereo. I didn't think it was right and had a word with an officer about where the stereo was. One or two others didn't like it either' (prisoner, fieldwork notes). This standpoint was consistent with their commitment to a collectivistic orientation among prisoners. Even if they did not actively enforce it, *stoics* conformed to and promoted a code of mutual loyalty and support.

Some prisoners—mainly *stoics* and *players*—expressed the norm against informing as a deeply engrained instinct. Grassing was 'not an option.... The thought never crosses my mind' (Kieran). The injunction against it was often learnt from an early age. Parents had emphasized the need for self-sufficiency—'my dad would say: "Beat him up, fuck the teachers, do it yourself, sort yourself out, you ain't no pushover"' (Callum)—and experience had taught the social penalties of divulging: 'If you opened your mouth [as a child] it played against ya. You were just seen as a threat, cos you were somebody that had talked so you weren't allowed within certain things' (Tyler; and see Irwin 1970). When norms were habituated into the psyche, they could be virtually intractable:

I could never do it, y'know, it's because I've grown up with that, it doesn't matter what happens to you, you go and sort it out yourself. You don't go into an office and you don't tell people's names, it doesn't happen, and for me that's something I won't ever be able to break. Sometimes I wish I could do it. I'd probably get a lot of things for it, but it's just something that I can't do. (Alexis)

I couldn't. I've not been brought up to be like that. Like, my upbringing you've just got to learn, no matter what happens, you've just got to take it on the chin. You can't grass no-one up. (Riz)

Prudential and normative reasons for not grassing were conjoined here. Informing was anathema to the self, it was *just not done*.

Institutional determinants of conflict

Previous chapters have shown how the prison's category, culture, and techniques of power shaped all aspects of its social life, and this was also the case in relation to forms of conflict. First, the prison's medium-security status influenced the *nature* of conflict. Lifers noted that, because the populations of longer-term, higher-security prisons were less transient than Cat-Cs, the violence that occurred in them was less commonplace but more severe. Tensions could less easily be ignored, since it was hard to live with indeterminate hostility, and, once started, disputes could not dissipate without clear resolution. Compared to prisons like Wellingborough, where minor scuffles were relatively common, casual violence was not worthwhile.

Second, the prison's incentive scheme influenced how conflicts were pursued. Jed noted that: 'You have to check yourself [now]. Years ago, you wouldn't give a fuck.' Tommy claimed that lower tensions in prison and the fact that 'everyone's working towards an end' had reduced incidents of violence and coercion. Max concurred that institutional incentives had altered how disputes were handled:

Years ago, you wouldn't care two hoots about what you said in front of who. If you've got a beef with someone now and you're on standard or enhanced, you don't want to lose that, so I would tend to pull someone to the side and then say something and try and sort it out that way.... It does make you think a bit more.

Some prisoners reported that offending behaviour courses had helped them think about modes of appropriate action. A minority rehearsed the teachings of cognitive skills classes in weighing up possibilities: 'consider the costs and the benefits'. On the whole though, it was the prison's web of incentives that fostered collective restraint. Although spontaneous punch-ups occurred fairly regularly, the terms by which conflicts developed were structured by a range of forces and considerations.

Conflict escalation, resolution, and prevention

To a large degree, by avoiding the informal economy, prisoners could significantly reduce their chances of conflict.[16] Yet fights were also sparked by apparently trivial issues, including noise,

[16] The language of 'assassins', 'strongarms', and 'bounty hunters' that some drug dealers employed (and which signalled their sense of ascendancy over their peers) had almost no meaning to those who were not involved in the drugs trade.

disputes about rival football teams, the escalation of play fights, refusals to give cigarette papers, and arguments over turn-taking on the telephones or pool tables. Tyler explained that most tensions were the outcomes of minor issues, and used an example of littering to illustrate how disputes could unfold:

'Here y'are mate, what you putting your stuff next to me door for? Don't take the piss'. That alone is a confrontation. He might say: 'What the fuck are you moaning about, you twat'. [You say:] 'Look, don't put your shit outside me door or I'll smash your fucking head in, don't take the piss yeah. It's your rubbish, don't put it outside my door'.

Disagreements over minor issues always risked being interpreted as personal affronts. As Chapter 6 noted, many prisoners were hypersensitive to perceptions that they were 'being talked down to' or 'taken for a dickhead'. Linguistic slights were therefore common causes of escalation. To call another prisoner a 'nob' or a 'muppet' could be perceived as disrespectful, even though such terms were largely considered 'everyday jail talk' (Martin). To casually label someone a 'grass' or a 'nonce' risked forcing them into counterattacks that locked both parties into linguistic combat.

This was particularly the case if disputes or accusations occurred in the presence of other prisoners, bringing public reputation into the frame. In such situations, tensions were ratcheted up by aggressive responses—'if you've got a problem, you know where my cell is'—primarily made to placate public audiences. While friends often advised prisoners against needless antagonism, other men often goaded them into hostile reprisals (often seeking the thrill of violent action)—'you're not gonna let him get away with that, are ya?!' Disputes were often then settled through peaceable private exchanges: 'I had a word with him. I said "you were laughing at me the other day", and he goes "nah", and apologized. And I just left it at that' (Morgan).

Few prisoners looked for fights if they could be avoided. Most merely wanted avenues out of confrontation that did not mean losing face. A range of pre-emptive strategies were therefore employed to try to avert conflict without appearing passive. 'Fronting' and 'putting on masks' were, for many prisoners, prudential strategies aimed at preventing greater problems in the future: 'everyone has to put on a front because otherwise someone is going to start trying to bully you and you'll end up scrapping all the fucking time' (prisoner, fieldwork notes). Many prisoners reported the need to present themselves far more aggressively than they desired. To maintain a macho façade and contain distress was itself experienced as a secondary pain of imprisonment (see Liebling and Maruna 2005: 6–7; Jewkes 2002, 2005):[17]

> I don't show no signs of weakness, no. You can't show no weaknesses. If someone cusses you, you cuss them back. You don't let somebody say 'you're a fucking idiot', or, you know, 'are you some kind of poof?' or something like that. You have to say: 'What's your problem, mate? You're more of a poof than I am, look at what you're wearing', stuff like that.... it's funny isn't it.... It is hard to be like that 24/7 for however many years. When I'm in my cell on my own I don't cry or nothing. But I look out of the window, and I probably do feel like crying. (Seb)

Other prisoners cultivated reputations as 'nutters' or 'tool merchants' (people prepared to use weapons) in order to ward off difficulties (see Sparks *et al.* 1996: 181):

> If I get in a fight with someone, win or lose, it's not just that fight there and then. I'd carry on coming back and back and back until I do win. So that's why I don't usually get any problems because they know they might kick hell out of me the first time but [I'm] going to carry on coming back and back and back.... And if I can't beat you with my two fists I'll beat you [with] something else. (Jordan)

These were defensive forms of aggression that collectively amplified frictions and took the risk of raising the stakes. There was a clear tension between the desire to avoid conflict and the need not to seem passive in the face of aggression. The result here—particularly among prisoners on parole sentences or on the VTU—was a culture of calibrated confrontation, with threats made in ways that communicated assertion without really demanding reactions. Thus, prisoners warned each other— 'stay out of my way' or 'don't speak to me'—slammed doors, and often mouthed off in front of their peers without taking further action. As Seb noted, these threats and moans were much more common than full confrontations: 'Instead of just going straight at it, they seem to warn people a lot more.'[18]

[17] The stressful and exhausting nature of putting on fronts is expressed most clearly by prisoners in therapeutic communities, who identify the freedom from putting on masks as one of the most liberating and transformative aspects of life on therapeutic wings (Shefer, in progress).

[18] The use of this strategy might explain why the culture on the VTU was perceived by officers as pettier and more childish than elsewhere in the prison.

Building oneself up physically was another mode of protective aggression, as a number of prisoners admitted: 'The bigger you are, the less men are going to want to fuck with you' (Wilson). Prison bodies served an important communicative function, with muscles warning other prisoners of violent potential. Most men worked almost exclusively on their upper bodies—some talked of developing a 'prison chest'—creating top-heavy bodies that looked like boxers' torsos sewn onto different legs. When prisoners collected their food from the servery and swaggered back to their cells in public view, the landings served as catwalks of masculine display. These performances helped place some prisoners 'above the line' of victimization. However, they could also make prisoners targets for those men seeking to build up their own reputations, particularly if they were perceived as needless bravado. Intelligent *players* like Stephen mocked the belief among some prisoners that 'if they're not in the gym every day they're some sort of pussy', and pointed to the advantages of being less visible: 'If you're pumping iron every day, the screws look at you nervously and that can have a bad effect. I've seen people get shipped out of jails just for being big and tough looking.' Conspicuous aggression could be counterproductive.

Experienced prisoners found less belligerent ways of avoiding conflict. They knew not to confront people who were coming off the phone or visits, when moods were often fraught, or when sitting with friends, when reputational concerns were heightened. They were careful with their words—even among friends—knowing that gossip about and criticisms of other prisoners could come back to haunt them. They modelled a culture of tense courtesy, recognizing that this was a collective means by which tensions could be neutralized and precluded:[19]

There's more politeness in prison than there is outside, because one little slight can cause a tear up in here. You bump into someone and you don't apologise and he'll turn round and 'Oi! Who [are] you fucking bumping into?' Next thing you know, you're fighting. (Alexis)

People are very careful not to bump into each other. If you stand on the central corridor one day, watch how people are very careful not to hit each other, bump into each other, they are very respectful of each other's

---

[19] It was mainly prisoners who were already 'above the line' who emphasized a code of politeness. More vulnerable prisoners were nervous that courtesy could be perceived as meek passivity.

personal space. And that is a manifestation of the stresses of being in close proximity.... It was one thing that struck me when I went out on town visits, people are bumping into you left, right and centre. For ten years I've never had that, and it was only then that I became aware, because I had something to contrast it to. I was like 'fucking hell, how rude people are!', because there is a level of politeness in prison that doesn't quite exist on the out. (Nathan)

While prison life could be tenser than life outside, it was thus, in some respects, less confrontational and more respectful. In describing their reactions to conflicts inside, some prisoners commented that they were more likely to exercise restraint in prison than in the community. Prison had taught them that conflicts could be resolved 'without you having to fight them.... Sometimes you just have to stick up for yourself and say: "Look, who do you think you are?", and they'll back away' (Martin). For some prisoners, reputation issues were no less important outside prison, where close-knit communities made status a less transient issue. But in comparison with the outside world, there was more to lose in prison. Conflicts developed momentum with dangerous speed, and there was less chance of getting away with violence:

I've just been looking for an excuse to give him a slap but there's no point. I really, really, really want to hurt this person but I can't. If he gets a slap it's going to come back to me.

Do you think he'll grass you up?

Yeah I know he will. The screws already know that I don't like him. You can't live in jail now without the fear of someone grassing you up. (Bradley)

Prison conflicts were dangerous both to ignore and to pursue, creating a highly strained culture of controlled but coiled aggression. Incarceration made prisoners more edgy, more frustrated, and more alert to potential victimization, yet generally more reluctant to engage in actual confrontation. It forced prisoners to be petty and assertive about minor issues at the same time as it required adaptability, tolerance, and self-restraint. The same was true in relation to the prison regime, which required patience at some times and persistence at others. The resulting tone was one of barely contained tension, a tone that hung in the daily ether. Many prisoners lived in constant fear of each other, and in constant tension with the environment.

How prisoners dealt with potential conflict varied according to their needs and aspirations. *Enthusiasts* in particular stated their preference for walking away from fights rather than putting their progression at risk. Luke reported not having retaliated after being assaulted because he wanted to avoid adding years to his sentence. He laughed off the notion of 'losing face', considering it an infantile concept used only by 'arseholes'. Some weaker *pragmatists* expressed similar concerns, fearing the loss of privileges or parole. As Dave suggested, prisoners who had little to lose relative to their adversaries could take advantage of this imbalance:

Some people snap back, knowing full well that the other person just wants to get out on their release date. Say you're due for parole, you're not going to have a major fight with someone and really injure them. [But] somebody who's already lost their parole, and they come up against that person, that person's not going to take none back: 'I'm not getting out no sooner', then *boom*!

For those men desperate to avoid jeopardy this did not mean submitting to others, but it required an ability to fend off demands without fuelling further antagonism: 'I'd say "you ain't getting nothing off me mate" and walk away' (Seb).

There was consensus that a prisoner could prevent further victimization by standing his ground (Jewkes 2005b). Anyone who fought back was not worth bullying, as Danny explained: 'people now know if they try anything, he's still gonna have a go.... They think twice about doing it because they know they're not gonna come out unscathed themselves; it's too much hassle, they'd rather go for an easier target.' Among *players* in particular, to show 'heart' or 'balls' was in itself worthy of respect (Edgar and O' Donnell 1998). Many *players* reported that they would have more admiration for a weaker prisoner who lost a fight but 'had a go' than for an aggressor who won. Indeed, VJ claimed that he would overturn the outcome of a dispute if he deemed the loser to be sufficiently brave: 'Win or lose, it don't matter. As long as you've tried your hardest to stop him. And then I'll go and say "man, put back his things", because you've tried, man, you've tried.' For these men, masculine status was a binary system, something that one either achieved or did not. Prisoners who were unwavering in the imposition of their will or in the defence of their integrity 'proved' the value of what they represented: to be prepared to fight for something validated both the cause and its defender. As Wilson illustrated, such notions were imported from gang culture in the community, where earning respect was about gaining masculine kudos through trials of self-assertion:

You've got to earn those stripes, got to make money, so people say you're a good hustler. [And] Take men out, don't necessarily kill them but you've got to stab them in the leg, some shit like that.... You respect [people] because they can handle themselves, they can hold their own. No man is going to fuck with that man, he's done his work, he's earned his stripes, he's been through the point where, and once you pass that level, someone else has to go through it, it just progresses.

Rules of fighting

It was significant that fights were not gauged only according to their ostensible outcomes, for their communicative functions mattered as much as their material consequences (Gambetta 2005). To fight signified bravery, assertiveness, and willingness not to submit, and these displays were important in themselves. This was not so much to stratify prisoners in a strict vertical hierarchy. Rather, it sorted prisoners into cruder categories of those who were and were not prepared to defend themselves through physical means. When officers shouted at prisoners to 'stop fighting', the speed with which hostilities were normally broken off evidenced the degree to which their primary purpose was often already served.[20] Only in situations of rare ferocity were prisoners keen to inflict serious injury.

There were also recognized rules about how fights should proceed. First, once a prisoner was clearly beaten, a fight should be stopped. This was partly because, at this stage, the fight had shown a clear winner. It was also to prevent unnecessary harm and related consequences. Few prisoners took pleasure in seeing another man beaten to a pulp, and most condemned the arbitrary, excessive, and illegitimate use of violence (Edgar *et al.* 2003). There were also pragmatic reasons to intervene in a fight: a man who was seriously injured was more likely to inform to staff, and a protracted fight was more likely to draw staff attention to the landings. As Danny argued, a self-contained fight was 'classed as a [success]: they've had the fight, nobody's been nicked for it, and then everyone's got away. If they get caught, they're gonna

---

[20] There were also advantages in being charged with 'fighting' rather than 'assault', the penalties for the latter being more severe.

spend more time in prison.' Second, prisoners who were clearly 'not fighters' or who showed genuine fear should not be forced to fight. Again, the reasons here were a complex combination of pity, prudence, and machismo—a certain amount of sympathy for the helpless; the knowledge that a weak prisoner was more likely to grass someone up; and a macho belief that there was nothing to be gained from fighting the weak or feminized.

Third, fights should be between two parties only ('straighteners'). Such arrangements were considered fairer than when associates joined in on behalf of their peers. They were also more likely to demonstrate a victor. This norm was at odds with expectations that prisoners should intervene to support friends. It kept in check the potential for interpersonal disputes to drag increasing numbers of prisoners into their orbit. 'If two people have a fight, that should be the end of it', said Aaron. Prisoners who fought in such circumstances often exchanged gestures of respect after the event, tacitly recognizing that an order of relative dominance was now clarified (Gambetta 2005).

An illustrative example is instructive here. On one wing, a fight was stopped at a point that one participant, and some observers, considered premature. The fighter approached the 'heads' on the wing to request a rematch, and was told that this was okay so long as the other prisoner agreed to it and friends did not get involved. With powerful prisoners standing at the end of the landing to stop anyone else from intervening, and to keep an eye out for staff, the fight was resumed until a winner was established. 'In the end, the situation was resolved fairly', Elliott commented. 'They both shook hands at the end of it, and that was the end of it.'

Although often sparked by trivial acts, fights were generally connected to interpersonal rivalries and matters of personal honour. Most prisoners were more preoccupied with the power relation between themselves and other, specific individuals than with an overall hierarchy on the wing (Edgar et al. 2003). However, the way that disputes unfolded was shaped by social factors, not least, the involvement of other prisoners as instigators, inhibitors and support, and the webs of affiliation that disputes brought into effect.[21] The prisoner hierarchy sometimes came into play in such

[21] It would be expected that the pattern and level of conflict within an establishment would relate to a number of sociostructural factors, such as the size of the informal economy, the number of organized gangs, the basis of order, and so on (see Sparks et al. 1996).

situations. Powerful prisoners could not demand fights, but they could arbitrate disputes and sanction the use of violence. Paul stopped the cell of a known informer being burnt out because he thought he had something to gain from befriending him instead. On another wing, after a minor interpersonal dispute in which a prisoner from Ashley's hometown had felt disrespected by a prisoner named Doug, Ashley had prevented other prisoners from attacking Doug because of a pragmatic connection he had formed with Doug's friend, Adrian, which ensured him a regular drug supply. Ashley explained:

If it wasn't for [Adrian], I'd have said: 'Yeah, fucking take them out'. But Adrian had a lot of heart. And I respected him. So I just stopped it, explained to my boys: 'Listen, he's my mate. If you want to beat him, wait till I'm gone'. Hold it down for four weeks.[22]

Ashley's intervention had been all the more impressive to other prisoners because, in order to prevent the attack, he had taken physical action against a man from his hometown. He had then used this act as leverage to procure a greater share of drugs from Adrian. In general though, prisoners with proven reputations, such as Paul and Ashley, neither needed nor wanted to engage in direct confrontation either with the system or with other prisoners. When their illicit activities required them to engage in violence, they did so without personal involvement, either paying other prisoners ('assassins') for acts of face-to-face retribution or using covert means of assault. The burning out of cells was in this respect an ideal strategy, because those who ordered such acts could ensure that they were off the wings or talking to officers when they occurred.

Interpersonal politics

Although interventions against bullying sometimes occurred, public condemnations were not always supported by action. Zack noted: 'They'll say they're not tolerated and people will sit there and they'll slag them off behind their backs, but no-one ever does nothing.' One reason for this was a reluctance to put

---

[22] After another incident a few days later, Adrian withdrew his support for Doug—'too much shit, mate'. Ashley had no further benefit in holding back his 'troops', and, in fear of a group assault, Doug placed himself in segregation for his own protection.

oneself at risk by intervening in interpersonal disputes. Another was that definitions of bullying were vague and contestable, allowing skilled prisoners to avoid being labelled as perpetrators. Most bullying was relatively 'low profile' (Callum): verbal harassment and low-level exploitation, rather than outright coercion.[23] Prisoners generally applied this latter, narrower definition, conceiving of bullying only in its more extreme forms.

The same prisoners who denounced 'out and out bullying' often admitted to less blatant forms of exploitation: ripping off other prisoners in drug deals (e.g. Martin, Tyler, Callum), using their presence to intimidate others (e.g. Cameron, Fin), and manipulating friendships for personal gain (e.g. Max, Tyler, Paul). Fin acknowledged the thin line between 'bullying' and manipulation or 'blagging':

I won't bully you out of it. I'd blag you out of it. In a sense, I am bullying you because of my size, and because of my demeanour. I'm not actually going to bully you. But if you've got a weakness I'm going to use that weakness.

Fin manipulated prisoners with little remorse, taking advantage of the wing's rapid turnover to find new victims: 'If you know they're getting [drugs], offer them two-s on a burn or cup of tea; pretend you're getting a visit soon and will pay them back.' In describing how he used his forcefulness and 'silver tongue' to get what he wanted, he provided a number of examples of how ideals could be harnessed and twisted for personal ends.[24] Some of his methods were clearly coercive. He rarely repaid debts, using his physicality and reputation for resolve to deter creditors from pursuing him: 'They'll have to come with tins of tuna and five or six of them and properly put me [in hospital] to get me off the wing.' One strategy was to 'show no fear ... never deviate from your stance'. Another

---

[23] Jordan identified the kinds of behaviours that were typical:

They verbally threaten him. He was [playing] football yesterday and they've deliberately just booted him all the time. He's got a PlayStation in his pad and since he's had that they've all piled into his pad and they've all booked a night. They basically just take the piss out of him all the time. They use his pad as a doss-hole.

Such actions were unambiguously classified as bullying by the prison authorities, as were acts such as name-calling and the enforcement of debts. This was despite the fact that such deals were normally entered into without pressure, and despite the fact that staff themselves often made bets with prisoners. It is also interesting to note that staff as well as prisoners employed a discourse of 'bullying', particularly in relation to treatment by management.

[24] 'That's one thing about criminals, you become such a fucking manipulator. You even manipulate your own memory. I've done it myself' (Fin).

technique was to employ prisoner norms to justify actions, even when these actions appeared to contravene accepted codes. If Fin disliked someone, he looked for excuses to assault or humiliate him that would have some credibility with other prisoners. It was illegitimate to do so simply on the basis of personal antipathy. However, if an adversary could be painted as having treated him disrespectfully, talked behind his back, or refused him customary forms of loyalty, such acts were easier to defend:

I say: 'Do you think I let some fucking prick talk to me like I'm a fucking idiot? If he hasn't got the fucking balls to come and tell me to my face, he's a prick and I'm going to treat him like a prick'. I'm justifying it...cutting down their options to do something about it.

In similar fashion, Fin had obtained drugs from two dealers on the wing by manipulating norms of personal treatment. Having explained that he had deliberately approached the weaker of the two, he expanded on his method as follows:

I put it on him, I said: 'Listen, my head's shot [i.e. I'm stressed]. Sort it out. My head's shot man, I don't want to lose it with you people'. I'm not saying to him I'm going to punch his face in, but [I'm] saying it's better to keep me happy. So basically he [said]: 'Yeah, OK, I'll just talk to my partner'. So then what I do is, I go to the partner and say: 'Listen, he's telling me yes'. I'm [effectively] saying: 'Well, your partner's agreed, if you don't agree, you've got to tell me to my face'. Divide and rule. Straight in his face. I'm making sure I'm facing him dead on, like a cobra, to give the biggest profile possible. It puts them on the spot.

Alongside barely veiled threats, Fin mobilized norms about mutual aid and frankness. Once the first dealer had effectively consented to selling Fin drugs, for the second to have refused would have left him open to accusations of personal prejudice and given grounds for offence.

Powerful prisoners often activated collective ideals for exploitative purposes, violating the same principles that they exerted against others. Codes of loyalty were used to pressure prisoners into storing goods, expectations of reciprocity were used to create unfair obligations, and rules against grassing were used to protect predatory behaviour from being exposed (Edgar and O'Donnell 1998). Such tactics were elaborated in Max's account of how he might 'blag' other prisoners to give him their possessions:

I'd be his best friend: 'Come up to my cell and have a cup of coffee'. He'd sit in here and he'll think: 'it's nice in here, I need some pictures'. I'll go: 'You want a few pictures, here you are mate', make him feel like he's [my] friend. He's not my fucking friend, I just want [his] trainers. 'You after anything else, mate?' 'Don't suppose you could sort us a couple of roll ups'. 'Here you go'. Then I'll bang it on him, as soon as he's smoked that, as soon as he's done: 'I fancy them trainers'. Then I'll start using my confidence, a bit of banter. If he's not as clued up as me, I could fucking get anything off him I wanted.... If the staff come to me then and say, 'leave him alone, let him have his trainers', I'd say, 'You're grassing me [up] to a screw'.

It was because of such moves that experienced prisoners were suspicious of kindness in others and were reluctant to accept gifts that could become obligations (Mauss 1990). Offers of tobacco one day could be turned into demands to fill flasks the next. As Paul summarized: 'There is a payback normally somewhere along the line.'

Grassing could be used for other strategic purposes. Max had placed himself on protection in a previous prison, and although he had claimed to others that he had smashed up his cell in anger rather than 'blocked himself off', he feared that rumours would catch up with him. If confronted by other prisoners, he explained how he would proceed:

If I didn't think I could do it by threats I would do it some other way. I might drop a note in the box saying, 'he's drug dealing', get one of them shipped out. Then I could use dirty tactics, I could go to a couple of the boys I know and say: 'Listen, I've just heard that cunt grassing up in the office'.

In similar fashion, grassing could be used to rid a wing of rivals in the drug trade, particularly if informers were smart enough to submit anonymous notes to staff over a period of weeks using different handwriting.

Intelligent prisoners knew how to use influence effectively and were able to manipulate men who were more impressionable. Bradley used his status to put weight on other prisoners to carry out attacks on his behalf, always choosing men from his home area in the knowledge that they were less likely to refuse or inform upon him if caught. Alfie took revenge on someone who had stolen from a friend by exploiting the antipathy of another prisoner on the wing:

There is another guy on the wing, a big guy, [who] I knew didn't like the thief, but because they never spoke to each other he had nothing to use as an argument. So I've noticed this and I've gone up to the big guy and said: 'I saw so-and-so come out of your pad earlier', that's all I said and then walked away. The next day, the thief had a black eye. It's just—use the right guy for the right job. I'm just a skinny man, but plant a seed and it will grow. If the situation warrants it, you do it.

The general point here is that the prisoner code—inasmuch as one could be defined—was not simply a collective means of mitigating the pains of imprisonment (Sykes 1958). It was also a tool of influence and a resource within interpersonal politics. Its terms were contestable, negotiable, and to some degree malleable, and its application was inconsistent. As Fin commented: 'There are written rules but there are exceptions and it's really hard to define, because there's no set pattern.' More specifically, norms and ideals were differentially mobilized in ways that reproduced prisoner hierarchies, with experienced, intelligent prisoners able to use the framework of principles to deflect trouble, define incidents, and assert their interests in ways that less confident and capable men could not manage. 'It can be [a game]', said Jordan, 'it's just a matter of how many pieces you've got at the time. Everybody is trying to play somebody for something.' For weaker prisoners, this very notion was alien: 'It's serious, it's not a game, it's your life you're gambling' (Elliott). To play games required some knowledge of the rules, and only some prisoners had the cultural capital to use the rules effectively.

Public Cultures and Private Beliefs

Life on the landings was hard to observe, with most cell doors pushed ajar during association periods. The privatization of social life meant that fewer than half of prisoners could be seen outside their cells at these times.[25] Most chose to socialize in small groups within cells, watching television, playing cards or chess, and chatting. Some were engaged in activities off the wings, such as evening education classes, gym, or chapel. Often, fewer than twenty prisoners used the communal rooms to play pool, darts, cards, and table tennis. Numbers were lower on canteen days, when prisoners consumed or exchanged the goods they had purchased. Likewise, most prisoners ate their meals in their cells rather than in the pods that were provided on A to D-wings to allow limited communal dining. E-wing and the VTU had no such space, but more room

[25] In some establishments, prisoners are not allowed to socialize in cells and are forced to mix on the landings during association periods.

and equipment for general association. Seating was provided on most wings around pool and table tennis tables.

Differences in design influenced social life on each wing in minor ways. The availability of casual seating at the ends of each landing on the VTU meant that older and more vulnerable prisoners were more visible on these wings, where they played cards or talked quietly. On E-wing, a higher proportion of prisoners socialized outside cells, primarily because they were yet to form stable social alliances. Public spaces throughout the prison tended to be dominated by younger, more boisterous men.

As Chapter 6 suggested, social structure was reflected in mundane activity. On E-wing, one pool table was dominated by 'the lads', while the other was used by newer, less powerful prisoners. Leon referred to the two tables as 'professional, where all the boys are, and amateur, [where] you get a lot of average lads'. On another wing, use of the two tables was split by race, and characterized by friendly rivalry: 'The pool on that table is phenomenal—I can't keep up!' (prisoner, fieldwork notes). Muslim prisoners on B-wing generally ate together on a specific table. Foreign national prisoners sat together playing cards on one landing on the VTU. On the exercise yards, many prisoners walked around in ethnically uniform groups or pairings. Most talked quietly, with their heads down. Some sat around the edges of the yard, leaning on wing buildings or the fence. One or two prisoners walked or jogged alone. Workshops and education classes reproduced the prison's general pattern of loose, partial segregation, with black and white prisoners often sitting in separate groups. This was not hostility or territorialism, 'they just don't come over here' (prisoner, fieldwork notes).

Mealtimes and unlock periods were on the whole calm and civil, particularly on D-wing, where prisoners collected food quietly and locked themselves up quickly at the end of the evening with unstated collective purpose. These acts aided the smooth flow of the regime in ways that benefited prisoners, reducing the need for staff to chivvy them along or begin the locking-up process as early as they did elsewhere in the prison. On all wings, association periods were used to place requests with staff, socialize, borrow goods, and put one's personal affairs in order:

I'll go and see a friend, I'll use the phone I'll have a shower, wash some clothing or I'll do a bit of ironing. By the time I've done that, sat upstairs, borrowed a TV guide, got the flask filled and spoke to a few people, association's done anyway. (Tyler)

[I] Try and get off [the wing] as much as possible. Stay in my pad a lot. If I do go out, I go up to Mickey's, play snooker, gamble on the snooker, and just buzz about till I get a bit of puff for that night.[26] That's basically it, really. (Darren)

Wings were places of public intimacy and domesticity (Crawley 2004a, 2004b). Prisoners cleaned their cells, took 'private moments' to sit drinking tea or smoking cigarettes, walked around in towels and flip-flops, preened themselves in preparation for visits and made private telephone calls, all within communal spaces. Games of pool and table-tennis were played in the glare of others, with staff as well as prisoners often standing around to observe and comment. Wing behaviour also had many ritual qualities. There were informal rules for joining queues—'Who's last? After you, yeah?'—and for the sharing of roll-ups among associates ('two-s on that'). Half-smoked cigarettes were passed wordlessly to friends: 'It's out of respect. I wouldn't smoke in front of someone and not give', one prisoner explained (fieldwork notes). Social warmth was acknowledged implicitly in these silent customs. Prisoners expected reciprocity in such ordinary acts, but they were expressions of friendship rather than just instrumental practices.

Rituals took the heat out of potentially knotty interactions, in an environment of relative strangers. Despite their outward tranquility, public settings were sites of wariness and suspicion. The need for caution and awareness was embedded in daily culture. On arrival on wings, prisoners learnt the need to 'stand back and look' (Den), to ask certain questions—what officers were like, how tightly the wing was policed, whether there were any drugs on the wing—and to observe certain interactions: 'Who's outspoken, who people defer to...who's going to whose pad, who's always shouting his mouth off, [who's] on a mission all the time [for drugs]' (Callum). Dishonesty and dangerousness were read from social tics and the signs of the body. Prisoners *felt* their way through the world as much as they scrutinized it consciously. For many prisoners, the requirement to be constantly alert was one of the most stressful and brutalizing aspects of imprisonment. Although violence was rare, the knowledge that, at any time, something *could* happen was profoundly destructive.

---

[26] 'Puff': cannabis.

Everyday conversation

Everyday conversation comprised topics both internal and external to the prison. Prisoners discussed other establishments and prison experiences ('that's a tough jail, that is'; 'that screw Mr Smith: he was a right bastard!'), and events within Wellingborough such as conflicts, ship-outs, and changes to the regime. Knowledge about courtroom politics and the prison system brought a certain amount of social prestige. Much conversation centred on decisions about home leave, parole, taggings, and recategorization—in particular, unfair decisions, the difficulties of getting paperwork in order, and the likely outcomes of impending verdicts. Plans for the future, including possible 'jobs' (both criminal and legitimate) and pledges to stay clean, also featured heavily in public discussion ('Getting out, that's the big topic', said Dave). Prisoners from the same areas talked about people and places they knew in common: 'who's been nicked, what's happening, who is going out with who, new pubs, new clubs...' (Jordan).

Drugs were a keystone of social discourse. Prison slang was replete with allusions to drug consumption and distribution, and many of the most commonly used identity labels were direct references to drugs. When prisoners stated 'I'm drug-free', the term was meant as an adjectival noun, a descriptor of the kind of person that they were, not just their current behaviour. This use of language highlighted the degree to which personal identity hinged on narcotic status. On the VTU in particular, the centrality of drugs in most prisoners' life histories contributed to a somewhat solipsistic, self-regarding culture in which many prisoners retreated into private thought about past deeds, personal projects of repair, and hopes of clean living.

Although they rarely went into depth about their families, prisoners also chatted about their upbringings ('I used to get beaten to go to church!') and shared observations and memories of their hometowns. 'Obviously you talk about prison a bit, but it's mostly outside you talk about.... Experiences we've had outside, really' (Connor). Younger prisoners often told stories about exploits with women and crime: 'We talk about women and getting out and what we've done to women and what experience we've had with women.... And we talk about our dodgy deals and who owes us this and who owes us that' (Cameron). Discussions of cars, sport, and tabloid gossip were also common.

Officers, often standing in doorways observing, were brought into debates about prison life and current affairs, or were subjected to light-hearted derision.

The tone of conversation was often highly performative. Prisoners mocked or outdid each other's assertions, punctured optimism about the future ('you'll be back on the gear in twenty minutes!'; 'you getting parole?! Don't talk shit!'), and ridiculed claims of physical and sexual potency, largely with good humour. One prisoner described the tendency for prisoners to boast about their wealth outside as 'Lear Jet' conversation, because of the manner in which prisoners made increasingly outlandish assertions about what they owned. While such exchanges served to boost self-esteem, others were aimed at diminishing the confidence of others.

Orientations to women

Women were largely absent from the prison, and yet they were hyperpresent in prisoner discourse. Views about women were highly polarized. Within public discourse, they were portrayed both as sexual objects and as untrustworthy sexual agents. As Nathan summarized:

Ninety-five per cent of the attitudes towards women you meet in prison are not good.... They're 'scum of the earth', 'root of all evil', you know what I mean. I've been betrayed since I've been in prison in the relationships that I've had. But it still doesn't make me class the whole of womanhood as bitches and evil scum, which seems to be a prevailing attitude.

Among younger prisoners in particular, tales of sexual experiences, fantasies, and intentions formed a great deal of conversational material. Women were often discussed in graphic (and sometimes violent) terms (see also Richards *et al.* 2003), as receptacles for male desire. Among some prisoners—in particular, *players* and younger *pragmatists*—they were expendable items of sexual exchange in relationships between men:

Just say that I've got a girlfriend. And us two, we hang about every day together. She comes to you, and you do whatever with her. I'd expect you to come back and say: 'You know what VJ, that girl's a [whore]'. If you come and told me that, I'd just break up [with her]. (VJ)

Female officers were often intrusively questioned about their personal lives and subjected to sexual commentary, either in person or in collective evaluations made in their absence. In such discussions, prisoners often explicitly acknowledged the impact of incarceration on sexual longing, claiming that their standards had been 'lowered' to include almost all women as objects of desire. Many described the deprivation of sexual activity as one of the key pains of imprisonment and used illicitly circulated pornography to self-stimulate. It was also common for prisoners to suggest that female staff struggled to contain their own sexual urges. Anyone who appeared successful in exposing hints of sexual interest was given cachet. Efforts to prove sexual magnetism and to sexualize and undermine the authority of female staff betrayed widespread feelings of sexual powerlessness. Not all prisoners engaged in or approved of such acts (see Crewe 2006a and Chapter 5), but they were publicly licensed, resulting in a culture of macho bravado.

Women were also widely depicted as dangerous agents of social and sexual treachery. 'Never put a woman before a good friend.... They're conniving people' VJ advised. In prisoners' life narratives, women regularly featured as corrupting influences: causes of criminal and narcotic downfall. In life stories, prisoners frequently portrayed their own infidelities as harmless accidents, proof of sexual potency, or evidence of the corrupting power of female sexuality. In contrast, women who had been unfaithful to them were castigated as callous, calculating, and promiscuous. Women's infidelities—whether sexual, social or financial—were considered unforgivable yet predictable.[27] Indeed, prisoners often taunted each other about the inevitability of being betrayed by wives and girlfriends, displacing their own insecurities about the vulnerabilities that imprisonment provoked.

However, alongside this public misogyny, imprisonment also fostered a spirit of sentimentality towards wives and girlfriends. Women were categorized in binary terms: 'There's two kinds: those who mess you about while you're inside, and those who are brilliant' (prisoner, fieldwork notes). Such distinctions were loaded with familiar tropes of purity and evil. Good women were virginal, self-sacrificing, and entirely non-criminal. Invariably,

---

[27] Perceived social betrayals could include going out beyond certain hours or with untrusted friends. Financial betrayals could include refusing to send in money or spending it without prior permission.

they were 'different from other girls', able to recognize and reveal prisoners' true identities, and save them from lives of crime.
Being valued by someone innocent, pure, and uncorrupted was a
reflection of one's own essential goodness, and offered a path to
spiritual redemption:

I've been a criminal through and through. My wife hasn't—she's hung
around criminals and whatnot, but she's not a criminal herself. She won't
do anything.... I had so much respect for her.... Because it was hard to
get [sex] off her, even if she wanted it so bad—I had to respect that. I
hadn't come across that before. But she was different.... I can honestly
say, I've never 'fucked' her. I've 'made love' to her every time. And that's
something I didn't have with any other woman.... And respect for her
was strengthened when she started to open my eyes about the way my
family had been towards me, the way my mother treated me, you know.
But this relationship, this Romeo and Juliet relationship, this best friend,
went out of the window, basically. I treated her like a cunt. I neglected
her. I'd choose the drugs over her all the time.... There's only one thing
[I regret in my life]: losing my wife. (Fin)

Women were thus represented as moral saviours as well as forces
of corruption. In their absence—and in certain spheres—those
female partners who did remain loyal were idealized as totems
of goodness and redemption. In cells, pictures of partners were
proudly displayed, sometimes alongside pornographic material.
Letters were cherished and read repeatedly, and were replied to
in a language of tender romanticism, often expressing regret for
past complacency and proposing idealistic plans for the future.
Cards, poems, pottery, and artwork also expressed sentiments of
romantic innocence. These statements of love and commitment
were not publicly disparaged, although they were sometimes
treated with scepticism.

This scepticism reflected the fact that feelings of devotion
often dissipated on release. It also recognized the difficulties of
sustaining relationships during long periods of incarceration.
These difficulties were partly practical, but they were fuelled by
pervasive anxieties about infidelity and emotional vulnerability
(Toch 1992). One fear was that partners would learn to cope on
their own, and would eventually seek independence. Another
was that partners would be unwilling to freeze or forego their
social and sexual needs. Prisoners were often paranoid about
sexual loyalty, interrogating their partners about their social
movements, asking friends outside to check on their activities,

and prohibiting them from mixing with certain people or in certain places. Unanswered phone calls or tense visits generated deep neurosis:

You find yourself going back to your cell and trying to find subtle things that you missed on the visit. You know: 'Why did she say that?' 'She wasn't very touchy-feely today, what's wrong?' [It's] a natural paranoia. Because she could be going out every night. She could have been sitting on a big fucking ten inch cock just before she come on a visit, you know. (Fin)

In suspicions of this kind, prisoners exposed their masculine insecurities and often projected upon women their own tendencies for guiltless sexual duplicity. 'Dear John' letters—apologetic terminations—were widely feared.

Many prisoners preferred to put an end to relationships when sentences began rather than cope with the stresses of trying to preserve them. Some claimed to do so selflessly, releasing their partners from the burdens of commitment. Others recognized that such acts were also self-serving, freeing them from emotional dependence. One prisoner commented that: 'Every man's weakness is his partner, and you've got to give yourself as easy bird as possible' (fieldwork notes). Other prisoners started relationships while in prison, obtaining phone numbers and addresses from friends or the partners of other prisoners, and building up from letters and phone calls to face-to-face visits.

The contrast between 'good' and 'bad' women was also striking in prisoners' descriptions of family members. Mothers and grandmothers in particular were venerated as figures of beauty, innocence, and integrity. For example:

My mum is the most beautifullest woman I know. The most loving, caring woman I know.... A brilliant mum...just a beautiful woman. Lovely, in every sense. Just my best mate. [My gran] was just so funny. So loving. She was kind of naïve in a funny sort of way as well. You know, she was a beautiful woman. Lovely. She'll help anyone, you know. She didn't discriminate against no-one. No matter what colour or creed, or whatever. She was just beautiful. (Kieran)

The unadulterated love conveyed in such descriptions was often an echo of the unconditional loyalty that these figures had themselves provided. It was also related to feelings of guilt about the anxieties and traumas that prisoners had imposed on the people who loved them. Kieran's mother had beaten him as a child, but she had also offered him unswerving support regardless of the pains he had caused her:

I can always remember my mum saying to me: 'Look, you are what you are. You are my first born and I love you to bits. The only thing I ask of you is tell me the truth. Never lie to me. Just tell me the truth and I'll be there for you'. And I respect her for that. And all the shit I've put her through as well.... And she's always there for me. Always sends my money. I love her to bits.

Given her unqualified support for him, it was significant that Kieran's mother was 'the only person I've got one hundred per cent faith in'. In contrast, in condemning his sister, Kieran's explanation revealed a common form of egotism:[28]

She started to smoke crack and that and she's a whore now and I hate her guts.... Because when I used to go to prison and secure units all over the country, she would come and visit me.... Now, it's totally, totally changed. Everything about her.... I truly hate what she's become. I've been here for three years, she's come to see me once.

High expectations of loyalty were common. While women who met these standards were idolized, those who did not were denounced in the fiercest terms. Most prisoners denied and disavowed dependency, but their demands for unconditional love implied low self-esteem. Male relatives were rarely portrayed in such strong, polar terms.[29]

Attitudes to women were not reducible to prisoners' life histories. However, there were clear links between orientations to female staff and past relationships with women (see Crewe 2006a; Crewe and Maruna 2006). Like Kieran, many prisoners struggled to maintain appropriate boundaries, seeking to establish pseudo-sexual relationships with female officers and then bridling when these women exercised authority. The switch from friendliness

[28] In describing why they were attracted to their girlfriends, prisoners often emphasized what the women did for them rather than their intrinsic characteristics. This apparent narcissism was no doubt fuelled by the culture of self-pity that imprisonment created.

[29] Four prisoners had almost identical, Oedipal life-narratives in which, after years of abuse, they had finally stood up to abusive fathers or stepfathers. The episodes in which they had done so—at which point the reign of the father figure had almost instantly collapsed—were the pivotal moments in their transitions from childhood to adult maturity, and in confirming their masculinities.

to discipline was regarded as 'two-faced', and a typically female betrayal. In such situations, female officers were often denounced as 'slags', the implication being that they were bad women as well as bad officers. These reactions showed the fragile nature of prisoners' strategies of masculine self-assertion.

For many prisoners, imprisonment amplified discourses of female protection and chivalry (Crewe 2006a and earlier chapters). An accepted rule among prisoners was that it was unacceptable to hit female staff without extremely severe provocation, if ever. Again, the connections with personal experiences were evident:

You don't hit a woman: put yourself back in a childhood state, and you see your dad doing that to your mum, you wanna kill him.... I'd kill someone who put a hand on my mum, cos that's the most precious thing to me. (Carlton)

Significantly though, it was when female officers stepped outside certain definitions of femininity—if they were perceived as too aggressive or unsympathetic—that they risked forfeiting their right to protection (Richards *et al.* 2003; Britton 2003; Crewe 2006a). The same terms were applied to women in general. Those who were old or childbearing were particularly sinless, but their moral purity could be easily polluted.

Given the prison's atmosphere of emotional suppression, it was unsurprising that female staff were lightning rods for forms of character and emotion that many prisoners did not exhibit in the presence of men. 'A lot shuts down when you're in prison. Women spark you up' one prisoner commented (fieldwork notes). Female officers were perceived as more open than male officers to displays of weakness and vulnerability, 'instead of that macho culture, stiff upper lip, not to cry, all that sort of thing' (Matt). In reference to the amount of emotion work she undertook, one female officer declared herself 'the mother of the wing' (fieldwork notes). Some teaching personnel were even more conspicuous as surrogate providers of feminine care, supplying informal counselling to prisoners who divulged their feelings: 'Sometimes I feel like ten people's wives and ten people's mothers!' one teacher commented (fieldwork notes). In classroom interactions, when prisoners deliberately provoked forms of nurture, sympathy, and affectionate censure, their cravings to be mothered were manifest.

Infantilization

As many prisoners acknowledged with embarrassment, the tedium of prison life incited a range of juvenile behaviours including pillow- and water-fights, mock arguments, and minor practical jokes (putting chillies in people's food; setting fire to hair, etc). 'Prison life turns you into a kid' (prisoner, fieldwork notes; see also Sykes 1958; Goffman 1961; Toch 1997). Other aspects of everyday life highlighted the ironies of trying to instil 'responsibility' in an environment that was intrinsically infantilizing. Prisoners had to ask staff for razors, bars of soap, and toilet paper, and took exception at the possibility of 'a grown man denying another man a drink' (prisoner, fieldwork notes) as they sought out hot water before evening lock-up. The existence of such fundamental dependencies, and the importance that became attached to Mars Bars and tobacco, seemed at odds with attempts to responsibilize prisoners.[30] As George noted trust and responsibility were defined in very limited ways:

There was a job for 'education cleaner' advertised the other week, and the notice said 'we see this as a very responsible job'. And basically all you're doing is pushing a broom up and down the corridor, y'know, so that's the level of responsibility you're given.

Further, the prison inadvertently encouraged some forms of deceit and dishonesty. The difficulty of getting pain relief when one needed it meant that prisoners feigned headaches to ensure they had reserves for the future. Prisoners with mild toothache exaggerated their pain to make sure they were considered emergencies. The environment of scarcity also encouraged some of the behaviours it purported to reform. As Isaac claimed, while trying to 'do his best' inside prison, you 'still have to be conniving. If I know I can get something for nothing, I'm going to grab it.... It's a survival thing. In the outside world...I've never stolen in my life!'

Views on imprisonment, politics, and government

Many prisoners expressed surprisingly punitive dispositions. Some declared their support for the death penalty, particularly for serious sexual offences (the idea that 'they should all be shot' was expressed

---

[30] You get excited: 'Oh yes, I'm owed five Mars Bars!' It's pathetic really, but it's just the way it is. If you were on the out, five Mars Bars is nothing. If you dropped £2.50 [outside] it wouldn't bother you. But in jail, £2.50 is a packet of burn. Small things become really important. (Rhys)

very frequently). Others asserted the need for prisons to be 'harder' and more austere. This stance was taken most often by veteran prisoners in the interests of their younger peers—to save them from the lives of serial imprisonment that they had experienced, or 'teach them some morals'. These prisoners pilloried prison managers for turning establishments from fearsome domains of discipline and hardship to 'holiday camps' that, they claimed, could have little deterrent effect. Such views were consistent with the widespread perception (even among prisoners with histories of addiction, abuse, deprivation, and mental illness) that criminal acts were, in essence, matters of cost-benefit analysis that could be discouraged if the penalties were sufficiently severe. Younger prisoners who publicly supported the idea of a harsher system did so for different reasons. There was macho credibility in claiming that one preferred 'real bird' or 'hard nicks' and could do time without the need for 'soft' luxuries.

It was significant that more punitive regimes had clearly not prevented those who advocated them from returning to crime. In promoting the idea of a harsher system, these prisoners revealed almost masochistic yearnings both to be punished for their repeated harm to others and—in their terms—to be 'cured' of their criminal tendencies.[31] Significantly too, when they decried the ineffectiveness of prison they signalled their sense of helplessness. Responsibility was shifted away from the self: 'It don't work', stated one prisoner, 'this is my twelfth sentence' (fieldwork notes). Calls for the prison to provide more 'help' and 'rehabilitation', with the terms defined rather vaguely, likewise conveyed desperation for wholesale solutions to be imposed on a hapless and powerless self. Harsh punishment was unlikely to help, but it presented itself as an easy solution.

At the same time, statements of agency dominated public discourse about crime, morality, and rehabilitation. As Chapter 4 indicated, it was important for prisoners of all kinds to feel that their adaptations were chosen independently of institutional imperatives, and that they alone were responsible for any decisions to 'reform'. 'Prisons can't change you', prisoners often declared, 'it's up to you to change yourself'. In a similar vein, prisoners consistently asserted that they had been 'raised to know the

---

[31] In his life story, Cameron repeatedly expressed regret that no one had ever fought back against him or 'taught him a lesson': 'I think I needed a real good hiding when I got out there. Just to try and calm me down'.

difference between right and wrong'. The implication was partly that they remained moral beings even if their behaviours violated conventional moral norms. At the same time, this view suggested that prisoners were responsible for their offending, and that neither moral deficiencies, parental failings, nor other environmental factors were accountable for their criminal behaviour. Indeed, in their explanations of their life paths, prisoners were deeply unsociological in their reasoning. Most emphasized choice and self-determination even as they detailed lives that were catalogues of social misfortune. Although Muslim prisoners presented a more theoretically informed view of crime, featuring references to inequality and deprivation, the prisoner community as a whole was deeply apolitical in its collective identity and self-description.

Another feature of prisoners' public discourse on crime and punishment was a pervasive cynicism about government intentions. Politicians and the judiciary were widely perceived as corrupt and self-interested (see Clemmer 1940). Many prisoners believed that the government had little interest in reducing crime because criminal justice agencies provided so much state employment. Such accusations were often directed at prison staff themselves: 'You want us to come back, you wouldn't have jobs otherwise.' Many prison policies were also viewed with suspicion. Prisoners repeatedly claimed that drug-testing had pushed prisoners from cannabis to heroin use, because opiates remained in the urine stream for less time than cannabinoids and were thus less easy to detect (see Crewe 2005b).[32] Some concluded that this was precisely the aim of drug testing—to turn more prisoners into heroin addicts in order to obtain more money for treatment programmes. More often, this consequence was regarded as being typical of systemic stupidity. Cannabis was considered a harmless drug that eased the pains of imprisonment with little financial or physical cost.[33] Staff confirmed that, when the drug of choice in prison was cannabis, officers had turned a blind eye to what had a 'calming effect' without generating significant debt or exploitation.

[32] Experienced prisoners noted that the amount of drugs in prison had decreased considerably since the early 1990s.

[33] Prisoners and staff agreed that the heroin economy was more volatile and its outcomes more significant. 'The consequences of heroin dealing bear no relation to the laid back attitude associated with cannabis [and] the dealers [are] qualitatively more businesslike and ruthless' (George, by letter).

Many other aspects of the regime were beheld with distrust, often with some justification. Televisions and PlayStations were viewed as devices designed to pacify and divide; the clandestine integration of some sex offenders into the mainstream prison population was seen as a strategy aimed at reducing trust between prisoners; and courses were dismissed as hollow interventions introduced only 'for government statistics' or to 'tick boxes', to provide an appearance of treatment. Uniformed staff often colluded in this cynicism, both about the folly of managerial policies and about the ineffectiveness of imprisonment.

Emotions, authenticity, and masculine identity

Despite the pervasive tendency for prisoners to put on 'masks' or 'fronts' as coping strategies (see also Schmid and Jones 1991; Jewkes 2005a), Wellingborough was considered less demanding of such performances than most other establishments. The tone here was set by staff. Prisoners explained that, in some prisons, the hostility that officers exuded translated not into solidarity between prisoners, but tension and mutual suspicion—a sense that one's guard needed to be up with both prisoners and staff (Liebling 2004: 364). Comments that it was easier to show kindness and emotion in Wellingborough than in other prisons pointed to the relatively relaxed atmosphere that staff helped to promote.

Discussions of identity affirmed a principle of authenticity. Fronting was a means of disguising weakness. To be seen as fronting was therefore in itself a mark of underlying insecurity. Paradoxically then, prisoners were tacitly exhorted both to be genuine and not to show weakness or fragility. *Players* were the prisoners most vocal in avowing that the person they were in prison was their authentic self, and that the prison stripped away rather than added layers of inauthenticity. It was in prison, they argued, when men were shorn of guns and gangs, that true bravery was exhibited. 'Everyone comes in standard', said Leon, borrowing institutional terminology to make his point: 'You judge them on what they're like inside, not what they've done.'[34] Boasts

---

[34] 'You get people going on about "I was a rogue, I'd do this and if I had my gun with me I'd do this to you" and I'd think "well you haven't got your gun, you're in prison. So what exactly are you saying?" And saying, "if I had my gun I'd do this and do that to you", really and truly they're weak. Without that they're nothing'. (VJ)

about acts of violence or drug deals outside prison, whether true or not, were dismissed as irrelevant to the prison environment, where craft and mettle were truly tested. These prisoners defined fronting as the making of idle or unsupportable proclamations. In general, these were men who projected threat and confidence, and were prepared to 'back up' their claims with violence. Although their public identities were, therefore, highly macho—the kinds that other prisoners considered phoney, puffed-up versions of masculinity—they were not conscious performances, but engrained aspects of masculine identity.

Other prisoners also endorsed the idea of authenticity, but presented more complex readings of personal and social identity. Men with prison experience mocked what they considered to be macho pretensions of confidence. They saw men who bragged about their crimes and connections as troublesome and immature. This category included young *pragmatists* who strutted and postured around the wings and *players* who in turn condemned *pragmatists* for being 'plastic gangsters'. *Enthusiasts* dismissed these 'jack-the-lads' as men who could not see their moral errors and faced lives of crime and prison. *Stoics* argued that their macho stylings went beyond what the environment necessitated and reflected deep-seated masculine insecurities. They recommended sincerity both for prudential reasons and because they believed that respect could be generated through confident authenticity:

I think it's important that you don't put fronts on, that you don't put masks on and try and be who you're not. It causes problems. I've seen lads come to prison, and they'll sit there and they'll tell you that they've committed this crime and that crime. And they're just trying to fit in. I would encourage anyone who comes to prison [to] just be yourself and take each day as it comes.... The golden rule I've always made is just be yourself in prison. And people will accept you for who you are. (Tommy)

Imagine I'm a first timer and we've padded up together, and I say to you: 'What are the rules that I need to know?' What would you say to me?

I'd just say, be yourself. That's it. That's all you can be, in prison. Just be yourself. (Den)

It was easy for prisoners who exuded confidence and experience to make these recommendations. Although it was true that being oneself was generally admired, this was especially the case if years of imprisonment had tailored one's character for the prison environment. For other prisoners, authenticity was sensible in principle, but could be dangerous in practice. Ian advised that one should not 'act big and hard' for prudential reasons—because being found out as a fake would be just cause for retribution. At the same time, prudence required him to put on some kind of 'prison face' rather than expose his frailties and sensitivities. Authenticity was harder for some prisoners than others.

Sexuality provided a case in point. Many prisoners claimed that gay men in prison would not face violence or persecution, and would be respected for being themselves. Others expressed anxiety or disgust about the prospect of being around gay men. At best, it was argued, gay prisoners would be tolerated providing that they 'controlled their urges' or 'don't bring it to my door' (Den). 'I've got no problem', said Kyle. 'As long as they don't try kissing me or touching me, they can do what the fuck they want, no discrimination at all about that on my part.' The fact that there were no openly gay prisoners in Wellingborough was indicative of concerns among those who did not fit standard prison moulds that authenticity was approved only within certain boundaries. Matt explained that the danger of outing himself was that he would not be able to stand by and let a prisoner mock him. Declaring his sexuality would therefore bring trouble upon himself. Likewise, for prisoners whose characters were naturally passive or sensitive, prison was a site where it was hazardous to act without some pretence. It was not just weaker prisoners, therefore, but also men who did not conform to certain kinds of masculine ideals who most often discussed the need to 'front'.

Other prisoners acknowledged that they could not express their full emotional range while in prison, and had become accustomed to regulating emotional expression:

You can't really express yourself like you can out there.... It's a cold place. You have to be kind of stone-faced. You only really show half of your emotions and feelings whilst you're inside. The other half is for outside.... Anything that's a weakness, you keep that to yourself.

So how do you deal with stress and sadness or being upset while you're in here?

To be honest, I don't really get upset whilst I'm in here. I just lock up any feelings that would get me into feeling sad or down or whatever, I just lock them away. As soon as I get sent down, they're locked away.... You're not really yourself in jail, you have to adjust to the environment you're in. Once you do that, it's just getting by. (Ewan)

A lot of people, even me, sometimes I don't even realise I'm doing it, it's just subconsciously you do it, your mind switches, you've got part of your brain that's designated for when you come to prison and it just turns on. (Kyle)

One function of these adjustments was to conceal emotion from other prisoners. Bradley talked of keeping his feelings 'on the inside, if you're really hurting.... Just carry on being yourself, then no one can say anything to you because they don't know what's going on in your head.' In this respect, emotional inhibition had preventive ends. Many prisoners knew that to display certain feelings could set in motion processes that would lead them into conflict. Ross was reluctant to express worries because he knew he would be called 'a pussy...and I'll get angry with them'. Leon sought to protect himself from his own backlash: 'If things happen, I wouldn't tell no-one, because I wouldn't want them to laugh behind my back. That could cause trouble if I find out about them, and then you're back to square one again.' Remaining in control of one's emotional reactions was a challenging part of the prison experience.

Another common strategy was to feign indifference in order to disguise one's hopes of progression:

Certain subjects will come up [and] walls will go straight up. Just what I'm like, [or] that I don't give a fuck about the jail and that I don't give a fuck about whether I get this or whether I get that. Or I don't care what happens, when really I do. (Ross)

Clearly though, prisoners were not always so cognisant of these strategies. Some served pre-consciously to avert disappointment and suppress emotions that threatened mental control. In prisoners' own terms, the prison was a 'place of negativity' (Tyler), which 'sever[ed] the nerve endings' and generated paranoia: 'You're on edge all the time, to a certain extent' (Luke). Some men noted the difficulty of showing their 'caring side' (Ronan), or described themselves as quieter or less lively inside prison than in the community. Imprisonment dulled and narrowed the positive end of the affective spectrum, while intensifying its negative frequencies. Going 'on autopilot' (prisoner, fieldwork notes) and learning to blank out feelings altogether were normal techniques of coping, to which some prisoners became oblivious. Asked if he felt that his prison persona was the same as his 'real identity', Max's response was telling: 'I don't even know if I know what the real me is, I've got that many masks covering up myself.'

Some prisoners struggled to maintain public performances of masculine stoicism (see also Jewkes 2002, 2005a). Those who strained to inure themselves to the prison's lacerating emotional climate had to secrete their feelings through alternative channels. Zack, an enthusiast with a forceful public persona, disclosed his need to cry 'twice a month, just to let the tension out. If I don't cry, I'm going to go fucking nuts.' Many prisoners emphasized the importance of the gym in 'releasing that aggression' (Wilson), relieving anxieties and aiding sleep: 'All the frustration I've gathered over a couple of days or months, I take it all out in the gym' (Cameron). Prisoners who self-harmed talked of the emotional functions of cutting the skin—its capacity both to remind them that their feelings still existed and to liberate them from the body: 'All that stress and tension, it flowed out with the blood' (Fin).

Although most prisoners claimed that prison had no impact on their masculine self-identity, the terms they used to describe their emotional adaptations often suggested otherwise. Imprisonment seemed to reinforce conventionally masculine identities either of blustering bravado or taciturn restraint. And while most prisoners denied their own affectations, they were quick to identify those of other men and to cite gender as a key determinant of prison culture:

It's just men, isn't it, macho bullshit. It's like Joe. Out there he's a good bloke, family man, top geezer. In here he has to put on a little bit of front to save face. I know that, he knows that, people that know him know that. We all know. We obviously don't verbally mention it. (Kyle)

Prisoners who knew each other outside prison colluded in each other's performances, in the knowledge that they too were enmeshed in a culture of emotional artifice.

Indeed, there was a striking and largely unspoken discrepancy between public actions and private acknowledgements. Prisoners who self-harmed received public disdain but also private compassion. When a prisoner in Wellingborough committed suicide, public pronouncements among some prisoners that the victim was a 'fraggle' were offset by widespread backstage sympathy and a publicly organized collection to buy flowers for his funeral. Almost everyone had an abstract appreciation of the private troubles of the strangers around them, and recognized that pain and insecurity were shared aspects of the prison experience. Yet almost all prisoners were complicit in reproducing a public culture of emotional denial.

This disjuncture between a public culture of masculine confidence and private feelings of anxiety and powerlessness has been widely reported in prison studies (Toch 1992; Newton 1994). Sykes (1958) argued that prisoners were 'figuratively castrated' by the deprivation of heterosexual relations, and that, in the absence of women, only those aspects of identity that were 'recognized or appreciated by men' derived public value. The prison's tense environment and its denial of normal markers of masculine status led to public enactments of toughness and resilience. These served as a shield against potential victimization and feelings of emasculation. Jewkes (2005a; 2002) describes the necessity of maintaining a 'hard' façade in order to survive the rigours of imprisonment. There are alternative ways of achieving masculinity, for example, in identities such as the 'scholar' and 'tradesman'. However, the hegemonic form of masculinity is one of 'controlled aggression', and this version is reinforced through the subjugation of less powerful versions of masculinity. Accounts of men's imprisonment have consistently identified these dynamics, describing cultures where homophobia is rampant, traces of weakness and 'femininity' are impugned, and prisoners appear engaged in perpetual battles to dominate others and prove their mettle (e.g. Scraton et al. 1991; Johnson 1987; Thurston 1996; Pollock 2004; Sabo et al. 2001).

Jewkes cites Gilmour's (1990: 224) claim that 'the harsher the environment and the scarcer the resources, the more manhood is stressed as inspiration and goal'. It follows, therefore, that the prisoner world in Wellingborough was not the arena of hyper-masculine aggression and ruthless brutality that studies of more depriving contexts have reported (for example, McVicar 1974; Boyle 1977; Scraton et al. 1991; Sabo et al. 2001). Certainly, imprisonment encouraged traits of emotional fortitude and physical self-reliance, and inhibited 'feminine' emotions such as compassion and care while licensing states of anger and apathy.[35] At the same time, Wellingborough's culture regulated 'excessive' masculinity, its hegemonic form was to some degree disputed, and prisoners could 'accomplish' credible masculinities through a variety of strategies and identities (see Messerschmidt 1993). As indicated above (and in Crewe 2006a), female staff played a

---

[35] That is, 'kicking off' was considered a viable way to express emotion, but crying was not.

variety of roles in these processes of masculine validation—on the whole unwittingly—as female objects against which identity could be defined and contrasted. Meanwhile, in providing parenting classes and small business training, the institution offered some alternative sources of masculine esteem.

Players exhibited a 'bad-ass' masculinity that objectified women and censured all expressions of weakness or femininity among men. Many younger *pragmatists* were self-described 'lads' who upheld notions of masculine status that venerated sexual promiscuity, drinking, expensive cars, and clothing; others sought out 'feminine comfort' to shore up masculine insecurities. *Stoics* and *retreatists* were more likely to present themselves as 'decent blokes'—resolute, upstanding, and emotionally self-contained. *Enthusiasts* exhibited a model of muscular citizenship, an unbending devotion to moral cause. These were all relatively traditional masculine roles, and all can be seen as ways of re-asserting masculine esteem in a culture that threatened and besieged it (Newton 1994). Nonetheless, it is important to emphasize the heterogeneity of these scripts and the fact that not all were defined by the callous brutality that accounts of prison life often present.

Emotion zones

Behaviours were also spatially structured. All social institutions have emotional economies of some kind: informal rules that sanction emotional expression, channel its possible forms and delimit where it can occur (see Crawley 2004b, in relation to officers). Wellingborough contained a number of 'emotion zones' that permitted a broader emotional register than most areas of the prison. One was the visits room, where prisoners showed forms of warmth and tenderness that were taboo on the landings. Men clucked over babies, dwelled in embraces with loved ones, and displayed open affection, as though their emotional identities had been awoken en route from the wings.[36] Indeed, once returned from visits, prisoners did not talk publicly about these displays or of the feelings that their visits exhumed. The emotional behaviour of other prisoners on visits was also (under normal circumstances)

---

[36] At the same time, a number of prisoners described the performative dimension of visits. Many sought to protect their families from anxiety, and therefore overstated their emotional health or reassured loved ones that they had no troubles or concerns.

disqualified knowledge: barred from use in the derision of others. To mock the appearance of someone else's loved ones was also a breach of unwritten rules.

Classrooms also harboured alternative emotional climates. Prisoners in cookery classes shared food and complimented each other's efforts; ingredients were exchanged without the rules that applied on the wings. In pottery lessons, men praised artistic ability, swapped tips, and shared pride and disappointment in their pottery products. In sociology lessons, they relaxed into student identities that allowed them to express hesitancy in their views, mock their own prejudices, and disclose some personal details. In the philosophy class, discussions of religion and politics took place between prisoners with wildly different perspectives without tension or reprisals. This atmosphere was cultivated by education staff and their particular attitude towards prisoners. In the same way, the chapel was described as 'an outlet from prison' whose more peaceful environment was a consequence of how staff and volunteers spoke to and respected prisoners. In Wilson's terms: 'It's a different atmosphere. The people there, they're more friendly towards you, they just talk to you differently and I reckon they listen a bit more.' In a range of environments, kindness, generosity, and emotional disclosure were permitted and there was some transient escape from the emotional side of penal domination. For most prisoners though, it was only when alone that they could discard public masks and truly be themselves (Jewkes 2002, 2005a). As one commented, 'as soon as that door hits, it's *my* time' (fieldwork notes). Pain, emotion, and fears for the future seeped out largely behind closed doors.

Private life

I'm always thinking about things. Never stop thinking.

What sort of things do you think about?

I don't know really, looking after me son and stuff and...but then I think about getting back into trouble. I'm always thinking about me family, me son. Me ex-girlfriend, I think about her a lot as well, I don't know.

So what do you do when you're banged up at eight, how do you then pass the rest of the evening?

I just watch telly, write a letter or something, listen to the radio. Go to bed about half ten, eleven o'clock. Sometimes it's two o'clock in the morning, depends, when I can't sleep. Weekends are the worst cos you're banged up at half four so you've got a lot of time. But then I can't sleep cos I'm always thinking about things. So, I just watch telly there's nothing else to do really.

Are there any times of the day or places in the jail where you do feel a bit more relaxed?

At eight 'o clock at night.

And how are you different at that time? How does that change you?

You just get behind the door and, I don't know, you're on your own aren't you. You've got time to think and it's on your own. I prefer night time in this place. I hate it when I have to get up in the morning, I hate it. The day's just begun hasn't it. I can't wait, in the morning I'm just looking forward to the night. Just to get banged up again. (Howard)

During the days, cells were only semi-private places. When locked shut, single cells were places of sanctuary, but also loneliness and regret. Cells were sites of reflection, where prisoners mulled over their lives and hatched plans of happier futures. Many reported having trouble sleeping, being haunted by memories of their crimes and the harms they had inflicted on others. Others worried endlessly about affairs outside prison that they were powerless to influence: partners in debt, ill children, dying parents, and so on. Indeed, many men claimed that prison itself was 'easy', but that the pain of practical helplessness to affect these external events was considerable. When informed that wives had requested divorces, or told on the phone by their own children that they had 'got a new daddy now' (prisoner, fieldwork notes), the anguish of confinement was palpable.

Worries centred on two other main areas. The first was time, space, and change. Many prisoners feared that lives outside would move on while theirs remained static. Time inside and outside worked at different paces.[37] Friends would settle down or forget about them; girlfriends would transfer affections; and communities might no longer be recognizable. One might return to a world where one's place was no longer clear. As Jewkes (2005b)

---

[37] Time also figured in a number of ways in discussions about adjustments to release: life outside seemed 'faster', especially the pace of traffic. The feeling that time had been lost led to compensations not just in terms of major life issues but everyday behaviours: 'You try moving and talking fast, you just seem to be in a rush everywhere' (Martin). Some prisoners also claimed that, having been socialized into the prison's timetable, they struggled on release to concentrate on anything for more than a two-hour time period.

has described, prisoners with long sentences expressed a sense of existing in a parallel time zone to the free world. Time slowed, leaving prisoners feeling trapped in a monotonous and unending present, with little sense of development. Some disclosed concerns not just about the denial of lifecourse opportunities—to form relationships or have children (Jamieson and Grounds 2005)—but also about losing the sense of their selfhood. As Chapter 5 noted, those who had maintained façades for years on end expressed fears that they could no longer split these social identities from their private selves (Jewkes 2002), and that the identities they had suspended on entering prison might no longer 'make sense'. For many men, incarceration provided too much opportunity to marinate in these existential thoughts on the nature of life, self, and society (see Goffman 1961; Cohen and Taylor 1972; Medlicott 2001). The sense of sheer boredom was pervasive.

A second fear for prisoners was returning to the lifestyles that had brought them to prison. This concern was particularly intense for ex-addicts, who dreaded submitting again to drug or alcohol use, particularly those who expected to be sent to hostels, where temptations were rife. For many men, these worries were constant preoccupations that made release a prospect of dread as well as excitement. Jacob said that staying away from drugs was his only concern: 'Because drugs bring me here'. Kieran was 'petrified of getting out . . . I'm scared of [crack] more than anything. It has a strong, strong, strong grip over me. Stronger than anything else.' Connor admitted being 'paranoid about getting out. . . . Obviously, I want to be out there. But it does worry me, what's going to happen. All it takes is one wrong move and I'm back on the drugs [and] coming to jail again pretty quickly.' Alfie's main worry was returning to heroin and never seeing his children: 'Cos I've neglected them for so long [and] I know for a fact I'll not survive another smack habit.'

More than anything else, these prisoners dreamed of remaining drug-free and knew that abstention was the key to contentment. But they were also realistic about their narcotic proclivities. As Kieran explained: 'If I don't smoke it I know I'll make money and I live a good life. But there's a little percentage of me that does want to smoke it, and that's all I need.' Ronan also recognized the ease with which he could descend once more into drug use:

One thing I'm worried about, Ben, is going back out there and getting like back into the drugs again. . . . I'm on the first couple of steps of a ladder, if you know what I mean, and it's so easy to fall back down to the bottom of the ladder when I get out. But what I want from life is a nice wife, couple of kids, nice house, nice car, and good job.

The ambitions outlined here were common, especially among men who defined themselves as drug abusers rather than professional criminals. Most prisoners did not express disdain for nine-to-five workers and mundane lifestyles. On the contrary, a large number longed for routine domesticity, a normal family life, and a legitimate job i.e. aspirations that sat within mainstream culture (Nightingale 1993). 'Since I've been coming into jails I've kind of always wanted a normal life', said Seb. 'A normal nuclear family.' Dreams of work centred on generative activity such as youth work and drug counselling (Maruna 2001), or self-employment (e.g. running cafes, barber shops, or fencing companies): work that appeared to offer some level of control and autonomy.

Cells were the closest that prisoners had to homes, and most attached considerable symbolic significance to their state and appearance. *Enthusiasts* took particular pride in the cleanliness of their cells, equating this with moral purity. *Players* emphasized the stocks and possessions that made their lifestyles more comfortable. A minority of prisoners protected themselves from becoming too comfortable in their cells, living in deliberate austerity and warning against confusing the prison with home, or becoming fixated on the internal environment: 'The minute you stop dreaming about the out, or your dreams are about prison, you're in trouble' (prisoner, fieldwork notes; and see Jewkes 2005b). For most men however, it was important to deck out the environment in a way that maximized comfort and conveyed identity.

Once locked up, prisoners watched television, wrote letters, read newspapers, books or magazines, drank tea and smoked cigarettes, and did 'pad workouts' (e.g. physical exercises). Some watched soap operas almost ritualistically, or developed comforting routines in which they rationed roll-ups and hot drinks for particular times of the evening. During day time lock-up periods, many played escapist, energetic dance music of a form that seemed deeply unsuited to the immediate environment but reminded them of better times. Music transported the self outside the walls of the prison, producing narcotic echoes and recollections of being out clubbing, or providing the elemental rush of vitality that imprisonment otherwise inhibited. Matt described his preference for pulsating guitar music: 'I wanna feel alive. Prison, it destroys your spirit, it destroys your soul, it destroys everything. It just destroys you as a personality.' Sentiments of this kind were rarely discussed openly, but they were frequently referred to in interviews, even by prisoners like Ashley, whose public identities were founded on self-confidence and mastery of the environment:

Just before you go to sleep, just before you nod off, that's when that lonely thing hits you: 'I'm here on my own', you know what I mean. 'I should have a woman, my family around'. Prison's a cold place. (Ashley)

Liberty, the quintessential deprivation of imprisonment, was missed most of all—although with some ambivalence for retreatists and other former addicts. The term itself was rarely used. Rather, prisoners expressed their loss of freedom in more mundane terms: the inability to 'pop down the corner-shop for a paper or a Mars Bar', to 'just go for a walk'.

Conclusion

It was possible in Wellingborough to identify a dominant system of norms. These norms can be summarized as follows: be straight and authentic with other prisoners—don't lie, boast, or exaggerate, don't be two-faced, don't fake it, be yourself; but don't show fear or emotional weakness and don't back down; don't trust anyone who you don't know well, don't give away private details, be wary and suspicious, but be respectful and don't present yourself as someone who thinks they are superior to other prisoners; take care of yourself, wear nice clothes, be hygienic and well turned-out; don't denigrate someone else's colour or culture, but stand up for your own people; don't let the system beat you, but be opportunistic, and take advantage of what it offers; don't borrow what you can't repay, don't get caught up with drugs if you can't take the risks; don't grass, except to protect yourself or others in extreme circumstances; objectify (most) females, but don't demean 'good women', and be respectful of old people and children.

These norms undoubtedly exerted some control over public behaviour. As Clemmer (1958: 152) noted, without them, the prisoner community would be harsher, more conflictual, and 'more woefully disorganized' than it already was. Yet, as prison researchers have suggested consistently, there was a striking gap between public ideals and actual behaviour. Norm violations were frequent, and, in private, ideological deviations from public statements were common. Prisoners held vastly different views about women, the morality of crimes, the acceptability of profiting from other prisoners, and the situations in which informing was legitimate. There was no consensus of values. Men who breached code prescriptions were not necessarily those 'on the border of two cultures' (1958: 110), with allegiances to groups outside the prison. More often, they were prisoners in search of personal gain or those with relatively long-held beliefs about moral behaviour.

Even in public, few norms were universally accepted, and their terms were not fixed or rigidly defined. Behaviour was guided less by a set of unbending stipulations than a set of conventions about appropriate action. As Clemmer (1958: 155) noted, there was 'no hard and fast code' and even those norms that were generally accepted were 'subject to different interpretations'. Few prisoners held themselves or others to the kinds of absolutist standards described by Sykes and Messinger. In all areas of principle and action, there were caveats, ambiguities, and mitigating circumstances.

That these conventions could be contested and negotiated also made them *resources* in interpersonal dynamics. They could be used to screen or justify exploitation, and to disguise behaviour that was potentially open to censure. Some prisoners were more skilled than others in defining norms in their favour—pushing other prisoners into storing goods on their behalf in the interests of 'loyalty', for example. Others, often men who had already 'proved' themselves, stepped outside ideals at the same time as they imposed them, working closely with officers without being seen as grasses, or intervening in other prisoners' lives while exhorting them to 'do their own time'. Norms were also enacted in different ways on different wings, creating distinctive localized cultures. On the VTU, for example, where a high proportion of prisoners sought to avoid the obligations of trade, the informal economy was less developed than elsewhere in the prison. There was also greater antipathy about drug dealing in this part of the prison.

Codes of conduct were sources of pain and exploitation as well as resolutions to common problems. The informal economy shored up deficiencies and offered narcotic means of coping, but most fights and pressures were linked to the debts and exchanges produced by trade. The defensive, prudential tone of many prisoner rules is worth noting. These were warnings about the perils of interpersonal relations as much as means of combating the essential pains of imprisonment. Many maxims were also contradictory, or, at least, they defined acceptable action in ways that made prison social life a matter of walking a tightrope— between the hazards of weakness, aggression, and inauthenticity, for example.

While the environment militated against many forms of empathy, solidarity, and emotional expression, it was also infused with moral codes and judgments. Between prisoners, there was 'casual cruelty' (Medlicott 2005), but also routine kindness. Violence was not celebrated uncritically and was bound by rules about its appropriate form and usage. Nor was it arbitrary, irrational or reducible to notions of pathological individuals (Edgar *et al.* 2003). Rather, it was shaped by interpersonal dynamics that were themselves structured by the terms of the regime. The everyday social world was atomized, but it was not a Hobbesian jungle of amorality, brutality, and ruthless individualism.

9
Concluding Comments

In 'The Penalisation of Policy and the Rise of the Neo-Liberalism', Loïc Wacquant suggests that, in Western Europe, the 'left hand' of the welfare state has been supplemented by a more punitive 'right hand' in the regulation of the working classes. A distinctive marriage of neo-liberalism, welfarism, and social authoritarianism has combined to aid and impel the urban underclass into specific kinds of acceptable citizenship. Both social *and* penal interventions have intensified. 'The invisible hand of the market and the iron fist of the state combine and complement each other to make the lower classes accept desocialized wage labour and the social instability it brings in its wake' (Wacquant 2001b: 404). The prison has returned 'to the frontline of institutions entrusted with maintaining social order' (ibid.), sweeping up those who pose threats to social security through their defiance of, or irrelevance to, the relentless passage of the service economy. In the US, Wacquant argues, where institutions of social welfare have already withered, or simply never existed, the solution to these social problems have been purely penal: 'all out carceralisation' (Wacquant 2001b: 406).

Wacquant is describing relatively long-term transformations in social and political management. It would be surprising if their techniques were duplicated in all institutions of the state. Prison systems are shaped by ebbs and flows in national and organizational tides, and have their own internal dynamics (Liebling 2004). However, law, order, and punishment have been prominent tropes in New Right ideology (Sparks 2007). The re-assertion of state authority, the belief in social discipline, and the critique of the liberal welfare state have shunted penality to the forefront of the social-political project while *also* refiguring the specific aims and strategies of imprisonment. Broadly, at least, modes of regulation within prisons seem to have reproduced those applied to 'problematic' populations outside.

In the US—although there is huge variation within its vast penal network—this has largely entailed punitive austerity. Within and outside the prison, it has meant increasing indifference to the conditions of the subordinate and a hands-*off* approach to the social causes of offending, alongside a highly authoritarian, firmly hands-*on* attitude to offenders themselves. Wacquant depicts the Los Angeles County Jail as little more than a concrete tomb (2002). California's prison system—the largest in the US, and larger than those of all European nations bar Russia and Ukraine—is likewise characterized as an idle and overcrowded zoo, dedicated only to containment and neutralization.

In the Prison Service of England and Wales, conditions are incomparably more humane, and the rehabilitative mission has not been abandoned. As this book has shown though, this is a particular version of rehabilitation. It has authoritarian as well as humanitarian features. It is more paternalistic than maternalistic, more pushy than caring, and more prescriptive than liberal. It insists on compliance and demands reform, and it rewards conditionally. Yet it also eschews conventional methods of paternal power. It is not experienced as 'an unrelenting imposition of authority' (Scraton *et al.* 1991: 63). Coercion, force and violence are not its most prominent characteristics. It polices indirectly and anonymously. Its policies are not the direct, obtrusive measures that 'chafe and vex' (Sparks *et al.* 1996: 323), as such. It is tight and intrusive, yet in some ways imperceptible; its grip is firm and enduring, yet its character is soft and light; and while its scope is wide, its source is diffuse. It has shifted up and out, but also moved more closely in. It is both dispersed and expanded. Instead of direct regulation, it affords space where autonomy can be exercised, albeit in limited forms, and 'responsible behaviour' can be exhibited. It makes itself visible and flexes its muscles only when this strategy fails (Hannah-Moffat 2005). As in the community then, assistance and authority are interlinked: the 'smack of firm government' (Sparks 2007: 85) is poised in the background to make sure that opportunity, support, and self-correction are grasped and pursued appropriately.

The pains of imprisonment and the managerial era

Penal power appears emblematic of the late-modern era. In its normal state, it is light and evanescent, rather than heavy and solid (Bauman 2000: 25). It is predominantly psychological rather than physical (Foucault 1977). Whether—as Foucault implied—it punishes more effectively but no more humanely than its institutional predecessors is arguable. It is important not be flippant about the fact that compared to only two decades ago, prisoners are much less likely to live with fear and hatred for their captors, be systematically brutalized, share cell-space with their own excrement, and be deprived for days on end of showers, fresh air, and clean clothing (see Jameson and Allison 1995). Critics of managerialism have a tendency to present a dystopian picture of criminal justice organizations that seems to disregard the degradations of the pre-reform era and ignore the improvements that modern management techniques have secured.

On the other hand, among some practitioners, there is a worrying assumption that the reformist battles have been won. Prisons are so clearly more decent, cleaner, more purposeful places—the argument goes—that there is no obvious manifesto for reform. This view underestimates the complex pains and new frustrations of the modern prison. Legitimacy has been raised in certain respects, and it is vital not to understate these improvements, but in other ways the prison experience has become harsher. Imprisonment has become 'deeper' and 'heavier' since the early 1990s. Movements are more restricted, security, has been tightened, and risk has become the trump-card of the system. Meanwhile, shifts in the way that power is organized and authority is exercised have created new weights and burdens, particularly around issues of powerlessness, autonomy, insecurity, and the meeting of personal needs. The carceral experience is less directly oppressive, but more gripping. It demands more and risks less. It is described by prisoners less in terms of weight than 'tightness'. Instead of brutalizing, destroying and denying the self, it grips, harnesses, and appropriates it for its own project. It turns the self into a vehicle of power rather than a place of last refuge. Although these pains seem unlikely to have the very long-term psychological consequences of brutalization, in the moment they may feel no less frustrating. What this suggests above all else is that, while penal pains can be reduced to some degree, pain is intrinsic to imprisonment, and it is much easier to change the mode of power and alter the pains than to evacuate pain and powerlessness from the prison experience.

The modern pains are not simply outcomes of the inherent conditions of imprisonment, many of which have been to some degree alleviated. Many of them are relatively invisible on the landings. They cannot be described by prisoners or understood by staff in the ways that missing one's wife or fearing for one's safety can be. Nor are they necessarily the fault of staff, unlike many of the privations of the past, which represented abuses of power or derelictions of managerial duty. Some are systemic, the consequences of bureaucratic inefficiency, overcrowding, and under resourcing. Some are the consequences of national strategies adopted in the interests of compliance and control. Others have little to do with the Prison Service specifically, and more to do with the nature of sentencing and the operation of psychological power in a climate that is increasingly risk-averse. For prison reformers, there are fewer clear enemies or easy targets.

In this context, power can be unwelcome for those who wield it as well as being corrosive for those who are subjected to its terms. Power-holders at all levels of the prison can feel alienated from the system they implement. Psychologists are discouraged from 'risking risk' and find themselves cast as captors; governors are forced to squeeze more prisoners into finite spaces. Almost nothing is known about the values and self-images of these occupational groups—how they feel about the power they exercise, whether they resist the demands that are made of them, and other such issues. Officers readily describe the difficulties of holding power and the increasing complexities of the job. Just as the task of being a prisoner has become more demanding, so has the job of being an officer. It is they who must get to grips with the complex terms of indeterminate sentences, with confusion over the fate of foreign national prisoners, with relaying to prisoners the opaque outcomes of conservative decision-making for which they hold no responsibility, and with handling prisoners whose frustrations they often cannot resolve. It is clear that how they do these things—how they use their power—defines the quality of life for prisoners to a very significant degree (Sparks et al. 1996; Liebling 2004; Cheliotis and Liebling 2006). Officers may not steer institutions or determine their techniques, but as the main mediators of institutional power, they can disrupt them considerably and make them markedly more or less punishing. Nowadays, it could be argued that they play a greater role in ensuring decency than compliance. This role makes them extremely influential, as Mathieson (1965) argued, but it also means that they feel rather less powerful than they seem, as Sykes (1958) noted. It should not be surprising that there are failings in their use of power when they are in this position.

Indeed, the achievement of legitimacy is difficult in part because there is so much distance and so many joins and divisions between the architects of power and its frontline representatives. For prisoners, there is little hope of tempering frustrations when the forces that produce them are outside the system or cannot be seen within it. In theory, and to external audiences, the prison has become more transparent and accountable. This does not necessarily translate into clarity or intelligibility on the landings. Power becomes less visible, less tangible, less challengeable and in some senses less accountable. This state is not at all unique to the prison. As Bauman (2000) notes, it is a widespread feature of contemporary life. When power can operate from a distance, direct engagement between the state and its subjects is unnecessary. In prison, however, the meaning of power and the consequences of its failings are intensified.

The question of whether and in what circumstances managerialism exacerbates or diminishes these tendencies is germane here. Most senior managers in the Prison Service report the same disquiet as academics. They recognize concerns that managerialism can too easily become an aim in itself, rather than a means to humanitarian ends; that it can fail to take seriously the sanctity of the individual (Feeley and Simon 1992); and that it can clamp the gaze of practitioners on narrow outputs and blind them to social and moral outcomes (Garland 1996). One danger is that modern managers fixate on 'performance' and smooth management at the expense of decency. The prison becomes a virtual entity, shrouded by a cloak of bureaucratic processes, and hamstrung by audits (and audits of audits). It becomes seen as a series of flowcharts, functions, and targets, while the actual, lived realities of the prison dissolve from managerial view. In some prisons, there is an astonishing discrepancy between the pronouncements of good health made by governors and the glaring deficits in treatment and legitimacy that can be picked up on a wing with only cursory attention. The fading of front-stage dissent makes it easy for managers to mistake quiescence for contentment, and lose sight of the difference between systemic efficiency and moral management.

A second possibility is that, in their preoccupation with process, prisons *perform* legitimacy but do not achieve justice. In many prisons, grievance procedures function smoothly, but very rarely yield (only adding to prisoners' feelings of powerlessness and illegitimacy). There are prisoner committees, but they are often discouraged from raising issues beyond food portions and canteen products because other issues are unchangeable or unpalatable.[1] Prisoners are treated respectfully, but often in instrumental ways (to stop things 'kicking off') that do not fully recognize their humanity and individuality. The landings are civilized, but in the interests of control. Indeed, a third danger is that decency is 'delivered' but in a manner that is faceless and impersonal. Qualities that are essential for the prison's redemptive aims—humanity, trust, faith, interest—and to which prisoners are highly sensitive are lost in the process. Whether procedural decency and effectiveness can be legitimizing principles, or whether they always tend towards these deficits, is extremely hard to judge.

Managers can too easily rely on weak solutions to the problem of order, as Chapter 5 discussed. The drawbacks of resigned fatalism among prisoners are hard for them to identify precisely because the condition of hopelessness does not proclaim itself loudly, in visible and vocal resistance. Furthermore, more legitimate bases of order are notoriously difficult to get right, particularly when historical events have eroded faith in their efficacy. As Liebling (2004) has argued, the escapes of the early 1990s rang the death knell for a model of penal order based principally on the quality of relationships, even though the model that was disavowed—one that confused decency for laxity, and led to an abdication of staff authority—was a misreading of the Woolf Report's recommendations. Instead of being fashioned in the liberal image of Woolf's original vision, relationships became associated with permissiveness and therefore risk. Situational control measures were ramped up significantly, and relationships, material improvements and rehabilitative opportunities were co-opted into a more repressive agenda of control.

The result is that, while positive relationships are central in the maintenance of decent and ordered regimes, the techniques that are intended to supplement them are instead liable to supplant them. Staff have sufficient power for legitimacy to take a backseat

---

[1] Prisoner representatives are often enhanced *enthusiasts*, who are already more positively disposed to the institution than many of their peers. By raising awareness of operational glitches, their contributions often assist smooth governance rather than the resolution of more significant concerns, such as poor staff-prisoner relations.

to other means of ensuring compliance. In some establishments, there is a sense that legitimacy is a matter for external parties: the Prisons Inspectorate, the Standards Audit Unit, and the Prisons Ombudsman (Drake 2007). The belief may be that there is less need for staff to legitimate their use of authority when these moral auditors are on hand to do so for them. Alternatively, staff believe that their relationships with prisoners are good—it is rare that they say otherwise—and are astounded and disappointed to discover that prisoners do not share this perception.

In terms of institutional stability, resignation is dangerous because it appears so stable, and because it may deepen and slip towards instability with little warning. The lines between blithe resignation, disengagement, and the utter desperation that can detonate collective unrest are difficult to decipher. It is hard to know whether recent disturbances have been caused by such sentiments—rather than brutality, poor conditions, or indifferent treatment, for example. Outsiders hear little about these episodes of 'concerted indiscipline'. The Prison Service has become skilled at containing incidents, both physically and in terms of their media coverage. They occur nonetheless, and there is growing concern that they have not been prefaced by traditional signs of forewarning. The fact that prisons are calm, and prisoners are compliant, for the vast majority of the time is no indication that they will not soon rupture.

Overcrowding intensifies all forms of discontent and germinates new frustrations. More prisoners share cells; staff time is stretched and officers become fraught; a smaller proportion of prisoners get onto the courses they must attend in order to progress; more are located far from home; movement through the system is slowed. As the system moves to bursting point, control becomes an increasing preoccupation of the prison authorities. Soft power hardens. Risk-aversion adds to these frustrations. Fewer prisoners are granted parole and home leave, and more are asked to sit courses that they have already taken or which take no account of who they feel they are. Giving up rather than giving in—disengaging from institutional efforts, refusing institutional incentives—becomes tempting, because it liberates the individual from self-management and the potential for disappointment. And as increasing numbers of prisoners begin sentences already embittered by huge or indeterminate sentences, it seems all the more likely that prisons will be characterized by feelings of powerlessness and resentment rather than normative commitment. If penal power is unforgiving, and the system becomes more risk-averse, feelings of injustice are bound to grow, even if cells are clean, exercise is regular, and officers are respectful. This is a fragile basis for order.

Historical accounts alert us that coercive regimes are also unlikely to achieve the reformative aims that they proclaim. The resocialization of beliefs is hard enough to achieve in prisons (Sparks *et al.* 1996: 321). When it occurs, it may be less because of the prison's efforts than because some prisoners enter the establishment already inclined to change. Nonetheless, the opportunities on offer for education, retraining, and treatment, and the moral climate in which they are offered, matter a great deal because they are the pivots around which identity can be reformed. Where they are made obligatory, they compromise their own potential. Prisoners—like everyone else—need to feel that they are agents in processes of change, and are making choices rather than being 'reprogrammed'. In its tone of insistence, the modern prison risks turning opportunities into obligations, and discouraging prisoners for whom self-determination is a matter of principle from taking up its offerings with any sincerity. To attach punitive consequences to decisions to refuse is likely to discourage many men who might otherwise welcome opportunities, and alienate those who need more time and space before they feel ready to change. Encouraging prisoners to take 'responsibility' for their lives is not intrinsically reactionary. Nor is the belief that prisoners should be challenged in their views of offending. Both carry dangers, however. It is one thing to help someone take control of their life, make informed choices and fulfil their potential, and another thing to remove much of their genuine autonomy, narrow down their options, and force them to conform to a predefined regime. As Crawford (2009) notes, in contractual forms of governance, choice tends to be reduced to a 'take it or leave it' exchange. There may be alternative models of rehabilitation that are less forceful, more democratic, and more genuinely empowering than those that currently dominate.

As it is, the prison already offers few spaces that do not feel carceral. Its expectations have shifted from suffering to repentance to compliance to commitment. As a result, sovereign zones have almost disappeared as self-regulation is expected for an expanding range of social and personal behaviour. Power seeps deeper into the cells and landings. The refuges from public performance that make imprisonment survivable have contracted (Jewkes 2002). The sense of autonomous identity on which psychological health relies is increasingly threatened. Prisoners need to perform in increasingly complex ways to staff as well as other prisoners. There is little room in these performances for the complications of the psyche, and little time for notions that the self can be damaged, conflicted, and contradictory. In its model of the self, governmental power does not seek to delve beyond the cognitive surface. It presupposes a rational agent who can weigh up appropriate decisions and who responds in predictable ways to incentives and disincentives. It presumes that responsible conduct can be recognized as such by those whose behaviours it steers. In working *through* the agency of the individual, it requires agency to be consistent and robust. And yet the criminal justice system spills over with people whose mental health problems make this simple notion of rationality even more problematic than it is for the psychologically healthy. These people elicit sympathy from staff, but the system itself can only deem them willfully ungovernable and punish them for their cognitive 'deficiencies', for they have spurned opportunities to self-govern responsibly. They are among the new losers of the system. Ironically too, many of the prisoners who do weigh up costs and benefits and take most responsibility for the consequences of their actions do so in ways that are anathema to institutional aims. *Players* perform all too well, while separating the process of self-monitoring from its official ambitions.

Social life, order, and institutional potential

The reconfiguration of penal power has multiple consequences for the social world of prisoners. The dominant plotline has been the controlled individualization of the prisoner community, a development consciously designed by the Prison Service as part of its recent 'compliance project'. In parallel with citizens at large (Beck 1992), prisoners have become relatively discrete, divided units. Collectively, they are an aggregate rather than a 'community'. The standardization of their experiences means that they have common interests, but not social solidarity as such. Their atomization has not been absolute and their world has not disintegrated into a state of granular anomie, but it has crumbled into a range of apathetic social cells with few collective bonds.

Alongside other strategies, this process of individualization has become the foundation of order. This is not government 'through the social' in the sense of the post-war American ethnographies, where prisoner leaders were recruited in the process of governance. It is government through the *dissolution of* the social. The splintering of interests creates a culture of atomized self-regulation, and supports an ethos of self-regarding fatalism. There seems little point in challenging collective issues when support cannot be relied upon. The collective negotiations between prisoners and staff that early theorists described are unlikely to develop when institutional policies address individual needs and insist upon self-governance. Moreover, while interests are individualized, the basis of individual self-interest is itself differentiated. The shards of individual compliance that comprise social order derive from different subjective needs and deprivations, different relationships with the institution, and differential experiences of power. Prisoners are in very different boats from each other, and reach freedom through a multitude of personal channels.

Cultural solidarity between prisoners has also atomized. Solidarity has rarely been identified in studies of imprisonment, but codes and claims of solidarity have been. These appear to have weakened, and this too seems to be related to the form and consequences of modern penal power. Many of the distinctive pains of modern imprisonment cannot easily be alleviated through collective norms or the comforts and cushions of social relations. Many—such as the various obligations to self-manage and engage appropriately—relate not to deficits or deprivations so much as *requirements*. They cannot easily be compensated for as such; rather, they must be fulfilled, pursued, performed, or ignored. There are few ways to manage them that do not reinforce institutional compliance. Those that do exist—the alternative certainties of disengagement or rebellion, for example—can be highly counter-productive if the aim is to be free. In this respect, not only does the prison officially promote individualized orientations to the institution, its unintended pains also promote individualized means of coping and adjustment.

Established 'deficits' remain in revised forms, mediated by institutional efforts to soften some of the inherent pains of imprisonment. These have different effects, tending to bind relationships rather than fracture them, albeit only loosely. Deprivations in moral and masculine status, safety, trust, privacy, autonomy, and emotional support generally *encourage* social allegiances, interactions, and commitments to codes of loyalty, respect and fortitude. For the individual prisoner, then, adaptation is an outcome of dual pressures: institutional imperatives that generally encourage processes of individualization, and structural imperatives (those that represent the more-or-less intrinsic conditions of incarceration) that mainly promote forms of social association. The relative strength of these forces depends on personal circumstances. For *stoics*, for example, the need to self-regulate is heightened by sentence conditions, while deficits in safety and material goods are diminished by the learned self-sufficiency that comes with prison experience. Institutional demands to conform and self-regulate exert a firmer grip than imperatives to form social bonds and get involved in trade. For *players*, the desire and skills to control the environment, accumulate power, and forge future contacts have the opposite effect. Other prisoners experience the prison as a place of danger or poverty or recovery or opportunity, and their social adaptations are shaped accordingly.

The prison's hierarchies, relationships, and norms are likewise moulded by these institutional and structural forces. As functional theorists of the prison argued (e.g. Sykes 1958; Cloward *et al.* 1960), there are relatively inherent absences, needs, and frustrations that structure the need for and nature of friendship, the basis of status and stigma, and the possibilities for emotional expression. But as situational theorists note (e.g. Kruttschnitt and Gartner 2005), they do so *alongside and in interaction with* the specific demands and mitigations of the modern institution: the loyalties, behaviours, and relationships that it increasingly seeks to regulate, the goods and opportunities it offers in return for compliance, and the frustrations it can or cannot relieve.

This book presents prisoner adaptations 'vertically' before it presents them 'horizontally' because the individual's relationship to institutional power is generally more significant in defining the experience of imprisonment than his or her relationships with other prisoners. In Sykes's 'society of captives', where the prison made few efforts to shape the prisoner social world or address and engage individual prisoners in its policies and practices, it was a prisoner's relationship with his peers that primarily defined his social existence. These relationships remain vital, and they do sometimes determine a prisoner's institutional orientation (for example, when a prisoner with strong loyalties to hometown associates is bound into a particular stance towards the institution). But the social world *as a whole* cannot be understood without an analysis of how institutional power has reached into, fractured, and reshaped the world of prisoners. For most prisoners, it is the personal orientation towards the institution that determines other social decisions.

Charting the prison's structural characteristics—its enduring social tendencies, its institutional features, and the precise terms of neo-paternalism—tells only half the story of the social world. Some establishments allow more trust than others, or reinforce less violent behaviour through the more careful and legitimate use of staff power. Some systems have relied more than others on coercion (Scraton *et al.* 1991), legitimacy (Sparks *et al.* 1996), or resigned fatalism (Carrabine 2004). The adaptations, hierarchies, and social relations that are more likely within these contexts can be predicted with some confidence. However, it is harder to know how different prisoners are oriented to staff, how their frustrations vary, the divergent reasons why they comply, or the precise pattern of social relations unless the other part of the story is explored: the needs, expectations and biographical arcs of the prisoners who enter it.

Prisoner typologies have typically focused on these imported characteristics without connecting them to structural and institutional characteristics. Studies of penal order have done the opposite, truncating their analysis before the level of the individual. When the two approaches are combined, it becomes harder to generalize about how the institution affects the individual, and how the individual shapes and navigates their environment. There is no simple model of prisonization. Like a fairground mirror, imprisonment exaggerates some aspects of identity and behaviour, while obscuring and suppressing others. But these distortions occur in different ways. Some prisoners willingly discard or redefine the identities with which they enter prison, and choose to cut off former ties. Some are overwhelmed by the social force of the institution. Others cling to their pre-carceral identities, and sweat to reproduce them, with varying degrees of success. The dynamic by which attributes are imported and obliterated is far from uniform.

This book has sought to take into account both individual, subjective experiences and structural obligations (Carrabine 2004). Its typology allows an embedded analysis of agency and constraint. In terms of resistance, for example, there are clear and important differences between gleefully subverting the prison in order to assert masculine power and engaging in illicit activity merely in order to subsist. It is only by seeing these acts in relation to personal aims and narratives, and the wider social context in which they are forged, that these distinctions can be appreciated. The typology also helps us think about how adaptations might be affected by enhancements or reductions in institutional legitimacy, and how specific policy decisions will differentially affect certain kinds of prisoners. A more authoritarian regime is likely to stimulate greater rebellion in *players*, and add to feelings of fatalism in other prisoners. Failures in service delivery and the limiting of privileges will agitate *pragmatists* disproportionately, and may push them towards disengagement. The ineffectiveness of formal grievance procedures, bureaucratic sclerosis, and an increased reliance on psychological power, will cause particular frustration for *stoics*. Where visits are difficult, opportunities restricted and officers disrespectful, *enthusiasts* may quickly turn into crusaders. Conversely, in showing faith, hope and understanding, a prison can help some wavering *players* in their quests to reshape their lives. By offering trust, opportunities, and meaningful incentives, it can offer narrative and material lifeboats to *pragmatists*, prisoners who are *disengaged*, and even some *retreatists*.

Some such shifts are more likely than others. Adaptations are not fixed, and prisoners can change as a result of imprisonment, but the prison's capacity to reform is limited by external cultures and experiences. It is important to question claims about its reformative potential, and to be sceptical of political claims that crime can be tackled by tweaking and reformulating the criminal justice system without paying attention to its social roots. However much the prison seeks to reduce its pains and offer avenues of personal reconstruction, individuals who enter prison defiled by abuse and addiction, or already deeply cynical about the agencies of the state, cannot easily be stitched up, repaired, and re-enchanted.

A luminous subtext here is drugs. Drugs permeate the prison society and have reshaped its structures. It is impossible to understand the prison experience without understanding the role of drugs in penal culture, personal biography, and criminal history. The question of how drugs and imprisonment are threaded into the 'fabric and lifecourse of the lower classes' (Wacquant 2002: 388), indeed, how they shape and reinforce each other's trajectories, is of vital concern. For men whose concepts of work and status barely extend beyond the drugs economy, imprisonment seems unlikely to expand horizons, particularly when prison work is so often so menial. For men enslaved to the appeal of drug consumption, the dismal irony is that the state of imprisonment may—in its immediate functions—be preferable to the state of addiction. It is uneasy to say, as Wacquant does (2002: 88), that:

Prison can also act, counterintuitively and within limits, as a stabilizing and restorative force for relations *already* deeply frayed by the pressures of life and labor at the bottom of the social edifice. For example, prisons extirpate abusive men from domestic space; interrupt for a time spirals of addiction; and provide some health care to derelicts who otherwise receive none.

The irony is dismal partly because instead of making people question how it can be that captivity, with all its horrors and consequences, can be a better state than certain modes of 'free living', it allows them to reassure themselves that prison is a benign institution. Politically, it is easier to extend the use of imprisonment as a perverse welfare agency than to propose more ambitious changes to social policy and social structure. In the face of a rapacious drug culture outside prison, to use imprisonment as the panacea for addiction is futile and disastrous. Drugs medicate pain, and imprisonment is unlikely to do more than provide temporary release from the pains of addiction while appending them with a new set of social handicaps that inhibit desistance from drugs and crime.

It has become less acceptable to express sympathy for offenders (Simon 2000; Liebling 2004). Writing about the American prison in the 1970s, Jacobs argued that prison reforms, the extension of juridical norms and rights to prisoners, and the bureaucratization of prison management made the institution increasingly *in step* with the standards and values of mainstream society. The prison moved 'from the periphery towards the center' of society (Jacobs 1977: 6), and prisoners were seen increasingly as part of the wider citizenry. Within two decades, it was clear that the role of the prison in political culture reinforced rather than erased distinctions between the 'criminal class' and the 'lawful public'. Through this bifurcation—what Garland (1996: 461) calls a 'criminology of the other'—offenders are distinguished in questionable ways from the 'law-abiding majority' and their interests are placed in direct opposition to those of 'the public', as if compassion is a finite resource and victimhood a binary concept. Despite their increasingly abject social profiles, offenders have apparently exhausted the sympathies even of the Left.[2] In political discourse, the big questions now are not about how prisoners should be treated, but when and on what basis they should be released (Sparks 2007). The focus shifts from prisoner rights towards a notion of public protection that is much more nebulous and politically manipulable. Prisoners as people become increasingly invisible in debates about imprisonment. Even in some attempts to promote decency, prisoners are somehow decentred from the rationale. When it is pointed out that 'every prisoner is someone's child' or argued that a good way to judge a prison is to ask whether you would feel satisfied if one of your family members were in it, the focus can slip away from the prisoner, towards his or her family. It appears to have become insufficient to argue that, whatever they have done, prisoners deserve humane treatment simply because they are human beings.

In the mainstream media, prisoners are presented as remorseless monsters. Meanwhile, prisons are depicted in ways that appear contradictory, but, in fact, represent different sides of the same discourse. Either they are 'holiday camps' that are not punitive enough for the creatures within them, or they are places whose relentless brutality provides confirmation that their inhabitants are ruthlessly amoral and inexorably violent. Many citizens are more likely to encounter the urban poor through these portrayals than through any kind of personal contact. Academics are in danger of sustaining these assumptions if they fail to fill the sociological gaps that explain the structural reasons why prisons *are* often places of exploitation and emotional indifference but are also places where morality and humanity survive *despite* the privations of imprisonment. Researchers can de-alienate the prison environment by bringing into focus the forces that produce its daily culture. To do this fully, and to observe the 'nether zones of social space' as a window on the state (Wacquant 2002: 389), it is essential to look beyond official portraits of the prison. Academics must break the crust of the prisoner world, and draw connections between the prison's mundane social realities—*what*

---

[2] Writing about the political climate in France, Wacquant (2001: 408) cites Lionel Jospin's use of the term 'sociological excuses' to capture this view that criminality should no longer be seen as a matter of social deprivation and the like.

it is like—and its institutional and political intentions—*what it is for* (Carrabine 2004; Kruttschnitt and Gartner 2005).

This has been a study of a single prison. Given prisoners' comments on the consistency of certain features of imprisonment across the system—drug culture, the difficulties of friendship, the atomized structure of the prisoner community—and considering the homogenization of management strategies in recent years, it seems likely that this account will be recognizable beyond its immediate location. Differences in security-category, in staff cultures, in the precise application of power, and in the composition of the prisoner population will account for variations in social conditions and adaptations. But I hope to have provided enough analytic description of these determinants for such variations to be explicable. Whether the analysis has wider application—for example, to the US's exceptional carceral climate—is less clear. It is interesting though to compare this account with studies from earlier decades: with the terms of hierarchy and the value system documented in *The Society of Captives* (Sykes 1958), with the descriptions of social relationships in *Pentonville* (Morris and Morris 1963), and with the 'closed emotional world' depicted in *Psychological Survival* (Cohen and Taylor 1972), for example. Much has changed, and much has stayed the same. Prisons retain totalitarian qualities, even if they may no longer be described as total institutions in the way that Goffman used the term. Adaptations take new forms, but certain outcomes endure: some prisoners manifest 'defeatism, quietism and resignation…to "escape" from the requirements of the society' (Merton 1938: 678), while others 'do reform' strategically (Boyle 1977). If there were ever any doubt that the prison has some basic properties, despite variations in context and function, Clemmer's words are striking. First published in 1940 to describe an American penitentiary, their terms are sadly familiar:

The prisoner's world is an atomized world. Its people are atoms interacting in confusion. It is dominated and it submits…. There are no definite communal objectives. There is no consensus for a common goal…. Trickery and dishonesty overshadow sympathy and cooperation. Such cooperation as exists is largely symbiotic in nature…. It is a world of individuals whose daily relationships are impersonalized…. Its people are thwarted, unhappy, yearning, resigned, bitter, hating, revengeful…. There is filth, stink, and drabness; there is monotony and stupor. There is disinterest in work. There is desire for love and hunger for sex. There is pain in punishment. Except for the few, there is bewilderment. (Clemmer 1940/1958: 297–8)

Appendix

Notes on the Research Process

It's difficult to tell the truth about how a book begins. The truth, as far as it can be presented to other people, is either wholly banal or too intimate. Public accounts tend to have a fictional texture—this is not to say they're untrue, but they are writerly explanations, fished from the sea that is the book itself. (Zadie Smith, *The Guardian* 15/7/06)

Just as authors of fiction are inclined to produce the 'writerly explanations' that Zadie Smith identifies, accounts of the research process tend to be glossed with academic paint. To be truthful about practical miscalculations and intellectual cul-de-sacs is hazardous. But self-conscious transparency should be recommended not just as a corrective to the accidental imposition of subjectivity onto the data (Gross 2000), but to ensure an account of the research that serves as an open guide rather than a defensive justification.

The genesis of the study was somewhat banal. My interest in prisons developed towards the end of my doctorate, when I attended a seminar by Eamonn Carrabine at Essex University that pointed to the significance of masculine discourses in the penal environment. I had been researching the role of gender identity in the production of popular media, and was drawn to the idea of exploring this issue in a different institutional context, one that was presented in popular discourse as a masculine arena *in extremis*.[1] The post-doctoral research proposal that I subsequently developed with Alison Liebling, rather grandly titled 'A New Society of Captives: Masculinity and Modern Penal Culture', married my ambition to explore prison masculinity with her enthusiasm to

---

[1] Initially, I wondered if the only significant link between my doctoral research and the prison study was a concern with masculinity and a preference for qualitative methods. My feeling now is that both projects were fundamentally concerned with issues of structure and agency, and with the relationship between institutional constraints and individual narratives.

see a revitalization of the tradition of prison ethnography that, at that time, was seen as a rather moribund enterprise (Simon 2000; Wacquant 2002; Morgan 2002).

Based on the proposal, I was awarded what was eventually a four-year Nuffield Foundation 'New Career Development Fellowship in the Social Sciences' (award NCF/00076/G). In the subsequent period, I received funding through the money contributed by the Prison Service to the Prisons Research Centre at the Cambridge Institute of Criminology. At no stage have my interests been directed or my findings suppressed. Indeed, the attitude of Prison Service senior managers towards my research has been enlightened and bears no relation to the more domineering, defensive, and manipulative attitudes that other researchers have reported (Wilson 2003; Hope 2004; and, Cohen and Taylor 1977). If this is making a pact with the devil, then, in my particular experience, he seems no less benign than the Research Council gods.

Access and Preparation

Wellingborough was chosen as a research site in consultation with senior practitioners, who decreed it an establishment with no obvious quirks or unusual characteristics but 'plenty of masculinity' (Wheatley 2002, pers. comm.). It was also a Category-C prison, and therefore more 'normal' (inasmuch as any one prison can be) than the higher-security prisons in which much recent research had taken place (e.g. Sparks *et al.* 1996; Liebling and Price 2001). Perhaps most importantly, Wellingborough's governor at the time, Peter Bennett, held a PhD in anthropology and understood the aims and requirements of ethnographic research. He was familiar with the prison sociology literature, citing it impressively and with ease. From the outset, Bennett was enthusiastic about hosting the research. In early discussions, he made clear that he would maintain a position of distanced support. There would be no expectations that I would 'report back' my observations or disclose confidential information, but he would be willing to comment on my findings and share his own perceptions. Assurances were given that an office would be set aside for the purposes of interviewing and note-taking, and that keys would be provided to allow full and unaccompanied access to all areas of the establishment.

Some months before the fieldwork phase began, a meeting was held with members of Wellingborough's senior management team, a principal officer, and a representative from the establishment's POA committee, at which I outlined the aims of the research and solicited views on its conduct. Feedback was positive, although I was warned that the prison environment would be cynical and forthright: 'People will tell you what you're like and what you're doing wrong. There's too much at stake for people to hold back' (fieldwork notes). A two-month pilot study was arranged at HMP Stafford, another Cat-C training prison, where I was given keys and let loose to familiarize myself with the environment and hone my research interests.

This was not my first experience of prison research—I had spent a few days in HMP Styal and HMP Manchester as part of another project—but the learning curve was still precipitous. Within a few days, I had been shown heroin, made the mistake of asking a prisoner for the inside story of a conflict between two other prisoners (and thus learnt how not to obtain information), been told by two prisoners that they were going to 'set a nigger on fire', and been approached in the gym by a huge, naked prisoner who demanded to know what I thought of his body.[2] To some degree, these incidents were tests, although they were checks on character rather than organized trials. Following the incident in the gym, prisoners encouraged me to lift weights with them and 'join us afterwards for the showers', an invitation designed to gauge my belief in assumptions about prison rape. I did not shower with prisoners subsequently, but neither did I react to their suggestion in a manner that suggested fear.[3]

Little of the prison literature that I had consumed had primed me for these encounters. Nor had the reading prepared me for many important empirical discoveries, such as the role of drugs within the prisoner society and the significance of regional identity. By the end of the pilot phase, it was also clear that although

[2] One female colleague complained that she had spent a decade doing research in prison but had '*never* seen a naked man' in prison during that period. The story was also, somehow, mistranslated so that a rumour emerged in my department that (for reasons that were unclear) *I* was the one who had stripped off in the prison gym.

[3] At the end of interviews, several prisoners expressed surprise that I had asked so few questions about rape and homosexual relations. When pushed as to why, they made clear that these were not significant issues in men's prisons, but that they had expected me to assume that they were.

men's prisons were suffused with masculine discourse, their social structure could not be reduced to themes of gender. As the study developed, its focus broadened, and while masculinity remained a sensitizing concept, its role in the analysis became less substantial. Having entered the environment fairly naively, I also learned that the prison was a safe environment, that it was not necessary to clutch my bag tightly, and that the most valuable research tools were sincerity and respect. None of these things should have caused surprise, but perhaps it says something about the moral status of prisoners and our decontextualized notions of crime and criminality that to some degree they did.

The research phase in HMP Wellingborough began in August 2002, when, with a team from the Institute of Criminology, I carried out a Quality of Prison Life survey with prisoners and a separate staff survey over a three-day period. This was seen as an opportunity to publicize the research plan, as well as to take a quantitative snapshot of the prison's moral condition. Staff surveys were handed out during a full-staff meeting, ensuring high visibility and maximum participation. Comments among staff that the results might make 'depressing reading' were portents of some of the cultural problems that became apparent once the fieldwork progressed. They also signalled a perception that the study was to some degree *evaluative*, which proved hard to shake off. For staff and prisoners, the key questions were about the prison's quality and practical outcomes rather than its social anatomy, and I had to stress repeatedly that my concerns were not directly of this nature. One hundred prisoners, selected randomly, also completed the questionnaires on the wings in groups of around twelve. When the main fieldwork period began in October, many prisoners remembered me from having taken part in these survey groups.

In the meantime, however, circumstances at the prison had changed and Peter Bennett had vacated the governor's post. As Jim Lewis began his first in-charge governing post, he was landed with a research project that had been agreed by his predecessor and might well feel like an evaluation of his competence. This was a difficult position for all parties, made all the more delicate by the fact that Lewis was in the middle of a two-year, part-time Masters course at the Institute of Criminology on which I occasionally taught.[4]

---

[4] In some seminars, I was discussing Wellingborough in front of its governor and his professional peer group, a situation that was rather unnerving for all involved.

Gamely and decently, he proclaimed himself happy to allow the study to continue along the same terms that had been originally agreed and retained a supportive stance throughout. Early during his tenure, Lewis requested some informal feedback on my impressions of Wellingborough's deceptively difficult staff culture, and this required some negotiation of terms (e.g. that I would not disclose anything said to me in confidence or talk specifically about individuals). Lewis anticipated and respected these ground-rules, and I did not feel compromised by anything that was discussed at the meeting that followed.

The Fieldwork Phase

Once the main fieldwork period began, I visited the prison no more than four days consecutively. In part, this was to give me some time back in my department to teach, digest findings, and write up notes. It was also because I found myself flagging after several days in what was an intense and demanding environment. I staggered the times at which I was present, doing occasional twelve-hour 'A-shifts', but more often staying from 8am–4.30pm or 12.30pm–8.30pm. My presence over several weekends, bank holidays, evenings, and on Christmas day were noted; indeed, they were often mocked, with some prisoners indignant rather than impressed that I was choosing to be in the prison when I could be 'down the pub' or 'with family'. Many scholars have argued that 'being there' is vital in prison research (for example, King 2000; Sparks *et al.* 1996), but it is also worth noting that being there all the time might not always garner respect.

Having consulted with colleagues, I chose to carry keys during the pilot study and in Wellingborough.[5] I experienced no resistance or surprise from prisoners about this. If anything, I felt that my autonomy and mobility were seen as indications that I was trusted and self-sufficient (see Jewkes 2002). From the start of the research, I wore a badge identifying my name and institution,[6] and carried a distinctive orange notebook (getting through nineteen by the end of the fieldwork) in which I scrawled contemporaneous notes. Only on one occasion was this approach

---

[5] These gave full access to all public areas of the prison, but not to cells.
[6] Officers did not wear name badges, so this strategy marked me out effectively.

problematic, when a handful of prisoners in an association room (all of whom had taken heroin that evening and were somewhat on edge) insisted that I show them what I was writing. Initially, I refused, explaining that if I exhibited the notebook I would be breaking promises of trust made to other prisoners I had been speaking to. Eventually, under some duress, I showed them the two or three pages on which I had been writing only about them. My notes were more or less verbatim and were descriptive rather than analytical, so there seemed more to gain than lose in display- ing their words back to them. My fears that other prisoners would start to make the same demands were not borne out.

Another important early decision was to take nothing into or out of the prison on behalf of prisoners (some researchers give away small amounts of tobacco, for example) and to make no promises of help that might make me vulnerable to exploitation or leave prisoners disappointed after an initial pledge of help.[7] In the end, I felt no compunction about taking home a small number of items that prisoners had given me: a written life story, a col- lection of poems, and a copy of a sociology project on which I had offered some guidance. Refusing requests from prisoners to bring in innocuous items such as books or music was much harder.[8] Although the idea was to avoid making power dispar- ities the main dynamic of emergent relationships, the effect was sometimes the opposite. My reluctance to do things for prisoners that would have been easy for me and of great value for them ac- tually brought disparities to the fore. As a result, I felt safe from being compromised and consistent in my treatment, but some- times rather callous.[9] Finding the right balance between mak- ing interactions with prisoners as egalitarian as possible without eliding evident discrepancies in power and liberty was a constant challenge.

As was consistent with my research stance, I did not offer any payment to prisoners either for talking on the wings or as an in- centive to be interviewed. Only one prisoner objected to this con- dition, arguing that 'no-one gets nothing for free in prison', and

---

[7] Some prisoners suggested that I could traffic drugs for them, although they did so in ways that could be defended as jokes.

[8] To have brought in anything would have constituted illegal trafficking.

[9] Consistency was vital because accusations of favouritism would have been very hard to disprove.

that I should not expect him to give up his time without pay of some kind. I maintained my position, confident that he would recognize its logic and that his repeated assertions that he would not talk to me concealed a strong desire to do so. This was a misjudgment. By the end of the study, he had become increasingly hostile, warning me that he did not trust me, that I was making him feel 'off-key', and that he would no longer interact with me at all. Significantly, two other prisoners on this wing (although none on any others, as far as I knew) also expressed hostility and cynicism towards me. One—a prisoner with some influence—accused me of being a 'spy' and refused even to hear me explain my position.[10] The other pointed out to me that hanging around on the landings was the equivalent of him coming to my house and standing in my living room.

It was hard to dismiss this observation. As Feldman notes, in 'a culture of surveillance, participant observation is ... a form of complicity with those outsiders who surveil (Feldman 1991: 12, cited in Rhodes 2001: 73; and see Wacquant 2002). I felt increasingly uncomfortable about my presence on the wings as an 'uninvited' observer. By this time, I had been chatting, joining in, hanging around, and taking notes for around three months (doing what Liebling (1999) calls 'reserved participation' and Owen (1998) refers to as 'quasi-ethnography'). Faced with this dilemma about 'intrusion', it seemed a good time to begin more formal interviews and to reduce the amount of time I spent on the wings. As one experienced researcher pointed out (Sparks, pers. comm.), many prisoners might interpret a long period of unstructured engagement as somewhat passive and might respect a more dynamic approach to fieldwork. Meanwhile, in an attempt to build trust and credibility on what was proving to be a difficult wing, I invited a prisoner for interview who I knew to have influence. This strategy seemed to work, and I experienced no subsequent problems of note anywhere in the prison.

Nevertheless, minor challenges and questions remained a daily and demanding occurrence. Many of these related to the basic aims of the research: who and what it was for. At first, I took these to be inquisitions about my independence, and would

[10] It was not clear who he thought I was spying for, but the accusation did make me reflect on the research role and the practical reality that a researcher *is* engaged in a certain kind of sociological espionage.

emphasize my university status and Nuffield Foundation funding as guarantees of my credibility and impartiality. It became apparent, however, that most prisoners wanted some sense that the study would 'make a difference' and was not just an exercise in intellectual curiosity. Many prisoners respected the notion that research was sometimes 'for your studies' or 'for a book', but for others this implied careerism and practical impotence. Negotiating such concerns was tricky. I did not want to mislead or promise too much by suggesting that academic research is always a source of transformation or that my work would lead to all of the changes that prisoners desired. Instead, I stressed that the trickle-down of academic knowledge was often slow, but that many practitioners as well as academics were (or would be) interested in my study. I also emphasized that the book hoped to provide a fuller and more accurate sense of the realities of imprisonment than was normally available.[11] Prisoners often responded most positively to this latter rationale, noting that members of the public had no idea what prison was really like and took their images from media portrayals that bore little relation to reality.

Questions about loyalties and 'whose side' I was on were raised surprisingly rarely, possibly because the research had no obvious policy focus. But I was often asked by prisoners what I thought of 'nonces'. My first response in such cases was to assert intellectual neutrality, that I was 'not judging anyone', but this was clearly inadequate given that the precise aim of the question was to probe my personal morality rather than my professional integrity. On several occasions, I reached an impasse with prisoners, where I insisted that offering opinions was beyond my role, while prisoners demanded a more personal engagement with their enquiry. Since I have always believed that researchers cannot expect personal disclosure without being prepared to give something

[11] Most prisoners were flabbergasted when I told them not to expect the book to be published for at least a couple of years, but they understood that research needed to be rigorous and took time to process. Several prisoners expressed an interest in reading the final product and gave me addresses to which I could send the manuscript or give notice of its publication. Draft copies of articles were sent for comment to two prisoners, and, at various times, to members of Wellingborough's senior management team and to Phil Wheatley, Director General of the Prison Service, as well as to academic peers. Practitioners were told that their comments would be taken into account in any re-drafting but that I offered no guarantee of making editorial changes except where they identified factual errors.

away of themselves, and since I had been open when asked about my marital status, politics, religion, and (most often) salary, there were limits to the immunity I could claim in other areas. The position on which I settled, and which fulfilled a need to be both honest and pragmatic, was to state that I did not like the offences committed by sex offenders, but that the same could be said about the crimes of lots of other prisoners, and that I did not believe that people who did bad things were necessarily bad people.

Other dilemmas raised conflicts about my ethical responsibilities. Many of the moments when I felt most confident of having penetrated the public impression of the prisoner community were also the times when I was placed in the most awkward situations. On the occasions when prisoners offered me hooch, smuggled food in front of me, blocked off a doorway to prevent officers from running to an incident in the visits room, and—without my full understanding of what was occurring—swung drugs on a line from one wing to another, my main reaction was to feel thrilled at being 'inside' the situation. Only later did I consider that knowledge of this kind could be dangerous, that it made me complicit in incidents that could have serious implications. It was hard to know whether they threatened the terms on which I had agreed the study. I was confident that governors understood that I could not be expected to report illicit activity, but I was less sure how officers would feel were they to know all of the things that I knew and had seen. Because they never asked me, I was able to exist in a convenient state of academic purgatory, where my knowledge remained in private storage where it was unprocessed and unjudged.

Of more concern was the potential for prisoners to associate me with disciplinary interventions. On one occasion, as I stood at the end of a spur chatting to three prisoners while they took turns to smoke heroin in a cell, an officer came into view and approached us with suspicion. Unconvincingly, the prisoners explained that they were doing nothing more than standing around talking. I maintained an awkward silence. The next day, two of the prisoners were called up for targeted drug tests, for which they tested positive and were placed on report. I emphasized to them the next day that I had said nothing to officers after the incident, but, despite their reassurances of faith, I was anxious for several days that they would think I had been pressured into disclosure or simply that my presence had drawn staff attention to the landing.

Research identity and loyalties

The incident—about four months into the research—precipitated a candid discussion with Callum about how I was perceived by prisoners at that time:

Not everybody is too sure about you. It's because you're an outsider. You know I got that piss test the morning after you saw me smoking that gear, people turned around and said: 'That was Ben'. I said: 'Really, no, it wasn't'; 'How do you know that?'; 'Trust me, Ben has seen me doing a lot of things that I *haven't* got into trouble for'.

Does that mean that when I'm on the landings people stop doing the things that they would be doing?

Some do. You know how people sit in their pad with the door open slightly and they're in there playing cards. [When] you go by, some people push the door to a little bit so you can't quite see what's going on. That's just the suspicious nature of inmates. Nobody is quite sure where you stand, you're not an inmate and you're not a screw, so what the fuck are you doing here? A lot of people can't understand why you're here and when you say you're writing a report they all think, 'Shit, the screws will read it'.

But it's not a report where I'm going to mention people's names..

...I know and I tell that to people but they're just suspicious. A lot of people are in here because they weren't suspicious enough. It's how it goes. Some people do tone it down when you're around. [You're] Trying to research something that don't really want to be researched.

Well, keep telling them on the wing I'm a good guy.

Tyler is fighting your case, [and] Tyler is a respected lad.

I'm surprised people talk about this.

We were talking about it this morning: what the fuck are you doing [it] for?! It's sad, man!

The exchange shone light on the kinds of backstage discussions that must occur in all research contexts. It also highlighted the intrinsic difficulties of conducting research in an environment where caution and mistrust are deeply embedded and where volunteering one's presence seems peculiar. Gaining trust was an iterative process. Prisoners like Tyler and Callum, who were among my early 'sponsors', tended to be among my first interviewees. Their willingness to be interviewed was based on observing my style and judging my credibility on the wings, as Tyler explained when I asked him why he had agreed to the interview:

I don't know, I spoke to you on the wing a few times, innit. Thought you were alright, not heard nobody say: 'Oh yeah he's said my business to somebody else'.... You know, it just happens that we've spoke a few times on the wing and I find you a pretty sensible fella. You know, so I don't really mind—we've spoke on the landing, I see how you've spoke with other people, I've seen how you've dealt with them: you've heard them, you've listened to them, you've got your own points of view.

By the end of the fieldwork phase, I felt very comfortable in the environment and familiar with a large proportion of prisoners. If I stood along the education corridor during movement to work and activities, around half of the prisoners who passed would give me acknowledgement of some kind ('How ya doing?', 'Wha g'wan Ben?!', or just a nodded hello). Most of the others I knew by face, if not name. I derived considerable satisfaction from this level of acceptance and from having such a clearly defined identity. Whether this represented *trust* was harder to tell, but I certainly felt I had become part of the prison's everyday furniture. When a prisoner who resembled me entered the prison after several months of my presence, he was given the nickname 'Ben junior'.[12]

Prisoners recognized that my class roots and experiences were very different from theirs. I was 'straight' (i.e. law-abiding), a 'college boy', and was often reminded that my accent and demeanour conveyed important social distinctions. When I asked questions using myself as an illustration, prisoners would often dismiss the plausibility of my examples: 'You're not the same as us, Ben!' (Danny); 'Street life is a whole different ball game to working a job from sixteen to thirty' (prisoner, fieldwork notes). Questions about my background often led to comical acknowledgements of the different worlds that we inhabited. When I told one prisoner that I had once lived in the Barbican, he responded with delight: 'The Barbican?! I used to burgle around the Barbican!' Another prisoner talked of the wonderful cheese that was served in King's

---

[12] I was not aware of being given any particular nickname, but was often scrutinized in terms of my clothes and research role. I received occasional compliments about my clothing, but was more often teased for looking like 'a student', in smart casual clothing, rather than the preferred style in prison of comfortable tracksuits or designer leisure wear. One governor suggested that I 'smarten up a little' in order to differentiate myself from prisoners. I was the same age as many of them and my hair was very short. However, I was keen not to look like a member of staff or seem uncomfortable in my appearance. On several occasions, staff briefly identified me as a prisoner, including me in head counts in education classes for example. Prisoners enjoyed such confusions, while staff were needlessly apologetic.

College, Cambridge, before admitting that he used to steal it from their kitchens. But these distinctions did not seem to be a barrier to disclosure or rapport, and they often allowed me to ask questions from the position of the informed outsider.[13]

Prisoners ascribed to me three main roles beyond my position as a researcher. The first of these was that of the 'expert': an advisor on matters about which I almost always had less expertise than they assumed, such as how to obtain housing or benefits on release. After interviews, a number of men asked me forlornly whether I thought there was anything 'really wrong' with them. I always said no to these questions, while pointing out that I did not have any psychological or psychiatric qualifications with which to provide reliable insight.[14] The second identity was that of the 'straight guy', someone whose views and ambitions were of value to men seeking to go straight. A number of prisoners enquired about the time and commitment it would take them to obtain further qualifications. Others asked questions about ethical dilemmas (such as the circumstances when informing to staff might be the right thing to do), using me as a benchmark of pro-social conduct. The final role was that of the 'fellow scholar' (Jewkes 2002), someone with whom personal theories of crime and criminality or broader intellectual interests could be discussed. My ignorance about some of these topics—which ranged from Shakespearian poetry to Nordic mythology—often came as a disappointment to prisoners, but I tried hard to provide a sounding board for men who were otherwise mentally isolated.

In relation to staff, my research identity was friendly but 'professional'. Officers certainly accepted me and were extremely welcoming, but there were limits to the degree that I was embraced by them. Unlike other researchers, I was not invited to birthday parties or retirement drinks, or confided in about personal issues. In truth, I was not especially eager to spend my free time at

---

[13] I suspect that my class identity also shielded me from being drawn into some of the kinds of misogynist discourse that other researchers have reported (e.g. Thurston 1996). I did encounter some very reactionary views, but perhaps fewer than I had expected. I was often asked about my own private life, but rarely in ways that felt intrusive. On the one occasion, on an exercise yard at HMP Stafford, when a prisoner began asking me explicit questions about when I had last had sex with my girlfriend, he was bundled out of conversation by his peers, who were both amused and embarrassed by the nature of his interrogation.

[14] Indeed, because of the mistrust that prisoners feel towards psychologists, I made a point of stressing as often as possible that I was a *sociologist*.

prison-related functions, but I certainly did not seek to place distance between myself and prison staff. Nor would they have perceived me as unfriendly, I am fairly sure. But officers rarely asked me questions about myself: my marital status or what I did with my weekends. I suspect that I was seen as a rather self-contained researcher, there above all to 'do a job'. In this respect, I think I was also fairly successful. Staff often joked that they had stopped noticing me and that I 'ghosted' across the wings. One senior officer, not known for readily giving praise, introduced me to a new member of staff as someone who 'we treated with the scepticism that we treat every outsider with, but who has earned our respect'. I had 'not pissed people off', which was unusual for a 'civilian', and, most importantly, I had 'known when to piss off –when you might be better off just leaving it'. No doubt, with more tenacity and bravery, I could have probed staff cultures and perceptions more deeply, but these were not my main concerns.

I had few moral anxieties about trying to uphold multiple loyalties and extending empathy both to the prison's sub- and super-ordinates (Liebling 2001), but I had some practical concerns about maintaining neutrality in such a binary environment. In fact, this was less problematic than I had expected. Prisoners recognized my reliance on staff goodwill, while staff knew that my primary interest was the world of prisoners. Both groups appreciated that I could not understand each without the other. Wellingborough's staff-prisoner relationships were not so antagonistic that they compelled the taking of sides. On occasions, however, the occupational culture of officers did test my ability to restrain my outrage. Early in the study, two officers joked in front of me about the recent suicide of a prisoner ('*Can I hang around for the morning?*'—'I wouldn't ask that on G-wing!'). On another occasion, when one officer moaned about having to check on a prisoner who was known as a prolific self-harmer, another joked that the prisoner might be busy 'having a slash'.[15] It is normal for researchers to have 'well-bitten tongues' (Gelsthorpe, pers. comm.), but at times I felt ashamed of the collusive silences that I

---

[15] The following discussion between officers occurred a few minutes later:
'Is he alright?'
'He's just manipulating staff. I don't think we should kowtow to him'.
'He's a wanker'. [senior officer]
'He doesn't even cut up properly, he just slashes'.

maintained. I found myself more at ease socially with the prison's teaching staff and management team than I did with basic grade staff. But like other researchers (Jewkes 2002), I also felt considerable sympathy for most officers given the emotional demands of the job, and marvelled at the patience and humanity with which many of them operated. When a member of Wellingborough's POA committee died suddenly during the fieldwork period, I was moved by the strength of camaraderie that officers displayed.[16]

In truth, I was far more comfortable interviewing than observing. I found the latter activity an intrusive and insecure form of fieldwork. Often, I felt that the 'real' prison was eluding me, that I was missing what was going on, and that the action was 'somewhere else'. In a prison with seven wings, plus workshops, classrooms, and other communal spaces, it was difficult to cover all areas without compromising the depth of understanding that makes ethnographic work distinctive. Meanwhile, the study's breadth meant that I had no obvious lens through which to concentrate my gaze, leaving my field of vision blurred and unfocused. I was also under no illusion that I was able to observe the prison in its 'natural state'. As my exchange with Callum (above) indicated, many prisoners modified their behaviour in my presence, even if only modestly.

Despite these difficulties, I have come to see the observational phase as a much more vital part of the study than it felt at the time. In terms of its analytic detail, this book is fairly reliant on interviews, but the tones and texture of prison life that it tries to convey required direct and sustained immersion. The observational period also laid the foundations on which the quality of the interviews was built. By the time they were conducted, I was familiar with prison language, rules, and rituals. Rapport and understanding were enhanced considerably by my having been present in certain locations, such as prisoners' cells, education classes, the visits room, and the segregation unit. These were places where prisoners showed aspects of themselves that they suppressed on the wings, and where experiences were so particular or intimate that they enabled discussions of personal

---

[16] I chose to attend the funeral because, to some degree, it was a prison event and an opportunity to show that I was more than just a research tourist. Nonetheless, it was difficult not to feel like something of an interloper given that I barely knew the man who had died.

issues such as family relationships, future hopes, and sentiments of pain or shame. I had paid particular attention to these areas at the beginning of the fieldwork, in order to become familiar to a small number of prisoners before entering the more impersonal and chaotic domains of the prison, such as the wings and workshops. This strategy seemed to pay dividends. In interviews, I frequently probed the discrepancies between public and private identities, and between stated identities and observed actions (see Crewe and Maruna 2006).

One of the claims of ethnography is that it makes possible a form of learning that is direct and experiential. It would be facile to claim that this is the norm in prison research, given the barriers to cultural assimilation, but prison researchers do soak up important aspects of the environment, albeit in diluted ways. Some experiences greatly accelerated and intensified my understanding of a world that I otherwise absorbed more remotely. On one occasion, having asked an officer to inform the prison gardener that I would be interviewing one of the prisoners who worked for him, I had a taste of the frustration that prisoners feel when officers make promises but do not deliver. The officer did not phone, and I was later called to the E-wing office to explain to an irate gardener why he was missing one of his prisoners.[17] A more instructive lesson came during an interview with Callum, with whom I had struck up rapport early in the fieldwork. As I returned from the hot water urn, where I had refilled our mugs, I apologized for the mistrust implied in my obligation to lock him out of my office during what was an absence of no more than a minute. The interview resumed, covering questions about Callum's background and identity. The following extract captures the difference between my and his understanding of our relationship, and my surprise at being confronted with social realities that most prisoners took for granted. This was a direct lesson in the limitations of prison 'friendship' and it attuned me to the prison's emotional economy:

I ain't under no illusions or nothing, I ain't Robin Hood, robbing the rich to feed the poor. I'm robbing every fucker to feed me. And even if I've got enough food in the cupboard, I'm still gonna rob ya. D'you know what I mean. [laughs] … if you'd have left me in here, while you'd gone down

[17] E-wing staff later commented that they were pleased to see me get some sense of the pressures they were under not to make mistakes.

to [the urn], I'd have looked at that [minidisc recorder]. I wouldn't have taken that, cos I'd know that you'd notice that as soon as you'd come back. I'd have looked at that [radio] and thought, right, you'd have noticed that when you'd come back. So I'd have gone through all the drawers, seen what was in there, d'you know what I mean. I might not have took anything, but I'd have looked anyway. And I'd have probably took half the coffee.

Even though...?

...Even though we're friends...? [laughs]

Well [stumbling], I wouldn't necessarily have assumed that, but we get on, y'know, we've talked a few times.

Mm-hm. But it's the circumstances I'm in, y'know, I'm in jail, my canteen don't come in till Friday, I ain't got no coffee. You've got a great big jar of it, you're not gonna miss half of it. I'm not gonna take the whole lot, because you're gonna notice that, and that would just bring trouble on me. But you're not gonna miss a couple of cups of it.

Right, okay, if I came back and saw that you'd nicked half my coffee, I wouldn't tell anyone, and it's not going to break my bank—it's only a bit of coffee. But I'd think: 'I thought we got on'. I'd feel like you'd broken our trust, or something like that. That's all. I'm not saying I don't understand ...

I know, I know exactly what you're saying.

[Joking] Or I'd come to your pad and steal some back....

I'd offer! Feel free, it's happening all the time.

What, pad-thieving?

I've had loads of stuff stolen out my cell cos of the open-door policy here. It's never big things though, cos you notice big things going missing and you'd go fucking mental. Say I've got a bag of sugar on the side, one of those ounce bags, next to it I'll have a little jar where I've been putting all my sachets.... I'll come back in a couple of days and open my sugar and it's: 'Hold on, I had about six in here, but now I've only got one serving'. You don't automatically think 'I've been robbed', you think: 'Fucking hell, what's happened there'. But what it is, is somebody next door, who you get along with, is sat there and he's thinking, 'Oh, I need a bit of sugar for this jug of tea—Callum's got a load', d'you know what I mean: 'Yeah, Callum won't mind. I'd better not touch [the big packet], better not open that, cos he'll probably go mad, but he keeps a bit in that barrel—yeah, yeah, take that'.... How did we get on to that?

We got on to that because we were talking about you stealing my coffee.

[Laughs] But it's nowt personal though, d'you know what I mean. It's nothing personal.

But it might feel personal.

You're never gonna look at me in the same light again, are you? [Laughs]

No, no, that's not true at all.

Obviously I'm not gonna leave you on your arse, cos, like I says, you're not gonna miss a couple of cups of coffee, but it'll make my life that much more bearable.

As Paul Rock (1979) suggests, researchers should acknowledge the uncomfortable truth that, to some degree, they are mining their respondents for their analytic yield. Prisoners know that this is the case. They are much more likely to open up to people who treat them as equals, but they are all too aware that their relationships with outsiders are fundamentally structured by the essential difference between being captive and being free.

Interviews

The inclusion of this extract is in part an attempt to provide an unpolished account of the interview process, a process that was most productive when it was messier and less disciplined than methodological textbooks tend to recommend. Rigid allegiance to an interview protocol is necessary in some contexts, but it is no substitute for the peculiar form of structured disorder that characterizes conversation. And while there are dangers in mistaking conversation for research or believing that equal exchange is likely in the research context, the skin of the environment is most likely to be pierced when the interview space approximates unfettered dialogue. Under such conditions, one has the feeling that 'findings' are evolving dynamically and collaboratively. The social experience is being *made sense of*, not simply downloaded from one person to another. Connections emerge naturally between apparently unrelated issues (low-level cell theft and friendship, for example), in ways that are theoretically significant. This requires some level of affective engagement, and it often means intervening to clarify meanings, push for elaboration and check responses against what has been observed in the field.[18]

---

[18] I felt very strongly that it was important not to appear morally judgmental, and yet there were times when it would have been not just difficult but also rather unnatural to have repressed surprise and shock, or to have withheld opinions when pushed to give them.

None of this precludes the interviewer from periodically consulting the schedule, nor from ensuring consistency in the content and approach of the interview. But there may always be some trade-off between strict scientific rigour and rapport, and thus between traditional notions of reliability and validity.

Interviews were conducted in a small office that had been converted from cell-space some years earlier on E-wing, the prison's induction unit. At my request, it contained a lockable filing cabinet (although, in fact, I removed all materials as I left the prison each day), a desk, two chairs, and a kettle, with which I was allowed to make tea or coffee for myself and prisoners during interviews. A small window looked out onto one of the prison's exercise yards, towards the VTU. A sign which read 'Dr Ben Crewe, Criminolgist [sic], Cambridge University' was placed on the door.[19] I did little at first to decorate the room, only choosing to spruce it up with posters after one interviewee described it as 'pretty fucking depressing' and another highlighted the connotations of having a room that was essentially bare:

I was surprised when I came in here—you've got eight shelves and the only thing that's on them is paint. I was shocked. If you came into my cell, and you seen me with the same sort of set up with nothing in there, you'd think to yourself: 'Hasn't he got any possessions?' If you've been in two years, if you've got nothing you're either not quite well in the head, a bit of a tramp, or you're just a dickhead. (Tyler)

Before interviews began, interviewees were asked to read and sign a consent form. I explained the aims of the research, my powerlessness to influence their sentence conditions, the terms of anonymity and data use, and my responsibilities in terms of confidentiality. As is standard, this meant stressing that I would be obliged to report any information relating to serious harm to self or others or a serious security breach (i.e. an escape). I had some concerns that this process formalized the interview situation unnecessarily, but was glad of terms that would offer protection and helped avoid compromising situations.

Two kinds of interviews were conducted with prisoners: a life-history interview and a prison interview. The former was conducted

---

[19] One day, I arrived to find 'all you screws can fuck off' scrawled on the sign, which I did not take personally (indeed, I did not think the comment was aimed at me, although it may have been) but which one of the prison governors was deeply apologetic about and insisted was removed immediately.

with forty prisoners, and generally built upon relationships already established during the observational stage of the research. The prison interview was conducted with all interviewees with the exception of two prisoners, one of whom was released before we could organize a follow-up to his life-history interview and one who, having participated in the life-history interview, asked to withdraw participation.

In all then, there were seventy-two prisoner interviewees, of whom forty were interviewed about their life stories and their prison experiences, two about their life stories only, and thirty about their prison experiences with only brief biographical description. Both kinds of interview lasted on average two and a half hours—the morning or afternoon time-slot—such that forty prisoners were interviewed for five hours or more overall and some for much longer once supplementary interviews are accounted for. Thirty-five interviewees were chosen based on personal relationships developed in the field. The others were selected randomly or according to a stratified sampling technique that sought to ensure some balance between prisoners from different wings and ethnic backgrounds. Ten interviewees were Afro-Caribbean, four were of South Asian descent, and three had mixed-race backgrounds.[20] Only two were foreign national prisoners, reflecting the low proportion of foreign nationals in the establishment.

The life history interviews were relatively unstructured. During the pilot study, I had used a modified version of the McAdams (1995) protocol, but had found the focus on events such as 'peaks' and 'turning points' too specific to capture the texture of prisoners' lives. Some interviewees had struggled to organize their life descriptions as a series of 'chapters'. Their lives had been chaotic, and imposing this framework constrained them into conceptual timeframes that did not capture their experiences. The format I therefore developed was more open and chronologically linear than the McAdams schedule. Before interviews began, I explained that we had the entire morning or afternoon available to talk, that I was interested in their *life* histories rather than their *criminal* histories, and that I was particularly keen to understand the key people and events in their lives so far. Interviewees were asked to start by describing their family lives and backgrounds, with

[20] Of course, many more prisoners from all these minority groups were talked to during informal interactions.

their responses used to help pace the rest of the interview (often, interviewees provided accelerated descriptions, upon which I then encouraged them to expand).

Subsequent questions focused on daily life, aims, personality, and key influences, with interviewees given relative freedom to elaborate as they saw fit and talk through their lives chronologically. Prompts were used primarily to encourage interviewees to reflect on their aims, motivations and key influences during significant life stages or events, and to cover questions around schooling, family and criminal career. Most interventions were clarifications, follow-up probes, or simply nods of encouragement and attempts at empathy. Towards the end of the interviews, a number of stand-alone questions were asked (some based on the McAdams schedule) about when interviewees felt they had become 'a man rather than a boy', what they were most proud of and most regretted in their lives, their current self-image, any key turning points, any social, political or religious issues which were important in them, and visions they had of the future.

The prison interviews were more structured and sought to cover a wide range of issues that would incorporate the concerns of the classic ethnographies, while taking account of the particularities of the institutional context, and some new concerns such as drug culture, relationships with female staff and masculinity. The main areas were: adaptive strategies and orientations, relationships with prison staff, social relationships, hierarchies and loyalties, everyday values and attitudes, drug culture, and the pains and problems of prison life. Inevitably, the interview schedule changed as questions were eliminated or rephrased. A form of language soon developed that translated abstract questions into more mundane terms. As is also usual, as I became more accustomed to certain pacings and patterns of response, I was more able to relax into the interview without nagging anxieties about whether all topics would be 'covered' within the limited timeframe provided by the prison routine.

Using a recording device undoubtedly altered the dynamics of the interaction. Some prisoners visibly formalized their demeanour when the minidisc player was switched on, and were clearly conscious of the microphone for an initial period. On a couple of occasions, when I announced the date and place as the interview began, prisoners joked that this reproduced the dynamics of the police station. Clearly, this was not the tone I was trying to create.

But interviewees quickly lost their self-consciousness and the benefits of verbatim transcription and being fully engaged within the interview room far outweighed the drawbacks of the initial hesitations that the recorder produced. Indeed, as other research-ers have reported (Jewkes 2002), prisoners were remarkably, sometimes disarmingly, candid, frequently disclosing histories of personal abuse within minutes of starting to talk, and without any prompting on my part.

As each interview began to wind down, I asked prisoners whether they had been surprised by anything they had said, whether there were issues they wanted to discuss further, and whether they had any questions for me. The responses at this stage fell into three patterns, each implying a different role that the interview appeared to play. For some prisoners, it was an interesting diversion, a rare opportunity to reflect on a world that they had come to take for granted: 'I know it might sound a bit daft', said Darren, 'but when you asked "what do you think of when you're banged behind that door at night?", I'd never thought about that really'. These prison-ers hoped that their contributions had been 'useful' or noted with satisfaction that the interview had given them new kinds of social insight.[21] A second common response was for prisoners to observe that the interview had provided them with some kind of personal insight into their current situation or future ambitions: 'It's made me look at where I am a lot more', said Isaac.

For a larger group, the interview seemed to have a therapeutic purpose. It was 'a good talk' (Ian), an opportunity 'to get things off your chest, to tell people how you feel, because it's a harsh environment really, it's not a caring environment' (Rhys). Many prisoners expressed surprise at their own candour, noting that they had 'never opened up to anyone like that before' (Kieran). Tyler commented that he had been in prison for ten years, 'and there's things I've told you today I ain't told no cunt, never. Cos I don't think I can trust them. Because they are part of the Prison Service.' A large proportion of prisoners said that there was

[21] Many prisoners expressed anxiety about whether their 'answers' were 'good enough' or what I was 'looking for'. Two interviews had to be halted for short periods, when prisoners said they were feeling paranoid and insecure. In such situ-ations, conventional notions of informed consent felt rather inadequate, but I did not believe that terminating the process entirely would have been any more helpful than continuing, with sensitivity.

no-one in the prison with whom they could 'fully relax' and talk about personal matters. It says more about the emotional deficits of the prison than about any skill on my part that my office seemed to be an oasis of relative trust. Prison researchers benefit in uncomfortable ways from their perceived neutrality and from their willingness to listen in an environment where information really is power, and sympathetic outlets are at a premium.

Once interviewees had left the wing, officers regularly offered their own views of them: 'the biggest drug dealer in the prison', 'a bully', or 'a good lad'. As institutional accounts of how prisoners were perceived, these were useful descriptions, and were often consistent with what prisoners had disclosed. When they were incongruous, I had no means of checking competing versions. I did not consult prison files for three reasons: because they are so often inaccurate, because prisoners' index offences and criminal histories were not especially relevant to my concerns, and because I felt it would betray prisoners if I were 'checking' written records behind their backs.

Leaving the Field and Writing Up

I was certainly affected by the research process, which was intense, consuming, and at times distressing. Good prison research demands considerable affective presence (Liebling 2001), and time is often (and rightly) spent putting one's research interests to one side while a prisoner describes how his parole hearing panned out or his anguish at losing custody of his children. Much of the distress in men's prisons is submerged beneath surface interactions, creating an environment that is superficially calm yet highly charged. This combination produces an oppressive consistency, whose basis is hard to identify, but whose effects I experienced as a sense of dread as I approached the prison and a sense of release as I drove away. It was the transition into the environment, from one world to another, which generated these feelings. Once I was inside the establishment, they quickly disappeared.

Watching my steps, justifying my presence, and trying to keep my practical and intellectual wits as sharp as possible was draining work. There were few opportunities for 'down-time'. Once established in the prison, I became a lightning rod for complaints and grievances from staff as well as prisoners. The prison's sociology and philosophy classes served as valuable 'rest zones', where I could re-charge energy and ideas without having to participate too actively in discussions. Outside the prison, I was often too tired to socialize on weekdays. At weekends, when letting off steam, I drank more than normal, and I was so hungry to make sense of my experiences that, in conversation, I leapt upon the slightest indication of genuine interest in my research.[22] I did not reach the point of compassion fatigue that some researchers report, but I was aware that, after a day in the prison conducting lengthy, personal interviews, my capacity to listen was depleted. My ego was hungry for its own attention. As it is for prisoners to a much, much greater degree, the prison was isolating and all-encompassing. It is still a total institution of sorts.

I left the field fairly suddenly, having let relevant staff and prisoners know that I was going. On one of my final visits, I presented E-wing staff with some matching mugs from Habitat, a present that overwhelmed them less than I had expected. Possibly, they were just not the sort of mugs that were appropriate to the environment—too small and too decorative. My intention was to return within a few weeks to conduct more staff interviews. In the medium term, I planned to maintain regular contact with the prison by reporting early findings to the sociology class and bringing in outside speakers for evening talks and discussions. Events and other demands intervened, but, in truth, once I returned to the routines of departmental life, the impetus to revisit the prison was lost. Normality was a relief. In the two years that followed, I negotiated research access for two MPhil students and organized several group visits, in which we toured the prison and discussed readings with the prisoner sociology class over tea and biscuits.[23] The events reinforced my memories of the warmth of

---

[22] Much of the interest I generated was sincere but ill-informed, or sought out only the 'juicy stories' about prison violence or brutality. It was worryingly easy to be tempted into rehearsing these tales. I also 'saw' crime and its consequences everywhere, or, at least, felt much more sensitized to suspicious activity and the visible signs of the drugs economy.

[23] In a letter that I received following a student visit, the prison tutor reported that her students were 'still buzzing about mixing with your students. I sensed that the whole event had a positive effect, but feedback has totally confirmed it—many aspire to continue studying sociology at a higher level. It appears that the visit made them realize what they were missing out on. It was quite a party and made a good afternoon "out" for them'. One prisoner had reported that, in all his time in prison, he had 'never experienced anything as bizarre' as what became a kind of mannered tea party, with one sixteen-stone armed robber volunteering to 'be mum' by taking charge of the teapot.

the environment, although the turnover of prisoners meant that there were few faces I recognized. The prison was no longer *mine*, and other establishments soon took over as the research sites of choice.

The subsequent lag between fieldwork and publication has been considerable, and is of some regret. As time has elapsed, the feel of the prison, its everyday noises, language, and rituals, have become less vivid. At times, I have worried that my ability to see the prison has weakened. It has become much harder to conjure up the prison's strange combination of stupor and vitality, tension and conviviality. But as immediate impressions have faded, their lines have been redrawn in terms that are less descriptive and more analytical, less anecdotal and more sociological. This is a different kind of vision, perhaps even a different form of knowledge, but it is what academic accounts are obliged to provide and it requires conceptual digestion and rumination. This was a highly inductive study, with few initial hypotheses and very broad objectives, and these characteristics slowed the process by which the conceptual meaning of the data became perceptible.

To avoid collusion in what Cohen and Taylor call the 'temporal fiction' by which research is normally presented, some comments should be offered about the route to the final text. Following the fieldwork period, interviews were transcribed in full and coded using NVivo software. Earlier publications based on this study illustrated the futility of trying to describe prison culture as a uniform entity, but at their time of writing, the typology that structures this book had not been developed.[24] Its emergence was sparked largely by the literature on penal order—in particular, Sparks *et al.* (1996), Carrabine (2004), Bosworth and Carrabine (2001)—and texts such as Abercrombie *et al.* (1990), Wrong (2002) and Scott (1990), all of which aided my reflections on issues of power, order, and resistance. Once the typology of adaptive styles emerged, it brought into relief the social fault-lines of the prisoner community.

Prisons are 'raw, and sometimes desperate, special places' (Liebling 1999: 152), and the language found in them—what Sykes and Messinger called the 'pungent argot of the dispossessed'

---

[24] I am referring in particular to Crewe 2005a and Crewe 2006b, in which attempts were made to differentiate prisoners' attitudes towards grassing and relationships with staff.

(1960: 11)—reflects these conditions. Terms are vibrant, direct, and decisive and, among prisoners in particular, they are unadorned by cliché. The extremity of the environment exposes values and priorities, and strips away extraneous and superficial forms of expression. Language is used economically, as if, by necessity, words really have to capture what they mean. It is curious that many of the classic prison ethnographies are written with minimal use of prisoner testimonies.[25] The liberal employment of direct quotations in this book is, to some degree, an ethical decision.[26] Prison researchers are rightly dismissive of prurient interests in the prison, but its intellectual attraction is undoubtedly linked to its *extremity*—the variation in human behaviour 'from compassion and wisdom to abuse and life-threatening violence' that it harbours (Liebling 1999: 152). The line between voyeuristic curiosity and ethical inquisition is not always clear, but one difference lies in the distinction between a tone that essentially distances and objectifies prisoners, and one that extends empathy and understanding (what Weber calls 'Verstehen'). The marginalization of prisoners from popular notions of citizenship means that their views have become disqualified knowledge (Morgan 1999). To convey their basic humanity and represent their experiences is a moral obligation.

The second aim of including so many excerpts is to evidence interpretations and give flesh to the more abstract conceptualizations that sociological analysis requires. It is for this reason too that interviewees are referred to throughout the text through pseudonymous names rather than abstract designations (e.g. 'male, 25, Midlands'). I hope that my use of case studies gives readers a sense of prisoners that goes beyond disembedded statements and demographic variables. No attempt has been made to disguise the identity of the prison, for I share King and Elliott's (1977) view

---

[25] *The Society of Captives*, for example, includes only a smattering of direct quotations, a decision which no doubt reflected the functionalist tendency to discount 'meaning'. The preference for objective language does not prevent Sykes from conveying the feel of the prison with remarkable clarity and sensitivity.

[26] Where quotations have been edited in minor ways—the removal of 'ums', 'ers' or incoherent digressions, for example—no indication is given within the text. Where more significant editing has occurred, this is denoted by a short line of dots (i.e. ....). Occasionally, excerpts from different stages of an interview have been spliced together in the same passage, but the integrity of meaning has not been altered.

that, in single-prison studies, guarantees of institutional anonymity are pointless.

I have been reluctant to foreground myself in the analysis itself, not because I think my identity was irrelevant to the study, but because my identity was not what the study was about. To some degree, no doubt, the slant of my findings and the nature of my interactions were shaped by my subjectivity and positioning, but I do not believe that they were merely outcomes of these things. It is important to avoid the 'reflexive spiral' where self-examination spills over into anecdotalism and apologetic subjectivism. When undertaken carefully and critically, qualitative research can go quite some way in uncovering the objective realities of the social world. There is too much to lose in self-indulgence. Likewise, there is too much at stake for research interests to remain at a level of intellectual abstraction. The prison is fascinating in part because of its social and interpersonal intensity—the manner in which it concentrates social life into such a compressed space, and creates iceberg identities whose appearances are deceptive and whose depths are submerged. The human costs of this environment are massive. We overuse prisons blindly, at our peril.

Written contact was maintained with three prisoners, all of whom feature heavily in this book. George wrote careful, rather formal letters as he moved towards release. Some described the simple joys of being in an open prison after many years in closed conditions: 'Being able to stroll through an avenue of trees with banks of wild grasses and flowers at either side down towards the lake to study the geese and ducks.' Others offered comment on the process of reintegration into a society that no longer exhibited the 'consensus/welfarism of pre-Thatcher days'. George's comments on the draft articles that I sent to him were tentative and humble, as reflected the self-effacing manner that long-term captivity had produced in him. By 2006, he had written to let me know that 'after being constrained to live half of my life in prison' he was 'finally a free man!', but contact was lost soon thereafter.

Like George, Nathan at first wrote mainly about the banal pleasures of a more open institution—walking on an uphill gradient, seeing the sky at night:

I sat out the back of the main housing unit, and stared into a cloudless night sky. There were stars. For the first time since I was nineteen, I could see the stars. Tension gone. Fear gone. The weight of the years... gone! I don't think the profundity of that moment will ever leave me.

Both George and Nathan were struck by how accustomed they had become to the effects of confinement. Nathan described closed conditions as 'an unmoving reality of oppressive greydom', and was struck by the feeling of a 'weight being lifted' on arrival in the Cat-D environment. Both men felt reawakened from the identities they had developed in conditions they now portrayed as 'tense' and 'infantilizing'. On release, Nathan returned to a supportive family and reintegrated with remarkable success, despite daily difficulties—not just in terms of finding employment or adjusting to a much-changed world, but in creating a plausible public narrative when strangers questioned him about his past. Still, the biggest surprise to him was that male toilets in pubs were no less revolting than when he had entered prison in the early 1990s.

Alfie and I corresponded only twice in the few months after the fieldwork before he was released. In his first letter, he described his family's doubts about his ability to stay drug-free in the community. The second letter struck a more positive tone, but, despite the pledge that he would write after a few weeks of his 'sojourn into the "real world"', nothing followed. With characteristic honesty, Alfie had told me that if ever I were to meet him on drugs in the community, I would hate him, so I had some ambivalence about the break in contact.[27] But I assume with great sadness that he is either back on drugs, back in prison, or no longer alive. I like to remember him with the optimism of the sign-off from his second letter, an excerpt from Max Ehrmann's *Desiderata*:

Go placidly amid the noise and haste, and remember what peace there may be in silence ...

With all its sham, drudgery and broken dreams,

it is still a beautiful world.

---

[27] On one occasion, I bumped into two Wellingborough ex-prisoners in Cambridge town centre. I had interviewed one of them at length, and he had stated with certainty that he would stay off drugs on release. Both he and his friend were clearly intoxicated and were deeply embarrassed to see me.

Bibliography

Aas, K.F. (2004) 'From narrative to database: Technological change and penal culture', *Punishment and Society*, 6(4) 379–393.

Abercrombie, N., Hill, S. and Turner, B. (1980) *The Dominant Ideology Thesis*. London: Allen and Unwin.

Aitken, J. (2003) *Pride and Perjury*. London: Continuum.

Akers, R.L., Hayner, N.S. and Gruninger, W. (1974) 'Homosexual and drug behavior in prison: A test of the functional and importation models of the inmate system', *Social Problems*, 21(3) 410–422.

Akers, R., Hayner, N. and Gruninger, W. (1977) 'Prisonization in five countries: Type of prison and inmate characteristic', *Criminology*, 14(4) 527–554.

Anderson, E. (1999) *The Code of the Street: Decency, Violence, and the Moral Life of the Inner City*. New York: W.W. Norton.

Archer, J. (2002) *Hell: A Prison Diary*. London: Macmillan.

Arnold, H. (2005) 'The effects of prison work', in A. Liebling and S. Maruna (eds) *The Effects of Imprisonment*. Cullompton: Willan, pp. 391–420.

—— (2008) 'The experience of prison officer training' in J. Bennett, B. Crewe and A. Wahidin (eds) *Understanding Prison Staff*. Cullompton: Willan, pp 399–418.

Atchley, R. and McCabe, P. (1968) 'Socialization in correctional communities: A replication', *American Sociological Review*, 33, 774–785.

Atherton, P. and Lloyd M. (1995) 'Tackling drug use at Long Lartin', *Prison Service Journal*, 99: 17–20.

Attrill, G. and Liell, G. (2007) 'Offenders; views on risk assessment', in N. Padfield (ed.) *Who to Release? Parole, Fairness and Criminal Justice*. Cullompton: Willan.

Bailey, K.D. (1994) *Typologies and Taxonomies: An Introduction to Classification Techniques*. Thousand Oaks: Sage.

Bauman, Z. (2000) *Liquid Modernity*. Cambridge: Polity Press.

Beck, U. (1992) *Risk Society: Towards a New Modernity*. New Delhi: Sage.

Becker, H. (1940) 'Constructive typology in the social sciences', in H.E. Barnes, H. Becker and F.B. Becker (eds) *Contemporary Social Theory*. New York: D Appleton Century.

Beckett, K. and Western, B. (2001) 'Governing social marginality', in D. Garland (ed.), Mass *Imprisonment: Social Causes and Consequences*. London: Sage.

Bennett J. and Wahidin A. (2008) 'Industrial relations in prison', in J. Bennett, B. Crewe, and A. Wahidin, (eds) *Understanding Prison Staff*. Cullompton: Willan.

Berlin, I. (1969) *Four Essays on Liberty*. London & New York: Oxford University Press.

Berk, B. (1966) 'Organizational goals and inmate organization', *American Journal of Sociology* 71(March): 522–524.

Bond, P., McGowan P. and Roger I. (1995) 'Drugs in prison: the Downview perspective', *Prison Service Journal*, 99: 32–35.

Bosworth, M. (1999) *Engendering Resistance: Agency and Power in Women's Prisons*. Aldershot: Dartmouth.

Bosworth, M. and Carrabine, E. (2000) 'Reassessing Resistance', *Punishment and Society*, 3(4): 501–515.

—— and Sparks, R. (2000) 'New Directions in Prison Studies: some introductory comments', *Theoretical Criminology*, 4(3): 259–264.

Bottoms, A.E. (1990) 'The aims of imprisonment', in D. Garland (ed.) *Justice, Guilt and Forgiveness in the Penal System*. Edinburgh: University of Edinburgh Centre for Theology and Public Issues, Occasional Paper No. 18.

—— (1995) 'The philosophy and politics of punishment and sentencing', in C.M.V. Clarkson and R. Morgan (eds) *The Politics of Sentencing Reform*, Oxford: Clarendon Press, pp. 17–49.

—— (1999) 'Interpersonal violence and social order in prisons', in M. Tonry and J. Petersilia (eds) *'Prisons', Crime and Justice: A Review of Research*, 26, 205–281.

—— (2002) 'Morality, crime, compliance and public policy' in A.E. Bottoms and M. Tonry (eds) *Ideology, Crime and Criminal Justice: A Symposium in Honour of Sir Leon Radzinowicz*. Cullompton: Willan.

—— (2003) 'Theoretical reflections on the evaluation of a penal policy initiative', in L. Zedner and A. Ashworth (eds) *The Criminological Foundations of Penal Policy: Essays in Honour of Roger Hood*. Oxford: Clarendon Press.

Bourdieu (1972, English Translation: 1977) *Esquisse d'une théorie de la pratique, précédé de trois études d'ethnologie kabyle*, full English translation as: *Outline of a Theory of Practice*. Cambridge: Cambridge University Press.

Bourdieu, P. (1984) *Distinction: A Social Critique of the Judgement of Taste* (translated by Richard Nice), London: Routledge.

Bowker, L.H. (1977) *Prisoner Subcultures*. Lexington, MA: Lexington Books.

Boyle, J. (1977) *A Taste of Freedom*. London: Pan Books.

—— (1984) *The Pain of Confinement: Prison Diaries*. Edinburgh: Canongate.

Bryans, S. (2007) *Managing Prisons in a Time of Change*. Cullompton: Willan.

Britton, D. (2003) *At Work in the Iron Cage: The Prison as Gendered Organization*. New York: New York University Press.

Brownlee, I. (1998) 'New Labour – new penology? Punitive rhetoric and the limits of managerialism in criminal justice policy', *Journal of Law and Society*, 25(3), 313–335.

Bukstel, L. and Kilman, P. (1980) 'Psychological effects of imprisonment on confined individuals', *Psychological Bulletin*, 88, 469–493.

Buntman, F.L. (2003) *Robben Island and Prisoner Resistance to Apartheid*. Cambridge: Cambridge University Press.

Butler, M. (2006) *Prisoner Confrontations: the role of shame, masculinity and respect*. Unpublished PhD thesis, Cambridge University.

Caird, R. (1974) *A Good and Useful Life: Imprisonment in Britain Today*. London: Hart-Davis.

Carlen, P. (1998) *Sledgehammer: Women's Imprisonment at the Millennium*. Basingstoke: Macmillan.

—— (2005) 'Imprisonment and the penal body politic: the cancer of disciplinary governance', in A. Liebling and S. Maruna (eds) *The Effects of Imprisonment*. Cullompton: Willan, pp. 421–441.

Carrabine, E. (2000) 'Discourse, governmentality and translation: towards a social theory of imprisonment', *Theoretical Criminology*, 4(3): 309–331.

—— (2004) *Power, Discourse and Resistance: A Genealogy of the Strangeways Prison Riot*. Dartmouth: Ashgate.

—— (2005) 'Prison riots, social order and the problem of legitimacy', *British Journal of Criminology*, 45, 896–913.

Carroll, L. (1974) *Hacks, Blacks and Cons: Race Relations in a Maximum Security Prison*. Lexington: D.C. Heath and Company.

Charlesworth, S. (1999) *A Phenomenology of Working-Class Experience*. Cambridge: Cambridge University Press.

Cheliotis, L. (2006) 'How iron is the iron cage of new penology? The role of human agency in the implementation of criminal justice policy', *Punishment and Society*, 8(3): 313–340.

—— (2008) 'Resisting the scourge of managerialism: on the uses of discretion in late-modern prisons', in J. Bennett, B. Crewe and A. Wahidin (eds) *Understanding Prison Staff*. Cullompton: Willan, pp. 247–261.

—— (2008) 'Governing through the looking-glass: Perception, morality and neo-liberal penality', PhD thesis, University of Cambridge.

—— and Liebling, A. (2006) 'Race matters in british prisons', *British Journal of Criminology*, 46, 286–317.

Clare, E., Bottomley, K., Grounds, A., Hammond, C.J., Liebling, A. and Taylor, C. (2001) *Evaluation of Close Supervision Centres*, London: Home Office.

Clark, D., Fisher, M. and McDougall, C. (1993) 'A new methodology for assessing the level of risk in incarcerated offenders', *British Journal of Criminology*, 33(3), 436–448.

—— (1999) 'Risk assessment in prisons and probation', in G. Towl and C. McDougall (eds) *What Do Forensic Psychologists Do? Current and Future Directions in the Prison and Probation Services.* Leicester: British Psychological Society.

Clemmer, D. (1940; second edition 1958) *The Prison Community.* New York: Holt, Rinehart and Winston.

Cloward, R., Grosser, G., McCleery, R., Ohlin, L., Sykes, G. and Messinger, S. (1960) *Theoretical Studies in Social Organization of the Prison.* New York: Social Science Research Council.

Cloward, R. and Ohlin, L. (1960) *Delinquency and Opportunity: A Theory of Delinquent Gangs.* Glencoe, IL: Free Press.

Cohen, S. and Taylor, L. (1972) *Psychological Survival: The Experience of Long-Term Imprisonment.* Harmondsworth: Penguin.

—— and —— (1977) 'Talking about Prison Blues', in C. Bell and H. Newby (eds) *Doing Sociological Research.* London: Allen & Unwin, pp 67–86.

Colvin, M. (1992) *The Penitentiary in Crisis: From Accommodation to Crisis in New Mexico.* Albany: State University of New York Press.

Cooke, D. (1989) 'Containing violent prisoners: an analysis of the Barlinnie Special Unit', *British Journal of Criminology,* 29, 129–143.

Cover, R. (1986) 'Violence and the Word', *Yale Law Journal,* 95, 1601–1629.

Crawford, A. (2009) 'Restorative justice and anti-social behaviour interventions as contractual governance: Constructing the citizen-consumer', in P. Knepper, J. Doak and J. Shapland (eds) *Urban Crime Prevention, Surveillance, and Restorative Justice: Effects of Social Technologies,* Taylor & Francis.

Crawley, E. (2004a) *Doing Prison Work: The public and private lives of prison officers.* Cullompton: Willan.

—— (2004b) 'Emotion and performance: prison officers and the presentation of self in prisons', *Punishment and Society,* 6(4): 411–427.

—— (2005) 'Institutional thoughtlessness in prisons and its impacts on the day-to-day prison lives of elderly men', in *Journal of Contemporary Criminal Justice,* Vol. 21, No. 4, 350–363 (2005).

Crawley, E. and Crawley, P. (2008) 'Understanding prison officers: culture, cohesion, and conflict', in J. Bennett, B. Crewe and A. Wahidin (eds) *Understanding Prison Staff.* Cullompton: Willan.

Cressey, D. (1958) 'Foreword' to D. Clemmer, *The Prison Community* (second edition). New York: Holt, Rinehart and Winston.

Crewe, B. (2005a) 'Codes and conventions: The terms and conditions of contemporary inmate values', in A. Liebling and S. Maruna, (eds) *The Effects of Imprisonment,* 177–208. Cullompton: Willan.

—— (2005b) 'The prisoner society in the era of hard drugs', *Punishment and Society,* 7(4), 457–481.

—— (2006a) 'Male prisoners' orientations towards female officers in an English prison', *Punishment and Society,* 8(4): 395–421.

—— (2006b) 'Prison drug dealing and the ethnographic lens', *The Howard Journal of Criminal Justice*, 45(4), 347–368.

—— (2007) 'Power, adaptation and resistance in the late-modern prison', *British Journal of Criminology*, 47(2): 256–275.

—— and Maruna, S. (2006) 'Self-narratives and ethnographic fieldwork', in D. Hobbs and R. Wright (eds) *The Handbook of Fieldwork*. Sage Publishing.

Crighton, D. (2005) 'Risk assessment', in D. Crighton and G. Towl (eds) *Psychology in Probation Services*. Oxford: Blackwell.

—— (2006) 'Methodological issues in psychological research in prisons', in G. Towl (ed) *Psychological Research in Prisons*. Oxford: Blackwell.

—— and Bailey, J. (2006) 'Psychological research into life sentence offenders', in G. Towl (ed) *Psychological Research in Prisons*. Oxford: Blackwell.

Darwall, S. (1977) 'Two kinds of respect', *Ethics* 88(1): 36–49.

Dean, M. (2006) (fourth edition) *Governmentality: Power and Rule in Modern Society*. London: Sage.

DiIulio, J. (1987) *Governing Prisons*. New York: The Free Press.

Dorn, N. and Nigel S. (eds.) (1987) *A Land Fit for Heroin? Drug Policies, Prevention and Practice*. Basingstoke: Macmillan.

Downes, D. (1988) *Contrasts in Tolerance*. Oxford: Clarendon Press.

Drake, D. (2007) 'A comparison of quality of life, legitimacy and order in two maximum-security prisons', unpublished PhD thesis, University of Cambridge.

Duke, K. (2003) *Drugs, Prisons and Policy-Making*, Basingstoke: Palgrave Macmillan.

Durkheim, E. (1933) *The Division of Labour in Society*. New York.

Dunbar, I. (1985) *A Sense of Direction*. London: Home Office.

Dymond-White, S. (2003) *The role of the Category-C prison*, unpublished MSt. thesis, Cambridge University.

Edgar, K. and O'Donnell, I. (1998) *Mandatory Drug Testing in Prisons: The Relationship between MDT and the Level and Nature of Drug Misuse* (Home Office Research and Statistics Directorate, Research Study 189), London: Home Office.

——, —— and Martin, C. (2003) *Prison Violence: The Dynamics of Conflict, Fear and Power*. Cullompton: Willan.

—— and Martin, C. (2004) *Perceptions of Race and Conflict: Perspectives of Minority Ethnic Prisoners and of Prison Officers*. Home Office Online Report 11/04.

Einat, T. (2004) 'Language, culture, identity and coping in Israeli prisons', paper presented at Cropwood Conference, 2004, *The Effects of Imprisonment: An International Symposium*, Robinson College, Cambridge, April 14–15th 2004.

—— and Einat, H. (2000) 'Inmate argot as an expression of prison subculture: The Israeli case', *The Prison Journal*, 80(3): 309–325.

Feeley, M.M. and Simon, J. (1992) 'The New Penology: Notes on the Emerging Strategy of Corrections and its Implications', *Criminology*, 30(4): 449–74.

Fielding, N. (1994) 'Cop canteen culture', in T. Newburn, and E.A. Stanko, (eds) *Just Boys Doing Business: Men, Masculinities and Crime*. London: Routledge.

Foucault, M. (1977) *Discipline and Punish: The Birth of the Prison*. Harmondsworth: Penguin.

—— (1978) *The History of Sexuality, Vol. 1: An Introduction*. Translated by Robert Hurley, New York: Pantheon.

—— (1982) 'The subject and power', in H.L. Dreyfus and P. Rabinow (eds) *Michel Foucault: Beyond Structuralism and Hermeneutics*, Chicago: Chicago University Press, pp. 208–226.

—— (1991) 'Governmentality', in G. Burchell, C. Gordon and P. Miller (eds) *The Foucault Effect*, Hemel Hempstead: Harvester Wheatsheaf, pp. 87–104.

Fox, K. (1999) 'Changing violent minds: Discursive correction and resistance in the cognitive treatment of violent offenders in prison', *Social Problems*, 46(1), 88–103.

Friendship, C., Blud. L., Erikson, M., Travers, R. (2002) *An Evaluation of Cognitive Behavioural Treatment for Prisoners*. Home Office Research Findings No. 161. London: Home Office.

Gambetta, D. (2005) 'Why prisoners fight', in D. Gambetta, *Crimes and Signs: Cracking the Codes of the Underworld*, Princeton, NJ: Princeton University Press.

Garabedian, P. (1963) 'Social roles and processes of socialization in the prison community', *Social Problems*, 11(Fall): 139–152.

Garfinkel, H. (1956) 'Conditions of successful degradation ceremonies', *American Journal of Sociology*, 61, 420–424.

Garland, D. (1996) 'The Limits of the Sovereign State: Strategies of Crime Control in Contemporary Society', *British Journal of Criminology*, 36, 445–471.

Garland, D. (1997) '"Governmentality" and the problem of crime: Foucault, criminology, sociology', *Theoretical Criminology*, 1, 173–214.

—— (2001a) *The Culture of Control Crime and Social Order in Contemporary Society*. Oxford: Oxford University Press.

—— (ed) (2001b) *Mass Imprisonment: Social Causes and Consequences*. London: Sage.

—— and Young, P. (1983) 'Towards a social analysis of penality', in D. Garland and P. Young (eds) *The Power to Punish: Contemporary Penality and Social Analysis*. Atlantic Highlands, NJ: Humanities Press.

Garofalo, J. and Clark, R. (1985) 'The inmate subculture in jails', *Criminal Justice and Behaviour*, 12(4): 415–434.

Genders, E. and Player, E. (1989) *Race Relations in Prisons*. Oxford: Oxford University Press.

—— (1995) *Grendon: A Study of a Therapeutic Prison*. Oxford: Clarendon Press.

Giddens, A. (1982) *Profiles and Critiques in Social Theory*. London: Macmillan Press.

—— (1991) *Modernity and Self-Identity: Self and Society in the Late Modern Age*. Stanford University Press.

—— (1984) *The Constitution of Society: Outline of the Theory of Structure*. Berkeley, CA: University of California Press.

Gilligan, J. (1996) *Violence: Our Deadly Epidemic and Its Causes*. Grosset/Putnam Books: New York.

Glaser, B. and Strauss, A. (1967) *The Discovery of Grounded Theory: Strategies for Qualitative Research*. Chicago: Aldine.

Goffman, E. (1961) *Asylums: Essays on the Social Situation of Mental Patients and Other Inmates*. Harmondsworth: Penguin.

Gross, R. (2000) 'The place of the personal and subjective in religious studies', in S.D. Moch and M.F. Gates (eds) *The Researcher Experience in Qualitative Research*. Thousand Oaks, CA: Sage, pp. 163–177.

Grusky, O. (1959) 'Organizational goals and the behaviour of informal leaders', *American Journal of Sociology*, 65(July): 59–67.

Halliday, J. (2001) *Making Punishment Work: Report of a Review of the Sentencing Framework for England and Wales*. London: Home Office Communication Directorate.

Halsey, M. (2006) 'Negotiating conditional release: Juvenile narratives of repeat incarceration', *Punishment and Society* 8(2): 147–181.

Haney, C., Banks, W. C., and Zimbardo, P. G. (1973) 'Interpersonal dynamics in a simulated prison', *International Journal of Criminology and Penology*, 1, 69–97.

Hannah-Moffat, K. (2001) *Punishment in Disguise: Penal Governance and Federal Imprisonment of Women in Canada*. Toronto: University of Toronto Press.

—— (2005) 'Criminality, need and the transformative risk subject: Hybridizations of risk/need in penality', in *Punishment and Society* 7:1, 29–51.

Harvey, J. (2007) *Young Men in Prison: Surviving and Adapting to Life Inside*. Cullompton: Willan.

Hassine, V. (1999) *Life Without Parole: Living in Prison Today*. Los Angeles: Roxbury Publishing.

HMCIP (2000) *Report on an Unannounced Inspection of HM Prison Wellingborough, 11–12 July 2000*.

—— *Report on a Full Announced Inspection of HM Prison Wellingborough, 4–8 August 2003*.

Home Office (2003) *Driving Delivery: A Strategic Framework for Psychological Services*. London: HM Prison Service, NPS, Home Office.

—— (2003) *The Prison Population in 2002: A Statistical Review*. London: Home Office.

HM Prison Standards Audit Unit (2002) *Final Report of a Combined Standards and Security Audit.*

Hope, T. (2004) 'Pretend it works: Evidence and governance in the evaluation of the reducing burglary initiative', *Criminal Justice*, 4(3): 287–308.

Hough, M. and Roberts, J. (1998) *Home Office Research Study 179, Attitudes to Punishment: Findings from the British Crime Survey.* London: Home Office Research, Development and Statistics Directorate.

Hutchinson, S. (2006) 'Countering catastrophic criminology: Reform, punishment and the modern liberal compromise', *Punishment and Society* 8(4), 443–467.

Irwin, J. (1970) *The Felon.* Englewood Cliffs, NJ: Prentice Hall.

—— (1980) *Prisons in Turmoil.* Chicago, Little Brown.

—— (1985) *The Jail.* Berkeley, CA: University of California Press.

—— (2005) *The Warehouse Prison: Disposal of the New Dangerous Classes.* Los Angeles: Roxbury.

—— and Austin, J. (1997) (second edition) *It's About Time: American's Imprisonment Binge.* Belmont, CA: Wadsworth.

—— and Cressey, D. (1962) 'Thieves, convicts and the inmate culture', *Social Problems*, 10, 142–155.

Jacobs, J. (1974) 'Street gangs behind bars', *Social Problems*, 21(3): 395–409.

—— (1977) *Stateville: The Penitentiary in Mass Society.* Chicago: University of Chicago Press.

—— (1983) *New Perspectives on Prisons and Imprisonment.* Ithaca: Cornell University Press.

James, E. (2003) *A Life Inside: A Prisoner's Notebook.* London: Atlantic.

Jameson, N. and Allison, E. (1995) *Strangeways 1990: A Serious Disturbance: The inside story of the biggest protest in the history of British prisons.*

Jamieson, R. and Grounds, A. (2005) 'Release and readjustment: Perspectives from studies of wrongfully convicted and politically motivated prisoners', in A. Liebling and S. Maruna (eds) *The Effects of Imprisonment.* Cullompton, Devon: Willan.

Jewkes, Y. (2002) *Captive Audience: Media, Masculinity and Power in Prisons.* Cullompton: Willan.

—— (2005a) 'Men behind bars: Doing masculinity as an adaptation to imprisonment', *Men and Masculinities*, 8, 44–63.

—— (2005b) 'Loss, liminality and the life sentence: Managing identity through a disruptive lifecourse', in A. Liebling and S. Maruna, (eds) *The Effects of Imprisonment*, Cullompton: Willan, pp. 366–388.

Johnson, R. (1976) *Culture and Crisis in Confinement.* Lexington: Lexington Books.

—— (1987) *Hard Time: Understanding and Reforming the Prison*. Pacific Grove, CA: Brooks/Cole Publishing.

Jones, T. and Newburn, T. (2006) 'Three strikes and you're out: Exploring symbol and substance in American and British crime control politics', *British Journal of Criminology*, 46, 781–802.

Kaminski, M. (2004) *Games Prisoners Play: The tragicomic worlds of Polish prison*. Princeton, NJ: Princeton University Press.

Kant, I. (1797/1991) *Die Metaphysik der Sitten* translated as *The Metaphysics of Morals*. Translation by M. Gregor, Cambridge: Cambridge University Press.

King, R. (2000) 'Doing research in prisons', in R. King and E. Wincup (eds.) *Doing Research on Crime and Justice*. Oxford: Oxford University Press.

—— (1991) 'Maximum-security custody in Britain and the USA: A study of Gartree and Oak Park Heights', *British Journal of Criminology*, 31, 126–152.

—— (1999) 'The rise and rise of supermax: An american solution in search of a problem?' *Punishment and Society*, 1(2): 163–186.

—— (2005) 'The effects of supermax custody', in A. Liebling and S. Maruna, (eds) *The Effects of Imprisonment*. Cullompton: Willan, pp. 118–145.

—— (2008) 'Prison staff: An international perspective', in J. Bennett, B. Crewe and A. Wahidin (eds) *Understanding Prison Staff*. Cullompton: Willan, pp. 30–48.

—— and Elliott, K. (1977) *Albany: Birth of a Prison, End of an Era*. London: Routledge and Kegan Paul.

—— and McDermott, K. (1989) 'British prisons 1970–1987: The ever-deepening crisis', *British Journal of Criminology*, 29: 107–128.

—— and McDermott, K. (1990) '"My geranium is subversive": Some notes on the management of trouble in prisons', *British Journal of Sociology*, 41(4): 445–471.

—— and McDermott, K. (1995) *The State of Our Prisons*. Oxford: Clarendon Press.

Koestler, A. (1940) *Darkness at Noon*. Bantam Books.

Kruttschnitt, C. and Gartner, R. (2005) *Marking Time in the Golden State: Women's Imprisonment in California*. Cambridge: Cambridge University Press.

Larner, J. and Ralph T. (1964) *The Addict in the Street*. Harmondsworth: Penguin.

Layder, D. (1998) *Sociological Practice: Linking Theory and Social Research*. London: Sage Publications.

Liebling, A. (1992) *Suicides in Prison*. London: Routledge Press.

—— (1999) 'Doing research in prison: breaking the silence?', *Theoretical Criminology* 3, 147–173.

—— (1999) 'Prison suicide and prisoner coping', in M. Tonry and J. Petersilia (eds) *Prisons, Crime and Justice: An Annual Review of Research*, 26, 283–360.

—— (2000) 'Prison officers, policing and the use of discretion', *Theoretical Criminology*, 4(3), 333–357.

—— (2001) 'Whose side are we on? Theory, practice and allegiances in prisons research', *British Journal of Criminology*, 41, 472–484.

—— (assisted by H. Arnold) (2004) *Prisons and Their Moral Performance: A Study of Values, Quality, and Prison Life*. Oxford: Clarendon Press.

——, Tait, S., Durie, L., Stiles, A., Harvey, J., assisted by Rose, G. (2005) *An Evaluation of the Safer Locals Programme*, Final Report (revised June 2005), Cambridge: Cambridge Institute of Criminology, Prisons Research Centre.

—— and Price, D. (2001) *The Prison Officer*. Winchester: Waterside Press.

—— Muir, G., Rose, G. and Bottoms, A.E. (1999) '*Incentives and Earned Privileges in Prison. Research Findings 87'*, London: Home Office Research, Development and Statistics Directorate.

Lipton, D., Martinson, R. and Wilks, J. (1975) *The Effectiveness of Correctional Treatment: A Survey of Treatment Evaluation Studies*. New York: Praeger.

Lipsky, M. (1980) *Street-Level Bureaucracy: Dilemmas of the Individual in Public Services*. New York: Russell Sage Foundation.

Lösel, F. (1995) 'Increasing consensus in the evaluation of offender rehabilitation? Lessons from recent research syntheses', *Psychology, Crime and Law*, 2 (1) 19–39

Lucken, K. (1998) 'Contemporary penal trends: Modern or postmodern?', *British Journal of Criminology*, 38(1): 106–23.

Lynch, M. (1998) 'Waste managers? The new penology, crime fighting, and parole agent identity', *Law & Society Review*, 32(4): 839–869.

MacDonald, D. and Sim, J. (1978) *Scottish Prisons and the Special Unit*. Glasgow: Scottish Council for Civil Liberties.

Mandela, N. (1994) *Long Walk to Freedom*. London: Little, Brown, and Co.

Marshall, S. (1997) 'Control in Category-C prisons', *Research Findings No. 54*, Home Office, HMSO.

Martinson, R. (1974) 'What works? Questions and answers about prison reform', *Public Interest*, 35, 22–54.

Maruna, S. (2001) *Making Good: How Ex-Convicts Reform and Rebuild Their Lives*. Washington DC: American Psychological Association Books.

—— and Mann, R. (2006) 'A fundamental attribution error? Rethinking cognitive distortions', *Legal and Criminological Psychology*, 11, 155–177.

Marx, K. (1938) *Capital. Vol 1*. Trans. Donna Torr. London: George Allen and Unwin.

Mathiesen, T. (1965) *The Defences of the Weak: A Sociological Study of a Norwegian Correctional Institution*. London: Tavistock.

Mauss, M. (1990) *The Gift: Forms and Functions of Exchange in Archaic Societies*. London: Routledge.

McAdams, D. (1995) 'The Life Story Interview' <http://www.sesp.northwestern.edu/docs/LifeStoryInterview.pdf>.

McCorkle, L. and Korn, R. (1954) 'Re-socialization within walls', *The Annals of the American Academy of Political and Social Sciences*, 293(May): 88–98.

McDermott, K. and King, R. (1988) 'Mind games: Where the action is in prisons', *British Journal of Criminology*, 28(3): 357–377.

McEvoy, K. (2001) *Paramilitary Imprisonment in Northern Ireland.* Oxford: Clarendon Press.

McGuire, J. (1995) 'Reviewing "what works": Past, present and future', in J. McGuire (ed.) *What Works: Reducing Reoffending.* Chichester: John Wiley.

McHugh, M., Heavens, J. and Baxter, K. (2008) 'Recruitment and assessment of prison staff', in J. Bennett, B. Crewe and A. Wahidin (eds) *Understanding Prison Staff.* Cullompton: Willan, pp. 369–385.

McKinney, J.C. (1954) 'Constructive typology in social research', in J.T. Doby, E.A. Suchmann, J.C. McKinney, R.G. Francis and J.P. Dean (eds) *An Introduction to Social Research*, Harrisburg, PA: Stackpole, pp. 139–198.

McLaughlin, E. and Muncie, J. (2000) 'The criminal justice system: New Labour's new partnerships', in J. Clarke *et al.* (eds) *New Managerialism, New Welfare?* London: Sage.

McLean, C. and Liebling, A. (2008) 'Prison Staff in the Public and Private Sector' , in J. Bennett, B. Crewe and A. Wahidin (2008) *Understanding Prison Staff.* Cullompton: Willan.

McVicar, J. (1974) *McVicar by Himself.* London: Hutchinson.

Medlicott, D. (2001) *Surviving The Prison Place: Narratives of Suicidal Prisoners.* Aldershot: Ashgate.

—— (2005) 'The unbearable brutality of being: Casual cruelty in prison and what this tells us about who we really are', in M.S. Breen (ed.) *Minding Evil: Explorations of Human Iniquity.* Amsterdam/New York, NY.

Merton, R. (1938) 'Social structure and anomie', *American Sociological Review*, 3, 672–682.

Messerschmidt, J.W. (1993) *Masculinities and Crime: Critique and Reconceptualization of Theory.* Lanham, Maryland: Rowman and Littlefield.

Milgram, S. (1963) 'Behavioural study of obedience', *Journal of Abnormal and Social Psychology*, 67(4): 371–378.

Morgan, R. (1991) Review of D. Garland's 'Punishment and Social Control', *British Journal of Criminology*, 31(4): 431–433.

—— (2002) 'Imprisonment: A brief history, the contemporary scene, and likely prospects', in M. Maguire, R. Morgan and R. Reiner (eds) *The Oxford Handbook of Criminology.* Oxford: Oxford University Press.

Morgan, S. (1999) 'Prison lives: Critical issues in reading prisoner autobiography', *Howard Journal of Criminal Justice*, 38(3), 328–340.

Morris, P. and Morris, T. (1963) *Pentonville: A Sociological Study of an English Prison*. London: Routledge.

Morrison, S. and O'Donnell, I. (1994). *Armed Robbery: A study in London*. Oxford: Centre for Criminological research, University of Oxford.

Mountbatten, Lord (1966) *Report of the Inquiry into Prison Escapes and Security*, HMSO, London.

Murdock, G. (1982) 'Large corporations and the control of the communications industries', in M. Gurevitch, T. Bennett, J. Curran and J. Woollacott (eds) *Culture, Society and the Media*. London: Routledge.

Narey, M. (2001) *Speech to the Prison Service Conference*, Nottingham, Feb. 2001.

Nellis, M. (2001). 'Community penalities in historical perspective' in A. E. Bottoms, L. Gelsthorpe, and S. Rex, *Community Penalities: Change and Challenges* Cullompton: Willan.

Newton, C. (1994) 'Gender theory and prison sociology: Using theories of masculinities to interpret the sociology of prisons for men', *The Howard Journal of Criminal Justice*, 33(3), 193–202.

Nightingale, C. (1993) *On The Edge*. New York: Basic Books.

O'Donnell, I. (2004) 'Prison rape in context', *The British Journal of Criminology*, 44, 241–255.

—— and Edgar, K. (1998), 'Routine victimisation in prisons', *The Howard Journal* 37(3): 266–279.

—— and Edgar, K. (1998) *Bullying in Prisons*, Occasional Paper No. 18. Oxford: Centre for Criminological Research.

O'Malley, P. (1999) 'Volatile and contradictory punishment', *Theoretical Criminology*, 3(2): 175–196.

Ohlin, J. (1956) *Sociology and the Field of Corrections*. New York: Social Science Council.

Owen, B. (1998) *In the Mix: Struggle and Survival in a Women's Prison*. Albany, NY: State University of New York Press.

Parker, T. (1990) *Life After Life*. London: Secker and Warburg.

Pearson, G. (1987) *The New Heroin Users*. Oxford, Blackwell.

—— and Hobbs, D. (2001) *Middle Market Drug Distribution*, Home Office Research, Development and Statistics Directorate, Research Study No. 227. London: Home Office.

Peckham, A. (1985) *A Woman in Custody: A Personal Account of One Nightmare Journey Through the English Penal System*. London: Fontana.

Phillips, C. (2008) 'Negotiating identities: Ethnicity and social relations in a young offenders' institution', *Theoretical Criminology*, 12(3), 313–331.

Pollock, J. (1997) *Prisons: Today and Tomorrow*. Sudbury, MA: Jones & Bartlett Publishers.

—— (2004) *Prisons and Prison Life: Costs and Consequences*. Los Angeles: Roxbury.

Pratt, J. (2002) *Punishment and Civilization: Penal Tolerance and Intolerance in Modern Society.* London: Sage.

Preble, E. and Casey, J. (1969) 'Taking care of business; the heroin user's life on the street', *The International Journal of the Addictions*, 4(1): 1–24.

Proshansky, H.M., Fabian, A.K. and Kaminoff, R. (1983) 'Physical worlds socialisation of the self', *Journal of Environment Psychology*, 3, 57–83.

Rhodes, L. (2001) 'Toward an anthropology of prisons', *Annual Review of Anthropology*, 30: 65–83.

—— (2004) *Total Confinement: Madness And Reason In The Maximum Security Prison.* California: University of California Press.

Richards, S.C., Terry, C.M. and Murphy, D.S. (2001) 'Lady hacks and gentleman convicts', in L.F. Alarid and P.F. Cromwell (eds) *Correctional Perspectives: Views from Academics, practitioners and Prisoners.* Roxbury: Los Angeles.

Robinson, G. (2002) 'Exploring risk management in probation practice: Contemporary developments in England and Wales', *Punishment and Society*, 4(1): 5–25.

—— (2008) 'Late-modern rehabilitation: The evolution of a penal strategy', *Punishment and Society.* 10(4):429–445.

Rock, P. (1979) *The Making of Symbolic Interactionism*, London: Macmillan.

Rose, N. (1999) (second edition) *Governing the Soul: The Shaping of the Private Self.* London: Free Association Books.

Sabo, D., Kupers, T. and London, W. (eds) (2001) *Prison Masculinities.* Philadelphia: Temple University Press.

Said, E. (1983) 'Criticism between culture and system', in E. Said, *The World, The Text and the Critic.* Cambridge, MA: Harvard University Press.

Sapp, A. and Vaughn, M. (1990) 'Juvenile sex offender treatment at state-operated correctional institutions', *International Journal of Offender Therapy and Comparative Criminology*, Vol. 34, No. 2, 131–146.

Schmid, T. and Jones, R. (1991) 'Suspended Identity: Identity Transformation in a Maximum Security Prison', *Symbolic Interaction*, 14, 415–432.

Schrag, C. (1944) '*Social types in a prison community*', Unpublished Master's thesis, University of Washington.

—— (1954) 'Leadership among inmates', *American Sociological Review*, 19, 37–42.

Scott, D. (2006) 'The caretakers of punishment: Prison officer personal authority and the rule of law', *Prison Service Journal*, 168, 14–19.

—— (2007) 'The changing face of the English prison: A critical review of the aims of imprisonment', in Y. Jewkes (ed) *Handbook on Prisons.* Cullompton: Willan, pp. 49–72.

—— (2008) 'Creating ghosts in the penal machine: Prison officer occupational morality and the techniques of denial', in J. Bennett,

B. Crewe and A. Wahidin, (eds) *Understanding Prison Staff.* Cullompton: Willan, pp. 168–186.

Scott, J. (1990) *Domination and the Arts of Resistance: Hidden Transcripts.* New Haven and London: Yale University Press.

Scott, J. (2001) *Power: Key Concepts.* Cambridge: Polity.

Scraton, P., Sim, J. and Skidmore, P. (1991) *Prisons Under Protest.* Milton Keynes: Open University Press.

Sennett, R. (1998) *The Corrosion of Character: The Personal Consequences of Work in the New Capitalism.* London: W.Norton.

Shannon, T and Morgan, C (1996) *The Invisible Crying Tree.* London: Doubleday.

Shefer, G. (in progress) *Doing rehabilitation in contemporary prisons – the case of therapeutic communities,* unpublished PhD thesis, University of Cambridge.

Sim, J. (1994a) 'Tougher than the rest? Men in prison', in T. Newburn and E. Stanko (eds), *Just Boys Doing Business,* London: Routledge.

—— (1994b) 'Reforming the penal wasteland: A critical reading of the Woolf report', in E. Player and M. Jenkins (eds) *Prisons After Woolf.* London: Routledge.

—— (2003) 'Whose side are we not on? Researching medical power in prisons' in S. Tombs and D. Whyte, (eds) *Unmasking the Crimes of the Powerful: Scrutinizing States and Corporations.* New York: Peter Lang.

—— (2008) 'An inconvenient criminological truth: pain, punishment and prison officers', in J. Bennett, B. Crewe and A. Wahidin (2008) *Understanding Prison Staff.* Cullompton: Willan, pp 187–209.

Simon, J. (1993) *Poor Discipline: Parole and the Social Control of the Underclass, 1890–1990.* Chicago: University of Chicago Press.

—— (2000) 'The "society of captives" in the era of hyper-incarceration', *Theoretical Criminology,* 4(3): 285–308.

—— (2007) *Governing Through Crime. How the War on Crime Transformed American Democracy and Created a Culture of Fear.* Oxford: Oxford University Press.

Smith, D. (2007) 'The foundations of legitimacy', in T. Tyler, (ed) *Legitimacy and Criminal Justice: International Perspectives.* New York: Russell Sage Foundation.

Smith, R. (2004) *A Few Kind Words and a Loaded Gun: The Auto-biography of a Career Criminal.* London: Penguin.

Smith, Z. (2006) 'On the beginning', *The Guardian,* 15/7/2006.

Sparks, R. (2002) 'Out of the 'Digger': The warrior's honour and the guilty observer', *Ethnography,* 3(4): 556–581.

—— (2007) 'The politics of imprisonment', in Y. Jewkes (ed.) *Handbook on Prisons.* Cullompton: Willan.

——, Bottoms, A. and Hay, W. (1996) *Prisons and the Problem of Order.* Oxford: Clarendon.

Street, D., Vintner, R. and Perrow, C. (1966) *Organization For Treatment.* New York: The Free Press.

Stockdale, J. and Stockdale, S. (1984) *In Love And War: The Story of a Family's Ordeal and Sacrifice During the Vietnam Years.* New York: Harper and Row.

Sykes, G. (1956) 'Men, merchants and toughs: A study of reactions to imprisonment', *Social Problems,* 4, 130–138.

—— (1958) *The Society of Captives: A Study of a Maximum-Security Prison.* Princeton, NJ: Princeton University Press.

—— (1995) 'The structural-functional perspective on imprisonment', in T. Blomberg and S. Cohen (eds) *Punishment and Social Control: Essays in Honor of Sheldon L. Messinger.* New York: Aldine de Gruyter.

—— and Messinger, S. (1960) 'The Inmate Social System', in R.A. Cloward *et al., Theoretical Studies in the Social Organization of the Prison.* New York: Social Science Research Council, pp. 5–19.

Sztompka, P. (1999) *Trust: A Sociological Theory.* Cambridge: Cambridge University Press.

Tait, S. (2008) 'Prison officer care for prisoners in one men's and one women's prison', unpublished PhD thesis. University of Cambridge.

Thomas, C. (1977) 'Theoretical perspectives on prisonization: A comparison of the importation and deprivation models', *Journal of Criminal Law and Criminology,* 68: 135–144.

Thomas, M. and Jackson, S. (2003) 'Cognitive-skills groupwork', in G. Towl (ed.) *Psychology in Prisons.*

Thurston, R. (1996) 'Are you sitting comfortably? Men's storytelling, masculinity, prison culture and violence', in M. Mac an Ghaill (ed.), *Understanding Masculinities,* Buckingham: Open University Press.

Thomas-Peter, B. (2006) 'The modern context of psychology in corrections: Influences, limitations and values of "what works"', in G. Towl (ed.) *Psychological Research in Prisons.* Oxford: Blackwell.

Toch, H. (1975) *Men in Crisis.* Chicago: Aldine.

—— (1992) *Living in Prison: The Ecology of Survival.* New York: The Free Press.

—— (1997) *Corrections: A Humanistic Approach.* New York: Harrow and Heston.

—— and Adams, K. (1989) *Coping: Maladaptation in Prisons.* New Brunswick, NJ: Transaction.

Tolson, A. (1977) *The Limits of Masculinity.* London: Tavistock.

Tong, J. and Farrington, D. (2006) 'How effective is the "Reasoning and Rehabilitation" programme in reducing reoffending? A meta-analysis of evaluations in four countries', *Psychology, Crime & Law,* 12:1, 3–24.

Towl, G. (ed.) (2003) *Psychology in Prisons.* Oxford: Blackwell.

—— (ed.) (2007) *Psychological Research in Prisons.* Oxford: Blackwell.

Tyler, T (1990) *Why People Obey The Law.* New Haven: Yale University Press

Useem, B. and Kimball, P. (1989) *States of Siege: US Prison Riots, 1971–1986.* Oxford: Oxford University Press.

Wacquant, L. (2000) 'The new "peculiar institution": On the prison as surrogate ghetto', *Theoretical Criminology*, 4(3): 377–389.

—— (2001a) 'Deadly symbiosis: Where ghetto and prison meet and merge', *Punishment and Society*, 3(1): 95–133.

—— (2001b) 'The penalisation of poverty and the rise of neo-liberalism', *European Journal on Criminal Policy and Research*, 9(4): 401–412.

—— (2002) 'The curious eclipse of prison ethnography in the age of mass incarceration', *Ethnography*, 3(4): 371–398.

Walker, P. (1995) 'New directions; tackling drug misuse at HM Prison Swaleside', *Prison Service Journal*, 99: 35–37.

Walker, S. and Worrall, A. (2000) 'Life as a woman: the gendered pains of indeterminate imprisonment', *Prison Service Journal*, 132, 27–37.

Walmsley, R. (2005) *World Prison Population List* (sixth edition), Home Office: HMSO.

Warr, J. (2008), 'Personal experiences of prison staff', in J. Bennett, B. Crewe, and A. Wahidin, (eds) *Understanding Prison Staff.* Cullompton: Willan.

Weber, M. (1949) *The Methodology of the Social Sciences.* Translated by E.A. Shils and H.A. Finch, Glencoe, Illinois: Free Press.

Wheatley, P. (2003) Interview with Phil Wheatley about Category-C prisons.

Wheeler, S. (1961) 'Socialization in correctional communities', *American Sociological Review*, 26, 697–712.

Wilkinson, J. (2005) 'Evaluating evidence for the effectiveness of the Reasoning and Rehabilitation programme', *The Howard Journal of Criminal Justice*, 44(1), 70–85.

Willmot, P. (1999) 'Working with life sentence prisoners', in G. Towl and C. McDougall (eds) *What Do Forensic Psychologists Do? Current and Future Directions in the Prison and Probation Services.* Leicester: British Psychological Society.

—— (2003) 'Working with lifers', in G. Towl. (ed) (2003) *Psychology in Prisons.* Oxford: Blackwell.

Wilson, D. (2003) '"Keeping Quiet" or "Going Nuts": Strategies used by young, black men in custody', *The Howard Journal of Criminal Justice*, 43(3), 317–330.

Woolf Report (1991) *Prison Disturbances April 1990: Report of an Inquiry by the Rt Hon. Lord Justice Woolf (Part I and II) and his Honour Judge Stephen Tumim (Part II)*, Cm. 1456, London: HMSO.

Wrong, D. (2002) *Power: Its Forms, Bases and Uses* (third edition). New Brunswick. Transaction Publishers.

Wyner, R. (2003) *From the Inside: Dispatches from a Women's Prison*. London: Aurum Press.

Zaitzow, B. and Thomas, T. (eds) (2003) *Women in Prison: Gender and Social Control*. Boulder, CO: Lynn Rienner Publishers.

Zamble, E. and Porporino, F.J. (1988) *Coping, Behaviour and Adaptation in Prisons Inmates*. Secaucus, NJ: Springer-Verlag.

Zedner, L. (2002) 'Dangers of dystopia in penal theory', *Oxford Journal of Legal Studies*, 22/2: 341–366.

—— (2007) 'Pre-crime and post-criminology?' *Theoretical Criminology*, Vol. 11, No. 2, 261–281.

Index